The Civil Mind

The Civil Mind

Margaret Earley Whitt
University of Denver

Janet L. Bland
Marietta College

THOMSON

WADSWORTH

Australia   Brazil   Canada   Mexico   Singapore   Spain   United Kingdom   United States

THOMSON
WADSWORTH

The Civil Mind
Margaret Earley Whitt/Janet L. Bland

Publisher: *Michael Rosenberg*
Development Editor: *Julie McBurney*
Managing Marketing Manager: *Mandee Eckersley*
Content Project Manager: *Karen Stocz*
Print Buyer: *Betsy Donaghey*
Text Designer: *Glenna Collett*

Photo Manager: *Sheri Blaney*
Photo Researcher: *Jill Engebretson*
Cover Designer: *Dutton & Sherman Design*
Printer: *West Group*
Compositor: *Graphic World Inc.*

Cover photos: top left: © Art Shay/Time & Life
Images/Getty; top right: © Jose Luis Pelaez,
Inc./CORBIS; bottom left: Jeff Mermelstein/Getty;
bottom right: © Bridget Besaw Gorman/AURORA;
background: © Bettman/Corbis

Library of Congress Control Number: 2006927722

ISBN 1-4130-1300-7

Thomson Higher Education
25 Thomson Place
Boston, MA 02210-1202

For more information about our products, contact us at:
Thomson Learning Academic Resource Center
1-800-423-0563

For permission to use material from this text or product,
submit a request online at
http://www.thomsonrights.com.
Any additional questions about permissions can be
submitted by e-mail to
thomsonrights@thomson.com.

Brief Contents

Contents

This chapter suggests that before we can write about issues of citizenship in the United States of America, we need to explore how we think and read about the people who call themselves American citizens. The United States is the most diverse nation on the planet, and how we employ this diversity determines how we both celebrate and resist our differences.

2 | Talking and Writing about Citizenship and Justice   46

This chapter explores the importance of purpose, voice, and audience when we talk about responsible citizenship. By verbalizing your ideas, you can clarify what you have written. You need to understand the necessary link between talking and writing about being a participating citizen. Purpose, voice, and audience shape who is included and who is left out of the discussion.

3   Before and after Writing: America and Democracy   **95**

This chapter asks you to consider your own writing style. Do you spend more time prewriting or rewriting? How do peers influence what you have to say?

Americans: Community, Communication, and Participation   142

This chapter explores the ways we communicate and participate in democracy. Part One considers patterns of inquiry, which are represented by different modes, the three appeals, and various genres. There are many genres, and each enhances understanding of the issue at hand and establishes an entry point for you when you want to join the conversation about an issue, event, or decision. Part Two broadens our discussion to explore the three spheres of communication—the public, private, and technical—and then considers how information moving across and among those spheres affects us as citizens.

PART TWO   CITIZENSHIP 101   187

This part includes a number of speeches and treatises (or excerpts) that have been an important part of the conversation about who we are and how we see ourselves as Americans.

**6   Point of Contact:
Immigration and the Changing Face of America   390**

**9   Point of Contact:
Terrorism and National Security   524**

10 Point of Contact: Technology, Internet Culture, and the Online Community   587

Appendix: Service Learning 645

WHAT IS THIS BOOK?

The Civil Mind is a book about writing and United States citizenship that allows students to engage in relevant national discourse by immersing themselves in some of the predominate conversations taking place in American culture. Issues of national concern such as race, religion, immigration, sexuality, technology, and terrorism are at the heart of writing instruction in *The Civil Mind,* so students are reading, thinking, talking, and writing in response to a wide variety of national debates. As students evaluate their cultural context in relation to such terms as privacy or racial profiling or gender roles, they can better understand and participate in that culture, no matter whether their opinions are conservative, liberal, or somewhere in between. There is a place for everyone in *The Civil Mind,* and the purpose of this text is to introduce students to elements of writing while exploring elements of the greater American conversation that is continually taking place across the nation.

 The Civil Mind brings a dynamic approach to writing—combining tried and true writing methods with up-to-date readings about what is happening in the world right now. This text offers opportunities to change the way writing and civic issues are taught and provides varied source material to support lively class discussions. *The Civil Mind* is a complete resource for writing teachers of all experience levels—from the beginner to the expert—and is flexible enough for success in classrooms at a variety of institutions—including community colleges and liberal arts colleges and universities. Below are a few comments from reviewers of the text, teachers of writing who had the opportunity to observe the development of the text from its first drafts to this final product.

 "The main strengths of *The Civil Mind* are its conceptual framework and its diverse selection of readings. This is especially true with respect to historical and cultural issues. In the process of advancing their writing skills, the book forces students to view themselves as part of a continuum or ongoing civic process and to make sense of past and current events."

      Jeffrey Lamar Coleman, St. Mary's College of Maryland

 "I would definitely consider adopting *The Civil Mind* for my classroom because its an excellent and responsible textbook containing content that will educate my students in ways much more important than can be gained by most 'average' class discussions, and it does so without ignoring the mechanical side of language. It gives students reason and occasion to write, teaching by examples both literal in form and passionate."

      Molly Chestnut Sides, Rock Valley College

"I anticipate the help offered by *The Civil Mind* to be greatly appreciated and useful for college students and professors alike."

Brian P. Ward, Valdosta State University

These colleagues see the strengths of *The Civil Mind,* and they want to bring those strengths into their classrooms. In the next few pages, you will see what elements the text contains, how those elements work together, and why this concept is unique. *The Civil Mind* is not just about ideas—*The Civil Mind* is about reading, thinking, talking, and writing about ideas. After all, shouldn't great ideas lead to great writing?

Writing is an assertive and profound act, a declaration of both existence and purpose that asserts again and again—I'm here, taking a stand or exploring an issue that matters. Writing is always in response to something, and there are many different areas of life where writing matters. In the academic world students and scholars are asked to document a position, the results of an experiment, the primary questions at hand in a controversy, and even the nature of human existence. It is through writing that we all come to a certain clarity about who we are and where we are in this American life.

One of the many remarkable things about American citizenship is its dynamic flexibility—just as there are many different ways to write, there are many ways to express and experience citizenship in the United States. If we examine our nation's past we easily find a chronological record of profound transformation in the nature of citizenship. Take, for instance, the famous phrase "all men are created equal" from the beginning of the *Declaration of Independence.* When that first group of American patriots sent their thoughts to the King of England, those words, which are at the heart of the American experience, must have seemed as profound as they were obvious—all men are equal. Since then we have revised and reconsidered what *all* encompasses (white, black, everyone?), what *men* includes (men and women, children and adults?), and exactly how we are going to interpret that elusive term *equal* (separate or all together, is there really such a thing?). So when we speak of citizenship in *The Civil Mind,* we are not speaking of a static state of being, something cold and unchanging forever carved in stone. American citizenship is alive with possibilities, forever on the brink of profound change and dynamic transformation. Such change is not simply a factor of time, however. Individuals may enter the American discussion, each in his or her way, in countless configurations, just as each student can address issues in his or her own writing.

WAYS TO USE THIS BOOK

With this vision of a transformational citizenship in mind, student and teacher alike are welcomed into *The Civil Mind* on their own terms. Beginning in the first chapters, which offer a variety of approaches in instructional rhetoric designed to further the writing skills and abilities of the college student, we have organized our approach to writing into a gradual, logical progression, accompanied by thematically grouped readings.

Chapter One.   As Chapter One provides an introduction to the United States, exploring where we all came from and just what we mean when we say "America," it also begins our discussion of writing by considering the poetry and prose of some well-known Americans. Beginning with a discussion of voice, the chapter moves through such topics as reader expectations, opinions, stereotypes, judgments and beliefs in argument, how to annotate an essay for better comprehension, and the use of humor in writing. Using a variety of written sources to consider and respond to, this chapter intends to set the stage for the student writer. Here is the big picture, the view through the wide-angle lens of how other writers think (and of course write) about America. This chorus of voices also sets the tone for the rest of the book, allowing for many opinions and experiences, including those who may have just arrived on our shores and in our classrooms.

Chapter Two.   This chapter considers the ways in which the writer begins to address a subject and starts writing. We begin with purpose, audience, and voice, moving quickly into tones and genres, finding a thesis, convincing beginnings and compelling endings, and constructing the paragraphs in between. Here student writers will find the major building blocks of essay writing. This is all accomplished within the context of race relations—specifically addressing the lives of African Americans. Although there are many racial concerns in America's past and present, the experiences of African Americans are both unique and profound in our national story and deserve such a focus.

Chapter Three.   This chapter focuses on a variety of writing techniques for *before* the first draft is written and *after* the first draft as students consider rewriting and editing. The many techniques outlined in this chapter allow student writers to customize their writing process, both for this class and throughout the rest of their college career. Techniques intended to facilitate the student *before* writing include restating information, brainstorming, free writing, and making lists, prewriting, summary, paraphrase, outlining, cubing, and mapping/clustering. Additional strategies explored here offer diverse approaches and considerations of writing as the writer works to refine and reconsider.

Topics covered that aid the student *after* the first draft is complete include expanding, deleting paragraphs, crafting, editing, and proofreading sentences; ten common errors to be aware of during proofreading; and peer revision. The thematic element of the readings takes a more historical approach, presenting examples from our nation's past. Such examples both widen the discussion (from issues of today to issues of yesterday) and establish common ground (between Americans of different eras) upon which we might consider the nature of the American life.

Chapter Four.   This chapter focuses on the nature of communication, addressing patterns of inquiry, the modes, Aristotle's three appeals, issues of community, determining authority through genre, group think and group dynamics, and using fiction to understand communities. Here student writers can begin to consider how their writing enters them into the communities they belong to. The readings in the chapter relate to elements of community participation, specifically the experience of sitting on a jury. With rights come responsibilities, and a citizen's right to a jury trial necessitates that some other citizens participate in the legal system.

Throughout these four chapters are the nuts and bolts of writing well, and while individual teachers and writers may use elements of the text to their own tastes, we feel there is a logical progression in working chronologically through these four chapters on writing.

What Is at Stake for Citizenship?

At the end of each chapter and Point of Contact, you will find a series of questions under the heading: "What Is at Stake for Citizenship?" Because citizenship is fluid and changeable, these questions provide regular opportunities throughout the text to pause and consider how the issues found in the material at hand may (or may not) change the terms of citizenship. Questions, at their most elementary level, introduce issues and demand consideration and response. Such consideration and response can logically lead student writers to a strong thesis or an interesting beginning to a paper. These questions may also serve as the inspiration for a great class discussion, an insightful paper topic, or just something to think about.

Citizenship 101

Citizenship 101 is a collection of important legislation and speeches (some abridged and some full text) at the heart of the American experience and is designed to offer background material to many of the issues raised in this text. This collection of documents is an integral part of *The Civil Mind,* providing not only a link to the past through a rich sampling of American voices but also profound evidence of the connections in our national life between the past and the present. The issues with which we struggle today—such as gender and race—are part of the greater rights and responsibilities of citizenship that have been issues of national focus for generations. Citizenship 101 reminds students of the process of national identity, spanning not just individual lives but many generations. Citizenship 101 encourages students to see that they are joining an ongoing national conversation and speaking for their generation.

This section might also serve as a starting point if students write a paper that requires some sort of research beyond the topics covered in this text. There are brief assignments throughout the first four chapters of the textbook that require a consultation of one or more documents in Citizenship 101.

This section is also presented as a model for how many people of many times have written about America and the American people. Student writers may consider form and style, context, and content—how best might we demand rights from a king or compose the language of legislation?—as they examine these texts. Taking into account the ideas of community and communication introduced in Chapter four, student writers are encouraged to consider the writers of Citizenship 101 their community of greater American writers and to strive to enter that community through their own writing.

Point of Contact Chapters

Point of Contact chapters appear in the last section of the book. These six points or issues include race, immigration, religion and public space, sexuality and identity, national security and terrorism, and technology. The Point of Contact chapters are crucial to the larger goals of *The Civil Mind,* providing a wide variety of topical opportunities for students to put into practice the primary issues of the first four chapters: citizenship and writing. The Point of Contact chapters provide both a breadth of topics and a depth of coverage—such that students may join the national conversation within the context of a multi-sided discussion. This section encourages our students to go from being readers to writers, to take into account their own feelings, thoughts, and opinions, and then strategize how they might persuade a reader to share them. Each Point of Contact contains a cluster of three casebooks that relate to some aspect of the issue—one casebook in each cluster is specifically a student-related concern. Each of the 18 casebooks has a selection of readings addressing various aspects of or opinions about the topic. For instance, in the National Security and Terrorism Point of Contact, one of the three casebooks, addresses the USA Patriot Act and contains readings that take a variety of positions (political and otherwise) on the success of the USA Patriot Act. Each of these topics is supported with introductory material and diverse opinions from many sources so that students may clearly see the field of discourse (who is taking what stand, what the terms of the argument are) before jumping into the discussion.

These casebooks are an invitation to writing and synthesis—an opportunity for student writers to read selections on a topic before writing on that topic themselves. Ideally, these many pieces of writing can be incorporated into students' writing, functioning as supporting evidence and background material. Each of the Point of Contact chapters has room for the student writer to enter the discourse; each of the 18 casebooks is missing one crucial piece of writing: the one the student will write.

Service Learning

Citizenship and writing are both communal acts—both require the context and relevance of community—and so we see these two acts as natural partners in the process of learning to communicate about our world. In the Appendix you will find information about service learning. As service learning comes of age in the twenty-first century, we look now to move beyond the idea of paternalism, beyond the notion that service learning is limited to college students helping disadvantaged people in an off-campus agency. Although there is a need for this traditional kind of community service, our notion of service learning is expanded to consider how community activism and participation (both online and in person) is service learning in the purest sense: learning by serving your community as an engaged and active citizen.

The most common way to evaluate the role of service learning in any composition class is to ask the student who is participating in the service learning to write about it. It is in the writing, where ideas are explored and experiences are reconsidered, that the value of good citizenship is truly realized.

From the very start, this book invites readers into a narrative of American history—encouraging students to consider where and how they wish to enter the story that rolls out before us. Reading and writing are inseparable—both for our purposes here in this textbook and in life. In *The Civil Mind*, the American experience is a narrative of many faces and voices, moving in many directions and through many times. To use the book effectively so that it mirrors all the dynamic qualities of citizenship, the story must be interrupted—a story read and then written—reconsidered and re-visioned by the student readers who stop the story (again and again) to begin rewriting it to include themselves and the miracle of their own lives.

ACKNOWLEDGMENTS

We would like to thank the talented Thomson Wadsworth staff for their support throughout the years of writing and production of *The Civil Mind*. This book was a real team effort, not only because there are two authors but also because we had so many people supporting us from the very start. We would first like to thank our good friend David Hall, who convinced us that we had a book before even one word was written, and Dickson Musslewhite, who worked so hard to get a green light for our book at Thomson Wadsworth. We want to thank Julie McBurney, who is indeed the world's best development editor. Her dedication to this project and her unfailing good humor made such a difference. We are also grateful to Karen Stocz, who capably and carefully oversaw the many details involved in the production process.

We would also like to thank our colleagues across the country who reviewed the book in all its incarnations and offered invaluable suggestions:

Scott Ash, *Nassau Community College*
Jeffrey Lamar Coleman, *St. Mary's College of Maryland*
Rebecca Flannagan, *Francis Marion University*
Margaret Harman, *Pfeiffer University*
Sharon Jaffe, *Santa Monica College*
Cynthia Kuhn, *Metropolitan State College of Denver*
Eleanor Lee, *Troy State University*
Meredith Love, *Francis Marion University*
Deborah Melnick, *Salem State College*
Michael Morris, *Eastfield College*
Beverly Neiderman, *Kent State University*
Ted Otteson, *University of Missouri–Kansas City*
Patricia Ralston, *Covenant College*
Gordon Reynolds, *Ferris State University*
Molly Chesnut Sides, *Rock Valley College*
Grant T. Smith, *Viterbo University*
Jennifer Thompson, *Embry-Riddle Aeronautical University*
Karen Toloui, *Diablo Valley College*
Brian P. Ward, *Valdosta State University.*

Finally we would like to thank our students; we had them in mind as we wrote each chapter, always asking ourselves: "How would they see this? What would they say? What might they write about it?"

On a personal note, we find ourselves looking into the past and the future for our inspiration. Janet would like to thank Mary Moskeland and Margaret Moskeland Bland, the first two great teachers she knew. Margaret would like to thank Spencer and Axel Whitt, who inspire hope in the future through their youthful exuberance for life and learning.

Margaret Earley Whitt
Janet L. Bland

America and Democracy:
A Rhetoric about Writing

CHAPTER 1

This chapter suggests that before we can write about issues of citizenship in the United States of America, we need to explore how we think and read about the people who call themselves American citizens. The United States is the most diverse nation on the planet, and how we employ this diversity determines how we both celebrate and resist our differences.

Thinking and Reading about America

NATION BUILDING: WHO WAS HERE AND WHO CAME

Give me your tired, your poor, Your huddled masses yearning to breathe free, The wretched refuse of your teeming shore. Send these, the homeless, the tempest-tost to me, I lift my lamp beside the golden door.
　　　　　—Emma Lazarus, from her poem "The New Colossus,"
　　engraved at the base of the Statue of Liberty National Monument

The old people in a new world, the new people made out of the old, that is the story I mean to tell, for this is what really is and what I really know.

—Gertrude Stein, *The Making of Americans*

If we want to talk about American citizenship, we might take a look at who we are and how we came to form this unique and powerful nation. One of the first questions we might consider as we talk about America and its citizens is where we're all from. Our diversity didn't just happen; rather, it's the result of human migration stretching back through time. Over the last four hundred years, people joined the American experiment in one of three primary ways. Native Americans were here since the Ice Age, having (according to one theory) crossed the Bering land bridge. The rest of America arrived, for better or worse, on their shore: Immigrants from around the world came here on a boat by choice; Africans were brought here on a boat by force. Since the middle of the twentieth century, that "boat" has more often been an airplane, but the idea is still the same. Every day different people from around the world come to America because they believe that this is the place where they can succeed. It's this ever-changing combination of people that makes our country uniquely challenged—leaving us both rich in our differences and often limited by our lack of acceptance of others. The story of America and its people is always an interesting story, but it's not always a happy one.

They Walked Here

Indians of North America—Osage, Iroquois, and Pawnee, by George Catlin.

The citizens who identify themselves as American Indians or Native Americans arrived here during the Ice Age some thirty thousand years ago, perhaps via the Bering land bridge. At the time of the first European contact, an estimated 10 million indigenous people lived north of Mexico. The land we think of as America was populated by numerous, distinct tribes and nations—each with its own language, culture, social structure, and system of spiritual beliefs. But by the time of the first permanent English settlement at Jamestown, Virginia, in 1607, their numbers had been drastically reduced through contact with Europeans in the form of war, forced labor, and epidemic disease. In the four hundred years that followed that first and much celebrated Thanksgiving, the people whom a lost explorer mistakenly called "Indians" have been pushed off their lands and had their sources of food destroyed through military action, expanded

*Manifest Destiny: The American philosophy that explains America's thirst for expansion and presents a defense for America's claim to all new territories. ". . . the right of our manifest destiny to over spread and to possess the whole of the continent which Providence has given us for the development of the great experiment of liberty."
—John O' Sullivan

*reservations: The result of vast expansion in the West by non-native settlers, reservations are tracks of land specified by treaty—between the tribe in question and the U.S. government—that determine where Native Americans may live and preserve their language and culture beyond many local and state laws and restrictions. While the original object was separation, today most Native Americans do not live on the reservations, and non-natives may live on leased reservation land.

settlement, and ranching. **Manifest Destiny***　left them contained on small patches of inferior land known as **reservations,***　where they are often unable to pursue a traditional lifestyle. Today the term "Native American" refers to a legal, governmentally determined status that involves official membership in a specific tribe or nation, such as the Hopi, Navajo, Iroquois, Seminole, Sioux, Ute, Walla Walla, and Ojibwa. The Citizenship Act of 1924 naturalized Indians born within the territorial limits of the United States, while the Indian Reorganization Act of 1934 recognized tribal governments as sovereign nations. Although over 50 percent of Native Americans live in urban settings, high rates of poverty, disease, and premature death on the reservations are a continuing national concern.

They Came by Choice

In 1620 a group of religious dissenters known as Pilgrims established the Plymouth Colony. Their Mayflower was just the first of countless ships, bringing immigrants from Great Britain who increased the population of those first settlements. Additional colonization would bring settlements of Swedes and the Dutch, while the ranks of the eighteenth-century immigrants would swell with the German and French.

The greatest influx of immigrants—over 37 million total—would arrive between the 1840s and the 1920s. Germans, the Irish (fleeing famine), Italians, more English, Scots, Welsh, Austro-Hungarians, Scandinavians, Russians, Poles, and other Slavs all came to America. With the settlement of the West came more immigrants who left their mark on the young nation. The Japanese brought their expertise in agriculture to California and Hawaii, while the Chinese built the railroad that would connect the continent. Throughout the continuing western expansion, people moved north from Mexico, bringing elements from their indigenous and Spanish cultures: food, music, language, architecture, and religion.

These millions of immigrants, while they might have been desperate, were also pragmatic. Although

Landing of the Puritans in America, 1620, Antonio Gisbert.

they brought all manner of religious faiths and political ideologies, fewer than 10 percent of immigrants specifically came to America for religious or political reasons. Jews, Catholics, and Protestants, anarchists, socialists, and communists—all came, and all were seeking the same opportunity, the same chance at a better life.

After World War II, a new status of immigrant, the refugee, was recognized, and after the conflict in Vietnam ended, immigrants from Vietnam, Laos, and Cambodia arrived in the 1970s. Today's immigrants are primarily from Latin America and Asia, although Middle Eastern and African communities continue to grow all around the country.

As each new wave of humanity arrived, the newcomers began at the bottom of the social and economic ladder. They were offered substandard housing and, as a matter of course, the hardest, dirtiest, most dangerous jobs. Yet they took those jobs, chasing an American dream that promised them something more for their hard work and perseverance. It commonly took more than a lifetime to move up in status, so often it was the immigrants' children, educated in public schools and free of the accents of the Old World, who would realize the American dream, not the immigrants themselves. More recently, concerns about population growth, the economic burden, and the proliferation of terrorism have threatened to stem the flow of new people coming to this land of immigrants.

They Came by Force

THE BLACK MAN'S LAMENT.   5

TORN FROM HIS FRIENDS.

Slave Traders, 1826. European slave traders separate a man from his family before putting them on board a slave ship. From *The Black Man's Lament; or How to Make Sugar,* by Amelia Opie.

The first African people brought against their will and sold as slaves in the colonies that would become the United States of America arrived in Virginia in 1619. During the next two hundred years, Africans were legally transported under the horrific conditions of the slave trade. When our founding fathers formed our new country and eventually wrote our Constitution, Africans (both enslaved and free) were denied citizenship. For the purposes of representational government in Congress, one African (enslaved or free) was equal to three fifths of one white person.

In 1808 the slave trade was outlawed in the United

*Jim Crow: (1870s to 1950s) Named for an old slave character (who embodied all negative stereotypes about blacks) who appeared in an 1829 minstrel song (sung by whites in blackface), Jim Crow was the system of laws that enforced the segregation of public spaces and places as "white only" and "colored only" in the American South. These laws were applied to all facets of southern life—including but not limited to schools, transportation, restaurants, parks, drinking fountains, and restrooms.

Brown v. Board of Education of Topeka: On May 17, 1954, the U.S. Supreme Court ruled unanimously that segregated schools are unconstitutional, putting an end to the doctrine of "separate but equal."

*civil rights movement: Beginning in 1954 with the Supreme Court's unanimous passage of *Brown v. Board of Education of Topeka,* the movement rallied black and white citizens to direct action to improve conditions for black citizens living in the southern states. The modern civil rights movement ended with the assassination of Martin Luther King Jr. in April 1968.

*genre: A distinctive type or style of composition.

States but continued illegally on a more limited basis until the Civil War (1861–1865). According to the 1860 census, almost 4 million Americans of African descent were held in slavery in the southern United States. Although the Civil War would decide the issue of slavery in the United States, little was done to determine the rights of the newly freed African Americans. Decades of disenfranchisement, racism, **Jim Crow*** segregation, and widespread lynching would follow. Not until 1948 would President Harry Truman desegregate the U.S. military. And it would not be for almost one hundred years after the Civil War, in 1954, that the U.S. Supreme Court, in ***Brown v. Board of Education of Topeka,*** * would find school segregation illegal. The **civil rights movement*** of the 1950s and 1960s would continue the fight for full citizenship of black Americans, but we have yet to achieve a fully equal society. Even as we begin the twenty-first century, nagging questions between black and white Americans and tensions on all sides threaten to tear us apart.

And yet, for all our history and past mistakes, we continue to be the richest, freest, and most diverse nation ever. We are loved, envied, hated, and targeted by other nations . . . but never ignored. Such is the power of our difference. Right now, all over the world, there are people whose greatest wish is to come to the United States and join this continual, controversial experiment in opportunity and democracy. The challenge, among Americans of all races, cultures, religions, and backgrounds, is to find the common ground of understanding and respect that allows us all, no matter how or when we arrived, to go forward into the future as full, equal, participating citizens.

This text will use a wide array of documents in many **genres*** about and creative responses to citizenship. As you make your way through this text and engage in class discussions about the selected readings, respond to the suggested assignments and exercises, and write your own essays about different elements of citizenship, you will have the opportunity to explore *how* writing works—for you as reader and as writer. As you engage in ideas pertinent to many American experiences, you will gain new insights about responsible citizenship, about the necessity of taking seriously the right to vote, and the role of justice and fair play in the American way of life.

THINKING ABOUT OUR COMPLEXITIES: VOICES IN THE CHORUS

Here is not merely a nation, but a teeming nation of nations.
—Walt Whitman

We will not be satisfied to take one jot or title less than our full manhood rights. We claim for ourselves every single right that belongs to a freeborn

American, political, civil, and social; and until we get these rights we will never cease to protest and assail the ears of America.

—W. E. B. Du Bois, Address to the Nation,
2nd annual meeting of Niagara Movement

The preceding quotes are two important statements from the late nineteenth and early twentieth centuries: One is a celebration of the individual, while the other is a declaration of community, with all the rights and responsibilities inherent in that membership. Together they embody a primary American paradox—the value of the individual who aspires to and expects nothing less than universal equality among fellow citizens.

When **Walt Whitman*** published his first edition of *Leaves of Grass* in 1855, he was attempting to define the American experience; he was also answering Ralph Waldo Emerson's 1843 essay, "The Poet," which called for a new and unique national poet— one who would sing of the country in a new voice. Whitman's poem "Song of Myself," which appeared in his now famous collection *Leaves of Grass*, is a celebration of being, a song of individuality and unity in one breath.

W. E. B. Du Bois* was one of the founders of the **Niagara Movement,*** which became the **NAACP***; he was also editor of *The Crisis*, the NAACP journal that promoted the creative work of young black talent. In his speech excerpted above, Du Bois draws attention to the natural state of equality among all Americans, regardless of race, and promises to fight for full extension of those rights until the very last person is declared equal and free.

Given earlier is an introductory line in Section 1 of "Song of Myself." In a slightly more complicated example on the next page, Whitman expands his poetic "voice" to sing of the multiplicity of American voices. Remember that as a poet, Whitman is very interested in capturing the big picture—a poetic line for Whitman will often exceed the width of a normal page. He also expands his subject matter beyond the socially acceptable limits of the day.

Can you picture him in New York City, walking through the streets trying to absorb all the sights and sounds he can for his new poetic voice in a new country? Do you sense the excitement with which he transcribes the "music" of America? As you read the poem, notice the image of an American orchestration—with each person playing his or her part in the great democratic symphony. The labor of individuals is also a part to be sung—how might that connect with the American idea of success through hard work? Is this the sound of a "successful" nation? Consider how the specific individuals add their own "sound" to the larger music of the American experience, how each individual is part of the overall sound but never lost in the music.

***Walt Whitman:** (1819–1892) A New York native and one of America's most famous poets, Whitman was not successful in his own time. In his struggle to support himself, he worked as a printer, teacher, self-taught writer and journalist, and later a government clerk, but he also served as a volunteer nurse for Union forces (including his own wounded brother) during the Civil War. He released several editions of *Leaves of Grass*, a collection of poems with a preface, beginning in 1855, but wouldn't receive substantial royalties until the 1882 edition.

***W. E. B. Du Bois:** (1868–1963) DuBois was one of the founders of the Niagara Movement, which became the NAACP. He was also editor of *The Crisis*, the NAACP journal, which promoted the creative work of young black talent. A scholar, scientist, and lifelong activist for civil rights, Du Bois was the first African American to earn a Ph.D. at Harvard.

***Niagara Movement:** Organized in 1905, and the forerunner of the NAACP, the leaders called for full and equal rights for black Americans.

***NAACP:** National Association for the Advancement of Colored People. Since its founding in 1909, the organization has been among the champions for equal rights for black Americans.

Walt Whitman

Song of Myself—Section 26

Now I will do nothing but listen,
To accrue what I hear into this song, to let sounds contribute toward it.
I hear bravuras of birds, bustle of growing wheat, gossip of flames, clack of sticks
    cooking my meals.
I hear the sound I love, the sound of the human voice,
5   I hear all sounds running together, combined, fused or following,
Sounds of the city and sounds out of the city, sounds of the day and night,
Talkative young ones to those that like them, the loud laugh of work—people at
    their meals,
The angry base of disjointed friendship, the faint tones of the sick,
The judge with hands tight to the desk, his pallid lips pronouncing a
    death-sentence,
10   The heave'etyo of stevedores unlading ships by the wharves, the refrain of the
    anchor-lifters.

The ring of alarm-bells, the cry of fire, the whirr of swift-streaking engines and
    hose-carts with premonitory tinkles and color'd lights,

The steam-whistle, the solid roll of the train of approaching cars,
The slow march play'd at the head of the association marching two and two,
(They go to guard some corpse, the flag-tops are draped with black muslin.)

15   I hear the violoncello, ('tis the young man's heart's complaint,)
I hear the key'd cornet, it glides quickly in through my ears,
It shakes mad-sweet pangs through my belly and breast.

I hear the chorus, it is a grand opera,
Ah this indeed is music—this suits me.

20   A tenor large and fresh as the creation fills me,
The orbic flex of his mouth is pouring and filling me full.
I hear the train'd soprano (what work with hers is this?)
The orchestra whirls me wider than Uranus flies.
It wrenches such ardors from me I did not know I possessed them,
25   It sails me, I dab with bare feet, they are lick'd by the indolent waves,
I am cut by bitter and angry hail, I lose my breath,
Steep'd amid honey'd morphine, my windpipe throttled in fakes of death,
At length let up again to feel the puzzle of puzzles,
And that we call Being.

Having read Whitman's collection of sounds and voices of America, how might you characterize your own contribution to the symphony? If you were going to write your own "American Symphony," what might you hear as you walked through your hometown and recorded the many sounds? Would you be included in your own symphony? What part do you play and how do you play it? Is Whitman's picture too big to be meaningful, or even too loud to be clear? Has he included all the voices you would? Who is missing? Or what?

In W. E. B. Du Bois's "Of the Dawn of Freedom," from *Souls of Black Folk*, here are the first and last paragraphs of Chapter 2. The first sentence is among the most often quoted line he wrote.

THE PROBLEM of the twentieth century is the problem of the color-line,—the relation of the darker to the lighter races of men in Asia and Africa, in America and the islands of the sea. It was a phase of this problem that caused the Civil War; and however much they who marched South and North in 1861 may have fixed on the technical points of union and local autonomy as a shibboleth, all nevertheless knew, as we know, that the question of Negro slavery was the real cause of the conflict. Curious it was, too, how this deeper question ever forced itself to the surface despite effort and disclaimer. No sooner had Northern armies touched Southern soil than this old question, newly guised, sprang from the earth,—What shall be done with Negroes? Peremptory military commands, this way and that, could not answer the query; the Emancipation Proclamation seemed but to broaden and intensify the difficulties; and the War Amendments made the Negro problems of to-day. . . .

For this much all men know: despite compromise, war, and struggle, the Negro is not free. In the backwoods of the Gulf States, for miles and miles, he may not leave the plantation of his birth; in well-nigh the whole rural South the black farmers are peons, bound by law and custom to an economic slavery, from which the only escape is death or the penitentiary. In the most cultured sections and cities of the South the Negroes are a segregated servile caste, with restricted rights and privileges. Before the courts, both in law and custom, they stand on a different and peculiar basis. Taxation without representation is the rule of their political life. And the result of all this is, and in nature must have been, lawlessness and crime. That is the large legacy of the Freedmen's Bureau, the work it did not do because it could not.

I have seen a land right merry with the sun, where children sing, and rolling hills lie like passioned women wanton with harvest. And there in the King's Highway sat and sits a figure veiled and bowed, by which the traveller's footsteps hasten as they go. On the tainted air broods fear. Three centuries' thought has been the raising and unveiling of that bowed human heart, and now behold a century new for the duty and the deed. The problem of the Twentieth Century is the problem of the color-line.

Du Bois says the problem of the twentieth century is the problem of the color-line. How would you define the "color-line" in today's world? Is there still such a thing? If you were writing an essay about justice (or injustice) in America, what would you say the problem of the twenty-first century is? Thinking back to Whitman, who includes everybody in his national chorus, does Du Bois include everybody? Reread the excerpt above and see if you can find a large group of people Du Bois is not talking about.

*Maxine Hong Kingston:
(1940–) The daughter of
Chinese immigrants, she is a
teacher and the author of
both fiction and nonfiction
primarily focused on the
Chinese American experience.
She earned her bachelor's
degree from Berkeley in 1962.

When we talk about the Voices in the Chorus, we also want to focus on individuals, offering them a solo, to allow us to hear one clear voice. In our next selection, **Maxine Hong Kingston,** * a Chinese American author and the daughter of Chinese immigrants, offers a brief explanation of the differences between Chinese voices and the soft, feminine voice she hears herself and other Chinese American girls adopt.

The following is an excerpt from her novel, *The Woman Warrior*, which may expand our discussion of the American voice.

How strange that the emigrant villagers are shouters, hollering face to face. My father asks, "Why is it I can hear Chinese from blocks away? Is it that I understand the language? Or is it that they talk loud?" They turn the radio up full blast to hear the operas, which do not seem to hurt their ears. And they yell over the singers that wail over the drums, everybody talking at once, big arm gestures, spit flying. You can see the disgust on American faces looking at women like that. It isn't just the loudness. It is the way Chinese sounds, chingchong ugly, to American ears, not beautiful like Japanese sayonara words with the consonants and vowels as regular as Italian. We make guttural peasant noise and have Ton Duc Thang names you can't remember. And the Chinese can't hear Americans at all; the language is too soft and western music unhearable. I've watched a Chinese audience laugh, visit, talk-story, and holler during a piano recital, as if the musician could not hear them. A Chinese-American, somebody's son, was playing Chopin, which has no punctuation, no cymbals, no gongs. Chinese piano music is five black keys. Normal Chinese women's voices are strong and bossy. We American-Chinese girls had to whisper to make ourselves American-feminine. Apparently we whispered even more softly than the Americans. Once a year the teachers referred my sister and me to speech therapy, but our voices would straighten out, unpredictably normal, for the therapists. Some of us gave up, shook our heads, and said nothing, not one word. Some of us could not even shake our heads. At times shaking my head is more self-assertion than I can manage. Most of us eventually found some voice, however faltering. We invented an American-feminine speaking personality, except for that one girl who could not speak up even in Chinese school.

Maxine Hong Kingston talks about the differences between languages, sounds, volume, music, and culture, but does she come to any conclusions? Are some cultures louder than others? Do languages sound louder when they are not the dominant language? Which is louder, language we speak or a language that is unfamiliar to us? How do accents matter? Is there an American sound that immigrants must conform to if they wish to be "real" Americans?

*Grace Paley: (1922–) The
daughter of Russian Jewish
immigrants, Paley is a well-
known political activist and the
first recipient of the Edith Wharton Citation of Merit; she is also
the highly acclaimed author of
three collections of short fiction
and three collections of poetry.

Grace Paley's * story, "The Loudest Voice," gives us yet another American voice and introduces the issue of religion—another American paradox—into the discussion of the American identity. On one hand, our Constitution promises freedom of religious expression; on the other hand, it also provides freedom from religion, forbidding the establishment of or support for a national religion through the separation of church and state. People of all faiths are free to practice their religion here, and atheists go about their daily lives without fear of official sanction. Despite all of this, we are largely a devout nation, attending religious services at a much higher rate than our European counterparts. The United States is primarily a Christian nation, despite the presence of many Muslim, Jewish, Buddhist, and Hindu Americans. Sacred Christian holidays become huge commercial events and government-sanctioned days off from work.

Paley's own childhood in a largely Jewish neighborhood in New York gave her a richly Jewish, if somewhat inaccurate, notion of the religious face of America: "I lived my childhood in a world so dense with Jews that I thought we were the great imposing majority and kindness had to be extended to the others because, as my mother said, everyone wants to live like a person. In school I met my friend Adele, who, together with her mother and father were not Jewish. Despite this they often seemed to be in a good mood." The humor of Paley's observations turn upon the obvious irony: America is not dense with Jews so much as with Christians—some of whom may be just a little surprised that Jews, who live without Jesus, are happy nonetheless. *As you read Paley's story, "The Loudest Voice," consider the tensions among the Jewish parents as their children participate in the Christmas play at school.*

Grace Paley

The Loudest Voice

There is a certain place where dumb-waiters boom, doors slam, dishes crash; every window is a mother's mouth bidding the street shut up, go skate somewhere else, come home. My voice is the loudest.

There, my own mother is still as full of breathing as me and the grocer stands up to speak to her. "Mrs. Abramowitz," he says, "people should not be afraid of their children."

"Ah, Mr. Bialik," my mother replies, "if you say to her or her father 'Ssh,' they say, 'In the grave it will be quiet.' "

"From Coney Island to the cemetery," says my papa. "It's the same subway; it's the same fare."

I am right next to the pickle barrel. My pinky is making tiny whirlpools in the brine. I   5
stop a moment to announce: "Campbell's Tomato Soup. Campbell's Vegetable Beef Soup. Campbell's S-c-otch Broth . . ."

"Be quiet," the grocer says, "the labels are coming off."

"Please, Shirley, be a little quiet," my mother begs me.

In that place the whole street groans: Be quiet! Be quiet! but steals from the happy chorus of my inside self not a tittle or a jot.

There, too, but just around the corner, is a red brick building that has been old for many years. Every morning the children stand before it in double lines which must be straight. They are not insulted. They are waiting anyway.

I am usually among them. I am, in fact, the first, since I begin with "A."   10

One cold morning the monitor tapped me on the shoulder. "Go to Room 409, Shirley Abramowitz," he said. I did as I was told. I went in a hurry up a down staircase to Room 409, which contained sixth-graders. I had to wait at the desk without wiggling until Mr. Hilton, their teacher, had time to speak.

After five minutes he said, "Shirley?"

"What?" I whispered.

He said, "My! My! Shirley Abramowitz! They told me you had a particularly loud, clear voice and read with lots of expression. Could that be true?"

15   "Oh yes," I whispered.

"In that case, don't be silly; I might very well be your teacher someday. Speak up; speak up."

"Yes," I shouted.

"More like it," he said. "Now, Shirley, can you put a ribbon in your hair or a bobby pin? It's too messy."

"Yes!" I bawled.

20   "Now, now, calm down." He turned to the class. "Children, not a sound. Open at page 39. Read till 52. When you finish, start again." He looked me over once more. "Now, Shirley, you know, I suppose, that Christmas is coming. We are preparing a beautiful play. Most of the parts have been given out. But I still need a child with a strong voice, lots of stamina. Do you know what stamina is? You do? Smart kid. You know, I heard you read 'The Lord is my shepherd' in Assembly yesterday. I was very impressed. Wonderful delivery. Mrs. Jordan, your teacher, speaks highly of you. Now listen to me, Shirley Abramowitz, if you want to take the part and be in the play, repeat after me, 'I swear to work harder than I ever did before.' "

I looked to heaven and said at once, "Oh, I swear." I kissed my pinky and looked at God.

"That is an actor's life, my dear," he explained. "Like a soldier's, never tardy or disobedient to his general, the director. Everything," he said, "absolutely everything will depend on you."

That afternoon, all over the building, children scraped and scrubbed the turkeys and the sheaves of corn off the schoolroom windows. Goodbye Thanksgiving. The next morning a monitor brought red paper and green paper from the office. We made new shapes and hung them on the walls and glued them to the doors.

The teachers became happier and happier. Their heads were ringing like the bells of childhood. My best friend Evie was prone to evil, but she did not get a single demerit for whispering. We learned "Holy Night" without an error. "How wonderful!" said Miss Glace, the student teacher. "To think that some of you don't even speak the language!" We learned "Deck the Halls" and "Hark! The Herald Angels". . . . They weren't ashamed and we weren't embarrassed.

25   Oh, but when my mother heard about it all, she said to my father: "Misha, you don't know what's going on there. Cramer is the head of the Tickets Committee."

"Who?" asked my father. "Cramer? Oh yes, an active woman."

"Active? Active has to have a reason. Listen," she said sadly, "I'm surprised to see my neighbors making tra-la-la for Christmas."

My father couldn't think of what to say to that. Then he decided: "You're in America! Clara, you wanted to come here. In Palestine the Arabs would be eating you alive. Europe you had pogroms. Argentina is full of Indians. Here you got Christmas. . . . Some joke, ha?"

"Very funny, Misha. What is becoming of you? If we came to a new country a long time ago to run away from tyrants, and instead we fall into a creeping pogrom, that our children learn a lot of lies, so what's the joke? Ach, Misha, your idealism is going away."

"So is your sense of humor."   30

"That I never had, but idealism you had a lot of."

"I'm the same Misha Abramovitch, I didn't change an iota. Ask anyone."

"Only ask me," says my mama, may she rest in peace. "I got the answer."

Meanwhile the neighbors had to think of what to say too.

Marty's father said: "You know, he has a very important part, my boy."   35

"Mine also," said Mr. Sauerfeld.

"Not my boy!" said Mrs. Klieg. "I said to him no. The answer is no. When I say no! I mean no!"

The rabbi's wife said, "It's disgusting!" But no one listened to her. Under the narrow sky of God's great wisdom she wore a strawberry-blond wig.

Every day was noisy and full of experience. I was Right-hand Man. Mr. Hilton said: "How could I get along without you, Shirley?"

He said: "Your mother and father ought to get down on their knees every night and   40 thank God for giving them a child like you."

He also said: "You're absolutely a pleasure to work with, my dear, dear child."

Sometimes he said: "For God's sakes, what did I do with the script? Shirley! Shirley! Find it."

Then I answered quietly: "Here it is, Mr. Hilton."

Once in a while, when he was very tired, he would cry out: "Shirley, I'm just tired of screaming at those kids. Will you tell Ira Pushkov not to come in till Lester points to that star the second time?"

Then I roared: "Ira Pushkov, what's the matter with you? Dope! Mr. Hilton told you five   45 times already, don't come in till Lester points to that star the second time."

"Ach, Clara," my father asked, "what does she do there till six o'clock she can't even put the plates on the table?"

"Christmas," said my mother coldly.

"Ho! Ho!" my father said. "Christmas. What's the harm? After all, history teaches everyone. We learn from reading this is a holiday from pagan times also, candles, lights, even Chanukah. So we learn it's not altogether Christian. So if they think it's a private holiday, they're only ignorant, not patriotic. What belongs to history, belongs to all men. You want to go back to the Middle Ages? Is it better to shave your head with a secondhand razor? Does it hurt Shirley to learn to speak up? It does not. So maybe someday she won't live between the kitchen and the shop. She's not a fool!"

I thank you, Papa, for your kindness. It is true about me to this day. I am foolish but I am not a fool.

That night my father kissed me and said with great interest in my career, "Shirley,   50 tomorrow's your big day. Congrats."

"Save it," my mother said. Then she shut all the windows in order to prevent tonsillitis.

In the morning it snowed. On the street corner a tree had been decorated for us by a kind city administration. In order to miss its chilly shadow our neighbors walked three blocks east to buy a loaf of bread. The butcher pulled down black window shades to keep the colored lights from shining on his chickens. Oh, not me. On the way to school, with both my hands I tossed it a kiss of tolerance. Poor thing, it was a stranger in Egypt.

I walked straight into the auditorium past the staring children. "Go ahead, Shirley!" said the monitors. Four boys, big for their age, had already started work as propmen and stage-hands.

Mr. Hilton was very nervous. He was not even happy. Whatever he started to say ended in a sideward look of sadness. He sat slumped in the middle of the first row and asked me to help Miss Glace. I did this, although she thought my voice too resonant and said, "Show-off!"

55   Parents began to arrive long before we were ready. They wanted to make a good impression. From among the yards of drapes I peeked out at the audience. I saw my embarrassed mother.

Ira, Lester, and Meyer were pasted to their beards by Miss Glace. She almost forgot to thread the star on its wire, but I reminded her. I coughed a few times to clear my throat. Miss Glace looked around and saw that everyone was in costume and on line waiting to play his part. She whispered, "All right. . . " Then:

Jackie Sauerfeld, the prettiest boy in first grade, parted the curtains with his skinny elbow and in a high voice sang out:

"Parents dear
We are here
To make a Christmas play in time.
It we give
In narrative
And illustrate with pantomine."

He disappeared.

My voice burst immediately from the wings to the great shock of Ira, Lester, and Meyer, who were waiting for it but were surprised all the same.

60   "I remember, I remember, the house where I was born . . ."

Miss Glace yanked the curtain open and there it was, the house—an old hayloft, where Celia Kornbluh lay in the straw with Cindy Lou, her favorite doll. Ira, Lester, and Meyer moved slowly from the wings toward her, sometimes pointing to a moving star and sometimes ahead to Cindy Lou.

It was a long story and it was a sad story. I carefully pronounced all the words about my lonesome childhood, while little Eddie Braunstein wandered upstage and down with his shepherd's stick, looking for sheep. I brought up lonesomeness again, and not being understood at all except by some women everybody hated. Eddie was too small for that and Marty Groff took his place, wearing his father's prayer shawl. I announced twelve friends, and half the boys in the fourth grade gathered round Marty, who stood on an orange crate while my voice harangued. Sorrowful and loud, I declaimed about love and God and Man, but because of the terrible deceit of Abie Stock we came suddenly to a famous moment. Marty, whose remembering tongue I was, waited at the foot of the cross. He stared desperately at the audience. I groaned, "My God, my God, why hast thou forsaken me?" The soldiers who were sheiks grabbed poor Marty to pin him up to die, but he wrenched free, turned again to the audience, and spread his arms aloft to show despair and the end. I murmured at the top of my voice, "The rest is silence, but as everyone in this room, in this city—in this world—now knows, I shall have life eternal."

That night Mrs. Kornbluh visited our kitchen for a glass of tea.

"How's the virgin?" asked my father with a look of concern.

"For a man with a daughter, you got a fresh mouth, Abramovitch."   65

"Here," said my father kindly, "have some lemon, it'll sweeten your disposition."

They debated a little in Yiddish, then fell in a puddle of Russian and Polish. What I understood next was my father, who said, "Still and all, it was certainly a beautiful affair, you have to admit, introducing us to the beliefs of a different culture."

"Well, yes," said Mrs. Kornbluh. "The only thing . . . you know Charlie Turner—that cute boy in Celia's class—a couple others? They got very small parts or no part at all. In very bad taste, it seemed to me. After all, it's their religion."

"Ach," explained my mother, "what could Mr. Hilton do? They got very small voices; after all, why should they holler? The English language they know from the beginning by heart. They're blond like angels. You think it's so important they should get in the play? Christmas . . . the whole piece of goods . . . they own it."

I listened and listened until I couldn't listen any more. Too sleepy, I climbed out of   70
bed and kneeled. I made a little church of my hands and said, "Hear, O Israel. . ." Then I called out in Yiddish, "Please, good night, good night. Ssh." My father said, "Ssh yourself," and slammed the kitchen door.

I was happy. I fell asleep at once. I had prayed for everybody: my talking family, cousins far away, passersby, and all the lonesome Christians. I expected to be heard. My voice was certainly the loudest.

What part is the young narrator asked to play? Is this a Christmas pageant or a Christian pageant? What might the names of the teachers and the names of the students tell you about this school? What does the narrator's mother mean when she calls Christian America "that creeping pogrom?" What if this story were about Muslim children? Since the terrorism of September 11, 2001, we are all suddenly much more aware of the American Muslim community. Many good American Muslim citizens went to great lengths to demonstrate their patriotism after the hijackings. How might they do that? What does it say about all Americans that Muslim Americans felt the need to prove themselves? What does it say in the story when all the Jewish parents permit their children to be in a play about Jesus?

READING ABOUT OUR DIVERSITIES: EXPECTATIONS AND CLUES

We black folk, our history and our present being, are mirror of all the manifold experiences of America. What we want, what we represent, what we endure is what America is.

—Richard Wright, *12 Million Black Voices*

For some time now I have been thinking about the validity or vulnerability of a certain set of assumptions conventionally accepted among literary historians and critics and circulated as "knowledge." This knowledge holds that traditional, canonical American literature is free of, uninformed, and unshaped by the four-hundred-year-old presence of, first, Africans and then African-Americans in the United States. [. . .] The contemplation of this black presence is central to any understanding of our national literature and should not be permitted to hover at the margins of the literary imagination.

—Toni Morrison, "Black Matters," *Playing in the Dark*

*Toni Morrison: (1931–)
Winner of the 1993 Nobel Prize for Literature (the only African American to do so), Morrison is the author of award-winning novels, plays, and critical essays; she has served as an editor for Random House and teaches at Princeton University.

Toni Morrison* is a Nobel Prize–winning American scholar and novelist who manages to remove all indicators of race from her short story "Recitatif." As a result, this story offers a great opportunity to consider how we define people without context, comparison, or opposition. In other words, when we lose the ability to say definitively who someone is, we also lose the ability to say who someone is not. This is not just a matter of who is black and who is white; rather, it is a matter of two crucial, opposing values in America—the importance of the individual to maintain identity through difference balanced against the importance of many individuals coming together as equals and forming one cohesive society. *As you read the story, be aware of your own responses to Twyla and Roberta.*

Toni Morrison

Recitatif

My mother danced all night and Roberta's was sick. That's why we were taken to St. Bonny's. People want to put their arms around you when you tell them you were in a shelter, but it really wasn't bad. No big long room with one hundred beds like Bellevue. There were four to a room, and when Roberta and me came, there was a shortage of state kids, so we were the only ones assigned to 406 and could go from bed to bed if we wanted to. And we wanted to, too. We changed beds every night and for the whole four months we were there we never picked one out as our own permanent bed.

It didn't start out that way. The minute I walked in and the Big Bozo introduced us, I got sick to my stomach. It was one thing to be taken out of your own bed early in the morning—it was something else to be stuck in a strange place with a girl from a whole other race. And Mary, that's my mother, she was right. Every now and then she would stop dancing long enough to tell me something important and one of the things she said was that they never washed their hair and they smelled funny. Roberta sure did. Smell funny, I mean. So when the Big Bozo (nobody ever called her Mrs. Itkin, just like nobody ever said St. Bonaventure)—when she said, "Twyla, this is Roberta. Roberta, this is Twyla. Make each other welcome." I said, "My mother won't like you putting me in here."

"Good," said Bozo. "Maybe then she'll come and take you home."

How's that for mean? If Roberta had laughed I would have killed her, but she didn't. She just walked over to the window and stood with her back to us.

"Turn around," said the Bozo. "Don't be rude. Now Twyla. Roberta. When you hear   5
a loud buzzer, that's the call for dinner. Come down to the first floor. Any fights and no
movie." And then, just to make sure we knew what we would be missing, "The Wizard
of Oz."

Roberta must have thought I meant that my mother would be mad about my being
put in the shelter. Not about rooming with her, because as soon as Bozo left she came
over to me and said, "Is your mother sick too?"

"No," I said. "She just likes to dance all night."

"Oh," she nodded her head and I liked the way she understood things so fast. So for
the moment it didn't matter that we looked like salt and pepper standing there and that's
what the other kids called us sometimes. We were eight years old and got F's all the time.
Me because I couldn't remember what I read or what the teacher said. And Roberta
because she couldn't read at all and didn't even listen to the teacher. She wasn't good at
anything except jacks, at which she was a killer: pow scoop pow scoop pow scoop.

We didn't like each other all that much at first, but nobody wanted to play with us
because we weren't real orphans with beautiful dead parents in the sky. We were dumped.
Even the New York City Puerto Ricans and the upstate Indians ignored us. All kinds of kids
were in there, black ones, white ones, even two Koreans. The food was good, though. At
least I thought so. Roberta hated it and left whole pieces of things on her plate: Spam, Sal-
isbury steak—even jello with fruit cocktail in it, and she didn't care if I ate what she wouldn't.
Mary's idea of supper was popcorn and a can of Yoo-Hoo. Hot mashed potatoes and two
weenies was like Thanksgiving for me.

It really wasn't bad, St. Bonny's. The big girls on the second floor pushed us around   10
now and then. But that was all. They wore lipstick and eyebrow pencil and wobbled their
knees while they watched TV. Fifteen, sixteen, even, some of them were. They were put-
out girls, scared runaways most of them. Poor little girls who fought their uncles off but
looked tough to us, and mean. God did they look mean. The staff tried to keep them separate from the younger children, but sometimes they caught us watching them in the
orchard where they played radios and danced with each other. They'd light out after us
and pull our hair or twist our arms. We were scared of them, Roberta and me, but neither of us wanted the other one to know it. So we got a good list of dirty names we could
shout back when we ran from them through the orchard. I used to dream a lot and almost
always the orchard was there. Two acres, four maybe, of these little apple trees. Hundreds
of them. Empty and crooked like beggar women when I first came to St. Bonny's but fat
with flowers when I left. I don't know why I dreamt about that orchard so much. Nothing
really happened there. Nothing all that important, I mean. Just the big girls dancing and
playing the radio. Roberta and me watching. Maggie fell down there once. The kitchen
woman with legs like parentheses. And the big girls laughed at her. We should have helped
her up, I know, but we were scared of those girls with lipstick and eyebrow pencil. Maggie
couldn't talk. The kids said she had her tongue cut out, but I think she was just born that
way: mute. She was old and sandy-colored and she worked in the kitchen. I don't know
if she was nice or not. I just remember her legs like parentheses and how she rocked
when she walked. She worked from early in the morning till two o'clock, and if she was
late, if she had too much cleaning and didn't get out till two-fifteen or so, she'd cut
through the orchard so she wouldn't miss her bus and have to wait another hour. She

wore this really stupid little hat—a kid's hat with ear flaps—and she wasn't much taller than we were. A really awful little hat. Even for a mute, it was dumb—dressing like a kid and never saying anything at all.

"But what if somebody tries to kill her?" I used to wonder about that. "Or what if she wants to cry? Can she cry?"

"Sure," Roberta said. "But just tears. No sounds come out."

"She can't scream?"

"Nope. Nothing."

15 "Can she hear?"

"I guess."

"Let's call her," I said. And we did.

"Dummy! Dummy!" She never turned her head.

"Bow legs! Bow legs!" Nothing. She just rocked on, the chin straps of her baby-boy hat swaying from side to side. I think we were wrong. I think she could hear and didn't let on. And it shames me even now to think there was somebody in there after all who heard us call her those names and couldn't tell on us.

20 We got along all right, Roberta and me. Changed beds every night, got F's in civics and communication skills and gym. The Bozo was disappointed in us, she said. Out of 130 of us state cases, 90 were under twelve. Almost all were real orphans with beautiful dead parents in the sky. We were the only ones dumped and the only ones with F's in three classes including gym. So we got along—what with her leaving whole pieces of things on her plate and being nice about not asking questions.

I think it was the day before Maggie fell down that we found out our mothers were coming to visit us on the same Sunday. We had been at the shelter twenty-eight days (Roberta twenty-eight and a half) and this was their first visit with us. Our mothers would come at ten o'clock in time for chapel, then lunch with us in the teachers' lounge. I thought if my dancing mother met her sick mother it might be good for her. And Roberta thought her sick mother would get a big bang out of a dancing one. We got excited about it and curled each others hair. After breakfast we sat on the bed watching the road from the window. Roberta's socks were still wet. She washed them the night before and put them on the radiator to dry. They hadn't, but she put them on anyway because their tops were so pretty—scalloped in pink. Each of us had a purple construction-paper basket that we had made in craft class. Mine had a yellow crayon rabbit on it. Roberta's had eggs with wiggly lines of color. Inside were cellophane grass and just the jelly beans because I'd eaten the two marshmallow eggs they gave us. The Big Bozo came herself to get us. Smiling she told us we looked very nice and to come downstairs. We were so surprised by the smile we'd never seen before, neither of us moved.

"Don't you want to see your mommies?"

I stood up first and spilled the jelly beans all over the floor. Bozo's smile disappeared while we scrambled to get the candy up off the floor and put it back in the grass.

She escorted us downstairs to the first floor, where the other girls were lining up to file into the chapel. A bunch of grown-ups stood to one side. Viewers mostly. The old biddies who wanted servants and the fags who wanted company looking for children they might want to adopt. Once in a while a grandmother. Almost never anybody young or anybody whose face wouldn't scare you in the night. Because if any of the real orphans had young relatives they wouldn't be real orphans. I saw Mary right away. She had on those green slacks I hated and hated even more now because didn't she know we were going to chapel? And that fur jacket with the pocket linings so ripped she had to pull to get her hands out of them. But her face was pretty—like always, and she smiled and waved like she was the little girl looking for her mother—not me.

I walked slowly, trying not to drop the jelly beans and hoping the paper handle would hold. I had to use my last Chiclet because by the time I finished cutting everything out, all the Elmer's was gone. I am left-handed and the scissors never worked for me. It didn't matter, though; I might just as well have chewed the gum. Mary dropped to her knees and grabbed me, mashing the basket, the jelly beans, and the grass into her ratty fur jacket.

"Twyla, baby. Twyla, baby!"

I could have killed her. Already I heard the big girls in the orchard the next time saying, "Twyyyyyla, baby!" But I couldn't stay mad at Mary while she was smiling and hugging me and smelling of Lady Esther dusting powder. I wanted to stay buried in her fur all day.

To tell the truth I forgot about Roberta. Mary and I got in line for the traipse into chapel and I was feeling proud because she looked so beautiful even in those ugly green slacks that made her behind stick out. A pretty mother on earth is better than a beautiful dead one in the sky even if she did leave you all alone to go dancing.

I felt a tap on my shoulder, turned, and saw Roberta smiling. I smiled back, but not too much lest somebody think this visit was the biggest thing that ever happened in my life. Then Roberta said, "Mother, I want you to meet my roommate, Twyla. And that's Twyla's mother."

I looked up it seemed for miles. She was big. Bigger than any man and on her chest was the biggest cross I'd ever seen. I swear it was six inches long each way. And in the crook of her arm was the biggest Bible ever made.

Mary, simple-minded as ever, grinned and tried to yank her hand out of the pocket with the raggedy lining—to shake hands, I guess. Roberta's mother looked down at me and then looked down at Mary too. She didn't say anything, just grabbed Roberta with her Bible-free hand and stepped out of line, walking quickly to the rear of it. Mary was still grinning because she's not too swift when it comes to what's really going on. Then this light bulb goes off in her head and she says "That bitch!" really loud and us almost in the chapel now. Organ music whining; the Bonny Angels singing sweetly. Everybody in the world turned around to look. And Mary would have kept it up—kept calling names if I hadn't squeezed her hand as hard as I could. That helped a little, but she still twitched and crossed and uncrossed her legs all through service. Even groaned a couple of times. Why did I think she would come there and act right? Slacks. No hat like the grandmothers and viewers, and groaning all the while. When we stood for hymns she kept her mouth shut. Wouldn't even look at the words on the page. She actually reached in her purse for a mirror to check her lipstick. All I could think of was that she really needed to be killed. The sermon lasted a year, and I knew the real orphans were looking smug again.

We were supposed to have lunch in the teachers' lounge, but Mary didn't bring anything, so we picked fur and cellophane grass off the mashed jelly beans and ate them. I could have killed her. I sneaked a look at Roberta. Her mother had brought chicken legs and ham sandwiches and oranges and a whole box of chocolate-covered grahams. Roberta drank milk from a thermos while her mother read the Bible to her.

Things are not right. The wrong food is always with the wrong people. Maybe that's why I got into waitress work later—to match up the right people with the right food. Roberta just let those chicken legs sit there, but she did bring a stack of grahams up to me later when the visit was over. I think she was sorry that her mother would not shake my mother's hand. And I liked that and I liked the fact that she didn't say a word about Mary groaning all the way through the service and not bringing any lunch.

Roberta left in May when the apple trees were heavy and white. On her last day we went to the orchard to watch the big girls smoke and dance by the radio. It didn't matter they said, "Twyyyyyla, baby." We sat on the ground and breathed. Lady Esther. Apple blossoms. I still go soft when I smell one or the other. Roberta was going home. The big cross and the big Bible was coming to get her and she seemed sort of glad and sort of not. I thought I would die in that room of four beds without her and I knew Bozo had plans to move some other dumped kid in there with me. Roberta promised to write every day, which was really sweet of her because she couldn't read a lick so how could she write anybody. I would have drawn pictures and sent them to her but she never gave me her address. Little by little she faded. Her wet socks with the pink scalloped tops and her big serious-looking eyes—that's all I could catch when I tried to bring her to mind.

35   I was working behind the counter at the Howard Johnson's on the Thruway just before the Kingston exit. Not a bad job. Kind of a long ride from Newburgh, but okay once I got there. Mine was the second night shift—eleven to seven. Very light until a Greyhound checked in for breakfast around six-thirty. At that hour the sun was all the way clear of the hills behind the restaurant The place looked better at night—more like shelter—but I loved it when the sun broke in, even if it did show all the cracks in the vinyl and the speckled floor looked dirty no matter what the mop boy did.

It was August and a bus crowd was just unloading. They would stand around a long while: going to the john, and looking at gifts and junk-for-sale machines, reluctant to sit down so soon. Even to eat. I was trying to fill the coffee pots and get them all situated on the electric burners when I saw her. She was sitting in a booth smoking a cigarette with two guys smothered in head and facial hair. Her own hair was so big and wild I could hardly see her face. But the eyes. I would know them anywhere. She had on a powder-blue halter and shorts outfit and earrings the size of bracelets. Talk about lipstick and eyebrow pencil. She made the big girls look like nuns. I couldn't get off the counter until seven o'clock, but I kept watching the booth in case they got up to leave before that. My replacement was on time for a change, so I counted and stacked my receipts as fast as I could and signed off. I walked over to the booth, smiling and wondering if she would remember me. Or even if she wanted to remember me. Maybe she didn't want to be reminded of St. Bonny's or to have anybody know she was ever there. I know I never talked about it to anybody.

I put my hands in my apron pockets and leaned against the back of the booth facing them.

"Roberta? Roberta Fisk?"

She looked up. "Yeah?"

40   "Twyla."

She squinted for a second and then said, "Wow."

"Remember me?"

"Sure. Hey. Wow."

"It's been a while," I said, and gave a smile to the two hairy guys.

"Yeah. Wow. You work here?"   45

"Yeah," I said. "I live in Newburgh."

"Newburgh? No kidding?" She laughed then a private laugh that included the guys but only the guys, and they laughed with her. What could I do but laugh too and wonder why I was standing there with my knees showing out from under that uniform. Without looking I could see the blue and white triangle on my head, my hair shapeless in a net, my ankles thick in white oxfords. Nothing could have been less sheer than my stockings. There was this silence that came down right after I laughed. A silence it was her turn to fill up. With introductions, maybe, to her boyfriends or an invitation to sit down and have a Coke. Instead she lit a cigarette off the one she'd just finished and said, "We're on our way to the Coast. He's got an appointment with Hendrix." She gestured casually toward the boy next to her.

"Hendrix? Fantastic," I said. "Really fantastic. What's she doing now?"

Roberta coughed on her cigarette and the two guys rolled their eyes up at the ceiling.

"Hendrix. Jimi Hendrix, asshole. He's only the biggest—Oh, wow. Forget it."   50

I was dismissed without anyone saying goodbye, so I thought I would do it for her.

"How's your mother?" I asked. Her grin cracked her whole face. She swallowed. "Fine," she said. "How's yours?"

"Pretty as a picture," I said and turned away. The backs of my knees were damp. Howard Johnson's really was a dump in the sunlight.

James is as comfortable as a house slipper. He liked my cooking and I liked his big loud family. They have lived in Newburgh all of their lives and talk about it the way people do who have always known a home. His grandmother has a porch swing older than his father and when they talk about streets and avenues and buildings they call them names they no longer have. They still call the A & P Rico's because it stands on property once a mom and pop store owned by Mr. Rico. And they call the new community college Town Hall because it once was. My mother-in-law puts up jelly and cucumbers and buys butter wrapped in cloth from a dairy. James and his father talk about fishing and baseball and I can see them all together on the Hudson in a raggedy skiff. Half the population of Newburgh is on welfare now, but to my husband's family it was still some upstate paradise of a time long past, a time of ice houses and vegetable wagons, coal furnaces and children weeding gardens. When our son was born my mother-in-law gave me the crib blanket that had been hers.

But the town they remembered had changed. Something quick was in the air. Mag-   55
nificent old houses, so ruined they had become shelter for squatters and rent risks, were bought and renovated. Smart IBM people moved out of their suburbs back into the city and put shutters up and herb gardens in their backyards. A brochure came in the mail announcing the opening of a Food Emporium. Gourmet food it said—and listed items the rich IBM crowd would want. It was located in a new mall at the edge of town and I drove out to shop there one day—just to see. It was late in June. After the tulips were gone and the Queen Elizabeth roses were open everywhere. I trailed my cart along the aisle tossing in smoked oysters and Robert's sauce and things I knew would sit in my cupboard for years. Only when I found some Klondike ice cream bars did I feel less guilty about spending James's fireman's salary so foolishly. My father-in-law ate them with the same gusto little Joseph did.

Waiting in the check-out line I heard a voice say, "Twyla!"

The classical music piped over the aisle had affected me and the woman leaning toward me was dressed to kill. Diamonds on her hand, a smart white summer dress. "I'm Mrs. Benson," I said.

"Ho. Ho. The Big Bozo," she sang.

For a split second I didn't know what she was talking about. She had a bunch of asparagus and two cartons of fancy water.

60   "Roberta!"

"Right."

"For heaven's sake. Roberta."

"You look great," she said.

"So do you. Where are you? Here? In Newburgh?"

65   "Yes. Over in Annandale."

I was opening my mouth to say more when the cashier called my attention to her empty counter.

"Meet you outside." Roberta pointed her finger and went into the express line.

I placed the groceries and kept myself from glancing around to check Roberta's progress. I remembered Howard Johnson's and looking for a chance to speak only to be greeted with a stingy "wow." But she was waiting for me and her huge hair was sleek now, smooth around a small, nicely shaped head. Shoes, dress, everything lovely and summery and rich. I was dying to know what happened to her, how she got from Jimi Hendrix to Annandale, a neighborhood full of doctors and IBM executives. Easy, I thought. Everything is so easy for them. The think they own the world.

"How long," I asked her. "How long have you been here?"

70   "A year. I got married to a man who lives here. And you, you're married too, right? Benson, you said."

"Yeah. James Benson."

"And is he nice?"

"Oh, is he nice?"

"Well is he?" Roberta's eyes were steady as though she really meant the question and wanted an answer.

75   "He's wonderful, Roberta. Wonderful."

"So you're happy."

"Very."

"That's good," she said and nodded her head. "I always hoped you'd be happy. Any kids? I know you have kids."

"One. A boy. How about you?

80   "Four."

"Four?"

She laughed. "Step kids. He's a widower."

"Oh."

"Got a minute? Let's have coffee."

85   I thought about the Klondikes melting and the inconvenience of going all the way to my car and putting the bags in the trunk. Served me right for buying all that stuff I didn't need. Roberta was ahead of me.

"Put them in my car. It's right here."

And then I saw the dark blue limousine.

"You married a Chinaman?"

"No," she laughed, "He's the driver."

"Oh, my. If the Big Bozo could see you now." 90

We both giggled. Really giggled. Suddenly, in just a pulse beat, twenty years disappeared and all of it came rushing back. The big girls (whom we called gar girls—Robert's misheard word for the evil stone faces described in a civics class) there dancing in the orchard, the ploppy mashed potatoes, the double weenies, the Spam with pineapple. We went into the coffee shop holding on to one another and I tried to think why we were so glad to see each other this time and not before. Once, twelve years ago, we passed like strangers. A black girl and a white girl meeting in a Howard Johnson's on the road and having nothing to say. One in a blue and white triangle waitress hat—the other on her way to see Hendrix. Now we were behaving like sisters separated for much too long. Those four short months were nothing in time. Maybe it was the thing itself. Just being there, together. Two little girls who knew what nobody else in the world knew—how not to ask questions. How to believe what had to be believed. There was politeness in that reluctance and generosity as well. Is your mother sick too? No, she dances all night. Oh—and an understanding nod.

We sat in a booth by the window and fell into recollection like veterans.

"Did you ever learn to read?"

"Watch." She picked up the menu. "Special of the day. Cream of corn soup. Entrees. Two dots and a wriggly line. Quiche. Chef salad, scallops . . . "

I was laughing and applauding when the waitress came up. 95

"Remember the Easter baskets?"

"And how we tried to *introduce* them?"

"Your mother with that cross like two telephone poles."

"And yours with those tight slacks."

We laughed so loudly heads turned and made the laughter harder to suppress. 100

"What happened to the Jimi Hendrix date?"

Roberta made a blow-out sound with her lips.

"When he died I thought about you."

"Oh, you heard about him finally?"

"Finally. Come on, I was a small-town country waitress." 105

"And I was a small-town country dropout. God, were we wild. I still don't know how I got out of there alive."

"But you did."

"I did. I really did. Now I'm Mrs. Kenneth Norton."

"Sounds like a mouthful."

"It is." 110

"Servants and all?"

Roberta held up two fingers.

"Ow! What does he do?"

"Computers and stuff. What do I know?"

"I don't remember a hell of a lot from those days, but Lord, St. Bonny's is as clear as 115 daylight. Remember Maggie? The day she fell down and those gar girls laughed at her?"

Roberta looked up from her salad and stared at me. "Maggie didn't fall," she said.

"Yes, she did. You remember."

"No, Twyla. They knocked her down. Those girls pushed her down and tore her clothes. In the orchard."

"I don't—that's not what happened."

120   "Sure it is. In the orchard. Remember how scared we were?"

"Wait a minute. I don't remember any of that."

"And Bozo was fired."

"You're crazy. She was there when I left. You left before me."

"I went back. You weren't there when they fired Bozo."

125   "What?"

"Twice. Once for a year when I was about ten, another for two months when I was fourteen. That's when I ran away."

"You ran away from St. Bonny's?"

"I had to. What do you want? Me dancing in that orchard?"

"Are you sure about Maggie?"

130   "Of course I'm sure. You've blocked it, Twyla. It happened. Those girls had behavior problems, you know."

"Didn't they, though. But why can't I remember the Maggie thing?"

"Believe me. It happened. And we were there."

"Who did you room with when you went back?" I asked her as if I would know her. The Maggie thing was troubling me.

"Creeps. They tickled themselves in the night."

135   My ears were itching and I wanted to go home suddenly. This was all very well but she couldn't just comb her hair, wash her face and pretend everything was hunky-dory. After the Howard Johnson's snub. And no apology. Nothing.

"Were you on dope or what that time at Howard Johnson's?" I tried to make my voice sound friendlier than I felt.

"Maybe, a little. I never did drugs much. Why?"

"I don't know; you acted sort of like you didn't want to know me then."

"Oh, Twyla, you know how it was in those days: black—white. You know how everything was."

140   But I didn't know. I thought it was just the opposite. Busloads of blacks and whites came into Howard Johnson's together. They roamed together then: students, musicians, lovers, protestors. You got to see everything at Howard Johnson's and blacks were very friendly with whites in those days. But sitting there with nothing on my plate but two hard tomato wedges wondering about the melting Klondikes it seemed childish remembering the slight. We went to her car, and with the help of the driver, got my stuff into my station wagon.

"We'll keep in touch this time," she said.

"Sure," I said. "Sure. Give me a call."

"I will," she said, and then just as I was sliding behind the wheel, she leaned into the window. "By the way. Your mother. Did she ever stop dancing?"

I shook my head. "No. Never."

145   Roberta nodded.

"And yours? Did she ever get well?"

She smiled a tiny sad smile. "No. She never did. Look, call me, okay?"

"Okay," I said, but I knew I wouldn't. Roberta had messed up my past somehow with that business about Maggie. I wouldn't forget a thing like that. Would I?

Strife came to us that fall. At least that's what the paper called it. Strife. Racial strife. The word made me think of a bird—a big shrieking bird out of 1,000,000,000 B.C. Flapping its wings and cawing. Its eye with no lid always bearing down on you. All day it screeched and at night it slept on the rooftops. It woke you in the morning and from the Today show to the eleven o'clock news it kept you an awful company. I couldn't figure it out from one day to the next. I knew I was supposed to feel something strong, but I didn't know what, and James wasn't any help. Joseph was on the list of kids to be transferred form the junior high school to another one at some far-out-of-the-way place and I thought it was a good thing until I heard it was a bad thing. I mean I didn't know. All the schools seemed dumps to me, and the fact that one was nicer looking didn't hold much weight. But the papers were full of it and then the kids began to get jumpy. In August, mind you. Schools weren't even open yet. I thought Joseph might be frightened to go over there, but he didn't seem scared so I forgot about it, until I found myself driving along Hudson Street out there by the school they were trying to integrate and saw a line of women marching. And who do you suppose was in line, big as life, holding a sign in front of her bigger than her mother's cross? MOTHERS HAVE RIGHTS TOO! it said.

I drove on, and then changed my mind. I circled the block, slowed down, and honked my horn.   150

Roberta looked over and when she saw me she waved. I didn't wave back, but I didn't move either. She handed her sign to another woman and came over to me where I was parked.

"Hi."

"What are you doing?"

"Picketing. What's it look like?"

"What for?"   155

"What do you mean, 'What for?' They want to take my kids and send them out of the neighborhood. They don't want to go."

"So what if they go to another school? My boy's being bussed too, and I don't mind. Why should you?"

"It's not about us, Twyla. Me and you. It's about our kids."

"What's more us than that?"

"Well, it is a free country."   160

"Not yet, but it will be."

"What the hell does that mean? I'm not doing anything to you."

"You really think that?"

"I know it."

"I wonder what made me think you were different."   165

"I wonder what made me think you were different."

"Look at them," I said. "Just look. Who do they think they are? Swarming all over the place like they own it. And now they think they can decide where my child goes to school. Look at them, Roberta. They're Bozos."

Roberta turned around and looked at the women. Almost all of them were standing still now, waiting. Some were even edging toward us. Roberta looked at me out of some refrigerator behind her eyes. "No, they're not. They're just mothers."

"And what am I? Swiss cheese."

"I used to curl your hair."   170

"I hated your hands in my hair."

The women were moving. Our faces looked mean to them of course and they looked as though they could not wait to throw themselves in front of a police car, or better yet, into my car and drag me away by my ankles. Now they surrounded my car and gently, gently began to rock it. I swayed back and forth like a sideways yo-yo. Automatically I reached for Roberta, like the old days in the orchard, when they saw us watching them and we had to get out of there, and if one of us fell the other pulled her up and if one of us was caught the other stayed to kick and scratch, and neither would leave the other behind. My arm shot out of the car window but no receiving hand was there. Roberta was looking at me sway from side to side in the car and her face was still. My purse slid from the car seat down under the dashboard. The four policemen who had been drinking Tab in their car finally got the message and strolled over, forcing their way through the women. Quietly, firmly they spoke. "Okay, ladies. Back in line or off the streets."

Some of them went away willingly; others had to be urged away from the car doors and the hood. Roberta didn't move. She was looking steadily at me. I was fumbling to turn on the ignition, which wouldn't catch because the gearshift was still in drive. The seats of the car were a mess because the swaying had thrown my grocery coupons all over it and my purse was sprawled on the floor.

"Maybe I am different now, Twyla. But you're not. You're the same little state kid who kicked a poor old black lady when she was down on the ground. You kicked a black lady and you have the nerve to call me a bigot."

175 The coupons were everywhere and the guts of my purse were bunched under the dashboard. What was she saying? Black? Maggie wasn't black.

"She wasn't black," I said.

"Like hell she wasn't, and you kicked her. We both did. You kicked a black lady who couldn't even scream."

"Liar!"

"You're the liar! Why don't you just go on home and leave us alone, huh?"

180 She turned away and I skidded away from the curb. The next morning I went into the garage and cut the side out of the carton our portable TV had come in. It wasn't nearly big enough, but after a while I had a decent sign: red spray-painted letters on a white background—AND SO DO CHILDREN!!!! I meant just to go down to the school and tack it up somewhere so those cows on the picket line across the street could see it, but when I got there, some ten or so others had already assembled—protesting the cows across the street. Police permits and everything. I got in line and we strutted in time on our side while Roberta's group strutted on theirs. That first day we were all dignified, pretending the other side didn't exist. The second day there was name calling and finger gestures. But that was about all. People changed signs from time to time, but Roberta never did and neither did I. Actually my sign didn't make sense without Roberta's. "And so do children what?" one of the women on my side asked me. Have rights, I said, as though it was obvious.

Roberta didn't acknowledge my presence in any way and I got to thinking maybe she didn't know I was there. I began to pace myself in the line, jostling people one minute and lagging behind the next, so Roberta and I could reach the end of our respective lines at the same time and there would be a moment in our turn when we would face each other. Still, I couldn't tell whether she saw me and knew my sign was for her. The next day I went early before we were scheduled to assemble. I waited until she got there before I exposed my new creation. As soon as she hoisted her MOTHERS HAVE RIGHTS TOO I began to wave my new one, which said, HOW WOULD YOU KNOW? I know she saw that one, but I had gotten addicted now. My signs got crazier each day, and the women on my side decided that I was a kook. They couldn't make heads or tails out of my brilliant screaming posters.

I brought a painted sign in queenly red with huge black letters that said, IS YOUR MOTHER WELL? Roberta took her lunch break and didn't come back for the rest of the day or any day after. Two days later I stopped going too and couldn't have been missed because nobody understood my signs anyway.

It was a nasty six weeks. Classes were suspended and Joseph didn't go to anybody's school until October. The children—everybody's children—soon got bored with that extended vacation they thought was going to be so great. They looked at TV until their eyes flattened. I spent a couple of mornings tutoring my son, as the other mothers said we should. Twice I opened a text from last year that he had never turned in. Twice he yawned in my face. Other mothers organized living room sessions so the kids would keep up. None of the kids could concentrate so they drifted back to The Price is Right and The Brady Bunch. When the school finally opened there were fights once or twice and some sirens roared through the streets every once in a while. There were a lot of photographers from Albany. And just when ABC was about to send a news crew, the kids settled down like nothing in the world had happened. Joseph hung my HOW WOULD YOU KNOW? sign in his bedroom. I don't know what became of AND SO DO CHILDREN!!!! I think my father-in-law cleaned some fish on it. He was always puttering around in our garage. Each of his five children lived in Newburgh and he acted as though he had five extra homes.

I couldn't help looking for Roberta when Joseph graduated from high school, but I didn't see her. It didn't trouble me much what she had said to me in the car. I mean the kicking part. I know I didn't do that, I couldn't do that. But I was puzzled by her telling me Maggie was black. When I thought about it I actually couldn't be certain. She wasn't pitch-black, I knew, or I would have remembered that. What I remember was the kiddie hat, and the semicircle legs. I tried to reassure myself about the race thing for a long time until it dawned on me that the truth was already there, and Roberta knew it. I didn't attack her; I didn't join in with the gar girls and kick that lady, but I sure did want to. We watched and never tried to help her and never called for help. Maggie was my dancing mother. Deaf, I thought, and dumb. Nobody inside. Nobody who would hear you if you cried in the night. Nobody who could tell you anything important that you could use. Rocking, dancing, swaying as she walked. And when the gar girls pushed her down, and started rough-housing, I knew she wouldn't scream, couldn't—just like me—and I was glad about that.

We decided not to have a tree, because Christmas would be at my mother-in-law's 185 house, so why have a tree at both places? Joseph was at SUNY New Paltz and we had to economize, we said. But at the last minute, I changed my mind. Nothing could be that bad. So I rushed around town looking for a tree, something small but wide. By the time I found a place, it was snowing and very late. I dawdled like it was the most important purchase in the world and the tree man was fed up with me. Finally I chose one and had it tied onto the trunk of the car. I drove away slowly because the sand trucks were not out yet and the streets could be murder at the beginning of a snowfall. Downtown the streets were wide and rather empty except for a cluster of people coming out of the Newburgh Hotel. The one hotel in town that wasn't built out of cardboard and Plexiglass. A party, probably. The men huddled in the snow were dressed in tails and the women had on furs. Shiny things glittered from underneath their coats. It made me tired to look at them. Tired, tired, tired. On the next corner was a small diner with loops and loops of paper bells in the window. I stopped the car and went in. Just for a cup of coffee and twenty minutes of peace before I went home and tried to finish everything before Christmas Eve.

"Twyla?"

There she was. In a silvery evening gown and dark fur coat. A man and another woman were with her, the man fumbling for change to put in the cigarette machine. The woman was humming and tapping on the counter with her fingernails. They all looked a little bit drunk.

"Well. It's you."

"How are you."

190 I shrugged. "Pretty good. Frazzled. Christmas and all."

"Regular?" called the woman from the counter.

"Fine," Roberta called back and then, "Wait for me in the car."

She slipped into the booth beside me. "I have to tell you something, Twyla. I made up my mind if I ever saw you again, I'd tell you."

"I'd just as soon not hear anything, Roberta. It doesn't matter now, anyway."

195 "No," she said. "Not about that."

"Don't be long," said the woman. She carried two regulars to go and the man peeled his cigarette pack as they left.

"It's about St. Bonny's and Maggie."

"Oh, please."

"Listen to me. I really did think she was black. I didn't make that up. I really thought so. But now I can't be sure. I just remember her as old, so old. And because she couldn't talk—well, you know, I thought she was crazy. She'd been brought up in an institution like my mother was and like I thought I would be too. And you were right. We didn't kick her. It was the gar girls. Only them. But, well I wanted to. I really wanted them to hurt her. I said we did it, too. You and me, but that's not true. And I don't want you to carry that around. It was just that I wanted to do it so bad that day—wanting to is doing it."

200 Her eyes were watery from the drinks she'd had, I guess. I know it's that way with me. One glass of wine and I start bawling over the littlest thing.

"We were kids, Roberta."

"Yeah. Yeah. I know, just kids."

"Eight."

"Eight."

205 "And lonely."

"Scared, too."

She wiped her cheeks with the heel of her hand and smiled. "Well, that's all I wanted to say."

I nodded and couldn't think of any way to fill the silence that went from the diner past the paper bells on out into the snow. It was heavy now. I thought I'd better wait for the sand trucks before starting home.

"Thanks, Roberta."

210 "Sure."

"Did I tell you? My mother, she never did stop dancing."

"Yes. You told me. And mine, she never got well." Roberta lifted her hands from that tabletop and covered her face with her palms. When she took them away she really was crying. "Oh, shit, Twyla. Shit, shit, shit. What the hell happened to Maggie?"

Now that you have read the story, look at what might be considered indications of race: Twyla's mother (Mary) had warned Twyla that "they"

- Never washed their hair.
- Smelled funny.

When Mary came to visit, she wore

- Green slacks, that "made her behind stick out."
- A ratty fur jacket.

When Roberta's mother came to visit, she

- Wore very large cross around her neck—six inches in each direction.
- Carried "the biggest Bible ever made."

Roberta's mother refuses to shake hands with Mary, and Mary calls her a "bitch" under her breath.

For lunch,

- Mary brings nothing.
- Roberta's mother brings chicken legs, ham sandwiches, oranges, chocolate-covered grahams, and milk.

At the Howard Johnson's, Roberta's description includes the following hints:

- Big and wild hair that hid her face.
- A powder blue halter and shorts outfit.
- Earrings "the size of bracelets."
- Heavy use of eyebrow pencil and lipstick.

A few years later, Roberta's description is very different:

- Her huge hair is sleek and smooth.
- Her clothes are those of a rich woman.
- She lives in a neighborhood of doctors and IBM executives.
- She has a limousine with a Chinese driver.

Twyla says about Roberta:

- "Everything is so easy for them. They think they own the world."

Look at the excerpted list above. As you read through the descriptions, are you able to determine which girl is what race? What happens to the experience of your reading this story when you cannot determine race? For readers who visualize characters when they read, Twyla and Roberta may become impossible to see clearly. Does it really matter who is black and who is white? Is the difference and division between black Americans and white Americans simply one of contrast? How might other Americans—for instance, those who are Latino or Asian—place themselves in the black versus white conflicts of today? Is the story about race at all? Or is the story grounded in a friendship that falters because of life situations that have separated the two girls into two distinct socioeconomic environments?

All reading requires a kind of readiness; various texts ask questions of us, and we approach them with a set of preconceived assumptions. As we read, clues emerge to direct us in what and how to think, and in how to examine those assumptions. Reading about the many faces and voices of citizenship requires us to ask questions about the author, audience, purpose, point of view, and tone (see Chapter 2).

SORTING OUT OPINIONS, STEREOTYPES, JUDGMENTS, AND BELIEFS

Unless we are pushed to be consciously deliberate in our thinking, we travel through our days equipped with a set of assumptions about how our world makes sense. Left alone, we rarely examine our assumptions because there is no need to do so. However, as we interact with others, we often find that our assumptions are tested, challenged, and questioned. We respond in two ways: by offering our opinions, which may be based in stereotypes, and by making judgments, which are shaped by our beliefs.

By definition, **opinions*** are weak arguing tools because they are not based on positive knowledge and depend on our impressions, which can be formed by our stereotypes. **Stereotypes*** are ideas that many people have about a thing or group of people that may be untrue or only partly true. One person may hold an opinion, but a stereotype is formed by a group. Stereotypes may be positive, but they are often negative. For example, the first time Tiger Woods won the Masters title in 1997, Fuzzy Zoeller, in what he thought was a joke, suggested that Woods refrain from ordering fried chicken and collard greens at the following year's Champions' dinner. (The winner of each year's Masters selects the menu for the coming year's dinner.) Zoeller's comment was widely quoted in the news media; was his comment an opinion or a stereotype? Zoeller had won the Masters title in 1979, when membership at the Augusta, Georgia, course was restricted to white males, a tradition left over from a time when the South believed that the only black men on a golf course were caddies.

A **judgment*** is usually an act of discernment that is the result of an individual's firmly held beliefs. Finally, **beliefs*** are rooted in a community's faith structure, creed, values, or sentiments. *Can you think of an example of a judgment you make? What about a belief you hold in common with the rest of your community?*

The following is an editorial from *Newsweek* written in support of The **Racial Privacy Initiative*** on the California ballot in November 2003. In "Dropping the 'One Drop' Rule," George Will argues why he believes all Americans should stop explaining

***opinion:** What a person may think about something, usually based in stereotypes, whim, or mood; insubstantial in argument.

***stereotype:** Something that one group of people believe about others who are different; may be partly true.

***judgment:** Weightier opinions based in a system of beliefs, usually arrived at by discernment.

***belief:** System of values rooted in a person's faith community; tenets, or creeds.

***Racial Privacy Initiative:** A 2003 California ballot measure that would, if passed, prevent government agencies in California from classifying individuals by race, ethnicity, color, or national origin for any purpose pertaining to public education, public contracting, or public employment.

where we are from and what our ethnic backgrounds are. You will notice as you read the editorial that there are questions in the margins. This sort of note taking while reading is called *annotation*. This is a good tool to use on a first reading. The questions will help you clarify what the author is trying to accomplish. A second type of annotation involves an analysis of the text through such elements as diction, tone, repetition, and allusion. As you read George Will's editorial, pay attention to the questions—are they the questions you would ask? Directly following the editorial is an analysis of the text using the second form of annotation.

George Will[1]

Dropping the 'One Drop' Rule

It is probably the most pernicious idea ever to gain general acceptance in America. No idea has done more, and more lasting, damage than the "one drop" rule, according to which if you have *any* admixture of black ancestry, you are black, period. This idea imparted an artificial clarity to the idea of race, and became the basis of the laws, conventions and etiquette of slavery, then of segregation and subsequently of today's identity politics, in which one's civic identity is a function of one's race[2] (or ethnicity, of gender, or sexual preference).

Today nothing more scaldingly reveals the intellectual bankruptcy and retrograde agenda of the institutionalized—fossilized, really—remnants of the civil-rights movement than this: those remnants constitute a social faction clinging desperately to the "one drop" rule, or some inchoate and unarticulated version of that old buttress of slavery and segregation. However, in California, where much of modern America has taken shape, a revolt is brewing—a revolt against the malignant legacy of that rule, and against identity politics generally, and in favor of a colorblind society.[3] The revolt is gathering strength—and signatures.

The signatures—1.1 million of them, by April 10—are required to put the Racial Privacy Initiative[4] on California's November ballot. If enacted, the RPI will prevent government agencies in California from classifying individuals by race, ethnicity, color or national origin for any purpose pertaining to public education, public contracting or public employment.

Who can object to the RPI 50 years after Ralph Ellison, in "Invisible Man," his great novel about black experience in America, wrote, "Our task is that of making ourselves individuals"? Who can object to the RPI 48 years after Thurgood Marshall, then an attorney representing the NAACP in *Brown v. Board of Education*, said, "Distinctions by race are so evil,[5] so arbitrary and invidious that a state bound to defend the equal protection of the laws must not involve them in any public sphere"? Who can object to the RPI 34 years after Martin Luther King died struggling for a society in which Americans "will not be judged by the color of their skin but by the content of their character"?

---

[1]Well-known political conservative.

[2]Why is civic identity connected to race?

[3]In a colorblind society, is anyone invisible?

[4]How can you keep race a secret?

[5]Is it evil to draw attention to race?

5   Who? Here is who: People who make their living by Balkanizing America[6] into elbow-throwing grievance groups clamoring for government preferment.[7] Such people include blacks in the civil-rights industry who administer today's racial spoils system of college admissions and contract set-asides, and white liberals who have a political stake in blacks forever thinking of themselves as permanently crippled by history and hence permanent wards of government.

But Ward Connerly says: Enough—actually, much too much—already. Connerly, the prime mover behind the RPI, is a successful businessman, a member of the University of California Board of Regents, and the man responsible for California voters enacting in 1996 Proposition 209 to eliminate government-administered racial preferences. He is black.[8]

At least, he is according to the "one drop" rule. Never mind that one of his grandparents was of African descent, another was Irish, another was Irish and American Indian, another was French Canadian. Furthermore, by the "one drop" rule, the children he and his Irish wife have had are black. And his grandchildren are black, even the two whose mother is half Vietnamese.[9]

A modest proposal: Instead of calling them, or grandfather Ward, blacks, why not call them Californians?[10] In California today more children are born to parents of different races than are born to two black parents. In a recent 15-year span (1982-97) multiracial births in California increased 40 percent. There has been a sharp increase in the number of applicants to the University of California who refuse to stipulate their race.[11]

The RPI follows the logic of the 2000 U.S. Census. The 1790 census classified Americans into five categories—white males 16 years and older, white males less than 16 years, white females, other white persons and slaves. In 1860 Chinese and American Indian were added as distinct races. By 1990 the census offered five major categories: white, black, Asian/Pacific Islander, American Indian/Native Alaskan and other. But births to black-white interracial parents nearly tripled in the 1990s. It is morally offensive and, the "one drop" rule notwithstanding, preposterous for a child of such a marriage to be required to choose to "be" the race of just one parent. And why should the alternative be "other"?[12]

10   So in 2000 the census expanded the available choices from five to 63. The 63 did not include the category Tiger Woods concocted for himself—"Cablinasian," meaning Caucasian, black, Indian and Asian. But the 63 threatened[13] those race-and-ethnicity entrepreneurs who toil to maximize their power and profits by maximizing the numbers they purport to speak for the numbers of people who supposedly are clearly this or than race or ethnicity. Hence the hysteria against the RPI.

The American Civil Liberties Union's chapter in Berkeley—of course—says the RPI would effectively return California to "pre-1964" status. That is, to before the law that

---

[6]What does this mean?

[7]Is there ever a good reason for preferential treatment?

[8]How does that matter?

[9]If Will is so into racial privacy, why did he just give this guy's whole family history?

[10]Millions of people can say this. Don't we want to be more specific about ourselves?

[11]How is this a problem?

[12]So what we really need is more categories?

[13]How?

guaranteed blacks access to voting booths and public accommodations. Orwellian language multiplies: Professional racemongers[14] denounce the RPI's ban on racial preferences as "racist," and people whose livelihood depends on dividing Americans into irritable clumps denounce the RPI as "divisive."

The RPI is sound social policy for a nation in which racial and ethnic boundaries are becoming wonderfully blurry.[15] This accelerating development should please Americans regardless of whether they accept, reject or are agnostic about the idea that the very concept of race is scientifically dubious, or is a mere convention—a "social construct."

By enacting the RPI, the one eighth of Americans who are Californians can help the other seven eighths put the "one drop" rule where it belongs—in a far corner of the mental attic where the nation puts embarrassments from its immaturity.

Is Will expressing an opinion or making a judgment? What is the difference?

Annotation

The editorial has been annotated to suggest how you might begin to enter conversation with a text by recording the questions that occur as you read.

The editorial has been annotated below in a second manner to suggest how you might approach talking back to a text. The first place to start is to understand the role of the genre that the writer has chosen. An **editorial*** is written for a newspaper or a magazine by an editor for the express purpose of giving to the public an informed opinion. The writer has some knowledge of the facts of the situation but wants to shape those facts to present readers with one particular way to think about them. An editorial is based in bias and is meant to champion a particular position. The writer wants you to agree, to see the issue his or her way.

Annotating an editorial should start with trying to determine the writer's position. Columnist George Will is a well-known political conservative. Though he never uses the words **"affirmative action"*** in his editorial, this controversial hot button is exactly what he is speaking against. First, let's look at his **diction*** as he builds his case for a "*colorblind society*." Those who are against a colorblind society are depicted this way:

They have entered "*intellectual bankruptcy*" and are following a "*retrograde agenda*" because they are "*fossilized remnants of the civil-rights movement*." Further, these people are "*clinging desperately*" to some "*inchoate and unarticulated version*" of some "*old buttress of slavery and segregation*." These people are the supporters of a "*malignant legacy*" who insist on "*Balkanizing America*" by being "*elbow-throwing grievance groups clamoring for government preferment*." Those who work for college admissions diversity are proponents of

> ***editorial:** An opinion piece that appears in newspapers and newsmagazines; attempts to sway the reader toward a particular point of view.
>
> ***affirmative action:** A program undertaken by government, employers, and educational institutions to redress the effects of past discrimination. The long-term goal is gender-free and color-blind laws bringing equal opportunity, but such a program may involve quotas, policies, and recruitment that recognize minority candidates who have been historically denied opportunity.
>
> ***diction:** Word choice.

---

[14]What is a racemonger?

[15]So does that mean we all look alike? Won't we still be different? What about multiculturalism?

a *"racial spoils system,"* and those who support minority quotas for a share of government projects support *"contract set-asides"*; in sum, people who would do all this see minorities as *"permanently crippled . . . permanent wards of government."* A close look at the italicized words above suggest negative connotations: These people are old and behind-the-times; they are stuck in the past and their behavior is childlike, to the point of throwing tantrums.

Will repeats the phrase "one drop" rule six times in his column, yet that language is not part of the RPI, which calls for California to stop classifying people by "race, ethnicity, color or national origin for any purpose pertaining to public education, public contracting or public employment." The "one drop" rule harkens back to a day when having "one drop" of black blood was enough to discriminate *against* an individual. Will repeats the term to provoke—the "one drop" rule does belong in "the mental attic where the nation puts embarrassments from its immaturity," but he uses the term to turn the meaning on its head; he makes a call for the abolishment of a legally sanctioned system intended to assure diversity and opportunity—on a level playing field—to a minority candidate. He does it all *without* using familiar language, without overtly saying: My position is solidly against affirmative action.

> ***allusion:** An indirect reference to a person or place in one text that solicits thoughts of that person or place in its original context.

He uses several **allusions*** that call the reader to understand a deeper message if that allusion is clear. For example, "a modest proposal" is a reference to Jonathan Swift's 1729 proposal of the same name, which called for preventing a famine in Ireland by having poor people eat their children. Swift's work is one of our language's great satires; Will's use of "a modest proposal," like Swift's, oversimplifies a complex situation and permits an easy summary: to call all people in California "Californians." He takes on the liberal American Civil Liberties Union and suggests that "Orwellian language multiplies." Here the allusion is to George Orwell's famous novel *1984*, which suggested a world where "Big Brother" was watching everybody's every move.

Annotation helps you determine the opinions and judgments that are being set forth by writers as they arrange the events of the news to make impressions on readers that are based in the writers' biases. As you look for writers' positions and purposes, you simultaneously must be thinking about their audiences. It is always possible to read any piece of writing and suddenly become aware that you might not be the intended audience for the piece. *Who is Will's audience? How is he convincing? Who does he use for expert opinion? Do you agree with him?*

> ***Sherman Alexie:** (1966–) A Spokane/Coeur d'Alene Indian and a graduate of Washington State University, Alexie is the author of poetry, short stories, novels, and screenplays. Alexie received the Washington State Arts Commission Poetry Fellowship in 1991 and the National Endowment for the Arts Poetry Fellowship in 1992.

Annotation is a helpful skill as you read various opinions in the process of forming your own. Start with questioning the text. Then move on to considering diction, tone, repetition, and allusion. *For practice, select one of the twentieth-century speeches from Citizenship 101 and annotate it both ways—first question the text, then address diction, tone, repetition, and allusion.*

Sherman Alexie* is a writer and a Spokane/Coeur d'Alene Indian. In the following interview, Alexie talks about being an Indian, a writer, and a man who is not working very hard to meet anyone's expectations. *While you read, keep in mind that, like you, Alexie understands voice, audience, and purpose. Who would you say is his intended audience? What voice does he use? And what is his purpose, beyond promoting his book, behind the things he says?*

Erik Himmelsbach

The Reluctant Spokesman

With the success of his new book, Sherman Alexie finds himself cast as the poster boy for all things American Indian. Trouble is, he's not much liked by his own tribe.

Sherman Alexie is ready to play cards with Satan.

The 30-year-old author is hunkered down at the Beverly Prescott, in town to discuss the film rights to his latest novel, "Indian Killer" (Atlantic Monthly Press), a slyly subversive potboiler about a serial murderer whose actions spark a modern battle of cowboys and Indians in Seattle. It may seem like perfect big-screen fodder, but Alexie, a Spokane Coeur d'Alene, harbors no illusions and is prepared for the inevitable raw deal from Hollywood.

"The real problem is that there's no white hero in my book," he says.

"They want loincloths. They want sweat lodges and vision guests. They want 'Dances With Wolves,' and I don't write that."

If producers aren't sensitive to the particulars of the late 20th century American Indian,   5
at least no one's mentioned Lou Diamond Phillips.

"I think he's done with the Indian thing," Alexie says with a grin. "He's done four or five of them, and they all flopped. Hopefully, he hasn't read the book and won't be interested."

While they're busy keeping Diamond Phillips off casting lists, Hollywood types also would be wise to avoid calling Alexie a "Native American." The author dismisses the term as meaningless, a product of liberal white guilt.

"I'm an Indian," he says. "I'll only use 'Native American' in mixed company.

"Indian Killer" is Alexie's second novel; the first was "Reservation Blues." (He's also written an acclaimed book of short stories, "The Lone Ranger and Tonto Fistfight in Heaven," and several volumes of poetry.)

It's a multilayered work. While it satisfied Alexie's desire to explore the mystery genre,   10
it also highlights the tenuous thread of civility that exists between white and American Indian cultures, how we are only a flash point away from igniting a racial powder keg—even in progressive Seattle, where Alexie lives with his wife, Diane.

"If you look at the history of the U.S. and chart what's happening, we are brewing a revolutionary stew," he says, comparing the present disparity among classes and races to France just before the French Revolution. "There's a tremendous level of anger out there, and the anger in the Indian community has not really been talked about. There's a huge open wound."

Healing would require apologies and reparations from the U.S. government, but Alexie isn't holding his breath. "It would change the whole myth of America, the rugged individual, the courageous pioneer, this whole American dream," he says. The government "would have to admit that there were terrible evils committed here, comparable to any evils ever."

Alexie has done his share of myth debunking. His earlier work, especially "Lone Ranger and Tonto," is notable for its honest and humorous character studies of modern tribal life. His stories are candid snapshots of a culture that has long been ignored.

In "Indian Killer" he leaves the reservation to examine the plight of the urban Indian, like himself, displaced from the tribe. He notes that 60% of the Indians in this country live in urban areas. But that presented new challenges, as Alexie struggled to develop some of the characters, especially white characters, whose life experiences are foreign to him.

15   "I grew up in a culture where you are taught that songs and stories have specific owners and you can't tell them without permission," he explains. "Growing up with those cultural constructs, the whole idea of the artist as the individual is totally outside my concept of who I am. I'm always operating with some sort of tribal responsibility, so here I am writing about people way outside my tribe, and it got uncomfortable."

While Alexie has enlightened the world at large about the contemporary American Indian experience, his tribe has essentially shunned him. Back at the Spokane Reservation in Wellpint, Wash., people have strong, often unfavorable opinions about the author who, as a child, often whiled away his days alone in his room playing Dungeons & Dragons or Nerf basketball.

"I was a divisive presence on the reservation when I was 7," he recalls. "I was a weird, eccentric, very arrogant little boy. The writing doesn't change anybody's opinion of me. If anything, it's intensified it."

Alexie says one tribal elder resents him not for anything he's written, but because he was a "ball hog" on the tribe's basketball team.

Part of the animosity stems from Alexie's decision to leave his tribal school and transfer to Reardan High, a virtually all-white school 20 miles from his home.

20   Alexie was terrified when he arrived at Reardan—he was the school's first and only Indian until his twin sisters joined him after a year. To assimilate, he had to abandon certain characteristics, including his reservation accent and some of his hair, which fell far below his shoulders.

"People think it's a trivial thing, and it's not," he says. "The physical act of cutting parts of yourself off to fit in, that's what it is."

Ultimately, though, Alexie succeeded at Reardan for the same reasons he was outcast by his tribe—his "insane ambition."

He drew on his experiences at the school when developing John Smith, a central character in "Indian Killer." Unlike Alexie, however, Smith was tormented by his lack of tribal identification: He was adopted by a white couple and never knew his heritage.

"Indian children adopted by non-Indian families have tremendous social problems," Alexie says.

25   Although ostracized by his tribe, Alexie has been embraced by many other American Indians, judging by the number of events and commencements he's asked to speak at.

He jokes that his "little books about one little reservation in Washington State" have come to represent all Indians everywhere. As such, he's not allowed to merely write books. He has had to become a poster boy.

"It's very interesting. Nobody ever asked Raymond Carver to speak for every white guy," Alexie says. "I end up having to be a spokesperson for Indian people. I've become a politician and a sociologist and psychologist and cultural critic, and all these jobs I have to fulfill simply based on the fact that I am an Indian writer getting a lot of attention."

Being selected as one of *Granta* magazine's "20 best American novelists under 40" has added to the author's laundry list of accolades, although he takes this sort of recognition with a grain of salt.

"There are hints I got on there because of some affirmative action policy," he says. "How many spots are reserved in the literary world for Indian people? None. If I was on there because of some newly invented Indian quota in the literary world, great. I hope we get lots more quotas."

While he doesn't shun his profile-building extracurricular responsibilities Alexie prefers   30
the solitude of his craft - "Writers and artists are by and large selfish bastards. It's isolated, individualistic. In that sense, it was a job I was perfectly suited for."

In this way, Alexie identifies with "Indian Killer's" Marie Polatkin, an angry, righteous Indian who will grant no quarter to the white intellectuals who think they understand the Native American experience.

But sharing his writing with the world has had a profound affect on this self-proclaimed selfish bastard. "I had no idea about the very quiet ways in which art works," he says, explaining the letters of support he receives from all over the country.

"I was in the Seattle airport, and this 10-year-old Indian boy came up to me and he said, 'I like your poem,' and he told me which poem he liked," Alexie says. "And at that moment, all the wonder and magic of what art is supposed to be about is contained there. For just a few moments, you forget about slogging through airport after airport. It sounds cliched and romantic and sentimental, and it is, but it's great. It's those little moments that save you."

As the day turns dark, and Hollywood's bright lights wink seductively at Alexie from his 11th-floor view at the Beverly Prescott, his thoughts suddenly turn from idyllic to pragmatic. Nothing, it seems, can save him from the dread of the meetings with the movie people. He'll hear about how his writing can be sliced and diced and marketed and compromised in the name of mass-market entertainment.

It's times like these that lie wraps himself in the security of what he considers his true   35
calling: poetry. (His latest book of poems, "The Summer of Black Widows" [Hanging Loose Press] was published in September.)

"There is no possible way to sell your soul because nobody's offering," he says with a laugh. "The devil doesn't care about poetry. No one wants to make a movie out of a poem."

Having read the interview, you should think about your own expectations. The title of the article is "The Reluctant Spokesman." What would make you think that Alexie is reluctant to be a spokesperson? Does this reluctance have more to do with how Native Americans are viewed by the rest of America, or with how the Indians back on the reservation view Sherman Alexie? What does it mean when the majority asks an individual to speak for all of his or her "people"? Have you ever been asked to be a "credit" to whatever group you might identify with, based on your race, religion, class, or ethnic background? How did that feel? For practice, reread "The Reluctant Spokesman" and anno-

tate it, using the skills you learned from the George Will editorial. Do your annotations help you answer any questions you might have about Sherman Alexie, and what he has to say, more clearly?

We all have differing views of America, our history here, and what should be considered important. Below are two poems, "On the Pulse of Morning" by **Maya Angelou*** and "Remember" by **Joy Harjo.*** These two poets, one African American and the other Native American, have taken up the same task, but the scope, the language, and the tone differ greatly.

In this excerpt from Maya Angelou's **inaugural poem,*** "On the Pulse of Morning," the narrator tells the story of America starting with the geological dawn of time and moving forward to January 20, 1993, when Angelou reads her poem at the first inauguration of President Bill Clinton. *As you read through these first few lines from the poem, follow the progression of the narrative as the poet begins to depict the history of America and her diverse people. Also note that the **narrator***—the voice in the poem—gives information and orders, telling the reader both how things have happened and what to think and do about those events.*

Maya Angelou reads at the Inauguration of President Clinton in 1993.

Maya Angelou

On the Pulse of Morning

A Rock, A River, A Tree
Hosts to species long since departed,
  Marked the mastodon.

The dinosaur, who left dry tokens
  Of their sojourn here   5
  On our planet floor,
  Any broad alarm of their hastening doom
  Is lost in the gloom of dust and ages.
But today, the Rock cries out to us, clearly, forcefully,
  Come, you may stand upon my   10
  Back and face your distant destiny,
  But seek no haven in my shadow.
I will give you no more hiding place down here.
  You, created only a little lower than
  The angels, have crouched too long in   15
  The bruising darkness,
  Have lain too long
  Face down in ignorance.

Your mouths spilling words
  Armed for slaughter.   20

The Rock cries out today, you may stand on me,
  But do not hide your face.

Joy Harjo's poem "Remember," from her book *She Had Some Horses*, is much shorter than Angelou's complete poem and far more directive. The narrator—the voice in the poem—presents what could almost be called a list of things to be remembered, thus implying their great importance. Although Harjo, through the great success of *She Had Some Horses*, is speaking to a national audience, she is not specifically speaking to the nation, as Angelou was when she read her poem at Clinton's inauguration. *How does that difference in purpose and audience affect "Remember"? Are we more aware of Harjo's background than Angelou's? Should we be?*

Joy Harjo

Remember

Remember the sky that you were born under,
  know each of the star's stories.
Remember the moon, know who she is. I met her
  in a bar once in Iowa City.

5   Remember the sun's birth at dawn, that is the
         strongest point of time. Remember sundown
         and the giving away to night.
       Remember your birth, how your mother struggled
         to give you form and breath. You are evidence of
10   her life, and her mother's, and hers.
       Remember your father. He is your life also.
       Remember the earth whose skin you are:
         red earth, black earth, yellow earth, white earth,
         brown earth, we are earth.
15   Remember the plants, trees, animal life who all have their
         tribes, their families, their histories, too. Talk to them,
         listen to them. They are alive poems.
       Remember the wind. Remember her voice. She knows the
         origin of the universe. I heard her singing Kiowa war
20   dance songs at the corner of Fourth and Central once.
       Remember that you are all people and that all people are you.
       Remember that you are this universe and that this universe is you.
       Remember that all is in motion, is growing, is you.
       Remember that language comes from this.
25   Remember the dance that language is, that life is.
       Remember.

> ***lyrical poem:** A lyrical poem tends to be short, lacks a cohesive or definite narrative, and clearly expresses a specific emotion or feeling.

Angelou's poem is a narrative and has the elements of plot or story within it, while Harjo's poem is more accurately called a **lyrical poem,*** as it is shorter, has no distinct sequence of events, and evokes a strong emotion or feeling. *How does this difference affect how each poet speaks to the people of America? Reading the complete text of Angelou's poem will help to answer this question.*

In this book, you will have the opportunity to read a number of different literary genres, as well as different styles of writing from the news media. Looking at American citizenship through a variety of artistic expressions enables you to explore your personal responses to the author. Whether you are faced with something you agree or disagree with, you will still need to "read" the piece, asking yourself questions about it and exploring the biases—the opinions and judgments—from which it has been produced.

DICTIONARY DEFINITION AND IMPLICATION

When you make sense of your thinking, you do so through choices in diction. You can choose words that are *denotative* or give a *dictionary definition*. Usually, these words do not invoke a passionate response; they are more likely to have a neutral effect on the reader. These word choices most closely signify the reality of the thing itself without calling up a number of various other possibilities, suggestions, or associations. You can also choose words that **connote,*** or offer by *implication*. When you

> ***connotation:** A meaning that suggests more than the word explicitly stated.

choose these words, they have a ripple effect; they offer shades of meaning, suggest more possibilities for interpretation, and color the argument being presented. Words with strong potential for many associations assist in developing the **tone*** of a piece. Tone should always support the writer's position and not work against it. Making lists of the words of these three parts of speech—adjectives, verbs, and nouns—is an important part of annotating your reading when you are analyzing tone.

Consider this speech by Robert F. Kennedy, made at a particularly tumultuous moment in American history. On the last day of March in 1968, President **Lyndon B. Johnson*** announced that he would not seek reelection. **Robert F. Kennedy*** was eager to test the waters to see if he might secure the Democratic nomination in August. On April 4, 1968, Martin Luther King, Jr. was assassinated in Memphis. Kennedy, in Indianapolis at a campaign rally, delivered the following remarks to an audience of African American citizens. Two months later Robert Kennedy, like his brother John and Martin Luther King before him, was assassinated.

> ***tone:** The sound of words, which conveys a meaning that might add to or take away from the words themselves; the attitude of a piece of writing; style or manner of expression.
>
> ***Lyndon B. Johnson:** (1908–1973) Thirty-sixth president of the United States (1963–1969). During his administration, most of the important civil rights legislation became law.
>
> ***Robert F. Kennedy:** (1925–1968) Attorney general in his brother John Kennedy's administration and senator from New York; assassinated in June 1968 when he was campaigning for president.

Ladies and Gentlemen - I'm only going to talk to you just for a minute or so this evening. Because. . .

I have some very sad news for all of you, and I think sad news for all of our fellow citizens, and people who love peace all over the world, and that is that Martin Luther King was shot and was killed tonight in Memphis, Tennessee.

Martin Luther King dedicated his life to love and to justice between fellow human beings. He died in the cause of that effort. In this difficult day, in this difficult time for the United States, it's perhaps well to ask what kind of a nation we are and what direction we want to move in.

For those of you who are black—considering the evidence evidently is that there were white people who were responsible—you can be filled with bitterness, and with hatred, and a desire for revenge.

We can move in that direction as a country, in greater polarization —black people amongst blacks, and white amongst

5

Martin Luther King, Jr. and Robert F. Kennedy.

whites, filled with hatred toward one another. Or we can make an effort, as Martin Luther King did, to understand and to comprehend, and replace that violence, that stain of bloodshed that has spread across our land, with an effort to understand, compassion and love.

For those of you who are black and are tempted to be filled with hatred and mistrust of the injustice of such an act, against all white people, I would only say that I can also feel in my own heart the same kind of feeling. I had a member of my family killed, but he was killed by a white man.

But we have to make an effort in the United States, we have to make an effort to understand, to get beyond these rather difficult times.

My favorite poet was Aeschylus. He once wrote: "Even in our sleep, pain which cannot forget falls drop by drop upon the heart, until, in our own despair, against our will, comes wisdom through the awful grace of God."

What we need in the United States is not division; what we need in the United States is not hatred; what we need in the United States is not violence and lawlessness, but is love and wisdom, and compassion toward one another, and a feeling of justice toward those who still suffer within our country, whether they be white or whether they be black.

10   (Interrupted by applause)

So I ask you tonight to return home, to say a prayer for the family of Martin Luther King, yeah that's true, but more importantly to say a prayer for our own country, which all of us love—a prayer for understanding and that compassion of which I spoke. We can do well in this country. We will have difficult times. We've had difficult times in the past. And we will have difficult times in the future. It is not the end of violence; it is not the end of lawlessness; and it's not the end of disorder.

But the vast majority of white people and the vast majority of black people in this country want to live together, want to improve the quality of our life, and want justice for all human beings that abide in our land.

(Interrupted by applause)

Let us dedicate ourselves to what the Greeks wrote so many years ago: to tame the savageness of man and make gentle the life of this world.

15   Let us dedicate ourselves to that, and say a prayer for our country and for our people. Thank you very much. (Applause)

As you did with the George Will editorial, notice what Kennedy chooses to repeat. Make lists of verbs, adjectives, and nouns that imply suggestions and help determine Kennedy's tone. Based on these brief remarks, what opinions do you think the speaker holds about the death of Martin Luther King, Jr.? Is Kennedy speaking about something besides King's death? How does knowing that Kennedy died violently just two months later affect your reading his words retrospectively? Does the speech take on a different weight because of its historical circumstances?

THE ROLE OF HUMOR

Often as Americans work toward acknowledging and understanding the differences between individual citizens, a natural yet complicated issue arises—we start to find these differences funny. And then we tell jokes about each other. We've all heard them: Polish jokes, black jokes, gay jokes, Jewish jokes, Italian jokes. This list could go on forever and is often something people disagree about. Some argue that jokes are healthy, a reasonable way to notice and respond to difference. Others say all jokes directed at one group or another are both unkind and discriminatory. Below is a discussion of jokes. *As you read through this section, think about what makes a joke funny, and why they are often so complicated to tell.*

In his editorial "Can We Laugh Now?" Brandt Ayers, publisher of the *Anniston (Alabama) Star*, asks if black and white Americans have gotten comfortable enough with each other to laugh together, and wonders if we might open our minds to see the value in something like "Amos and Andy," a radio show now thought to be politically incorrect. *See if you agree with the points he makes.*

Brandt Ayers

Can We Laugh Now?

Early last Saturday morning, I went down to the bus station to greet an old friend passing through. We embraced, as old friends do when they haven't seen each other for a long, long time.

I started to say old friends who had "soldiered together" in a good cause, but that would put me on an undeserved level with a national—and personal—hero: Congressman John Lewis of Atlanta.

Lewis has suffered physical and emotional injuries that would embitter a saint: As a leader of the sit-in movement to integrate lunch counters in the '60s, as a Freedom Rider, as a leader gravely clubbed by Alabama State Troopers at the Edmund Pettus Bridge on March 7, 1965.

Yet he spoke here, on the 40th anniversary of the 1961 bus-burning, as he always does. He spoke of building "the Beloved Community," one that encompasses you and me, whoever "you" may be. He is a saint.

Do saints have a sense of humor? At least one does. As autograph-seekers crowded around him, I suggested they were there, not because of his fame, but his "good looks." His half-shy smile said, "I'm not vain about my looks."   5

Forty years he's been at this business of building the beloved community. Where are we now, two generations down the road?

Far enough for white businessmen in some communities to take an interest in improving majority-black schools. Far enough for the moral core of the civil rights movement to weaken and the indictment "racist" to become an all-purpose complaint. Far enough for all the obvious indignities of segregation to vanish into an unimaginable past. But not far enough to solve all the riddles of the human heart.

How comfortable are the two races who came together in conflict, as strangers, two generations ago? Are we easy enough, self-confident enough in each other's company to take a joke, to laugh with each other as we take our mutual pratfalls in the human comedy?

Have we made courtesy a tyrant and political correctness a religion that requires excommunication from the human race for a Caucasion who laughs at Amos 'n Andy or any African-American who chuckles at an episode of *Lum 'n' Abner's Jot 'Em' Down Store?*

10   Segments from each in the 1940s dealt with singing contests. In Jot 'Em' Down Store's mythical country store of Pine Ridge, Ark., Abner's dotty father, Phinus, tells (for the umpteenth time) the tale of losing the singing contest because his shoes were too tight to put back on for his stage debut.

An African-American with a goofy grandfather, lost in a reminiscent fog, would find the show mildly amusing, and certainly familiar. The writing, however, can't compare with *Amos 'n' Andy*, a show whose popularity on radio and TV lasted from the 1920s to the 1960s.

The two expatriate Alabamians in Chicago are constantly in amiable conflict, with Amos, the "Kingfish" of the Mystic Knights of the Sea Lodge, perpetually trying to outwit his friend Andy Brown.

In this episode, the recital has to be delayed because Andy is stricken with stage fright, termed "buck fever" by the local paper. Andy proclaims himself "regusted" by the media exposure.

He says, "Wait until the newspaper cricket hear me sing." Amos tells Andy that it was the newspaper's "cricket" who wrote the story and warns him not to argue with the press, "The pen is mightier than the sword." "I'd rather be stuck by a pen," says Andy. The King-fish replies, "You been stuck by one."

15   I agree with the African-American columnist for *The Miami Herald*, Leonard Pitts, who hated the show until he finally saw a few and wrote, "I looked and I laughed. These people were rich beyond stereotypes."

Probably we've moved past those two shows with white-trash comedy, *The Dukes of Hazzard*, black idiots such as "JJ" on *Good Times*, and most of all, the universal, everyman humor of Bill Cosby.

But are we still too awkward with each other to keep the wisdom of Uncle Remus from our children? Surely not, or we would have to erase great slices of both African and American culture.

Banish Br'er Rabbit and the Tar-Baby to the closet? We should rise in unanimous protest at the wisdom untaught, the lost delight in "tricksters" whose roots stretch all the way back to east and central Africa.

Hide that dumb fox and that crafty rabbit and we would lose values too personal and important: The animals upon which we project our own fears, dreams and ideals—in whom we see ourselves at our cleverest.

20   The return of the Freedom Riders was a solemn occasion, but the intervening 40 years reminds us we will never be secure in the "beloved community" until we are healthy enough to laugh at ourselves.

Comedian Chris Rock delivered the following jokes in his role as host of the 2005 Academy Awards. *Are his jokes funny or insulting? What is the role of stereotypes and beliefs?*

On the world:
"You know the world is going crazy when the best rapper is a white guy, the best golfer is a black guy, the tallest guy in the NBA is a Chinese guy, the Swiss hold the America's Cup, France is accusing the U.S. of arrogance, Germany doesn't want to go to war, and the three most powerful men in America are named 'Bush,' 'Dick' and 'Colon.' Need I say more?"

On black movies:

"Black movies don't have real names, they have names like Barbershop. That's not a name, it's just a location."

Chris Rock is one of the most in-demand young comics performing today. His work is popular, but the controversy that surrounds him is based on his frequent use of obscenity, not his racial jokes. In the first joke, the humor is embedded in the ironic idea that the world is crazy without familiar stereotypes. *Do you agree with Rock's assessment of our dependence on those stereotypes?* In the second joke, Rock makes a sweeping statement about black movies. It's a funny thing to say when Rock says it, but would the joke still be funny if a white comic told it?

As you can see, considerations of America and her people pose many more questions than answers. In this chapter we hope to begin the discussion, to think about who is here and how they got here. We heard some voices and began to think about the music of the American Symphony. By reading and thinking about the many faces of America, you can begin to understand how your responses to the various genres help you to consider critically your own assumptions about race, ethnicity, color, and national origin, and what effects they have on your personal definition of good citizenship.

What Is at Stake for Citizenship?

1. What can happen in a democracy when individuals are not treated equally?
2. Should we be concerned about injustices of the past, or just move forward?
3. How should religion function in a democracy?
4. Do we need to be able to see people in order to form ideas about them?
5. What does a "good American" do and say?
6. Are you aware of stereotypes and beliefs that prevent you from thinking fairly about other people?
7. How do language, sound, accent, and speech matter in our multicultural society?
8. How many ways are there to tell the history of America, and who should tell it?
9. What is the easiest thing about being an American, and what is the hardest?
10. How do we define ourselves as Americans *and* keep our identity?

CHAPTER 2

This chapter explores the importance of purpose, voice, and audience when we talk about responsible citizenship. By verbalizing your ideas, you can clarify what you have written. You need to understand the necessary link between talking and writing about being a participating citizen. *Purpose, voice, and audience* shape who is included and who is left out of the discussion.

Talking and Writing about Citizenship and Justice

Though not all [white shoe shine customers in New Orleans], by any means, were so open about their purposes, all of them showed us how they felt about the Negro, the idea that we were people of such low morality that nothing could offend us. . . .When they paid me, they looked as though I were a stone or a post. They looked and saw nothing.
—John Howard Griffin, *Black Like Me*

STARTING THE CONVERSATION

*John Howard Griffin:
(1920–1980) White author of
1961 *Black Like Me;* turned
his skin dark and traveled
throughout South as a black
man.

Before any of us is ready to write about participating in a twenty-first-century democracy, we need to begin a conversation about the subject. Back in 1959, **John Howard Griffin,** * a syndicated columnist and author, decided to act on an idea that had been in his mind for years. He wanted answers to these questions: "If a white man became a Negro in the Deep South, what adjustments would he have to make? What is it like to experience discrimination based on skin color, something over which one has no control?"[1] After he made arrangements with the owner of an African American magazine for financial support in return for articles about his experience, he went home to tell his wife.

Try to imagine the conversation that took place that night in his home when he explained that he wanted to chemically alter his white skin so that he could pass as a black man in the South so that he could understand what it felt like to be a black man.

Griffin's book *Black Like Me* (1961), now considered a classic, records his experiences as a black man as he roamed the city streets and country roads of the segregated South.

Through the early 1960s, first-class citizenship in the United States appeared to be based on pigmentation: White people had no problems registering to vote; black people were often denied the same right. When Griffin spent a night at the Trappist monastery in Conyers, Georgia, he was invited by a young English instructor to visit noted southern author Flannery O'Connor, an opportunity he declined. In a letter

---

[1]John Howard Griffin, *Black Like Me* (New York: Signet, 1962), 7.

to a priest about the potential visit, O'Connor had this to say: "If John Howard Griffin gets to Georgia again, we would be delighted to see him; but not in blackface. I don't in the least blame any of the people who cringed when Griffin sat down beside them. He must have been a pretty horrible-looking object."[2] O'Connor knew about Griffin's project, but she made this comment (in a letter dated October 28, 1960) before *Black Like Me* was published. *Why would O'Connor be horrified of Griffin as a black man?*

In the following excerpt from *Black Like Me*, Griffin is hitchhiking in the early evening hours on his way toward Montgomery, Alabama, when a black man stops to offer him a ride. *After you read the excerpt, talk with your classmates about your feelings about both Griffin and the family with whom he spends the night. Pay attention to how your own race shapes your thoughts about both the hosts and the guest. Try to imagine yourself in either role.*

Griffin's *Black Like Me*.

I walked down the highway into the darkness again, carrying both duffel bags in my left hand and feeding myself the tasteless pineapple fried pie with my right.

A distant hum behind me caught my attention. I turned to see a yellow glow on the road's horizons. It grew stronger and headlights appeared. Though I dreaded riding with another white man, I dreaded more staying on the road all night. Stepping out into full view, I waved my arms. An ancient car braked to a halt and I hurried to it. To my great relief, the reflections from the dash light showed me the face of a young Negro man.

We discussed my problem. He said he lived back in the woods, but had six kids and only two rooms. He wouldn't even have a bed to offer me. I asked him about some other house in the area where I might rent a bed. He said there were none any better than what he had to offer.

However, we could find no other solution.

---

[2]Flannery O'Connor, *Habit of Being* (New York: Farrar, Straus and Giroux, 1979), 414.

5   "You can't stand out here all night. If you don't mind sleeping on the floor, you're welcome to come with me," he said finally.

"I don't mind sleeping on the floor," I said. "I just wouldn't want to put you to any trouble."

As we drove several miles down a lane into the forest, he told me he was a sawmill worker and never made quite enough to get out from under his debts. Always, when he took his check to the store, he owed a little more than the check could cover. He said it was the same for everyone else; and indeed I have seen the pattern throughout my travels. Part of the Southern white's strategy is to get the Negro in debt and keep him there.

"It makes it hard, doesn't it?" I said.

"Yeah, but you can't stop," he answered quickly. "That's what I tell the men at the mill. Some of them are willing just to sit there. I told them, 'Okay, so you're going to give up just because you get no butter with your bread. That's no way to act. Go ahead and eat the bread—but work, and maybe someday we'll have butter to go with it.' I tell them we sure ain't going to get it any other way."

10   I asked him if he could not get together with some of the others and strike for better wages. He laughed with real amusement.

"Do you know how long we'd last, doing something like that?"

"Well, if you stuck together, they sure couldn't kill you all."

"They could damn sure try," he snorted. "Anyway, how long could I feed my kids? There's only a couple of stores in twenty miles. They'd cut off credit and refuse to sell to us. Without money coming in, none of us could live."

He turned off the lane into a rutted path that led through dense underbrush up to a knoll. The headlights fell on a shanty of unpainted wood, patched at the bottom with a rusting Dr Pepper sign. Except for the voices of children, a deep silence hung over the place. The man's wife came to the door and stood silhouetted against the pale light of a kerosene lamp. He introduced us. Though she appeared embarrassed, she asked me in.

15   The subdued babble of children mounted to excited shouts of welcome. They ranged in age from nine years to four months. They were overjoyed to have company. It must be a party. We decided it was.

Supper was on the makeshift table. It consisted entirely of large yellow beans cooked in water. The mother prepared mashed beans and canned milk for the infant. I remembered the bread and offered it as my contribution to the meal. Neither parent apologized for the meagerness of the food. We served ourselves on plastic dishes from the table and sat where we could find places, the children on the floor with a spread-out newspaper for a tablecloth.

I congratulated them on such a fine family. The mother told me they had been truly blessed. "Ours are all in good health. When you think of so many people with crippled or blind or not-right children, you just have to thank God." I praised the children until the father's tired face animated with pride. He looked at the children the way another looks at some rare painting or treasured gem.

Closed into the two rooms, with only the soft light of two kerosene lamps, the atmosphere changed. The outside world, outside standards disappeared. They were somewhere beyond in the vast darkness. In here, we had all we needed for gaiety. We had shelter, some food in our bellies, the bodies and eyes and affections of children who were not yet aware of how things were. And we had treats. We cut the Milky Way bars into thin slices for dessert. In a framework of nothing, slices of Milky Way become a great gift. With almost rabid delight, the children consumed them. One of the smaller girls salivated so heavily the chocolate dribbled syruplike from the corner of her mouth. Her mother wiped it off with her fingertip and unconsciously (from what yearning?) put it in her own mouth.

After supper, I went outside with my host to help him carry water from a makeshift boarded well. A near full moon shone above the trees and chill penetrated as though brilliance strengthened it. We picked our way carefully through fear of snakes down a faint footpath to the edge of the trees to urinate. The moon-speckled landscape exhaled its night rustlings, its truffle-odor of swamps. Distantly, the baby cried. I listened to the muffled rattle of our waters against damp leaf loam. A fragment of memory returned—recollection of myself as a youngster reading Lillian Smith's *Strange Fruit*, her description of the Negro boy stopping along a lonely path to urinate. Now, years later, I was there in a role foreign to my youth's wildest imaginings. I felt more profoundly than ever before the totality of my Negro-ness, the immensity of its isolating effects. The transition was complete from the white boy reading a book about Negroes in the safety of his white living room to an old Negro man in the Alabama swamps, his existence nullified by men but reaffirmed by nature, in his functions, in his affection.

"Okay?" my friend said as we turned back. Moonlight caught his protruding cheek- 20 bones and cast the hollows beneath into shadow.

"Okay," I said.

The house stood above us, rickety, a faint light at the windows. I could hear the whites say, "Look at that shanty. They live like animals. If they wanted to do better they could. And they expect us just to accept them? They *like* to live this way. It would make them just as miserable to demand a higher standard of living as it would make us miserable to put us down to that standard."

I mentioned this to my host. "But we can't do any better," he said. "We work just for that . . . to have something a little better for the kids and us."

"Your wife doesn't seem to get down in the dumps," I remarked.

"No—she's good all the way through. I'll tell you—if we don't have meat to cook with 25 the beans, why she just goes ahead and cooks the beans anyhow." He said this last with a flourish that indicated the grandness of her attitude.

We placed buckets of water on the cast-iron wood stove in the kitchen so we could have warm water for washing and shaving. Then we returned outside to fill the wood-box.

"Are there really a lot of alligators in these swamps?" I asked.

"Oh God yes, the place is alive with them."

"Why don't you kill some of them? The tails make good meat. I could show you how. We learned in jungle training when I was in the army."

"Oh, we can't do that," he said. "They stick a hundred-dollar fine on you for killing a 30 gator. I'm telling you," he laughed sourly, "they got all the loopholes plugged. There ain't a way you can win in this state."

"But what about the children?" I asked. "Aren't you afraid the gators might eat one of them?"

"No . . ." he said forlornly, "the gators like turtle better than they do us."

"They must be part white," I heard myself say.

His laugher sounded flat in the cold air. "As long as they keep their bellies full with turtles, they're no danger to us. Anyway, we keep the kids close to the house."

35   The cheerful and fretful noises of children being readied for bed drifted to us as we returned to the kitchen. Physical modesty in such cramped quarters was impossible, indeed in such a context it would have been ridiculous. The mother sponge-bathed the children while the husband and I shaved. Each of the children went to the toilet, a zinc bucket in the corner, since it was too cold for them to go outside.

Their courtesy to me was exquisite. While we spread tow sacks on the floor and then feed sacks over them, the children asked questions about my own children. Did they go to school? No, they were too young. How old were they then? Why, today is my daughter's fifth birthday. Would she have a party? Yes, she'd certainly had a party. Excitement. Like we had here, with the candy and everything? Yes, something like that.

But it was time to go to bed, time to stop asking questions. The magic remained for them, almost unbearable to me—the magic of children thrilled to know my daughter had a party. The parents brought in patchwork quilts from under the bed in the other room and spread them over the pallets. The children kissed their parents and then wanted to kiss Mr. Griffin. I sat down on a straight-back chair and held out my arms. One by one they came, smelling of soap and childhood. One by one they put their arms around my neck and touched their lips to mine. One by one they said and giggled soberly, "Good night, Mr. Griffin."

I stepped over them to go to my pallet near the kitchen door and lay down fully dressed. Warning the children he did not want to hear another word from them, the father picked up the kerosene lamp and carried it into the bedroom. Through the doorless opening I saw light flicker on the walls. Neither of them spoke. I heard the sounds of undressing. The lamp was blown out and a moment later their bedspring creaked.

Fatigue spread through me, making me grateful for the tow-sack bed. I fought back glimpses of my daughter's birthday party in its cruel contrasts to our party here tonight.

40   "If you need anything, Mr. Griffin, just holler," the man said.

"Thank you. I will. Good night."

"Good night," the children said, their voices locating them in the darkness.

"Good night," again.

"Good night, Mr. Griffin."

45   "That's enough," the father called out warningly to them.

I lay there watching moonlight pour through the crack of the ill-fitting door as everyone drifted to sleep. Mosquitoes droned loudly until the room was a great hum. I wondered that they should be out on such a cold night. The children jerked in their sleep and I knew they had been bitten. The stove cooled gradually with almost imperceptible interior pops and puffings. Odors of the night and autumn and the swamp entered to mingle with the inside odors of children, kerosene, cold beans, urine and the dead incense of pine ashes. The rots and the freshness combined into a strange fragrance—the smell of poverty. For a moment I knew the intimate and subtle joys of misery.

And yet misery was the burden, the pervading, killing burden. I understood why they had so many children. These moments of night when the swamp and darkness surrounded them evoked an immense loneliness, a dread, a sense of exile from the rest of humanity. When the awareness of it strikes, a man either suffocates with despair or he turns to cling to his woman, to console and seek consolation. Their union is momentary escape from the swamp night, from utter hopelessness of its ever getting better for them. It is an ultimately tragic act wherein the hopeless seek hope.

Thinking about these things, the bravery of these people attempting to bring up a family decently, their gratitude that none of their children were blind or maimed, their willingness to share their food and shelter with a stranger—the whole thing overwhelmed me. I got up from bed, half-frozen anyway, and stepped outside.

A thin fog blurred the moon. Trees rose as ghostly masses in the diffused light. I sat on an inverted washtub and trembled as its metallic coldness seeped through my pants.

I thought of my daughter, Susie, and of her fifth birthday today, the candles, the cake and party dress; and of my sons in their best suits. They slept now in clean beds in a warm house while their father, a bald-headed old Negro, sat in the swamps and wept, holding it in so he would not awaken the Negro children.

I felt again the Negro children's lips soft against mine, so like the feel of my own children's good-night kisses. I saw again their large eyes, guileless, not yet aware that doors into wonderlands of security, opportunity and hope were closed to them.

It was thrown in my face. I saw it not as a white man and not as a Negro, but as a human parent. Their children resembled mine in all ways except the superficial one of skin color, as indeed they resembled all children of all humans. Yet this accident, this least important of all qualities, the skin pigment, marked them for inferior status. It became fully terrifying when I realized that if my skin were permanently black, they would unhesitatingly consign my own children to this bean future.

Assume the role of a black male parent who lives with his family in an isolated area. Would you pick up another black man walking on the roadside in the evening? Would you invite this stranger to your home, share your limited food supplies with him, and then make a bed for him on the floor? As a black man, would you have stopped for a man whose skin color was different from your own and offered the same hospitality?

Now assume the role of a poor Asian man who lives in an isolated area. Would you pick up another Asian man and offer him hospitality? Would you do so if the hitchhiker had been African American, and/or disabled in some way, or Latino/Latina? Would cleanliness make a difference to you? As the hitchhiker, would you have had any trouble accepting the hospitality of a complete stranger—one different from yourself or similar to you in ethnicity or race?

In the reading, Griffin moves toward his realization that pigmentation is the only thing that separates the two men. As you were thinking about what you would have done in both roles, how big a part would pigmentation have played in your decisions?

Now consider what you would do as a woman. Do you think gender is more or less important than race or ethnicity in this scenario?

In today's world, it is hard to imagine the likelihood of finding yourself in such an isolated area, much less a swamp filled with gators! The above was an exercise in your imaginative powers. Realistically, let's move the questions to apartment renting.

Imagine yourself renting an apartment to someone ethnically, racially, or physically different from yourself. What qualities in a would-be renter would prohibit you from sealing the deal? Would it matter to you that there are laws preventing discrimination in housing? Are you more comfortable with people who are like you? Why or why not?

MUSIC AND ISSUES OF JUSTICE

Justice stubbed her big toe on Mandela
And Liberty was misquoted by the Indians
Slavery was just a learning phase, forgotten without a verdict
While Justice is on a rampage
For endangered surviving black males
I mean really; if anyone REALLY valued life
And cared about the masses
                    —Tupac Shakur, "Lady Liberty Needs Glasses"

> justice is lost/justice is raped/justice is gone
> pulling your strings/justice is done
> seeking no truth/winning is all
> find it so grim/so true/so real
>   —Metallica, "And Justice for All"

Opinions about music often run strong. In some families, music divides generations—making it impossible to find common ground. Often the issues that spark the greatest controversy are race related. We often expect, though, that people within a certain age and race feel similarly about a particular kind of music. In the following column by Roland S. Martin, he speaks against "the brother" in support of "the sisters." *Do you agree with his position? Is it likely that the brother would find Martin a traitor to the (his) cause? Is the issue larger than gender-support related?*

Roland S. Martin

Thumbs Up to the Sisters at Spelman

Fannie Lou Hamer, a civil rights activist from Mississippi, coined the term, "I'm sick and tired of being sick and tired," nearly 40 years ago. Yet that profound statement still rings true today and was best exemplified recently by a group of black college women in Atlanta.

Sick and tired of the degradation of women in rap videos, these women from the historically black, all-female college—along with some men from nearby colleges—shut down a bone marrow drive on their campus by rap artist Nelly. The lack of minority bone marrow donors is a huge problem, and Nelly, through his non-profit foundation, 4Sho4Kids, wanted to bring some attention to the problem after his sister was diagnosed with leukemia.

All he ended up doing was bringing more attention to the exploitation of women, namely black women, in rap music.

What sent the Spelman women over the edge? Nelly's latest video, "Tip Drill." As usual, women prance, dance, shake it and back that thang up on camera, but in one scene, Nelly has his credit card and uses the butt of a woman as if it's an ATM machine.

5   Nelly, was that a sho4kids to watch on BET or MTV?

Here is how his staff responded to the outrage in a story in The *Atlanta-Journal Constitution*:

—"We're about the business of saving lives," said Chalena Mack, executive director of 4Sho4Kids.

—"To cancel it (the drive) because of this issue is a shame. And to put him in this position is not right. There's a work image, and then there's a human being who loves his sister and is trying to do a good thing," said Juliette Harris, Nelly's publicist with Alliance Management Group.

He loves his sister? What about the woman in his video?! Would he be happy to see his sister in a rap video and have someone slide a credit card down her butt?

Rappers are always talking about how they love their mommas and their sisters, but they are quick to degrade the women in somebody else's family. I heard this sadistic attitude once before at the 1993 national convention of the National Association of Black Journalists.

Under questions from journalists, Bushwick Bill, formerly of the rap group The Geto Boys, said, "I'm sorry if I talk about what I've experienced in my lifetime. I call women b-----s and 'hos because all the women I've met since I've been out here are b-----s and 'hos."

A female reporter responded, "And what do you call your mother?"   10

"I call her 'woman,' but I'm not f---ing my mother. If I was f---ing you, you'd be a b---h."

The place erupted, and a ton of folks stormed out of the room in protest.

Nelly wasn't as crass to make such a statement verbally, but his actions pretty much say the same thing.

His publicist tried to juxtapose his "work image" with that of his non-profit activities. Yeah, right. A drug dealer makes some money in the daytime by poisoning the community, but is willing to buy turkeys and toys at Thanksgiving and Christmas. I guess we're supposed to overlook his job because of his philanthropic moments.

It's fair to compare a rapper to a drug dealer because their "work" is destroying the   15
community. People all over the world who have never met a young black woman are judging them as being scantily-clad-buck-wild freaks who are quick to get their groove on for a shot of Cristal champagne.

I'm not like the Bill O'Reillys of the world who denounce all of rap music. There are many songs that I enjoy because of the rapturous beats. Yet there comes a time when you have to say enough is enough.

Rap impresario Russell Simmons, in response to the criticism that rap music is obscene, often says, "poverty is obscene." He's right. But why can't we say both are obscene?

The Spelman women and men who joined them in protest deserve our praise. Maybe if more folks in black America stand up for righteousness, Nelly and his cohorts will stop the visual destruction of the sisterhood.

Does doing something positive—in this case, supporting a bone marrow drive— outweigh the devaluing of the female body? For whom is Martin writing this column? Are you part of his audience? Are some people intentionally left out? What do you think is Martin's purpose? What action do you think he is seeking? Do you find yourself agreeing or disagreeing with Martin's position?

What is the most appropriate place to start when deciding what your position will be? Is this a simple case of somebody being right and somebody being wrong? Make a list *purpose: In a writing assignment, the reason and intended goal.

*audience: The person or group of people to which a piece of writing is directed.

*of questions you have about Nelly and about the Spelman students and their male supporters. Once you have listed the questions, think about your **purpose***and **audience**.**

CONSIDERING PURPOSE, DETERMINING AUDIENCE, AND PRODUCING VOICE

*voice: Deliberate choices in diction and syntax to support **purpose**.

*reader: The person who reads the assignment for a grade; the reader and audience may well be different people.

Purpose and audience go together; neither can be relegated to the backseat. When talking or writing about citizenship, you need to think about to whom you are speaking or writing, and for what purpose. Once you know purpose and audience, you produce a voice to make you successful in reaching your audience for a desired purpose. You, as speaker/writer, control this rhetorical triangle: One point is **voice**.* How will your style or manner of expression help you accomplish your goals? What words will you choose? At another point is the *purpose* of your words. What do you want them to accomplish? What is your goal? Why are you writing/speaking? At the third point is the *audience,* the people you have in mind who need to hear the message, who need to respond to the goal. How much about your message do they already know? Are they already on your side, or are they perhaps a hostile group?

In real-world writing, we always have an audience. And it is likely your reader is also your intended audience. In classroom writing, we always have a teacher. The teacher will read your work but may not necessarily be the intended audience. The teacher may often serve as your writing advocate, helping you to be more effective in reaching your intended audience. It is important to realize the distinction between a **reader*** and an audience.

What are all the things you need to know about the audience? What are you trying to accomplish?

The following are two reviews of Eminem's 2001 Grammy-winning *The Marshall Mathers LP.* It became the fastest-selling rap album in history. Both reviewers try to understand both Eminem and the CD-buying public's overwhelmingly positive response to him. Richard Kim's review stresses Eminem's use of the word "faggot"— Eminem's repetitive targeting of the homosexual world. On the other hand, Fuchs's review retells Eminem's familiar tough childhood story and then tries to figure out why our culture rewards him for his derogatory and wholesale slams. *After you read and* **annotate*** *the reviews, determine Kim's and Fuchs's* audiences. *What are they trying to accomplish by writing these reviews? Do both have the same* purpose? *How does race play a role in our response to Eminem?*

> ***annotate**: To add critical commentary or explanatory notes to an existing text.

Richard Kim

Eminem—Bad Rap?

Does *The Marshall Mathers LP*—in which great white hip-hop hope **Eminem*** fantasizes about killing his wife, raping his mother, forcing rival rappers to suck his dick and holding at knife-point faggots who keep "eggin' [him] on"—deserve Album-of-the-Year honors? This is the question before members of the National Academy of Recording Arts and Sciences (NARAS), who have, since nominating Eminem for four Grammy awards, received unsolicited advice from a bizarre constellation of celebrities, journalists and activists ranging from Charles Murray to British pop singer (and Eminem collaborator) Dido.

Bob Herbert of the *New York Times* took the opportunity to deplore not just Eminem's lyrics but the entire genre of rap music for "infantile rhymes" and "gibberish." In a more nuanced report, *Teen* magazine asked, Eminem: angel or devil? and discovered that 74 percent of teenage girls surveyed would date him if they could. The Ontario attorney general even attempted to bar Eminem from entering the country for violating the "hate propaganda" section of the Canadian Criminal Code.

But the most vociferous and persistent criticism of Eminem has come from an odd combination of activists: gay rights groups like the Gay and Lesbian Alliance Against Defamation (GLAAD) and family-values right-wingers like James Dobson's Focus on the Family. They all argue that Eminem's album threatens not only the objects of his violent lyrical outbursts but also, in GLAAD's words, the "artist's fan base of easily influenced adolescents who emulate Eminem's dress, mannerisms, words and beliefs."

In the face of all this attention to Eminem's "hate speech," even the usually taciturn NARAS is doing some public soul-searching. The academy's president, Michael Greene, recently said, "There's no question about the repugnancy of many of his songs. They're nauseating in terms of how we as a culture like to view human progress. But it's a remarkable recording, and the dialogue that it's already started is a good one."

As I have been forced to sit through all this Eminem-inspired hand-wringing over the physical and psychological well-being of faggots like myself, I've wondered just how good that dialogue really is. For one thing, so much of what has been said and written about Eminem has been political grandstanding. For example, **Lynne Cheney,*** not usually known as a feminist, singled out Eminem as a "violent misogynist" at a Senate committee

> ***Eminem**: (1972–) Born Marshall Mathers, Eminem burst onto the rap scene in the late 1990s, exploiting his poor white background as the subject matter for his lyrics. His *The Marshall Mathers LP* won a Grammy for Best Rap Album in 2001, selling nearly 2 million copies in the first week.
>
> ***Lynne Cheney**: (1941–) Married to Vice President Richard Cheney since 1964, Mrs. Cheney has a Ph.D in English from the University of Wisconsin. She has served as chair (1986–1993) of the National Endowment for the Humanities and has been a force in writing and speaking about the importance of historical knowledge in the education of children.

5

hearing on violence and entertainment. Eminem's lyrics, she argued, pose a danger to children, "the intelligent fish swimming in a deep ocean," where the media are "waves that penetrate through the water and through our children . . . again and again from this direction and that." Pretty sick stuff. Maybe it comes from listening to *Marshall Mathers*, but maybe it's the real Lynne Cheney, of lesbian pulp-fiction fame, finally standing up.

GLAAD, for its part, argues that Eminem encourages anti-gay violence, and it has used the controversy over Eminem's lyrics to fuel a campaign for hate-crimes legislation. While GLAAD and Cheney have different motives, both spout arguments that collapse the distance between speech and action—a strategy Catharine MacKinnon pioneered in her war against pornography. Right-wingers like Cheney and antiporn feminists like MacKinnon have long maintained such an unholy alliance, but you would think gay activists would be more cautious about making such facile claims. After all, if a hip-hop album can be held responsible for anti-gay violence, what criminal activities might the gay-friendly children's book *Daddy's Roommate* inspire? Because the lines between critique and censorship, dissent and criminality, are so porous and unpredictable, attacking Eminem for promoting "antisocial" activity is a tricky game.

Thankfully, GLAAD stops short of advocating censorship; instead it asks the entertainment industry to exercise "responsibility." GLAAD launched its anti-Eminem crusade by protesting MTV's heavy promotion of *Marshall Mathers*, which included six Video Music Award nominations and a whole weekend of programming called "Em-TV." After meeting with GLAAD representatives in June, MTV's head of programming, Brian Graden, piously confessed, "I would be lying to you if I didn't say it was something we struggled with." Liberal guilt aside, MTV nonetheless crowned Eminem with Video of the Year honors and then, in an attempt to atone for its sins, ran almost a full day of programming devoted to hate crimes, starting with a mawkish after-school special on the murder of Matthew Shepard, called *Anatomy of a Hate Crime*, and concluding with a seventeen-hour, commercial-free scrolling catalogue of the kind of horrific and yet somehow humdrum homophobic, misogynous and racist incidents that usually don't make it into the local news.

Perhaps understandably, Eminem's detractors still weren't satisfied, but given the fact that Eminem is one of the bestselling hip-hop artists of all time, what exactly did they expect from MTV and the Grammys but hypocrisy and faithless apology? And what do they really expect from Eminem—a recantation? Does anyone remember the homophobic statements that Sebastian Bach of Skid Row and Marky Mark made a decade ago? Point of fact: Marky Mark revamped his career by becoming that seminal gay icon, the Calvin Klein underwear model, and Bach, long blond locks still in place, recently starred in the Broadway musical *Jekyll and Hyde*. All of which just goes to show, if hunky (and profitable) enough, you can always bite the limp-wristed hand that feeds you. Meanwhile, the dialogue among Eminem's fans has been equally confusing. Some, like gay diva Elton John (who's scheduled to perform a duet with Eminem at the Grammys) and hip-hop star Missy Elliot, praise Eminem's album as hard-hitting reportage from the white working-class front. They argue that his lyrics are not only excusable but laudable, because they reflect the artist's lived experiences. This is, as London *Guardian* columnist Joan Smith pointed out, a "specious defence."

Should we excuse Eminem because he is, after all, sincere? Should we ignore his own genuinely violent acts—like pistol-whipping a man he allegedly caught kissing his wife? Others, like *Spin* magazine, have defended him as a brilliant provocateur. Far from being about realness, they argue, *Marshall Mathers* is parody, a horror show of self-loathing and other-loathing theater, a sick joke that Eminem's fans are in on. They point to how he peppers his rants with hyperbole, denials and reversals, calling into question not only the sincerity of his words but also their efficacy. For example, he raps about how he "hates fags" and then claims he's just kidding and that we should relax—he "likes gay men."

I don't know if Eminem really likes gay men, although I'd sure like to find out. What is clear from listening to *Marshall Mathers* is that he needs gay men. When asked by MTV's Kurt Loder about his use of the word "faggot," Eminem said, "The lowest degrading thing that you can say to a man when you're battling him is to call him a faggot and try to take away his manhood. Call him a sissy, call him a punk. 'Faggot' to me doesn't necessarily mean gay people. 'Faggot' to me just means taking away your manhood." Of course, using the word "faggot" has this effect only through its association with homosexuality and effeminacy, but there, really, you have it. Homosexuality is so crucial to Eminem's series of self-constructions (he mentions it in thirteen of eighteen tracks) that it's hard to imagine what he would rap about if he didn't have us faggots.

Eminem is, in his own words, "poor white trash." He comes from a broken home; he used to "get beat up, peed on, be on free lunch and change school every 3 months." So who does he diss in order to establish his cred as a white, male rapper? The only people lower on the adolescent totem pole than he is—faggots. This strategy of securing masculinity by obsessively disavowing homosexuality is hardly Eminem's invention, nor is it unique to male working-class culture or hip-hop music. Indeed, Eminem's lyrics may be more banal than exceptional in the way they invoke homophobic violence.

Marshall Mathers reworks the classic Western literary trope of homosexuality, which manifests itself as at once hysterical homophobia and barely submerged homoeroticism. It reflects the kind of locker-room antics that his white, male, suburban audience is well acquainted with. So too were Matthew Shepard's killers, Aaron McKinney and Russell Henderson, and the perpetrators of the hate crimes MTV listed (who were, not so incidentally, almost all white men), and, for that matter, the Supreme Court, which recently held in the Boy Scouts' case that homophobic speech is so essential to boyhood that it's constitutionally protected. Herein may lie the real brilliance of Eminem as an artist and as a businessman. In a political culture dominated by vacuous claims to a fictive social unity—tolerance, compassionate conservatism, reconciliation—he recognizes that pain and negativity, of the white male variety in particular, still sell.

Marshall Mathers, aka Eminem.

10

So does *Marshall Mathers* deserve Album of the Year? Well, I probably wouldn't vote for it, but if it does win, that would be perfectly in keeping with Grammy's tradition of rewarding commercial success. And where might a really good dialogue on homophobia, violence and entertainment begin? It might look at why *The Marshall Mathers LP* proved to be so pleasurable for so many, not despite but rather because of its violent themes. It might start by seeing Eminem not as an exception but as the rule—one upheld not just by commercial entertainment values but by our courts, schools, family structures and arrangements of public space. As Eminem says, "Guess there's a Slim Shady in all of us. Fuck it, let's all stand up."

Cynthia Fuchs

Eminem: *The Marshall Mathers LP* (Aftermath/Interscope)

Murdering Rhymes

I murder a rhyme one word at a time.
You never heard of a mind as perverted as mine.
You better get rid of that nine, it ain't gonna help.
What good's it gonna do against a man that strangles himself.
                                        —Eminem, "I'm Back"

Eminem, you can melt in my mouth anytime.
                    —Eminem fan, homemade poster

Eminem had a hard life coming up, violent and traumatic. He felt abandoned by his single mother, watched a lot of TV, was beaten into a coma by classmates, quit school after three tries at the ninth grade, and flipped burgers for a spell. In between, he paid his MC dues at local contests and on all kinds of stages. This much you know from the bijillion and one interviews the 27-year-old Detroit native has done since turning out two multiplatinum records within a year. And yes, homeboy's come out on top: however dreadful his childhood, he's learned to work his demons. Check the lyrics quoted above, off his new album, *The Marshall Mathers LP*: what's more awful than a man who will do damage to himself? Or these lyrics, from the song "Under The Influence": "Some bitch asked for my autograph/I called her a whore, spit beer in her face and laughed/I drop bombs like I was in Vietnam/All bitches is hos, even my stinkin' ass mom." (This would be the same mom who has famously hit him with a $10 million slander suit.) Eminem deploys his bad experiences like artillery, rat-a-tat, and doesn't mind displaying his pissed-at-the-planet mania like some kind of medal he's awarded to himself: good job, asshole, you've survived.

Angry and sad, boastful and self-disparaging, Em follows many artists who've emerged from bad beginnings, maybe a little surprised that he's made it, but also resentful and looking for payback. Most accounts of Eminem focus on his true survivor status, because, you know, authenticity is important for credibility, not to mention sales. In the star profiles and the feature stories, Em comes off as really angry, really crazy, really belligerent, and, even better, really having reasons to be all of that. Those reasons make him good copy. And his whiteness makes him simultaneously terrifying and unscary, the perfect pop product. As the flavor of the minute, he's the cover boy for *Spin, The Source, Muzik, Stress,* and *XXL*. He's touring with Dre and Snoop for Up in Smoke, partying hard and causing trouble, just like he's supposed to. Mad at his detractors, he accuses them of hypocrisy, of not accepting him as he thinks he is. In "Bitch Please II," he spews, "So when you see me, dressin' up like a nerd on TV/Or heard the CD usin' the fag word so freely/It's just me being me; here, want me to tone it down?/Suck my fuckin' dick, you faggot." You see the pattern, and it's not news.

That Eminem's imagination takes him to dark and disagreeable places is predictable; that he exhibits it so relentlessly and so profitably is something else. When people fret about Eminem's wickedness or call him out for writing misogynistic and homophobic lyrics, they're only stating the obvious, what he and his fans already know. And he's ready with an answer. Or better, he *is* the answer, a walking-and-talking cultural symptom. In "The Way I Am," Eminem expounds, "Since birth I've been cursed with this curse to just curse/And just blurt this berserk and bizarre shit that works/And it sells and it helps in itself to relieve/All this tension, dispensin' these sentences." So there it is: he's performing therapy. And the culture in turn rewards him for being "outrageous," for marking its limits. Undoubtedly, these limits are familiar. Eminem is no different from other wild-white-boy celebrities who punch out paparazzi, crash their cars, or dis their girls in public; sometimes they even smoke dope and carry concealed weapons. But they're never so alarming as black men with guns. Not even. Eminem's anger confined to specific targets and characters and often funny in its delivery is somehow understandable, even when it's whiny. Listeners can assume he's not talking about them ("I'm not a bitch!"). He claims to speak for social and political victims, kids who don't get respect, who are pissed off and afraid (for instance, on the new record, the Columbine shooters, verbally abused by their classmates). He says he speaks for those who can't speak for themselves (excepting, of course, those "bitches" and "fags," who apparently don't deserve to speak anyway). True, he's no longer disenfranchised, but he remembers it well enough, at least for the moment, to act like he is.

This is, of course, the standard dilemma for artists whose currency is being—or seeming—real. There's no way to win at this game: the industry loves authentic artists and immediately turns them not-authentic (the dreaded sell-out). Which means that even those performers who don't claim authenticity (say, 'N Sync), eventually succumb to its demands, assuming songwriting or producing duties on their albums, even if they're not equipped. Eminem is working very hard to maintain his measure of realness. But it's an uphill struggle. For all his raging and cursing, he's adorable. Girls and boys love him on *TRL*, voting him into the same countdown as the Backstreet Boys and Christina Aguilera (and, to be fair, those rebels Limp Bizkit and Korn). Hilariously, the kids vote him in even though his video is all about hating the consuming conformity exemplified by Britney, et. al. (And in fact, we've been here before, with Blink-182's "All the Small Things," a dis of popstars that made them popstars).

In a number of songs on the new album, including the current single, "The Real Slim Shady," Eminem slams his "enemies" with comic book intensity. In the video, he wears a superhero costume and an insane asylum straitjacket while rapping, "I'm sick of you little

5

girl and boy groups, all you do is annoy me/So I have been sent here to destroy you/And there's a million of us just like me/Who cuss like me; who just don't give a fuck like me/Who dress like me; walk, talk and act like me/And just might be the next best thing, but not quite me!" Of course, the irony is built into the song: Eminem's signature style the bleached blond hair, pale skin, humungous T-shirt has spawned droves of lookalikes and wannabes. Voila, he's a teen idol. Poor Em, can't win for losing.

Perhaps this is just desserts. As *XXL* and *Salon*, among others, have noted, Eminem's targets are easy and have been hit previously by other social critics. On *The Marshall Mathers LP*, he repeatedly disses the usual suspects: Britney, Carson Daly, the Insane Clown Posse, his mother. These aren't exactly folks who have done or will do him harm, and they don't cost him much; most of his fans (and others) are openly delighted to see the Christina fuck-me doll caught between Fred Durst and someone who vaguely looks like Carson. You know, it's like, awesome.

And so, that these days, Marshall Mathers is doing battle with himself, spitting venom and verse like there's no tomorrow. He's remade himself between the two albums: the first was named for the "real" Slim Shady, the new one for the "real" Marshall Mathers, as if either of them is "real." Still, the concerns on the two records are not so different: he remains mad at his wife for cheating on him, the pop industry for being crass and commercial, homosexuals for threatening his manhood (or something like that). And yet, as hardheaded and fucked up as he is when in performance mode—which appears to be continuous—Eminem is nothing if not self-conscious of his own artifice and extremity. There may be some irony in his current circumstances: after a couple of scuffles, he's been charged with assault and carrying a concealed weapon. Ever-ready to talk about himself, he's now telling interviewers that his fame has turned into a "nightmare," that all he ever wanted was a "career in hip-hop," as if this is a simple and straightforward desire. More often than not, such a career involves controversy and noise. And so Eminem, demonically clever white boy, brings it.

What's most notable about all this hasn't been much noted in the press. He's termed inane and offensive, clever and ignorant. But he's not called representative, not for his race, generation, genre, or gender, not even for his class (whatever that may be at this point). No one is saying that Eminem's vile language or violent imagery typifies the white race or even the young urban white male. In part this is a function of his own acerbic self-censure, which allows him a comedic, almost Woody-Allen-style cut-and-run. And in part it's because he's hanging with Dre and them: he doesn't "act white." But the more immediate and discomforting reason is precisely this: he is white. And white boys don't have to represent.

When we determine audience, we become more acutely aware of who's included and who's excluded. *Are you part of Kim's audience? Are you part of Fuchs's audience? Now that you have read the reviews, would you be more inclined to call them responses than reviews? How much attention is directed to the music and how much to the cultural phenomenon that Eminem has become in the early years of the new century? Do Eminem's lyrics have any relevancy or consequences for issues of justice?*

The following third response is a review of the CD itself. *How would you describe Massey's audience and purpose? How are they different from the two review-responses above? Do you find anything about the following short review disturbing?*

Chris Massey

Eminem: *The Marshall Mathers LP*

I love this CD. I picked it up because I thought it might be "decent." I had "The Real Slim Shady" stuck in my head, playin' over and over, after watching the video on good ole MTV. So . . . I took the plunge . . . handed over my 15 bucks . . . and headed home to spin it. Little did I know what was in store. I'm a latecomer to the whole Eminem craze. I didn't expect the sporadic genius of *The Marshall Mathers LP*, that's for sure.

The Marshall Mathers LP is certainly not for the squeamish or the young, and well deserves the "Explicit Content" sticker on its front. Unlike most rap artists who talk about gangs and cars and guns and bitches, Eminem talks more about domestic violence, gays, crime and himself (okay, the latter is certainly integral to the music of any rap artist).

Much of the material is based on his life, and his abuse at the hands of his father, and some none-too-pleasant remarks about his mother, who is even now suing him for something like $10 million. The album is riddled with profanity. From "Puffy" Combs to Britney Spears to boy bands, no one is safe under the scrutiny of Eminem's pen. There's been much controversy over the lyrics since the album was released, especially concerning Eminem's apparent hatred of gays, and the controversy is certainly warranted, but for my two cents his lyrics hardly detract from the album more than the derogatory lyrics about bitches and such do from any other rap album. It's expected.

The beats are awesome, taken from both the Dr. Dre camp and Eminem's own. They provide a different background for each track and avoid sounding as though they're all in the same vein. This is good—we're going to hear this album on every street this summer, so diversity of rhythm is certainly a good thing. The rhythm of Slim Shady's delivery is also diverse. Every song has him switching up and sounding entirely different. From the talking/rhyming of "Stan" to the relentless rhyme of "The Way I Am," Eminem is anything but boring. His rhythms are smart and interesting.

The most disturbing track is "Kim," a song about his wife and the mother of his child, Hallie. The song is a six-minute tirade, Eminem screaming at his wife as she cries and pleas with him—a brutal glance into the dark halls of domestic violence that never fails to give chills. 5

The album is brilliant, for the most part, and I've been spinning it continuously for weeks, just as I listened to Dr. Dre's *2001* for weeks straight last year. The content may be disturbing, and Eminem may be dangerous, but the album as a whole is a major work from a skinny boy from Detroit.

The following lyrics are from a song called "Criminal" on the fast-selling, award-winning Marshall Mathers LP. How do the review-responses above prepare you for reading the words of one of Eminem's songs?

Eminem

Criminal

A lot of people ask me . . . stupid fuckin questions
A lot of people think that . . . what I say on records
or what I talk about on a record, that I actually do in real life
or that I believe in it

5   Or if I say that, I wanna kill somebody, that . . .
       I'm actually gonna do it
       or that I believe in it
       Well, shit . . . if you believe that
       then I'll kill you
10   You know why?
       Cuz I'm a
       CRIMINAL
       CRIMINAL
       You god damn right
15   I'm a CRIMINAL
       Yeah, I'm a CRIMINAL

       My words are like a dagger with a jagged edge
       That'll stab you in the head
       whether you're a fag or lez
20   Or the homosex, hermaph or a trans-a-vest
       Pants or dress - hate fags? The answer's "yes"
       Homophobic? Nah, you're just heterophobic
       Starin at my jeans, watchin my genitals bulgin (Ooh!)
       That's my motherfuckin balls, you'd better let go of em
25   They belong in my scrotum, you'll never get hold of em
       Hey, it's me, Versace
       Whoops, somebody shot me!
       And I was just checkin the mail
       Get it? Checkin the 'male'?
30   How many records you expectin to sell
       after your second LP sends you directly to jail?
       C'mon!—Relax guy, I like gay men
       Right, Ken? Give me an amen (AAA-men!)
       Please Lord, this boy needs Jesus
35   Heal this child, help us destroy these demons
       Oh, and please send me a brand new car
       And a prostitute while my wife's sick in the hospital
       Preacher preacher, fifth grade teacher
       You can't reach me, my mom can't neither
40   You can't teach me a goddamn thing cause
       I watch TV, and Comcast cable
       and you ain't able to stop these thoughts
       You can't stop me from toppin these charts
       And you can't stop me from droppin each March
45   with a brand new cd for these fuckin retards
       Duhhh, and to think, it's just little ol' me
       Mr. "Don't Give A Fuck," still won't leave

       I'm a CRIMINAL

Cuz every time I write a rhyme, these people think it's a crime
to tell em what's on my mind—I guess I'm a CRIMINAL
but I don't gotta say a word, I just flip em the bird
and keep goin, I don't take shit from no one

My mother did drugs—malt liquor, cigarettes, and speed
The baby came out— disfigured, ligaments indeed
It was a seed who would grow up just as crazy as she
Don't dare make fun of that baby cause that baby was me
I'm a CRIMINAL—an animal caged who turned crazed
But how the fuck you sposed to grow up when you weren't raised?
So as I got older and I got a lot taller
My dick shrunk smaller, but my balls got larger
I drink malt liquor to fuck you up quicker
than you'd wanna fuck me up for sayin the word . . .
My morals went thhbbppp when the president got oral
Sex in his Oval Office on top of his desk
Off of his own employee
Now don't ignore me, you won't avoid me
You can't miss me, I'm white, blonde-haired
And my nose is pointy
I'm the bad guy who makes fun of people that die
in plane crashes and laughs
As long as it ain't happened to him
Slim Shady, I'm as crazy as Eminem and Kim combined—*kch* the maniac's in
Replacin the doctor cause Dre couldn't make it today
He's a little under the weather, so I'm takin his place
(Mm-mm-mmm!) Oh, that's Dre with an AK to his face
Don't make me kill him too and spray his brains all over the place
I told you Dre, you should've kept that thang put away
I guess that'll teach you not to let me play with it, eh?
I'm a CRIMINAL . . .
Windows tinted on my ride when I drive in it
So when I rob a bank, run out and just dive in it
So I'll be disguised in it
And if anybody identifies the guy in it
I'll hide for five minutes
Come back, shoot the eyewitness
Fire at the private eye hired to pry in my business
Die, bitches, bastards, brats, pets
This puppy's lucky I didn't blast his ass yet
If I ever gave a fuck, I'd shave my nuts
tuck my dick in between my legs and cluck
You motherfuckin chickens ain't brave enough
to say the stuff I say, so this tape is shut
Shit, half the shit I say, I just make it up

50

55

60

65

70

75

80

85

90

To make you mad so kiss my white naked ass
95   And if it's not a rapper that I make it as I'm a be
a fuckin rappist in a Jason mask

Who is the audience for this rap song? Does the audience understand the song's purpose? Is it possible that someone not in the intended audience might not understand the purpose? Is it possible there are multiple purposes? Does the voice match the purpose for the intended audience? What happens when the music is removed from the words? How is it possible to interpret the purpose of the song for someone not in its intended audience? Are you a member of the audience? Are your parents? Your younger siblings?

LISTENING FOR VOICE AND INTERPRETING TONE

The Constitution, the black men came to understand, was the white boys' Bible; and the lawyers quoted it often, chapter and verse, taking secular pleasure in its ornate language every bit as much as the rural people relished the antiquated resonance of biblical thou shalts and wherefores and cometh and goeths. But was this religion, or was this fact?

—Melissa Fay Greene, *Praying for Sheetrock*

Once a speaker/writer has considered purpose and determined audience, he or she will then produce a *voice* in which to accomplish the desired results. The most important aspect of voice is the **tone,** or style or manner of expression. The accent or inflection of various words expresses differences of meaning and connects with emotional responses. Tone can be warm and inviting; it can also be ironic and distant. Tone can be calculating and cold, demeaning and dismissive. When tone fails to connect with the reader/listener, the speaker/writer may fail miserably in accomplishing the purpose and winning over all the audience. Perhaps only part of the audience is won over; someone is left out and insulted. In prose, tone is perfectly pitched when it is fine-tuned to support the purpose and address the intended audience.

*tone: The sound of words, which convey a meaning that might add to or take away from the words themselves; the attitude of a piece of writing; style or manner of expression.

*Queen Latifah: (1970–) Born Dana Elaine Owens and winner of one Grammy, Queen Latifah at the start of the twenty-first century is the most well known female rapper.

There are many ways to enter a discussion about tone, but for our purposes here we turn to rap lyrics. In rap music, voice comes across even in the written word. Rapsters and anger often go hand-in-hand. The tone in rap music either invites you in or dismisses you quickly. In rap music, the purpose may well be to offend and demean, and we have to take a second look at how tone works to support not the intended audience but some other group or people who may be the "target" of the song.

Oddly, the subjects of both Eminem's song earlier in the chapter and **Queen Latifah's*** song on the following page—violence, misogyny, sex, and so forth—are used by the music industry, perhaps in different ways. *How would you compare Eminem's lyrics from "Criminal" with those of Queen's lyrics (more recently sung by Queen Latifah) for "Sleeping on the Sidewalk"? Is the audience the same? Is the purpose the same? Is the voice the same? In looking at one beside the other, do both songs* *come into a sharper perspective? Is one more effective in reaching its goals than the other? How do the songs explore the issue of justice?*

Sleeping on the Sidewalk

I was nothin' but a city boy
My trumpet was my only toy
I've been blowin' my horn
Since I knew I was born
But there ain't nobody wants to know   5

I've been
Sleepin' on the sidewalk
Rollin' down the road
I may get hungry
But I sure don't want to go home   10

So round the corner comes a limousine
And the biggest grin I've ever seen
Come on sonny won't you sign
Right along the dotted line
What you sayin' Are you playin'   15
Sure you don't mean me?

Sleepin' on the sidewalk
Rollin' down the road
I may get hungry
But I sure don't wanna go home   20

(tell you what happened . . .)
They took me to a room without a table
They said "blow your trumpet into here"
I played around as well as I was able
And soon we had the record of the year   25
I was a legend all through the land
I was blowin' to a million fans
Nothin' was a-missin'
All the people want to listen
You'd have thought I was a happy man   30

And I was
Sleepin' like a princess
Never touch the road
I don't get hungry
And I sure don't want to go home   35

(have to have some fun . . .)
Now they tell me that I ain't so fashionable
An' I owe the man a million bucks a year
So I told 'em where to stick the fancy label
40   It's just me and the road from here

Back to playin' and layin'
I'm back on the game
Sleepin' on the sidewalk
Rollin' down the road
45   I sure get hungry and I
Sure do wanna go home

In this final selection by Korn, the subject of these lyrics—violence against the homosexual male—has also been a prime reason for "hate crime" legislation in our courts. *After reading "Faget," discuss with others in a group how this piece helps or hurts homosexuals. What is the tone here? Defiance? If so, who is defying whom? Is there a double message in the singer's words? In how many ways might the lyrics of this song be misunderstood?*

Korn

Faget

Him!

Here I am different in this normal world
Why did you tease me? Made me feel upset
Fucking stereotypes feeding their heads
5   I am ugly. Please just go away.

Him!
I can see inside you fine!
This blessing in disguise
Him!
10   Why do you treat me this way?
Made to hate to stay (Made the hurt to stay)

I sound like I can never seem to escape
All the laughing, all the pain
If you were me, what would you do?
15   Nothing, probably. You'd just throw me away.

Faget!

I'm just a pretty boy, whatever you call it
You wouldn't know a real man if you saw it
It keeps going on day after day, son

You fake, if we don't want none   20
I'm sick and tired of people treating me this way everyday
Who gives a fuck?!
Right now I got something to say to all the people that think
I'm strange and I should be out here locked up in a cage
You don't know what the hell is up now anyway   25
You got this pretty-boy feeling
Like I'm enslaved to a world that never
Appreciated shit
You can suck my dick and fucking like it!!!

He had my gun but he had to find the money   30
(He might come, but he has a body mighty)
Any say, anyway, don't wanna say, anyway, any say,
Going away, don't wanna say, anyway

I'm just a pretty boy, I'm not supposed to fuck a girl
I'm just a pretty boy, living in this fucked up world   35

All my life, who am I?

I'm just a faget!
Faget!
I'm a faget!
Faget!   40
I'm not a faget
What am I?
Faget!
You mother fucking queers!

Bring your own examples of rap lyrics to class and take a look at how tone works for and against particular audiences. Some people whisper and some people scream to make their points. Rap and issues of justice make odd bedfellows.

CONTRASTING TONES IN DIFFERENT GENRES

In the following **short story,** written in the 1950s by Alice Childress (1920–1994), a domestic worker amuses her friend Marge on the bus by recounting an exchange with her new employer about a "health card." Today, when people ask to see your health card, they are asking for proof of insurance; when the

> *short story: A narrative form of fiction, shorter than forty pages that has characters and a plot in which they act or exist.

employer asks to see a health card in this story, what kind of proof is she asking for? *Determine how, as the title of the story, this health card becomes the subject around which the author develops her tone. After you read the story, discuss purpose, audience, and voice. Which component is easiest to address first? By interpreting the tone of the story, decide if you are included in or excluded from the audience. Have a discussion with another classmate whose position is the opposite of yours. How does the voice of the story support the purpose and its audience? Underline words and phrases that contribute to producing the voice. What are the best words to describe the* tone *of the story? How does a definition of "health card" make itself clear through the author's tone?*

Alice Childress

Health Card

Well, Marge, I started an extra job today . . . . Just wait, girl. Don't laugh yet. Just wait till I tell you . . . . The woman seems real nice . . . . Well, you know what I mean . . . . She was pretty nice, anyway. Shows me this and shows me that, but she was real cautious about loadin' on too much work the first morning. And she stopped short when she caught the light in my eye.

Comes the afternoon, I was busy waxin' woodwork when I notice her hoverin' over me kind of timid-like. She passed me once and smiled and then she turned and blushed a little. I put down the wax can and gave her an inquirin' look. The lady takes a deep breath and comes up with, "Do you live in Harlem, Mildred?"

Now you know I expected something' more than that after all the hesitatin'. I had already given her my address so I didn't quite get the idea behind the question. "Yes, Mrs. Jones," I answered, "that is where I live."

Well, she backed away and retired to the living room and I could hear her and the husband just a-buzzin'. A little later on I was in the kitchen washin' glasses. I looks up and there she was in the doorway, lookin' kind of strained around the gills. First she stuttered and then she stammered and after beatin' all around the bush she comes out with, "Do you have a health card, Mildred?"

5   That let the cat out of the bag. I thought real fast. Honey, my brain was runnin' on wheels. "Yes, Mrs. Jones, " I says, "I have a health card." Now Marge, this is a lie. I do not have a health card. "I'll bring it tomorrow," I add real sweet-like.

She beams like a chromium platter and all you could see above her taffeta house coat is smile. "Mildred," she said, "I don't mean any offense, but one must be careful, mustn't one?"

Well, all she got from me was solid agreement. "Sure," I said, "indeed *one* must, and I am glad you are so understandin,' 'cause I was just worryin' and studyin' on how I was goin' to ask you for yours, and of course you'll let me see one from your husband and one for each of the three children."

By that time she was the same color as the housecoat, which is green, but I continue on: "Since I have to handle laundry and make beds, you know . . ." She stops me right there and after excusin' herself she scurries from the room and has another conference with hubby.

Inside fifteen minutes she was back. "Mildred, you don't have to bring a health card. I am sure it will be all right."

10   I looked up real casual kind-of and said, "On second thought, you folks look real clean, too, so . . ." And then she smiled and I smiled and then she smiled again . . . . Oh, stop laughin' so loud, Marge, everybody on this bus is starin'.

The narrator tells the story to Marge, but is the audience larger than Marge? With whom do you sympathize—the narrator who has been asked for her health card or the employer who does the asking? The narrator controls the short story; we hear nothing about why the employer feels as she does. Do you think the employer has a good reason for asking for the health card? Is it possible she may be concerned about a communicable disease? By reading the story, is it possible to describe the characters by race or ethnicity? Once you identify and/or describe the characters, does this new knowledge help you to feel either excluded from or included in the audience?

How does the tone of the story welcome you or exclude you?

In the 1930s, the Carnegie Corporation funded a full-scale study of black-white relations in the United States. In charge of this massive undertaking was **Gunnar Myrdal,*** a Swedish economist with an international reputation. The resulting study, *An American Dilemma*, over 1,500 pages, was published in 1944. The central thesis was that white Americans, nurtured by Christian beliefs and egalitarian rhetoric, were haunted by their treatment of black Americans, and this dilemma would eventually result in significant changes in race relations.

> ***Gunnar Myrdal:** (1898–1987) A 1974 Swedish Nobel Prize winner in economics. He was commissioned in 1938 by the Carnegie Corporation to study the "American Negro Problem." His findings were published in 1944 as *An American Dilemma: The Negro Problem and Modern Democracy.*

The following paragraphs open the introduction of the first edition of *An American Dilemma. Read carefully to determine purpose, voice, and audience. Also, notice what happens to the tone when the genre is not creative fiction but a sociological treatise. Setting aside the fact that you were not born in the 1930s, do you think you are included in or excluded from the audience of this serious study?*

Gunnar Myrdal

The Negro Problem as a Moral Issue

There is a "Negro problem" in the United States and most Americans are aware of it, although it assumes varying forms and intensity in different regions of the country and among diverse groups of the American people. Americans have to react to it, politically as citizens and, where there are Negroes present in the community, privately as neighbors.

To the great majority of white Americans the Negro problem has distinctly negative connotations. It suggests something difficult to settle and equally difficult to leave alone. It is embarrassing. It makes for moral uneasiness. The very presence of the Negro in America; his fate in the country through slavery, Civil War and Reconstruction; his recent career and his present status; his accommodation; his protest and his aspiration; in fact his entire biological, historical and social existence as a participant American represent to the ordinary white man in the North as well as in the South an anomaly in the very structure of American society. To many, this takes on the proportion of a menace—biological, economic, social, cultural, and, at times, political. This anxiety may be mingled with a feeling of individual and collective guilt. A few see the problem as a challenge to statesmanship. To all it is a trouble.

These and many other mutually inconsistent attitudes are blended into none too logical a scheme which, in turn, may be quite inconsistent with the wider personal, moral, religious, and civic sentiments and ideas of the Americans. Now and then, even the least sophisticated individual becomes aware of his own confusion and the contradiction in his attitudes. Occasionally he may recognize, even if only for a moment, the incongruence of his state of mind and find it so intolerable that the whole organization of his moral pre-cepts is shaken. But most people, most of the time, suppress such threats to their moral integrity together with all of the confusion, the ambiguity, and inconsistency which lurks in the basement of man's soul. This, however, is rarely accomplished without mental strain. Out of the strain comes a sense of uneasiness and awkwardness which always seems attached to the Negro problem.

Think about the tone in this piece. Underline some of the word choices that help you to understand the tone. Is the tone effective in reaching the author's intended audience? Take a look at the Constitution of the United States and the Declaration of Independence. Do either of these two documents shed any light on Myrdal's treatise?

Over sixty years have passed since Myrdal wrote his landmark study. In a more recent survey conducted by the Gallup Organization for the American Association of Retired People (AARP) and the Leadership Conference on Civil Rights, surprising progress was discovered from the 2,002 people who responded to a telephone survey in late 2003. The following article places the findings in context.

Adam Goodheart

Change of Heart

The rural Maryland county where I live, barely an hour from the Washington, D.C., Beltway, is a place whose soul is not just divided but fractured. There are still small towns here that feel like the Old South, where whites talk about "colored people" and blacks in their late 40s remember such things as farming with mules and horses and attending seg-regated schools. But there are newer communities, too: sprawling tracts of identical sub-urban houses whose middle-class residents—black as well as white—think little about the past and care even less. In their midst, a small but growing Hispanic population has started to thrive, drawn by the economic opportunities that change has brought.

Many parts of our country today look something like this. When President Lyndon Johnson's Kerner Commission famously prophesied in 1968 a future of "two societies, one black, one white," it was wrong. What we have now is a multiplicity of Americas, often sharing the same neighborhood, but rarely the same mindset.

The good news is that in the 50 years since the Supreme Court ruled in favor of school desegregation in the case of *Brown* v. *Board of Education*, there have been some dramatic changes in Americans' attitudes toward race and equality. Today, most Americans—55 percent—think that the state of race relations is either very or somewhat good, according to a landmark telephone survey of 2,002 people conducted last November and December by the Gallup Organization for AARP and the Leadership Conference on Civil Rights (LCCR). Yet disheartening divisions between the races persist. Such is the complicated picture painted by "Civil Rights and Race Relations," the largest and most comprehensive race-relations sur-vey of blacks, Hispanics, and whites that Gallup has ever undertaken.

The most astonishing progress has been made in two areas that hit closest to home for most Americans: interracial relationships and the neighborhoods we live in. Consider that 70 percent of whites now say they approve of marriage between whites and blacks, up from just 4 percent in a 1958 Gallup poll. Such open-mindedness extends across racial lines: 80 percent of blacks and 77 percent of Hispanics also said they generally approve of interracial marriage. Perhaps even more remarkable, a large majority of white respondents—66 percent—say they would not object if their own child or grandchild chose a black spouse. Blacks (86 percent) and Hispanics (79 percent) were equally accepting about a child or grandchild's marrying someone of another race.

When it comes to choosing neighbors, an inclusive spirit again prevails: majorities of blacks, whites, and Hispanics all say they would rather live in racially mixed neighborhoods than surround themselves with only members of their own group. "It's hard now to imagine the level of fear and anxiety that Americans felt about these issues just a few decades ago," says Taylor Branch, who won a Pulitzer Prize in 1989 for his history of the Civil Rights Movement, *Parting the Waters: America in the King Years, 1954–1963.* "The idea [among whites] that you might have a black colleague or customer or neighbor has now become relatively commonplace except in a few scattered pockets." Similarly, slight majorities of whites and Hispanics and a little less than half of blacks think that minorities should try to blend in with the rest of American culture rather than maintain their own separate identities.

The data did show a significant generation gap: young Americans (ages 18–29) of all races were more likely than older respondents (65-plus) to favor the retention of distinctive cultures. But this is not necessarily a step backward. "Younger people are more likely to have been exposed in school to the idea that multiculturalism is a positive thing, that it's not necessarily bad when certain groups desire to be among their own kind," suggests the eminent Harvard sociologist William Julius Wilson. "This is a phenomenon of just the last couple of decades."

When it comes to future expectations, however, in certain respects the picture is as bleak as ever. Sixty-three percent of Americans think that race relations will always be a problem for our country—a view that varies little whether the respondents are white, black, or Hispanic. That's up sharply from the 42 percent who felt similarly in a study done in 1963, when most Americans were seeing television images of African Americans withstanding police dogs and fire hoses but believed the Civil Rights Movement would eventually prevail. (Indeed, respondents over 65, who remember the 1960s well, were the ones most likely to remain optimistic, while those under 30—of all races—were the least hopeful.)

"There was a sense then that eventually truth and justice would win out," recalls Julian Bond, who as a founder of the Student Nonviolent Coordinating Committee (SNCC) led some of the earliest sit-ins and is now chairman of the National Association for the Advancement of Colored People (NAACP). "Maybe people are looking back and realizing we haven't come as far as we'd hoped."

A large majority of Americans of all ages and races does agree that the 20th-century crusade for civil rights was a watershed in our nation's history. In addition, most people of all backgrounds also believe that the movement has benefited not just blacks and other minorities but all Americans. This is a remarkable degree of unanimity for an issue that violently divided so many families and communities just a generation or two ago.

"The Civil Rights Movement has had enormous collateral effects for everyone from gays to members of religious minorities, and especially for women," Branch says. "These effects have been felt in every university, every corporation, and even, I'd venture to say, almost every American household, down to the level of who does the dishes and changes the diapers."

But when it comes to gauging the ultimate success or failure of the struggle, members of different races diverge sharply. While 56 percent of whites say they believe that "all or most" of the goals of Dr. Martin Luther King Jr. and the 1960s Civil Rights Movement have been achieved, only 21 percent of blacks agree with them. A similar margin divides whites' and blacks' opinions on how much of a role the movement will continue to have: 66 percent of blacks think it will be "extremely important" to the United States in the future, compared with only 23 percent of whites. "Many whites have a misconception of the Civil Rights Movement as something with a few limited goals that have already been achieved," Branch suggests.

Similarly, the AARP-LCCR survey found vast gulfs between different groups' percep- tions of how minorities are treated today. Seventy-six percent of white respondents think that blacks are treated "very fairly" or "somewhat fairly," but only 38 percent of blacks agree with them; nearly one-third, in fact, say that members of their race are treated "very unfairly." (Hispanics fall in the middle: they are more or less evenly divided about the treat- ment of their own group as well as that of blacks.) And while 61 percent of whites believe that blacks have achieved equality in the realm of job opportunities, just 12 percent of African Americans concur.

How is it that we can all share the same land, the same history, and yet reach such different conclusions? The disparities start to make sense when you look at the most fun- damental measure of each group's current happiness: economic prosperity.

Blacks are more than twice as likely as whites to say that their personal finances are in "poor shape"; they are also more than twice as likely to say they worry constantly about whether their family's income will be enough to pay the bills. Hispanics appear to be feel- ing similar or even greater degrees of financial stress. And indeed, their concerns are legit- imate: nationally, the median household income is $35,500 among blacks, $40,000 among Hispanics, and $55,318 among whites, according to the most recent figures avail- able from the U.S. Census Bureau.

15   "Were we to have solved all the problems that we tried to take on, there would be rel- ative parity today," Bond says. "The fact that there is still an enormous wealth gap between blacks and whites is evidence of the continuing legacy of segregation and even of slavery."

What explains these persistent economic disparities? Continued prejudice, plain and simple. Half a century after *Brown*, a minuscule 8 percent of African Americans could claim that they had ever in their lives been denied admittance to a school on account of race. Yet other forms of discrimination persist. A third reported that they had been passed over for a job because they are black, a third said they had been blocked from promotion, and a quarter said they had been denied an opportunity to rent or buy hous- ing. Only slightly fewer Hispanics said they had experienced similar forms of prejudice.

Even more than such dramatic instances of racism, it is the less obvious, day-to-day examples of prejudice that are a continuing, grinding burden on minorities in America. Nearly half of all blacks reported having experienced at least one form of discrimination in the last 30 days, in settings ranging from stores (26 percent) to restaurants and theaters (18 percent) to public transportation (10 percent). The figures for Hispanics were at nearly the same level. Perhaps most troubling of all, a surprising 22 percent of blacks and 24 per- cent of Hispanics said they had, in the past month, been the victims of prejudice in an interaction with the police.

For the record, a significant number of white Americans maintain that they, too, are sometimes penalized on the basis of race: 21 percent report that they have been the victims of reverse discrimination, especially in the workplace. And many seem unaware or even dismissive of continuing prejudice against other groups: nearly half insist that society treats them no better than blacks. But the majority of whites—52 percent—say they support affirmative action for blacks, as do 81 percent of blacks and 66 percent of Hispanics. So while an uncomfortably large number of Americans remain in denial about persistent discrimination against minorities, an even larger percentage, it seems, want to do the right thing.

Like the American countryside, the AARP-LCCR survey results are a landscape of layers: old outlooks and new perceptions, 20th-century memories and 21st-century expectations. One of the most unexpected results came when the polltakers asked participants to consider the prediction that by 2050 the majority of Americans will be nonwhite. Only about 13 percent of each group said this would be a bad thing; most Americans said it simply won't matter.

So, as their country changes, perhaps Americans—more than they are often given credit for—are ready to change along with it. Indeed, the revolution that *Brown* started will likely continue through the next 50 years and beyond. "We did much," Bond says, "but there's much left to do."   20

1. Would not object to a child or grandchild's marrying someone of another race:
   Overall   71%
   Hispanic   79%
   White   66%
   Black   86%
2. Prefer to live in a neighborhood that is mostly mixed:
   Hispanic   61%
   White   57%
   Black   78%
3. Believe race relations will always be a problem in the United States:
   Overall   63%
   Hispanic   60%
   White   62%
   Black   72%
4. Think all or most of the goals of Dr. Martin Luther King, Jr., and the Civil Rights Movement have been achieved:
   Overall   50%
   Hispanic   38%
   White   56%
   Black   21%
5. Have been denied a rental or an opportunity to buy a home:
   Hispanic   19%
   White   2%
   Black   24%

Statistics referred to in the text of Goodheart's article have been extracted for a clearer referencing above. *How do your answers to the questions above correspond with your group's percentages? Are you included in the data collection pool? Who has been left out? Do you find any statistics that surprise you? Does any conclusion that Myrdal arrived at back in 1944 help you understand the responses to question 3 above: Most people questioned believe that race relations will always be a problem in the United States.*

*didactic: Intended to teach a moral lesson.

*treatise: A systematic exposition or argument.

*thesis: A position maintained by a sustained argument; a controlling idea.

In the three examples above—an easy-to-follow, humorous, and **didactic*** short story and a weighty, classic historical **treatise*** and a news article about *statistical data*—you might not notice on a first reading that each can shed light on the meaning of the others. Myrdal suggests that white America represses guilt, while Childress's domestic serves as a means to mock Mrs. Jones's discomfort in asking Mildred for her health card. The language of the historical treatise suggests a vocabulary you can use to write about a serious and important issue; the language of the light-hearted story provides an example you can use to understand more readily the abstract concepts of the treatise. While both pieces of prose can stand on their own, when put together a complicated topic is illuminated. The article containing statistical data brings Myrdal's excerpt into contemporary times. Further, the ability to rewrite or paraphrase the content of each piece helps you to identify the **thesis**,* point of view, argument, or controlling idea of the prose pieces.

FINDING THE THESIS AND UNIFYING THE WHOLE

So there must have been dozens of times that *nigger* was spoken in front of me before I reached the third grade. But I didn't "hear" it until it was said by a small pair of lips that had already learned it could be a way to humiliate me. That was the word I went home and asked my mother about. And since she knew that I had to grow up in America, she took me in her lap and explained.
—Gloria Naylor, "A Word's Meaning Can Often Depend on Who Says It"

Being able to successfully find the *thesis* of any piece of writing, no matter the genre, will help you read with better comprehension. A thesis can best be explained as a proposition or position that a person advances and maintains by a sustained argument. Some writers place the thesis in the first paragraph, but others depend on you to pick up the controlling idea within the first several pages of the piece. There is no right, dependable, or sure place to search for a thesis. After reading a piece, it may be helpful to talk with someone about what each of you thought the piece was about. Pay close attention to the beginning of Gloria Naylor's short fifteen-paragraph essay.

Gloria Naylor

A Word's Meaning Can Often Depend on Who Says It

Language is the subject. It is the written form with which I've managed to keep the wolf away from the door and, in diaries, to keep my sanity. In spite of them, I consider the written word inferior to the spoken, and much of the frustration experienced by novelists is the awareness that whatever we manage to capture in even the most transcendent passages falls short of the richness of life. Dialogue achieves its power in the dynamics of a fleeting moment of sight, sound, smell, and touch.

I'm not going to enter the debate here about whether it is language that shapes reality or vice versa. That battle is doomed to be waged whenever we seek intermittent reprieve from the chicken and egg dispute. I will simply take the position that the spoken word, like the written word, amounts to a nonsensical arrangement of sounds or letters without a consensus that assigns "meaning." And building from the meaning of what we hear, we order reality. Words themselves are innocuous; it is the consensus that gives them true power.

I remember the first time I heard the word *nigger*. In my third-grade class, our math tests were being passed down the rows, and as I handed the papers to a little boy in back of me, I remarked that once again he had received a much lower mark than I did. He snatched his test from me and spit out that word. Had he called me a nymphomaniac or a necrophiliac, I couldn't have been more puzzled. I didn't know what a nigger was, but I knew that whatever it meant, it was something he shouldn't have called me. This was verified when I raised my hand, and in a loud voice repeated what he had said and watched the teacher scold him for using a "bad" word. I was later to go home and ask the inevitable question that every black parent must face—"Mommy, what does *nigger* mean?"

And what exactly did it mean? Thinking back, I realize that this could not have been the first time the word was used in my presence. I was part of a large extended family that had migrated from the rural South after World War II and formed a close-knit network that gravitated around my maternal grandparents. Their ground-floor apartment in one of the buildings they owned in Harlem was a weekend mecca for my immediate family, along with countless aunts, uncles, and cousins who brought along assorted friends. It was a bustling and open house with assorted neighbors and tenants popping in and out to exchange bits of gossip, pick up an old quarrel, or referee the ongoing checkers game in which my grandmother cheated shamelessly. They were all there to let down their hair and put up their feet after a week of labor in the factories, laundries, and shipyards of New York.

Amid the clamor, which could reach deafening proportions—two or three conversations going on simultaneously, punctuated by the sound of a baby's crying somewhere in the back rooms or out on the street—there was still a rigid set of rules about what was said and how. Older children were sent out of the living room when it was time to get into the juicy details about "you-know-who" up on the third floor who had gone and gotten herself "p-r-e-g-n-a-n-t!" But my parents, knowing that I could spell well beyond my years, always demanded that I follow the others out to play. Beyond sexual misconduct and death, everything else was considered harmless for our young ears. And so among the anecdotes of the triumphs and disappointments in the various workings of their lives, the word *nigger* was used in my presence, but it was set within contexts and inflections that caused it to register in my mind as something else.

In the singular, the word was always applied to a man who had distinguished himself in some situation that brought their approval for his strength, intelligence, or drive:

"Did Johnny *really* do that?"

"I'm telling you, that nigger pulled in $6,000 of overtime last year. Said he got enough for a down payment on a house."

When used with a possessive adjective by a woman—"my nigger"—it became a term of endearment for her husband or boyfriend. But it could be more than just a term applied

5

to a man. In their mouths it became the pure essence of manhood—a disembodied force that channeled their past history of struggle and present survival against the odds into a victorious statement of being: "Yeah, that old foreman found out quick enough—you don't mess with a nigger."

10   In the plural, it became a description of some group within the community that had overstepped the bounds of decency as my family defined it. Parents who neglected their children, a drunken couple who fought in public, people who simply refused to look for work, those with excessively dirty mouths or unkempt households were all "trifling niggers." This particular circle could forgive hard times, unemployment, the occasional bout of depression—they had gone through all of that themselves—but the unforgivable sin was a lack of self-respect.

A woman could never be a "nigger" in the singular, with its connotation of confirming worth. The noun *girl* was its closest equivalent in that sense, but only when used in direct address and regardless of the gender doing the addressing. *Girl* was a token of respect for a woman. The one-syllable word was drawn out to sound like three in recognition of the extra ounce of wit, nerve, or daring that the woman had shown in the situation under discussion.

"G-i-r-l, stop. You mean you said that to his face?"

But if the word was used in a third-person reference or shortened so that it almost snapped out of the mouth, it always involved some element of communal disapproval. And age became an important factor in these exchanges. It was only between individuals of the same generation, or from any older person to a younger (but never the other way around), that *girl* would be considered a compliment.

I don't agree with the argument that use of the word *nigger* at this social stratum of the black community was an internalization of racism. The dynamics were the exact opposite: the people in my grandmother's living room took a word that whites used to signify worthlessness or degradation and rendered it impotent. Gathering there together, they transformed *nigger* to signify the varied and complex human beings they knew themselves to be. If the word was to disappear totally from the mouths of even the most liberal of white society, no one in that room was naïve enough to believe it would disappear from white minds. Meeting the word head-on, they proved it had absolutely nothing to do with the way they were determined to live their lives.

15   So there must have been dozens of times that *nigger* was spoken in front of me before I reached third grade. But I didn't "hear" it until it was said by a small pair of lips that had already learned it could be a way to humiliate me. That was the word I went home and asked my mother about. And since she knew that I had to grow up in America, she took me in her lap and explained.

In the opening two paragraphs, Naylor drives each of her sentences toward this last sentence of the second paragraph: *"Words themselves are innocuous; it is the consensus that gives them true power."* In these two paragraphs, each sentence promises us that Naylor is going to privilege the spoken word over the written word. We need to be clear on this point before we read the rest of the essay, but if we were satisfied with summing up the essay by this statement—words spoken mean more than words written—we would be doing a disservice to what follows. While Naylor's *thesis* is now clear to us, we don't have much to be excited about. In fact, we might have thought of this very premise ourselves, so we may feel underchallenged.

The first sentence in paragraph three looms large: "I remember the first time I heard the word *nigger*." The remaining thirteen paragraphs, the bulk of the essay, explore Naylor's recollection of the consensus of this moment. Only with the additional knowledge that Naylor is going to write about this explosive epithet does her thesis take on its distinctive slant, for the essay is controlled by a full exploration of how *nigger* sounds in the mouths of family, friends, or enemies, about what happens to *nigger* when it is heard in various contexts. To say that sound makes words matter is not so nearly interesting because the thesis remains *abstract;* once we have the example, *nigger,* we have added the *concrete,* and now we know what means Naylor will use to control her idea.

Sometimes a thesis and a controlling idea may be the same; sometimes a writer will use a controlling idea to expand or give concrete existence to an abstract thesis. Naylor's essay is an example of a separation between a thesis and a controlling idea; the latter becomes an extension of the former. Further, the fact that Naylor does not expand beyond the many uses and sounds of *nigger* is her way of unifying the whole. She provides for the reader a clear thesis with a controlling idea guided by one riveting concrete example satisfactorily explored.

So when you sit down to write a thesis for your next paper, think about the context of the thesis. For Naylor, the thesis is about language in the context of race. For

Halle Berry with her Oscar for Best Actress, 2002.

instance, if you wanted to write about anti-Semitism, that subject could easily become too broad to be focused into a usable thesis. But if you found a specific context for your thesis (writing about the containment wall in Israel), you could make your thesis and paper more immediate and effective.

Sometimes a thesis is not explicitly stated, but in such cases, the piece has a controlling idea that is so prevailing that it makes the thesis obvious, and it becomes an easy task to state it in your own words. Look at the following speech to see an example of a controlling idea where the thesis is clear—yet not explicitly stated.

The movie industry's highest awards, the Academy of Motion Picture Arts and Sciences Awards, familiarly called the Oscars, have been presented annually since the spring of 1929. Ten years later, in 1939, Hattie McDaniel won the Oscar for Best Supporting Actress for her role in *Gone with the Wind.* She was the first African American to win that award. Over fifty years later, Whoopi Goldberg became the second African American female to win in that category for her performance in *Ghost* (1990). When Halle Berry's name was called for Best Actress in 2002, it was an historical moment for the Academy of Motion Picture Arts and Sciences. The following is the speech Halle Berry gave when she accepted her Oscar for her performance in *Monster's Ball. As you read the speech, determine its thesis. Is it separate from or the same as its* controlling idea? *Does Berry assume her audience already knows that she is making history? Who is her audience? Are you included? Is her audience race based?*

Oscar Thank You for Best Actress Award, Halle Berry (acceptance speech)

Oh, my God. Oh, my God. I'm sorry. This moment is so much bigger than me. This moment is for Dorothy Dandridge, Lena Horne, Diahann Carroll. It's for the women that stand beside me, Jada Pinkett, Angela Bassett, Vivica Fox. And it's for every nameless, faceless woman of color that now has a chance because this door tonight has been opened. Thank you. I'm so honored. I'm so honored. And I thank the Academy for choosing me to be the vessel for which His blessing might flow. Thank you.

I want to thank my manager, Vincent Cirrincione. He's been with me for twelve long years and you fought every fight and you've loved me when I've been up, but more importantly you've loved me when I've been down. You have been a manager, a friend, and the only father I've ever known. Really. And I love you very much.

I want to thank my mom who's given me the strength to fight every single day, to be who I want to be and given me the courage to dream, that this dream might be happening and possible for me. I love you, Mom, so much. Thank you. My husband, who is just a joy of my life, and India [her daughter], thank you for giving me peace because only with the peace that you've brought me have I been allowed to go to places that I never even knew I could go. Thank you. I love you and India with all my heart.

I want to thank Lions Gate. Thank you. Mike Paseornek, Tom Ortenberg for making sure everybody knew about this little tiny movie. Thank you for believing in me. Our director Marc Forster, you're a genius. You're a genius. This moviemaking experience was magical for me because of you. You believed in me; you trusted me, and you gently guided me to very scary places. I thank you. I want to thank Ivana Chubic. I could have never figured out who the heck this lady was without you. I love you. Thank you. I want to thank Lee Daniels, our producer. Thank you for giving me this chance, for believing that I could do it. And now tonight I have this. Thank you.

5   I want to thank my agents—CAA, Josh Lieberman especially. I have to thank my agents—Kevin Huvane, thank you. Thank you for never kicking me out and sending me somewhere else. Thank you. I, I, I, who else? I have so many people that I know I need to thank. My lawyers—Neil Meyer, thank you. Okay, wait a minute. I got to take . . . seventy-four years here!! Ok. I got to take this time! I got to thank my lawyer, Neil Meyer, for making this deal. Doug Stone. I need to thank lastly and not leastly, I have to thank Spike Lee for putting me in my very first film and believing in me. Oprah Winfrey for being the best role model any girl can have. Joel Silver, thank you. And thank you to Warren Beatty. Thank you so much for being my mentors and believing in me.

Thank you! Thank you! Thank you!

Think of an award that you would like to win. Before you begin your acceptance speech, consider the purpose and audience for your speech—and then make sure your voice assists you in accomplishing your goals. Will your thesis and controlling idea be the same—or different?

In the following opinion column, what kind of thesis and/or controlling idea does Mark Pino use to make his point? Identify the thesis and/or controlling idea. Who is the audience for this piece? Are you included?

Mark Pino

If Hispanics Want a Voice, They Must Vote

It's a straightforward political formula, V=P. That's votes equal power.

The more votes, the more power.

It's a power that Osceola's Hispanic community is still trying to tap.

It's a power that many current leaders give lip service to because it hasn't manifested itself. But like the tides, it is only a matter of time before the churning surf changes the lay of the land. It's a power that's already lapping at the edge of political landscape.

And it's a power that could tip the scales one way or another in this year's elections.   5
In a state where every vote counts, Hispanics have clout—if they turn out and vote.

Registering Hispanics and getting them to the polls is the goal of a massive voter-education and registration drive that is the mastermind of the government of Puerto Rico.

Right off the bat, some people are going to be suspicious of the effort. Others will be angry about an effort to motivate Hispanics, mainly Puerto Ricans living on the mainland, to do something so basic.

Those folks are threatened because they know votes mean power.

Votes give voice to people. Hispanics in the country need a voice. Cubans form a part of that voice already. As U.S. citizens, Puerto Ricans—more than 3 million on the main-land—form another part of that bloc. And in Florida, they could help decide who sits in the White House. If only everyone could hear Mari Carmen Aponte, executive director of the Puerto Rico Federal Affairs Administration. The arm of the Puerto Rican government is lead-ing the effort to register 300,000 new Hispanic voters. They're close, and count 37,000—enough to decide a national race—new voters in Florida.

Aponte is a passionate apostle for getting out the vote. As citizens, she said, Puerto   10
Ricans have a duty to vote and give voice to Latinos living here who don't have that privi-lege. I've never heard anything that stirring from local leaders.

The "Que Nada Nos Detenga!" campaign—Spanish for "Let Nothing Stop Us!"—is a nonpartisan effort. Both parties win if Latinos vote, though Puerto Ricans have traditionally tended to vote for Democrats. But that doesn't always hold true. In Central Florida, John Quinones of Kissimmee was elected to the state House as a Republican.

Quinones was one of only a handful of elected officials at last week's event. Osceola Sheriff Charlie Aycock, Public Defender Bob Wesley and state Sen. Gary Siplin, D-Orlando, were the only non-Hispanic officeholders I spotted.

I don't know if you would call it a snub, but members of Osceola's Anglo power struc-ture were missing. That doesn't come as a surprise to me, though leaders openly court Latino support—when it's convenient.

Still, Hispanics haven't shown they are a force in local politics. Only one Hispanic has been elected to local office. (I put Quinones in a different category, because he holds state office.) The late Robert Guevara broke the barrier when he was elected to the County Commission in 1996. But if he was the Jackie Robinson of local politics, nearly 10 years later there has been no Willie Mays—or others—to follow him.

15   That will only change when Hispanics recognize the power that voting brings.

How far into the lead did you have to read before you were clear about the thesis? Remember that a thesis is more than the subject of the article; a thesis is the position a writer takes about a subject. It is a point of view.

> *news feature story:
> A signed news story that slants the news toward the writer's bias.

A common genre in newspapers is the **news feature story.*** A writer delivers a particular attitude about a current topic. A feature story does not necessarily state the thesis word for word, but it delivers the message through a deliberate arrangement of events through a particular choice of words. It is up to the reader to determine the thesis and state it in his or her own words. Once you know the attitude of the writer, your appreciation will be affected either negatively or positively, and your comprehension will deepen.

You should notice that different genres deliver theses in different ways. The above examples indicate that in an essay, you are more likely to find a thesis stated word for word; the writer makes it easy and accessible for the reader. In a speech, the writer delivers the thesis not explicitly but implicitly by expecting the audience to share in the greater context. In an opinion column or feature story, you cannot always assume, of course, that the writer's position will be your own. However, a well-constructed piece of writing will always have a thesis or controlling idea, and whatever it turns out to be will be the means through which the whole of the piece is unified. Writing works best when one piece succeeds at delivering one unified and sustained argument.

When it is your turn to develop a thesis, you might try starting with these questions:

- *Where?* Are you taking sides or exploring several positions?
- *What?* What are the points where opinions may be formed? Are you for it? Against it?
- *Why?* Why includes the supporting points that form the body of your paper.

Here is yet another way to think about a thesis. A thesis will contain a SUBJECT, a VERB, and a POINT OF VIEW (S+V+PoV). An example: I will immerse myself in the issues of the upcoming election in order to cast an informed vote because I believe that voting does equal power.

In addition, use this guideline to check your thesis in the following ways:

- Is it *specific?* The more specific the thesis, the more easily you can control your focus.
- Is it *narrow?* A thesis should narrow the subject to a manageable size, a size appropriate to the length of your paper. One central idea is sufficient.
- Is it *arguable?* A valid thesis states a position over which reasonable people could possibly disagree.
- Is it *interesting?* A thesis should try for the unexpected point of view.

Read the following news story, which appeared in the Washington Post on July 2, 2004, and develop a thesis about why Bill Cosby is an appropriate man to make this strong statement about America's black children. If you are not familiar with Cosby's background other than his appearance in the popular television situation comedy that bears his name, do some brief research on the Internet.

Don Babwin

Bill Cosby Gets a Little More off His Chest

CHICAGO, July 1—Bill Cosby delivered another tirade against the black community Thursday, telling a room full of activists that black children are running around not knowing how to read or write and "going nowhere."

He also had harsh words for struggling black men, telling them: "Stop beating up your women because you can't find a job."

Cosby drew criticism in May when, at a commemoration of the anniversary of the *Brown v. Board of Education* desegregation decision, he upbraided some poor blacks for their grammar and accused them of squandering opportunities the civil rights movement gave them. He shot back Thursday, saying his detractors were trying in vain to hide the black community's "dirty laundry." "Let me tell you something, your dirty laundry gets out of school at 2:30 every day, it's cursing and calling each other [racial epithets] as they're walking up and down the street," Cosby said during an appearance at the Rainbow/PUSH Coalition & Citizenship Education Fund's annual conference. "They think they're hip," the entertainer said. "They can't read; they can't write. They're laughing and giggling, and they're going nowhere."

Comedian Bill Cosby.

Cosby elaborated on his previous comments in a talk interrupted several times by applause. He castigated some blacks, saying that they cannot simply blame whites for problems such as teen pregnancy and high school dropout rates.

"For me there is a time . . . when we have to turn the mirror around," he said. "Because for me it is almost analgesic to talk about what the white man is doing against us. And it keeps a person frozen in their seat, it keeps you frozen in your hole you're sitting in."

He also chastised black men who missed out on opportunities and are now angry about their lives. "You've got to stop beating up your women because you can't find a job, because you didn't want to get an education and now you're [earning] minimum wage," Cosby said.

Cosby appeared with the Rev. Jesse Jackson, founder and president of the education fund, who defended the entertainer's statements. "Bill is

5

saying let's fight the right fight, let's level the playing field," Jackson said. "Drunk people can't do that. Illiterate people can't do that."

Cosby also said many young people are failing to honor the sacrifices made by those who struggled and died during the civil rights movement. "Dogs, water hoses that tear the bark off trees, Emmett Till," he said, naming the black youth who was tortured and murdered in Mississippi in 1955, for allegedly whistling at a white woman. "And you're going to tell me you're going to drop out of school? You're going to tell me you're going to steal from a store?"

*Rainbow/PUSH Coalition:
A merger of Operation PUSH (1971) and the National Rainbow Coalition (1985). Headquartered in Chicago, the founder and president is Jesse Jackson Sr. The organization fights for social, racial, and economic justice with a multiracial, international membership.

Don Babwin reports what Bill Cosby said at the **Rainbow/PUSH Coalition*** & Citizenship Education Fund's annual conference. *Does the author's position in this piece support or challenge your own? What is his thesis? How would you describe the audience to whom he is writing? What purpose do you think he wants to accomplish?*

While this piece is labeled as a news story, Babwin has used a large number of adjectives and verbs that deliver an attitude toward and about the subject of the story. While not quite a "feature," it comes close. *Keep in mind that Babwin does not share Cosby's position. Underline some of the words that deliver the author's tone.*

BEGINNING—FINDING THE HOOK

Gerica McCrary said she cried when she heard about the decision to hold a separate white-only prom only a year after she helped bring black and white students together in her rural high school's first integrated prom.
—"Georgia High School Students Plan White-Only Prom,"
Associated Press, May 2, 2003

The pool of prospective jurors in the O.J. Simpson civil trial split along racial lines Tuesday, with whites saying Simpson was probably guilty of murder and African-Americans saying he is innocent.
—CNN: O.J. Simpson Home Page

Police abuse has never been evenly distributed throughout American society; it has always disproportionately victimized people of color.
—American Civil Liberties Union Home Page

First sentences are never easy, but once you have something, anything, down on the paper or the screen, you will have narrowed considerably the possibilities for the second sentence. As the paragraph develops, you should move your sentences in increasingly smaller circles, tightening the grip on your reader. One of the sentences above comes from an unsigned news story, the other two from the front pages of two authoritative websites. In the first sentence, you are not likely to know Gerica McCrary, but you know she cried when she heard the news and that she has some history in her school that has now been overturned. As a reader, you have questions right away to which you want answers. The most important are two: In this new century, *why* did the school decide to segregate the prom? And, is it possible that the school's *first* and *only* integrated prom took place in 2002? Effective beginnings hint at information that is to come and that you, as readers, feel compelled to know more about.

The next sentence reminds the reader of the strong racial underpinnings of O. J. Simpson's lengthy televised trial. Once a second trial, a civil trial, was on the docket, the possible jurors fell into two camps; you might be curious about *why* this black-and-white view of Simpson's first verdict would color his second trial as well. In the last example, you might pause on the use of "police abuse," but then you read on to determine that "people of color" are likely to experience it more than "white people," or in a parallel term, "people of no color." Each example, in different genres, creates a desire for more information. These beginning sentences are effective hooks.

In each case, the focus is on one person or group of people, but the subject is part of a larger world, and you immediately want to understand more about the subject's context. The subject, then, becomes a vehicle to take the reader along for the ride. Besides moving from the specific example, a concrete representative, into a greater more complex abstract idea, you might use the following means to write effective hooks:

- Personal or fictional *anecdote*
- Startling *statistic*
- Logical three-part *syllogism*
- Open-ended question
- Unusual *analogy*
- Spirited *quotation*
- Extended *simile* or *metaphor*

Common to all effective beginnings is the use of strong, active verbs and some moment of engagement.

The following examples come from people's responses to the jubilee celebration of the most important Supreme Court case of the twentieth century, *Brown v. Board of Education of Topeka. Read the following opening sentences and underline the strong verbs and identify the elements that surprise you as a reader. Can you also name the tool that contributes to creating the hook?*

1. I was born in 1954 just four months after the Supreme Court decision in *Brown v. Board of Education* outlawed the "separate but equal" doctrine of school segregation. That fact has shaped my life immeasurably. —"Building a Road to a Diverse Society," Beverly Daniel Tatum (*Chronicle of Higher Education*, B6, April 2, 2004).

2. For the first decade of my legal career, I, like most civil-rights professionals, believed with an almost religious passion that the *Brown* decision was the equivalent of the Holy Grail of racial justice. And why not? —"The Real Lessons of a 'Magnificent Mirage,'" Derrick Bell (*Chronicle of Higher Education*, B10, April 2, 2004).

3. We weren't proud of having roaches, but we were kind of proud that they helped hook the bass and catfish that ended up battered and fried on white supper tables. It was a funny kind of line that connected the roaches to the fish, the

blacks to the whites and my neighborhood to the rest of the world.
  —"A Dream Is a Good Place to Start," Endesha Ida Mae Holland, *My Soul Looks Back in Wonder*. Ed. Juan Williams (New York: Sterling, 2004. p. 25).

4. I woke up sick on Tuesday, and by Saturday I was totally paralyzed. I have lupus, and doctors think that's what caused a blood clot to manifest on my spinal cord.
  —"Wheels of Progress," Michelle Steger, *My Soul Looks Back in Wonder*. Ed. Juan Williams (New York: Sterling, 2004. p. 178).

5. The Gay Movement was clearly inspired by the Civil Rights Movement. Many gay people who had participated in the summer of '64 began to say, "Okay, we're next now." The rhetoric, the arguments have substantial overlap.
  —"Threads in the Civil Rights Quilt," Congressman Barney Frank, *My Soul Looks Back in Wonder*. Ed. Juan Williams (New York: Sterling, 2004. p. 182).

6. With every passing decade since 1954 we continue to ask ourselves how much the South and the nation have changed since the *Brown v. Board of Education of Topeka* decision ended "separate but equal" education in public schools. The hallowed words of Thomas Jefferson that "all men are created equal," proclaimed at the nation's founding 178 years before *Brown*, seemed finally to include black men, women, and children, at least insofar as public schooling was concerned.
  —"Black, White, and *Brown*," Neil Foley, *The Journal of Southern History*, 70 (May 2004): p. 343.

7. *Brown v. Board of Education of Topeka* tolled the bell for Jim Crow America.
  —"From *Brown* to *Green* and Back: The Changing Meaning of Desegregation," Raymond Wolters, *The Journal of Southern History*, 70 (May 2004): p. 317.

From the above beginnings, talk with a classmate about what you might expect the next sentence to be. Try writing the next sentence, matching your tone with that established in the beginning. How does one sentence prepare a reader for what is to follow?

ENDING—DROPPING THE CURTAIN

"But I went to a black prom and I had fun," she added. "It didn't kill me, so I tell my son, 'Just go to the prom and have fun. Don't come out hating anyone.'"
  —"Georgia High School Students Plan White-Only Prom,"
  Associated Press, May 2, 2003

In all, 17 jurors have passed the phases to weed people out for hardship and bias from media reports. Fujisaki will seat a final panel of 12 jurors and eight alternates.
The jury selection process was to continue Wednesday.
Unlike the criminal trial, there will be no sequestration.
  —Greg Lamotte and Associated Press, CNN: OJ Simpson's Home Page

And the ACLU's Capital Punishment Project works against the discriminatory application of the death penalty in this country, where the color of a defendant and victim's skin plays a crucial and unacceptable role in determining who will be sentenced to death.
  —ACLU Home Page

Just as you need to think consciously about beginning a paper, you also need to apply that same kind of attention to ending a paper. When you attend a theatrical performance that has succeeded in figuratively transporting you to another world and then the curtain drops, you are likely to sit silent and stunned in your seat for the briefest moment before the sound of applause returns you to the theater where you have literally been all evening. A good closing sentence is a bit like this. You finish reading a piece, and for just an instant in time, you sit quietly, maybe head down, maybe rereading the end because it is that good. And you want to stay inside the reading experience, to prolong it, if only for a moment.

The sentences above end the pieces that are referred to in the "Beginning" section. In the news story, the pronoun is identified in a preceding paragraph, but the speaker's message is a vital one. Though she is a black woman who had attended an all-black prom, and the vote to segregate the event once more was moving backwards into history, the woman's words—simple and without rancor—serve to elevate her to a higher moral plane: "Don't come out hating anyone." It is a thought that gives pause.

The second closing comes from CNN's O. J. Simpson website and reminds the reader of that criminal trial, the one widely watched on television, and that this civil trial will be different. One difference spelled out is the "no sequestration," and now, after that trial has done its work, a different verdict as well. Finally, the opening about "police abuse" on the ACLU website concludes with a chilling reminder that the color of a person's skin plays a "crucial and unacceptable role" in determining if that person will live or die.

Each of these closings, in closely related genres, are effective curtain drops; each succeeds in creating the moment of silence before moving on to the next piece you plan to read. Closing with a logical conclusion, a moral lesson, or specific word choices that focus the reader's attention are three ways to consider ending a piece of writing. You might consider the following other ways of writing a sentence that gives the feel of a curtain dropping:

- Return to an image or reference from the first paragraph.
- Use a metaphor or simile to evoke the essence of the whole.
- Place a short, simple sentence with punch after a longer, more complicated one.
- Arrange two sentences that suggest an odd juxtaposition with each other.
- Let the last words be straight from the mouth of a person in the piece.

Read the following closing sentences and determine what about each of them makes for an effective end.

1. Although some progress has been made, the road to racial equality is not complete. Supreme Court Associate Justice Sandra Day O'Connor suggested in her judicial opinion in the Michigan case that perhaps in 25 years affirmative-action programs would no longer be needed or allowed. We will all have to intensify our building efforts if we expect to meet that construction deadline. —"Building a Road to a Diverse Society," Beverly Daniel Tatum (*Chronicle of Higher Education*, B7, April 2, 2004).
2. These divisions have been exploited to enable an uneasy social stability, but at a cost that is not less onerous because it is all too obvious to blacks and all but invisible to a great many whites.

—"The Real Lessons of a 'Magnificent Mirage,'" Derrick Bell (*Chronicle of Higher Education*, B10, April 2, 2004).

3. Somebody with a powerful hate in their heart had burned my Mama to death. They were after me, but they got my mama.

    After that, I had to leave Greenwood [Mississippi]. I remembered my vow on The University of Minnesota campus . . . twenty years after leaving the Mississippi Delta—I received my Ph.D. in American studies.

    —"A Dream Is a Good Place to Start," *My Soul Looks Back in Wonder*. Ed. Juan Williams (New York: Sterling, 2004. p. 30).

4. We are surprisingly populous as a minority group. You can't voluntarily join a different race, but anybody can join the disabled at any time. If we could band together to wield that power, we could get whatever we want.

    —"Wheels of Progress," Michelle Steger, *My Soul Looks Back in Wonder*. Ed. Juan Williams (New York: Sterling, 2004. p. 180).

5. Given what racism had done, if you grow up in the city and are walking alone at night in some areas and two or three young, roughly dressed black guys come walking by, you're a little apprehensive. Even Jesse Jackson has said he felt that. But if you were walking at night in Mississippi and you heard voices, you hoped that they were black, not white. If they were blacks, you said, "Oh, thank God." If they were whites, it was "Let's hide." I've realized there's nothing inherent about racism; it's always contextual.

    —"Threads in the Civil Rights Quilt," Congressman Barney Frank, *My Soul Looks Back in Wonder* Ed. Juan Williams (New York: Sterling, 2004. p. 185).

6. If our nation is ever to move beyond race to a colorblind future, and I think it must, it will have to begin by euthanizing white privilege in the collective unconscious of America and reckoning with that "strange career" that still lingers in the sad story of seventy-eight-year-old Essie Mae Washington-Williams, who met her white father [Strom Thurmond] for the first time when she was sixteen and out of respect would not reveal the secret that would have destroyed his career and challenged the white supremacist convictions on which it was built.

    —"Black, White and *Brown*," Neil Foley, *The Journal of Southern History*, 70 (May 2004): p. 350.

7. Once again the federal courts are interpreting "desegregation" to mean what most people thought it meant when *Brown* was handed down in 1954 and what Congress intended when it enacted the Civil Rights Act of 1964: the prohibition of official racial discrimination, not the prohibition of racially neutral policies that have racially disproportionate effects.

    —"From *Brown* to *Green* and Back: The Changing Meaning of Desegregation," Raymond Wolters, *The Journal of Southern History*, 70 (May 2004): p. 326.

How do these endings match the list of suggestions of possible curtain droppings listed above? Do you think any of them succeed in making you pause before moving on to your next activity? Go back and read the first sentence (from the previous section) and the last sentence together. Along with the title of the piece, can you imagine what kinds of topics are explored in between? Think of a moment where you have been witness to an act of injustice. How would you conclude your story?

BUILDING THE BRIDGE—PARAGRAPHS AS PLANKS

While you may not write the beginning and ending first and then write the body of your paper, it makes good sense to check the ending with your beginning to see how they connect with each other—and then to think of the body as the bridge that brings both the beginning and ending together. Bridges are built by the careful positioning of planks, deciding what we think will fit best where, when we need a thick and long plank and when just a thin and short one will do. These paragraph planks are held together by a careful choice of **transitions*** and *repetitions*, based on some logical, rhetorical, or emotional design. The goal is to create a bridge that spans the necessary distance with clarity.

> *transitional markers: Specific words used to show the connection and/or relationship of one paragraph or sentence to another.
>
> **Jackson Advocate:* Since 1938, Mississippi's oldest African American newspaper has published stories not covered significantly or sufficiently by white-owned presses. It has been the target of numerous acts of vandalism and has been firebombed at least three times, the latest incident occurring in 1998.

In January 1998, the ***Jackson Advocate,**** Mississippi's oldest African American newspaper and the largest weekly in the state, was firebombed, destroying the paper's archived materials. In the following eight-paragraph online news story about the event, the paragraphs have been rearranged to demonstrate both how paragraphs may fit together in more than one way and how, in places, transitional words and logic demand a specific order. The numbering of the paragraphs indicates the author's ordering:

Center for Living Democracy
Jackson Advocate Rises from the Ashes

4. The latest arson, preceded by an anonymous and "chilling" telephone death threat ("They told me they were going to kill me when I stepped outside," said the editor.), resulted in an estimated $100,000 in damage. "My wife's computer had a complete melt-down."

7. Past writers for *The Jackson Advocate* have included David DuBois, who follows in the footsteps of his stepfather W.E.B. DuBois in overseeing the Encyclopedia Africana in Ghana, and who lectures regularly at the University of Massachusetts in Amherst, Mass.

1. While *The New York Times* and *The Washington Post* are filing stories on the fire-bombing Monday morning of a black weekly newspaper in Jackson, Miss., the national television news cameras have yet to arrive, according to Charles Tisdale, editor of *The Jackson Advocate.* "The only exception is BET [Black Entertainment Television], which is airing a story tonight," Tisdale told me late Wednesday evening.

3. Then on January 16, [1982,] we were firebombed again and machine gunned." Police apprehended the men responsible for both bombings, identifying them as "ex-Klansmen." "How they knew they were ex-Klan, I don't know," said Tisdale.

6. *The Jackson Advocate* is recognized overseas as an independent media outlet and an outspoken voice of dissent. "Our circulation numbers 20,000, only 7,400 of whom are local," said Tisdale. "Many of our subscribers are in Germany. The German news magazine *Der Spiegel* recently did a four-page story on us, and we've been featured in *Le Monde* and in other leading publications in Holland and England."

5

2. Among the 20 incidents of vandalism against his paper, Tisdale recalled two incidents in particular. "This is not the first time I've been bombed," he said. "On December 22, 1981, we were bombed."

5. Yet from the ashes, the paper continues its publication schedule. "Oh yes, we're coming out with an edition tomorrow," said Tisdale. "I know we'll have to move to new offices, though."

8. As a show of solidarity, The American News Service is donating to the African-American owned newspaper a subscription to its national wire service on solutions news. About 20 percent of ANS stories focus on community-based efforts to improve race relations.

Peace, Jonathan J. Hutson, Acting Director, Interracial Democracy Program Center for Living Democracy

Read the article as it appears above. Identify the problems you notice as you are reading. Then, read the article a second time, rearranging the paragraphs into their numbered order. Seeing the paragraphs out of order is a way to call attention to the importance of repeating words and transitional markers.

Here is a list of transitional markers that you may find helpful in linking paragraphs together. The list is meant to be suggestive rather than exhaustive.

When you want to make an *addition:*
> again, also, and then, besides, equally important, finally, first (second, third, etc.), further, furthermore, in addition, last, likewise, moreover, next, too

When you want to show *cause and effect:*
> accordingly, consequently, hence, in short, then, therefore, thus, truly

When you want to show *comparison:*
> in a like manner, likewise, similarly

When you want to *acknowledge another possibility:*
> after all, although this may be true, at the same time, even though, I admit, naturally, of course, and yet, at the same time, but, for all that, however, in contrast, in spite of, nevertheless, notwithstanding, on the contrary, on the other hand, still, yet

When you want to show a *connection or relationship in time:*
> after a short time, afterwards, as long as, as soon as, at last, at length, at that time, at the same time, before, earlier, immediately, in the meantime, lately, later, meanwhile, of late, presently, shortly, since, soon, temporarily, thereafter, thereupon, until, when, while

The order that paragraphs take in any given piece depends on your purpose and audience and in what genre you write. That order can be dictated by the words you select and the promise that each paragraph makes in relationship both to itself and to the paragraphs that come before and after it. While a transitional word in the first sentence often connects what is to come with the paragraph you have just completed, sentences within a paragraph function in a tighter manner. Each sentence must predict what will follow while making clear the connection to what has just been written. Sometimes each sentence will suggest a question for the reader, which will be answered in the next sentence.

A close examination of the following short paragraphs will illustrate how and why the paragraphs connect and also how the sentences within them deliver on their one coherent promise. In the summer of 2004, the country had the opportunity to both mourn the loss and celebrate the life of three men whose diverse contributions changed the way Americans thought about the concept of freedom: singer **Ray Charles*** (1930–2004), President **Ronald Reagan*** (1911–2004), and actor **Marlon Brando*** (1924–2004). In "America, Ray Charles Style" columnist William Raspberry takes a close look at how Charles's rendition of "America the Beautiful" made him see the country through a more hopeful lens.

You see, I always cherished America—even if I acknowledged it only as the too-seldom played B-side of my consciousness. Charles's "America" invited me to turn the record over.

Charles could do that. He had a way of cutting through the confusions and mixed emotions and preconceptions, and reaching us at our core. The genius that made it possible for him to universalize the blues and spirituals and country—anything he touched— made it possible for him to universalize patriotism, too.

But if Ray Charles changed the Fourth of July with his "America the Beautiful," he also changed the song. "God done shed His grace on thee! He crowned thy good, yes he did, in a brotherhood."

The shift isn't merely from Katharine Lee Bates's elegant lyric to the black vernacular; it is a shift in meaning.

As Kenneth Moynihan noted in a recent commentary in the *Worcester (Mass.) Telegram & Gazette*, Bates penned a prayer: "[May] God shed his grace on thee and crown thy good with brotherhood." Ray made it a *fait accompli*.

As Moynihan put it, "A fervent hope for the future has been turned into a happy fact of the present."

*Ray Charles: (1930–2004) Born in poverty and blind at seven years old, Charles went on to win twelve Grammys and be named to the Halls of Fame in Rhythm and Blues, Jazz, and Rock and Roll.

*Ronald Reagan: (1911–2004) The fortieth president of the United States (1981–1989); his legacy is his contribution to the fall of communism and his swelling of the ranks of government bureaucracy after declaring that "government is the problem."

*Marlon Brando: (1924–2004) Considered by many other actors as the actor who taught them the most about freedom, Brando mastered the "method approach" in which an actor draws on the motivations of the character to determine what actions should be emphasized. His career fluctuated between brilliance— in such roles as Stanley Kowalski in Tennessee Williams's *A Streetcar Named Desire* and as the Godfather—and disappointingly squandered talent.

*eulogy: On the occasion of someone's death, a tribute offering praise and commendation.

Raspberry is writing a newspaper column, and journalistic style favors short paragraphs—even one-sentence paragraphs. Raspberry made six paragraphs out of what could be only one substantial paragraph. *Try taking the sentences above and combining them into one or two paragraphs. What do you gain (and or lose) in shifting the sentences into different paragraph planks?*

The following are the first three paragraphs of a **eulogy*** for President Reagan from his Polish friend Lech Walesa, who led the anticommunist trade union Solidarity and was instrumental in organizing free trade unions and leading shipyard strikes. Walesa gained attention and worldwide support for his efforts. He won the Nobel Peace Prize in 1983 and was president of Poland from 1990 until he was defeated in 1995.

GDANSK, Poland—When talking about Ronald Reagan, I have to be personal. We in Poland took him so personally. Why? Because we owe him our liberty. This can't be said often enough by people who lived under oppression for half a century, until communism fell in 1989.

Poles fought for their freedom for so many years that they hold in special esteem those who backed them in their struggle. Support was the test of friendship. President Reagan was such a friend. His policy of aiding democratic movements in Central and Eastern Europe in the dark days of the Cold War meant a lot to us. We knew he believed in a few simple principles such as human rights, democracy and civil society. He was someone who was convinced that the citizen is not for the state, but vice-versa, and that freedom is an innate right.

I often wondered why Ronald Reagan did this, taking the risks he did, in supporting us at Solidarity, as well as dissident movements in other countries behind the Iron Curtain, while pushing a defense buildup that pushed the Soviet economy over the brink. Let's remember that it was a time of recession in the U.S. and a time when the American public was more interested in their own domestic affairs. It took a leader with a vision to convince them that there are greater things worth fighting for. Did he seek any profit in such a policy? Though our freedom movements were in line with the foreign policy of the United States, I doubt it.

The first paragraph of Walesa's tribute to Reagan begins on a personal note; Reagan becomes the embodiment of Polish liberty. The "we in Poland" of the first paragraph becomes the "Poles" of the second paragraph. The thankfulness for liberty in the first paragraph is explained in the second paragraph. Reagan becomes the friend because he supported their efforts. This idea of the second paragraph is expanded in the third. But why, when it might not have been the best time domestically for Reagan to support Poland, did he do it? Walesa ends this paragraph with a suggestion that Reagan did not offer the support that he did to profit from doing so. We might expect the eulogy to continue by exploring why politicians make the decisions they do.

Effective paragraphs should connect with both those that come before and those that follow. A reader should be able to ask questions about what has been said and then discover some answers in the following paragraph.

Finally, here are five paragraphs from Joal Ryan's obituary on Marlon Brando, who was both acclaimed as the greatest actor of his time and dismissed as an insulting, overweight ogre. Most all would agree, though, that he introduced to the stage and screen a freedom in acting that had not been seen, heard, or felt before.

Talk with a classmate about why these paragraphs should follow this order. List the transitions and repetitions that make the order easy to follow. Is it possible to merge any of these paragraphs so that the sense of the whole is still maintained?

In his prime, Brando was a two-time Oscar winner (for *On the Waterfront* and *The Godfather*), and an eight-time nominee. But because Brando was never particularly interested in being a movie star, he was also famously a one-time Oscar rejector. In 1973, he famously dispatched would-be Native American Sacheen Littlefeather (aka Mexican-American actress Maria Cruz) to the Oscar ceremonies to decline his Academy Award for playing Don Vito Corleone in *The Godfather*.

For the last 25 years, Brando's girth loomed as large as his name. In the mid-1990s, he reportedly tipped the scales at 400 pounds.

Weight, age and agonizing family dramas eroded the movie-star looks that brought him beefcake status in the 1950s ("He's a walking hormone factory," a producer said of him then). But Brando's reputation, though sullied in stinkers like *The Island of Dr. Moreau*, was never diminished. He earned $3 million for just three weeks work on *The Score*. Even in down times (and despite dismissively referring to director Frank Oz as "Miss Piggy"), the Brando brand name was still gold.

"Brando is just the best actor in the world today," director Eliza Kazan said in 1954. Kazan's sentiment met with little disagreement.

The length of paragraphs, their order, and the transitions and repetitions that tie them together all contribute to building the bridge that takes the reader from the thoughtful beginning to the curtain-dropping end.

The following two essays respond to two of the documents in Citizenship 101. The first is an essay that appeared on July 4, 2004, and uses Franklin Roosevelt's Four Freedoms to express concern about the administration of President George W. Bush and remind Americans that the freedoms we enjoy should never be taken for granted. The second is a response to the fortieth anniversary of the Civil Rights Act of 1964, reminding us that women were legally discriminated against before the passage of this law. *As you read the essays, pay particular attention to how the writers develop their paragraphs. Underscore the transitional markers and the repeating words. By looking closely at how sentences are hooked together, determine why and how each is necessary in contributing to the promise of each paragraph.*

George Yates

America's 'Four Freedoms' Aren't Quite So Robust This July 4

"The pursuit of Happiness" is one of the three inalienable rights listed in our Declaration of Independence. Note that this right does not guarantee that each of us will actually achieve complete Happiness. What it does guarantee is that our government cannot arbitrarily restrict our right to seek Happiness.

But what did Thomas Jefferson mean by "the pursuit of Happiness"? Most people would suggest that pursuing Happiness basically means being free to pursue a desirable lifestyle. It is probable that we would share a common focus on possessing physical goods, societal respect and family relationships—our "second level" benefits.

However, our primary focus should actually be on the "first level" rights that make possible our pursuit of Happiness. These rights are mandated by our Declaration of Independence and our Constitution. It was only six decades ago that Americans were sacrificing their second level benefits to protect their first level rights. Indeed, World War II was a harsh reminder that we cannot take those rights for granted.

Therefore, it is most appropriate that on this July 4, the 228th celebration of our Independence Day, we evaluate our current ability to pursue Happiness. The challenge to making such a determination is to select a standard capable of evaluating our first level rights. Fortunately, an appropriate evaluative standard does exist—the "Four Freedoms."

On Jan. 6, 1941, in his State of the Union address, President Franklin D. Roosevelt described four "essential human freedoms": freedom of speech, freedom of religion, freedom from want, and freedom from fear. He warned that they had to be protected against the threat of German fascism and Japanese militarism.   5

The Four Freedoms are as critical to our ability to pursue Happiness today as they were 63 years ago. And though we enjoy a high level of access to them, it is a fact that in recent years the trend has been to restrict their availability. The end result is that too many of us are being denied a full opportunity to pursue Happiness.

Freedom of Speech

Few of us would consider intrusive censorship of our freedom of speech as being compatible with the pursuit of Happiness. Yet that practice is prevalent in our society. It occurs, for example, when we exercise our constitutional right to criticize the behaviors and policies of the current administration. Its loyalists allege we are: unpatriotic, disloyal to our nation, aiding the enemy and failing to support our troops. These allegations are slanderous and illegitimate, intended only to coerce us into silence.

Freedom of Religion

10   There is no more intensely personal behavior than that involved in following our religious and moral beliefs. It is essential to our pursuit of Happiness. That is why our Constitution specifically requires the separation of government and religion. Yet in recent years there has been a concerted effort by religious conservatives to impose their own beliefs on our nation's laws.

These intrusions, for example, include laws and presidential executive orders that restrict a woman's choice, discussion of birth control and the creation of new stem cell lines. The current administration is attempting to pass a constitutional amendment to ban same-sex marriages. Such actions only highlight the extent of our government's religious bias.

Freedom from Want

For many Americans, it has become difficult in recent years to pursue Happiness due to the poorly performing economy. One example is that most of the government-supported social, cultural, health and education programs have, and are being, significantly reduced. This is occurring because major reductions in federal funding have forced local governments to reduce their services for the public.

Federal funding is scarce to a large extent because of the immense tax cuts recently given primarily to wealthy individuals and large corporations. The Iraq war has further drained well over $140 billion from the federal government's treasury in less than two years.

15   Freedom from Fear

Fear may be real or perceived, but its negative impact on our pursuit of Happiness is obvious. For example, surveys indicate that a majority of Americans have a greater fear of terrorist attacks now than shortly after Sept. 11, 2001. This may seem surprising, given the billions of dollars spent since then on the Iraq war and on domestic security systems. But it is due mainly to the government's continuing emphasis on publicizing fear.

Actually, our greatest fear should be that the other three freedoms will steadily become even more restricted.

Given the foregoing evaluation, it might seem that for the vast majority of Americans the pursuit of Happiness is likely to be unrewarding. This conclusion is simply not acceptable.

We must increase the ability of all Americans to more successfully pursue Happiness by restoring the full availability of our Four Freedoms.

Ellen Goodman

A Forty-Year Search for Equality

BOSTON—And now for a small story from the Latter-Day Annals of Working Womanhood. Fresh out of college in 1963, I got my first job at *Newsweek* magazine. In those days, women were hired as researchers and men were hired as writers . . . and that was that.

It was, as we used to say, a good job *for a woman*. If we groused about working *for* the men we studied *with* in college, we did it privately. It was the way things were.

I don't share my garden-variety piece of personal history as a lament or gripe. Woe isn't me. Nor am I one to regale the younger generation with memories of the bad old days when I walked four miles in the snow to school. They already know that women were treated as second-class citizens.

But what they don't know, I have found, is that this was *legal*.

It was legal to have segregated ads that read "male wanted" and "female wanted." It was legal to fire a flight attendant if she got married. It was legal to get rid of a teacher when she became pregnant. 5

If a boss paid a woman less because she was a woman, he was unapologetic. If he didn't want to hire a woman for a "man's job," he just didn't.

We sometimes forget that the lives of men and women didn't just passively evolve. But on July 2 we celebrate the 40th anniversary of a powerful engine of this social change, the Civil Rights Act of 1964.

One unexpected word was tucked into Title VII of that landmark legislation banning racial segregation and discrimination: sex.

Legend has it that Rep. Howard W. Smith, a Virginian and head of the House Rules Committee, introduced sex as a joke. He was trying to ridicule the idea that you could legislate social behavior.

But the segregationist was just half of an odd couple. The other half were feminists. 10 The National Women's Party had been trying to get such a law long before they brought it to Smith. After he introduced the sex discrimination amendment to ripples of laughter, Rep. Martha Griffiths of Michigan, one of only nine women in Congress, argued for it fiercely.

Omitting sex, she said, would protect only African American males from discrimination. And if blacks were protected, the only unprotected class left would be white women.

When President Johnson signed the bill, it became illegal for the first time to discriminate in employment on the grounds of sex. What had seemed to many a "natural" way of treating men and women differently because of their roles in the family and society became what the courts now call "invidious."

"This is the act that put meaning into the word discrimination," says historian Alice Kessler-Harris, who remembers when she was forced to sign a paper promising to tell her employer if she became pregnant. "Title VII legitimized women's search for equality in the workforce."

This 40-year "search" has seen enormous success stories. In the first Title VII case, the Supreme Court ruled that it was illegal to refuse to hire a woman because she had small children. Under pressure, newspapers stopped segregating their employment pages. Women tiptoed into some "male jobs" and took hold in others.

15   Today's working women sometimes wonder whether we've won the booby prize—the right to be treated like men. We haven't yet figured out the next phase, how to get support for family and work.

But there are still plenty of reminders that the bad old days are not so old. They may be alive and well and living in your workplace.

Just last Tuesday a federal court allowed a class-action suit on behalf of 1.6 million women employees of Wal-Mart. The plaintiffs' statistics and anecdotes could fill a volume in another generation's Annals of Working Womanhood.

When a single mother discovered that her male counterpart made $23,000 more, her Wal-Mart boss replied, "he has a wife and two children to support." When a woman wanted to sell hardware, she was sent to sell baby clothes. And another woman looking for a promotion confronted a store manager who said, "Men are here to make a career and women aren't." "What we see with Wal-Mart and other cases," says Marcia Greenberg of the National Women's Law Center, "is an everyday struggle to make sure the promise of the law really becomes a reality."

When the old feminists lobbied the old segregationist to include sex, Smith said mischievously and maybe maliciously, "I don't think it can do any harm . . . maybe it can do some good."

20   He was joking. But they were left smiling.

Using these two essays as examples, select another document from Citizenship 101 and write a response to a current controversial issue where you see justice being denied. For example, how do these lines from Winthrop's "Model of Christian Charity" address our involvement in Iraq: "For we must consider that we shall be as a city upon a hill. The eyes of all people are upon us. So that if we shall deal falsely with our God in this work we have undertaken, and so cause Him to withdraw His present help from us, we shall be made a story and a by-word through the world."

What Is at Stake for Citizenship?

1. Should pigmentation determine a person's rights?
2. Is there a difference between segregation and "separate but equal"?
3. Should employers be held to the same standards of health and conduct as their employees?
4. How is it a "problem" when our founding government documents call for justice and equality for all, and we discriminate against some faction or privilege one race over another?
5. Do you think that words have no meaning until they are spoken? Can ugly words be spoken in such a way that they appear to be positive words?
6. Should musical lyrics that target and demean specific groups be protected by freedom of speech?
7. Is segregation of anything in the public domain ever appropriate?
8. How should hate crimes—such as firebombings—be punished?

This chapter asks you to consider your own writing style. Do you spend more time prewriting or rewriting? How do peers influence what you have to say?

CHAPTER

Before and after Writing: America and Democracy

. . . our American Constitution is the steel frame that holds this great skyscraper we call democracy firmly to the earth.

—Lillian Smith, *Now Is the Time*

What the people want is very simple. They want an America as good as its promise.

—Barbara Jordan, Harvard University Commencement Address, June 1977

BEFORE WRITING

Prewriting consists of all the ways that you get ready to write. We spoke in earlier chapters about the role of reading, thinking, and talking; now let's focus on actually getting random ideas down on paper. College writing—in all your courses—often starts with a piece (or a number of pieces) of writing that are not your own but to which you are asked to respond. To do so, you must first, of course, understand what you are reading.

Asking questions, restating difficult or unfamiliar information, and paying attention to language choices are ways to comprehend what you have read. You might think of these activities as a rough kind of paraphrase or summary activity. This is step one. After you have a clearer understanding of the content of your reading, you are now ready to *brainstorm, free write*, or *make lists*. While free writing might be a kind of stream of consciousness in complete sentences, brainstorming and making lists are less concerned with making connections and more concerned with helping you make sense of what you will write. This is step two. Sometimes you might want to start out with one of these methods and then move to another. Form does not matter as much as just getting some ideas about what you are reading down on paper. Organizing your written thoughts is step three. These steps are illustrated in a response to the following speech.

In the summer of 1972, five men broke into the Democratic National Committee's headquarters in the Watergate complex in Washington, D.C. The burglars were later found to have ties with the highest level of the Republican Party. Thus began

*Watergate: This complex in Washington, D.C. housed the Democratic National Committee's headquarters. With ties to the highest level of the Republican Party, five men broke into the headquarters, and thus began a series of scandals–known as "Watergate"–that eventually forced Nixon to resign the first sitting president in our country's history to do so.

*Richard Nixon: (1913–1994) The thirty-seventh president of the United States. Nixon's involvement in the coverup of the Watergate scandals of 1974 ultimately forced him to resign the presidency. He was later given a full pardon by President Gerald Ford, who believed the nation needed to put Watergate to rest and move forward with other business of the country.

*impeachment: According to the Constitution, the House of Representatives has the charge of impeaching high-ranking government officials when they abuse the powers of their office. Impeachment is not dismissal from office; it is accusation. The Senate has the power to dismiss. Two presidents have been impeached–Andrew Johnson and William Clinton; neither was dismissed from office. Impeachment proceedings began for Richard Nixon, but he resigned from office before the proceedings could follow their natural course.

*Barbara Jordan: (1936–1996) A three-term congresswoman from Texas who came into the national spotlight for her televised speech during the impeachment proceedings of Richard Nixon. She delivered the keynote address at the Democratic National Convention in 1976 and 1992.

what has become known as **Watergate,*** an unfolding of scandals that in August 1974 resulted in the first resignation of a sitting president in our country's history. Before **Richard Nixon's*** resignation, the House Judiciary Committee was beginning the work of **impeachment*** of the president. A junior member of that committee, **Barbara Jordan,*** a Democrat from Texas elected in 1972, gave a speech on July 25, 1974, that propelled her into the national limelight. Jordan, along with Congressman Andrew Young of Georgia, was the first African American southerner to go to Congress since **Reconstruction.*** The following is thenow-famous speech she made that day. *As you read the speech, annotate in the margins to help you keep track of your response.*

Barbara Jordan, July 25, 1974
Speech to House Judiciary Committee

Mr. Chairman:

1. I join in thanking you for giving the junior members of this committee the glorious opportunity of sharing the pain of this inquiry. Mr. Chairman, you are a strong man and it has not been easy but we have tried as best we can to give you as much assistance as possible.

2. Earlier today, we heard the beginning of the Preamble to the Constitution of the United States, "We, the people." It is a very eloquent beginning. But when the document was completed on the seventeenth of September 1787 I was not included in that "We, the people." I felt somehow for many years that George Washington and Alexander Hamilton just left me out by mistake. But through the process of amendment, interpretation and court decision I have finally been included in "We, the people."

Former Congresswoman Barbara Jordan (1936–1996).

3. Today, I am an inquisitor; I believe hyperbole would not be fictional and would not overstate the solemnness that I feel right now.

My faith in the Constitution is whole, it is complete, it is total. I am not going to sit here and be an idle spectator to the diminution, the subversion, the destruction of the Constitution.

*Reconstruction: The reorganization and reestablishment of the seceded states in the Union after the American Civil War.

4. The subject of its jurisdiction are those offenses which proceed from the misconduct of public men. That is what we are talking about. In other words, the jurisdiction comes from the abuse or violation of some public trust. It is wrong, I suggest, it is a misreading of the Constitution, for any member here to assert that for a member to vote for an article of impeachment means that that member must be convinced that the President should be removed from office.

5. The Constitution doesn't say that. The powers relating to impeachment are an essential check in the hands of this body, the legislature, against and upon the encroachment of the Executive. In establishing the division between the two branches of the legislature, the House and the Senate, assigning to the one the right to accuse and to the other the right to judge, the framers of this Constitution were very astute. They did not make the accusers and the judges the same person.

6. We know the nature of impeachment. We have been talking about it awhile now. It is chiefly designed for the President and his high ministers to somehow be called into account. It is designed to "bridle" the Executive if he engages in excesses. It is designed as a method of national inquest into the conduct of public men. The framers confined in the Congress the power, if need be, to remove the President in order to strike a delicate balance between a President swollen with power and grown tyrannical and preservation of the independence of the Executive. The nature of impeachment is a narrowly channeled exception to the separation of powers maxim; the federal convention of 1787 said that. It limited impeachment to high crimes and misdemeanors and discounted and opposed the term, "maladministration." "It is to be used only for great misdemeanors," so it was said in the North Carolina ratification convention. And in the Virginia ratification convention: "We need one branch to check the others."

7. The North Carolina ratification convention: "No one need to be afraid that officers who commit oppression will pass with immunity.

8. "Prosecutions of impeachments will seldom fail to agitate the passions of the whole community," said Hamilton in the *Federalist Papers,* number 65. "And to divide it into parties more or less friendly or inimical to the accused." I do not mean political parties in that sense.

9. The drawing of political lines goes to the motivation behind impeachment; but impeachment must proceed within the confines of the constitutional term, "high crime and misdemeanors."

10. Of the impeachment process, it was Woodrow Wilson who said that "nothing short of the grossest offenses against the plain law of the land will suffice to give them speed and effectiveness. Indignation so great as to overgrow party interest may secure a conviction; but nothing else can."

11. Common sense would be revolted if we engaged upon this process for petty reasons. Congress has a lot to do: Appropriations, tax reform, health insurance, campaign finance reform, housing, environmental protection, energy sufficiency, mass transportation. Pettiness cannot be allowed to stand in the face of such overwhelming

5

10

problems. So today we are not being petty. We are trying to be big, because the task we have before us is a big one.

12. This morning, in a discussion of the evidence, we were told that the evidence which purports to support the allegations of misuse of the CIA by the President is thin. We are told that that evidence is insufficient. What that recital of the evidence this morning did not include is what the President did know on June 23, 1972. The President did know that it was Republican money, that it was money from the Committee for the Re-election of the President, which was found in the possession of one of the burglars arrested on June 17.

13. What the President did know on June 23 was the prior activities of E. Howard Hunt, which included his participation in the break-in of Daniel Ellsberg's psychiatrist, which included Howard Hunt's participation in the Dita Beard ITT affair, which included Howard Hunt's fabrication of cables designed to discredit the Kennedy Administration.

14. We were further cautioned today that perhaps these proceedings ought to be delayed because certainly there would be new evidence forthcoming from the President of the United States. There has not even been an obfuscated indication that this committee would receive any additional materials from the President. The committee subpoena is outstanding and if the President wants to supply that material, the committee sits here. The fact is that on yesterday, the American people waited with great anxiety for eight hours, not knowing whether their President would obey an order of the Supreme Court of the United States.

15. At this point, I would like to juxtapose a few of the impeachment criteria with some of the President's actions.

16. Impeachment criteria: James Madison, from the Virginia ratification convention. "If the President be connected in any suspicious manner with any person and there is grounds to believe that he will shelter him, he may be impeached."

17. We have heard time and time again that the evidence reflects payment to the defendants of money. The President had knowledge that these funds were being paid and that these were funds collected for the 1972 presidential campaign. We know that the President met with Mr. Henry Petersen twenty-seven times to discuss matters related to Watergate, and immediately thereafter met with the very persons who were implicated in the information Mr. Petersen was receiving and transmitting to the President. The words are, "If the President be connected in any suspicious manner with any person and there be grounds to believe that he will shelter that person, he may be impeached."

18. Justice Story: "Impeachment is intended for occasional and extraordinary cases where a superior power acting for the whole people is put into operation to protect their rights and rescue their liberties from violations."

19. We know about the Houston plan. We know about the break-in of the psychiatrist's office. We know that there was absolute, complete direction in August 1971 when the President instructed Ehrlichman to "do whatever is necessary." This instruction led to a surreptitious entry into Dr. Fielding's office. "Protect their rights." "Rescue their liberties from violation."

20. The South Carolina ratification convention impeachment criteria: Those are impeachable "who behave amiss or betray their public trust."

21. Beginning shortly after the Watergate break-in and continuing to the present time, the President has engaged in a series of public statements and actions designed to thwart the lawful investigation by government prosecutors. Moreover, the President has made public announcements and assertions bearing on the Watergate case which the evidence will show he knew to be false. These assertions, false assertions; impeachable, those who misbehave. Those who "behave amiss or betray their public trust."

22. James Madison, again at the constitutional convention: "A President is impeachable if he attempts to subvert the Constitution."

23. The Constitution charges the President with the task of taking care that the laws be faithfully executed, and yet the President has counseled his aides to commit perjury, willfully disregarded the secrecy of grand jury proceedings, concealed surreptitious entry, attempted to compromise a federal judge while publicly displaying his cooperation with the process of criminal justice. "A President is impeachable if he attempts to subvert the Constitution."

24. If the impeachment provision in the Constitution of the United States will not reach the offenses charged here, then perhaps that eighteenth century Constitution should be abandoned to a twentieth century paper shredder.

25. Has the President committed offenses and planned and directed and acquiesced in a course of conduct which the Constitution will not tolerate? This is the question. We know that. We know the question.

26. We should now forthwith proceed to answer the question.

27. It is reason, and not passion, which must guide our deliberations, guide our debate, and guide our decision.

28. Mr. Chairman, I yield back the balance of my time.

Restating Difficult or Unfamiliar Information

Step one, activities that help you make sense of what you have read—asking questions, restating difficult information in your own words, paying attention to language choices—may look something like the following. The numbered information responds to the numbered paragraphs of Jordan's speech. The more you can say about what you have read, the more the information can become your own.

1. Barbara Jordan is a junior member of the committee in a place where seniority matters. She defers to those who are senior members of the committee, giving praise to the chairman of the committee. She appears to understand the political world.

2. Dates of the original Constitution. She was not a part of that document; she had been left out. Speaks in groups of threes: "amendment, interpretation and court decision." Is this effective?

3. Now, she is a part of the Constitution. Uses three terms again and balances a positive with a negative. In a powerful sentence, she proclaims, "My faith in the Constitution is whole, it is complete, it is total." All three words mean roughly the same thing, but the inclusion of all three adds a verbal exclamation to her pleasure in being included among those who are protected and guided by the Constitution. She won't be a part of its "diminution, the subversion, the destruction."

4. (This might be a good place to check the Constitution for the wording of the information about impeachment.) She clarifies the meaning of impeachment. You don't have to be convinced the president should be removed from office to support impeachment.

5. The accusers and the judges are not the same. She applauds the framers of the Constitution for dividing the duties between the two branches of the legislature: the House accuses; the Senate judges.

6. Notice the language choices here surrounding the president (the head of the executive branch), who will be called to account by the legislators—a system of checks and balances: Impeachment will "bridle" the executive—what else is bridled? A horse? An animal that needs to be brought under control? Is President Nixon dehumanized in this moment? She continues to go back to the framers of the Constitution—using the language in her speech that would have echoed how the framers responded to the break with England— "a President swollen with power and grown tyrannical." In the long history of the English monarchy, the word "tyrannical" or its root word would have been associated with kings. Impeachment was meant to be used in a "narrow" channel, one reserved for "high crimes and misdemeanors" or "great misdemeanors," she points out. Jordan uses historical support here.

7 and 8. More historical references to impeachment.

9. A reference to parties in (8) is clarified here as not being "political parties." She repeats that impeachment is about high crimes and misdemeanors—this is at the root of their business. Has President Nixon committed high crimes and misdemeanors? One-third of the way through her speech, she is reminding her colleagues and clarifying for them (and a national audience who is watching on television) the charge of the House Judiciary committee.

10. Language from Woodrow Wilson she finds useful: "nothing short of grossest offenses against the plain law of the land."

11. Here she uses repetition, contrasting "petty" with "big." Congress has important things to do, so this impeachment proceeding better not be petty; it is big.

12. Now, finally, she directs her attention to a review of what is known about President Nixon. That morning the committee had learned that the evidence against the president was "thin" and "insufficient." *But,* she states overtly what had been left out of the morning's presentation: what the President *did* know on the morning of June 23, 1972: It was Republican money from the Committee for the Re-election of the President that was found on one of the arrested burglars.

13. More about what the president knew—about E. Howard Hunt—and his criminal participation in clandestine activities to discredit the Kennedy administration.

14. President Nixon has not offered the committee any additional information to help them understand his role or participation or lack thereof. The day before, the American people waited to see if their president would obey an order of the Supreme Court. When she alludes to the third branch of the government—the judiciary—she now has put forth a subtle reminder about the checks and balances of all three branches with each other.

15. With both an understanding of what impeachment is and what the president did know, she matches one with the other to try to help herself and the committee see whether impeachment (the accusation of wrongdoing) is in order.

16. She returns to history again—this time James Madison (known as the Father of the Constitution), who said, "if the President is connected in any suspicious manner . . . he may be impeached."

17. She sees a fit—the president knew that funds collected for the 1972 presidential campaign were being used as hush money for the burglars. She then connects President Nixon's behavior directly to Madison's quote. The words aren't hers, Jordan seems to be saying, they are the words of the Constitution and words about the Constitution that come from the framers themselves.

18. From the justice story: a connection between impeachment and "extraordinary cases."

19. And then coming forward, more about what President Nixon knew—going back to before the Watergate break-in.

20. And back in time to yet another ratification convention, bringing up another definition: Impeachment is for those "who behave amiss or betray their public trust."

21. Then she ties this definition to what the president knew to be false while making public announcements about it. Again the actions of the president and the definitions of impeachment from history are successfully connected.

22. In a final connection, she returns to James Madison and quotes his point that a president may not "subvert the Constitution."

23. She lists the president's wrongdoings in language that makes clear that he has indeed subverted the Constitution, but *without* saying so explicitly: The president has counseled others to commit perjury and has willfully disregarded, concealed, and compromised the truth. Then she simply repeats Madison's definition—as though to say, draw your own conclusions, but what possibly could you draw except to see the substantial reason for voting for impeachment of this president. And all without saying so explicitly.

24. Rather than overtly stating her support of impeachment, she brings the past and present together in an office-spun image: If you don't see these connections, then perhaps the eighteenth-century Constitution should be abandoned to the twentieth-century paper shredder.

25. She closes by repeating the question—in short, Should this president be impeached. And then she says twice more: We know the question.

26. So we should answer the question.

27. And returns to the use of three terms to close: reason should guide deliberations, debate, and decision.

28. In what is a congressional convention, she then yields the floor to the chair.

Brainstorming, Free Writing, Making Lists

Step two, the activity that helps you make sense of what you will write—by brainstorming, free writing, or making lists—may look like the following. The order of the paragraphs in the speech matters less at this point than first efforts at putting your thoughts down on paper in a way that helps you organize possible ideas you do want to express in writing.

Free writing

Barbara Jordan had been in the House of Representatives only two years when President Nixon's choices elevated her into the limelight. Nixon was in trouble for lying to the American public, and the House Judiciary Committee was deciding whether to impeach him. At this time, we had only impeached one president, Andrew Johnson, and that had been a hundred years earlier (find out exact dates). Now, all of America looked on as this formidable (how do I know she is formidable—I better show how I know this) black woman took the microphone to speak. (Do I need to try to hear what she sounds like? I could add that to my response.) (If I heard her, I would know if "formidable" is the right word to describe her!)

Making lists

Her connection to the political system

Her use of diction—punctuating her comments in threes

Her knowledge of history

Making history and the present match

Good use of specific details

Never says *yes* we should impeach Nixon

She just puts forth the information to do so

The committee and then the full house needs to accuse

She lets the committee know this is *big*, not petty.

Barbara Jordan shows her respect for and faith in the Constitution—"it is whole, it is complete, it is total"—in her speech to the House Judiciary Committee on July 25, 1974. Impeachment of President Richard Nixon appears to be imminent, but before that can happen, the president decides to resign from office. He does so on August 8, 1974, just over two weeks from the date of Jordan's speech, becoming the first president to ever resign in disgrace from the highest office in the land.

Brainstorming

1. Why is the speech famous? How was it important then? Does it have any relevance for today? What about Clinton's impeachment?
2. Does it matter that Jordan casts herself as an outsider—who has recently become a part of the people governed by the Constitution?
3. Was she ever right about being excluded from the Constitution?
4. Was she left out of the Constitution because she was female? Because she was black?
5. If she is black and female and these happenstances of her existence caused her to be left out, then what was it that made her now feel a sense of belonging?
6. Does she now feel she belongs because of her role in the House? Her intelligence? Her understanding of history?
7. Does it matter that she impresses again and again on her audience that this is a seriously important and *big* moment?

8. Does the repetition make her rhetoric more weighted with the serious nature of the situation?
9. Would she be as effective if she had not done her historical homework?
10. Is delivering the historical quotes necessary?
11. Does the history add an urgency to Nixon's predicament?
12. What about the tone in this speech? Is it dignified? Is it hostile toward Nixon? Toward the presidency? Toward her audience?

Where or how you get started is of less importance than where you conclude. In this example of step two, you could start with the brainstorming questions and then move to the list, and finally to free writing. The goal is to find a way to become familiar with unfamiliar material. Before you can respond to the single speech or synthesize materials—for example, the speech plus parts of the Constitution—you need to become totally comfortable with what the material itself is all about. It is difficult and often painful to write a response to something you do not understand. Much of the material you will face in your college classes will be unfamiliar.

Using Barbara Jordan's speech, try out the techniques of step two to move toward an understanding of how you might respond to one of these three questions.

- *How is this speech relevant to us today?*
- *Is knowing and using history important to make a stand on today's issues?*
- *Jordan's speech is* implicit *in her position on Nixon's impeachment. Is this technique more or less effective than if she had been* explicit?

Although you may be more familiar with the impeachment of Bill Clinton, it was not the first in our nation's history. Following Barbara Jordan's example of using history to better understand today, consider the story of Andrew Johnson, the seventeenth president of the United States.

The first successful impeachment in our country's history was that of President **Andrew Johnson,** who took office after the assassination of President **Abraham Lincoln.** In the days of Reconstruction, political opinions from the North and South often reflected positions that were to have been settled by the outcome of the Civil War. The Thirteenth Amendment abolished slavery from within the United States. Congress wanted to pass a law that said all persons born in the United States would be citizens. Johnson vetoed this legislation, but Congress overrode his veto. The following year, in 1867, Congress passed a series of **Reconstruction Acts,** which put the former Confederate states under military rule. Johnson discovered that his secretary of war, **Edwin M. Stanton,** was helping the opposition, so he fired him. This act was in violation of the

*Andrew Johnson: (1808–1875) The seventeenth president of the United States and the first president to be successfully impeached. He remained in office by a slim one-vote margin. After Lincoln's assassination and the end of the Civil War, Johnson was at odds with congressional leaders, who wanted to control the southern states.

*Abraham Lincoln: (1809–1865) The sixteenth president of the United States, who served during the trying days of our country's War Between the States. He was assassinated at Ford's Theatre in Washington, D.C., by John Wilkes Booth.

*Reconstruction Acts: In the spring of 1867, the South was divided into military districts, and the states that had seceded from the Union had to agree to certain conditions in order to be reinstated. Among the requirements was ratification of the Fourteenth and Fifteenth Amendments to the Constitution.

*Edwin M. Stanton: (1814–1869) The secretary of war under President Andrew Johnson, who removed him from office and spurred the House of Representatives to begin impeachment proceedings. Congress wanted Stanton to stay in office so that the military rule of the South after the Civil War would continue without interruption. Johnson was in violation of the Tenure of Office Act.

> **Tenure of Office Act: The president was not to remove any federal office holder without the approval of the Senate. Johnson dismissed Edwin Stanton, and the legislative branch was up in arms. The act was eventually declared unconstitutional.*

Tenure of Office Act* (later found to be unconstitutional), which prohibits the president from firing a high-ranking official without Senate approval. This was the impetus for the impeachment. By only one vote, Johnson remained in office.

Practicing Prewriting Techniques

I intend to stand by the Constitution, as the chief ark of our safety, as the palladium of our civil and religious liberty. Yes, let us cling to it as the mariner clings to the last plank when the night and the tempest close around him!
—*Andrew Johnson, impromptu speech to his supporters on the occasion of his impeachment, February 22, 1868*

The following excerpts from the debate in the Senate represent positions both for and against Johnson's removal from office. *Read the various positions and determine which way each Senator will cast his vote. Then write a response in which you argue for the most persuasive position of the four Senators. Before you write your response, experiment with some of the prewriting techniques explained above: free writing, brainstorming, making lists.*

Senator John Sherman, Ohio

Instead of cooperating with Congress, by execution of laws passed by it, he has thwarted and delayed their execution, and sought to bring the laws and the legislative power into contempt. Armed by the Constitution and the laws, with vast powers, he has neglected to protect loyal people in the rebel States, so that assassination is organized all over those States, as a political power to murder, banish and maltreat loyal people, and to destroy their property. All these he might have ascribed to alleged want of power, or to difference of opinion in questions of policy, and for these reasons no such charges were exhibited against him, though they affected the peace and safety of the nation. When he adds to those political offenses the willful violations of a law by the appointment of a high officer during the session of the Senate, and without its consent, and with the palpable purpose to gain

THE HIGH COURT OF IMPEACHMENT IN SESSION IN THE SENATE CHAMBER, MONDAY, MARCH 23, 1868
Benjamin R. Curtis of the counsel for the President is reading the answer to the articles of impeachment. At the table in the middleground are seated the Committee of Managers of the House of Representatives.

The high court of impeachment in session at the Senate, Washington. March 23, 1868.

possession of the Department of War, for an indefinite time, a case is made not only within the express language of the law a high misdemeanor, but one which includes all the elements of a crime, to wit: a violation of express law, willfully and deliberately done with the intent to subvert the constitutional power of the Senate, and having the evil effect of placing in the hands of the President unlimited power over all the officers of the Government.

This I understand to be the substance of the eleventh article. It contains many allegations which I regard in the nature of the inducement, but it includes within it the charge of the willful violation of law more specifically set out in the second, third, seventh, and eighth articles, and I shall therefore vote for it.

The power of impeachment of all the officers of the Government, vested in the Senate of the United States, is the highest trust reposed in any branch of our Government. Its exercise is indispensable at times to the safety of the nation, while its abuse, especially under political excitement, would subordinate the executive and the judiciary to the legislative department. The guards against such a result are in the love of justice inherent in the people who would not tolerate an abuse of power, and also in the solemn appeal each of us have made to Almighty God to do impartial justice in this cause. We dare not for any human consideration disregard this oath, but guided by conscience and reason will, no doubt, each for himself, render his verdict upon these charges according to the law and the testimony, and without bias from personal, political, or popular influence. This done we may disregard personal consequences and leave our judgment and conduct in this great historical trial to the test of time.

Senator James W. Grimes, Iowa

I have thus, as briefly as possible, stated my views of this case. I have expressed no views upon any of the questions upon which the president has been arraigned at the bar of public opinion outside of the charges. I have no right to travel out of the record.

Mr. Johnson's character as a statesman, his relations to political parties, his conduct as a citizen, his efforts at reconstruction, the exercise of his pardoning power, the character of his appointments, and the influences under which they were made, are not before us on any charges, and are not impugned by any testimony.

Nor can I suffer my judgment of the law governing this case to be influenced by political considerations. I cannot agree to destroy the harmonious working of the Constitution for the sake of getting rid of an unacceptable President. Whatever may be my opinion of the incumbent, I cannot consent to trifle with the high office he holds. I can do nothing which, by implication, may be construed into an approval of impeachments as a part of future political machinery.

However widely, therefore, I may and do differ with the President respecting his political views and measures, and however deeply I have regretted, and do regret, the difference between himself and the Congress of the United States, I am not able to record my vote that he is guilty of high crimes and misdemeanors by reason of those differences. I am acting in a judicial capacity, under conditions whose binding obligation can hardly be exceeded, and I must act according to the best of my ability and judgment, and as they require. If, according to their dictates, the President is guilty, I *must* say so; if, according to their dictates the President is not guilty, I *must* say so.

5   In my opinion the President has not been guilty of an impeachable offense by reason of anything alleged in either of the articles preferred against him at the bar of the Senate by the House of Representatives.

Senator Lyman Trumbull, Illinois

Painful as it is to disagree with so many political associates and friends whose conscientious convictions have led them to a different result, I must, nevertheless, in the discharge of the high responsibility under which I act, be governed by what my reason and judgment tell me is the truth, and the justice and the law of this case. What law does this record show the President to have violated? Is it the tenure of office act? I believe in the constitutionality of that act, and stand ready to punish its violators; but neither the removal of that faithful and efficient officer, Edwin M. Stanton, which I deeply regret, nor the *ad interim* designation of Lorenzo Thomas, were, as has been shown, forbidden by it. Is it the reconstruction acts? Whatever the facts may be, this record does not contain a particle of evidence of their violation. Is it the conspiracy act? No facts are shown to sustain such a charge, and the same may be said of the charge of a violation of the appropriation act of March 2d 1867; and these are all the laws alleged to have been violated. It is, however, charged that Andrew Johnson has violated the Constitution. The fact may be so, but where is the evidence of it to be found in this record? Others may, but I cannot find it. To convict and depose the Chief Magistrate of a great nation, when his guilt was not made palpable by the record, and for insufficient cause, would be fraught with far greater danger to the future of the country than can arise from leaving Mr. Johnson in office for the remaining months of his term, with powers curtailed and limited as they have been by recent legislation.

Once set the example of impeaching a President for what, when the excitement of the hour shall have subsided, will be regarded as insufficient causes, as several of those now alleged against the President were decided to be by the House of Representatives only a few months since, and no future President will be safe who happens to differ with a majority of the House and two thirds of the Senate on any measure deemed by them important, particularly if of a political character. Blinded by partisan zeal, with such an example before them, they will not scruple to remove out of the way any obstacle to the accomplishment of their purposes, and what then becomes of the checks and balances of the constitution, so carefully devised and so vital to its perpetuity? They are all gone. In view of the consequences likely to flow from the day's proceedings, should they result in conviction on what my judgment tells me are insufficient charges and proofs, I tremble for the future of my country. I cannot be an instrument to produce such a result; and at the hazard of the ties even of friendship and affection, till calmer times shall do justice to my motives, no alternative is left me but the inflexible discharge of duty.

Senator Charles Sumner, Ohio

This is one of the last great battles with slavery. Driven from these legislative Chambers; driven from the field of war, this monstrous power has found a refuge in the Executive Mansion, where, in utter disregard of the Constitution and laws, it seeks to exercise its ancient far-reaching sway. All this is very plain. Nobody can question it. Andrew Johnson is the impersonation of the tyrannical Slave Power. In him it lives again. He is the lineal ancestor of John C. Calhoun and Jefferson Davis. And he gathers about him the same supporters. Original partisans of slavery North and South; habitual compromisers of great principles; maligners of the Declaration of Independence politicians without heart; lawyers, for whom a technicality is everything, and a promiscuous company who at every stage of the battle have set their faces against Equal Rights—these are his allies. It is the old troop of slavery, with a few recruits, ready as of old for violence—cunning in device and heartless in quibble. With the President at their head, they are now entrenched in the Executive Mansion.

Not to dislodge them is to leave this country a prey to one of the most hateful tyrannies of history. Especially is it to surrender the Unionists of the rebel States to violence and bloodshed. Not a month, not a week, not a day should be lost. *The safety of the Republic requires action at once*. The lives of innocent men must be rescued from sacrifice.

I would not in this judgment depart from that moderation which belongs to the occasion; but God forbid that, when called to deal with so great an offender, I should affect a coldness which I cannot feel. Slavery has been our worst enemy, murdering our children, filling our homes with mourning, and darkening the land with tragedy; and now it rears its crest anew with Andrew Johnson as its representative. Through him it assumes once more to rule the Republic and to impose its cruel law. The enormity of his conduct is aggravated by his barefaced treachery. He once declared himself the Moses of the colored race. Behold him now the Pharaoh. With such treachery in such a cause there can be no parley. Every sentiment, every conviction, every vow against slavery must now be directed against him. Pharaoh is at the bar of the Senate for judgment.

The formal accusation is founded on certain recent transgressions, enumerated in articles of impeachment, but it is wrong to suppose that this is the whole case. It is very wrong to try this impeachment merely on these articles. It is unpardonable to higgle over words and phrases when for more than two years the tyrannical pretensions of this offender, now in evidence before the Senate, as I shall show, have been manifest in their terrible, heartrending consequences.

On the Internet, find some pro and con responses to President Bill Clinton's impeachment proceedings. How does the language of over a hundred years ago compare with how we write and talk today? Is it more complicated to determine the position of Johnson's or Clinton's contemporaries? After reading the above commentary on Johnson and doing your research on Clinton, what do these two events have in common? Using Citizenship 101, *find the specific reference to impeachment in the Constitution and use that information to support your argument, and then write an essay exploring how one of these impeachments might inform your understanding of the other.*

Summary

A **summary*** is a condensing of a longer piece of writing. The first sentence should include the author and title. The thesis should be included in your summary as soon as it is clear to you. If the thesis is not overtly stated, you might find it useful to state the thesis at the conclusion of your summary. Try to reduce each paragraph to one sentence. Think carefully about what you might want to

> ***summary:** Reducing the whole of another's work by carefully reading and restating the main idea of each paragraph into a sentence. An effective summary is objective, not evaluating how or why something is written, but comprehending what is written.*

quote directly from the piece; use word groupings that appear to go to the heart of the material and express a point in language that you would like to preserve.

The purpose of a summary is not to include what you think about what you are reading but to try, with as much distance as possible, to indicate what the piece conveys. When you read nonfictional material, writing a summary is one way to be in active dialogue with the text; you are asking that text—paragraph by paragraph— what is important. To reduce a paragraph to a sentence, you first have to understand the paragraph. Summary is an important way to gain greater understanding of a text and an effective way to refer to another text in your own writing.

The following piece comes from an anthology called *Dream Me Home Safely: Writers on Growing Up in America. After you read this essay, write your own summary of "Toadstools." Then see how your work differs from the summary provided at the end of the essay.*

Bich Minh Nguyen

Toadstools

We live in a neighborhood of Vanderveens and Hoekstras, with ranch houses, Sears siding, and rec room basements. My sister and I have tagged two houses as "rich": the blue split-level on the corner with a wide sloping lawn and the one with the swimming pool. It's a real pool, not one of those aboveground tubs covered with a tarp. In the summer that in-ground pool glistens as pure and fenced and untouchable as the old white couple who own it. They invite no one but our next-door neighbors, and from a distance we imagine their pale heads shining wet; we hear the splashes they make while we run through the sprinklers in our yard.

My grandmother's voice rises above all others in the neighborhood, calling my siblings and me home for lunch. Every day we have feasts: bowls of pho, stewed shrimp with rice. Homemade French fries are nestled under garlic-seared minute steaks. One day I bring over a friend so she can get in on the action too. But my friend shrinks back. She takes a couple of fries and refuses anything more. She shakes her head, blond curls quivering. She says, "Your house smells funny."

And like that my world divides in half. Outside I climb trees, ride bicycles around the block, chase down ice cream trucks with the girls in the neighborhood. We are friends in certain hours, the interstices between our real lives. When they go off for Vacation Bible School I go back home, where our driveway is patchy with motor oil. There are junk drawers, junk cabinets, a junk garage. In the kitchen Noi is opening cans of lychee and serving the fruit in teacups; she carves apples and mangoes clean of skin. She spends her days knitting sweaters and blankets, reading up on the news from Vietnam, working in the kitchen. When she turned in to *Another World* and a language she doesn't understand I sit beside her, reading library books that pile around me and never get returned on time.

On the weekends my family goes to the Saigon Market, where the shelves are crammed with rice paper and tea. My father spends hours talking to the storeowner; they go over business, relatives, the latest ones to arrive. He buys my sister and me bags of dried cuttlefish and plums, and we go outside to look in the windows of the Waterbed

Gallery next door. There's always broken glass in the parking lot, and we wonder where it comes from. On 28th Street all cars are going fast, headlights winking on toward darkness. Sometimes we're allowed to walk to Meijer's and buy an orange crush. The fluorescent aisles hold stories of other people's houses: Hamburger Helper, Shake n' Bake, gravies made by Knorr; meatloaves, casseroles, pork chops with applesauce.

Before falling asleep at night I go to Noi's room and ask for permission. *Grandmother, good night; may I go to sleep now?* She sits cross-legged, working on a puzzle, and some-times her long silver hair is down, pooled around her like a cape. She might let me go with a wave of her hand. She might say no, so I'll stay and have an apple. Once in a while I help with a puzzle; I sit beside her and read the same books to stamp them in my mind. There are times I return again and again, barging in on her late-night meditations to ask the same question until my parents yell at me to be quiet and go to bed.

The truth is that the neighborhood has been going downhill. Our next-door neighbors can no longer ignore the silent man who lives alone and never mows his lawn. They move carefully past the divorced woman—absent ex-husband never mentioned—who lives with her two kids and a deaf cat. They speak in frightened whispers about the "hyper" boy down the street. My family's arrival has signaled a turning point. We are a pieced-together lot, not white, not Republican, not Christian. My stepmother is Latina and has declined to change her last name; my father works shirtless in the yard. My stepsister has been caught smok-ing; my sister has threatened to beat up a girl who made fun of her clothes. My brother leads big-wheel parades around the block; my uncles blast Santana from the basement. And I am always lurking, making up gossip. We are funny-looking. Funny-smelling. Our souls are not saved.

And on days after rain when toadstools bloom in our yard my grandmother goes out and digs up each one. The kids in the neighborhood see this and screw up their faces. "Are you gonna eat them for supper?" they call out, laughing, their Kool-Aid mouths wide.

It takes me years to understand what Noi is doing. The realization begins on the night of a school play in sixth grade. Everyone will go except my grandmother, who has decided that her presence would be an embarrassment. She wouldn't wear her *ao dai* and endure my eyes cast downward. So we leave for the play and I am bothered the whole time. I want to go back and tell her that I never meant to be ashamed of us; I never meant to absorb that point of view. I want to say so much, but I do not.

So I say this now: I know why she dug up the toadstools. Here is a woman with imag-ination, who supplies her own meanings to soap operas she doesn't really comprehend. I think she must have pictured my siblings and me stealing away with the toadstools, putting their foreign substance in our mouths. She never acknowledged the neighborhood chil-dren laughing, their cheeks puffed with derision. When she knelt in the yard she pulled up the toadstools to save us.

We owe our childhoods to other people. In 1975 my father and grandmother gath-ered up their family and fled from Vietnam to start over on the other side of the world. I wonder what Noi must have thought that first winter in Michigan. The breathless cold, falling ice, drifts of snow so high months would pass before we'd see the yard again. From her bedroom window the streetlamps cast an eerie glow on the neighborhood. I wonder now when I stopped asking her for permission. How many nights did I return, lonely and wide awake, saying *Grandmother, may I go to sleep now?*

Write your own summary before reading this one provided below.

Using one sentence for each of the ten paragraphs, a summary of "Toadstools" could look like this ten-sentence paragraph:

In Bich Minh Nguyen's "Toadstools," she begins by describing her family as isolated from others in the neighborhood; the rich have a swimming pool, but she and her sister can only run through their sprinklers. Her grandmother calls them home for lunch—a feast of bowls of pho, stewed shrimp with rice—but when a friend comes too, she won't eat the food and says, "Your house smells funny." Nguyen realizes that she lives in two worlds—on the outside she rides bikes and chases down the ice cream truck, but once inside, she eats different food and spends time with her grandmother, who watches television but doesn't understand the language. When she goes to the Saigon Market with her family, she recognizes that the location, on a busy street, with broken glass in the parking lot, is a walk away from Meijer's where she buys an orange crush and notices that aisles are filled with the food of other people's houses, such as Hamburger Helper. When she goes to bed at night, she always goes to her grandmother's room and asks for permission to go to sleep. The neighborhood is going downhill—people's differences cannot be ignored: divorced woman, "hyper" boy, silent man; nobody is exactly like anyone else, but they remain funny-looking and funny-smelling. When it rains, the toadstools grow, and her grandmother digs up every one. It is years later that she understands why her grandmother digs up the toadstools, but on the night of a school play, she realizes her grandmother thinks she will embarrass her and decides not to attend, and Nguyen wants to tell her this would not be the case, but she can't. Her grandmother, she decides, pulls up the toadstools to save her from eating them because she is a woman of imagination and toadstools could be dangerous. The family has come from Vietnam to start anew in Michigan, and Nguyen realizes as an adult that we "owe our childhoods to other people"; in her case, to her grandmother who she still wants to ask permission to go to sleep.

THESIS: By first showing how she is different from her rich neighbors, she gradually comes to understand that each neighbor is different from the next, and that her grandmother, whose differences embarrassed her as a child, becomes the person to whom she owes her childhood.

What was your childhood experience of growing up in America? As you think about your own experience, use some of the prewriting techniques discussed above to prepare for writing about your childhood. What are the differences in your writing when you are responding to a piece of writing and when you are responding to your own experiences and observations? What can you learn from Nguyen to get you started in the prewriting of your own experience? You might want to make a list or brainstorm about what Nguyen does to make her essay successful.

Many of Nguyen's points—being different from others, being embarrassed by her grandmother, summer activities of childhood, eating special foods, taking trips with her father—are universal abstracts to which Nguyen has added her own concrete specific examples. You might use a summary or a list to discover another's points and substitute your own concrete examples in place of theirs. For instance, can you remember feeling different? What concrete specifics make the answer to this question your own story? Do you and Nguyen share the same America?

Paraphrase

A **paraphrase*** is a restating of someone else's writing in your own words. Usually, you will summarize longer pieces and paraphrase shorter pieces. Read the sentences you want to paraphrase, look away from them, think about what you have just read, and then restate the information in your own words. Paraphrasing is not the place to use quotes from the original material.

> ***paraphrase:** Restating another's words in your own unique fashion, while giving the author credit.

Read the following selected sentences from "Toadstools" and paraphrase them. When you have written your own paraphrase, see how it compares to the one provided below.

In 1975 my father and grandmother gathered up their family and fled from Vietnam to start over on the other side of the world. I wonder what Noi must have thought that first winter in Michigan. The breathless cold, falling ice, drifts of snow so high months would pass before we'd see the yard again. From her bedroom window the streetlamps cast an eerie glow on the neighborhood.

Over a quarter century ago, my family, specifically my father and grandmother, left Vietnam for Michigan. The contrast between the tropical weather of Vietnam and the freezing temperatures and mountains of snow in Michigan must have been staggering for my grandmother. As she looked from the house out into the streetlamps at night, Noi must have been both scared and mystified by their haunting light.

Outlining

All papers can be outlined. If you do not use this tool as a prewriting technique, you might want to use it after you have finished your paper as a means of checking for balance in your organization. You may associate the activity of writing an **outline*** with the necessity of writing in complete sentences or phrases and having a capital B for every A and a Roman numeral II for every I. You may also think of an outline as a less formal structure, more like a list. After you have made the list, then you can see if certain points fall under other points. Or it might be clearer to you that certain points need to be grouped together under a missing larger point.

> ***outline:** A listing of points contained in a prose piece; suggests order, context, and connection of ideas to each other. An outline may be used either before or after writing.
>
> ***Thomas Jefferson:** (1743–1826) The third president of the United States, whose work on our country's founding documents was essential to establishing how we see ourselves as a nation.
>
> ***Sally Hemings:** (1773–1853) Thomas Jefferson's Negro slave, who historians believe gave birth to several of his children. Some of the black and white descendants of Jefferson today remain at odds with each other over the legitimacy of the birth claims.

It does not take an impeachment to make history matter in current issues. Consider the case of Thomas Jefferson, whose actions two centuries ago still resonate today in American culture. Some historians believe **Thomas Jefferson*** had children by his slave **Sally Hemings,*** and, as a result of this knowledge, many people are interested in how to reconcile the man who penned the words "all men are created equal" with the man who owned slaves, did not free them in his life or upon his death, and also stated in *Notes on the State of Virginia* that whites are superior.

Read the following essay about Thomas Jefferson and Sally Hemings and see how Gordon-Reed's points would look in an informal outline, provided below. Then take the information provided and see if you can sharpen the outline and its focus presented in the essay in a more formal outline structure. Does moving from an informal to a more formal outline seem helpful to you?

Annette Gordon-Reed

Was the Sage a Hypocrite?

Thomas Jefferson, American president. Jefferson (1743–1826) was the primary author of the Declaration of Independence and one of the major figures of early American political history. After serving as the nation's first secretary of state (1790–1793) and as vice-president to John Adams (1797–1801), he was elected the third president of the USA, holding office from 1801 to 1809.

Of all the Founding Fathers, it was Thomas Jefferson for whom the issue of race loomed largest. In the roles of slaveholder, public official and family man, the relationship between blacks and whites was something he thought about, wrote about and grappled with from his cradle to his grave. Jefferson's first memory was of being carried on a pillow by a slave when he was two years old; on his deathbed, the last face he saw was that of the slave who attended him in his final hour. The interest in Jefferson's racial views, long the subject of scrutiny, has reached a crescendo in our time. As Americans attempt to build a more egalitarian, multiracial future, we crave a better understanding of what the man credited with most eloquently expressing the American creed felt about race. What did Jefferson think about black people? How does his relationship with Sally Hemings complete our picture of him? How should we, in a more racially enlightened era, interpret what we know about his thoughts and actions?

Two documents authored by Jefferson have served as templates for examining his racial beliefs. The Jefferson we know from the Declaration of Independence pronounced "all men are created equal," a phrase that provided a central argument for ending slavery and bringing blacks into citizenship, and it still offers the best hope for conquering the doctrine of white supremacy. As unbelievable as it may seem to modern observers who have a knee-jerk sensitivity to signs of Jeffersonian hypocrisy, this language genuinely alarmed many of Jefferson's contemporaries. Even though Jefferson was a slaveholder, the sentiments in the Declaration, when added to his well-known antislavery stance and his support for the hierarchy-shattering French Revolution, made his seem a radical bent on leveling the social order. Whether he truly believed in the equality of mankind or not, they argued, it was dangerous for him to express the thought—people would get ideas. They were exactly right. People did get ideas, and continue to do so.

Then there's the Jefferson of the *Notes on the State of Virginia*, who in the time-honored fashion—"I'm no racist but . . ."—proclaimed whites' superior beauty and ventured his "suspicion" that although racial intermixture improved them, blacks were intellectually inferior to whites. Although he qualified his disparaging remarks because he hadn't observed blacks in their natural state of freedom in Africa, Jefferson's presentation leaves no doubt that he, like a typical white person of the 18th century, believed in white supremacy. Consider Abigail Adams, who upon seeing *Othello* expressed her "disgust and horror" at the thought of a black man touching a white woman. And the Jefferson-Hemings connection places Jefferson firmly within the world of Southern plantation society, where the rules of the game featured public denunciations of "amalgamation" but private practice of it at all levels of white society.

Perhaps most challenging to America's present aspirations is Jefferson's belief that blacks and whites could never coexist as equal citizens of the U.S. Whites, he said, would never give up their prejudices against blacks, and blacks would never forgive what whites had done to them. This is often cited as another example of how wrong Jefferson could be about the future of the American experiment. In reality, it shows that Jefferson had a deeper understanding of the true nature of America's racial dilemma than many are comfortable admitting. Yes, blacks are citizens. But look what it took to achieve that status and maintain it: a civil war followed by an endless procession of lawsuits, legal initiatives, commissions and efforts at social engineering, all designed to prop up blacks' civil and social rights.

It has been a hard road, and the Jefferson of the *Notes* would be astounded that we have come this far. The Jefferson of the Declaration, who at the end of his life voiced the hope that the document's mandate would one day apply "to all," would understand that we still have ground to cover.

5

Informal outline of "Was the Sage a Hypocrite?"

Jefferson and Race

Slaveholder, public official, family man

His memories of relationships between blacks and whites

Our memories of Jefferson

Declaration of Independence

"all men are created equal"

Its meaning at the time

Its meaning today

Notes on the State of Virginia

Whites superior and blacks intellectually inferior

Jefferson as "typical" white 18th century man

White man—black woman = OK

Abigail Adams as "typical" white 18th century woman

Black man—white woman = not OK

Race continues as problem

Jefferson's thoughts: Could whites and blacks co-exist?

Some progress, but not there yet

Cubing

A cube has six sides to it. You remember the feel of wooden blocks, a pair of dice, an ice cube. As you toss the cube up and down in your hand or as you turn it from side

> *cubing: The activity of looking at subject matter through a variety of lenses: describing, comparing, associating, analyzing, applying, and arguing.

to side, perhaps a color, a message, a number, or a symbol of some kind on the block gave you a new something to think about. So it is with **cubing*** a subject matter or an issue. If you track your issue through the six sides of the critical thinking cube, your topic will open up and offer you different possibilities of entering the material by writing about it.

1. Describe it: What does this issue look like? How does it feel? What shape can it take?
2. Compare and/or contrast it: What is this issue similar to or different from?
3. Associate it: How does this issue connect with other issues?
4. Analyze it: What is this issue composed of? What are its parts? How do the parts fit together?
5. Apply it: How can you use this issue? What might it be good for? How can it help you understand other issues?
6. Argue for or against it: What makes you want to support this issue? Why is the issue not worth supporting?

In the spring of 2004, word and graphic photos reached the American press about mistreatment of prisoners in Abu Ghraib. In an early response to the horrific reports, Anne Applebaum of the *Washington Post* suggests trying to understand the situation through the eyes of the American soldiers—one who was photographed with the prisoners and another who blew the whistle.

As you read the essay, outline its main ideas so that you will have a quick reference to which to refer. Then in classroom groups have each group select one side of the cube. What new ways of thinking about the prisoner torture at Abu Ghraib occur to you? Which cubing question is the most helpful in illuminating the issue for you? How might it direct your writing?

Anne Applebaum

What Would You Do?

Turn the clock back six months. Imagine yourself on the other side of the world, in the soldiers' quarters at Abu Ghraib prison. Conditions are primitive: There is no mess hall, everyone sleeps in former cellblocks, it's impossible to escape the heat. As one of 450 military

Fort Hood, Texas: PFC Lynndie R. England arrives at the military courthouse at Fort Hood, Texas, with her attorneys on the first day of her trial in the Abu Ghraib prison scandal in Iraq. May 2, 2005.

police in charge of 7,000 inmates, you wear 60 pounds of body armor at all times, and serve in shifts lasting up to 18 hours. You don't know who the prisoners really are, but you do know that any one of them might attack you, and that all of them might riot at any moment. During the day, you're tense and sweaty. At night insurgents fire over the prison walls.

Now imagine you have been told that military intelligence wants some of the prisoners "softened up" for interrogation. What do you do?

Don't argue that you would be forced to obey. For despite the heat and the stress, the soldiers who faced this situation at Abu Ghraib six months ago were not completely deprived of choices. Clearly Pfc. Lynndie R. England, whose face now stares out at us almost daily from the newspaper front pages—cigarette in hand, grinning behind a pile of naked men, pulling an Iraqi prisoner by a dog collar—had a choice: She chose to pose for the photographs, despite the fact that her clerk's job required little contact with detainees. By contrast, Spec. Joseph M. Darby, whose picture we've hardly seen at all, had a choice too: He chose to place an anonymous note under the door of a superior describing the abuse. Later he chose to make a sworn statement, setting off the investigation.

But don't argue that anything—your religion, your education, your material background—would automatically make you accept or reject that order either. In hindsight, it seems clear that Pfc. England is a villain, and that Spec. Darby is a hero. Yet nothing in the biography of either predicts those labels. England's lawyer describes her as a "20-year-old farm girl from West Virginia who lives in a trailer park"—almost the same socioeconomic profile as Jessica Lynch. England's friends have described her as normal, happy, well-adjusted. "It's not like her to be like that," a family friend says of the photos. "She's a caring person." According to her mother, Lynndie England joined the army to pay for college: She loved thunderstorms, and wanted to be a meteorologist.

But if England's biography contains no clues, neither does that of Darby. He, too, lived in a coal town, in a household headed by a disabled stepfather. To make ends meet, he

5

worked the night shift at Wendy's. If that sounds potentially heroic, look closer. It seems Darby was well known, in his days at North Star High School in southwest Pennsylvania, for punching out paper towel dispensers. His former girlfriend remembers him "pounding" on someone who insulted him on a school bus. When a *Washington Post* reporter told one of Darby's other high school friends of his heroic decision to protest the mistreatment of prisoners, the man shook his head and said, "That don't sound like Joe."

The lesson, if there is one, is that no one's behavior in extreme circumstances is predictable. Childhood poverty is no more an excuse or an explanation for villainy than it is a necessary component of heroism. Neither love of thunderstorms nor a penchant for destroying paper towel dispensers provides a clue to how a person will behave when, as at Abu Ghraib, all of the rules are removed. Evil is a mystery. So is heroism.

Over the next few months, many will claim otherwise. Inevitably, and perhaps understandably, the characters of the soldiers involved in abuse will become part of the argument over who is to blame. Staff Sgt. Ivan "Chip" Frederick's family has already posted Web photographs of their son, one of those under arrest, with his arm around Iraqi children—as if a child-loving patriot could not be responsible for prisoner abuse. At the same time, Army superiors have spoken of the soldiers at Abu Ghraib as a "rogue unit"—as if no ordinary soldiers could do such things, as if the explanation for these events lies only in their psyches and not in the system created over many months.

As I say, this kind of talk is inevitable, perhaps understandable. But it should be kept in perspective. The best way to do that is to keep reminding yourself that the only possible answer to the question "What would you do" in such a situation has to be: "I don't know."

Now that you have used the prewriting technique of cubing to respond to an essay, start with an idea and see how cubing may be helpful when you have only the idea/issue/question you may want to write about. Here are some topics that you might address first by cubing the subject matter:

- *My role as a prison guard*
- *Being "American" overseas*
- *Fair and equitable treatment*
- *For what causes would I blow the whistle?*

Mapping or Clustering

map or cluster: A visual means of linking ideas on paper with the use of circles and lines.

When you **map or cluster*** an idea, issue, or topic, you provide for yourself a visual component that may help you "see" what you will write before you start writing. Start with the primary or main idea and put that inside a circle at the center of your paper. Then think about the kinds of things you want to say about that main idea. Just write them down as they come to you, putting a circle around each one. Then think of what you might say about the secondary or supporting ideas. Put down these tertiary ideas, which may be examples, illustrations, or anecdotes, and circle each one of them. Now your map is likely to be a mess, so just start organizing by drawing lines from the main idea to the supporting idea to the examples.

Once you have the lines drawn, then start anew. This time, put the main idea at the top or side of the page. Under or next to that put a row of the supporting ideas going across or down the page. Finally, under or next to that row, put another row with the examples. Use the circles and use lines to connect as you map out your writing plan.

In a brief article in *The New Yorker* (June 28, 2004), Richard Reid, the shoe bomber, who is serving life in prison in Colorado, had his public defender call the person in charge of the letters to the editor for *Time* magazine. When Reid's *Time* arrived, the letters had been removed. The FBI was in fact cutting them out because Reid, who has acknowledged his ties to Al Qaeda, might be receiving a coded message within someone's letter to the editor. Reid will not receive the back copies of the missing pages. The topic is an intriguing one because in post-9/11 America we find ourselves taking extra precautions. What other ways might a magazine be censored for prison inmates? Mapping is a good way to think through the topic.

Your two maps might look something like this:

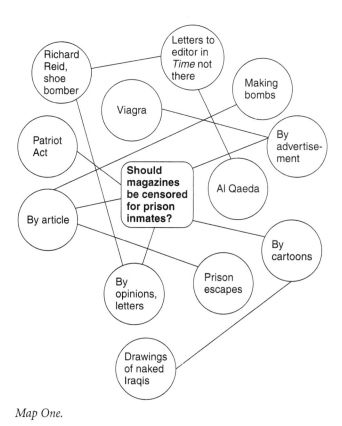

Map One.

Map Two.

Writing is most often generated from what we read, what we observe, and what we experience. In your college classes, most writing assignments will be generated in response to what you have read. Try the prewriting technique of mapping by responding to Applebaum's column on the prison guards at Abu Ghraib. Perhaps some aspect of that column that you cubed will now be ready for mapping/clustering.

AFTER WRITING

After your writing is finished, you need to look again and decide if, indeed, you are really finished—or might there be something that calls out to be rewritten. If you spend relatively little time prewriting, you might need to spend more time rewriting.

You need to think about your own particular style. If you are a person who gets a writing assignment and then spends a good deal of time getting started, you may well be a person who prefers prewriting. Remember that simply *thinking* about your paper is always the first step in the prewriting process. If you just jump in and begin writing, these *rewriting* activities may be helpful for you.

Expanding

In the summer of 2004, **Michael Moore's*** documentary made history when *Fahrenheit 9/11* surpassed $100 million in ticket sales. People either loved or hated the movie—usually, depending on their feelings about President George W. Bush. While the film itself was controversial, so was the labeling of it—was it really a documentary? Was it a satire? Was it an "attack" movie?

National Review, a conservative news weekly, offers a regular feature called "The Week." Here is what the editors had to say about Moore's movie:

> *Michael Moore: (1954–)
Moore won his first academy award for best documentary in 2003 for *Bowling for Columbine.* His *Fahrenheit 9/11,* a stinging rebuke of President George W. Bush, was the first documentary to gross over $100 million.

National Review

Moore and His Friends

Michael Moore, Director, Fahrenheit 9/11.

Michael Moore's *Fahrenheit 9/11* is the biggest-selling documentary in movie history. Compared with normal Hollywood fare, that may be like being the best team in Canadian football. But it would be foolish to underestimate the film's potential impact. Moore has created a new form of media, the attack movie, which follows blogs, talk radio, and cable TV among recent arrivals.

Like remoras following a shark, Moore's critics have been cleaning up his errors and distortions. They have a busy task. Moore says the Bush family is enmeshed with the Saudis, having received over a billion dollars of Saudi business. This refers to a Saudi purchase in the mid-'90s from BDM, a defense contractor owned by the Carlyle Group, on one of whose advisory boards George H. W. Bush sat. But the Carlyle Group sold BDM five months before the elder Bush joined its board. Moore says that George W. Bush went to war in Afghanistan to ice a deal for a natural-gas pipeline with Unocal, a Texas company. But Unocal had dropped its pipeline idea in 1998. Moore shows a pre-invasion Iraq of happy children flying kites. Yes, and Germany hosted an exuberant Olympics in 1936 (filmed, come to think of it, by Leni Riefenstahl).

The real response to Moore and the mindset he addresses is not fact-checking, but questioning. If American ties to the Saudi regime have been too close, and they have, what is the remedy? Pulling out American bases (which the Bush administration has now done)? Should there be other pressures? What kind? If it was a failure to have let Osama bin Laden escape in Tora Bora, then should the United States have committed more troops? If we should not have sent any troops at all to Iraq, then what should be our policy toward rogue states with sophisticated armies, who are also sponsors of terror? Mothers bewail the deaths of their sons in battle, as Lila Lipscomb does in *Fahrenheit 9/11*. But so do they in all wars? Is pacifism the answer?

Michael Moore can dismiss or evade these questions, because he considers them unimportant. He wishes only to accomplish his goal, which is to have the United States withdraw from the world (and perhaps hope that the world withdraws from us). But they are also questions for his mainstream well-wishers. Sen. Tom Daschle voted for the Iraq war, but attended the Washington opening of *Fahrenheit 9/11*, and reportedly sucked up to the filmmaker. Former Clinton operatives Chris Lehane and Mark Fabiani are running Moore's "war room," responding to his critics. The chairman of the Democratic National Committee, Terry McAuliffe, told NR's Byron York that he "believes" Moore's pipeline theory about Afghanistan. The sometimes-sensible William Raspberry and the rabid Paul Krugman have written columns admitting Moore's mistakes and irresponsibility, but saying that they are justified in the greater cause of running down Bush. After taking power with such allies and under such auspices, how do liberals propose to govern?

The above commentary is four paragraphs. To expand what has been said, take the piece and put one paragraph on each page. First, you will need to annotate the sentences to determine if each one delivers the information satisfactorily. Does it satisfy the purpose of the whole? Does it speak to the intended audience? Since this piece is the work of a professional writer, the most we can do is use it as an example of where we might want to expand if the piece were our own.

Michael Moore's *Fahrenheit 9/11 (Do Michael Moore and his movie need any more context? Other movies? How this one is different? Do we need to say anything about length? Point of view? Assumes audience knows enough to say no more)* is the biggest-selling documentary *(Do you want to call it a documentary here when below you call it an "attack movie"—would it be better to call it an "attack movie" from the beginning?)* in movie history. Compared with normal *(What is normal? Is this the best word?)* Hollywood fare, that may be like being the best team in Canadian football *(Does this football analogy work well here? Is this the best way to hold up Hollywood fare—by Canadian football?)* it would be foolish to underestimate the film's potential impact. *(The impact on what? The Presidential election of 2004? On Bush? On Kerry?)* Moore has created a new form of media, the attack movie *(Is Moore's the first movie ever to attack? Is it really a new genre?)*, which follows blogs *(Does a blog need to be defined?)*, talk radio, and cable TV *(Are talk radio and cable TV recent arrivals—should these three genres be linked or explored and expanded separately?)* among recent arrivals.

Are there other movies, television shows, or books that you have seen or read that attack some aspect of America or democracy? The Manchurian Candidate, Wag the Dog, Amish in the City, Who Wants to Marry My Dad?, Super Size Me, Fast Food Nation, and Nickel and Dimed: On (Not) Getting by in America *would be some examples. Write a four-paragraph response to one that you have seen or read. Then put one paragraph on each page and see what kind of depth or context you can give your piece by asking questions about it. Is the expanded piece better than your original?*

Deleting Paragraphs

Is it possible that you have written too much? First, start with your paragraphs. Does each paragraph address the thesis of the whole piece. Finding and taking out whole paragraphs is often easier than the attention necessary to craft effective sentences.

In the following writing sample, which paragraph(s) do not move forward the review of Michael Moore's Fahrenheit 9/11? *Another way to think of deleting paragraphs is to ask yourself if the point can be made in a more condensed way. Is each paragraph essential?*

Mary Corliss/Cannes
A First Look at *Fahrenheit 9/11*

1. A few years ago, Michael Moore spoke with then-Governor George W. Bush, who told the muckraker: "Behave yourself, will ya? Go find real work." Moore has made trouble for so many powerful people he has become a media power of his own. He can even make celebrities of mere movie reviewers: When his latest cinematic incendiary device, "Fahrenheit 9/11," had its first press screening Monday morning, American critics emerging from the theater were besieged by a convoy of TV and radio crews from networks around the world who wanted to know what they thought of Moore's blast at the Bush Administration.

2. Disney, for one, was not impressed. Earlier this month, the company ordered its subsidiary, Miramax Films, not to release the film. Moore says that his lawyer was told by Disney CEO Michael Eisner that distributing it would harm the company's negotiations for favorable treatment for its Florida theme parks from that state's governor, one Jeb Bush. Harvey Weinstein, co-chair of Miramax, is now trying to buy the film back from Disney and to fashion his own coalition of the willing—other distributors happy to profit from Disney's timidity. The result of this internal agitation will be to raise the profile and, most likely, the profitability of Moore's film, which he still hopes will open on the July 4th weekend.

3. So much for the controversy. How is it as a movie? "Fahrenheit 9/11"—the title is a play on the Ray Bradbury novel (and Francois Truffaut film) "Fahrenheit 451," about a future totalitarian state where reading, and thus independent thinking, has been outlawed—has news value beyond its financing and distribution tangles. The movie, a brisk and entertaining indictment of the Bush Administration's Middle East policies before and after September 11, 2001, features new footage of abuse by U.S. soldiers: a Christmas Eve 2003 sortie in which Iraqi captives are publicly humiliated.

4. Though made over the past two years, the film has scenes that seem ripped from recent headlines. Last week, Defense Secretary Donald Rumsfeld visited Iraq and, to the cheers of his military audience, defiantly called himself "a survivor" (a word traditionally reserved for those who have lived through the Holocaust or cancer, not for someone enduring political difficulties). In the film, a soldier tells Moore's field team: "If Donald Rumsfeld was here, I'd ask for his resignation."

5   5. Moore's perennial grudge is against what President Eisenhower called the military-industrial complex: the collusion of big corporations and bad government to exploit the working class, here and abroad, for their own gain and in the process deprive citizens of their liberties. The Bush Administration's Iraq policy is handmade for Moore's grievances. Bush and his father have enjoyed a long and profitable relationship with the ruling families of Saudi Arabia, including the bin Ladens. The best-seller "House of Bush, House of Saud" by Craig Unger, whom Moore interviews, estimates that the Saudis have enriched the Bushes and their closest cronies by $1.4 billion.

6. Politicians reward their biggest contributors, and the Bushes are no exceptions. Fifteen of the 19 September 11th hijackers were Saudis; but when Prince Bandar, the Saudi ambassador who is close to the First Family, dined with the President in the White House two days after the attacks, the mood was collegial, not angry. In the Iraqi ramp-up and occupation, the Administration has rewarded its Saudi and Texas supporters with billions in rebuilding contracts. As Blaine Ober, president of an armored vehicle company, tells Moore: the Iraqi adventure is "good for business, bad for the people."

7. Bad for the people of Iraq, Ober means. But, Moore argues, bad for Americans as well. As he sees it, 9/11 was a tragedy for America, a career move for Bush. The attacks allowed the President to push through Congress restrictive laws that would have been defeated in any climate but the "war on terror" chill. "Fahrenheit 9/11" shows some tragicomic effects of the Patriot Act: a man quizzed by the FBI for casually mentioning at his health club that he thought Bush was an "asshole"; a benign peace group in Fresno, Cal., infiltrated by an undercover police agent.

8. Two Bush quotes in the film indicate the Administration's quandary in selling repression to the American people. One: "A dictatorship would be a heck of a lot easier, no doubt about it." The other: "They're not happy they're occupied. I wouldn't be happy if I were occupied either." Moore's argument is that the U.S. is currently being occupied by a hostile, un-American force: the quintet of Bush, Rumsfeld, Dick Cheney, John Ashcroft and Paul Wolfowitz.

9. Moore is usually the front-and-center star of his own films. Here, his presence is mostly that of narrator and guiding force, though he does make a few piquant appearances. While chatting with Unger across the street from the Saudi embassy in Washington, he is approached and quizzed by Secret Service agents. Hearing from Rep. John Conyers that no member of Congress had read the complete Patriot Act before voting for it, he hires a Mister Softee truck and patrols downtown D.C. reading the act to members of Congress over a loudspeaker. Toward the end, he tries to get Congressmen to enlist their sons in the military. Surprise: no volunteers.

10   10. The film has its longueurs. The interviews with young blacks and a grieving mother in Moore's home town of Flint, Michigan, are relevant and poignant, but they lack the propulsive force and homespun indignance of the rest of the film. "Fahrenheit 9/11" is at its best when it provides talking points for the emerging majority of those opposed to the Iraq incursion. In sum, it's an appalling, enthralling primer of what Moore sees as the Bush Administration's crimes and misdemeanors.

11. "Fahrenheit 9/11" may be seen as another example of the liberal media preaching to its own choir. But Moore is such a clever assembler of huge accusations and minor peccadilloes (as with a shot of Wolfowitz sticking his pocket comb in his mouth and sucking on it to slick down his hair before a TV interview) that the film should engage audiences of all political persuasions.

12. In one sense, Michael Moore took George W. Bush's advice. He found "real work" deconstructing the President's Iraq mistakes. "Fahrenheit 9/11" is Moore's own War on Error.

Take another look at paragraph 2 above. Is this paragraph necessary to a review of the movie itself? The paragraph treats the Disney response to the movie but does not mention a single detail about the movie. Is it necessary to helping you understand what you will encounter when you see the movie? How does the review set you up to watch the Bush–Saudi Arabia connection? Notice the level of context in the review. Do you need more information or less?

When rewriting, it is necessary to pay attention to what you have written sentence by sentence. The following four categories might be helpful in giving you a new way to think about your sentences: by types, by images, by balance, and by strong verbs.

Crafting Sentences: TIBS

Types of sentences

The English language offers four ways to construct a sentence:

- **Simple:** includes one subject group PLUS one verb group and expresses a complete thought (S+V). This grouping may also be called an independent clause.
- **Compound:** includes two subject groups PLUS two verb groups. The two groups are separated by one of the FANBOYS or a semicolon. The two groups may be called two independent clauses. Without the connectors, they would appear as two simple sentences. FANBOYS are the coordinate conjunctions:

   (S+V [*FANBOYS* or ;] S+V)

   - For
   - And
   - Nor
   - But
   - Or
   - Yet
   - So

- **Complex:** includes one subject group plus one verb group that stands alone PLUS one subject group plus one verb group preceded by a WASAWBI or other subordinate conjunction or one of the four relative pronouns—*who, which, that, what*. WASAWBI are the most commonly used words in dependent clauses:

   ([*WASAWBI*]S+V+S+V) or (S+V+[*WASAWBI*]+S+V)

   - When
   - Although
   - Since
   - As
   - While

- Because
- If

- **Compound-Complex:** includes a combination of the two described above, with the possibility of a total of only three subject groups PLUS three verb groups

$$(S+V[FANBOYS \ or \ ;]+S+V+[WASAWBI]+S+V+S+V)$$

In the following article by Jonathan Alter, his writing style has much to teach us about crafting sentences. *After reading the complete piece, talk with a classmate about the types of sentences he uses.* You will find examples from his work used to illustrate pertinent points.

Jonathan Alter

The Art of the Closing Argument

At a gala fund-raiser in Los Angeles recently, comedian Billy Crystal told John Kerry, "If you're having a good time, John, tell your face." Kerry laughed, and a few days later Longface—showing a commendable sense of security—picked the Smiling Populist as his running mate. By late last week the chemistry was working a little too well, with jokes popping up about how much John and John touched each other in public. What John Kerry can learn from John Edwards is not just how to grin but how to talk—how to frame a message that penetrates. If he succeeds at that, Edwards won't have to carry any states for him because Kerry will have already won.

Language is the most underappreciated force in politics. If you don't believe so, ask yourself this: why does the rest of the world so dislike President Bush? It's not Iraq alone; the contempt for the American president—even in countries sending troops to Iraq—predates the invasion. The answer is the cowboy language that Bush uses: "Axis of Evil." "Either you're with us, or you are with the terrorists." "Bring it on." When he blurs 9/11 and Saddam Hussein or hypes WMD or says ominously of suspected but unconvicted terrorists, as he did in his 2003 State of the Union Message, "Let's put it this way—they are no longer a problem to the United States and our friends and allies," the words don't disappear in the ether, they bounce off satellites for years. For all the fuss over "Fahrenheit 9/11," the more farsighted recent documentary is "Control Room," which takes viewers behind the scenes of Al-Jazeera. The folks who work at the Arab network don't hate us for who we are—as one admits, he'd even work for Fox News if he could. They hate us—more specifically, our government—for what we say. "With words, we govern," as Benjamin Disraeli put it.

Bush may mangle the language, but he understands its importance, and manages, with the help of his first-rate speechwriter, Mike Gerson, to speak in ways that have worked at home politically even as they alienate the world. Kerry understands the point abstractly: he has recently been taking a page from the moderate Democratic playbook and talking at every stop about "values." But with the exception of a few new lines ("We're all in the same boat" connects well to his Navy biography), his language is still too overblown, impersonal and unmemorable. In his book *The Tipping* Point, Malcolm Gladwell writes that for good ideas to break through and succeed, they must be "sticky," with some sort of fresh paste that adheres to the brain. Kerry's oratory isn't.

Which brings us back to Edwards. His presence on the podium has already lifted Kerry's rhetorical game a notch. Every reporter covering the primaries agreed that Edwards was the star stump speaker. And in question-and-answer sessions with voters, Edwards can drive the ball 500 feet over the center-field wall. When pressed about trial lawyers, for instance, he explains with great conviction how he has fought "all my life" for poor and middle-class people against powerful corporate interests like HMOs and insurance companies. It works, and will boomerang on Dick Cheney in a debate if Cheney brings up the trial-lawyer business.

There's a reason only two United States senators in the 20th century (Harding and Kennedy) moved directly from the Senate to the White House. If they serve long enough, even sometimes eloquent orators like Kerry eventually begin using Legis-speak. No one cares about this bill or that, only about where the country is going and who can take them there. Edwards has resisted learning Legis-speak because he has long been fluent in another, superior language. To be a first-rank trial lawyer, the kind that other lawyers travel miles to see, as they did Edwards, you must speak perfectly idiomatic American.

Most lawyers and lawyer-politicians have never seen the inside of a courtroom. If they ventured in (or at least watched more Court TV), they would observe the great overlap between juries and voters. A good political speech should resemble a good closing argument by a prosecutor (which Kerry was) or plaintiff's attorney (Edwards), where the case builds slowly and quietly—without hectoring—to a devastating conclusion about the defendant. The key is converting negative arguments into positive feelings toward the lawyer's client, in the case of John Kerry. The election may turn on whether voters want a new president and vice president who sound more like trial attorneys than laconic cowboys. As much as we love to hate lawyers, it's been a long time since a Western was a hit.

These sentences appear together at the start of the second paragraph in Alter's essay:

1. **Language** <u>is</u> the most underappreciated force in politics. (simple sentence)
2. *If* you <u>do</u>n't <u>believe</u> so, [you] <u>ask</u> yourself this: why <u>does</u> the **rest** of the world so <u>dislike</u> President Bush? (complex-compound sentence)
3. <u>It's</u> not Iraq alone; the **contempt** for the American president—even in countries sending troops to Iraq—<u>predates</u> the invasion. (compound sentence)
4. The **answer** <u>is</u> the cowboy language *that* **Bush** <u>uses</u>: "Axis of Evil." (complex sentence)

These sentences comprise the closing paragraph of the same essay. *First, identify the type of sentence Alter uses, then identify the subject and verb groups and the WASAWBI words.*

1. Most lawyers and lawyer-politicians have never seen the inside of a courtroom.
2. If they ventured in (or at least watched more Court TV), they would observe the great overlap between juries and voters.
3. A good political speech should resemble a good closing argument by a prosecutor (which Kerry was) or plaintiff's attorney (Edwards), where the case builds

slowly and quietly—without hectoring—to a devastating conclusion about the defendant.

4. The key is converting negative arguments into positive feelings toward the lawyer's client, in this case John Kerry.

5. The election may turn on whether voters want a new president and vice president who sound more like trial attorneys than laconic cowboys.

6. As much as we love to hate lawyers, it's been a long time since a Western was a hit.

Successful writers use a variety of types of sentences. When you can hear a monotonous beat in the rhythm of a group of sentences, there is a good chance that the sentence pattern is being repeated too often. Stop and take a look at the types that are present in your own prose or in a reading assignment.

The ideas below also come from Alter's article, but they are not his sentences. *Rewrite these repetitive-sounding sentences to show a variety of types. When you do that, you will also be showing the connection of ideas, one to another. This connectivity is the main reason you should use a variety of sentence types.*

*figures of speech: The various means by which we use language creatively.

*allusion: An indirect reference to a person or place in one text that solicits thoughts of that person or place in its original context.

*metaphor: A figure of speech in which one word is used in place of another to suggest similarity between the two.

*simile: A figure of speech in which two unlike things are compared with the use of *like* or *as*.

*hyperbole: An exaggeration or overstatement.

*personification: The representation of an inanimate object with the qualities of a living being.

*alliteration: Two or more words close together with the same initial sounds.

*metonymy: The use of an associated feature to suggest something not stated.

*synecdoche: Using one part of something to signify the whole.

- Bush mangles the language.
- He understands its importance.
- His speechwriter, Mike Gerson, helps him to be popular at home.
- He alienates the rest of the world, though.
- Kerry understands this point.
- He has been using "values" more often.
- His language is overblown.
- It is impersonal.
- It is unmemorable.
- Good oratory must stick to the brain.
- Kerry's does not.

Images

English works well when it offers us a way to actually see what is being said. Among the many **figures of speech,** **allusion,** **metaphor,** **simile,** **hyperbole,** **personification,** **alliteration,** **metonymy,** and **synecdoche** are among the most common and effective in helping us to see what is being said. These figures of speech are generally associated with creative literature—fiction, poetry, drama, and the personal essay—but they can be used successfully in academic writing as well.

Twenty years after the Supreme Court passed *Brown v. Board of Education of Topeka,* Alice Walker wrote a fable about a little boy's first day of attendance at a formerly all-white school. Sentence by sentence, Walker makes good use of the figures of speech catalog. At the end of the story, these terms are defined and illustrated by examples from the story. Groups of words in **bold** are figures of speech.

Alice Walker

The First Day (A Fable after *Brown*): A Short Story

Stanley marched to the edge of **the jungle**, took a deep breath, then plunged in. The morning sun was already high in the **September sky**. The humid **air drew** a delicate film of perspiration to his brow. He walked a few yards across red **burning** sand and the **perspiration ran** into his eyes. It was very hot. He reached up timidly and loosened his collar. He was cramped in his clothes and as he breathed outward, his **shirt**, under the armpits and down along the ribs, **strained** inward against him. He was not dressed for the jungle, for he was wearing everything new. New **white** shirt, new **blue** suit, new **black** shoes, **red** socks and **red** tie. His shoes were hard and stiff; the **starch** in his shirt was beginning to **melt into his skin**.

Into such dense foliage and lush **green grass** Stanley had never been before. He was more used to plain dry sand and a barren view. He looked with apprehension at the gorgeous and **riotous flowers** around him and his steps were cautious, **quiet**, and **quick**, on the **soft springy** floor of the woods. His attentive ears caught the sound of **animals** roaming about in the forest. Two of them **bounded** up to him. They began running to and fro on both sides of him. He kept walking. One of the animals, a **small lion cub, snarled** at him. The **cub's father** hit him across the eyes with his tail. Wiping at his eyes, Stanley began to run. Then he remembered something his mother had told him: that human beings should not show their fear of animals. If you don't let them know they scare you, she had said, you can walk right past them and they will not attack. Accordingly, Stanley deliberately slowed his pace, and when the **big lion** roared and his foul breath rolled out into his face, he pretended not to notice but stared and walked straight ahead.

He wished fervently that he had taken his father's gun, then he could send them all scattering. But he was just a small boy, and his father would never have allowed him to take the gun. His father had told him he must learn not to fear the jungle animals. He said if he was afraid of them he would never leave **their yard**, and would grow up to be a timid little man who jumped when anyone said "boo!"

He was going somewhere he had never gone before, and that made it hard; most of the animals running alongside him he had never seen before. He had been given direction how to get there. He had been told that the animals themselves would provide the surest guide; and it was true, all the animals of the jungle kept going by him. **Some snarled** fiercely, some **barked**, and some hit at him with their tails. Those with good teeth **bared** them, and he had to look away quickly or risk being tempted to run.

The closer he got where he was going the more furious the animals became. A **lioness** who could not contain herself **leapt** forward and **drove her claws** down the side of his face. When the other animals saw the blood they began to **prance** around, sniffing at the blood and wanting more. Hesitantly, then boldly, because he did not want them to think he was afraid, Stanley took out his clean white handkerchief and wiped the blood away. But even after he put the handkerchief back into his pocket the **red stripes** kept dripping and his new white shirt was ruined.

But he had almost reached his destination. He walked up, up, up, while the animals pressed forward and gathered in behind him. A **hyena** bumped against him, almost knocking him over. She was mangy and thin, hungry-looking and smelly, **laughing a crazy laugh**. Stanley felt sick. The perspiration from his **face fell** in **droplets down** through the red tracks of the lioness' claws and rolled through the ground in noiseless **scarlet splashes**.

As he approached the opening through which he must pass, he was horrified to see a **line of fat blue vultures standing shoulder to shoulder** across it. He wondered if he had come so far for nothing. But he would not turn around now, nor could he, for behind him the animals had pressed fast and thick. **Muttering and milling** about, spitting and practically cursing with fury, the pack behind him began to advance. There was nothing for him to do but press forward.

Squaring his shoulders, and concentrating on his **multiplication tables**—which he had started to learn the summer before—Stanley pushed his way through. As he ducked under the wings of the vultures he felt a stunning crash at the back of his head and then a searing burn across the back of his neck. Once inside he did not turn to look back at them; he know they stood pressed around the entrance, momentarily without a leader to follow in after him. His **head hurt** terribly, his knees felt weak. His clothes had been slashed and he was bleeding profusely from the nose.

There was no one inside to meet him. He stood **limply** against the long cool wall of the corridor, a **small dark shadow** beneath electric lights. He was all alone. Suddenly he began to cry. He wanted his mother. He wanted his father. He could not recall the correct sequence of his multiplication tables, and all thought except for peace and home deserted him. He was paralyzed by this first excursion away from home, and **wanted arms around him**.

10   But in the empty school building, which belonged to him too there was no one; only a new, shiny **white water cooler** to offer him comfort. And suddenly, because he had never done so before, he was afraid to drink from it.

Allusion. Walker begins her story with a character named Stanley, who is heading into a "jungle" for the first time. This is an allusion to journalist Henry Morton Stanley, who was sent by his newspaper into the jungles of Africa to find the Scottish missionary Dr. David Livingstone ("Dr. Livingstone, I presume"). Both Stanleys were going where they had not gone before.

Metaphor. Walker uses an extended metaphor throughout the short story, where one thing is compared to another thing, so that you may see the likenesses in separate entities. Here "jungle" is really the new school. "Animals" are various white people—both students and their parents, who are specifically called "small lion cub," "cub's father," "big lion," "lioness," "hyena." These "animals" make appropriate sounds: They "snarl," "roar," "bark," "bare" their teeth, "leap," "prance around," bear their claws, and laugh a "crazy laugh." The "line of fat blue vultures" are policemen who guard the school against the entry of young Stanley. "Their yard" is the world of the white people. The "red stripes" are his blood and the "scarlet splashes" are the blood-tinged sweat drops that strike the floor.

Simile. Though Walker uses none in this piece, a simile is like a metaphor except one thing is compared to another by the use of "like" or "as."

Hyperbole. Walker employs hyperbole, an impossible exaggeration of fact, when she refers to the starch of Stanley's shirt, which "melts into his skin," and the "burning" sand. The shirt may go limp, as she later declares that it does, but it does not melt into his skin. The sand may be hot, but it does not burn his feet.

Personification. Walker instills in inanimate objects the ability to behave as human. Personification is often achieved by a verb attributing a human action to a nonhuman, such as perspiration that "runs," the humid air that "draws," and the shirt that "strains." In other places, an adjective may give lifelike gestures to an inhuman object, such as, "riotous flowers."

Alliteration. Walker knows that repeating initial sounds of words works best when they do not call attention to themselves: "September sky" (which also lets us know it is the start of school), "green grass," "quiet . . . quick," "soft springy," "some snarled," "face fell," "droplets down," "scarlet splashes," "muttering . . . milling," "squaring . . . shoulders," "head hurt," "white water."

Metonymy. Walker uses words to suggest other words she chooses not to use. For example, Stanley's clothes are red, white, and blue, the colors of America, where all men are created equal. In this metonymical usage, Stanley becomes a symbol of America herself as he attempts to integrate the school. Walker mentions Stanley's efforts at the "multiplication tables" twice, suggesting larger numbers of young students who will have to face what he is facing on this day, and how many there will be is unknown because even Stanley cannot "recall the correct sequence." As an ever-present tribute to segregation, the water cooler also suggests the baptismal fount from which, on this day, Stanley will not partake.

Synecdoche. Walker uses a part to signify the whole in such expressions as Stanley becoming "a small dark shadow," his self being temporarily replaced "beneath the electric lights," and when he desperately wants his mother and father beside him, Walker reduces the need to "arms around him."

Notice in these three sentences from Alter's essay that he uses both alliteration and metonymy effectively. Identify both figures of speech and explain how they work.

1. His presence on the podium has already lifted Kerry's rhetorical game a notch.
2. Every reporter covering the primaries agreed that Edwards was the star stump speaker.
3. And in question-and-answer sessions with voters, Edwards can drive the ball 500 feet over the center-field wall.

Using Walker's short fable as a model, try writing your own fable about a particular challenge of living in America where you see democracy either celebrated or denied. Then rewrite your fable deliberately using some of the figures of speech explained above.

Balance

Remember the old seesaws of your elementary school playgrounds? You and a friend on the seesaw kept it going up and down, but if you did not have the board in the right place and your weights did not balance, then the seesawing didn't happen. One of you was up in the air; the other, down on the ground. When things worked on the balance, you could sit for a while—still—both of you in midair. When you can find that kind of balance in a sentence, where it hangs comfortably complete in midair, there is a satisfaction in such a creation, just as there is in being able to find that place on the seesaw that lets you just sit awhile.

Balance in sentences works best in two ways. Unless otherwise noted, examples come from Martin Luther King, Jr.'s "Letter from a Birmingham Jail." Though King was a master at the balanced sentence, you can take the suggestions below and develop your own thoughtful sentences.

- An abstract term is answered by a concrete example (ex. 2) or perhaps the concrete expression moves towards an abstract concept (ex. 1).

  1. But more basically, I am in **Birmingham** because **injustice** is here.
  2. The nations of Asia and Africa are moving with **jet-like speed** toward gaining **political independence**, but we still **creep at horse-and-buggy pace** toward gaining **a cup of coffee at a lunch counter.**

- What is offered or asked in one half of the sentence is met in the second half by a suitable answer. A play of words with each other causes a reader to think again about the opposite meanings, many times in the same root word.

  1. **Injustice anywhere** is a threat to **justice everywhere.**
  2. Whatever affects **one directly**, affects **all indirectly.**
  3. **Lukewarm acceptance** is much more bewildering than **outright rejection.**
  4. Those who talk about **family values** should start **valuing families.** —John Kerry, acceptance speech for Democratic presidential nomination, 2004
  5. And so, my fellow Americans: ask not **what your country can do for you—** ask what **you can do for your country.** —John F. Kennedy, Inaugural Address, January 20, 1961

Applying the suggestions above, rewrite a few of your sentences in a completed assignment so that you have achieved a balance of abstract and concrete or in suitable wordplay.

Strong action verbs

To sustain our reader's attention, we need to search for verbs that make a commanding appearance in the sentence. All too often, we settle for linking verbs that merely connect without attitude or passion.

In the summer of 2004, 1970s singing sensation Linda Ronstadt performed in Las Vegas. During the show she made a political comment that got her escorted off-stage and out of the resort. As you read Erin Cox's commentary on the event, think about your own position on the role of celebrities making political remarks in an entertainment venue. Cox's verb choices have all been put in bold. *What do you think her choices add to the effectiveness of her remarks?*

Erin Cox

Our Pop Culture Doesn't Want Musical Artists to Actually Have Something to Say

There**'s** just something about an election year that **draws** out the unexpected and the bizarre. **Consider** singer Linda Ronstadt in both categories.

Ronstadt recently **crawled** out from whatever enormous rock she's been under the last few decades and **emerged** to join other vocal Americans supporting a regime change with Election 2004. Nothing wrong with a little soapbox mounting. The problem with Linda **is**, she**'s** got bad judgment of good timing.

Ronstadt, a superstar of the '70s, **seized** the moment during her recent tour while **performing** at the Aladdin hotel-casino in Las Vegas. While **finishing** her encore performance with a rendition of the Eagles' "Desperado," Ronstadt **dedicated** the song to controversial filmmaker Michael Moore. The singer **praised** Moore as a "great American patriot" and **urged** the audience to view his documentary "Fahrenheit 9/11."

Perhaps it **was** the two-drink minimum that night, but Ronstadt's little speech **did**n't **settle** too well. Accounts **vary**, but reportedly some of the 4,500 audience members **stormed** out, **ripping** down concert posters and **tossing** cocktails around. The Aladdin president **refused** to allow Ronstadt back into her hotel suite and **escorted** her off the property. Whoopsy-daisy. **Looks** like Ronstadt's 1989 Grammy-winning duet with Aaron Neville **predicted** it. She **"Do**n't **Know** Much" about the political climate in her own country.

Did she not **get** the memo? It **looked** a little something like this.   5
From: The American People
To: All Celebrities (Actors, musicians, et al.)
Re: Your Political Voice
Memo Text: You **have** no political voice.

Where **were** the Dixie Chicks when she **needed** them? Ronstadt **should have known** better. In a vanilla, mid-grade arena such as a Vegas showroom, no white-bread audience **will go** for some liberal stink-raising from a what's-her-name entertainer a tinge-bit past her prime. Especially at a time when tensions **are** high and the stakes **are** even higher. She **should have saved** that for the House of Blues.

Ronstadt **joins** the ranks of other celebrities who**'ve been dumped** for their political views. The diet-shake corporation Slim Fast recently **terminated** its contract with actress/comic Whoopi Goldberg, relieving her as company spokesperson. This action **coincided** with her controversial appearance at a Sen. John Kerry fundraiser. Poor Whoopi. No more Diet Mocha Shakes. She**'s got** nowhere to go but up.

If famous persons **seek** a place to have their say, they **should consider going** abroad. A well known musician such as Bonnie Raitt **can travel** to Sweden on her European summer tour and freely **speak** her mind. While performing at the Stockholm Jazz Festival, Raitt **told** the crowd, "We're **gonna sing** this for George Bush because he**'s** out of here, people" as she **tore** into her song "Your Good Thing (Is About To End)." Raitt **received** no criticism or gin and tonics **thrown** in her face for her remarks, as Sweden **was** one of the numerous countries that **refused** to support the Iraq invasion in 2003.

Critics **may argue** that musicians **are paid** to entertain, not sermonize. People **pay** good money to hear the tunes they **danced, romanced** and **grew** up with. They **want** to feel nice and relaxed, not agitated.

10   If we as Americans **demanded** less of our singers and entertainers, we **would be robbed** of some excellent work. There **would be** no Marian Anderson, Pete Seeger, Woody Guthrie, Paul Simon or Stevie Wonder. Willie Nelson, Bob Dylan, Joni Mitchell, Marvin Gaye, Neil Young or Nina Simone **would have been unemployed**.

My parents **grew** up in a world where mainstream radio **played** politically and socially-amped songs in heavy rotation during an equally turbulent era. They **had** Bob Dylan, John Lennon and Joan Baez. They **had** "Blowin' in the Wind" and "Revolution." Unless we **listen** to public radio 24/7, my generation **has** to ingest MTV, **saturated** with "artists" such as Britney Spears or 50 Cent, to provide us with sociopolitical commentary. The current popular culture **doesn't promote** politics, unless politics **come** with a push-up bra or a 9mm.

When **asked** by CBS news why she **took** a political stance in Las Vegas, Ronstadt **replied**, "This **is** an election year. I **want** people to get their heads up out of the mashed potatoes and **learn** something about the issues and **go** vote."

Good luck, Linda. Those **are** some mighty thick taters.

Try your hand at writing a letter to the college newspaper about a decision to dismiss or applaud an entertainer you have hired for a campus event. When your letter is complete, go back and pay attention to TIBS. Have you varied your sentence types, used figures of speech in some sentences, attempted to balance one or two, and checked to see that your strong, active verbs outnumber your linking verbs at least three to one?

Editing Sentences: For Clarity

Among the most common problems in sentence clarity are overwriting or obfuscating. The writer has obscured sentence sense by being *wordy* or by being *vague*. Syndicated columnist James Kilpatrick has been writing about writing for many years. In this column, he speaks to redundancies. *As you read his column, note the redundancies he uses in the title and opening paragraph to point out their all too pervasive presence in the things we read.*

James Kilpatrick

Free Gifts, Old Adages

In the preparation of sermons—or the writing of syndicated columns—writers tend to say the exact same thing time after time. They revert back to previous pronouncements. They often continue on with their harangues after their really essential point has been made. And so on.

Yes, today's topic is the redundant word or phrase. Two years have passed since we last denounced such repugnancies as "exact same," "revert back," "continue on" and "really essential." For too long we have neglected "2 a.m. in the morning" and the odious "free gift." It is time to recur to fundamentals (but not to basic fundamentals) in discussing this aspect of the writing art.

The adjective "redundant" is rooted in the Latin "unda," wave. Thus a redundant phrase is "overflowing, excessive." For writers, the crime of redundancy involves the use of more words than are necessary to serve a writer's purpose, whether the purpose is to inform, to educate, to arouse, to mollify, or simply to amuse. In his justly famous "little book," Professor William Strunk long ago ordered his students to "omit needless words." He said:

> "Vigorous writing is concise. A sentence should contain no unnecessary words, a paragraph no unnecessary sentences, for the same reason that a drawing should have no unnecessary lines and a machine no unnecessary parts. This requires not that the writer make all his sentences short, or that he avoid all detail and treat his subjects only in outline, but that every word tell."

Strunk's Rule 13 lies at the heart of the writing art. The art comprises two elements, clarity and style. Let me leave the little dog tricks of "style" for another day. Without clarity, our labors are wasted. What words are "unnecessary"? What words make such a contribution to "clarity" that their technical redundancy may be excused?

These are judgment calls. If we are writing for an audience of lawyers, it would be redundant to quote a "sworn affidavit" or identify a "convicted felon." An affidavit is not an affidavit until it is sworn, and a felon is not a felon until he has been convicted of a felony. For an audience of laymen, the adjectives "sworn" and "convicted" may not be "needless" at all. They may contribute usefully to the goal of clarity.

In his "Modern American Usage," Bryan Garner says that adept editors should be alert to 33 redundancies that he finds especially offensive. For examples, he cites absolute necessity, actual fact, advance planning, basic fundamentals, brief respite, collaborate together, general consensus of opinion, fellow colleagues, few in number, free gift, future plans, interact with each other, merge together, and mutual advantage of both.

Also, new recruit, pair of twins, pause for a moment, poisonous venom, reason is because, re-elected for another term, regress back, the same identical, still continues to, surrounded on all sides, temporary reprieve, throughout the entire, and visible to the eye.

Garner's anathema did not embrace such old targets as "small hamlet," "component parts" and "very unique." He is a strict tutor, but he has his moments of leniency; he now regards "old adage" as merely a venial sin, and he surrenders on "the hoi polloi." (The "the" is technically redundant, "but the three-word phrase predominates and ought to be respected.")

I mellow with advancing age. In times past I have roundly denounced "four short years," "nape of the neck" and "hot water heater." Now the padded phrases strike me as Benign Redundancies. They are not "unnecessary." They contribute to clarity. Other "needless" words may serve a different purpose: They contribute to style. In Professor Strunk's exception, these are words that "tell." Let us not condemn them without good cause.

Too wordy

Either strike through the words that impede or rewrite for clarity in the sentences below:

1. Time and again, I often find myself referring to the tried and true method of checking the Supreme Court's decisions by reading and searching the Constitution in order to come to understand why my interpretation is not the same as their interpretation.

2. After a brief respite in time, we can hope for a general consensus of opinion from our fellow colleagues about whether or not we should reflect back on the country's record of successful impeachment proceedings.

Too vague

Sharpen the focus of fuzzy pronoun references.

> Vague: *This* will be a good time to put *this* into our plans.

> (A common error is to use the word "this" without a clear reference. In the sentence above, we are not sure what is being put into the plans. The first "this" suggests a meaning of "now"; the sentence would be more clear if the repetition of the word did not occur.)

> Clear: *Now* will be a good time to put *this action* into our plans.

1. After the teachers suggested and the students demanded, the trustees asked for more time to respond to *their* requests.

> (The pronoun "their" provides an example of ambiguous reference. We are not sure whose requests—the teachers'? the students'? both?)

Proofreading: Ten Common Errors

1. *Spelling:*

Today we depend on the spell checker function of our computers to let us know when something is misspelled. But the spell checker does not know how to differentiate a *deer* from a *dear, to* from *too,* or *principle* from *principal,* and it is useless with typos, such as *on* for *one* or *ton* for *tone.* If you consider yourself a good speller, then read your paper *out loud* to see if you pick up on the typos. Another good check is to read your paper *backwards.* If you already know that you need help with spelling, then have someone else read behind you to check for your spelling. Your campus may have a writing center. Take advantage of the tutoring services provided there. Tutors are most likely to be more efficient with your time and theirs when you can tell them exactly what you need help with.

2. *Commonly confused words:*

Here is a list of words that are the most commonly interchanged. Each has been used correctly in a sentence. A good rule of thumb to remember is that possessive pronouns NEVER take apostrophes. If you use an apostrophe with ANY pronoun, it will be a contraction.

a. *Its, it's*

   i. The old dog wagged *its* tail.

   ii. *It's* only a few more months until the general election. Or *it's* been a long time since the last election.

   Note: Its'—Not a word. No such thing.

  b. Whose, who's

      i. *Whose* book is on the table?

      ii. *Who's* going with us tonight to the political caucus? Or *Who's* been with us in the past week? (*who is; who has*)

    Note: Whos'—Not a word. No such thing.

  c. There, their, they're

      i. *There* are no more battles to be waged.

      ii. *Their* books were left on the table.

      iii. *They're* planning to host the next conference.

    Note: There're—If you tried to pronounce this word, you would feel the problem in your tongue! No such word.

  d. To, too, two

      i. I want *to warn* you about the late hour. (infinitive—to + a verb)

      ii. Steer the boat *to the shore*. (preposition—to + its object)

      iii. Ask the captain if you can come *too*. (meaning also)

      iv. Ask the captain if *too* much water has entered the deck. (meaning excessive)

      v. The twins were limited to *two* bites of their sandwich.

  e. Your, you're, yours

      i. *Your* ball game will start in 20 minutes.

      ii. *You're* not going to leave the meeting early.

      iii. *Yours* was always the agenda I planned to follow.

    Note: Yours'—Not a word. Does not exist.

3. *Active and passive voice:*

In an active sentence, the subject actually does the action of the verb. In a passive sentence, the subject does NOT perform the action of the verb. In effective sentences, careful writers choose the active voice.)

Action: The bus **driver sped** towards home. (the driver is doing the speeding)

Passive: The **bus was driven** by the man who exceeded the limit. (the bus is not doing the driving)

4. *Sexist language:*

Treat men and women equally in your sentences. If it is not appropriate to talk about what a man is wearing then do not talk about what a woman is wearing. If it is not appropriate to identify marital status for women, do not do so for men. Resist using diminutive terms or reductive adjectives for either men or women. Use *"he or she"* or *"she or he"* in sentences when you are not sure about the gender of the person in question. Do not use only *he* or only *she;* never rotate the pronouns: *she* in one paragraph, *he* in the next. Use both and feel comfortable doing so. Do not use the plural "their" when a singular is needed.

a. Visiting her physician for the first time, Martha wondered if her ailments would be taken seriously. Waiting for *her or him* to enter the examining room, she realized she had not bothered to ask if Dr. Jones were male or female!

b. Kobe Bryant appeared in court this afternoon wearing a teal scarf around his neck. (Is this a fashion report or a report on his courtroom date?)

5. *Repetition:*

Sometimes key terms are repeated when synonyms or pronouns might easily substitute.

Money was always tight in the Nelson household, so they spoke constantly about *money. Money* was on everyone's tongue so much that you might have thought they would tire of the talk of *money* long before they actually did so. *Money* guided everything they purchased, of course, but *money* also controlled their lives, their thoughts, their leisure time.

Rewrite these sentences for clarity and variety.

6. *Sentence fragments or run-on sentences or comma splices:*

A *fragment* lacks either a subject or a verb, which makes the sentence incomplete. A *run-on* has too much—usually two sentences have been inappropriately merged. A *comma splice* occurs when you link two sentences together with a comma, when a semicolon or a conjunction (FANBOYS) and a comma are necessary.

a. *Fragment:* On the day that was suggested John who dropped charges against her for defrauding the insurance company.

b. *Run-on:* When you called last night, I got excited that you might be coming home I didn't know you meant that it would still be at least four months from now.

c. *Comma Splice:* I asked you not to appear one hour before our appointed time, you came early anyway.

7. *Subject-verb agreement:*

Subjects and verbs must agree in number (singular or plural). Placing your verb next to the subject makes for a tighter sentence, and it is less likely you will make an error in agreement. Problems usually occur when the subject and verb are separated from each other by a clause or phrase.

Loose Structure: **Each** of the apples you left on my desk this morning **was rotten** to the core.

Tight Structure: The **apples were rotten** that you left on my desk this morning.

8. *Pronoun-antecedent agreement:*

An antecedent is the word that comes before the pronoun and serves as the word to which the pronoun refers. These words must agree in number.

 a. *Everybody* has been given a test to match *his or her* ability.
 b. The *Committee* wants to make sure that *its* job is properly explained before assigning responsibilities.

9. *Dangling participles and misplaced modifiers:*

When you dangle a participle you leave out the word that is doing the action. Word groups need to be as close as possible in the sentence to the words they were intended to modify.

Incorrect: Looking out the ninth-floor window, the mountains were covered with clouds. (This would suggest the mountains were looking out the window, which would not make sense.)

Correct: Looking out the ninth-floor window, I noticed the mountains were covered with clouds. ("I" am now doing the action, and the participle no longer dangles.)

Unclear: The couple shared the cake on Saturday evening with nuts. (This sentence asks its readers to determine what role the nuts play—are they the couple's friends or are they inside the cake?)

Clear: The couple shared the cake with nuts on Saturday evening. (Most likely, this rearrangement is the intended meaning.)

10. *Parallelism:*

Sentences work well in English when words or word groups on both sides of the conjunction adhere to the same grammatical construction. To check yourself, start with the conjunction (usually "and") and see what you have used to the left and the right. Problems in parallelism can usually be heard when you read the sentence aloud. Also, if you are reading the paper and you lose the meaning, the problem is often that of parallelism.

 a. Before submitting the take-home exam, she studied her paper thoroughly— reading it aloud and backwards, editing it for clarity, *and* proofing her sentences for those common errors.
 b. When it was time to sit for the LSAT exam, the eager students prepared earnestly, waited patiently, *and* concentrated intensely—thus demonstrating their commitment to the profession.

PEER REVISION

When you have the opportunity to talk about and read your peers' papers before they are handed in, you can be helpful to each other. Peer revision is a crucial step between you and the person who will give you a grade. When you read each other's work it is a good reminder that all writing is a public act and that your audience is always larger than your grader. Think about ways to use more than one kind of peer revision.

Alphabet Game

The alphabet game uses various letters as a way of sending messages to each other about where problems may occur. Another student will read your paper and mark in the left-hand margin beside each paragraph one of the following letters: RASS. Rearrange (sentence level); Add (need more examples); Subtract (too many examples); Substitute (word level). If these letters do not work for you, think of some others that would: maybe CUT. Cut (too much information); Unclear (vague at the sentence level); Tighten (consider the paragraphs—are there too many?). All students cannot do everything well, but each of you has a particular strength; peer revision should play toward your own individual strengths. Sometimes students feel more comfortable with larger issues—like organization, thesis, word choice, strength of examples, flow, and conclusion.

Each peer group of two or three or four should decide what kinds of things you want to mark on another's paper. The whole group need not mark the same letters or issues, but each person in the group needs to be clear about what his or her responsibility is going to be. The group should then write the definitions of the terms they plan to use so that each student will understand the feedback given beside each paragraph. Maybe one student feels most confident in spelling and only wants to check that area. So the S, or maybe SP, all would agree, represents "Spelling." The checker does not need to correct the spelling error, only indicate that it exists. Maybe another person is very comfortable dealing with word choice, and the group agrees that something like WC indicates a need for the author to reconsider word choice.

Peer reading groups should never be busywork for you but should provide helpful information given from one student to another about an area about which the student is comfortable giving his or her expertise. Often students feel uncomfortable at first, thinking that the other people in the group will criticize their work. A successful peer review is not about exposing the errors of one writer but rather a pooling of the writing talents and writing comfort zones of the entire group.

Writing Partners

After the first paper has been assigned, graded, and returned, your instructor may assign you a writing partner. Having a writing partner works well in many ways. The two of you can hold each other accountable for the work in the class for the rest of the term. You will meet with each other on the day the writing assignment has been handed out to talk about your topic and how you plan to handle the various stages of the writing process. You will meet a second time to show each other some of your prewriting activities and your first paragraph. Two days before the paper is due, you meet a third time to read each other's papers and give advice as you best know how to do so. What may be the most helpful here is that your writing partner can let you know if what you are trying to say is clear.

When you meet with your partner three times on each assignment, you will learn your own ways of dealing with each other. Playing to your individual strengths will give you the opportunity as well to know and care about someone else's grade. You should know the work of your writing partner by the end of the term almost as well as you know your own work. This partnership in writing might also serve as a model for you to use in your other classes. Even one more person doubles the check and the concern about your writing.

Thesis or First-Paragraph-Only Workshop

On a given day, your instructor might assign three or four of you, depending on class length, to bring your first paragraph with you to workshop with the whole class. This can be done by projecting the paragraph from your laptop to the whole class if the classroom is networked, by placing the paragraph on an overhead projector, or by simply handing out your paragraph on paper to each student. After the student reads his or her paragraph aloud to the class, the instructor will lead the discussion by asking pertinent questions about what the class thinks is the thesis or controlling idea, about its clarity, about where the class expects the paper to go from this point.

Sometimes the student whose paragraph is being workshopped does not talk but takes notes on what is being said. Sometimes the student may have the opportunity to explain what he or she wanted to say and ask specific questions about how to get there. What becomes clear instantly to all the students is how much easier it is to learn from a workshop when you can clearly articulate what you want to argue in your paper. What a wonderful opportunity to have a classroom full of people actively considering your work!

While each student cannot be individually helped for each writing assignment, each student should have the opportunity to be helped in a large group at least one time. Questions that the instructor asks about someone else's paper may be helpful in your thinking about your work. When the class agrees that someone has arrived at an excellent thesis, you may be able to use that person's success as a model for your own writing.

Prewriting/Talking Workshop

Even if you have a writing partner, a workshop in class where you meet in small groups of three or four on the day the assignment is handed out can be an effective way to get started. First, it discourages you from putting the assignment into your notebook and not thinking about it until the night before the paper is due. If you have the opportunity to listen, think, and talk about what you might want to write about— and how you might go about writing, you are already at work on the assignment.

Talking workshops are a good place to review with others the purpose and audience for the assignment and what voice you will need to use. In talking about the purpose of the assignment, you have the opportunity to try out your thesis. As others in your group talk about what they will be doing, you can use the time actively listening—maybe mapping out your own ideas or making a list of questions you want to ask yourself or others at this time.

You may think of writing as a solitary activity, but the more you participate in peer revision groups, the more you will see how important you can be to each other as you develop your own writing effectiveness. *Below you will find a sample student essay, perhaps similar to something you might come across as you participate in peer review. As you read the student essay, play the alphabet game (listed under peer review) and decide what "code" or collection of letters you will use, or select the important issues you wish to mark in the essay. You are not trying to correct or "fix" the essay; you are simply using a code (agreed upon in your group) to indicate points in the essay that the writer might want to revisit.*

Rusty Hellis

Public Monuments

In America today we have a lot of public monuments, and people wonder if we should have more of them or if they are good. I have seen a lot of public monuments and I think they are very serious things; the reason being is that monuments are for sadness, tragedies, and other stuff we would like not to know about but because of the monuments, we are forced to pay attention. I suppose that's a good idea for the people who suffered, but in a way it makes the rest of us suffer too. Which is sad. Maybe instead of a monument we could try to change the things that caused the negative thing to happen in the first place?

When I went with my family to Europe two summers ago, we took a walking tour in Munich that showed lots of stuff from Hitler and World War II. The guide showed us this memorial to Jews killed by the Nazis, and it was totally ignored, a triangle of weeds between these busy streets. That was a bad memorial. It was for a really bad thing but no one cared about it—there weren't even any crosswalks to get to it. Then he showed us a school for art students. It was the old office building for all the big wigs in the Nazi party. The students in that school studied the kind of art Hitler would have hated. So that was a great memorial.

In New York everyone is having a fight about what the Ground Zero sight is going to be like. Some people want it to be a hole in the ground and other people want a garden and others just say leave it a lone and give us some buildings. Because a tragic thing happened there, we have to mark it with a memorial. In a way it would be like a large gravestone, which really matter to people, even if no one is buried there. My uncle died in a small plane crash when I was a freshman in high school. He had told my grandparents that if he died he wanted his ashes scattered over a certain part of California, so my family all got together and did it from a plane. It was sad but it was also cool, putting yourself out into the world. Then my grandmother got upset that there was no gravestone to put flowers on, so she got one. He's not buried there but it has his name on it and we put flowers there. That's what memorials do, I think, give you somewhere to put flowers.

What Is at Stake for Citizenship?

1. What does it mean for a citizen to say: "My faith in the Constitution is whole, it is complete, it is total"?
2. What kinds of "great misdemeanors" should be impeachable offenses in the world we live in today? What would you consider the "grossest offenses"?
3. Does knowing history help us to be better citizens?
4. Do you think impeachment should be used as a political tool? Do you think it has been used this way in the past?
5. What is essential in defining a growing-up-in-America story? Should we all share certain things in common? If so, what are they?
6. Do you think we should know about the intimate details of our elected leaders' lives? Does it matter to the office that Thomas Jefferson had children by his slave?
7. Do you think "documentaries" about sitting presidents are important in a democracy?
8. How can language be a force in politics? Should it matter how well or effectively our leaders speak?

CHAPTER 4

This chapter explores the ways we communicate and participate in democracy. Part One considers patterns of inquiry, which are represented by different modes, the three appeals, and various genres. There are many genres, and each enhances understanding of the issue at hand and establishes an entry point for you when you want to join the conversation about an issue, event, or decision. Part Two broadens our discussion to explore the three spheres of communication—the public, private, and technical—and then considers how information moving across and among those spheres affects us as citizens.

Americans: Community, Communication, and Participation

Town meeting.

In Maycomb, grown men stood outside in the front yard for only two reasons: death and politics. I wondered who had died. Jem and I went to the front door, but Atticus called, "Go back in the house."
> —Harper Lee, *To Kill a Mockingbird*

The lottery was conducted—as were the square dances, the teen-age club, the Halloween program—by Mr. Summers, who had time and energy to devote to civic duties.
> —Shirley Jackson, "The Lottery"

Citizenship is not an isolated incident, but rather a communal relationship, and the clearest way we have of expressing the terms of our American citizenship is by considering the relationships we are part of within our communities. The freedoms we hold most dear—freedom of the press, speech, assembly, and religion, to name a few—are about the right of individuals to express or act on their beliefs within their communities. If you think about it, freedom is all about what we do in public: we publish articles, we speak our minds, we sign petitions, we march for a cause, or we worship as we please—all in the open without fear of government intervention. That's the nature of our freedom—by definition it protects the rights of individual expression in public while ensuring that each person is afforded equal opportunity. The right to bear arms, the right to a speedy trial and a jury of one's peers, the right to vote, the right to privacy—all make it possible for individual opinion to be expressed and acted on within a larger community—a city, state, region, or the nation itself. In the end, citizenship is both an individual right and a community responsibility.

PART ONE

Patterns of Inquiry

Although you may share beliefs, customs, interests, and experiences with the people around you, those commonalities don't mean you aren't an individual with your own positions and opinions and your own way of expressing them. Depending on the context, you may choose any number of ways to share information or make your point. Similarly, when you are writing, you will employ different means to accomplish different goals. Once you know WHAT you want to say (your subject), and TO WHOM you want to say it (your audience), these different means or **modes*** are the stylistic tools that determine HOW you send your message (your voice).

> ***modes**: System of organization that categorizes context-specific forms of language.
>
> ***invention**: The process by which ideas are transformed into argument.

Modes are context-specific forms, unique tools for inquiry that allow you to claim the space required for **invention.*** You can employ individual modes of inquiry (and the relationships between them) in many different ways. A clearer understanding of what modes do and how they work may help students understand the strengths and applications of each form. Before you can focus exclusively on the content of your writing, this consideration of different genres will expand the writing process and encourage you to treat audience and purpose as crucial variables that determine which genre will likely lead you to writing success.

Below is a list of important modes—*description, narration, example, definition, classification, comparison/contrast, cause and effect,* and *argument.* As you read about them, consider how you might employ them in your own writing. Each is accompanied by examples from the chapter readings.

Description

This mode employs primarily sense perceptions to quantify and qualify a person, a place, or situation. Description is an account that deals most often with issues of how things look, sound, feel, seem, taste, smell, or are arranged—documenting human perceptions to set one person or situation or thing apart from all possible persons, situations, and things. Description is about specificity—with a goal of transmitting a distinct mental image or impression through language.

Example: The morning of June 27th was clear and sunny, with the fresh warmth of a full-summer day; the flowers were blossoming profusely and the grass was richly green. The people of the village began to gather in the square, between the post office and the bank, around ten o'clock. ("The Lottery," Shirley Jackson)

Example from Your Own Writing.   If you were writing an essay about serving on a jury, you might want to use description to show the reader what the courtroom looked like from your point of view in the jury box.

Narration

Unlike the rest of the approaches covered here, narration relies on the qualities and expectations of story. Think plot, characters, conflict, and setting. Often narration appears in the form of an introductory anecdote—a brief, exemplary story that introduces a topic with compelling detail. Narration also appears in the form of case studies to introduce medical, sociological, or scientific subjects by putting a human face on a topic, and as a running commentary for a video or other performance. (This is not to be confused with the sort of narrator we find when we read fiction— the voice in the story that tells us what's happening.) Narration is an effective tool when balanced with argument in a paper.

Example: I wasn't sure what to expect back on Sept. 29 when potential jurors shuttled across lower Manhattan's Centre Street for jury selection. Along the way, one man asked a court office if it was for the Kozlowski case. As a writer-reporter for *Sports Illustrated*, I wondered whether Atlanta Falcons tight end Brian Kozlowski had got into a legal scrape. Of course, the defendants were actually Dennis Kozlowski, the CEO of Tyco International, and ex-CFO Mark Swartz. Through a series of ever larger acquisitions throughout the '90s, the two built Tyco into a $36 billion conglomerate and made themselves exceedingly wealthy in the process. ("One Angry Man," Pete McEntegart)

Example from Your Own Writing.   If you wanted to write about how people under the age of twenty-five use the Internet as a primary research tool, you might give a brief narration of your own online research experiences at the beginning of your essay.

Example

To give an example is to employ the tools of representation and sample, where one thing suggests many. Examples, positive or negative, serve as a representative of many persons, events, positions, and behaviors. Examples offer a case or situation that serves as a precedent or model for other things that are similar. They also come in the form of a sample problem or exercise that can illustrate a specific method or principle. Often using numerous examples is a powerful way to support an argument.

Example: The prospective juror sitting next to me claimed with undue pride that he could neither read nor write; I can only assume he was hoping to be dismissed. He was. Others had pressing health concerns, or were new citizens whose

English skills were not up to the technical jargon of the case, or in the instance of one man, worked as a fire fighter and his possible technical knowledge might affect his opinions. An older man sitting next to me started quietly ranting against "the system" when the judge asked him about his situation. One woman was 75 and had already served on four juries and felt she had already done her duty. A college freshman asked to be let off as he too was just beginning his spring break and had hoped for some time off. Another man offered so many intimate details about his distressing medical condition (which made it impossible for him to sit for long periods of time) that other members of the pool rolled their eyes. And in one ironic case, a woman appealed to the judge to release her from the jury because her husband was one of those charged in the Enron case and all of his energy (and hers) was going toward defending himself against numerous charges in his own upcoming trial. ("A Few Thoughts on Not Doing My Civic Duty," Janet Bland)

Example from Your Own Writing.   If you were writing about a local citizens' group involved in environmental issues, you could give several examples of local polluters in the area who have done damage to a particular stream.

Definition

By stating a precise significance or meaning, making clear and distinct the meaning of language, action, or situation, you create definition. To define is to limit and specify, to reach for the denotation, not the connotation of a word. Keep in mind the secondary but related meaning of definition as it refers to the clarity of a signal (radio or television) or image. Definition determines meaning.

> ***Groupthink:** A reductive pattern of thought within problem-solving groups that forces agreement over correct solutions.

Example: **Groupthink.*** Groupthink is a term that describes the all-to-common phenomenon where, in search of a decision or solution, members of a group:

1. seek group concurrence excessively
2. convince themselves that the group's position must be correct to the exclusion of all other positions
3. suppress dissent that would threaten the harmony of the group or undermine adherence to either of the first two points.

Groupthink can often lead groups to quickly embrace poor decisions and prevent them from exploring alternatives. (Explanatory chapter material)

Example from Your Own Writing.   If you were writing about gun laws, you could define the meaning of a term such as "concealed carry permit" or "waiting period."

Classification

The act or result of arranging and/or organizing according to category creates separate classes. Classification separates items into classes or groups based on shared characteristics or traits, thus designating what something is based on what group or subset it belongs to. Classification determines how individual pieces fit into groups with other similar pieces to form general meanings and understandings.

Example: The public sphere of communication is just that: public, and includes such things as speeches, press releases, web logs, media articles and editorials, advertisements, and slogans on t-shirts. If a message is directed at the general public, it's in the public sphere—the content can be specific but the audience is as wide as possible. Public communication best expresses the things you say to the world, and once made public usually stays public. (Explanatory chapter material)

Example from Your Own Writing.   If you were writing an essay on preservation of wildlife in local wetlands, you could use classification to limit your discussion to endangered species.

Comparison/Contrast

The examination of two or more items, events, actions, or situations in terms of each other expresses meaning through the presence and/or absence of difference. Without relying on additional context or meaning, comparison/contrast is the process qualifying and quantifying one item by another, a search for meaning through relationship. You can compare, or contrast, or both, depending on the nature of the items being evaluated.

Example: We were far from ready to vote on any of the charges (there were 24 against each defendant), but we went around the room that first day to express our general views. About half the panel essentially said the prosecution's case was baseless and the men weren't guilty of anything except perhaps bad taste in furnishings. . . . On the other hand, a few jurors felt from the start that these guys were crooks. I expressed the view, shared by at least one fellow juror, that while I didn't buy much of the prosecution's case, I was troubled by the four bonuses charged as separate grand larcenies—totaling about $145 million—that the two divvied up. ("One Angry Man," Pete McEntegart)

Example from Your Own Writing.   If you were writing an essay about voter registration, you could compare/contrast the efforts of the Democrats and the Republicans to increase their support with new voters.

Cause and Effect

Considering two or more items, events, actions, or situations in terms of the chronology they share, with a focus on how the first precipitated the second, is to establish a cause-and-effect relationship. Relying primarily upon time, cause and effect explains how one item or event is led to or created by another item or event. Great care must be taken when employing this mode, for while all cause and effect relationships occur in time, the mere passage of time—when one thing happens and then another—does not automatically indicate cause and effect.

Example: Having watched countless hours of "The Practice" and "Law and Order" and "Judge Judy" and "LA Law," my fellow prospective jurors spoke fluent television lawyer drama-talk. In the course of the Q & A period, several people asked, much to the judge's chagrin, if they might approach the bench, a woman inquired if there would be a 15 minute recess where she might speak to the judge, and one befuddled man attempted to object. Except for the elderly veteran of four previous trials, few of my fellow citizens had been in a real courtroom, one that existed outside their television screens. As we all thrashed about in our attempts to find something that would get us out of the courtroom, many employed terminology as if they had regularly spent time in front of a judge. And suddenly it seemed to me that the legal system was something we wanted to watch on television, but not actually be part of in our real lives. We could talk the talk, but none of us wanted to walk the walk. ("A Few Thoughts on Not Doing My Civic Duty," Janet Bland)

Example from Your Own Writing. If you were writing an essay about economic policy, you could explore the cause-and-effect relationship between tax cuts and economic growth.

Argument

Unlike exposition, which explores and informs, argument seeks to prove a point and convince an audience. Argument is adversarial but not exclusive, and several positions on one topic may well exist equally. The art of argument is to put forth a position and its motivations in hopes of convincing others to adopt that view. Without good support, no argument can be successful.

Example: I am a strong believer in the courts as a place for ordinary people to be heard, often when other institutions have failed them. People have criticized the jury system, saying juries can't be trusted to consider the facts. I couldn't disagree more. Juries are a vital example of democracy in action. The people who sit on juries are the same people who decide who the president should be. People who are entrusted to choose the leader of the free world are capable of weighing evidence in a courtroom—and they do, every day across America. I found again and again and again that they take their service seriously, and follow the law even when the law is at odds with what they personally believe. ("Juries: Democracy in Action," John Edwards)

Example for Your Writing. If you were writing an essay about religion and public schools, you could make an argument for (or against) school prayer.

The examples above (from the chapter and for essays you could write) present each mode individually for clarity. Keep in mind, however, that it's not their individual use that makes these modes effective but rather how they are used in concert with one another. Good writers, writers who want to present their opinions in a dynamic and successful manner, often use more than one mode in a piece of writing.

Combining the Modes

In the following essay, "The Great Obligation," Anna Quindlen uses several of the modes mentioned above to argue for professional journalistic standards based on the idea that a good journalist can and must empathize with the subject of the story. *As you read Quindlen's work, note the annotations that point out how different modes are employed throughout.*

Anna Quindlen

The Great Obligation

In 1981 I interviewed a couple named Stanley and Julie Patz. Perhaps the last name rings a bell. Twenty-five years ago, their 6-year old son, Etan, left his family's lower Manhattan loft for the school bus stop two blocks away and vanished. This was before pictures on milk cartons, or Amber Alerts, or even the National Center for Missing and Exploited Children, which Etan's disappearance helped create. Stan Patz is a photographer, and a picture he had taken of his son, bright eyes, long bangs, became iconic overnight. Etan Patz: the most famous missing child since the Lindbergh baby.

"We're not interested in publicity anymore," Stan Patz said when I called.

He didn't remember the story I had done: I've never forgotten it. The couple's loss, their need, their grief, made me feel that I had to lift the level of my game to meet the level of their bereavement. This was impossible, but I was moved to try.

I have often thought about the effect the Patzes had on me as some reporters brought disgrace upon the profession. And it has made me wonder whether good journalists always have that moment in their background, the moment that merges humanity and story in an indelible way. Or the opposite: are the frauds always of character, not craft? Skimming Jayson Blair's sloppy and unrepentant book about his confabulations at *The New York Times*, I sensed no concern for the people he covered. His emphasis was on quantity, how many stories could he shoehorn into the shortest span of days. The individuals in his stories were never more than the means to a careerist end.

5   How else to explain the actions of Jack Kelley, the *USA Today* star reporter who resigned amid an investigation that concluded he had invented significant parts of at least eight articles? One of his suspect stories—an account of an escape from Cuba in a small boat under a crescent moon that was not out on the night in question amid a storm that never occurred—was illustrated with a photo Kelley had taken of a woman he called Yacqueline. (The name of the alleged human beings changed several times as Kelley worked on his draft.) In his account, Yacqueline and her young son tragically drowned. In real life, the woman in the photograph is alive and living in the United States, a legal immigrant. No boat, no moon. Not quite so page one, that.

Reporters are often asked about their obligation to readers, but perhaps the most important obligation is the one we owe the subjects of our stories, whose lives are limned by our words, for better or for worse. David Halberstam, the best-selling author who won a Pulitzer telling the truth about Vietnam, says it was writing obituaries as a young man at the *Nashville Tennessean* that made this clear to him. "For most people it was the one time they got their name in print," he recalled. "If you got something wrong you could cause enormous pain to ordinary people."

Tom Brokaw, the NBC anchorman, remembers a young black woman who decided to march in the streets of Americus, GA., during dangerous racial unrest there. "I'm often asked to name my most memorable interview," Brokaw says, "and I suppose most people think I'll say Dr. Martin Luther King or Bobby Kennedy or Gorbachev or Mandela or

Margaret Thatcher or some other big name. But honestly, I always bring up that young woman. I was just 25 at the time and she taught me so much that night."

Perhaps that sort of learning curve is harder now. Ordinary people too often are turned into celebrities, so that Jessica Lynch, whose story was one of those Blair phonied up, went from a soldier to a national figure faster than you could say "made-for-TV movie." The Patzes predate the strafe heartbreaker, the human-interest stories transmuted into all-pathos-all-the-time, their protagonists hurtling from one news magazine to another until they seem less like people and more like talking heads. And talking heads never inspire compassion.

All this makes you wonder if journalism schools should teach not just accuracy but empathy. But the truth is, you really get that by covering stories, not studying them, by imagining yourself in the place of the people you interview. All these years later, and I still apologized to Stan for talking about his son in the past tense. "I got over that a long time ago," he said. "He's gone."

He's not looking for publicity anymore. His son has been declared legally dead by the courts; Stan Patz believes Etan was murdered by a convicted child molester now in jail in Pennsylvania. Still there's a pad by the phone for taking notes when someone calls, most recently a woman who believes her former husband is Etan. Still he clips the stories out of habit. The original impulse is gone: "To create a history for Etan." If you're a reporter, I leave you with that image for those times when you think what you do is fleeting. The closest thing this man has to the body of his son is the body of your work. If that doesn't make you want to do better, find another job.

10

Paragraph 1—Here the author begins with a **narrative**,* a story from her life that presents her main point—that good reporters have an obligation to the people in their stories—in an interesting and concrete manner.

Paragraphs 2–5—Quindlen expands her **narrative** into an **example*** of being a good reporter. She then makes her **argument**,* one of **cause and effect**,* that caring about the people in the story results in good, truthful reporting. Conversely, she believes that dishonest reporting is the result of bad character and not caring about people. Her **example** of this relationship is Jayson Blair. Here she begins to build a **definition*** of both honest and dishonest reporting.

Paragraph 6—Quindlen cites another **example,** Jack Kelley, of the **cause-and-effect** relationship between not really caring about people and dishonest reporting.

Paragraph 7—Here is another **example** of the **cause-and-effect** relationship between caring about people and truthful reporting. Notice how each **example** leads to a clear **classification*** as one sort of reporter or another.

Paragraph 8—Here Tom Brokaw is used as an **example** of the **cause-and-effect** relationship between caring about people and honest reporting, but it's presented in a **narrative** form,

***narrative:** This mode relies upon the qualities and expectations of story.

***example:** To give an example is to employ the tools of representation and sample where one thing suggests many.

***argument:** Unlike exposition, which explores and informs, argument seeks to prove a point and convince an audience.

***cause and effect:** Considering two or more items, events, actions, or situations in terms of the chronology they share, with a focus on the ways in which the first thing precipitated the second, is to establish a cause-and-effect relationship.

***definition:** By stating a precise significance or meaning, making clear and distinct the meaning of language, action, or situation, you create definition.

***classification:** Classification separates items into classes or groups based on shared characteristics or traits, thus designating what something is based on what group or subset it belongs to.

> *comparison/contrast: The examination of two or more items, events, actions, or situations in terms of each other expresses meaning through the presence and/or absence of difference.

with quotations from Brokaw. Through this series of **examples**, the author is hoping to present a **definition** of good reporting and good reporters who care about people—in addition to offering a subtle **comparison/contrast*** between good and bad reporters.

Paragraphs 9–10—The **argument** is expanded and we return to touch upon the original **narrative**, the story of Etan.

Paragraph 11—Here Quindlen returns to her own **narrative** and experience, her own **example** of how good reporting works. And like any good **narrative**, we get the important details at the end. Further, there is a sense of **definition**, as we are left with a clear impression of how things are today for Etan Patz's family.

Quindlen's writing is complex and her point is convincing because of her fluid integration of the modes. She often uses several of these tools within the same paragraph. She makes an argument about reporters and manages to give a clear picture of both her own writing and the writing of those in the field—both those she admires and those who have been revealed as dishonest. In a matter of a few paragraphs, she says something relevant about herself, her field, our culture, honesty, and the human character. That's a lot of work for a rather short essay. The reason she accomplishes so much is that she employs all the modes effectively.

Having read the essay by Quindlen, can you imagine writing one similar to it? What might you say about yourself and your community while you argue about how character is manifested in people?

Write an essay that considers a time when you were an example of something, either positive or negative. Who would you compare/contrast yourself with (in your essay) to best define who you are? What narrative might you tell to begin an essay about yourself and your community?

> *annotate: To add critical commentary or explanatory notes to an existing text.

"Teaching Apathy?", by Marina Krakovsky, explores the connections between student government in high school and voter apathy. Krakovsky employs many of the modes discussed above and seen in Quindlen's essay. *As you read "Teaching Apathy?"* **annotate*** *the essay and note where and how different modes are used to support a thesis.*

Marina Krakovsky

Teaching Apathy?

"It doesn't seem to make any difference who gets elected—nothing changes. Why should I care?" This could be the voice of any of a hundred million or so adults over 18 in the United States who won't cast a ballot on November 2. Turnout for federal elections has steadily declined from 1960—when 63.6 percent of the voting-age population voted—to 2000, when the figure was 51.3 percent.

But the same sentiment applies to growing numbers of high school students. In last year's annual survey of college freshmen sponsored by the American Council on Education and UCLA, only 21.5 percent reported voting frequently in high school elections—a slight

drop from the previous year and a plummet from the record 78.7 percent in 1968.

Adults' apathy toward the electoral process is often explained by widespread cynicism about politicians' vested interests and Beltway power broking. Could it be that those attitudes take shape long before people are old enough to vote?

Daniel McFarland, an assistant professor of education and (by courtesy) sociology, and graduate student Carlos Starmanns are studying student councils in hundreds of high schools across the country. Their preliminary findings suggest that, at their best, student councils can fulfill the lofty aims of well-meaning administrators: to promote community spirit, give students a voice and train future leaders. Frequently, though, there are grounds for the cynical view that councils are little more than puppets of school administrations; that school elections are empty popularity contests; and that students who run for office care more about impressing college admissions committees than serving their classmates.

Student government "is a really important socialization environment," says McFarland, but in many cases it may be doing more harm than good. "It's [students'] first experience of representative government, and if it's a joke and it doesn't matter and has no authority or influence, what are they learning?"

McFarland and Starmanns began their study by examining the written constitutions of 207 public and 66 private high schools. They plan to continue with interviews and a rigorous analysis of the effects the high school experience has on adult political participation.

In public schools, the Stanford researchers found a striking correlation between student power and a school's socioeconomic level (determined using the percentage of students eligible for free or reduced-price lunches). By and large, students in more affluent districts have councils with influential student participation, while councils in poorer, minority schools wield no influence.

Student representatives in wealthier schools are far likelier to have the power to raise and spend money, make recommendations to the faculty and, with enough votes, even override faculty vetoes of their decisions. In one well-to-do New Hampshire public school, McFarland learned that students served on the committee to select the new principal, passed changes to disciplinary procedures and proposed a schedule of special events for Martin Luther King Day. When the principal vetoed the proposal, the student council members considered appealing the decision to the district, but decided against it, in part to preserve their relationship with the principal.

McFarland and Starmanns also found a great disparity along socioeconomic lines in the quality of written constitutions. Poor schools tend to have skimpy documents with only

5

a vague description of the council's purpose and procedures and the powers of each office. Wealthier schools generally have well-defined written frameworks. One 20-page constitution, complete with a preamble clearly modeled after the American Constitution ("We the students . . ."), lists strict attendance guidelines, spells out what to do in cases of conflict, describes each office's powers and responsibilities in exhaustive detail, and specifies precise requirements for amending the constitution. It reads very much like a living document, open to change and relevant to the life of the school.

10   McFarland's current research substantiates patterns he first noticed in yearlong field studies of two schools in the Midwest. He found, for example, that in the poor, rural school, few students even bothered to run for student council. In one grade, every candidate ran uncontested. And candidates ran without any kind of platform or campaign, just as you'd expect in a government without real power.

Whatever the reasons for the lack of meaningful student government in impoverished schools—principals' fear of students, more pressing claims on meager resources, or attitudes students may bring from home—these findings distress educators who believe public schools ought to empower future citizens and help level society's playing field.

Abundant research "exposes the differences in educational quality in this country between public schools in affluent and in poor neighborhoods," says Eamonn Callan, an associate dean at the School of Education and author of the 1997 book *Creating Citizens: Political Education and Liberal Democracy.* "What I find revealing and troubling in Dan's work is that opportunities for civic engagement within the school are also distributed differentially."

"One could say that poorer schools are likely to create apathetic citizens," Starmanns reasons. Political apathy is one of the social-cognitive "loops" identified by psychology professor Albert Bandura in his book *Self-Efficacy: The Exercise of Control* (1997). Simply put, powerlessness discourages participation, and failure to participate ensures lack of impact. But if educators effectively engage students in school government, students should come to see themselves as people who can make a difference.

William Damon, director of the Stanford Center for the Study of Adolescence and a senior fellow at the Hoover Institution, notes that while young people are quite involved with their families and friends—and to a lesser extent their schools—the picture changes in matters of citizenship. "When it comes to what it means to participate in a democracy or even to be an American or someone who imagines herself as one of the future leaders of this country, that's where we see the radar screen being kind of blank," he says. Since 1972—the first year 18-year-olds could vote in a national election—voter turnout in presidential elections among those in the 18- to 24-year-old group has shown a downward trend, the main exception being 1992.

15   Alternative schools—charter, magnet or private—seem to offer opportunities for meaningful political participation greater than even the wealthiest public schools. Student councils typically consist of 20 to 40 officers, regardless of school size, so these generally smaller schools enable a greater percentage of students to hold office. And because alternative schools tend to have a clear mission, their constitutions try to uphold school values—by encouraging the election of moral exemplars, for example. However, alternative schools also tend to give faculty tighter control over students (including reins on elections), leading McFarland and Starmanns to wonder whether such schools raise citizens who are not used to thinking for themselves.

Nearly two centuries ago, visiting Frenchman Alexis de Tocqueville observed that Americans tended to belong to voluntary associations, and he argued that this "associationalism" taught us civic virtues indispensable to self-government. Today, social scientists such as Harvard's Robert Putnam have noticed a disturbing trend in the past several decades: Americans no longer seem to be a nation of joiners. In his book *Bowling Alone: The Collapse and Revival of American Community,* Putnam gives examples of sharply declining membership in organizations from bridge clubs to charities, service groups to school PTAs and even bowling leagues. He cites dwindling involvement in activities such as working for a political party, attending a political rally or running for office. An erosion in civic engagement, Putnam believes, may weaken the glue that binds our democratic society.

Tocqueville showed that a foreign eye sometimes can see what is invisible to locals. Similarly, McFarland says although most high schools think they should have student councils, social scientists haven't bothered to study the institution. "People think of student government as a frill, like band and art," says Callan. Callan was born in Ireland and lived for 20 years in Canada, so he is well acquainted with civil tensions that can threaten to tear a democracy apart. Starmanns, who spent most of his life in Spain, Germany and Argentina before coming to the United States to study political philosophy, says that while the American system of student government is probably the most advanced in the world, that doesn't necessarily mean students here have better chances to participate.

But socioeconomic differences don't explain everything that ails American schools, in Damon's view. He cites Columbine High School—"a place that was reeking of disengagement," he says—as a stark example of a spiritual poverty that can coexist with material wealth. (In Putnam's terms, divisive cliques work against "bridging social capital," the stuff that ties a society together across racial, cultural, religious and class lines.) Conversely, Damon points out that there are inner-city schools where students actively participate because principals have faith in their charges. Under the best leadership, he insists, economics need not be destiny.

Some would disagree, and discussions of American education have a way of quickly turning political—especially when the subject is politics itself. But scholars can probably all agree on one thing: all students deserve a good education and appropriate opportunities to engage in civic life.

Think about your own level of participation in high school. Were you involved in student government? Do you see any elements of your high school in this essay? Write an essay considering Krakovsky's main points and taking your own experiences into account. Argue for or against the idea that high school involvement determines our level of civic engagement.

Aristotle's Three Appeals

When writers want to make a point or further an argument, they use specific **rhetorical strategies*** to appeal to their audiences. Connections can be made with an audience in many ways, but Aristotle divided such strategies into three distinct appeals— *ethos, the ethical appeal; pathos, the emotional appeal;* and *logos, the logical appeal.* As you read about them, consider how you

***rhetorical strategies:** Any conscious choice—including but not limited to issues of vocabulary, form, voice, and construction—intended to strengthen an argument and better convince a reader.

might employ them in your own writing. Each is accompanied by examples from the chapter readings.

Ethos—the ethical appeal

This rhetorical strategy is based on the character of the speaker and is designed to appeal to the readers' shared values. Writers who employ and emphasize their expertise, their gravitas, and their system of values as they further an argument are making an ethical appeal.

Example: Abundant research "exposes the differences in educational quality in this country between public schools in affluent and in poor neighborhoods," says Eamonn Callan, an associate dean at the School of Education and author of the 1997 book *Creating Citizens: Political Education and Liberal Democracy.* "What I find revealing and troubling in Dan's work is that opportunities for civic engagement within the school are also distributed differentially." ("Teaching Apathy?" Marina Krakovsky)

Example from Your Own Writing.   If you were writing an essay about college-level student athletes, you could formulate an argument based on your own experiences as a student athlete and speak as an expert on the subject.

Pathos—the emotional appeal

This rhetorical strategy is directed toward the feelings and emotions of the reader and is designed to move the audience on a visceral level. Writers who strive to engage and arouse such feelings as empathy, fear, and rage are making an emotional appeal.

Example: I'll never forget the first time I met Jennifer Campbell. A charming, determined 5-year-old, she couldn't walk or feed herself, and still needed a playpen. Because of a doctor's terrible mistake, she was born with permanent brain damage. I met her loving, determined parents, who were hoping for a way to help pay for her costly care, and to make sure other families wouldn't suffer as they had. ("Juries: Democracy in Action," John Edwards)

Example from Your Own Writing. If you were writing an essay about homelessness, you could make an argument based on the tragic circumstances of one homeless family you have come in contact with while volunteering at a shelter.

Logos—the logical appeal

This rhetorical strategy is directed toward the readers' intellectual capabilities and is designed to privilege reason supported by evidence. Writers who argue with facts and other evidence to work toward a well-reasoned conclusion are making a logical appeal.

*Miranda v. Arizona: (1966) Landmark U.S. Supreme Court case that ruled that police officers were required to inform suspects of certain legal rights, commonly known as Miranda rights.

Example: Simply put, rights that you don't know about are rights you don't have. That's why we have what are known as Miranda Rights. In ***Miranda v. Arizona,**** the Supreme Court ruled that self-incriminating statements cannot be used against a suspect unless that suspect has been informed of the right not to self-incriminate. Today, many citizens know their Miranda rights: those who commit crimes or who are accused of crimes hear them when they are arrested, and law abiding citizens hear them every night on their favorite television shows. (Explanatory chapter material)

Example from Your Own Writing.   If you were writing an essay about the death penalty, you could support your argument with facts and statistics concerning how many people currently sit on death row and how much those inmates cost taxpayers each year.

In the same way modes are most successfully employed when used together, appeals are most effective in concert. Ethical appeals often need some elements of a logical appeal to round out the argument. Emotional appeals are generally considered to be the least effective, but when used as support for the other two, they can have a powerful impact upon a reader. *Just for practice, write the same two-hundred-word essay asking to borrow your parents' car three times, using a different appeal each time. By making the same argument to borrow the car in three different ways, you can more easily see how one argument can be shaped in three different ways based on the appeals.*

Issues of Community and Citizenship

Anna Quindlen is writing about one of the many communities she belongs to. She might have chosen to write about being a mother or a New Yorker—two of her other communities—but instead she chose to write about being a reporter. Like Quindlen, we all belong to many communities. And it is within these communities—the neighborhood, the residence hall, the church group, the rowing club—that we find ourselves acting and reacting as citizens. For as was mentioned in the beginning of this chapter, citizenship is a communal effort, something that exists when we interact with others. Democracy is participatory, and that participation is expressed in many different ways, depending on the nature of the community.

In 1948, Shirley Jackson's famous short story "The Lottery" was published in *The New Yorker* magazine. Many readers expressed outrage and disbelief that the community portrayed in Jackson's story could exist; several readers demanded to know where in America this evil town could be found and why nothing had been done to stop the residents of this terrible place. Although the story was clearly presented as a work of fiction, readers around the country believed that the village (and its inhabitants) portrayed in "The Lottery" were real. Such is the power of narrative. *When you read the story, keep in mind that this is a community following what it feels to be its civic duties. Pay attention to the tone of the piece, and as you read about how the town goes about its civic duty, compare/contrast the story with events or occasions in your own communities.*

Shirley Jackson

The Lottery

The morning of June 27th was clear and sunny, with the fresh warmth of a full-summer day; the flowers were blossoming profusely and the grass was richly green. The people of the village began to gather in the square, between the post office and the bank, around ten o'clock; in some towns there were so many people that the lottery took two days and had to be started on June 26th, but in this village, where there were only about three hundred people, the whole lottery took less than two hours, so it could begin at ten o'clock in the morning and still be through in time to allow the villagers to get home for noon dinner.

The children assembled first, of course. School was recently over for the summer, and the feeling of liberty sat uneasily on most of them; they tended to gather together quietly for a while before they broke into boisterous play, and their talk was still of the classroom and the teacher, of books and reprimands. Bobby Martin had already stuffed his pockets full of stones, and the other boys soon followed his example, selecting the smoothest and roundest stones; Bobby and Harry Jones and Dickie Delacroix—the villagers pronounced this name "Dellacroy"—eventually made a great pile of stones in one corner of the square and guarded it against the raids of the other boys. The girls stood aside, talking among themselves, looking over their shoulders at the boys, and the very small children rolled in the dust or clung to the hands of their older brothers or sisters.

Soon the men began to gather. Surveying their own children, speaking of planting and rain, tractors and taxes. They stood together, away from the pile of stones in the corner, and their jokes were quiet and they smiled rather than laughed. The women, wearing faded house dresses and sweaters, came shortly after their menfolk. They greeted one another and exchanged bits of gossip as they went to join their husbands. Soon the women, standing by their husbands, began to call to their children, and the children came reluctantly, having to be called four or five times. Bobby Martin ducked under his mother's grasping hand and ran, laughing, back to the pile of stones. His father spoke up sharply, and Bobby came quickly and took his place between his father and his oldest brother.

The lottery was conducted—as were the square dances, the teen club, the Halloween program—by Mr. Summers, who had time and energy to devote to civic activities. He was a round-faced, jovial man and he ran the coal business, and people were sorry for him, because he had no children and his wife was a scold. When he arrived in the square, carrying the black wooden box, there was a murmur of conversation among the villagers, and he waved and called. "Little late today, folks." The postmaster, Mr. Graves, followed him, carrying a three-legged stool, and the stool was put in the center of the square and Mr. Summers set the black box down on it. The villagers kept their distance, leaving a space between themselves and the stool, and when Mr. Summers said, "Some of you fellows want to give me a hand?" there was a hesitation before two men, Mr. Martin and his oldest son, Baxter, came forward to hold the box steady on the stool while Mr. Summers stirred up the papers inside it.

5   The original paraphernalia for the lottery had been lost long ago, and the black box now resting on the stool had been put into use even before Old Man Warner, the oldest

man in town, was born. Mr. Summers spoke frequently to the villagers about making a new box, but no one liked to upset even as much tradition as was represented by the black box. There was a story that the present box had been made with some pieces of the box that had preceded it, the one that had been constructed when the first people settled down to make a village here. Every year, after the lottery, Mr. Summers began talking again about a new box, but every year the subject was allowed to fade off without anything's being done. The black box grew shabbier each year; by now it was no longer completely black but splintered badly along one side to show the original wood color, and in some places faded or stained.

Mr. Martin and his oldest son, Baxter, held the black box securely on the stool until Mr. Summers had stirred the papers thoroughly with his hand. Because so much of the ritual had been forgotten or discarded, Mr. Summers had been successful in having slips of paper substituted for the chips of wood that had been used for generations. Chips of wood, Mr. Summers had argued, had been all very well when the village was tiny, but now that the population was more than three hundred and likely to keep on growing, it was necessary to use something that would fit more easily into the black box. The night before the lottery, Mr. Summers and Mr. Graves made up the slips of paper and put them in the box, and it was then taken to the safe of Mr. Summers' coal company and locked up until Mr. Summers was ready to take it to the square next morning. The rest of the year, the box was put way, sometimes one place, sometimes another; it had spent one year in Mr. Graves's barn and another year underfoot in the post office, and sometimes it was set on a shelf in the Martin grocery and left there.

There was a great deal of fussing to be done before Mr. Summers declared the lottery open. There were the lists to make up—of heads of families, heads of households in each family, members of each household in each family. There was the proper swearing-in of Mr. Summers by the postmaster, as the official of the lottery; at one time, some people remembered, there had been a recital of some sort, performed by the official of the lottery, a perfunctory, tuneless chant that had been rattled off duly each year; some people believed that the official of the lottery used to stand just so when he said or sang it, others believed that he was supposed to walk among the people, but years and years ago this part of the ritual had been allowed to lapse. There had been, also, a ritual salute, which the official of the lottery had had to use in addressing each person who came up to draw from the box, but this also had changed with time, until now it was felt necessary only for the official to speak to each person approaching. Mr. Summers was very good at all this; in his clean white shirt and blue jeans, with one hand resting carelessly on the black box, he seemed very proper and important as he talked interminably to Mr. Graves and the Martins.

Just as Mr. Summers finally left off talking and turned to the assembled villagers, Mrs. Hutchinson came hurriedly along the path to the square, her sweater thrown over her shoulders, and slid into place in the back of the crowd. "Clean forgot what day it was," she said to Mrs. Delacroix, who stood next to her, and they both laughed softly. "Thought my old man was out back stacking wood," Mrs. Hutchinson went on, "and then I looked out the window and the kids was gone, and then I remembered it was the twenty-seventh and came a-running." She dried her hands on her apron, and Mrs. Delacroix said, "You're in time, though. They're still talking away up there."

Mrs. Hutchinson craned her neck to see through the crowd and found her husband and children standing near the front. She tapped Mrs. Delacroix on the arm as a farewell and began to make her way through the crowd. The people separated good-humoredly to let her through: two or three people said, in voices just loud enough to be heard across the crowd, "Here comes your, Missus, Hutchinson," and "Bill, she made it after all." Mrs. Hutchinson reached her husband, and Mr. Summers, who had been waiting, said cheerfully, "Thought we were going to have to get on without you, Tessie." Mrs. Hutchinson said grinning, "Wouldn't have me leave m'dishes in the sink, now, would you, Joe?," and soft laughter ran through the crowd as the people stirred back into position after Mrs. Hutchinson's arrival.

10   "Well, now," Mr. Summers said soberly, "guess we better get started, get this over with, so's we can go back to work. Anybody ain't here?"

"Dunbar" several people said. "Dunbar, Dunbar."

Mr. Summers consulted his list. "Clyde Dunbar," he said. "That's right. He's broke his leg, hasn't he? Who's drawing for him?"

"Me. I guess," a woman said, and Mr. Summers turned to look at her. "Wife draws for her husband," Mr. Summers said. "Don't you have a grown boy to do it for you, Janey?" Although Mr. Summers and everyone else in the village knew the answer perfectly well, it was the business of the official of the lottery to ask such questions formally. Mr. Summers waited with an expression of polite interest while Mrs. Dunbar answered.

"Horace's not but sixteen yet," Mrs. Dunbar said regretfully. "Guess I gotta fill in for the old man this year."

15   "Right." Mr. Summers said. He made a note on the list he was holding. Then he asked, "Watson boy drawing this year?"

A tall boy in the crowd raised his hand. "Here," he said. "I m drawing for my mother and me." He blinked his eyes nervously and ducked his head as several voices in the crowd said things like "Good fellow, Jack," and "Glad to see your mother's got a man to do it."

"Well," Mr. Summers said, "guess that's everyone. Old Man Warner make it?" "Here," a voice said, and Mr. Summers nodded.

A sudden hush fell on the crowd as Mr. Summers cleared his throat and looked at the list. "All ready?" he called. "Now, I'll read the names—heads of families first—and the men come up and take a paper out of the box. Keep the paper folded in your hand without looking at it until everyone has had a turn. Everything clear?"

The people had done it so many times that they only half listened to the directions; most of them were quiet, wetting their lips, not looking around. Then Mr. Summers raised one hand high and said, "Adams." A man disengaged himself from the crowd and came forward. "Hi, Steve," Mr. Summers said, and Mr. Adams said, "Hi, Joe." They grinned at one another humorlessly and nervously. Then Mr. Adams reached into the black box and took out a folded paper. He held it firmly by one corner as he turned and went hastily back to his place in the crowd, where he stood a little apart from his family, not looking down at his hand.

20   "Allen" Mr. Summers said. "Anderson . . . Bentham."

"Seems like there's no time at all between lotteries any more" Mrs. Delacroix said to Mrs. Graves in the back row. "Seems like we got through with the last one only last week."

"Time sure goes fast," Mrs. Graves said.

"Clark . . . Delacroix."

"There goes my old man," Mrs. Delacroix said. She held her breath while her husband went forward.

25   "Dunbar," Mr. Summers said, and Mrs. Dunbar went steadily to the box while one of the women said, "Go on, Janey," and another said, "There she goes."

"We're next," Mrs. Graves said. She watched while Mr. Graves came around from the side of the box, greeted Mr. Summers gravely and selected a slip of paper from the box. By now, all through the crowd there were men holding the small folded papers in their large hands, turning them over and over nervously. Mrs. Dunbar and her two sons stood together, Mrs. Dunbar holding the slip of paper.

"Harburt . . . Hutchinson."

"Get up there, Bill," Mrs. Hutchinson said, and the people near her laughed.

"Jones."

"They do say," Mr. Adams said to Old Man Warner, who stood next to him, "that over in the north village they're talking of giving up the lottery." 30

Old Man Warner snorted. "Pack of crazy fools," he said. "Listening to the young folks, nothing's good enough for *them*. Next thing you know, they'll be wanting to go back to living in caves, nobody work any more, live *that* way for a while. Used to be a saying about 'Lottery in June, corn be heavy soon.' First thing you know, we'd all be eating stewed chickweed and acorns. There's *always* been a lottery," he added petulantly. "Bad enough to see young Joe Summers up there joking with everybody."

"Some places have already quit lotteries," Mrs. Adams said.

"Nothing but trouble in *that*," Old Man Warner said stoutly. "Pack of young fools."

"Martin." And Bobby Martin watched his father go forward. "Overdyke . . . Percy."

"I wish they'd hurry," Mrs. Dunbar said to her older son. "I wish they'd hurry." 35

"They're almost through," her son said.

"You get ready to run tell Dad," Mrs. Dunbar said.

Mr. Summers called his own name and then stepped forward precisely and selected a slip from the box. Then he called, "Warner."

"Seventy-seventh year I been in the lottery," Old Man Warner said as he went through the crowd. "Seventy-seventh time."

"Watson." The tall boy came awkwardly through the crowd. Someone said, "Don't be nervous, Jack," and Mr. Summers said, "Take your time, son." 40

"Zanini."

After that, there was a long pause, a breathless pause, until Mr. Summers, holding his slip of paper in the air, said, "All right, fellows." For a minute, no one moved, and then all the slips of paper were opened. Suddenly, all the women began to speak at once, saying, "Who is it?," "Who's got it?," "Is it the Dunbars?," "Is it the Watsons?" Then the voices began to say, "It's Hutchinson. It's Bill," "Bill Hutchinson's got it."

"Go tell your father," Mrs. Dunbar said to her older son.

People began to look around to see the Hutchinsons. Bill Hutchinson was standing quiet, staring down at the paper in his hand. Suddenly, Tessie Hutchinson shouted to Mr. Summers, "You didn't give him time enough to take any paper he wanted. I saw you. It wasn't fair!" "Be a good sport, Tessie," Mrs. Delacroix called, and Mrs. Graves said, "All of us took the same chance."

"Shut up, Tessie," Bill Hutchinson said. 45

"Well, everyone," Mr. Summers said, "that was done pretty fast, and now we've got to be hurrying a little more to get done in time." He consulted his next list. "Bill," he said, "you draw for the Hutchinson family. You got any other households in the Hutchinsons?"

"There's Don and Eva," Mrs. Hutchinson yelled. "Make them take their chance!"

"Daughters draw with their husbands' families, Tessie," Mr. Summers said gently. "You know that as well as anyone else."

"It wasn't *fair*," Tessie said.

50

"I guess not, Joe." Bill Hutchinson said regretfully. "My daughter draws with her husband's family, that's only fair. And I've got no other family except the kids." "Then, as far as drawing for families is concerned, it's you," Mr. Summers said in explanation, "and as far as drawing for households is concerned, that's you, too. Right?"

"Right," Bill Hutchinson said.

"How many kids, Bill?" Mr. Summers asked formally.

"Three," Bill Hutchinson said. "There's Bill, Jr., and Nancy, and little Dave. And Tessie and me."

"All right, then," Mr. Summers said. "Harry, you got their tickets back?" Mr. Graves nodded and held up the slips of paper. "Put them in the box, then," Mr. Summers directed. "Take Bill's and put it in."

55

"I think we ought to start over," Mrs. Hutchinson said, as quietly as she could. "I tell you it wasn't *fair*. You didn't give him time enough to choose. *Every*body saw that."

Mr. Graves had selected the five slips and put them in the box, and he dropped all the papers but those onto the ground, where the breeze caught them and lifted them off.

"Listen, everybody," Mrs. Hutchinson was saying to the people around her.

"Ready, Bill?" Mr. Summers asked, and Bill Hutchinson, with one quick glance around at his wife and children, nodded.

"Remember," Mr. Summers said, "take the slips and keep them folded until each person has taken one. Harry, you help little Dave." Mr. Graves took the hand of the little boy, who came willingly with him up to the box. "Take a paper out of the box, Davy," Mr. Summers said. Davy put his hand into the box and laughed. "Take just one paper," Mr. Summers said. "Harry, you hold it for him." Mr. Graves took the child's hand and removed the folded paper from the tight fist and held it while little Dave stood next to him and looked up at him wonderingly.

60

"Nancy next," Mr. Summers said. Nancy was twelve, and her school friends breathed heavily as she went forward, switching her skirt, and took a slip daintily from the box. "Bill, Jr.," Mr. Summers said, and Billy, his face red and his feet over-large, nearly knocked the box over as he got a paper out. "Tessie," Mr. Summers said. She hesitated for a minute, looking around defiantly, and then set her lips and went up to the box. She snatched a paper out and held it behind her.

"Bill," Mr. Summers said, and Bill Hutchinson reached into the box and felt around, bringing his hand out at last with the slip of paper in it.

The crowd was quiet. A girl whispered, "I hope it's not Nancy," and the sound of the whisper reached the edges of the crowd.

"It's not the way it used to be," Old Man Warner said clearly. "People ain't the way they used to be."

"All right," Mr. Summers said. "Open the papers. Harry, you open little Dave's."

65

Mr. Graves opened the slip of paper and there was a general sigh through the crowd as he held it up and everyone could see that it was blank. Nancy and Bill, Jr., opened theirs at the same time, and both beamed and laughed, turning around to the crowd and holding their slips of paper above their heads.

"Tessie," Mr. Summers said. There was a pause, and then Mr. Summers looked at Bill Hutchinson, and Bill unfolded his paper and showed it. It was blank.

"It's Tessie," Mr. Summers said, and his voice was hushed. "Show us her paper, Bill."

Bill Hutchinson went over to his wife and forced the slip of paper out of her hand. It had a black spot on it, the black spot Mr. Summers had made the night before with the heavy pencil in the coal company office. Bill Hutchinson held it up, and there was a stir in the crowd.

"All right, folks," Mr. Summers said. "Let's finish quickly."

Although the villagers had forgotten the ritual and lost the original black box, they still   70
remembered to use stones. The pile of stones the boys had made earlier was ready; there were stones on the ground with the blowing scraps of paper that had come out of the box. Mrs. Delacroix selected a stone so large she had to pick it up with both hands and turned to Mrs. Dunbar. "Come on," she said. "Hurry up."

Mrs. Dunbar had small stones in both hands, and she said, gasping for breath, "I can't run at all. You'll have to go ahead and I'll catch up with you."

The children had stones already. And someone gave little Davy Hutchinson a few pebbles.

Tessie Hutchinson was in the center of a cleared space by now, and she held her hands out desperately as the villagers moved in on her. "It isn't fair," she said. A stone hit her on the side of the head.

Old Man Warner was saying, "Come on, come on, everyone." Steve Adams was in the front of the crowd of villagers, with Mrs. Graves beside him.

"It isn't fair, it isn't right," Mrs. Hutchinson screamed, and then they were upon her.   75

Consider the festive community atmosphere of the stoning, like a holiday or a barn raising, and consider what else we might call the actions of the village. Was this like an election? Or more like being drafted to serve your country? Is it like a public execution? Is it vigilante justice? Or is it more like a jury of Tessie's peers? Are the townspeople murderers, or more like volunteer firefighters who come together to take care of a dangerous task before returning to their private lives? What's important to this community? Are those the same things that are important where you grew up? Compare/contrast the value system of your hometown and this village. You might be surprised how much they have in common, except (obviously) for stoning Tessie. All communities have rules, traditions, and customs that their members must follow.

Write an essay about the values of your community. Do you agree with those values or not? Has there ever been a time where you stood up against your community?

When considering the nature of a community, it can be interesting to consider what sorts of freedoms a community considers essential. In Citizenship 101, you will find the Declaration of Independence and the Declaration of Sentiments—both documents define important freedoms. After reading both declarations, write your own "Declaration" that outlines the sorts of rights and freedoms you think are absolutely essential to the survival and prosperity of your community.

Determining Authority through Genre

Often we can find similar ideas in very different genres. We may also see the same information in two differing genres but give one source more credence than the other, even though they both raise the same questions. In the next reading, an encyclopedia entry, you will be introduced to Stanley Milgram, a famous psychologist who studied the effects of conformity on average people.

As you read, think about what connections you might make between this entry and the short story "The Lottery." Is Milgram studying the same thing that Jackson is writing about? Which genre, short story or encyclopedia entry, do you think has more authority in a discussion of human behavior?

Encarta Encyclopedia 2004

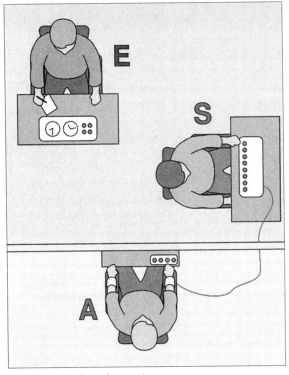

Diagram of Milgram's experiment.

During the 1960s, American psychologist Stanley Milgram studied a form of social influence stronger than conformity: obedience to authority. In a famous series of experiments that attracted controversy about human research ethics, Milgram put each of 1,000 subjects into a situation in which they were ordered by an experimenter to administer painful electric shocks to a confederate (who did not actually receive any shocks). The subjects in these studies were led to believe that they were acting as "teachers" in a study of the effects of punishment on learning. Each time the "learner" made a mistake on a memory test, the subject was supposed to deliver a shock. The intensity of the shocks was to increase, beginning at 15 volts and continuing in 15-volt increments to 450 volts. In most situations, the subjects could not actually see the learner, but they could hear an audiotaped response that sounded increasingly serious with each successive shock. The learner's protests would begin with grunts of pain, progress to shouting and sometimes even complaints of heart trouble, and eventually turn to agonized screams of "Let me out of here!" After the teacher passed the 330-volt level, the learner would fall silent and give no further responses. Yet at each step, an experimenter ordered the subject to raise the level of shock to the learner.

Many of the subjects in the experiment felt extreme anguish over the pain they thought they were inflicting. They sweated, trembled, bit their lips, or broke into fits of nervous laughter. Despite their distress, an astonishing 65 percent of subjects in Milgram's initial study delivered the final punishment of 450 volts. Other social psychologists conducting similar experiments later observed comparable levels of obedience among men and women all over the world. Apparently, many otherwise decent people will cause intense suffering to others rather than disobey authority.

Milgram designed this experiment in order to understand the obedience of Nazi soldiers and officials in killing millions of Jews and others during World War II. When interviewed after the experiment, many of Milgram's subjects said that they had obeyed largely because they thought the experimenter would bear responsibility for any harm to the learner. Similarly, Nazi death camp administrator Adolf Eichmann, when tried for murdering thousands of innocent people, attributed his behavior to the fact that he was merely following the orders of his superiors.

People were surprised at Shirley Jackson's story. Were you surprised at how people acted in Milgram's experiments? Obedience plays a role in both pieces; which do you think does a better job explaining obedience? Which genre would you prefer to read? Is it possible to stand up to a community? Under what circumstances have you stood up against a majority value or decision in your own community? How did it feel? What happened?

Not all group dynamics lead to electric shock or stoning. Many pressures and issues are present in almost every group, and it is usually easier to "go with the flow" than to differentiate one's self. This is quite common when groups are asked to solve a problem or come up with a solution or course of action. It would seem that if several individuals came together to solve something, the group would move logically toward the best course of action, benefiting from the talents and experiences of each group member. But it's not quite that simple to come to the right decision in a group. Individuals acting in a group often fall victim to something called *groupthink*. Groupthink is a term that describes the all-too-common phenomenon where, in search of a decision or solution, members of a group:

1. seek group concurrence excessively,
2. convince themselves that the group's position must be correct to the exclusion of all other positions,
3. suppress dissent that would threaten the harmony of the group or undermine adherence to either of the first two points.

Groupthink can often lead groups to quickly embrace poor decisions and prevent them from exploring alternatives. People from all walks of life can fall victim to this limiting and unsuccessful group dynamic. It's the power of the group. It's the nature of human society.

Consider the information you have about Jackson's story, Milgram's research, and the phenomenon of groupthink, and then write an essay comparing and contrasting the three. Of these three human behaviors, which seems the most problematic to you? Which is the most dangerous to society? Does the nature of our source material change our ideas about a topic?

*Harper Lee: (1926–) Author of the Pulitzer Prize–winning novel (1960) *To Kill a Mockingbird,* her only book.

*lynch: To hang or otherwise execute as punishment a presumed criminal for cultural (racial) offense, carried out by mobs, without any due process of law. Lynchings were most common in the South, and after the Civil War, the victims were almost exclusively African Americans. Lynchings were a tool to support white supremacy and subvert civil rights.

*court-appointed attorney: Every defendant has the right to legal counsel. Court-appointed attorneys are hired by the courts to defend those without means to hire a lawyer.

Using Fiction to Understand Communities

Fiction is often an excellent mirror of society, and through narrative we are often able to find the terms of our own lives and communities. Both short stories and novels can offer us a glimpse inside our own worlds, worlds we have inhabited so long we almost fail to notice the terms of our existence. In this excerpt from **Harper Lee's*** *To Kill a Mockingbird,* Tom Robinson (a black man falsely accused of raping a white woman) has been moved back into the town jail before his trial, and some of the white citizens of Maycomb feel justice would be best served if they dragged Tom out of jail and **lynched*** him in the middle of the night. Atticus Finch, his **court-appointed attorney,*** must act to protect not only Tom's right to a trial by a jury of his peers but also Tom's life. Into this dangerously charged situation jump three children: Jem, Dill, and Scout (Jean Louise), our narrator. *Consider as you read the excerpt how ideas of community and justice are working with and against each other in this story.*

From *To Kill a Mockingbird*

Harper Lee

Atticus Finch (played by Gregory Peck) *faces the mob of vigilantes outside the jail while the children look on.*

Next day was Sunday. In the interval between Sunday School and Church when the congregation stretched its legs, I saw Atticus standing in the yard with another knot of men. Mr. Heck Tate was present, and I wondered if he had seen the light. He never went to church. Even Mr. Underwood was there. Mr. Underwood had no use for any organization but *The Maycomb Tribune,* of which he was the sole owner, editor, and printer. His days were spent at his linotype, where he refreshed himself occasionally from an ever-present gallon jug of cherry wine. He rarely gathered news; people brought it to him. It was said that he made up every edition of *The Maycomb Tribune* out of his own head and wrote it down on the linotype. This was believable. Something must have been up to haul Mr. Underwood out.

I caught Atticus coming in the door, and he said that they'd moved Tom Robinson to the Maycomb jail. He also said, more to himself than to me, that if they'd kept him there in the first place there wouldn't have been any fuss. I watched him take his seat on the third row from the front, and I heard him rumble, "Nearer my God to thee," some notes behind the rest of us. He never sat with Aunty, Jem and me. He liked to be by himself in church.

The fake peace that prevailed on Sundays was made more irritating by Aunt Alexandra's presence. Atticus would flee to his office directly after dinner, where if we sometimes looked in on him, we would find him sitting back in his swivel chair reading. Aunt Alexandra composed herself for a two-hour nap and dared us to make any noise in the yard, the neighborhood was resting. Jem in his old age had taken to his room with a stack of football magazines. So Dill and I spent our Sundays creeping around in Deer's Pasture.

Shooting on Sundays was prohibited, so Dill and I kicked Jem's football around the pasture for a while, which was no fun. Dill asked if I'd like to have a poke at Boo Radley. I said I didn't think it'd be nice to bother him, and spent the rest of the afternoon filling Dill in on last winter's events. He was considerable impressed.

We parted at suppertime, and after our meal Jem and I were settling down to a routine evening, when Atticus did something that interested us; he came into the living room carrying a long electrical extension cord. There was a light bulb on the end.   5

"I'm going out for a while," he said. "You folks'll be in bed when I come back, so I'll say good night now."

With that, he put his hat on and went out the back door.

"He's takin' the car," said Jem.

Our father had a few peculiarities: one was, he never ate desserts; another was that he liked to walk. As far back as I could remember, there was always a Chevrolet in excellent condition in the carhouse, and Atticus put many miles on it in business trips, but in Maycomb he walked to and from his office four times a day, covering about two miles. He said his only exercise was walking. In Maycomb, if one went for a walk with no definite purpose in mind, it was correct to believe one's mind incapable of definite purpose.

Later on, I bade my aunt and brother good night and was well into a book when I heard Jem rattling around in his room. His go-to-bed noises were so familiar to me that I knocked on his door: "Why ain't you going to bed?"   10

"I'm goin' downtown for a while." He was changing his pants.

"Why? It's almost ten o'clock, Jem."

He knew it, but he was going anyway.

"Then I'm goin' with you. If you say no you're not, I'm goin' anyway, hear?"

Jem saw that he would have to fight me to keep me home, and I suppose he thought   15
a fight would antagonize Aunty, so he gave in with little grace.

I dressed quickly. We waited until Aunty's light went out, and we walked quietly down the back steps. There was no moon tonight.

"Dill'll wanta come," I whispered.

"So he will," Jem said gloomily.

We leaped over the driveway wall, cut through Miss Rachel's side yard and went to Dill's window. Jem whistled bob-white. Dill's face appeared at the screen, disappeared, and five minutes later he unhooked the screen and crawled out. An old campaigner, he did not speak until we were on the sidewalk. "What's up?"

20   "Jem's got the look-arounds," an affliction Calpurnia said all boys caught at his age.

"I've just got this feeling," Jem said, "just this feeling."

We went by Mrs. Dubose's house, standing empty and shuttered, her camellias grown up in weeds and Johnson grass. There were eight more houses to the post office corner.

The south side of the square was deserted. Giant monkey-puzzle bushes bristled on each corner, and between them an iron hitching rail glistened under the street lights. A light shone in the country toilet, otherwise that side of the courthouse was dark. A larger square of stores surrounded the courthouse square; dim lights burned from deep within them.

Atticus's office was in the courthouse when he began his law practice, but after several years of it he moved to quieter quarters in the Maycomb Bank building. When we rounded the corner of the square, we saw the car parked in front of the bank. "He's in there," said Jem.

25   But he wasn't. His office was reached by a long hallway. Looking down the hall, we should have seen *Atticus Finch, Attorney-at-Law* in small sober letters against the light from behind the door. It was dark.

Jem peered in the bank door to make sure. He turned the knob. The door was locked. "Let's go up the street. Maybe he's visiting Mr. Underwood."

Mr. Underwood not only ran *The Maycomb Tribune,* he lived in it. That is, above it. He covered the courthouse and jailhouse news simply by looking out his upstairs window. The office building was on the northwest corner of the square, and to reach it we had to pass the jail.

The Maycomb jail was the most venerable and hideous of the county's buildings. Atticus said it was like something Cousin Joshua St. Clair might have designed. It was certainly someone's dream. Starkly out of place in a town of square-faced stores and steep-roofed houses, the Maycomb jail was a miniature Gothic joke one cell wide and two cells high, complete with tiny battlements and flying buttresses. Its fantasy was heightened by its red brick façade and the thick steel bars at its ecclesiastical windows. It stood on no lonely hill, but was wedged between Tyndal's Hardware Store and *The Maycomb Tribune* office. The jail was Maycomb's only conversation piece: its detractors said it looked like a Victorian privy; its supporters said it gave the town a good solid respectable look, and no stranger would ever suspect that it was full of niggers.

As we walked up the sidewalk, we saw a solitary light burning in the distance. "That's funny," said Jem, "jail doesn't have an outside light."

30   "Looks like it's over the door," said Dill.

A long extension cord ran between the bars of a second floor window and down the side of the building. In the light from its bare bulb, Atticus was sitting propped against the front door. He was sitting in one of his office chairs, and he was reading, oblivious of the nightbugs dancing over his head.

I made to run but Jem caught me. "Don't go to him," he said, "he might not like it. He's all right, let's go home. I just wanted to see where he was."

We were taking a short cut across the square when four dusty cars came in from the Meridian highway, moving slowly in a line. They went around the square, passed the bank building, and stopped in front of the jail.

Nobody got out. We saw Atticus look up from his newspaper. He closed it, folded it deliberately, dropped it in his lap, and pushed his hat to the back of his head. He seemed to be expecting them.

"Come on," whispered Jem. We streaked across the square, across the street, until   35
we were in the shelter of the Jitney Jungle door. Jem peeked up the sidewalk. "We can get closer," he said. We ran to Tyndal's Hardware door—near enough, at the same time discreet.

In ones and twos, men got out of the cars. Shadows became substance as light revealed solid shapes moving toward the jail door. Atticus remained where he was. The men hid him from view.

"He in there, Mr. Finch?" a man said.

"He is," we heard Atticus answer, "and he's asleep. Don't wake him."

In obedience to my father, there followed what I later realized was a sickeningly comic aspect of an unfunny situation: the men talked in near-whispers.

"You know what we want," another man said. 'Get aside from the door, Mr. Finch."   40

"You can turn around and go home again, Walter," Atticus said pleasantly. "Heck Tate's around here somewhere."

"The hell he is," said another man. "Heck's bunch's so deep in the woods they won't get out till mornin'."

"Indeed? Why so?"

"Called 'em off on a snipe hunt" was the succinct answer. "Didn't you think a' that, Mr. Finch?"

"Thought about it, but didn't believe it. Well then," my father's voice was still the same,   45
"that changes things, doesn't it?"

"It do," another deep voice said. Its owner was a shadow.

"Do you really think so?"

This was the second time I heard Atticus ask that question in two days, and it meant somebody's man would get jumped. This was too good to miss. I broke away from Jem and ran as fast as I could to Atticus.

Jem shrieked and tried to catch me, but I had a lead on him and Dill. I pushed my way through the dark smelly bodies and burst into the circle of light.

"Hey, Atticus!"   50

I thought he would have a fine surprise, but his face killed my joy. A flash of plain fear was going out of his eyes, but returned when Dill and Jem wriggled into the light.

There was a smell of stale whiskey and pigpen about, and when I glanced around I discovered that these men were strangers. They were not the people I saw last night. Hot embarrassment shot through me: I had leaped triumphantly into a ring of people I had never seen before.

Atticus got up from his chair, but he was moving slowly, like an old man. He put the newspaper down very carefully, adjusting its creases with lingering fingers. They were trembling a little.

"Go home, Jem," he said. "Take Scout and Dill home."

55   We were accustomed to prompt, if not always cheerful acquiescence to Atticus's instructions, but from the way he stood Jem was not thinking of budging.

"Go home, I said."

Jem shook his head. As Atticus's fists went to his hips, so did Jem's, and as they faced each other I could see the resemblance between them: Jem's soft brown hair and eyes, his oval face and snug-fitting ears were our mother's, contrasting oddly with Atticus's graying black hair and square-cut features, but they were somehow alike. Mutual defiance made them alike.

"Son, I said go home."

Jem shook his head.

60   "I'll send him home," a burly man said, and grabbed Jem roughly by the collar. He yanked Jem nearly off his feet.

"Don't you touch him!" I kicked the man swiftly. Bare-footed, I was surprised to see him fall back in real pain. I intended to kick his shin, but aimed too high.

"That'll do, Scout." Atticus put his hand on my shoulder. "Don't kick folks. No—" he said, as I was pleading justification.

"Ain't nobody gonna do Jem that way," I said.

"All right, Mr. Finch, get 'em outa here," someone growled. "You got fifteen seconds to get 'em outa here."

65   In the midst of this strange assembly, Atticus stood trying to make Jem mind him. "I ain't going," was his steady answer, to Atticus's threats, requests, and finally, "Please Jem, take them home."

I was getting a bit tired of that, but felt Jem had his own reasons for doing as he did, in view of his prospects once Atticus did get him home. I looked around the crowd. It was a summer's night but the men were dressed, most of them, in overalls and denim shirts buttoned up to their collars. I thought they must be cold-natured, as their sleeves were unrolled and buttoned at the cuffs. Some wore hats pulled firmly down over their ears. They were sullen-looking, sleepy-eyed men who seemed unused to late hours. I sought once more for a familiar face, and at the center of the semi-circle I found one.

"Hey, Mr. Cunningham."

The man did not hear me, it seemed.

"Hey, Mr. Cunningham. How's your entailment gettin' along?"

70   Mr. Walter Cunningham's legal affairs were well known to me; Atticus had once described them at length. The big man blinked and hooked his thumbs in his overall straps. He seemed uncomfortable; he cleared his throat and looked away. My friendly overture had fallen flat.

Mr. Cunningham wore no hat, and the top half of his forehead was white in contrast to his sunscorched face, which led me to believe that he wore one most days. He shifted his feet, clad in heavy work shoes.

"Don't you remember me, Mr. Cunningham? I'm Jean Louise Finch. You brought us some hickory nuts one time, remember?" I began to sense the futility one feels when unacknowledged by a chance acquaintance.

"I go to school with Walter," I began again. "He's your boy, ain't he? Ain't he, sir?"

Mr. Cunningham was moved to a faint nod. He did know me after all.

"He's in my grade," I said, "and he does right well. He's a good boy," I added, "a real   75
nice boy. We brought him home for dinner one time. Maybe he told you about me, I beat
him up one time but he was real nice about it. Tell him hey for me, won't you?"

Atticus had said it was the polite thing to talk to people about what they were
interested in, not about what you were interested in. Mr. Cunningham displayed no
interest in his son, so I tackled his entailment once more in a last-ditch effort to make
him feel at home.

"Entailments are bad," I was advising him, when I slowly awoke to the fact that I was
addressing the entire aggregation. The men were all looking at me, some had their mouths
half-open. Atticus had stopped poking at Jem: they were standing together beside Dill.
Their attention amounted to fascination. Atticus's mouth, even, was half-open, an attitude
he had once described as uncouth. Our eyes met and he shut it.

"Well, Atticus, I was just sayin' to Mr. Cunningham that entailments are bad an' all, but
you said not to worry, it takes a long time sometimes . . . that you all'd ride it out together
. . . " I was slowly drying up, wondering what idiocy I had committed. Entailments seemed
all right enough for living room talk.

I began to feel sweat gathering at the edges of my hair; I could stand anything but a
bunch of people looking at me. They were quite still.

"What's the matter?" I asked.   80

Atticus said nothing. I looked around and up at Mr. Cunningham, whose face was equally
impassive. Then he did a peculiar thing. He squatted down and took me by both shoulders.

"I'll tell him you said hey, little lady," he said.

Then he straightened up and waved a big paw. "Let's clear out," he called. "Let's get
going, boys."

As they had come, in ones and twos the men shuffled back to their ramshackle cars.
Doors slammed, engines coughed, and they were gone.

I turned to Atticus, but Atticus had gone to the jail and was leaning against it with his   85
face to the wall. I went to him and pulled his sleeve. "Can we go home now?" He nodded, produced his handkerchief, gave his face a going-over and blew his nose violently.

"Mr. Finch?"

A husky voice came from the darkness above: "They gone?"

Atticus stepped back and looked up. "They've gone," he said. "Get some sleep, Tom.
They won't bother you anymore."

From a different direction, another voice cut crisply through the night: "You're damn
tootin' they won't. Had you covered all the time, Atticus."

Mr. Underwood and his double-barreled shotgun were leaning out of his window   90
above *The Maycomb Tribune* office.

It was long past my bedtime and I was growing quite tired; it seemed that Atticus
and Mr. Underwood would talk for the rest of the night, Mr. Underwood out the window
and Atticus up at him. Finally Atticus returned, switched off the light above the jail door, and
picked up his chair.

"Can I carry it for you, Mr. Finch?" asked Dill. He had not said a word the whole time.

"Why, thank you, son."

Walking toward the office, Dill and I fell into step behind Atticus and Jem. Dill was
encumbered by the chair, and his pace was slower. Atticus and Jem were well ahead of
us, and I assumed that Atticus was giving him hell for not going home, but I was wrong.

As they passed under a streetlight, Atticus reached out and massaged Jem's hair, his one gesture of affection.

In the excerpt, there are two different groups of citizens, each group acting to support its own ideas about justice. It's easy to see where they disagree, but can you find any values the two hold in common? Compare/contrast the goals of these two groups. Although she doesn't really understand how or why, Scout manages to defuse a very dangerous situation. How do you think that happened? What does this excerpt say, if anything, about community involvement?

Write an essay about the different communities you belong to, and how you are involved in those communities. Consider which is your most important community. Do the various communities conflict with each other?

PART TWO

Communication: Spheres of Communication

Communication can happen between many individuals and groups and in a variety of situations, so the term "communication" is often more general than we would like it to be. But if we wish to begin considering on a more specific level the differing types of communication, we can rely upon a system that organizes communication into three areas called **Spheres of Communication.*** By classifying language as belonging in either the public, the private, or the technical sphere, its intentions and deeper meanings can be considered in a variety of contexts.

> *Spheres of communication: Communication can be categorized by the sphere—the area, conditions, and audience—it occurs within, primarily the public, the private, and the technical spheres.

The **public sphere** of communication is just that: public. It includes such media as speeches, press releases, web logs, media articles and editorials, advertisements, and slogans on T-shirts. If a message is directed at the general public, it's in the public sphere. The content can be specific, but the audience is as wide as possible. Public communication best expresses the things you say to the world, and once made public it usually stays public.

The **private sphere** is much more limited in scope and audience, and it includes such media as personal letters, private thoughts or feelings shared with another select person, and intimate details. Private communication is based on and usually stays within a relationship: within a friendship, a marriage, or a family. It can also take place between lawyer and a client, a doctor and a patient, a member of the clergy and a follower of that faith. If the audience is limited in scope, and the message specifically not meant for a general audience because of issues of intimacy and privacy, it's a private communication.

The **technical sphere** of communication covers all means of technical or specialized conversation. It's how experts in any given field—from astronomy to coal mining to medical research—talk to one another in their shared, specialized language. Technical communication involves complex, specific vocabulary that is shared among those experts and crucial to the exchange of technical information. The audience is limited here, but because of issues of specialization and expertise, the message is not private or intimate.

These spheres can exist in pure form, but they often overlap or combine. Think for instance of the secret recipe for Coca-Cola; it's a secret recipe that would only be shared in the most private situation, but likely expressed in rather technical language that would be clearest to those in the beverage industry. Yet the existence of this "secret recipe" (much like Colonel Sanders's "Eleven Herbs and Spices") is public knowledge. Everyone knows they exist, but if such recipes were ever made public, the companies that keep this information private would be destroyed by copycat competition.

The excerpt from *To Kill a Mockingbird* is also an excellent example of over-lapping communication spheres. If, as was mentioned above, overlapping modes (narrative put together with argument, for instance) create dynamic writing, then overlapping spheres of communication are no less intense. Consider how you might feel if you told your best friend a very personal secret (private sphere) and that friend made that information available on your school website (public sphere)! That overlap would elicit a variety of emotions, not all of them positive. In *To Kill a Mockingbird,* Scout takes a public, impersonal, and dangerous situation—where a group of white men show up to lynch a black man before he can have his day in court—and makes it private and intimate by reminding Mr. Cunningham that his son has played at the Finches' house and eaten at their table. Cunningham is willing to hurt Atticus until Scout reminds Cunningham that he and Atticus are both fathers, and that Atticus has helped the Cunninghams with their legal problems. Scout takes the public and makes it personal—with dramatic emotional results.

In their own twisted and racist way, Mr. Cunningham and his group thought they were doing their civic duty . . . even if they were denying Tom his right to a speedy trial by a jury of his peers. This right to a jury trial is crucial to our system of justice, but it depends on a willing group of citizens to allow those juries to do their jobs. Justice also depends on the willingness of regular citizens to serve on those juries, despite any inconvenience or hardship.

Overlapping the Spheres

In the essay that follows, "A Few Thoughts on Not Doing My Civic Duty," Janet Bland uses **narrative*** and **example*** to explore the problems of finding willing people to serve on these juries. *As you read, consider what the author is trying to do—is she telling a story or trying to make a point?*

> ***narrative:** This mode relies upon the qualities and expectations of story.
>
> ***example:** To give an example is to employ the tools of representation and sample where one thing suggests many.

Janet L. Bland

A Few Thoughts on Not Doing My Civic Duty

A jury listens as evidence is presented.

I recently received a summons to jury duty in the mail. It would be dishonest to suggest that I greeted this opportunity to participate in the American system of justice with anything other than irritation. It was spring break at the university where I teach, but I was busy correcting final papers from winter quarter, writing a presentation for a conference the following week, and preparing for spring quarter teaching. Quite frankly, I didn't have the time. Nevertheless, Monday morning at eight o'clock, I arrived at the Denver County Courthouse, turned in my paperwork in the Jury selection room, and then took a seat among several hundred of my fellow citizens who were also waiting to see if they would be selected to serve on a jury.

Crowded together in what amounted to a holding pen for the disgruntled, everyone around me was exchanging reasons for not serving. The brief wait seemed to increase the anxiety in the room. And then, with little preamble, a video appeared on multiple monitors around the large room; it was comprised mainly of real people telling us that, after they stopped struggling against the idea of serving on a jury, it wasn't so bad after all. Rewarding even. When one interviewee on the video casually mentioned she was a jury member on a murder trial that lasted over nine weeks, an audible shudder ran through the crowd. Collectively we braced ourselves for the worst.

The selection lottery began quickly. In random batches of 25, numbers (not names) were called and people began filing toward the front of the room to stand near the clerks who had come to lead them to the courtrooms. My number was called and very quickly I found myself in the jury box answering questions about myself that would be used by the court, the plaintiff, and the defendant in the civil case before us. The case was a lawsuit brought by the owner of a fire fighting equipment manufacturer against a former employee and another manufacturer. Before the questions to the jury began, the judge estimated the trial would take eight days. The jury pool, for lack of a better term, winced. This is the part that you don't see on television, the part where no one wants to serve on the jury.

Popular courtroom dramas don't include scenes of jury selection; it would be too time-consuming and depressing . . . even for television. I suppose it's much the same in a real criminal trial. Imagine coming into a courtroom as the defendant, ready to fight for your future, and your life depends on a group of irritated people who really don't want to be there. I don't know if the defendants are present during a criminal trial jury selection, but all the parties of this particular lawsuit were sitting right there as person after person in the pool clarified his or her own personal hardship. With millions at stake, it couldn't have made them feel good to listen to us trying to squirm our way out of the finest legal system in the world.

The prospective juror sitting next to me claimed with undue pride that he could nei-   5
ther read nor write; I can only assume he was hoping to be dismissed. He was. Others had pressing health concerns, or were new citizens whose English skills were not up to the technical jargon of the case, or in the instance of one man, worked as a fire fighter and his possible technical knowledge might affect his opinions. An older man sitting next to me started quietly ranting against "the system" when the judge asked him about his situation. One woman was 75 and had already served on four juries and felt she had already done her duty. A college freshman asked to be let off as he too was just beginning his spring break and had hoped for some time off. Another man offered so many intimate details about his distressing medical condition (which made it impossible for him to sit for long periods of time) that other members of the pool rolled their eyes. And in one ironic case, a woman appealed to the judge to release her from the jury because her husband was one of those charged in the Enron case and all of his energy (and hers) was going toward defending himself against numerous charges in his own upcoming trial.

There was something dreary about the whole process; I was at once embarrassed to be part of the avoidance techniques and worried I might be selected to serve. And I couldn't help thinking at the time that I certainly wouldn't want any of those people serving on my jury if I were ever charged with a crime. Serving on a jury of one's peers may well renew faith in the justice system but sitting there through the selection process does entirely the opposite. It was nothing like television.

And perhaps that was the problem. Having watched countless hours of "The Practice" and "Law and Order" and "Judge Judy" and "LA Law," my fellow prospective jurors spoke fluent television lawyer drama-talk. In the course of the Q & A period, several people asked, much to the judge's chagrin, if they might approach the bench. A woman inquired if there would be a fifteen-minute recess where she might speak to the judge, and one befuddled man attempted to object. Except for the elderly veteran of four previous trials, few of my fellow citizens had been in a real courtroom, one that existed outside their television screens. As we all thrashed about in our attempts to find something that would get us out of the courtroom, many employed terminology as if they had regularly spent time in front of a judge. And suddenly it seemed to me that the legal system was something we wanted to watch on television, but not actually be part of in our real lives. We could talk the talk, but none of us wanted to walk the walk.

Democracy can be a tiresome, inconvenient business. Only about half of us who are legally eligible to vote bother to do so, and it seems that we want to serve on a jury even less. But a justice system that guarantees the right to a trial by a jury of one's peers requires that those peers be made to serve as jurors, however unenthusiastically. People who live in non-democratic nations are never called to jury duty; they are instead often subject to verdicts rendered in secret without right of appeal. It seems obvious however, and not a little patronizing, to mention the horrors of totalitarianism when faced with the irritations of democracy, particularly when I didn't serve on the jury myself.

Based on dismissals from the judge and both parties of the lawsuit, 18 of the original 25 member pool were eventually released–those who were highly educated, those with strong opinions about email privacy at work, or who were suing their former employers, or who expressed some interest in conspiracy theories or a strong dislike for the government, or had previous personal experience as a party to a lawsuit. Some had never even made it into the jury box for questioning and had sat silently in the front of the courtroom. All they needed in the end was six jurors and an alternate, so most of the original group might be freed.

10   Having offered clear opinions about lawsuits, and having been involved in one that I spoke of at length, I was the first person the defense excused from the jury box. When they called my name and I exchanged my hot seat in the jury box for a place at the back of the courtroom, I felt a great rush of both relief and guilt—happy that I could go back to my busy life and embarrassed that I had failed to do my civic duty. When so little is asked of us, it seems pathetic to avoid such a small but crucial task. And yet we did. Those who joined me at the back of the courtroom could barely contain their glee. The judge released us and quietly we slipped out of the courtroom while the judge began to address the sitting jury and wheels of justice began once again to slowly turn without us.

> *free rider: Describes the phenomenon within a free society where compliance is preferred or even required but not enforceable. The free rider takes advantage of everyone else's compliance.

This essay is about the public and the private—both the public experience of appearing for jury duty and the private thoughts of one person who wanted to avoid serving. In what other ways do the public and the private seem to overlap in this essay? Democracy has always suffered from the **"free rider"*** problem—where those who do not do their civic duty (vote, pay taxes, serve on juries, buy fishing licenses) take advantage of those who do. A free rider is always part of the burden on the system.

When our author got out of jury duty, was she acting as a free rider? Or was she just lucky? Write an essay in which you take a position on whether or not citizenship has obligations. Are we obligated to participate? Are we required to be good citizens? You might use an example from your own experiences, perhaps a time where you were asked to volunteer for something. How do rights and responsibilities work together in a community?

In the essay above, the author also notes how much technical language the prospective jurors had gleaned from television and were attempting to use in the courtroom as they communicated with the judge. Technical legal language used to be employed primarily by those in the legal system—judges, lawyers, and other court employees, and police or probation officers. Just a generation ago few people knew the technical language of the system, while the rest of the population had little or no access to the terminology. This led to problems because although people accused of crimes had rights, such as the right to an attorney, they were not aware that they should or could ask for one.

Simply put, rights that you don't know about are rights you don't have. That's why we have what are known as Miranda Rights. In *Miranda v. Arizona*, the U.S. Supreme Court ruled that self-incriminating statements cannot be used against a suspect unless that suspect had been informed of the right not to self-incriminate. Today, many people know their Miranda rights: Those who commit crimes or who are accused of crimes hear them when they are arrested, and law-abiding citizens hear them every night on their favorite television shows: *You have the right to remain silent. Anything you say can and will be used against you in a court of law. You have the right to an attorney. If you cannot afford an attorney, one will be provided for you at no cost. Do you understand these rights?* This was once a purely technical communication, but thanks to *Miranda v. Arizona* and several decades of police dramas on TV, this technical language has been brought into the public sphere. The clarification of these rights has even become a new verb: Police "mirandize" a suspect, meaning they read the person his or her rights before proceeding with questioning and arrest.

In the case of *Miranda*, the transformation across the spheres of language of technical communication to public communication has had an invaluable result: The vast majority of Americans, even those who will never be arrested, are aware of their rights during criminal arrest and can recite them from memory. If the government had mailed a letter to every household in America to tell us of these specific rights, few of us would have read it and even fewer would have remembered them. But when presented in the form of compelling narrative—all those thousands of hours of police dramas and crime shows—we can recite our rights as readily as we can the Pledge of Allegiance. And we have seen, through story after story, how those rights work and what those rights really mean. The average person gained, through narrative, some knowledge and comprehension of the once purely technical language.

But in the case of the essay "A Few Thoughts on Not Doing My Civic Duty," the use of technical courtroom language by prospective jurors was not a positive event. Familiar as they were with how it worked on TV, the people described in the essay tried unsuccessfully to use the language of *Perry Mason* in the real world. Although we amateurs might comprehend on the surface what it means when one lawyer objects, the grounds for those objections and the legal precedents involved remain purely technical communication—those are the kinds of details you can't get from a narrative. Narrative, the kind we use in television shows, just isn't real, and so its limits in transmitting technical information are profound. You may remember how at the end of every *Perry Mason* episode the real killer breaks down and confesses on the stand. That rarely happens in real life, in a real courtroom . . . if only because most criminals, thanks to *Miranda v. Arizona*, know their right not to self-incriminate.

Does this mean that we all know our rights and are able to assert them in all circumstances? Of course not. Life is rarely that simple. In our post-9/11 world, the balance between our safety and our civil rights is a complex and precarious process. Americans want terrorists arrested before they can kill any more innocent people. How this is to be accomplished is the question. Some say that if we throw all our civil rights out the window in pursuit of our enemies, we will have lost what makes America great—our freedom. Others counter that there will be nothing left to protect if we don't take strong steps to find those who wish to harm us, even if a few innocent people are inconvenienced along the way. In the next article, "Teaching the Silent Treatment," the conflict between these two positions is considered. *As you read, be aware of how technical language is being used by all parties.*

Making the Technical Public

Amy Herdy

Teaching the Silent Treatment

As activist Mark Cohen pointed to the phrases on the dry-erase board, dozens of men and women of various ages and styles of dress repeated them in a single loud chorus: "I intend to remain silent. I wish to speak to an attorney."

"Those are the magic words," Cohen, a member of the human-rights group the Dandelion Center, told the audience. He said if any of them was detained by the police or federal agents. "Don't forget them."

Cohen's advice was part of a presentation called "Know Your Rights," sponsored by the American Friends Service Committee, or AFSC, and the Dandelion Center. The presentation, given Thursday evening in Denver, was in response to federal agents calling activists and community organizers recently in Denver and across the country.

Denver FBI spokeswoman Monique Kelso said the visits and phone calls by members of the Joint Terrorism Task Force were designed to gather intelligence on any plans for violence at the political conventions or the presidential inauguration. And, she said, they would continue.

5   "We have an obligation to talk to people in this circumstance," Kelso said.

Agents were questioning those "expected to have specific details of people in groups planning criminal acts," Kelso said.

Yet many believe the encounters have nothing to do with pre-emptive police work and everything to do with intimidating those who have a history of protest in order to prevent activities that are protected under the First Amendment.

"The kinds of questions asked of these activists . . . not the kind of questions being asked in good faith to elicit information on criminal activity," said Mark Silverstein, legal director of the American Civil Liberties Union Foundation of Colorado.

Across the country, the questions are more or less the same, Silverstein said: "Are you planning to commit any crimes? Do you know anyone who plans to commit any crimes? Do you know that withholding such knowledge from us is a crime?"

10   Sarah Bardwell, a 21-year-old intern for the AFSC in Denver who has protested against the war in Iraq, said the agents who appeared at her house and questioned her and four roommates did not seem to expect answers.

"They didn't wait, after asking one question, for any of us to reply," said Bardwell, who described the encounter as "snotty chitchat."

"We said, 'You should leave our porch,' and they said, 'We'll leave your porch when we want to,'" recalled Bardwell, who said she does not have a history of violence and believes the purpose of the visit was to frighten her and the others.

Kelso, who recognized the three questions but would not confirm them as protocol, said the interviews were not "scare tactics" and no one was under obligation to cooperate.

"They can talk, or if they don't feel confident talking, they can have their attorney present, or they can just ask us to go away," said Kelso (the third option was echoed repeatedly at the training at the AFSC office). Kelso also added that the FBI would not hold a grudge against someone for refusing to answer questions.

15   "We wouldn't look negatively on that at all," she said.

Bardwell said that was not the reaction of the agents she met. "When we wouldn't answer their questions, they said they would make more intrusive efforts to do their job," she said.

The encounter left her angry, confused and upset, Bardwell said, but more determined than ever to be active in her community.

"I feel even more inspired," she said.

Ms. Kelso (the FBI spokesperson) and Ms. Bardwell (the activist who was questioned) have two very different views of how asserting one's rights would go over with FBI agents. Review the article and make a few notes for yourself on what each woman thinks about this assertion of rights and how the authorities might respond to it. As good citizens, which is more important, for us to cooperate or to know our right not to? Does it make any difference that the agents are looking for terrorists? What do you think about this situation, and how would you answer if tomorrow these agents came to your door?

Write an essay about a time where you asserted your rights, or the rights of another. Consider how difficult that was, and how the people around you responded.

In the next essay **John Edwards,*** U.S. senator and the 2004 Democratic candidate for vice president, writes about the jury system from his own point of view—that of a former trial lawyer. *As you read his essay, consider the role Edwards played in the courtroom.*

> ***John Edwards:** (1953–) A State senator from North Carolina and former personal injury lawyer, Edwards was the Democratic vice presidential candidate in 2004.

John Edwards

Juries: "Democracy in Action"

I'll never forget the first time I met Jennifer Campbell. A charming, determined 5-year-old, she couldn't walk or feed herself, and still needed a playpen. Because of a doctor's terrible mistake, she was born with permanent brain damage. I met her loving, determined parents, who were hoping for a way to help pay for her costly care, and to make sure other families wouldn't suffer as they had. Back then, in 1985, I was a young North Carolina lawyer starting to build a name as someone willing to take cases others rejected as long shots. This case was exactly that. The insurance companies were skilled at making cases like this "go away." The Campbells had no money, and the trial would be long, complicated and expensive. If we lost, neither the Campbells nor I would receive a dime.

But there was no question that these were risks worth taking for Jennifer. The other side was counting on the Campbells to walk away intimidated, but they were wrong. A jury eventually agreed, and awarded the Campbells enough to make sure Jennifer's parents would never have to worry about her care.

These days it's fashionable for people to complain that the courts are clogged with frivolous lawsuits, and to dismiss the legal profession as a bastion of greed. In a nation as large as ours, it isn't difficult to find an outrageous case here and there. They draw publicity, and it's easy to come away with the impression that the court system is hopelessly broken.

I can tell you from long experience that it is not. Before I was elected to the United States Senate, I spent nearly two decades as a lawyer standing up for people who needed a voice. During that time, I worked on hundreds of cases, big and small. I'm proud of the work I did, and the people I represented. There was nothing frivolous about the families who came to me for help. Like the Campbells, many were in very difficult places in their lives. Often, they found themselves up against powerful opposition—insurance companies, large corporations—who had armies of lawyers to represent them. Giving them a chance for justice was very important to me. I was more than just their lawyer. I cared about them. Their cause was my cause.

5   And that's what good lawyers—I would say most lawyers—do for their clients all the time. I am a strong believer in the courts as a place for ordinary people to be heard, often when other institutions have failed them. People have criticized the jury system, saying juries can't be trusted to consider the facts. I couldn't disagree more. Juries are a vital example of democracy in action. The people who sit on juries are the same people who decide who the president should be. People who are entrusted to choose the leader of the free world are capable of weighing evidence in a courtroom—and they do, every day across America. I found again and again and again that they take their service seriously, and follow the law even when the law is at odds with what they personally believe.

That's not to say the system is perfect. Frivolous lawsuits waste good people's time and hurt the real victims. That's why I have proposed to prevent them: Lawyers in medical-malpractice lawsuits, for example, should have to bring their cases to independent experts who certify that the complaints have merit before they are filed. And lawyers who bring frivolous cases should face tough, mandatory sanctions, with a "three strikes" penalty.

The solution isn't to restrict access to the courts, or to cap awards. Those steps won't stop the bad cases. They would leave modest families like the Campbells struggling to pay for the negligence of others.

But it isn't just about money. Lawsuits often have results that reach well beyond the courtroom. Just one example of many: because of the Campbell's case, hospitals in North Carolina began changing their procedures to make sure the kind of mistakes that injured Jennifer were less likely to happen again. By any measure, you can certainly call that justice.

As a very successful personal injury lawyer, Edwards was an expert and spoke the technical language of the legal system, but he was well known for winning large judgments in personal injury cases by using his "down-home charm" with the jury.

Edwards relies heavily on narration and example to make his argument. Do you think he is successful in making his point about juries, especially when we hear so much about frivolous lawsuits that cost us all so much money? Which sort of communication do you think would be most effective with a jury—public, private, or technical? Why?

How do you think he views the jury system, and why? Write an essay in which you argue against a widely held perception (such as the idea that all lawsuits are frivolous) by using specific examples of people. Your goal is to argue against the rule by writing about the exception.

When the Private Becomes Public

In this next essay, "Twelve Anonymous Men," Barney Gimbel focuses on a different aspect of the jury system—jury selection as legal tactic. Serving on a jury is a public gesture that has, until recently, been something of a private action. Unless you served on a jury when famous people were on trial, your role on the jury was rather anonymous, and you were not supposed to discuss the evidence with anyone until deliberations began, and then only with the other members of the jury. The judgment of one's fellow citizen was a confidential process. There were questions in the selection process that allowed both sides to guess at how you might vote, but your privacy largely remained intact.

Recently, however, if you served on a jury when the defendant was someone famous, or very wealthy, or both, suddenly what little anonymity you might have felt sitting among your fellow jurors can evaporate. Today the media is often barred from publishing names of jurors before a trial ends, but public interest in a trial often translates to public interest in the jury members. As you read "Twelve Anonymous Men," consider what expectations of privacy you might have if you served on a jury and whether or not those expectations are realistic.

Barney Gimbel

Twelve Anonymous Men

Keith Rohman can't remember the last time he had to tail an unfaithful husband. These days, the Los Angeles-based private investigator spends much of his time checking into another group of unlucky souls: jurors. Even before they step into the jury box, he often knows the value of their home, how much debt they are carrying and if they've ever been charged with a crime. "Every bit of information about a juror helps," he says. "After all, it only takes one to throw a case."

Being called to serve on a jury used to be, at worst, an inconvenience. But the fall-out from high-profile cases like Martha Stewart's and Dennis Kozlowski's is just beginning. Last week the lawyers of former star investment banker Frank Quattrone asked a federal judge for an anonymous jury in his retrial, arguing that they didn't want a replay of the Tyco mistrial that was prompted by the press's publishing the name of Juror No. 4. The broader impact: experts say that without the promise of anonymity, many potential jurors may do everything they can to be eliminated—all at a time when the courts need them, with the upcoming showcase trials of former executives at Enron, WorldCom and HEALTHSOUTH. "There's going to be a reluctance for people to put themselves under that kind of media scrutiny," says jury consultant Richard Gabriel, who worked on the O.J. Simpson case. "What juror wants their face on the front page of the newspaper?"

The problem with anonymous juries is that they typically protect privacy only while the trial is underway. At some point, jurors are vulnerable to media scrutiny. Lawyers, of course, have an early start. Consider the Martha Stewart case. Even before the verdict, Stewart's attorneys hired private investigators to look into the jurors' personal lives—checking out anything they might have lied about before the trial and thus might be grounds for appeal. A month after the guilty verdicts, they alleged that juror Chappell Hartridge had lied on his juror questionnaire when he failed to acknowledge a 1997 arrest for assaulting a girlfriend as well as other legal troubles. The failure to answer those questions honestly, the lawyers argued, deprived Stewart of her right to a fair trial. (Prosecutors counter that Stewart would be unable to show that accurate responses would have required his dismissal.)

There's no law against checking into juror's lives—as long as no one contacts the jurors directly during or before the trial. "It's not just what happens in the jury room," says

Rohman, the private investigator. "Your whole life is fair game." And with so many public records on the Internet, it's easy to piece together someone's life history in minutes. At this rate, jurors may start to wonder who's really on trial.

Do you think jurors should remain anonymous to all parties throughout the process of a trial, or is this an unrealistic expectation for jurors? Should jurors have the right to protect their personal information from private investigators, or should defense lawyers be able to pick the best jury for their clients, based on private information? Is this the jury system envisioned by the first leaders of our country?

Write an essay arguing that something now private or secret should be made public. Or write an essay in which you explore a public event or situation where there should be more privacy. No matter which you argue for, consider who or what benefits from privacy.

This next essay, "One Angry Man," is the story of Pete McEntegart, a juror who served in the trial of Tyco executives. After months of the trial and deliberations, the judge declared a **mistrial.*** *As you read the story of how it was for the jury in this situation, imagine what you might have felt or experienced in McEntegart's position. Consider what "unanimous" means, and if you think that is too much to ask of twelve strangers.*

> ***mistrial:** A judge declares a mistrial in criminal court when errors or events in the trial are such that the trial cannot proceed, or when a jury cannot agree on a verdict. A mistrial is the ending of one proceeding with the possibility to go to trial again, without double jeopardy being attached.

One Angry Man

Pete McEntegart

Sketch of the Tyco jury.

The dust had barely settled since the Tyco jury was sent home after a mistrial was declared. I was Juror No. 11, and I'm not at all sure how I feel. Numb, mostly. Disappointed. Angry. Could I really have just spent six months of my life on one of the signature corporate-fraud cases of the Wall Street bubble only to have the judge rule that it must be started again from scratch, like some do-over in a childhood kickball game? How did it come to this?

I wasn't sure what to expect back on Sept. 29 when potential jurors shuttled across lower Manhattan's Centre Street for jury selection. Along the way, one man asked a court office if it was for the Kozlowski case. As a writer-reporter for *Sports Illustrated*, I wondered whether Atlanta Falcons tight end Brian Kozlowski had got into a legal scrape. Of course, the defendants were actually Dennis Kozlowski, the CEO of Tyco International, and ex-CFO Mark Swartz. Through a series of ever larger acquisitions throughout the '90s, the two built Tyco into a $36 billion conglomerate and made themselves exceedingly wealthy in the process.

I was shocked when I was placed on the panel, since I'd once worked as an investment banker. I didn't think the prosecution would want a juror who had been active on Wall Street during a go-go era and might well see nothing wrong with the fat bonuses and lavish parties for men generating great wealth for the company. I certainly did not enter the case with a vendetta against the defendants, who were accused of taking tens of millions of dollars in unauthorized bonuses and essentially using Tyco assets as a giant piggy bank to fund their lavish lifestyles. In fact, their whole defense was that whatever money they took to fund their spending habits, they took it with the board's knowledge and consent. They pleaded greedy, but not guilty.

The prosecution's case was that these men lied to, cheated and stole from investors and directors. But prosecutors made a major miscalculation in spending so much time putting Kozlowski's excesses on trial. There were vivid accounts and video of the now famous $2 million bash Kozlowski threw in Sardinia for his wife that featured singer Jimmy Buffett and his over-the-top purchases of items like $6,000 shower curtains. These seemed to be the activities that most titillated the media, judging by the marked jump in attendance on those days of testimony in an otherwise boring trial. But the jury spent almost no time during deliberations on those topics, and rightfully so. Much of what these two men did might have been unseemly, even unethical—but illegal beyond a reasonable doubt? Not to us. Instead, several jury members expressed disgust that the prosecution had wasted our time on all this. The case was supposed to last three months, but it stretched on and on, through 48 witnesses, more than 700 exhibits and 12,000-plus pages of testimony. Eventually, some jurors essentially tuned out, and, really, it was hard to blame them.

Lost amid all the white noise—much of it generated by two high-powered teams of talented defense lawyers—was damning evidence on a few specific charges. That, I realized, is why juries deliberate, to sift through mountains of evidence to find the facts. It was clear from the start of the deliberations, more than two weeks ago, that this would be a difficult process. We were far from ready to vote on any of the charges (there were 24 against each defendant), but we went around the room that first day to express our general views. About half the panel essentially said the prosecution's case was baseless and the men weren't guilty of anything except perhaps bad taste in furnishings.

One juror offered her view that when things went to hell at Tyco, the Ivy League-educated, Waspy board closed ranks and served up, in her words, the "Polack and the Jew" on a platter for a D.A. eager to make an example of somebody—anybody—for the corporate greed of the late '90s. (Never mind that there was no testimony about Kozlowski's roots, or that Swartz is even Jewish.) That was the first indication that the soon-to-be-infamous Juror No. 4, Ruth Jordan, wasn't going to make our job any easier. Jordan, a law-school grad and former teacher, seemed to be at war with herself. Whenever she reached the precipice of a guilty vote on any count, she recoiled as if she had touched a hot stove. She was the one who allegedly flashed an O.K. signal to the defendants one day during deliberations as she left the court. The other jurors and I were unaware at the time that any such gesture had taken place.

On the other hand, a few jurors felt from the start that these guys were crooks. I expressed the view, shared by at least one fellow juror, that while I didn't buy much of the prosecution's case, I was troubled by the four bonuses charged as separate grand larcenies—totaling about $145 million—that the two divvied up. I felt fairly certain after checking the financial documents during deliberations that three of those bonuses were illegal. They were supposed to be approved by the board's compensation committee; they were not. And the reasons offered by Swartz on the stand for why they were legitimate seemed to be fabrications, repeated over and over in a virtuoso performance.

If there was a white noise in the courtroom, though, there was a real racket in the jury room. The first day we instituted a policy of standing before speaking because we were talking over one another. The stand-and-speak policy was only partly effective. Yet, slowly and surely, we did make progress by focusing especially on the bonuses and on a $20 million payment that the defendants made to the fellow director (Frank Walsh) without informing the rest of the board for six months.

The first bonus, taken in 1999 in the form of a loan forgiveness totaling $37.5 million for the executives, was in many ways the clearest. During a mind-numbing nine days on the stand, Swartz said that payment was necessary to correct for accounting charges brought about by two acquisitions. He even sketched out an elaborate calculation that he claimed explained the size of the payments. It didn't hold water. Their bonus formula had in fact been properly adjusted for the accounting changes. The calculation he performed on that stand? Complete nonsense, wrong on so many levels as to be laughable—if it hadn't proved so convincing initially to much of the jury.

10 As for the three other bonuses, Swartz stated repeatedly that they were early payouts from the annual-bonus formula and thus legitimate. When the payouts were made, however, the defendants sought a special accounting treatment for the bonuses as "direct and incremental." The justification for such a classification included declaring that they were specifically not early payouts of the annual-bonus plan. In other words, they were just another helping of remuneration. Swartz signed memos at the time stating exactly that. On the stand, his explanation was the exact opposite, and when confronted about the contradiction he performed a dizzying tap dance. The fourth bonus, however, had been approved after the fact by the compensation committee, which did raise reasonable doubt.

After about a week, all the jurors but one (yes, No. 4) seemed ready to convict on the bogus-bonus charges. That was when the jury broke down and one juror, speaking for most of us, sent a letter to the judge about the "poisonous" atmosphere in the room. Charges of closed-mindedness and even corruption were being hurled about the room like spitballs. Eleven of us had become convinced that the 12th juror would never agree to a guilty verdict on any count, no matter how compelling the evidence. We saw no reason to continue under such circumstances and no plausible benefit in doing so. For two days, we practically begged the judge to declare a mistrial due to a hung jury. Miraculously, on the following Monday we seemed to have a breakthrough. Jordan said she had had a change of heart and believed that her view of reasonable doubt was perhaps extreme. There was skepticism about her sudden turnabout. We were worried that she was giving in to the group without actually being convinced by the evidence. We didn't want that kind of decision. But when she was able to state legitimate reasons for her change of views, we plowed ahead. We still had nearly half the charges to consider. By Wednesday morning, we had finished hearing a rereading of Swartz's testimony, and it was clear to all of us that he had not been honest on the stand. Even Jordan conceded that. She then said something that still stuns me: that she was "disappointed in the defendants." She had, it seems, made a great emotional investment in her belief that the defendants were not guilty, and now she realized that they had lied to her. They had let her down.

The deliberations continued to be difficult and, in many ways, dysfunctional. Yet by Thursday afternoon, we had reached a strong consensus for guilty verdicts on the final two counts, conspiracy and securities fraud. Now we had to start again from the top to finalize our verdicts or decide to leave some counts hung, and we raced to finish that afternoon. Jordan wavered again and again before acceding to any guilty verdicts, though there was a consensus just as strong in the opposite direction on more than half of the charges. Still, it seemed we might complete the task. Before we left for the day, Juror No. 5 reasonably suggested that we ask the court for an extra half-hour to finally put this all to rest. Jordan, in particular, objected. She needed an extra night to think it over. Uh-oh.

And that was basically that. On Friday, as we started to deliberate, we were abruptly stopped by court officers. We couldn't get the extra hour or so that it would probably have taken to reach a verdict on most of the charges. No doubt we would have been hung on some of them. Jordan, who had unconscionably been outed by name by the *Wall Street Journal* and the *New York Post*, had received a threatening letter. The judge declared a mistrial. It was particularly frustrating that the mistrial was caused, in the end, by events outside the courtroom. Lord knows we had enough problems inside the jury room. We had come together, however uneasily, only to have the marathon canceled just as we were staggering the final yards. I can't say for certain that we would have reached a verdict. It was forever a moving target, like Charlie Brown lining up a placekick with Lucy as his holder. But I am incensed that we didn't get the chance to try.

I certainly hope there will be a retrial. I believe that the defendants committed crimes and that the law demands that they be held accountable. If it's all the same with the state, though, I'm going to sit the next one out. I've served my time.

The Tyco mistrial was the result of both long deliberations and the loss of anonymity of one juror who claimed that her innocent hand gesture was misinterpreted. *Should this perceived loss of privacy be reason enough for a mistrial? How might publishing the names and addresses of jurors in the newspaper—something that happened in several famous murder trials in the first half of the twentieth century—be a problem? Who might be harmed, a defendant or a juror? The author also reveals the inner workings of the jury room, a private sphere of conversation, to the public. Do you think he was right to give so much information, or was he careful to protect the privacy of his fellow jurors?*

Write an essay in which you tell of a long or difficult process that ended unsatisfactorily. If this essay is your one chance to tell your side of the story, what details can you reveal that will clarify the situation for someone who was not there?

Beyond the Spheres—The Power of Celebrity

What if someone famous gets called to jury duty? It's one thing for a private citizen to want to protect his or her privacy while serving on a jury, but what about a public figure? In the following article, Oprah Winfrey—arguably the most famous

*Oprah Winfrey: (1954–) Talk show host and actor, she is famous for her award-winning, nationally syndicated television program.

woman in America—is called to jury duty and chosen to be part of a jury in a murder trial. As with any good media figure, the cameras follow her everywhere, even to the courthouse. *As you read this, consider the ways Oprah's presence on this jury might have changed the process for everyone involved. And think about how the spheres of communication are overlapping as the very public* **Oprah Winfrey*** *joins her fellow citizens in the jury room.*

Mike Colias

Winfrey, Jury Convict Man of Murder

A jury that included talk show host Oprah Winfrey convicted a man of murder Wednesday after a trial that turned into a media frenzy because of the billionaire in the jury box.

Jurors deliberated for more than two hours before convicting 27-year-old Dion Coleman of first-degree murder in the February 2002 shooting death of 23-year-old Walter Holley. Coleman is scheduled to be sentenced in September and he could face 45 years to life in prison.

"It's a huge reality check, there's a whole other world going on out there . . . When your life intersects with others in this way, it is forever changed," Winfrey said outside the courtroom, flanked by other jurors.

Winfrey, who was paid $17.20 a day for her civic duty, said she plans to do a show about the trial next week with other jurors. Winfrey's selection as a juror Monday drew loads of attention to the trial. Television cameras chronicled her moves outside and inside the bustling lobby of the Cook County Criminal Courts Building because cameras weren't allowed in the courtroom. Filling many of the seats in the cramped courtroom were more than a dozen reporters and sketch artists.

5   Even her lunches were the subject of coverage, from her failed quest to find a breadless turkey sandwich at the courthouse cafeteria to Wednesday's court provided meal of jerk chicken and scalloped potatoes.

Winfrey called all the attention distracting. "This is not good for the victim's family. . . This is not about Oprah Winfrey, the fact is a man has been murdered," Winfrey said.

Before she was chosen, Winfrey said she thought she was too opinionated to be picked as a juror, but lawyers on both sides approved of her serving.
"She was accepted by both parties and we want fair intelligent jurors on a jury whether it's Miss Winfrey or anyone else," Prosecutor Kathy Van Kampen said.

Assistant Public Defender Cynthia Brown said she thought Winfrey would be a good juror because she has been a civil lawsuit defendant before and might better understand what it's like to be accused of something. In 1998, a Texas jury acquitted Winfrey in a defamation case brought by cattlemen over comments about eating beef that she and a vegetarian activist made on a 1996 show. A second lawsuit against Winfrey filed shortly after the first trial lingered until its dismissal in 2002.

Van Kampen said all the hoopla had no effect on the trial. Juror Suzanne Goodman of Arlington Heights agreed. "It was a lot of fun, it was like being on her show," said Goodman, who plans to appear on Winfrey's show. (Associated Press writer Anna Johnson contributed to this report.)

There seems to be a real focus on money, media, and food in this article. Is that what's to be expected when a talk show host joins a jury? Who is the audience for this article—is it Oprah's audience? Oprah says all the attention is "distracting" and not good for the victim's family; what about the accused and his family? This case would never have made it to the national spotlight if not for Oprah. Is that fair? Do you think her presence on the jury helped or hurt the accused? Is celebrity a force powerful enough to change the way the rest of us communicate?

Write an essay in which you put yourself in the defendant's place. Would you want someone famous helping decide your fate if you were on trial? Who would that person be, and why? Remember, what makes someone famous—a talent for singing or acting or playing a sport, for instance—may not be what you would want in a juror.

Community, Communication, and Participation— Summing It All Up

Serving on a jury is just one way we may be called on to do our civic duty. While it is not without its hardships and difficulties, as jurors must often neglect their jobs and families to play a part in the process of American justice, it is crucial to maintaining the fair and impartial legal system we have enjoyed for more than two hundred years. It is very difficult to be an active citizen without taking action or being part of a community—both of which require some sort of communication. If called to jury duty, or while participating in any other community event, you should pay attention to how the public, private, and technical spheres of communication regularly come into play and often overlap each other in dynamic and often emotional ways.

When authors sit down to write about issues of community, communication, and participation, the different modes are often employed to accomplish differing goals. Description, narration, example, definition, classification, compare/contrast, cause and effect, and argument are all used in concert with one another throughout the writing to communicate key ideas. Which modes are chosen and how they are combined is up to the individual writer, and the awareness of such choices should be at the front of your mind as you express your ideas on paper. Narration is always compelling, but it cannot stand alone. Description, example, definition, classification, and argument are brought in to build a defendable position from facts, statistics, and groups. Comparison/contrast and cause and effect are employed to determine relationships between elements. By mastering the use of all the modes, you may join the discussion around whatever topic is of interest.

Whenever you write you are making choices about rhetorical strategies— including ethical, emotional, and logical appeals. Ethical appeals are strong, but sometimes student writers have few areas of expertise they can use to support an argument. Emotional appeals are powerful but are never enough to support an argument alone. Logical appeals are always well supported, but too many statistics and your prose might get dry for your reader. The strongest arguments rely on a combination of appeals. It's always important to be aware of the choices you make and to evaluate your success as you learn and grow as a dynamic and persuasive writer.

What Is at Stake for Citizenship?

1. Are we still a democracy if we must compel our citizens to participate in that democracy—as we compel people to serve on juries?
2. Do individuals have the right to act as "free riders," or do they have a responsibility to participate?
3. How much privacy can a juror expect, and is that expectation realistic?
4. Is there ever a time when justice is best served by taking the law into your own hands?
5. Is there ever a time when courts do not bring justice to individuals? If so, what can be done about it?
6. How do we define a good citizen?
7. Do civil rights matter if we don't know what they are?
8. Do citizens of a democracy have a responsibility to learn what their rights are?
9. What does it mean when we say "a jury of your peers"—does that mean all the jurors have to be just like the defendant in race, religion, income, education, age, or political beliefs?
10. Is there really such a thing as the right to privacy in a community activity?

The Mayflower Compact, 1620

Led by **William Bradford,** *who would go on to serve as governor of the* **Plymouth Colony** *for thirty years, passengers aboard the* **Mayflower** *wrote and agreed to this compact. Pledging to consider themselves a "civil body politick," they agreed to write laws and obey them for the general good of the whole colony. The 102 passengers who arrived at Plymouth Rock in 1620 included about a third Separatists, who were aboard the* **Mayflower** *to escape religious persecution in England. A majority signed the compact, establishing* **the first basis for written laws in the New World.** *Almost half of the passengers did not make it through the first year, but those that did went on to prosper.*

"In the name of God, Amen. We, whose names are underwritten, the Loyal Subjects of our dread Sovereign Lord, King James, by the Grace of God, of England, France and Ireland, King, Defender of the Faith, e&.

Having undertaken for the Glory of God, and Advancement of the Christian Faith, and the Honor of our King and Country, a voyage to plant the first colony in the northern parts of Virginia; do by these presents, solemnly and mutually in the Presence of God and one of another, covenant and combine ourselves together into a civil Body Politick, for our better Ordering and Preservation, and Furtherance of the Ends aforesaid; And by Virtue hereof to enact, constitute, and frame, such just and equal Laws, Ordinances, Acts, Constitutions and Offices, from time to time, as shall be thought most meet and convenient for the General good of the Colony; unto which we promise all due submission and obedience.

In Witness whereof we have hereunto subscribed our names at Cape Cod the eleventh of November, in the Reign of our Sovereign Lord, King James of England, France and Ireland, the eighteenth, and of Scotland the fifty-fourth. Anno Domini, 1620."

John Winthrop

From *A Model of Christian Charity*, 1630

John Winthrop *was elected the first governor of the* **Massachusetts Bay Colony** *before the* **Arbella** *left port in England. While still on board, Winthrop set forth the Puritan vision for the New World. He saw their purpose—their laws and government—within the greater framework of God's plan for them. They were to be an example to others—***"as a city upon a hill."** *Winthrop added a warning as well: They could not deal falsely with their God or their ways would be known throughout the world. From the theological pulpit and onto the political podium, the metaphor of the United States as a "city upon a hill" has been used by presidents and presidential hopefuls since the early days of the Republic—from John Adams to John Kerry, who is distantly related to John Winthrop.*

Now the only way to avoid this shipwreck, and to provide for our posterity, is to follow the counsel of Micah, to do justly, to love mercy, to walk humbly with our God. For this end, we must be knit together, in this work, as one man. We must entertain each other in brotherly affection. We must be willing to abridge ourselves of our superfluities, for the supply of others' necessities. We must uphold a familiar commerce together in all meekness, gentleness, patience and liberality. We must delight in each other; make others' conditions our own; rejoice together, mourn together, labor and suffer together, always having before our eyes our commission and community in the work, as members of the same body. So shall we keep the unity of the spirit in the bond of peace. The Lord will be our God, and delight to dwell among us, as His own people, and will command a blessing upon us in all our ways, so that we shall see much more of His wisdom, power, goodness and truth, than formerly we have been acquainted with. We shall find that the God of Israel is among us, when ten of us shall be able to resist a thousand of our enemies; when He shall make us a praise and glory that men shall say of succeeding plantations, "may the Lord make it like that of New England." For we must consider that we shall be as a city upon a hill. The eyes of all people are upon us. So that if we shall deal falsely with our God in this work we have undertaken, and so cause Him to withdraw His present help from us, we shall be made a story and a by-word through the world. We shall open the mouths of enemies to speak evil of the ways of God, and all professors for God's sake. We shall shame the faces of many of God's worthy servants, and cause their prayers to be turned into curses upon us till we be consumed out of the good land whither we are going.

And to shut this discourse with that exhortation of Moses, that faithful servant of the Lord, in his last farewell to Israel, Deut. 30. "Beloved, there is now set before us life and death, good and evil," in that we are commanded this day to love the Lord our God, and to love one another, to walk in his ways and to keep his Commandments and his ordinance and his laws, and the articles of our Covenant with Him, that we may live and be multiplied, and that the Lord our God may bless us in the land whither we go to possess it. But if our hearts shall turn away, so that we will not obey, but shall be seduced, and worship other Gods, our pleasure and profits, and serve them; it is propounded unto us this day, we shall surely perish out of the good land whither we pass over this vast sea to possess it.

Therefore let us choose life, that we and our seed may live, by obeying His voice and cleaving to Him, for He is our life and our prosperity.

Virginia Slave Laws, 1660s

*Although **Africans** were present in the **New World,** their legal status was often more fluid than is commonly thought. Some blacks were held in lifelong bondage, while others were held (as many whites were) in indentured servitude—able to own property, testify against white colonists in court, and then freed after a specified period of time. Others held in servitude claimed their freedom through Christian baptism, although that was a limited option. These complexities of status continued until the mid-1660s, when white indentured servants became less common and Africans enslaved for life became more common. Through the 1660s, the Virginia colonies began passing laws that expanded the rights of white slave owners and more severely limited the rights and the abilities of Africans (and those of African descent) to escape slavery. These laws paved the way in the colonies for slavery to be a permanent condition reserved exclusively for blacks who had no civil or moral rights.*

December 1662

Whereas some doubts have arisen whether children got by any Englishman upon a Negro woman should be slave or free, *be it therefore enacted and declared by this present Grand Assembly,* that all children born in this country shall be held bond or free only according to the condition of the mother; and that if any Christian shall commit fornication with a Negro man or woman, he or she so offending shall pay double the fines imposed by the former act.

September 1667

Whereas some doubts have risen whether children that are slaves by birth, and by the charity and piety of their owners made partakers of the blessed sacrament of baptism, should by virtue of their baptism be made free, *it is enacted and declared by this Grand Assembly, and the authority thereof,* that the conferring of baptism does not alter the condition of the person as to his bondage or freedom; that diverse masters, freed from this doubt may more carefully endeavor the propagation of Christianity by permitting children, though slaves, or chose of greater growth if capable, to be admitted to that sacrament.

October 1669

Whereas the only law in force for the punishment of refractory servants resisting their master, mistress, or overseer cannot be inflicted upon Negroes, nor the obstinacy of many of them be suppressed by other than violent means, *be it enacted and declared by this Grand Assembly* if any slave resists his master (or other by his master's order correcting him) and by the extremity of the correction should chance to die, that his death shall not be accounted a felony, but the master (or that other person appointed by the master to punish him) be acquitted from molestation, since it cannot be presumed that premeditated malice (which alone makes murder a felony) should induce any man to destroy his own estate.

The Declaration of Independence of the Thirteen Colonies, 1776

After the battles of Lexington and Concord, where in open revolt the Minutemen fought British troops, and the publication of **Thomas Paine's** *pro-independence pamphlet* **Common Sense***, the Second Continental Congress convened in Philadelphia and began debating what course of action the colonies should take. On June 7, 1776, Richard Henry Lee, representative from the colony of Virginia, proposed a resolution "that these united colonies are and of right ought to be free and independent States." A committee was formed to draft a formal declaration, but* **Thomas Jefferson** *wrote the bulk of the text of the first draft, which was edited by* **John Adams** *and* **Benjamin Franklin***. On July 2, 1776, the Congress voted for independence, and then began debating the language of the declaration—removing Jefferson's accusation that the British encouraged the slave trade. The final form of the document—**a three-part argument addressing the rights of man, the terms of the grievances against King George III, and a formal assertion of independence**—was adopted on July 4, 1776. This document, with its soaring language and remarkable claim that "all men are created equal" became the blueprint for people seeking freedom and equality for the next 230 years.*

In CONGRESS, July 4, 1776

The unanimous Declaration of the thirteen United States of America,

When in the Course of human events, it becomes necessary for one people to dissolve the political bands which have connected them with another, and to assume among the powers of the earth, the separate and equal station to which the Laws of Nature and of Nature's God entitle them, a decent respect to the opinions of mankind requires that they should declare the causes which impel them to the separation.

We hold these truths to be self-evident, that all men are created equal, that they are endowed by their Creator with certain unalienable Rights, that among these are Life, Liberty and the pursuit of Happiness.—That to secure these rights, Governments are instituted among Men, deriving their just powers from the consent of the governed,—That whenever any Form of Government becomes destructive of these ends, it is the Right of the People to alter or to abolish it, and to institute new Government, laying its foundation on such principles and organizing its powers in such form, as to them shall seem most likely to effect their Safety and Happiness. Prudence, indeed, will dictate that Governments long established should not be changed for light and transient causes; and accordingly all experience has shown, that mankind are more disposed to suffer, while evils are sufferable, than to right themselves by abolishing the forms to which they are accustomed. But when a long train of abuses and usurpations, pursuing invariably the same Object evinces a design to reduce them under absolute Despotism, it is their right, it is their duty, to throw off such Government, and to provide new Guards for their future security.—Such has been the patient sufferance of these Colonies; and such is now the necessity which constrains them to alter their former Systems of Government. The history of the present King of Great Britain [George III] is a history of repeated injuries and usurpations, all having in direct object the establishment of an absolute Tyranny over these States. To prove this, let Facts be submitted to a candid world.

He has refused his Assent to Laws, the most wholesome and necessary for the public good. 5

He has forbidden his Governors to pass Laws of immediate and pressing importance, unless suspended in their operation till his Assent should be obtained; and when so suspended, he has utterly neglected to attend to them.

He has refused to pass other Laws for the accommodation of large districts of people, unless those people would relinquish the right of Representation in the Legislature, a right inestimable to them and formidable to tyrants only.

He has called together legislative bodies at places unusual, uncomfortable, and distant from the depository of their public Records, for the sole purpose of fatiguing them into compliance with his measures.

He has dissolved Representative Houses repeatedly, for opposing with manly firmness his invasions on the rights of the people.

He has refused for a long time, after such dissolutions, to cause others to be elected; 10 whereby the Legislative powers, incapable of Annihilation, have returned to the People at large for their exercise; the State remaining in the mean time exposed to all the dangers of invasion from without, and convulsions within.

He has endeavored to prevent the population of these States; for that purpose obstructing the Laws for Naturalization of Foreigners; refusing to pass others to encourage their migrations hither, and raising the conditions of new Appropriations of Lands.

He has obstructed the Administration of Justice, by refusing his Assent to Laws for establishing Judiciary powers.

He has made Judges dependent on his Will alone, for the tenure of their offices, and the amount and payment of their salaries.

He has erected a multitude of New Offices, and sent hither swarms of Officers to harass our people, and eat out their substance.

15   He has kept among us, in times of peace, Standing Armies without the consent of our legislatures.

He has affected to render the Military independent of and superior to the Civil power.

He has combined with others to subject us to a jurisdiction foreign to our constitution and unacknowledged by our laws; giving his Assent to their Acts of pretended Legislation:

For Quartering large bodies of armed troops among us:

For protecting them, by a mock Trial, from punishment for any Murders which they should commit on the Inhabitants of these States:

20   For cutting off our Trade with all parts of the world:

For imposing Taxes on us without our Consent:

For depriving us, in many cases, of the benefits of Trial by Jury:

For transporting us beyond Seas to be tried for pretended offences:

For abolishing the free System of English Laws in a neighboring Province, establishing therein an Arbitrary government, and enlarging its Boundaries so as to render it at once an example and fit instrument for introducing the same absolute rule into these Colonies:

25   For taking away our Charters, abolishing our most valuable Laws, and altering fundamentally the Forms of our Governments:

For suspending our own Legislatures, and declaring themselves invested with power to legislate for us in all cases whatsoever.

He has abdicated Government here, by declaring us out of his Protection and waging War against us.

He has plundered our seas, ravaged our Coasts, burnt our towns, and destroyed the lives of our people.

He is at this time transporting large Armies of foreign Mercenaries to complete the works of death, desolation and tyranny, already begun with circumstances of Cruelty and perfidy scarcely paralleled in the most barbarous ages, and totally unworthy the Head of a civilized nation.

30   He has constrained our fellow Citizens taken Captive on the high Seas to bear Arms against their Country, to become the executioners of their friends and Brethren, or to fall themselves by their Hands.

He has excited domestic insurrections amongst us, and has endeavored to bring on the inhabitants of our frontiers, the merciless Indian Savages, whose known rule of warfare, is an undistinguished destruction of all ages, sexes and conditions.

In every stage of these Oppressions We have Petitioned for Redress in the most humble terms: Our repeated Petitions have been answered only by repeated injury. A Prince whose character is thus marked by every act which may define a Tyrant, is unfit to be the ruler of a free people. Nor have We been wanting in attentions to our British brethren. We have warned them from time to time of attempts by their legislature to extend an unwarrantable jurisdiction over us. We have reminded them of the circumstances of our emigration and settlement here. We have appealed to their native justice and magnanimity, and we have conjured them by the ties of our common kindred to disavow these usurpations, which, would inevitably interrupt our connections and correspondence. They too have been deaf to the voice of justice and of consanguinity. We must, therefore, acquiesce in the necessity, which denounces our Separation, and hold them, as we hold the rest of mankind, Enemies in War, in Peace Friends.

We, therefore, the Representatives of the United States of America, in General Congress, Assembled, appealing to the Supreme Judge of the world for the rectitude of our intentions, do, in the Name, and by the Authority of the good People of these Colonies, solemnly publish and declare, That these United Colonies are, and of Right ought to be Free and Independent States; that they are Absolved from all Allegiance to the British Crown, and that all political connection between them and the State of Great Britain, is and ought to be totally dissolved; and that as Free and Independent States, they have full Power to levy War, conclude Peace, contract Alliances, establish Commerce, and to do all other Acts and Things which Independent States may of right do. And for the support of this Declaration, with a firm reliance on the protection of divine Providence, we mutually pledge to each other our Lives, our Fortunes and our sacred Honor.

The Constitution of the United States of America, 1787

*The federal convention convened in the state house in Philadelphia in the spring of 1787 for the **purpose of rewriting the Articles of Confederation**. Soon it became apparent that the Articles would have to be scrapped and a new effort would have to be launched. General **George Washington** was elected president of the Constitutional Convention. **James Madison,** whom history would label **"The Father of the Constitution,"** advocated for **more power for a central government** in order to provide order and stability to the individual states. The Constitution was the work of 55 elected men, who cooperated and compromised to develop the end product. Though Jefferson and Adams were overseas, **Benjamin Franklin,** at 81, was the senior statesman present. Through James Madison's daily notes about the proceedings, historians have been able to construct an account of the many negotiations that made this document possible. A first draft was completed at the end of the summer 1787, and a year later, in July 1788, the Constitution was ratified by the requisite number of states and became the foundation of our democratic government. (See **Bill of Rights** at the head of the First Amendment.)*

We the People of the United States, in Order to form a more perfect Union, establish Justice, insure domestic Tranquility, provide for the common defense, promote the general Welfare, and secure the Blessings of Liberty to ourselves and our Posterity, do ordain and establish this Constitution for the United States of America.

Article. I.

Section 1.

All legislative Powers herein granted shall be vested in a Congress of the United States, which shall consist of a Senate and House of Representatives.

Section. 2.

Clause 1: The House of Representatives shall be composed of Members chosen every second Year by the People of the several States, and the Electors in each State shall have the Qualifications requisite for Electors of the most numerous Branch of the State Legislature.

Clause 2: No Person shall be a Representative who shall not have attained to the Age of twenty five Years, and been seven Years a Citizen of the United States, and who shall not, when elected, be an Inhabitant of that State in which he shall be chosen.

5   Clause 3: Representatives and direct Taxes shall be apportioned among the several States which may be included within this Union, according to their respective Numbers, which shall be determined by adding to the whole Number of free Persons, including those bound to Service for a Term of Years, and excluding Indians not taxed, three fifths of all other Persons. The actual Enumeration shall be made within three Years after the first Meeting of the Congress of the United States, and within every subsequent Term of ten Years, in such Manner as they shall by Law direct. The Number of Representatives shall not exceed one for every thirty Thousand, but each State shall have at Least one Representative; and until such enumeration shall be made, the State of New Hampshire shall be entitled to choose three, Massachusetts eight, Rhode-Island and Providence Plantations one, Connecticut five, New-York six, New Jersey four, Pennsylvania eight, Delaware one, Maryland six, Virginia ten, North Carolina five, South Carolina five, and Georgia three.

Clause 4: When vacancies happen in the Representation from any State, the Executive Authority thereof shall issue Writs of Election to fill such Vacancies.

Clause 5: The House of Representatives shall choose their Speaker and other Officers; and shall have the sole Power of Impeachment.

Section. 3.

Clause 1: The Senate of the United States shall be composed of two Senators from each State, chosen by the Legislature thereof, for six Years; and each Senator shall have one Vote.

Clause 2: Immediately after they shall be assembled in Consequence of the first Election, they shall be divided as equally as may be into three Classes. The Seats of the Senators of the first Class shall be vacated at the Expiration of the second Year, of the second Class at the Expiration of the fourth Year, and of the third Class at the Expiration of the sixth Year, so that one third may be chosen every second Year; and if Vacancies happen by Resignation, or otherwise, during the Recess of the Legislature of any State, the Executive thereof may make temporary Appointments until the next Meeting of the Legislature, which shall then fill such Vacancies.

10   Clause 3: No Person shall be a Senator who shall not have attained to the Age of thirty Years, and been nine Years a Citizen of the United States, and who shall not, when elected, be an Inhabitant of that State for which he shall be chosen.

Clause 4: The Vice President of the United States shall be President of the Senate, but shall have no Vote, unless they be equally divided.

Clause 5: The Senate shall choose their other Officers, and also a President pro tempore, in the Absence of the Vice President, or when he shall exercise the Office of President of the United States.

Clause 6: The Senate shall have the sole Power to try all Impeachments. When sitting for that Purpose, they shall be on Oath or Affirmation. When the President of the United States is tried, the Chief Justice shall preside: And no Person shall be convicted without the Concurrence of two thirds of the Members present.

Clause 7: Judgment in Cases of Impeachment shall not extend further than to removal from Office, and disqualification to hold and enjoy any Office of honor, Trust or Profit under the United States: but the Party convicted shall nevertheless be liable and subject to Indictment, Trial, Judgment and Punishment, according to Law.

Section. 4.

Clause 1: The Times, Places and Manner of holding Elections for Senators and Representatives, shall be prescribed in each State by the Legislature thereof; but the Congress may at any time by Law make or alter such Regulations, except as to the Places of choosing Senators.

Clause 2: The Congress shall assemble at least once in every Year, and such Meeting shall be on the first Monday in December, unless they shall by Law appoint a different Day.

Section. 5.

Clause 1: Each House shall be the Judge of the Elections, Returns and Qualifications of its own Members, and a Majority of each shall constitute a Quorum to do Business; but a smaller Number may adjourn from day to day, and may be authorized to compel the Attendance of absent Members, in such Manner, and under such Penalties as each House may provide.

Clause 2: Each House may determine the Rules of its Proceedings, punish its Members for disorderly Behavior, and, with the Concurrence of two thirds, expel a Member.

Clause 3: Each House shall keep a Journal of its Proceedings, and from time to time publish the same, excepting such Parts as may in their Judgment require Secrecy; and the Yeas and Nays of the Members of either House on any question shall, at the Desire of one fifth of those Present, be entered on the Journal.

Clause 4: Neither House, during the Session of Congress, shall, without the Consent of the other, adjourn for more than three days, nor to any other Place than that in which the two Houses shall be sitting.

Section. 6.

Clause 1: The Senators and Representatives shall receive a Compensation for their Services, to be ascertained by Law, and paid out of the Treasury of the United States. They shall in all Cases, except Treason, Felony and Breach of the Peace, be privileged from Arrest during their Attendance at the Session of their respective Houses, and in going to and returning from the same; and for any Speech or Debate in either House, they shall not be questioned in any other Place.

Clause 2: No Senator or Representative shall, during the Time for which he was elected, be appointed to any civil Office under the Authority of the United States, which shall have been created, or the Emoluments whereof shall have been increased during such time; and no Person holding any Office under the United States, shall be a Member of either House during his Continuance in Office.

Section. 7.

Clause 1: All Bills for raising Revenue shall originate in the House of Representatives; but the Senate may propose or concur with Amendments as on other Bills.

Clause 2: Every Bill which shall have passed the House of Representatives and the Senate, shall, before it become a Law, be presented to the President of the United States; If he approve he shall sign it, but if not he shall return it, with his Objections to that House in which it shall have originated, who shall enter the Objections at large on their Journal, and proceed to reconsider it. If after such Reconsideration two thirds of that House shall agree to pass the Bill, it shall be sent, together with the Objections, to the other House, by which it shall likewise be reconsidered, and if approved by two thirds of that House, it shall become a Law. But in all such Cases the Votes of both Houses shall be determined by yeas and Nays, and the Names of the Persons voting for and against the Bill shall be entered on the Journal of each House respectively. If any Bill shall not be returned by the President within ten Days (Sundays excepted) after it shall have been presented to him, the Same shall be a Law, in like Manner as if he had signed it, unless the Congress by their Adjournment prevent its Return, in which Case it shall not be a Law.

25   Clause 3: Every Order, Resolution, or Vote to which the Concurrence of the Senate and House of Representatives may be necessary (except on a question of Adjournment) shall be presented to the President of the United States; and before the Same shall take Effect, shall be approved by him, or being disapproved by him, shall be repassed by two thirds of the Senate and House of Representatives, according to the Rules and Limitations prescribed in the Case of a Bill.

Section. 8.

Clause 1: The Congress shall have Power To lay and collect Taxes, Duties, Imposts and Excises, to pay the Debts and provide for the common Defense and general Welfare of the United States; but all Duties, Imposts and Excises shall be uniform throughout the United States;

Clause 2: To borrow Money on the credit of the United States;

Clause 3: To regulate Commerce with foreign Nations, and among the several States, and with the Indian Tribes;

Clause 4: To establish an uniform Rule of Naturalization, and uniform Laws on the subject of Bankruptcies throughout the United States;

30   Clause 5: To coin Money, regulate the Value thereof, and of foreign Coin, and fix the Standard of Weights and Measures;

Clause 6: To provide for the Punishment of counterfeiting the Securities and current Coin of the United States;

Clause 7: To establish Post Offices and post Roads;

Clause 8: To promote the Progress of Science and useful Arts, by securing for limited Times to Authors and Inventors the exclusive Right to their respective Writings and Discoveries;

Clause 9: To constitute Tribunals inferior to the supreme Court;

35   Clause 10: To define and punish Piracies and Felonies committed on the high Seas, and Offences against the Law of Nations;

Clause 11: To declare War, grant Letters of Marque and Reprisal, and make Rules concerning Captures on Land and Water;

Clause 12: To raise and support Armies, but no Appropriation of Money to that Use shall be for a longer Term than two Years;

Clause 13: To provide and maintain a Navy;

Clause 14: To make Rules for the Government and Regulation of the land and naval Forces;

Clause 15: To provide for calling forth the Militia to execute the Laws of the Union, suppress Insurrections and repel Invasions;

Clause 16: To provide for organizing, arming, and disciplining, the Militia, and for governing such Part of them as may be employed in the Service of the United States, reserving to the States respectively, the Appointment of the Officers, and the Authority of training the Militia according to the discipline prescribed by Congress;

Clause 17: To exercise exclusive Legislation in all Cases whatsoever, over such District (not exceeding ten Miles square) as may, by Cession of particular States, and the Acceptance of Congress, become the Seat of the Government of the United States, and to exercise like Authority over all Places purchased by the Consent of the Legislature of the State in which the Same shall be, for the Erection of Forts, Magazines, Arsenals, dock-Yards, and other needful Buildings;—And

Clause 18: To make all Laws which shall be necessary and proper for carrying into Execution the foregoing Powers, and all other Powers vested by this Constitution in the Government of the United States, or in any Department or Officer thereof.

Section. 9.

Clause 1: The Migration or Importation of such Persons as any of the States now existing shall think proper to admit, shall not be prohibited by the Congress prior to the Year one thousand eight hundred and eight, but a Tax or duty may be imposed on such Importation, not exceeding ten dollars for each Person.

Clause 2: The Privilege of the Writ of Habeas Corpus shall not be suspended, unless when in Cases of Rebellion or Invasion the public Safety may require it.

Clause 3: No Bill of Attainder or ex post facto Law shall be passed.

Clause 4: No Capitation, or other direct, Tax shall be laid, unless in Proportion to the Census or Enumeration herein before directed to be taken.

Clause 5: No Tax or Duty shall be laid on Articles exported from any State.

Clause 6: No Preference shall be given by any Regulation of Commerce or Revenue to the Ports of one State over those of another: nor shall Vessels bound to, or from, one State, be obliged to enter, clear, or pay Duties in another.

Clause 7: No Money shall be drawn from the Treasury, but in Consequence of Appropriations made by Law; and a regular Statement and Account of the Receipts and Expenditures of all public Money shall be published from time to time.

Clause 8: No Title of Nobility shall be granted by the United States: And no Person holding any Office of Profit or Trust under them, shall, without the Consent of the Congress, accept of any present, Emolument, Office, or Title, of any kind whatever, from any King, Prince, or foreign State.

Section. 10.

Clause 1: No State shall enter into any Treaty, Alliance, or Confederation; grant Letters of Marque and Reprisal; coin Money; emit Bills of Credit; make any Thing but gold and silver Coin a Tender in Payment of Debts; pass any Bill of Attainder, ex post facto Law, or Law impairing the Obligation of Contracts, or grant any Title of Nobility.

Clause 2: No State shall, without the Consent of the Congress, lay any Imposts or Duties on Imports or Exports, except what may be absolutely necessary for executing it's inspection Laws: and the net Produce of all Duties and Imposts, laid by any State on Imports or Exports, shall be for the Use of the Treasury of the United States; and all such Laws shall be subject to the Revision and Controul of the Congress.

Clause 3: No State shall, without the Consent of Congress, lay any Duty of Tonnage, keep Troops, or Ships of War in time of Peace, enter into any Agreement or Compact with another State, or with a foreign Power, or engage in War, unless actually invaded, or in such imminent Danger as will not admit of delay.

Article. II.

Section. 1.

55   Clause 1: The executive Power shall be vested in a President of the United States of America. He shall hold his Office during the Term of four Years, and, together with the Vice President, chosen for the same Term, be elected, as follows

Clause 2: Each State shall appoint, in such Manner as the Legislature thereof may direct, a Number of Electors, equal to the whole Number of Senators and Representatives to which the State may be entitled in the Congress: but no Senator or Representative, or Person holding an Office of Trust or Profit under the United States, shall be appointed an Elector.

Clause 3: The Electors shall meet in their respective States, and vote by Ballot for two Persons, of whom one at least shall not be an Inhabitant of the same State with themselves. And they shall make a List of all the Persons voted for, and of the Number of Votes for each; which List they shall sign and certify, and transmit sealed to the Seat of the Government of the United States, directed to the President of the Senate. The President of the Senate shall, in the Presence of the Senate and House of Representatives, open all the Certificates, and the Votes shall then be counted. The Person having the greatest Number of Votes shall be the President, if such Number be a Majority of the whole Number of Electors appointed; and if there be more than one who have such Majority, and have an equal Number of Votes, then the House of Representatives shall immediately choose by Ballot one of them for President; and if no Person have a Majority, then from the five highest on the List the said House shall in like Manner choose the President. But in choosing the President, the Votes shall be taken by States, the Representation from each State having one Vote; A quorum for this Purpose shall consist of a Member or Members from two thirds of the States, and a Majority of all the States shall be necessary to a Choice. In every Case, after the Choice of the President, the Person having the greatest Number of Votes of the Electors shall be the Vice President. But if there should remain two or more who have equal Votes, the Senate shall choose from them by Ballot the Vice President.

Clause 4: The Congress may determine the Time of choosing the Electors, and the Day on which they shall give their Votes; which Day shall be the same throughout the United States.

Clause 5: No Person except a natural born Citizen, or a Citizen of the United States, at the time of the Adoption of this Constitution, shall be eligible to the Office of President;

neither shall any Person be eligible to that Office who shall not have attained to the Age of thirty five Years, and been fourteen Years a Resident within the United States.

Clause 6: In Case of the Removal of the President from Office, or of his Death, Res- 60 ignation, or Inability to discharge the Powers and Duties of the said Office, the Same shall devolve on the Vice President, and the Congress may by Law provide for the Case of Removal, Death, Resignation or Inability, both of the President and Vice President, declaring what Officer shall then act as President, and such Officer shall act accordingly, until the Disability be removed, or a President shall be elected.

Clause 7: The President shall, at stated Times, receive for his Services, a Compensation, which shall neither be increased nor diminished during the Period for which he shall have been elected, and he shall not receive within that Period any other Emolument from the United States, or any of them.

Clause 8: Before he enter on the Execution of his Office, he shall take the following Oath or Affirmation:—"I do solemnly swear (or affirm) that I will faithfully execute the Office of President of the United States, and will to the best of my Ability, preserve, protect and defend the Constitution of the United States."

Section. 2.

Clause 1: The President shall be Commander in Chief of the Army and Navy of the United States, and of the Militia of the several States, when called into the actual Service of the United States; he may require the Opinion, in writing, of the principal Officer in each of the executive Departments, upon any Subject relating to the Duties of their respective Offices, and he shall have Power to grant Reprieves and Pardons for Offences against the United States, except in Cases of Impeachment.

Clause 2: He shall have Power, by and with the Advice and Consent of the Senate, to make Treaties, provided two thirds of the Senators present concur; and he shall nominate, and by and with the Advice and Consent of the Senate, shall appoint Ambassadors, other public Ministers and Consuls, Judges of the supreme Court, and all other Officers of the United States, whose Appointments are not herein otherwise provided for, and which shall be established by Law: but the Congress may by Law vest the Appointment of such inferior Officers, as they think proper, in the President alone, in the Courts of Law, or in the Heads of Departments.

Clause 3: The President shall have Power to fill up all Vacancies that may happen dur- 65 ing the Recess of the Senate, by granting Commissions which shall expire at the End of their next Session.

Section. 3.

He shall from time to time give to the Congress Information of the State of the Union, and recommend to their Consideration such Measures as he shall judge necessary and expedient; he may, on extraordinary Occasions, convene both Houses, or either of them, and in Case of Disagreement between them, with Respect to the Time of Adjournment, he may adjourn them to such Time as he shall think proper; he shall receive Ambassadors and other public Ministers; he shall take Care that the Laws be faithfully executed, and shall Commission all the Officers of the United States.

Section. 4.

The President, Vice President and all civil Officers of the United States, shall be removed from Office on Impeachment for, and Conviction of, Treason, Bribery, or other high Crimes and Misdemeanors.

Article. III.

Section. 1.

The judicial Power of the United States, shall be vested in one supreme Court, and in such inferior Courts as the Congress may from time to time ordain and establish. The Judges, both of the supreme and inferior Courts, shall hold their Offices during good Behavior, and shall, at stated Times, receive for their Services, a Compensation, which shall not be diminished during their Continuance in Office.

Section. 2.

Clause 1: The judicial Power shall extend to all Cases, in Law and Equity, arising under this Constitution, the Laws of the United States, and Treaties made, or which shall be made, under their Authority;—to all Cases affecting Ambassadors, other public Ministers and Consuls;—to all Cases of admiralty and maritime Jurisdiction;—to Controversies to which the United States shall be a Party;—to Controversies between two or more States;—between a State and Citizens of another State;—between Citizens of different States,—between Citizens of the same State claiming Lands under Grants of different States, and between a State, or the Citizens thereof, and foreign States, Citizens or Subjects.

70   Clause 2: In all Cases affecting Ambassadors, other public Ministers and Consuls, and those in which a State shall be Party, the Supreme Court shall have original Jurisdiction. In all the other Cases before mentioned, the Supreme Court shall have appellate Jurisdiction, both as to Law and Fact, with such Exceptions, and under such Regulations as the Congress shall make.

Clause 3: The Trial of all Crimes, except in Cases of Impeachment, shall be by Jury; and such Trial shall be held in the State where the said Crimes shall have been committed; but when not committed within any State, the Trial shall be at such Place or Places as the Congress may by Law have directed.

Section. 3.

Clause 1: Treason against the United States, shall consist only in levying War against them, or in adhering to their Enemies, giving them Aid and Comfort. No Person shall be convicted of Treason unless on the Testimony of two Witnesses to the same overt Act, or on Confession in open Court.

Clause 2: The Congress shall have Power to declare the Punishment of Treason, but no Attainder of Treason shall work Corruption of Blood, or Forfeiture except during the Life of the Person attainted.

Article. IV.

Section. 1.

Full Faith and Credit shall be given in each State to the public Acts, Records, and judicial Proceedings of every other State. And the Congress may by general Laws prescribe the Manner in which such Acts, Records and Proceedings shall be proved, and the Effect thereof.

Section. 2.

Clause 1: The Citizens of each State shall be entitled to all Privileges and Immunities   75
of Citizens in the several States.

Clause 2: A Person charged in any State with Treason, Felony, or other Crime, who shall flee from Justice, and be found in another State, shall on Demand of the executive Authority of the State from which he fled, be delivered up, to be removed to the State having Jurisdiction of the Crime.

Clause 3: No Person held to Service or Labor in one State, under the Laws thereof, escaping into another, shall, in Consequence of any Law or Regulation therein, be discharged from such Service or Labor, but shall be delivered up on Claim of the Party to whom such Service or Labor may be due.

Section. 3.

Clause 1: New States may be admitted by the Congress into this Union; but no new State shall be formed or erected within the Jurisdiction of any other State; nor any State be formed by the Junction of two or more States, or Parts of States, without the Consent of the Legislatures of the States concerned as well as of the Congress.

Clause 2: The Congress shall have Power to dispose of and make all needful Rules and Regulations respecting the Territory or other Property belonging to the United States; and nothing in this Constitution shall be so construed as to Prejudice any Claims of the United States, or of any particular State.

Section. 4.

The United States shall guarantee to every State in this Union a Republican Form of   80
Government, and shall protect each of them against Invasion; and on Application of the Legislature, or of the Executive (when the Legislature cannot be convened) against domestic Violence.

Article. V.

The Congress, whenever two thirds of both Houses shall deem it necessary, shall propose Amendments to this Constitution, or, on the Application of the Legislatures of two thirds of the several States, shall call a Convention for proposing Amendments, which, in either Case, shall be valid to all Intents and Purposes, as Part of this Constitution, when ratified by the Legislatures of three fourths of the several States, or by Conventions in three fourths thereof, as the one or the other Mode of Ratification may be proposed by the Congress; Provided that no Amendment which may be made prior to the Year One thousand eight hundred and eight shall in any Manner affect the first and fourth Clauses in the Ninth Section of the first Article; and that no State, without its Consent, shall be deprived of its equal Suffrage in the Senate.

Article. VI.

Clause 1: All Debts contracted and Engagements entered into, before the Adoption of this Constitution, shall be as valid against the United States under this Constitution, as under the Confederation.

Clause 2: This Constitution, and the Laws of the United States which shall be made in Pursuance thereof; and all Treaties made, or which shall be made, under the Authority of the United States, shall be the supreme Law of the Land; and the Judges in every State shall be bound thereby, any Thing in the Constitution or Laws of any State to the Contrary notwithstanding.

Clause 3: The Senators and Representatives before mentioned, and the Members of the several State Legislatures, and all executive and judicial Officers, both of the United States and of the several States, shall be bound by Oath or Affirmation, to support this Constitution; but no religious Test shall ever be required as a Qualification to any Office or public Trust under the United States.

Article. VII.

85   The Ratification of the Conventions of nine States, shall be sufficient for the Establishment of this Constitution between the States so ratifying the same done in Convention by the Unanimous Consent of the States present the Seventeenth Day of September in the Year of our Lord one thousand seven hundred and Eighty seven and of the Independence of the United States of America the Twelfth. In witness whereof We have hereunto subscribed our Names,

Bill of Rights

During the state debates about whether to ratify the Constitution, many expressed concern about the **protection of individual rights** *and feared the possible tyranny of a strong central government. The citizens were apprised of detailed information through a series of Federalist Papers, in which James Madison, John Jay, and Alexander Hamilton encouraged support for the Constitution. A number of states ratified the Constitution on the condition that these individual rights would be included. In September 1789, twelve Articles were introduced to the states, and* **by 1791, the first ten Amendments** *were approved and became known as the Bill of Rights.*

Amendment I (1791)

Congress shall make no law respecting an establishment of religion, or prohibiting the free exercise thereof; or abridging the freedom of speech, or of the press; or the right of the people peaceably to assemble, and to petition the government for a redress of grievances.

Amendment II (1791)

A well regulated militia, being necessary to the security of a free state, the right of the people to keep and bear arms, shall not be infringed.

Amendment III (1791)

No soldier shall, in time of peace be quartered in any house, without the consent of the owner, nor in time of war, but in a manner to be prescribed by law.

Amendment IV (1791)

The right of the people to be secure in their persons, houses, papers, and effects, against unreasonable searches and seizures, shall not be violated, and no warrants shall issue, but upon probable cause, supported by oath or affirmation, and particularly describing the place to be searched, and the persons or things to be seized.

Amendment V (1791)

No person shall be held to answer for a capital, or otherwise infamous crime, unless on a presentment or indictment of a grand jury, except in cases arising in the land or naval forces, or in the militia, when in actual service in time of war or public danger; nor shall any person be subject for the same offense to be twice put in jeopardy of life or limb; nor shall be compelled in any criminal case to be a witness against himself, nor be deprived of life, liberty, or property, without due process of law; nor shall private property be taken for public use, without just compensation.

Amendment VI (1791)

In all criminal prosecutions, the accused shall enjoy the right to a speedy and public trial, by an impartial jury of the state and district wherein the crime shall have been committed, which district shall have been previously ascertained by law, and to be informed of the nature and cause of the accusation; to be confronted with the witnesses against him; to have compulsory process for obtaining witnesses in his favor, and to have the assistance of counsel for his defense.

Amendment VII (1791)

In suits at common law, where the value in controversy shall exceed twenty dollars, the right of trial by jury shall be preserved, and no fact tried by a jury, shall be otherwise re-examined in any court of the United States, than according to the rules of the common law.

Amendment VIII (1791)

Excessive bail shall not be required, nor excessive fines imposed, nor cruel and unusual punishments inflicted.

Amendment IX (1791)

The enumeration in the Constitution, of certain rights, shall not be construed to deny or disparage others retained by the people.

Amendment X (1791)

The powers not delegated to the United States by the Constitution, nor prohibited by it to the states, are reserved to the states respectively, or to the people.

Amendment XI (1798)

The judicial power of the United States shall not be construed to extend to any suit in law or equity, commenced or prosecuted against one of the United States by citizens of another state, or by citizens or subjects of any foreign state.

Amendment XII (1804)

The electors shall meet in their respective states and vote by ballot for President and Vice-President, one of whom, at least, shall not be an inhabitant of the same state with themselves; they shall name in their ballots the person voted for as President, and in distinct ballots the person voted for as Vice-President, and they shall make distinct lists of all persons voted for as President, and of all persons voted for as Vice-President, and of the number of votes for each, which lists they shall sign and certify, and transmit sealed to the seat of the government of the United States, directed to the President of the Senate;—The President of the Senate shall, in the presence of the Senate and House of Representatives, open all the certificates and the votes shall then be counted;—the person having the greatest number of votes for President, shall be the President, if such number be a majority of the whole number of electors appointed; and if no person have such majority, then from the persons having the highest numbers not exceeding three on the list of those voted for as President, the House of Representatives shall choose immediately, by ballot, the President. But in choosing the President, the votes shall be taken by states, the representation from each state having one vote; a quorum for this purpose shall consist of a member or members from two-thirds of the states, and a majority of all the states shall be necessary to a choice. And if the House of Representatives shall not choose a President whenever the right of choice shall devolve upon them, before the fourth day of March next following, then the Vice-President shall act as President, as in the case of the death or other constitutional disability of the President. The person having the greatest number of votes as Vice-President, shall be the Vice-President, if such number be a majority of the whole number of electors appointed, and if no person have a majority, then from the two highest numbers on the list, the Senate shall choose the Vice-President; a quorum for the purpose shall consist of two-thirds of the whole number of Senators, and a majority of the whole number shall be necessary to a choice. But no person constitutionally ineligible to the office of President shall be eligible to that of Vice-President of the United States.

Amendment XIII (1865)

Section 1.

Neither slavery nor involuntary servitude, except as a punishment for crime whereof the party shall have been duly convicted, shall exist within the United States, or any place subject to their jurisdiction.

Section 2.

Congress shall have power to enforce this article by appropriate legislation.

Amendment XIV (1868)

Section 1.

All persons born or naturalized in the United States, and subject to the jurisdiction thereof, are citizens of the United States and of the state wherein they reside. No state shall make or enforce any law which shall abridge the privileges or immunities of citizens of the United States; nor shall any state deprive any person of life, liberty, or property, without due process of law; nor deny to any person within its jurisdiction the equal protection of the laws.

Section 2.

Representatives shall be apportioned among the several states according to their respective numbers, counting the whole number of persons in each state, excluding Indians not taxed. But when the right to vote at any election for the choice of electors for President and Vice President of the United States, Representatives in Congress, the executive and judicial officers of a state, or the members of the legislature thereof, is denied to any of the male inhabitants of such state, being twenty-one years of age, and citizens of the United States, or in any way abridged, except for participation in rebellion, or other crime, the basis of representation therein shall be reduced in the proportion which the number of such male citizens shall bear to the whole number of male citizens twenty-one years of age in such state.

Section 3.

No person shall be a Senator or Representative in Congress, or elector of President and Vice President, or hold any office, civil or military, under the United States, or under any state, who, having previously taken an oath, as a member of Congress, or as an officer of the United States, or as a member of any state legislature, or as an executive or judicial officer of any state, to support the Constitution of the United States, shall have engaged in insurrection or rebellion against the same, or given aid or comfort to the enemies thereof. But Congress may by a vote of two-thirds of each House, remove such disability.

Section 4.

The validity of the public debt of the United States, authorized by law, including debts incurred for payment of pensions and bounties for services in suppressing insurrection or rebellion, shall not be questioned. But neither the United States nor any state shall assume or pay any debt or obligation incurred in aid of insurrection or rebellion against the United States, or any claim for the loss or emancipation of any slave; but all such debts, obligations and claims shall be held illegal and void.

Section 5.

The Congress shall have power to enforce, by appropriate legislation, the provisions of this article.

Amendment XV (1870)

Section 1.

The right of citizens of the United States to vote shall not be denied or abridged by the United States or by any state on account of race, color, or previous condition of servitude.

Section 2.

The Congress shall have power to enforce this article by appropriate legislation.

Amendment XVI (1913)

The Congress shall have power to lay and collect taxes on incomes, from whatever source derived, without apportionment among the several states, and without regard to any census of enumeration.

Amendment XVII (1913)

The Senate of the United States shall be composed of two Senators from each state, elected by the people thereof, for six years; and each Senator shall have one vote. The electors in each state shall have the qualifications requisite for electors of the most numerous branch of the state legislatures.

When vacancies happen in the representation of any state in the Senate, the executive authority of such state shall issue writs of election to fill such vacancies: Provided, that the legislature of any state may empower the executive thereof to make temporary appointments until the people fill the vacancies by election as the legislature may direct.

This amendment shall not be so construed as to affect the election or term of any Senator chosen before it becomes valid as part of the Constitution.

Amendment XVIII (1919)

Section 1.

After one year from the ratification of this article the manufacture, sale, or transportation of intoxicating liquors within, the importation thereof into, or the exportation thereof from the United States and all territory subject to the jurisdiction thereof for beverage purposes is hereby prohibited.

Section 2.

The Congress and the several states shall have concurrent power to enforce this article by appropriate legislation.

Section 3.

This article shall be inoperative unless it shall have been ratified as an amendment to the Constitution by the legislatures of the several states, as provided in the Constitution, within seven years from the date of the submission hereof to the states by the Congress.

Amendment XIX (1920)

The right of citizens of the United States to vote shall not be denied or abridged by the United States or by any state on account of sex.

Congress shall have power to enforce this article by appropriate legislation.

Amendment XX (1933)

Section 1.

The terms of the President and Vice President shall end at noon on the 20th day of January, and the terms of Senators and Representatives at noon on the 3d day of January, of the years in which such terms would have ended if this article had not been ratified; and the terms of their successors shall then begin.

Section 2.

The Congress shall assemble at least once in every year, and such meeting shall begin at noon on the 3d day of January, unless they shall by law appoint a different day.

Section 3.

If, at the time fixed for the beginning of the term of the President, the President elect shall have died, the Vice President elect shall become President. If a President shall not have been chosen before the time fixed for the beginning of his term, or if the President elect shall have failed to qualify, then the Vice President elect shall act as President until a President shall have qualified; and the Congress may by law provide for the case wherein neither a President elect nor a Vice President elect shall have qualified, declaring who shall then act as President, or the manner in which one who is to act shall be selected, and such person shall act accordingly until a President or Vice President shall have qualified.

Section 4.

The Congress may by law provide for the case of the death of any of the persons from whom the House of Representatives may choose a President whenever the right of choice shall have devolved upon them, and for the case of the death of any of the persons from whom the Senate may choose a Vice President whenever the right of choice shall have devolved upon them.

Section 5.

Sections 1 and 2 shall take effect on the 15th day of October following the ratification of this article.

Section 6.

This article shall be inoperative unless it shall have been ratified as an amendment to the Constitution by the legislatures of three-fourths of the several states within seven years from the date of its submission.

Amendment XXI (1933)

Section 1.

The eighteenth article of amendment to the Constitution of the United States is hereby repealed.

Section 2.

The transportation or importation into any state, territory, or possession of the United States for delivery or use therein of intoxicating liquors, in violation of the laws thereof, is hereby prohibited.

Section 3.

This article shall be inoperative unless it shall have been ratified as an amendment to the Constitution by conventions in the several states, as provided in the Constitution, within seven years from the date of the submission hereof to the states by the Congress.

Amendment XXII (1951)

Section 1.

No person shall be elected to the office of the President more than twice, and no person who has held the office of President, or acted as President, for more than two years of a term to which some other person was elected President shall be elected to the office of the President more than once. But this article shall not apply to any person holding the office of President when this article was proposed by the Congress, and shall not prevent any person who may be holding the office of President, or acting as President, during the term within which this article becomes operative from holding the office of President or acting as President during the remainder of such term.

Section 2.

This article shall be inoperative unless it shall have been ratified as an amendment to the Constitution by the legislatures of three-fourths of the several states within seven years from the date of its submission to the states by the Congress.

Amendment XXIII (1961)

Section 1.

The District constituting the seat of government of the United States shall appoint in such manner as the Congress may direct:

A number of electors of President and Vice President equal to the whole number of Senators and Representatives in Congress to which the District would be entitled if it were a state, but in no event more than the least populous state; they shall be in addition to those appointed by the states, but they shall be considered, for the purposes of the election of President and Vice President, to be electors appointed by a state; and they shall meet in the District and perform such duties as provided by the twelfth article of amendment.

Section 2.

The Congress shall have power to enforce this article by appropriate legislation.

Amendment XXIV (1964)

Section 1.

The right of citizens of the United States to vote in any primary or other election for President or Vice President, for electors for President or Vice President, or for Senator or Representative in Congress, shall not be denied or abridged by the United States or any state by reason of failure to pay any poll tax or other tax.

Section 2.

The Congress shall have power to enforce this article by appropriate legislation.

Amendment XXV (1967)

Section 1.

In case of the removal of the President from office or of his death or resignation, the Vice President shall become President.

Section 2.

Whenever there is a vacancy in the office of the Vice President, the President shall nominate a Vice President who shall take office upon confirmation by a majority vote of both Houses of Congress.

Section 3.

Whenever the President transmits to the President pro tempore of the Senate and the Speaker of the House of Representatives his written declaration that he is unable to discharge the powers and duties of his office, and until he transmits to them a written declaration to the contrary, such powers and duties shall be discharged by the Vice President as Acting President.

Section 4.

Whenever the Vice President and a majority of either the principal officers of the executive departments or of such other body as Congress may by law provide, transmit to the President pro tempore of the Senate and the Speaker of the House of Representatives their written declaration that the President is unable to discharge the powers and duties of his office, the Vice President shall immediately assume the powers and duties of the office as Acting President. Thereafter, when the President transmits to the President pro tempore of the Senate and the Speaker of the House of Representatives his written declaration that no inability exists, he shall resume the powers and duties of his office unless the Vice President and a majority of either the principal officers of the executive department or of such other body as Congress may by law provide, transmit within four days to the President pro tempore of the Senate and the Speaker of the House of Representatives their written declaration that the President is unable to discharge the powers and duties of his office. Thereupon Congress shall decide the issue, assembling within forty-eight hours for that purpose if not in session. If the Congress, within twenty-one days after receipt of the latter written declaration, or, if Congress is not in session, within twenty-one days after Congress is required to assemble, determines by two-thirds vote of both Houses that the President is unable to discharge the powers and duties of his office, the Vice President shall continue to discharge the same as Acting President; otherwise, the President shall resume the powers and duties of his office.

Amendment XXVI (1971)

Section 1.

The right of citizens of the United States, who are 18 years of age or older, to vote, shall not be denied or abridged by the United States or any state on account of age.

Section 2.

The Congress shall have the power to enforce this article by appropriate legislation.

Amendment XXVII (1992)

No law varying the compensation for the services of the Senators and Representatives shall take effect until an election of Representatives shall have intervened.

Farewell Address, September 17, 1796

George Washington (1732–1799).

*The most famous speech of the first president of the United States was never delivered orally. After some collaborative input from James Madison and Alexander Hamilton, the speech appeared first in a newspaper in Philadelphia and a week later in a Boston paper. He chose to use this forum **to announce his retirement from public life, to express his gratitude to the nation, and to offer advice about the future of the country.** He praises the Constitution for its checks and balances and encourages that it be "sacredly maintained." He suggests that our liberty is closely connected to our Union—to love one is to love the other, advice that mattered to Abraham Lincoln during the days of the Civil War. What future Americans should be cognizant of are these three pertinent and still relevant areas: the fury of party spirit, the dangers of foreign intrigue and entangling alliances, and the deception of pretended patriotism.*

To the People of the United States.
FRIENDS AND FELLOW-CITIZENS:

1. The period for a new election of a citizen, to administer the executive government of the United States, being not far distant, and the time actually arrived, when your thoughts must be employed designating the person, who is to be clothed with that important trust, it appears to me proper, especially as it may conduce to a more distinct expression of the public voice, that I should now apprize you of the resolution I have formed, to decline being considered among the number of those out of whom a choice is to be made.

2. I beg you at the same time to do me the justice to be assured that this resolution has not been taken without a strict regard to all the considerations appertaining to the relation which binds a dutiful citizen to his country; and that in withdrawing the tender of service, which silence in my situation might imply, I am influenced by no diminution of zeal for your future interest, no deficiency of grateful respect for your past kindness, but am supported by a full conviction that the step is compatible with both.

3. The acceptance of, and continuance hitherto in, the office to which your suffrages have twice called me, have been a uniform sacrifice of inclination to the opinion of duty, and to a deference for what appeared to be your desire. I constantly hoped, that

it would have been much earlier in my power, consistently with motives, which I was not at liberty to disregard, to return to that retirement, from which I had been reluctantly drawn. The strength of my inclination to do this, previous to the last election, had even led to the preparation of an address to declare it to you; but mature reflection on the then perplexed and critical posture of our affairs with foreign nations, and the unanimous advice of persons entitled to my confidence impelled me to abandon the idea.

4. I rejoice, that the state of your concerns, external as well as internal, no longer renders the pursuit of inclination incompatible with the sentiment of duty, or propriety; and am persuaded, whatever partiality may be retained for my services, that, in the present circumstances of our country, you will not disapprove my determination to retire.

5. The impressions, with which I first undertook the arduous trust, were explained on the proper occasion. In the discharge of this trust, I will only say, that I have, with good intentions, contributed towards the organization and administration of the government the best exertions of which a very fallible judgment was capable. Not unconscious, in the outset, of the inferiority of my qualifications, experience in my own eyes, perhaps still more in the eyes of others, has strengthened the motives to diffidence of myself; and every day the increasing weight of years admonishes me more and more, that the shade of retirement is as necessary to me as it will be welcome. Satisfied, that, if any circumstances have given peculiar value to my services, they were temporary, I have the consolation to believe, that, while choice and prudence invite me to quit the political scene, patriotism does not forbid it.

6. In looking forward to the moment, which is intended to terminate the career of my public life, my feelings do not permit me to suspend the deep acknowledgment of that debt of gratitude, which I owe to my beloved country for the many honors it has conferred upon me; still more for the steadfast confidence with which it has supported me; and for the opportunities I have thence enjoyed of manifesting my inviolable attachment, by services faithful and persevering, though in usefulness unequal to my zeal. If benefits have resulted to our country from these services, let it always be remembered to your praise, and as an instructive example in our annals, that under circumstances in which the passions, agitated in every direction, were liable to mislead, amidst appearances sometimes dubious, vicissitudes of fortune often discouraging, in situations in which not unfrequently want of success has countenanced the spirit of criticism, the constancy of your support was the essential prop of the efforts, and a guarantee of the plans by which they were effected. Profoundly penetrated with this idea, I shall carry it with me to my grave, as a strong incitement to unceasing vows that Heaven may continue to you the choicest tokens of its beneficence; that your union and brotherly affection may be perpetual; that the free constitution, which is the work of your hands, may be sacredly maintained; that its administration in every department may be stamped with wisdom and virtue; than, in fine, the happiness of the people of these States, under the auspices of liberty, may be made complete, by so careful a preservation and so prudent a use of this blessing, as will acquire to them the glory of recommending it to the applause, the affection, and adoption of every nation, which is yet a stranger to it.

7. Here, perhaps I ought to stop. But a solicitude for your welfare which cannot end but with my life, and the apprehension of danger, natural to that solicitude, urge me, on an occasion like the present, to offer to your solemn contemplation, and to recommend to your frequent review, some sentiments which are the result of much reflection, of no inconsiderable observation, and which appear to me all-important to the permanency of your felicity as a people. These will be offered to you with the more freedom, as you can only see in them the disinterested warnings of a parting friend, who can possibly have no personal motive to bias his counsel. Nor can I forget, as an encouragement to it, your indulgent reception of my sentiments on a former and not dissimilar occasion.

8. Interwoven as is the love of liberty with every ligament of your hearts, no recommendation of mine is necessary to fortify or confirm the attachment.

9. The unity of Government, which constitutes you one people, is also now dear to you. It is justly so; for it is a main pillar in the edifice of your real independence, the support of your tranquility at home, your peace abroad; of your safety; of your prosperity; of that very Liberty, which you so highly prize. But as it is easy to foresee, that, from different causes and from different quarters, much pains will be taken, many artifices employed, to weaken in your minds the conviction of this truth; as this is the point in your political fortress against which the batteries of internal and external enemies will be most constantly and actively (though often covertly and insidiously) directed, it is of infinite moment, that you should properly estimate the immense value of your national Union to your collective and individual happiness; that you should cherish a cordial, habitual, and immovable attachment to it; accustoming yourselves to think and speak of it as of the Palladium of your political safety and prosperity; watching for its preservation with jealous anxiety; discountenancing whatever may suggest even a suspicion, that it can in any event be abandoned; and indignantly frowning upon the first dawning of every attempt to alienate any portion of our country from the rest, or to enfeeble the sacred ties which now link together the various parts.

10. For this you have every inducement of sympathy and interest. Citizens, by birth or choice, of a common country, that country has a right to concentrate your affections. The name of American, which belongs to you, in your national capacity, must always exalt the just pride of Patriotism, more than any appellation derived from local discriminations. With slight shades of difference, you have the same religion, manners, habits, and political principles. You have in a common cause fought and triumphed together; the Independence and Liberty you possess are the work of joint counsels, and joint efforts, of common dangers, sufferings, and successes.

11. But these considerations, however powerfully they address themselves to your sensibility, are greatly outweighed by those, which apply more immediately to your interest. Here every portion of our country finds the most commanding motives for carefully guarding and preserving the Union of the whole.

12. The North, in an unrestrained intercourse with the South, protected by the equal laws of a common government, finds, in the productions of the latter, great additional resources of maritime and commercial enterprise and precious materials of manufacturing industry. The South, in the same intercourse, benefiting by the agency of the North, sees its agriculture grow and its commerce expand. Turning partly into its own channels the seamen of the North, it finds its particular navigation invigorated; and,

while it contributes, in different ways, to nourish and increase the general mass of the national navigation, it looks forward to the protection of a maritime strength, to which itself is unequally adapted. The East, in a like intercourse with the West, already finds, and in the progressive improvement of interior communications by land and water, will more and more find, a valuable vent for the commodities which it brings from abroad, or manufactures at home. The West derives from the East supplies requisite to its growth and comfort, and, what is perhaps of still greater consequence, it must of necessity owe the secure enjoyment of indispensable outlets for its own produc-tions to the weight, influence, and the future maritime strength of the Atlantic side of the Union, directed by an indissoluble community of interest as one nation. Any other tenure by which the West can hold this essential advantage, whether derived from its own separate strength, or from an apostate and unnatural connection with any for-eign power, must be intrinsically precarious.

13. While, then, every part of our country thus feels an immediate and particular interest in Union, all the parts combined cannot fail to find in the united mass of means and efforts greater strength, greater resource, proportionably greater security from external danger, a less frequent interruption of their peace by foreign nations; and, what is of inestimable value, they must derive from Union an exemption from those broils and wars between themselves, which so frequently afflict neighboring countries not tied together by the same governments, which their own rivalships alone would be suffi-cient to produce, but which opposite foreign alliances, attachments, and intrigues would stimulate and embitter. Hence, likewise, they will avoid the necessity of those overgrown military establishments, which, under any form of government, are inaus-picious to liberty, and which are to be regarded as particularly hostile to Republican Liberty. In this sense it is, that your Union ought to be considered as a main prop of your liberty, and that the love of the one ought to endear to you the preservation of the other.

14. These considerations speak a persuasive language to every reflecting and virtuous mind, and exhibit the continuance of the union as a primary object of Patriotic desire. Is there a doubt, whether a common government can embrace so large a sphere? Let experience solve it. To listen to mere speculation in such a case were criminal. We are authorized to hope, that a proper organization of the whole, with the auxiliary agency of governments for the respective subdivisions, will afford a happy issue to the exper-iment. It is well worth a fair and full experiment. With such powerful and obvious motives to Union, affecting all parts of our country, while experience shall not have demonstrated its impracticability, there will always be reason to distrust the patriotism of those, who in any quarter may endeavor to weaken its bands.

15. In contemplating the causes, which may disturb our Union, it occurs as matter of seri-ous concern, that any ground should have been furnished for characterizing parties by Geographical discriminations, Northern and Southern, Atlantic and Western; whence designing men may endeavor to excite a belief, that there is a real difference of local interests and views. One of the expedients of party to acquire influence, within particular districts, is to misrepresent the opinions and aims of other districts. You can-not shield yourselves too much against the jealousies and heart-burnings, which spring from these misrepresentations; they tend to render alien to each other those, who ought to be bound together by fraternal affection. The inhabitants of our

western country have lately had a useful lesson on this head; they have seen, in the negotiation by the Executive, and in the unanimous ratification by the Senate, of the treaty with Spain, and in the universal satisfaction at that event, throughout the United States, a decisive proof how unfounded were the suspicions propagated among them of a policy in the General Government and in the Atlantic States unfriendly to their interests in regard to the Mississippi; they have been witnesses to the formation of two treaties, that with Great Britain, and that with Spain, which secure to them every thing they could desire, in respect to our foreign relations, towards confirming their prosperity. Will it not be their wisdom to rely for the preservation of these advantages on the union by which they were procured? Will they not henceforth be deaf to those advisers, if such there are, who would sever them from their brethren, and connect them with aliens?

16. To the efficacy and permanency of your Union, a Government for the whole is indispensable. No alliances, however strict, between the parts can be an adequate substitute; they must inevitably experience the infractions and interruptions, which all alliances in all times have experienced. Sensible of this momentous truth, you have improved upon your first essay, by the adoption of a Constitution of Government better calculated than your former for an intimate Union, and for the efficacious management of your common concerns. This Government, the offspring of our own choice, uninfluenced and unawed, adopted upon full investigation and mature deliberation, completely free in its principles, in the distribution of its powers, uniting security with energy, and containing within itself a provision for its own amendment, has a just claim to your confidence and your support. Respect for its authority, compliance with its laws, acquiescence in its measures, are duties enjoined by the fundamental maxims of true Liberty. The basis of our political systems is the right of the people to make and to alter their Constitutions of Government. But the Constitution which at any time exists, till changed by an explicit and authentic act of the whole people, is sacredly obligatory upon all. The very idea of the power and the right of the people to establish Government presupposes the duty of every individual to obey the established Government.

17. All obstructions to the execution of the Laws, all combinations and associations, under whatever plausible character, with the real design to direct, control, counteract, or awe the regular deliberation and action of the constituted authorities, are destructive of this fundamental principle, and of fatal tendency. They serve to organize faction, to give it an artificial and extraordinary force; to put, in the place of the delegated will of the nation, the will of a party, often a small but artful and enterprising minority of the community; and, according to the alternate triumphs of different parties, to make the public administration the mirror of the ill-concerted and incongruous projects of faction, rather than the organ of consistent and wholesome plans digested by common counsels, and modified by mutual interests.

18. However combinations or associations of the above description may now and then answer popular ends, they are likely, in the course of time and things, to become potent engines, by which cunning, ambitious, and unprincipled men will be enabled to subvert the power of the people, and to usurp for themselves the reins of government; destroying afterwards the very engines, which have lifted them to unjust dominion.

19. Towards the preservation of your government, and the permanency of your present happy state, it is requisite, not only that you steadily discountenance irregular opposi-tions to its acknowledged authority, but also that you resist with care the spirit of inno-vation upon its principles, however specious the pretexts. One method of assault may be to effect, in the forms of the constitution, alterations, which will impair the energy of the system, and thus to undermine what cannot be directly overthrown. In all the changes to which you may be invited, remember that time and habit are at least as necessary to fix the true character of governments, as of other human institutions; that experience is the surest standard, by which to test the real tendency of the existing constitution of a country; that facility in changes, upon the credit of mere hypothesis and opinion, exposes to perpetual change, from the endless variety of hypothesis and opinion; and remember, especially, that, for the efficient management of our com-mon interests, in a country so extensive as ours, a government of as much vigor as is consistent with the perfect security of liberty is indispensable. Liberty itself will find in such a government, with powers properly distributed and adjusted, its surest guardian. It is, indeed, little else than a name, where the government is too feeble to withstand the enterprises of faction, to confine each member of the society within the limits pre-scribed by the laws, and to maintain all in the secure and tranquil enjoyment of the rights of person and property.

20. I have already intimated to you the danger of parties in the state, with particular ref-erence to the founding of them on geographical discriminations. Let me now take a more comprehensive view, and warn you in the most solemn manner against the baneful effects of the spirit of party, generally.

21. This spirit, unfortunately, is inseparable from our nature, having its root in the strongest passions of the human mind. It exists under different shapes in all governments, more or less stifled, controlled, or repressed; but, in those of the popular form, it is seen in its greatest rankness, and is truly their worst enemy.

22. The alternate domination of one faction over another, sharpened by the spirit of revenge, natural to party dissension, which in different ages and countries has perpe-trated the most horrid enormities, is itself a frightful despotism. But this leads at length to a more formal and permanent despotism. The disorders and miseries, which result, gradually incline the minds of men to seek security and repose in the absolute power of an individual; and sooner or later the chief of some prevailing faction, more able or more fortunate than his competitors, turns this disposition to the purposes of his own elevation, on the ruins of Public Liberty.

23. Without looking forward to an extremity of this kind, (which nevertheless ought not to be entirely out of sight,) the common and continual mischiefs of the spirit of party are sufficient to make it the interest and duty of a wise people to discourage and restrain it.

24. It serves always to distract the Public Councils, and enfeeble the Public Administra-tion. It agitates the Community with ill-founded jealousies and false alarms; kindles the animosity of one part against another, foments occasionally riot and insurrection. It opens the door to foreign influence and corruption, which find a facilitated access to the government itself through the channels of party passions. Thus the policy and the will of one country are subjected to the policy and will of another.

25. There is an opinion, that parties in free countries are useful checks upon the admin-istration of the Government, and serve to keep alive the spirit of Liberty. This within

certain limits is probably true; and in Governments of a Monarchical cast, Patriotism may look with indulgence, if not with favor, upon the spirit of party. But in those of the popular character, in Governments purely elective, it is a spirit not to be encouraged. From their natural tendency, it is certain there will always be enough of that spirit for every salutary purpose. And, there being constant danger of excess, the effort ought to be, by force of public opinion, to mitigate and assuage it. A fire not to be quenched, it demands a uniform vigilance to prevent its bursting into a flame, lest, instead of warming, it should consume.

26. It is important, likewise, that the habits of thinking in a free country should inspire caution, in those entrusted with its administration, to confine themselves within their respective constitutional spheres, avoiding in the exercise of the powers of one department to encroach upon another. The spirit of encroachment tends to consolidate the powers of all the departments in one, and thus to create, whatever the form of government, a real despotism. A just estimate of that love of power, and proneness to abuse it, which predominates in the human heart, is sufficient to satisfy us of the truth of this position. The necessity of reciprocal checks in the exercise of political power, by dividing and distributing it into different depositories, and constituting each the Guardian of the Public Weal against invasions by the others, has been evinced by experiments ancient and modern; some of them in our country and under our own eyes. To preserve them must be as necessary as to institute them. If, in the opinion of the people, the distribution or modification of the constitutional powers be in any particular wrong, let it be corrected by an amendment in the way, which the constitution designates. But let there be no change by usurpation; for, though this, in one instance, may be the instrument of good, it is the customary weapon by which free governments are destroyed. The precedent must always greatly overbalance in permanent evil any partial or transient benefit, which the use can at any time yield.

27. Of all the dispositions and habits, which lead to political prosperity, Religion and Morality are indispensable supports. In vain would that man claim the tribute of Patriotism, who should labor to subvert these great pillars of human happiness, these firmest props of the duties of Men and Citizens. The mere Politician, equally with the pious man, ought to respect and to cherish them. A volume could not trace all their connections with private and public felicity. Let it simply be asked, Where is the security for property, for reputation, for life, if the sense of religious obligation desert the oaths, which are the instruments of investigation in Courts of Justice? And let us with caution indulge the supposition, that morality can be maintained without religion. Whatever may be conceded to the influence of refined education on minds of peculiar structure, reason and experience both forbid us to expect, that national morality can prevail in exclusion of religious principle.

28. It is substantially true, that virtue or morality is a necessary spring of popular government. The rule, indeed, extends with more or less force to every species of free government. Who, that is a sincere friend to it, can look with indifference upon attempts to shake the foundation of the fabric?

29. Promote, then, as an object of primary importance, institutions for the general diffusion of knowledge. In proportion as the structure of a government gives force to public opinion, it is essential that public opinion should be enlightened.

30. As a very important source of strength and security, cherish public credit. One method of preserving it is, to use it as sparingly as possible; avoiding occasions of expense by cultivating peace, but remembering also that timely disbursements to prepare for danger frequently prevent much greater disbursements to repel it; avoiding likewise the accumulation of debt, not only by shunning occasions of expense, but by vigorous exertions in time of peace to discharge the debts, which unavoidable wars may have occasioned, not ungenerously throwing upon posterity the burden, which we ourselves ought to bear. The execution of these maxims belongs to your representatives, but it is necessary that public opinion should cooperate. To facilitate to them the performance of their duty, it is essential that you should practically bear in mind, that towards the payment of debts there must be Revenue; that to have Revenue there must be taxes; that no taxes can be devised, which are not more or less inconvenient and unpleasant; that the intrinsic embarrassment, inseparable from the selection of the proper objects (which is always a choice of difficulties), ought to be a decisive motive for a candid construction of the conduct of the government in making it, and for a spirit of acquiescence in the measures for obtaining revenue, which the public exigencies may at any time dictate.

31. Observe good faith and justice towards all Nations; cultivate peace and harmony with all. Religion and Morality enjoin this conduct; and can it be, that good policy does not equally enjoin it? It will be worthy of a free, enlightened, and, at no distant period, a great Nation, to give to mankind the magnanimous and too novel example of a people always guided by an exalted justice and benevolence. Who can doubt, that, in the course of time and things, the fruits of such a plan would richly repay any temporary advantages, which might be lost by a steady adherence to it ? Can it be, that Providence has not connected the permanent felicity of a Nation with its Virtue? The experiment, at least, is recommended by every sentiment which ennobles human nature. Alas! is it rendered impossible by its vices?

32. In the execution of such a plan, nothing is more essential, than that permanent, inveterate antipathies against particular Nations, and passionate attachments for others, should be excluded; and that, in place of them, just and amicable feelings towards all should be cultivated. The Nation, which indulges towards another an habitual hatred, or an habitual fondness, is in some degree a slave. It is a slave to its animosity or to its affection, either of which is sufficient to lead it astray from its duty and its interest. Antipathy in one nation against another disposes each more readily to offer insult and injury, to lay hold of slight causes of umbrage, and to be haughty and intractable, when accidental or trifling occasions of dispute occur. Hence frequent collisions, obstinate, envenomed, and bloody contests. The Nation, prompted by ill-will and resentment, sometimes impels to war the Government, contrary to the best calculations of policy. The Government sometimes participates in the national propensity, and adopts through passion what reason would reject; at other times, it makes the animosity of the nation subservient to projects of hostility instigated by pride, ambition, and other sinister and pernicious motives. The peace often, sometimes perhaps the liberty, of Nations has been the victim.

33. So likewise, a passionate attachment of one Nation for another produces a variety of evils. Sympathy for the favorite Nation, facilitating the illusion of an imaginary common interest, in cases where no real common interest exists, and infusing into one

the enmities of the other, betrays the former into a participation in the quarrels and wars of the latter, without adequate inducement or justification. It leads also to concessions to the favorite Nation of privileges denied to others, which is apt doubly to injure the Nation making the concessions; by unnecessarily parting with what ought to have been retained; and by exciting jealousy, ill-will, and a disposition to retaliate, in the parties from whom equal privileges are withheld. And it gives to ambitious, corrupted, or deluded citizens, (who devote themselves to the favorite nation,) facility to betray or sacrifice the interests of their own country, without odium, sometimes even with popularity; gilding, with the appearances of a virtuous sense of obligation, a commendable deference for public opinion, or a laudable zeal for public good, the base or foolish compliances of ambition, corruption, or infatuation.

34. As avenues to foreign influence in innumerable ways, such attachments are particularly alarming to the truly enlightened and independent Patriot. How many opportunities do they afford to tamper with domestic factions, to practice the arts of seduction, to mislead public opinion, to influence or awe the Public Councils! Such an attachment of a small or weak, towards a great and powerful nation, dooms the former to be the satellite of the latter.

35. Against the insidious wiles of foreign influence (I conjure you to believe me, fellow-citizens,) the jealousy of a free people ought to be constantly awake; since history and experience prove, that foreign influence is one of the most baneful foes of Republican Government. But that jealousy, to be useful, must be impartial; else it becomes the instrument of the very influence to be avoided, instead of a defense against it. Excessive partiality for one foreign nation, and excessive dislike of another, cause those whom they actuate to see danger only on one side, and serve to veil and even second the arts of influence on the other. Real patriots, who may resist the intrigues of the favorite, are liable to become suspected and odious; while its tools and dupes usurp the applause and confidence of the people, to surrender their interests.

36. The great rule of conduct for us, in regard to foreign nations, is, in extending our commercial relations, to have with them as little political connection as possible. So far as we have already formed engagements, let them be fulfilled with perfect good faith. Here let us stop.

37. Europe has a set of primary interests, which to us have none, or a very remote relation. Hence she must be engaged in frequent controversies, the causes of which are essentially foreign to our concerns. Hence, therefore, it must be unwise in us to implicate ourselves, by artificial ties, in the ordinary vicissitudes of her politics, or the ordinary combinations and collisions of her friendships or enmities.

38. Our detached and distant situation invites and enables us to pursue a different course. If we remain one people, under an efficient government, the period is not far off, when we may defy material injury from external annoyance; when we may take such an attitude as will cause the neutrality, we may at any time resolve upon, to be scrupulously respected; when belligerent nations, under the impossibility of making acquisitions upon us, will not lightly hazard the giving us provocation; when we may choose peace or war, as our interest, guided by justice, shall counsel.

39. Why forego the advantages of so peculiar a situation? Why quit our own to stand upon foreign ground? Why, by interweaving our destiny with that of any part of Europe,

entangle our peace and prosperity in the toils of European ambition, rivalship, interest, humor, or caprice?

40. It is our true policy to steer clear of permanent alliances with any portion of the foreign world; so far, I mean, as we are now at liberty to do it; for let me not be understood as capable of patronizing infidelity to existing engagements. I hold the maxim no less applicable to public than to private affairs, that honesty is always the best policy. I repeat it, therefore, let those engagements be observed in their genuine sense. But, in my opinion, it is unnecessary and would be unwise to extend them.

41. Taking care always to keep ourselves, by suitable establishments, on a respectable defensive posture, we may safely trust to temporary alliances for extraordinary emergencies.

42. Harmony, liberal intercourse with all nations, are recommended by policy, humanity, and interest. But even our commercial policy should hold an equal and impartial hand; neither seeking nor granting exclusive favors or preferences; consulting the natural course of things; diffusing and diversifying by gentle means the streams of commerce, but forcing nothing; establishing, with powers so disposed, in order to give trade a stable course, to define the rights of our merchants, and to enable the government to support them, conventional rules of intercourse, the best that present circumstances and mutual opinion will permit, but temporary, and liable to be from time to time abandoned or varied, as experience and circumstances shall dictate; constantly keeping in view, that it is folly in one nation to look for disinterested favors from another; that it must pay with a portion of its independence for whatever it may accept under that character; that, by such acceptance, it may place itself in the condition of having given equivalents for nominal favors, and yet of being reproached with ingratitude for not giving more. There can be no greater error than to expect or calculate upon real favors from nation to nation. It is an illusion, which experience must cure, which a just pride ought to discard.

43. In offering to you, my countrymen, these counsels of an old and affectionate friend, I dare not hope they will make the strong and lasting impression I could wish; that they will control the usual current of the passions, or prevent our nation from running the course, which has hitherto marked the destiny of nations. But, if I may even flatter myself, that they may be productive of some partial benefit, some occasional good; that they may now and then recur to moderate the fury of party spirit, to warn against the mischiefs of foreign intrigue, to guard against the impostures of pretended patriotism; this hope will be a full recompense for the solicitude for your welfare, by which they have been dictated.

44. How far in the discharge of my official duties, I have been guided by the principles which have been delineated, the public records and other evidences of my conduct must witness to you and to the world. To myself, the assurance of my own conscience is, that I have at least believed myself to be guided by them.

45. In relation to the still subsisting war in Europe, my Proclamation of the 22d of April 1793, is the index to my Plan. Sanctioned by your approving voice, and by that of your Representatives in both Houses of Congress, the spirit of that measure has continually governed me, uninfluenced by any attempts to deter or divert me from it.

46. After deliberate examination, with the aid of the best lights I could obtain, I was well satisfied that our country, under all the circumstances of the case, had a right to take, and

was bound in duty and interest to take, a neutral position. Having taken it, I determined, as far as should depend upon me, to maintain it, with moderation, perseverance, and firmness.

47. The considerations, which respect the right to hold this conduct, it is not necessary on this occasion to detail. I will only observe, that, according to my understanding of the matter, that right, so far from being denied by any of the Belligerent Powers, has been virtually admitted by all.

48. The duty of holding a neutral conduct may be inferred, without any thing more, from the obligation which justice and humanity impose on every nation, in cases in which it is free to act, to maintain inviolate the relations of peace and amity towards other nations.

49. The inducements of interest for observing that conduct will best be referred to your own reflections and experience. With me, a predominant motive has been to endeavor to gain time to our country to settle and mature its yet recent institutions, and to progress without interruption to that degree of strength and consistency, which is necessary to give it, humanly speaking, the command of its own fortunes.

50. Though, in reviewing the incidents of my administration, I am unconscious of intentional error, I am nevertheless too sensible of my defects not to think it probable that I may have committed many errors. Whatever they may be, I fervently beseech the Almighty to avert or mitigate the evils to which they may tend. I shall also carry with me the hope, that my Country will never cease to view them with indulgence; and that, after forty-five years of my life dedicated to its service with an upright zeal, the faults of incompetent abilities will be consigned to oblivion, as myself must soon be to the mansions of rest.

51. Relying on its kindness in this as in other things, and actuated by that fervent love towards it, which is so natural to a man, who views it in the native soil of himself and his progenitors for several generations; I anticipate with pleasing expectation that retreat, in which I promise myself to realize, without alloy, the sweet enjoyment of partaking, in the midst of my fellow-citizens, the benign influence of good laws under a free government, the ever favorite object of my heart, and the happy reward, as I trust, of our mutual cares, labors, and dangers.

Elizabeth Cady Stanton
Declaration of Sentiments—The Seneca Falls Convention, 1848

*Abolitionist and mother of the **Suffragists Movement, Elizabeth Cady Stanton** modeled her Declaration of Sentiments after the **Declaration of Independence** for the occasion of the first women's rights convention in America, held in Seneca Falls, New York, which marked the beginning of the struggle for the vote for women in America. Along with **Lucretia Mott** (another abolitionist and proponent of women's rights), Cady Stanton organized her convention for women after being denied admittance to an antislavery convention in London. The early suffragist movement was closely tied to **abolition,** and **Frederick Douglass** was one of the attendees in Seneca Falls.*

1. Declaration of Sentiments

When, in the course of human events, it becomes necessary for one portion of the family of man to assume among the people of the earth a position different from that which they have hitherto occupied, but one to which the laws of nature and of nature's God entitle them, a decent respect to the opinions of mankind requires that they should declare the causes that impel them to such a course.

We hold these truths to be self-evident: that all men and women are created equal; that they are endowed by their Creator with certain inalienable rights; that among these are life, liberty, and the pursuit of happiness; that to secure these rights governments are instituted, deriving their just powers from the consent of the governed. Whenever any form of government becomes destructive of these ends, it is the right of those who suffer from it to refuse allegiance to it, and to insist upon the institution of a new government, laying its foundation on such principles, and organizing its powers in such form, as to them shall seem most likely to effect their safety and happiness. Prudence, indeed, will dictate that governments long established should not be changed for light and transient causes; and accordingly all experience hath shown that mankind are more disposed to suffer. While evils are sufferable, than to right themselves by abolishing the forms to which they are accustomed. But when a long train of abuses and usurpations, pursuing invariably the same object, evinces a design to reduce them under absolute despotism, it is their duty to throw off such government, and to provide new guards for their future security. Such has been the patient sufferance of the women under this government, and such is now the necessity which constrains them to demand the equal station to which they are entitled. The history of mankind is a history of repeated injuries and usurpations on the part of man toward woman, having in direct object the establishment of an absolute tyranny over her. To prove this, let facts be submitted to a candid world.

- He has never permitted her to exercise her inalienable right to the elective franchise.
- He has compelled her to submit to laws, in the formation of which she had no voice.
- He has withheld from her rights which are given to the most ignorant and degraded men—both natives and foreigners.
- Having deprived her of this first right of a citizen, the elective franchise, thereby leaving her without representation in the halls of legislation, he has oppressed her on all sides.
- He has made her, if married, in the eye of the law, civilly dead. He has taken from her all right in property, even to the wages she earns.
- He has made her, morally an irresponsible being, as she can commit many crimes with impunity, provided they be done in the presence of her husband.
- In the covenant of marriage, she is compelled to promise obedience to her husband, he becoming, to all intents and purposes, her master, the law giving him power to deprive her of her liberty, and to administer chastisement.
- He has so framed the laws of divorce, as to what shall be the proper causes, and in case of separation, to whom the guardianship of the children shall be given, as to be wholly regardless of the happiness of women, the law, in all cases, going upon a false supposition of the supremacy of man, and giving all power into his hands.
- After depriving her of all rights as a married woman, if single, and the owner of property, he has taxed her to support a government which recognizes her only when her property can be made profitable to it.

- He has monopolized nearly all the profitable employments, and from those she is permitted to follow, she receives but a scanty remuneration. He closes against her all the avenues to wealth and distinction which he considers most honorable to himself. As a teacher of theology, medicine, or law, she is not known.
- He has denied her the facilities for obtaining a thorough education, all colleges being closed against her.
- He allows her in Church, as well as State, but a subordinate position, claiming Apostolic authority for her exclusion from the ministry, and, with some exceptions, from any public participation in the affairs of the Church.
- He has created a false public sentiment by giving to the world a different code of morals for men and women, by which moral delinquencies which exclude women from society, are not only tolerated, but deemed of little account in man.
- He has usurped the prerogative of Jehovah himself, claiming it as his right to assign for her a sphere of action, when that belongs to her conscience and to her God.
- He has endeavored, in every way that he could, to destroy her confidence in her own powers, to lessen her self-respect and to make her willing to lead a dependent and abject life.

Now, in view of this entire disfranchisement of one-half the people of this country, their social and religious degradation, in view of the unjust laws above mentioned, and because women do feel themselves aggrieved, oppressed, and fraudulently deprived of their most sacred rights, we insist that they have immediate admission to all the rights and privileges which belong to them as citizens of the United States.

5   In entering upon the great work before us, we anticipate no small amount of misconception, misrepresentation, and ridicule; but we shall use every instrumentality within our power to effect our object. We shall employ agents, circulate tracts, petition the State and National legislatures, and endeavor to enlist the pulpit and the press in our behalf. We hope this Convention will be followed by a series of Conventions embracing every part of the country.

2. Resolutions

WHEREAS, the great precept of nature is conceded to be, that "man shall pursue his own true and substantial happiness." Blackstone in his Commentaries remarks, that this law of Nature being coeval with mankind, and dictated by God himself, is of course superior in obligation to any other. It is binding over all the globe, in all countries and at all times; no human laws are of any validity if contrary to this. And such of them as are valid, derive all their force. And all their validity, and all their authority, mediately and immediately, from this original; therefore,

Resolved,

That such laws as conflict, in any way with the true and substantial happiness of woman, are contrary to the great precept of nature and of no validity, for this is superior in obligation to any other.

Resolved,

That all laws which prevent woman from occupying such a station in society as her conscience shall dictate, or which place her in a position inferior to that of man, are contrary to the great precept of nature, and therefore of no force or authority.

Resolved,

That woman is man's equal, was intended to be so by the Creator, and the highest good of the race demands that she should be recognized as such.

Resolved,

That the women of this country ought to be enlightened in regard to the laws under   10
which they live, that they may no longer publish their degradation by declaring themselves satisfied with their present position, nor their ignorance, by asserting that they have all the rights they want.

Resolved,

That inasmuch as man, while claiming for himself intellectual superiority, does accord to woman moral superiority. It is pre-eminently his duty to encourage her to speak and teach. As she has an opportunity, in all religious assemblies.

Resolved,

That the same amount of virtue, delicacy, and refinement of behavior that is required of woman in the social state, should also be required of man, and the same transgressions should be visited with equal severity on both man and woman.

Resolved,

That the objection of indelicacy and impropriety, which is so often brought against woman when she addresses a public audience, comes with a very ill-grace from those who encourage, by their attendance, her appearance on the stage, in the concert. Or in feats of the circus.

Resolved,

That woman has too long rested satisfied in the circumscribed limits which corrupt customs and a perverted application of the Scriptures have marked out for her, and that it is time she should move in the enlarged sphere which her great Creator has assigned her.

Resolved,

That it is the duty of the women of this country to secure to themselves their sacred   15
right to the elective franchise.

Resolved,

That the equality of human rights results necessarily from the fact of the identity of the race in capabilities and responsibilities.

Resolved, therefore.

That, being invested by the creator with the same capabilities, and the same consciousness of responsibility for their exercise, it is demonstrably the right and duty of woman, equally with man, to promote every righteous cause by every righteous means; and especially in regard to the great subjects of morals and religion, it is self-evidently her right to participate with her brother in teaching them, both in private and in public, by writing and by speaking. By any instrumentalities proper to be used, and in any assemblies proper to be held; and this being a self evident truth growing out of the divinely implanted principles of human nature, any custom or authority adverse to it, whether modern or wearing the hoary sanction of antiquity, is to be regarded as a self-evident falsehood, and at war with mankind.

Resolved,

That the speedy success of our cause depends upon the zealous and untiring efforts of both men and women, for the overthrow of the monopoly of the pulpit, and for the securing to women an equal participation with men in the various trades, professions, and commerce.

The "Ain't I a Woman?" Speech

Sojourner Truth

Sojourner Truth (1797–1883).

Sojourner Truth gave her famous "Ain't I a Woman?" speech at the 1851 Women's Rights Convention in Akron, Ohio. (The women's rights movement grew in large part out of the antislavery movement.) No formal record of the speech exists, but Frances Gage, an abolitionist and president of the convention, recounted Truth's words. There is debate about the accuracy because Gage did not record the account until 1863, and her record differs somewhat from newspaper accounts of 1851. However, it is Gage's report that endures, and it is clear that, whatever the exact words, "Ain't I a Woman?" made a great impact at the convention and has become a classic expression of women's rights.

The Classic Report

Several ministers attended the second day of the Woman's Rights Convention, and were not shy in voicing their opinion of man's superiority over women. One claimed "superior intellect", one spoke of the "manhood of Christ," and still another referred to the "sin of our first mother."

Suddenly, Sojourner Truth rose from her seat in the corner of the church.

"For God's sake, Mrs. Gage, *don't* let her speak!" half a dozen women whispered loudly, fearing that their cause would be mixed up with Abolition.

Sojourner walked to the podium and slowly took off her sunbonnet. Her six-foot frame towered over the audience. She began to speak in her deep, resonant voice: "Well, children, where there is so much racket, there must be something out of kilter, I think between the Negroes of the South and the women of the North—all talking about rights— the white men will be in a fix pretty soon. But what's all this talking about?"

Sojourner pointed to one of the ministers. "That man over there says that women   5
need to be helped into carriages, and lifted over ditches, and to have the best place every- where. Nobody helps *me* any best place. *And ain't I a woman?*"

Sojourner raised herself to her full height. "Look at me! Look at my arm." She bared her right arm and flexed her powerful muscles. "I have plowed, I have planted and I have gathered into barns. And no man could head me. *And ain't I a woman?*"

"I could work as much, and eat as much as man—when I could get it—and bear the lash as well! *And ain't I a woman?* I have borne children and seen most of them sold into slavery, and when I cried out with a mother's grief, none but Jesus heard me. *And ain't I a woman?*"

The women in the audience began to cheer wildly.

She pointed to another minister. "He talks about this thing in the head. What's that they call it?"

"Intellect," whispered a woman nearby.   10

"That's it, honey. What's intellect got to do with women's rights or black folks' rights? If my cup won't hold but a pint and yours holds a quart, wouldn't you be mean not to let me have my little half-measure full?"

"That little man in black there! He says women can't have as much rights as men. 'Cause Christ wasn't a woman." She stood with outstretched arms and eyes of fire. "Where did your Christ come from?"

"*Where did your Christ come from?*" she thundered again. "From God and a Woman! Man had nothing to do with him!"

The entire church now roared with deafening applause.

"If the first woman God ever made was strong enough to turn the world upside down   15
all alone, these women together ought to be able to turn it back and get it right-side up again. And now that they are asking to do it the men better let them."

Or . . . .

Well, children, where there is so much racket there must be something out of kilter. I think that 'twixt the negroes of the South and the women at the North, all talking about rights, the white men will be in a fix pretty soon. But what's all this here talking about?

That man over there says that women need to be helped into carriages, and lifted over ditches, and to have the best place everywhere. Nobody ever helps me into carriages, or over mud-puddles, or gives me any best place! And ain't I a woman? Look at me! Look at my arm! I have ploughed and planted, and gathered into barns, and no man could head me! And ain't I a woman? I could work as much and eat as much as a man—when I could get it—and bear the lash as well! And ain't I a woman? I have borne thirteen children, and seen most all sold off to slavery, and when I cried out with my mother's grief, none but Jesus heard me! And ain't I a woman?

Then they talk about this thing in the head; what's this they call it? [member of audience whispers, "intellect"] That's it, honey. What's that got to do with women's rights or negroes' rights? If my cup won't hold but a pint, and yours holds a quart, wouldn't you be mean not to let me have my little half measure full?

Then that little man in black there, he says women can't have as much rights as men, 'cause Christ wasn't a woman! Where did your Christ come from? Where did your Christ come from? From God and a woman! Man had nothing to do with Him.

20   If the first woman God ever made was strong enough to turn the world upside down all alone, these women together ought to be able to turn it back, and get it right side up again! And now they is asking to do it, the men better let them.

Obliged to you for hearing me, and now old Sojourner ain't got nothing more to say.

Or . . . .

A Contemporaneous Account

From the *Anti-Slavery Bugle,* Salem, Ohio, June 21, 1851.

One of the most unique and interesting speeches of the Convention was made by Sojourner Truth, an emancipated slave. It is impossible to transfer it to paper, or convey any adequate idea of the effect it produced upon the audience. Those only can appreciate it who saw her powerful form, her whole-souled, earnest gesture, and listened to her strong and truthful tones. She came forward to the platform and addressing the President (Frances Gage) said with great simplicity:

May I say a few words? Receiving an affirmative answer, she proceeded; I want to say a few words about this matter. I am for woman's rights. I have as much muscle as any man, and can do as much work as any man. I have plowed and reaped and husked and chopped and mowed, and can any man do more than that? I have heard much about the sexes being equal; I can carry as much as any man, and can eat as much too, if I can get it. I am as strong as any man that is now.

As for intellect, all I can say is, if woman have a pint and a man a quart—why can't she have her little pint full? You need not be afraid to give us our rights for fear we will take too much—for we won't take more than our pint will hold.

25   The poor men seem to be all in confusion and don't know what to do. Why children, if you have woman's rights give it to her and you will feel better. You will have your own rights, and there won't be so much trouble.

Frederick Douglass

The Meaning of July Fourth for the Negro, July 5, 1852

One of the leaders of the abolitionist movement, **Frederick Douglass** *was the most well-known* **lecturer on the evils of slavery** *in the decade before the Civil War. He served as an advisor to President Abraham Lincoln during the war and fought for the adoption of Amendment 15 to the Constitution, the right to vote for the black man. At an* **event commemorating the signing of the Declaration of Independence,** *held in the Corinthian Hall of Rochester, New York, Douglass unleashed some of his most provocative rhetoric as he asked the crowd: "What, to the American slave, is your 4th of July?" Douglass points out the* **hypocrisy of a nation that celebrates liberty when a large number of its**

Frederick Douglass (1818–1895).

people are enslaved*. Some historians have called this rebuke the most powerful and moving of Douglass's oratory.*

Fellow Citizens, I am not wanting in respect for the fathers of this republic. The signers of the Declaration of Independence were brave men. They were great men, too—great enough to give frame to a great age. It does not often happen to a nation to raise, at one time, such a number of truly great men. The point from which I am compelled to view them is not, certainly, the most favorable; and yet I cannot contemplate their great deeds with less than admiration. They were statesmen, patriots and heroes, and for the good they did, and the principles they contended for, I will unite with you to honor their memory . . . .

. . . Fellow-citizens, pardon me, allow me to ask, why am I called upon to speak here to-day? What have I, or those I represent, to do with your national independence? Are the great principles of political freedom and of natural justice, embodied in that Declaration of Independence, extended to us? and am I, therefore, called upon to bring our humble offering to the national altar, and to confess the benefits and express devout gratitude for the blessings resulting from your independence to us?

Would to God, both for your sakes and ours that an affirmative answer could be truthfully returned to these questions! Then would my task be light, and my burden easy and delightful. For who is there so cold, that a nation's sympathy could not warm him? Who so obdurate and dead to the claims of gratitude that would not thankfully acknowledge such priceless benefits? Who so stolid and selfish, that would not give his voice to swell the hallelujahs of a nation's jubilee, when the chains of servitude had been torn from his limbs? I am not that man. In a case like that, the dumb might eloquently speak, and the "lame man leap as an hart."

But such is not the state of the case. I say it with a sad sense of the disparity between us. I am not included within the pale of glorious anniversary! Your high independence only reveals the immeasurable distance between us. The blessings in which you, this day, rejoice, are not enjoyed in common. The rich inheritance of justice, liberty, prosperity and independence, bequeathed by your fathers, is shared by you, not by me. The sunlight that brought light and healing to you, has brought stripes and death to me. This Fourth of July is yours, not mine. You may rejoice, I must mourn. To drag a man in fetters into the grand illuminated temple of liberty, and call upon him to join you in joyous anthems, were inhuman mockery and sacrilegious irony. Do you mean, citizens, to mock me, by asking me to speak today? If so, there is a parallel to your conduct. And let me warn you that it is dangerous to copy the example of a nation whose crimes, towering up to heaven, were thrown down by the breath of the Almighty, burying that nation in irrevocable ruin! I can today take up the plaintive lament of a peeled and woe-smitten people!

5   "By the rivers of Babylon, there we sat down. Yea! we wept when we remembered Zion. We hanged our harps upon the willows in the midst thereof. For there, they that carried us away captive, required of us a song; and they who wasted us required of us mirth, saying, Sing us one of the songs of Zion. How can we sing the Lord's song in a strange land? If I forget thee, O Jerusalem, let my right hand forget her cunning. If I do not remember thee, let my tongue cleave to the roof of my mouth."

Fellow-citizens, above your national, tumultuous joy, I hear the mournful wail of millions! whose chains, heavy and grievous yesterday, are, today, rendered more intolerable by the jubilee shouts that reach them. If I do forget, if I do not faithfully remember those bleeding children of sorrow this day, "may my right hand forget her cunning, and may my tongue cleave to the roof of my mouth!" To forget them, to pass lightly over their wrongs, and to chime in with the popular theme, would be treason most scandalous and shocking, and would make me a reproach before God and the world. My subject, then, fellow-citizens, is American slavery. I shall see this day and its popular characteristics from the slave's point of view. Standing there identified with the American bondman, making his wrongs mine, I do not hesitate to declare, with all my soul, that the character and conduct of this nation never looked blacker to me than on this 4th of July! Whether we turn to the declarations of the past, or to the professions of the present, the conduct of the nation seems equally hideous and revolting. America is false to the past, false to the present, and solemnly binds herself to be false to the future. Standing with God and the crushed and bleeding slave on this occasion, I will, in the name of humanity which is outraged, in the name of liberty which is fettered, in the name of the constitution and the Bible which are disregarded and trampled upon, dare to call in question and to denounce, with all the emphasis I can command, everything that serves to perpetuate slavery—the great sin and shame of America! "I will not equivocate; I will not excuse"; I will use the severest language I can command; and yet not one word shall escape me that any man, whose judgment is not blinded by prejudice, or who is not at heart a slaveholder, shall not confess to be right and just.

But I fancy I hear some one of my audience say, "It is just in this circumstance that you and your brother abolitionists fail to make a favorable impression on the public mind. Would you argue more, and denounce less; would you persuade more, and rebuke less; your cause would be much more likely to succeed." But, I submit, where all is plain there is nothing to be argued. What point in the anti-slavery creed would you have me argue? On what branch of the subject do the people of this country need light? Must I undertake to prove that the slave is a man? That point is conceded already. Nobody doubts it. The slaveholders themselves acknowledge it in the enactment of laws for their government. They acknowledge it when they punish disobedience on the part of the slave. There are seventy-two crimes in the State of Virginia which, if committed by a black man (no matter how ignorant he be), subject him to the punishment of death; while only two of the same crimes will subject a white man to the like punishment. What is this but the acknowledgment that the slave is a moral, intellectual, and responsible being? The manhood of the slave is conceded. It is admitted in the fact that Southern statute books are covered with enactments forbidding, under severe fines and penalties, the teaching of the slave to read or to write. When you can point to any such laws in reference to the beasts of the field, then I may consent to argue the manhood of the slave. When the dogs in your streets, when the fowls of the air, when the cattle on your hills, when the fish of the sea, and the reptiles that crawl, shall be unable to distinguish the slave from a brute, then will I argue with you that the slave is a man!

For the present, it is enough to affirm the equal manhood of the Negro race. Is it not astonishing that, while we are ploughing, planting, and reaping, using all kinds of mechanical tools, erecting houses, constructing bridges, building ships, working in metals of brass, iron, copper, silver and gold; that, while we are reading, writing and ciphering, acting as clerks, merchants and secretaries, having among us lawyers, doctors, ministers, poets, authors, editors, orators and teachers; that, while we are engaged in all manner of enterprises common to other men, digging gold in California, capturing the whale in the Pacific, feeding sheep and cattle on the hill-side, living, moving, acting, thinking, planning, living in families as husbands, wives and children, and, above all, confessing and worshipping the Christian's God, and looking hopefully for life and immortality beyond the grave, we are called upon to prove that we are men!

Would you have me argue that man is entitled to liberty? that he is the rightful owner of his own body? You have already declared it. Must I argue the wrongfulness of slavery? Is that a question for Republicans? Is it to be settled by the rules of logic and argumentation, as a matter beset with great difficulty, involving a doubtful application of the principle of justice, hard to be understood? How should I look to-day, in the presence of Americans, dividing, and subdividing a discourse, to show that men have a natural right to freedom? speaking of it relatively and positively, negatively and affirmatively. To do so, would be to make myself ridiculous, and to offer an insult to your understanding. There is not a man beneath the canopy of heaven that does not know that slavery is wrong for him.

What, am I to argue that it is wrong to make men brutes, to rob them of their liberty, to work them without wages, to keep them ignorant of their relations to their fellow men, to beat them with sticks, to flay their flesh with the lash, to load their limbs with irons, to hunt them with dogs, to sell them at auction, to sunder their families, to knock out their teeth, to burn their flesh, to starve them into obedience and submission to their masters? Must I argue that a system thus marked with blood, and stained with pollution, is wrong? No! I will not. I have better employment for my time and strength than such arguments would imply.

What, then, remains to be argued? Is it that slavery is not divine; that God did not establish it; that our doctors of divinity are mistaken? There is blasphemy in the thought. That which is inhuman, cannot be divine! Who can reason on such a proposition? They that can, may; I cannot. The time for such argument is passed.

At a time like this, scorching irony, not convincing argument, is needed. O! had I the ability, and could reach the nation's ear, I would, to-day, pour out a fiery stream of biting ridicule, blasting reproach, withering sarcasm, and stern rebuke. For it is not light that is needed, but fire; it is not the gentle shower, but thunder. We need the storm, the whirlwind, and the earthquake. The feeling of the nation must be quickened; the conscience of the nation must be roused; the propriety of the nation must be startled; the hypocrisy of the nation must be exposed; and its crimes against God and man must be proclaimed and denounced.

What, to the American slave, is your 4th of July? I answer; a day that reveals to him, more than all other days in the year, the gross injustice and cruelty to which he is the constant victim. To him, your celebration is a sham; your boasted liberty, an unholy license; your national greatness, swelling vanity; your sounds of rejoicing are empty and heartless; your denunciation of tyrants, brass fronted impudence; your shouts of liberty and equality, hollow mockery; your prayers and hymns, your sermons and thanksgivings, with all your religious parade and solemnity, are, to Him, mere bombast, fraud, deception, impiety, and hypocrisy—a thin veil to cover up crimes which would disgrace a nation of savages. There is not a nation on the earth guilty of practices more shocking and bloody than are the people of the United States, at this very hour.

Go where you may, search where you will, roam through all the monarchies and despotisms of the Old World, travel through South America, search out every abuse, and when you have found the last, lay your facts by the side of the everyday practices of this nation, and you will say with me, that, for revolting barbarity and shameless hypocrisy, America reigns without a rival . . . .

15 . . . Allow me to say, in conclusion, notwithstanding the dark picture I have this day presented, of the state of the nation, I do not despair of this country. There are forces in operation which must inevitably work the downfall of slavery. "The arm of the Lord is not shortened," and the doom of slavery is certain. I, therefore, leave off where I began, with hope. While drawing encouragement from "the Declaration of Independence," the great principles it contains, and the genius of American Institutions, my spirit is also cheered by the obvious tendencies of the age. Nations do not now stand in the same relation to each other that they did ages ago. No nation can now shut itself up from the surrounding world and trot round in the same old path of its fathers without interference. The time was when such could be done. Long established customs of hurtful character could formerly fence themselves in, and do their evil work with social impunity. Knowledge was then confined and enjoyed by the privileged few, and the multitude walked on in mental darkness. But a change has now come over the affairs of mankind. Walled cities and empires have become unfashionable. The arm of commerce has borne away the gates of the strong city. Intelligence is penetrating the darkest corners of the globe. It makes its pathway over and under the sea, as well as on the earth. Wind, steam, and lightning are its chartered agents. Oceans no longer divide, but link nations together. From Boston to London is now a holiday excursion. Space is comparatively annihilated.—Thoughts expressed on one side of the Atlantic are distinctly heard on the other.

The far off and almost fabulous Pacific rolls in grandeur at our feet. The Celestial Empire, the mystery of ages, is being solved. The fiat of the Almighty, "Let there be Light," has not yet spent its force. No abuse, no outrage whether in taste, sport or avarice, can now hide itself from the all-pervading light. The iron shoe, and crippled foot of China must be seen in contrast with nature. Africa must rise and put on her yet unwoven garment. "Ethiopia shall stretch out her hand unto God." In the fervent aspirations of William Lloyd Garrison, I say, and let every heart join in saying it:

God speed the year of jubilee
The wide world o'er!
When from their galling chains set free,
Th' oppress'd shall vilely bend the knee,
And wear the yoke of tyranny
Like brutes no more.
That year will come, and freedom's reign,
To man his plundered rights again
    Restore.

God speed the day when human blood
Shall cease to flow!
In every clime be understood,
The claims of human brotherhood,
And each return for evil, good,
Not blow for blow;
That day will come all feuds to end,
And change into a faithful friend
Each foe.

God speed the hour, the glorious hour,
When none on earth
Shall exercise a lordly power,
Nor in a tyrant's presence cower;
But to all manhood's stature tower,
By equal birth!
That hour will come, to each, to all,
And from his Prison-house, to thrall
Go forth.

Until that year, day, hour, arrive,   20
With head, and heart, and hand I'll strive,
To break the rod, and rend the gyve,
The spoiler of his prey deprive—
So witness Heaven!
And never from my chosen post,
Whate'er the peril or the cost,
Be driven.

Abraham Lincoln

The Gettysburg Address, November 19, 1863

*Brief yet eloquent, this famous speech was given by **President Abraham Lincoln** on November 19, 1863, at the dedication of Gettysburg National Cemetery in Gettysburg, Pennsylvania, to commemorate the crucial Union victory and memorialize the dead. He was not the featured speaker, but followed a two-hour speech by Edward Everett, a popular speaker of the day whose words were highly praised while Lincoln's were hardly commented upon at the time. The **Battle of Gettysburg,** fought in July 1863, is thought to be the turning point in the Civil War, after which the **Confederacy** would fight a largely defensive war against the invading Union troops. Contrary to popular myth, Lincoln's remarkable speech was not written at the last minute, a few jottings on the back of an envelope, but rather went through several drafts.*

Abraham Lincoln (1809–1865).

Four score and seven years ago our fathers brought forth on this continent, a new nation, conceived in Liberty, and dedicated to the proposition that all men are created equal.

Now we are engaged in a great civil war, testing whether that nation, or any nation so conceived and so dedicated, can long endure. We are met on a great battle-field of that war. We have come to dedicate a portion of that field, as a final resting place for those who here gave their lives that that nation might live. It is altogether fitting and proper that we should do this.

But, in a larger sense, we can not dedicate—we can not consecrate—we can not hallow—this ground. The brave men, living and dead, who struggled here, have consecrated it, far above our poor power to add or detract. The world will little note, nor long remember what we say here, but it can never forget what they did here. It is for us the living, rather, to be dedicated here to the unfinished work which they who fought here have thus far so nobly advanced. It is rather for us to be here dedicated to the great task remaining before us—that from these honored dead we take increased devotion to that cause for which they gave the last full measure of devotion—that we here highly resolve that these dead shall not have died in vain—that this nation, under God, shall have a new birth of freedom—and that government of the people, by the people, for the people, shall not perish from the earth.

The Emancipation Proclamation, January 1, 1863
Abraham Lincoln

After three years of a divisive and bloody civil war, **Abraham Lincoln** *offered a final version of the Emancipation Proclamation,* **offering freedom to all slaves then dwelling in states that had seceded from and were in rebellion with the union.** *Though the proclamation was limited—it did not affect slavery in the border states or those states already under Union control—it served to deny the Confederacy slave labor and to bring additional men into the service of the Union military. Its lasting reality was contingent on Union military victory. Historians have called the proclamation the crowning achievement of Lincoln's presidency. Before signing the final version, Lincoln reportedly said, "I never, in my life, felt more certain that I was doing right than I do in signing this paper."*

A Proclamation.

Whereas, on the twenty-second day of September, in the year of our Lord one thousand eight hundred and sixty-two, a proclamation was issued by the President of the United States, containing, among other things, the following, to wit:

"That on the first day of January, in the year of our Lord one thousand eight hundred and sixty-three, all persons held as slaves within any State or designated part of a State, the people whereof shall then be in rebellion against the United States, shall be then, thenceforward, and forever free; and the Executive Government of the United States, including the military and naval authority thereof, will recognize and maintain the freedom of such persons, and will do no act or acts to repress such persons, or any of them, in any efforts they may make for their actual freedom.

"That the Executive will, on the first day of January aforesaid, by proclamation, designate the States and parts of States, if any, in which the people thereof, respectively, shall then be in rebellion against the United States; and the fact that any State, or the people thereof, shall on that day be, in good faith, represented in the Congress of the United States by members chosen thereto at elections wherein a majority of the qualified voters of such State shall have participated, shall, in the absence of strong countervailing testimony, be deemed conclusive evidence that such State, and the people thereof, are not then in rebellion against the United States."

Now, therefore I, Abraham Lincoln, President of the United States, by virtue of the power in me vested as Commander-in-Chief, of the Army and Navy of the United States in time of actual armed rebellion against the authority and government of the United States, and as a fit and necessary war measure for suppressing said rebellion, do, on this first day of January, in the year of our Lord one thousand eight hundred and sixty-three, and in accordance with my purpose so to do publicly proclaimed for the full period of one hundred days, from the day first above mentioned, order and designate as the States and parts of States wherein the people thereof respectively, are this day in rebellion against the United States, the following, to wit:

Arkansas, Texas, Louisiana, (except the Parishes of St. Bernard, Plaquemines, Jefferson, St. John, St. Charles, St. James Ascension, Assumption, Terrebonne, Lafourche, St. Mary, St. Martin, and Orleans, including the City of New Orleans) Mississippi, Alabama, Florida, Georgia, South Carolina, North Carolina, and Virginia, (except the forty-eight counties designated as West Virginia, and also the counties of Berkley, Accomac, Northampton, Elizabeth City, York, Princess Ann, and Norfolk, including the cities of Norfolk and Portsmouth), and which excepted parts, are for the present, left precisely as if this proclamation were not issued.

And by virtue of the power, and for the purpose aforesaid, I do order and declare that all persons held as slaves within said designated States, and parts of States, are, and henceforward shall be free; and that the Executive government of the United States, including the military and naval authorities thereof, will recognize and maintain the freedom of said persons.

And I hereby enjoin upon the people so declared to be free to abstain from all violence, unless in necessary self-defense; and I recommend to them that, in all cases when allowed, they labor faithfully for reasonable wages.

And I further declare and make known, that such persons of suitable condition, will be received into the armed service of the United States to garrison forts, positions, stations, and other places, and to man vessels of all sorts in said service.

And upon this act, sincerely believed to be an act of justice, warranted by the Constitution, upon military necessity, I invoke the considerate judgment of mankind, and the gracious favor of Almighty God.

10   In witness whereof, I have hereunto set my hand and caused the seal of the United States to be affixed.

Done at the City of Washington, this first day of January, in the year of our Lord one thousand eight hundred and sixty three, and of the Independence of the United States of America the eighty-seventh.

By the President: ABRAHAM LINCOLN
WILLIAM H. SEWARD, Secretary of State.

Booker T. Washington

Atlanta Exposition Speech, September 18, 1895

Booker T. Washington (1856–1915).

The founder of Tuskegee Institute in Alabama and one of the leaders in education for African Americans, **Booker T. Washington** *was invited to give* **a speech at the Atlanta Exposition, a trade show,** *to a predominantly white audience. The speech was enormously well received on the day he gave it, but a backlash occurred when more black people became aware of what many considered to be too many concessions. The speech was dubbed "The Atlanta Compromise" by W. E. B. Du Bois, who became the leading voice for the other side of the debate. (See Du Bois's position.) Presenting the view of accommodation,* **Washington encouraged his people to "cast down their buckets" where they were, supporting, for the most part, industrial and trade schools.** *Washington eased the southern white man's mind when he offered to work in concert with white men in all things essential to mutual progress but "for all things that are purely social we can be as separate as the fingers," espousing the status quo for social segregation.*

Mr. President and Gentlemen of the Board of Directors and Citizens:

One-third of the population of the South is of the Negro race. No enterprise seeking the material, civil, or moral welfare of this section can disregard this element of our population and reach the highest success. I but convey to you, Mr. President and Directors, the sentiment of the masses of my race when I say that in no way have the value and manhood of the American Negro been more fittingly and generously recognized than by the managers of this magnificent Exposition at every stage of its progress. It is a recognition that will do more to cement the friendship of the two races than any occurrence since the dawn of our freedom.

Not only this, but the opportunity here afforded will awaken among us a new era of industrial progress. Ignorant and inexperienced, it is not strange that in the first years of our new life we began at the top instead of at the bottom; that a seat in Congress or the state legislature was more sought than real estate or industrial skill; that the political convention or stump speaking had more attractions than starting a dairy farm or truck garden.

A ship lost at sea for many days suddenly sighted a friendly vessel. From the mast of the unfortunate vessel was seen a signal, "Water, water; we die of thirst!" The answer from the friendly vessel at once came back, "Cast down your bucket where you are." A second time the signal, "Water, water; send us water!" ran up from the distressed vessel, and was answered, "Cast down your bucket where you are." And a third and fourth signal for water was answered, "Cast down your bucket where you are." The captain of the distressed vessel, at last heeding the injunction, cast down his bucket, and it came up full of fresh, sparkling water from the mouth of the Amazon River. To those of my race who depend on bettering their condition in a foreign land or who underestimate the importance of cultivating friendly relations with the Southern white man, who is their next-door neighbor, I would say: "Cast down your bucket where you are"—cast it down in making friends in every manly way of the people of all races by whom we are surrounded.

Cast it down in agriculture, mechanics, in commerce, in domestic service, and in the professions. And in this connection it is well to bear in mind that whatever other sins the South may be called to bear, when it comes to business, pure and simple, it is in the South that the Negro is given a man's chance in the commercial world, and in nothing is this Exposition more eloquent than in emphasizing this chance. Our greatest danger is that in the great leap from slavery to freedom we may overlook the fact that the masses of us are to live by the productions of our hands, and fail to keep in mind that we shall prosper in proportion as we learn to dignify and glorify common labor, and put brains and skill into the common occupations of life; shall prosper in proportion as we learn to draw the line between the superficial and the substantial, the ornamental gewgaws of life and the useful. No race can prosper till it learns that there is as much dignity in tilling a field as in writing a poem. It is at the bottom of life we must begin, and not at the top. Nor should we permit our grievances to overshadow our opportunities.

To those of the white race who look to the incoming of those of foreign birth and strange tongue and habits for the prosperity of the South, were I permitted I would repeat what I say to my own race, "Cast down your bucket where you are." Cast it down among the eight millions of Negroes whose habits you know, whose fidelity and love you have tested in days when to have proved treacherous meant the ruin of your firesides. Cast down your bucket among these people who have, without strikes and labor wars, tilled your fields, cleared your forests, build your railroads and cities, and brought forth treasures from the bowels of the earth, and helped make possible this magnificent representation of the progress of the South. Casting down your bucket among my people, helping and encouraging them as you are doing on these grounds, and to education of head, hand, and heart, you will find that they will buy your surplus land, make blossom the waste places in your fields, and run your factories. While doing this, you can be sure in the future, as in the past, that you and your families will be surrounded by the most patient, faithful, law-abiding, and unresentful people that the world has seen. As we have proved our loyalty to you in the past, in nursing your children, watching by the sick-bed of your mothers and fathers, and often following them with tear-dimmed eyes to their graves, so in the future, in our humble way, we shall stand by you with a devotion that no foreigner can approach, ready to lay down our lives, if need be, in defense of yours, interlacing our industrial, commercial, civil, and religious life with yours in a way that shall make the interests of both races one. In all things that are purely social we can be as separate as the fingers, yet one as the hand in all things essential to mutual progress.

There is no defense or security for any of us except in the highest intelligence and development of all. If anywhere there are efforts tending to curtail the fullest growth of the Negro, let these efforts be turned into stimulating, encouraging, and making him the most useful and intelligent citizen. Effort or means so invested will pay a thousand per cent interest. These efforts will be twice blessed—blessing him that gives and him that takes. There is no escape through law of man or God from the inevitable:

The laws of changeless justice bind Oppressor with oppressed;
And close as sin and suffering joined We march to fate abreast . . .

10   Nearly sixteen millions of hands will aid you in pulling the load upward, or they will pull against you the load downward. We shall constitute one-third and more of the ignorance and crime of the South, or one-third [of] its intelligence and progress; we shall contribute one-third to the business and industrial prosperity of the South, or we shall prove a veritable body of death, stagnating, depressing, retarding every effort to advance the body politic.

Gentlemen of the Exposition, as we present to you our humble effort at an exhibition of our progress, you must not expect overmuch. Starting thirty years ago with ownership here and there in a few quilts and pumpkins and chickens (gathered from miscellaneous sources), remember the path that has led from these to the inventions and production of agricultural implements, buggies, steam-engines, newspapers, books, statuary, carving, paintings, the management of drug stores and banks, has not been trodden without contact with thorns and thistles. While we take pride in what we exhibit as a result of our independent efforts, we do not for a moment forget that our part in this exhibition would fall far short of your expectations but for the constant help that has come to our educational life, not only from the Southern states, but especially from Northern philanthropists, who have made their gifts a constant stream of blessing and encouragement.

The wisest among my race understand that the agitation of questions of social equality is the extremest folly, and that progress in the enjoyment of all the privileges that will come to us must be the result of severe and constant struggle rather than of artificial forcing. No race that has anything to contribute to the markets of the world is long in any degree ostracized. It is important and right that all privileges of the law be ours, but it is vastly more important that we be prepared for the exercise of these privileges. The opportunity to earn a dollar in a factory just now is worth infinitely more than the opportunity to spend a dollar in an opera-house.

In conclusion, may I repeat that nothing in thirty years has given us more hope and encouragement, and drawn us so near to you of the white race, as this opportunity offered by the Exposition; and here bending, as it were, over the altar that represents the results of the struggles of your race and mine, both starting practically empty-handed three decades ago, I pledge that in your effort to work out the great and intricate problem which God has laid at the doors of the South, you shall have at all times the patient, sympathetic help of my race; only let this be constantly in mind, that, while from representations in these buildings of the product of field, of forest, of mine, of factory, letters, and art, much good will come, yet far above and beyond material benefits will be that higher good, that, let us pray God, will come, in a blotting out of sectional differences and racial animosities and suspicions, in a determination to administer absolute justice, in a willing obedience among all classes to the mandates of law. This, coupled with our material prosperity, will bring into our beloved South a new heaven and a new earth.

W. E. B. Du Bois

Of Mr. Booker T. Washington and Others, 1903

W. E. B. DuBois (1868–1963).

The renaissance man of African American letters during the first fifty years of the twentieth century and the founder of black studies in American academic life, **W. E. B. Du Bois** *also played a pivotal role in the establishment of the National Association for the Advancement of Colored People (NAACP). In this third chapter of* **Souls of Black Folks,** *Du Bois responds to Booker T. Washington's Atlanta Exposition speech, referring to it as the Atlanta Compromise (see Washington's position). Du Bois argues with what he sees as too narrow a plan, too much conciliation and submission to the white man. Du Bois champions these three issues in particular:* **the necessity of political power embodied in the right to vote, insistence on civil rights, and the importance of higher education for Negro youth, beyond industrial training.**

Easily the most striking thing in the history of the American Negro since 1876 is the ascendancy of Mr. Booker T. Washington. It began at the time when war memories and ideals were rapidly passing; a day of astonishing commercial development was dawning; a sense of doubt and hesitation over—took the freedmen's sons,—then it was that his leading began. Mr. Washington came, with a simple definite programme, at the psychological moment when the nation was a little ashamed of having bestowed so much sentiment on Negroes, and was concentrating its energies on Dollars. His programme of industrial education, conciliation of the South, and submission and silence as to civil and political rights, was not wholly original; the Free Negroes from 1830 up to war-time had striven to build industrial schools, and the American Missionary Association had from the first taught various trades; and Price and others had sought a way of honorable alliance with the best of the Southerners. But Mr. Washington first indissolubly linked these things; he put enthusiasm, unlimited energy, and perfect faith into his programme, and changed it from a by-path into a veritable Way of Life. And the tale of the methods by which he did this is a fascinating study of human life.

It startled the nation to hear a Negro advocating such a programme after many decades of bitter complaint; it startled and won the applause of the South, it interested and won the admiration of the North; and after a confused murmur of protest, it silenced if it did not convert the Negroes themselves.

To gain the sympathy and cooperation of the various elements comprising the white South was Mr. Washington's first task; and this, at the time Tuskegee was founded, seemed, for a black man, well-nigh impossible. And yet ten years later it was done in the word spoken at Atlanta: "In all things purely social we can be as separate as the five fingers, and yet one as the hand in all things essential to mutual progress." This "Atlanta Compromise" is by all odds the most notable thing in Mr. Washington's career. The South interpreted it in different ways: the radicals received it as a complete surrender of the demand for civil and political equality; the conservatives, as a generously conceived working basis for mutual understanding. So both approved it, and to-day its author is certainly the most distinguished Southerner since Jefferson Davis, and the one with the largest personal following.

Next to this achievement comes Mr. Washington's work in gaining place and consideration in the North. Others less shrewd and tactful had formerly essayed to sit on these two stools and had fallen between them; but as Mr. Washington knew the heart of the South from birth and training, so by singular insight he intuitively grasped the spirit of the age which was dominating the North. And so thoroughly did he learn the speech and thought of triumphant commercialism, and the ideals of material prosperity, that the picture of a lone black boy poring over a French grammar amid the weeds and dirt of a neglected home soon seemed to him the acme of absurdities. One wonders what Socrates and St. Francis of Assisi would say to this.

5   And yet this very singleness of vision and thorough one-ness with his age is a mark of the successful man. It is as though Nature must needs make men narrow in order to give them force. So Mr. Washington's cult has gained unquestioning followers, his work has wonderfully prospered, his friends are legion, and his enemies are confounded. To-day he stands as the one recognized spokesman of his ten million fellows, and one of the most notable figures in a nation of seventy millions. One hesitates, therefore, to criticize a life which, beginning with so little, has done so much. And yet the time is come when one may speak in all sincerity and utter courtesy of the mistakes and shortcomings of Mr. Washington's career, as well as of his triumphs, without being thought captious or envious, and without forgetting that it is easier to do ill than well in the world. The criticism that has hitherto met Mr. Washington has not always been of this broad character. In the South especially has he had to walk warily to avoid the harshest judgments,—and naturally so, for he is dealing with the one subject of deepest sensitiveness to that section. Twice—once when at the Chicago celebration of the Spanish-American War he alluded to the color-prejudice that is "eating away the vitals of the South," and once when he dined with President Roosevelt—has the resulting Southern criticism been violent enough to threaten seriously his popularity. In the North the feeling has several times forced itself into words, that Mr. Washington's counsels of submission overlooked certain elements of true manhood, and that his educational

programme was unnecessarily narrow. Usually, however, such criticism has not found open expression, although, too, the spiritual sons of the Abolitionists have not been prepared to acknowledge that the schools founded before Tuskegee, by men of broad ideals and self-sacrificing spirit, were wholly failures or worthy of ridicule. While, then, criticism has not failed to follow Mr. Washington, yet the prevailing public opinion of the land has been but too willing to deliver the solution of a wearisome problem into his hands, and say, "If that is all you and your race ask, take it."

Among his own people, however, Mr. Washington has encountered the strongest and most lasting opposition, amounting at times to bitterness, and even today continuing strong and insistent even though largely silenced in outward expression by the public opinion of the nation. Some of this opposition is, of course, mere envy; the disappointment of displaced demagogues and the spite of narrow minds. But aside from this, there is among educated and thoughtful colored men in all parts of the land a feeling of deep regret, sorrow, and apprehension at the wide currency and ascendancy which some of Mr. Washington's theories have gained. These same men admire his sincerity of purpose, and are willing to forgive much to honest endeavor which is doing something worth the doing. They cooperate with Mr. Washington as far as they conscientiously can; and, indeed, it is no ordinary tribute to this man's tact and power that, steering as he must between so many diverse interests and opinions, he so largely retains the respect of all.

But the hushing of the criticism of honest opponents is a dangerous thing. It leads some of the best of the critics to unfortunate silence and paralysis of effort, and others to burst into speech so passionately and intemperately as to lose listeners. Honest and earnest criticism from those whose interests are most nearly touched,—criticism of writers by readers,—this is the soul of democracy and the safeguard of modern society. If the best of the American Negroes receive by outer pressure a leader whom they had not recognized before, manifestly there is here a certain palpable gain. Yet there is also irreparable loss,— a loss of that peculiarly valuable education which a group receives when by search and criticism it finds and commissions its own leaders. The way in which this is done is at once the most elementary and the nicest problem of social growth. History is but the record of such group-leadership; and yet how infinitely changeful is its type and character! And of all types and kinds, what can be more instructive than the leadership of a group within a group?— that curious double movement where real progress may be negative and actual advance be relative retrogression. All this is the social student's inspiration and despair.

Now in the past the American Negro has had instructive experience in the choosing of group leaders, founding thus a peculiar dynasty which in the light of present conditions is worth while studying. When sticks and stones and beasts form the sole environment of a people, their attitude is largely one of determined opposition to and conquest of natural forces. But when to earth and brute is added an environment of men and ideas, then the attitude of the imprisoned group may take three main forms,—a feeling of revolt and revenge; an attempt to adjust all thought and action to the will of the greater group; or, finally, a determined effort at self-realization and self-development despite environing opinion. The influence of all of these attitudes at various times can be traced in the history of the American Negro, and in the evolution of his successive leaders.

Before 1750, while the fire of African freedom still burned in the veins of the slaves, there was in all leadership or attempted leadership but the one motive of revolt and revenge,—typified in the terrible Maroons, the Danish blacks, and Cato of Stono, and veiling all the Americas in fear of insurrection. The liberalizing tendencies of the latter half of the eighteenth century brought, along with kindlier relations between black and white, thoughts of ultimate adjustment and assimilation. Such aspiration was especially voiced in the earnest songs of Phyllis, in the martyrdom of Attucks, the fighting of Salem and Poor, the intellectual accomplishments of Banneker and Derham, and the political demands of the Cuffes.

10   Stern financial and social stress after the war cooled much of the previous humanitarian ardor. The disappointment and impatience of the Negroes at the persistence of slavery and serfdom voiced itself in two movements. The slaves in the South, aroused undoubtedly by vague rumors of the Haytian revolt, made three fierce attempts at insurrection,—in 1800 under Gabriel in Virginia, in 1822 under Vesey in Carolina, and in 1831 again in Virginia under the terrible Nat Turner. In the Free States, on the other hand, a new and curious attempt at self-development was made. In Philadelphia and New York color-prescription led to a withdrawal of Negro communicants from white churches and the formation of a peculiar socio-religious institution among the Negroes known as the African Church—an organization still living and controlling in its various branches over a million of men.

Walker's wild appeal against the trend of the times showed how the world was changing after the coming of the cotton-gin. By 1830 slavery seemed hopelessly fastened on the South, and the slaves thoroughly cowed into submission. The free Negroes of the North, inspired by the mulatto immigrants from the West Indies, began to change the basis of their demands; they recognized the slavery of slaves, but insisted that they themselves were freemen, and sought assimilation and amalgamation with the nation on the same terms with other men. Thus, Forten and Purvis of Philadelphia, Shad of Wilmington, Du Bois of New Haven, Barbadoes of Boston, and others, strove singly and together as men, they said, not as slaves; as "people of color," not as "Negroes." The trend of the times, however, refused them recognition save in individual and exceptional cases, considered them as one with all the despised blacks, and they soon found themselves striving to keep even the rights they formerly had of voting and working and moving as freemen. Schemes of migration and colonization arose among them; but these they refused to entertain, and they eventually turned to the Abolition movement as a final refuge.

Here, led by Remond, Nell, Wells-Brown, and Douglass, a new period of self-assertion and self-development dawned. To be sure, ultimate freedom and assimilation was the ideal before the leaders, but the assertion of the manhood rights of the Negro by himself was the main reliance, and John Brown's raid was the extreme of its logic. After the war and emancipation, the great form of Frederick Douglass, the greatest of American Negro leaders, still led the host. Self-assertion, especially in political lines, was the main programme, and behind Douglass came Elliot, Bruce, and Langston, and the Reconstruction politicians, and, less conspicuous but of greater social significance, Alexander Crummell and Bishop Daniel Payne.

Then came the Revolution of 1876, the suppression of the Negro votes, the changing and shifting of ideals, and the seeking of new lights in the great night. Douglass, in his old age, still bravely stood for the ideals of his early manhood,—ultimate assimilation through self-assertion, and on no other terms. For a time Price arose as a new leader, destined, it seemed, not to give up, but to re-state the old ideals in a form less repugnant to the white South. But he passed away in his prime. Then came the new leader. Nearly all the former ones had become leaders by the silent suffrage of their fellows, had sought to lead their own people alone, and were usually, save Douglass, little known outside their race. But Booker T. Washington arose as essentially the leader not of one race but of two,—a compromiser between the South, the North, and the Negro. Naturally the Negroes resented, at first bitterly, signs of compromise which surrendered their civil and political rights, even though this was to be exchanged for larger chances of economic development. The rich and dominating North, however, was not only weary of the race problem, but was investing largely in Southern enterprises, and welcomed any method of peaceful cooperation. Thus, by national opinion, the Negroes began to recognize Mr. Washington's leadership; and the voice of criticism was hushed.

Mr. Washington represents in Negro thought the old attitude of adjustment and submission; but adjustment at such a peculiar time as to make his programme unique. This is an age of unusual economic development, and Mr. Washington's programme naturally takes an economic cast, becoming a gospel of Work and Money to such an extent as apparently almost completely to overshadow the higher aims of life. Moreover, this is an age when the more advanced races are coming in closer contact with the less developed races, and the race-feeling is therefore intensified; and Mr. Washington's programme practically accepts the alleged inferiority of the Negro races. Again, in our own land, the reaction from the sentiment of war time has given impetus to race-prejudice against Negroes, and Mr. Washington withdraws many of the high demands of Negroes as men and American citizens. In other periods of intensified prejudice all the Negro's tendency to self-assertion has been called forth; at this period a policy of submission is advocated. In the history of nearly all other races and peoples the doctrine preached at such crises has been that manly self-respect is worth more than lands and houses, and that a people who voluntarily surrender such respect, or cease striving for it, are not worth civilizing.

In answer to this, it has been claimed that the Negro can survive only through submission. Mr. Washington distinctly asks that black people give up, at least for the present, three things,— 15

First, political power,

Second, insistence on civil rights,

Third, higher education of Negro youth,—and concentrate all their energies on industrial education, and accumulation of wealth, and the conciliation of the South. This policy has been courageously and insistently advocated for over fifteen years, and has been triumphant for perhaps ten years. As a result of this tender of the palm-branch, what has been the return? In these years there have occurred:

1. The disfranchisement of the Negro.
2. The legal creation of a distinct status of civil inferiority for the Negro.
3. The steady withdrawal of aid from institutions for the higher training of the Negro.

These movements are not, to be sure, direct results of Mr. Washington's teachings; but his propaganda has, without a shadow of doubt, helped their speedier accomplishment. The question then comes: Is it possible, and probable, that nine millions of men can make effective progress in economic lines if they are deprived of political rights, made a servile caste, and allowed only the most meagre chance for developing their exceptional men? If history and reason give any distinct answer to these questions, it is an emphatic

NO. And Mr. Washington thus faces the triple paradox of his career:

1. He is striving nobly to make Negro artisans business men and property-owners; but it is utterly impossible, under modern competitive methods, for workingmen and property-owners to defend their rights and exist without the right of suffrage.
2. He insists on thrift and self-respect, but at the same time counsels a silent submission to civic inferiority such as is bound to sap the manhood of any race in the long run.
3. He advocates common-school and industrial training, and depreciates institutions of higher learning; but neither the Negro common-schools, nor Tuskegee itself, could remain open a day were it not for teachers trained in Negro colleges, or trained by their graduates.

This triple paradox in Mr. Washington's position is the object of criticism by two classes of colored Americans. One class is spiritually descended from Toussaint the Savior, through Gabriel, Vesey, and Turner, and they represent the attitude of revolt and revenge; they hate the white South blindly and distrust the white race generally, and so far as they agree on definite action, think that the Negro's only hope lies in emigration beyond the borders of the United States. And yet, by the irony of fate, nothing has more effectually made this programme seem hopeless than the recent course of the United States toward weaker and darker peoples in the West Indies, Hawaii, and the Philippines,—for where in the world may we go and be safe from lying and brute force? The other class of Negroes who cannot agree with Mr. Washington has hitherto said little aloud. They deprecate the sight of scattered counsels, of internal disagreement; and especially they dislike making their just criticism of a useful and earnest man an excuse for a general discharge of venom from small-minded opponents. Nevertheless, the questions involved are so fundamental and serious that it is difficult to see how men like the Grimkes, Kelly Miller, J. W. E. Bowen, and other representatives of this group, can much longer be silent. Such men feel in conscience bound to ask of this nation three things:

1. The right to vote.
2. Civic equality.
3. The education of youth according to ability.

They acknowledge Mr. Washington's invaluable service in counselling patience and courtesy in such demands; they do not ask that ignorant black men vote when ignorant whites are debarred, or that any reasonable restrictions in the suffrage should not be applied; they know that the low social level of the mass of the race is responsible for much discrimination against it, but they also know, and the nation knows, that relentless color-prejudice is more often a cause than a result of the Negro's degradation; they seek the abatement of this relic of barbarism, and not its systematic encouragement and pampering by all agencies of social power from the Associated Press to the Church of Christ. They advocate, with Mr. Washington, a broad system of Negro common schools supplemented by thorough industrial training; but they are surprised that a man of Mr. Washington's insight cannot see that no such educational system ever has rested or can rest on any other basis than that of the well-equipped college and university, and they insist that there is a demand for a few such institutions throughout the South to train the best of the Negro youth as teachers, professional men, and leaders.

This group of men honor Mr. Washington for his attitude of conciliation toward the   20
white South; they accept the "Atlanta Compromise" in its broadest interpretation; they recognize, with him, many signs of promise, many men of high purpose and fair judgment,
in this section; they know that no easy task has been laid upon a region already tottering
under heavy burdens. But, nevertheless, they insist that the way to truth and right lies in
straightforward honesty, not in indiscriminate flattery; in praising those of the South who
do well and criticizing uncompromisingly those who do ill; in taking advantage of the
opportunities at hand and urging their fellows to do the same, but at the same time in
remembering that only a firm adherence to their higher ideals and aspirations will ever
keep those ideals within the realm of possibility. They do not expect that the free right to
vote, to enjoy civic rights, and to be educated, will come in a moment; they do not expect
to see the bias and prejudices of years disappear at the blast of a trumpet; but they are
absolutely certain that the way for a people to gain their reasonable rights is not by voluntarily throwing them away and insisting that they do not want them; that the way for a
people to gain respect is not by continually belittling and ridiculing themselves; that, on the
contrary, Negroes must insist continually, in season and out of season, that voting is necessary to modern manhood, that color discrimination is barbarism, and that black boys
need education as well as white boys.

In failing thus to state plainly and unequivocally the legitimate demands of their
people, even at the cost of opposing an honored leader, the thinking classes of American
Negroes would shirk a heavy responsibility,—a responsibility to themselves, a responsibility
to the struggling masses, a responsibility to the darker races of men whose future depends
so largely on this American experiment, but especially a responsibility to this nation,—this
common Fatherland. It is wrong to encourage a man or a people in evil-doing; it is wrong
to aid and abet a national crime simply because it is unpopular not to do so. The growing
spirit of kindliness and reconciliation between the North and South after the frightful difference of a generation ago ought to be a source of deep congratulation to all, and especially to those whose mistreatment caused the war; but if that reconciliation is to be
marked by the industrial slavery and civic death of those same black men, with permanent
legislation into a position of inferiority, then those black men, if they are really men, are
called upon by every consideration of patriotism and loyalty to oppose such a course by
all civilized methods, even though such opposition involves disagreement with Mr. Booker
T. Washington. We have no right to sit silently by while the inevitable seeds are sown for
a harvest of disaster to our children, black and white.

First, it is the duty of black men to judge the South discriminatingly. The present
generation of Southerners is not responsible for the past, and they should not be blindly
hated or blamed for it. Furthermore, to no class is the indiscriminate endorsement of the
recent course of the South toward Negroes more nauseating than to the best thought of
the South. The South is not "solid"; it is a land in the ferment of social change, wherein
forces of all kinds are fighting for supremacy; and to praise the ill the South is today per-
petrating is just as wrong as to condemn the good. Discriminating and broad-minded criticism
is what the South needs,—needs it for the sake of her own white sons and daughters, and
for the insurance of robust, healthy mental and moral development.

Today even the attitude of the Southern whites toward the blacks is not, as so many
assume, in all cases the same; the ignorant Southerner hates the Negro, the workingmen
fear his competition, the money-makers wish to use him as a laborer, some of the

educated see a menace in his upward development, while others—usually the sons of the masters—wish to help him to rise. National opinion has enabled this last class to maintain the Negro common schools, and to protect the Negro partially in property, life, and limb. Through the pressure of the money-makers, the Negro is in danger of being reduced to semi-slavery, especially in the country districts; the workingmen, and those of the educated who fear the Negro, have united to disfranchise him, and some have urged his deportation; while the passions of the ignorant are easily aroused to lynch and abuse any black man. To praise this intricate whirl of thought and prejudice is nonsense; to inveigh indiscriminately against "the South" is unjust; but to use the same breath in praising Governor Aycock, exposing Senator Morgan, arguing with Mr. Thomas Nelson Page, and denouncing Senator Ben Tillman, is not only sane, but the imperative duty of thinking black men.

It would be unjust to Mr. Washington not to acknowledge that in several instances he has opposed movements in the South which were unjust to the Negro; he sent memorials to the Louisiana and Alabama constitutional conventions, he has spoken against lynching, and in other ways has openly or silently set his influence against sinister schemes and unfortunate happenings. Notwithstanding this, it is equally true to assert that on the whole the distinct impression left by Mr. Washington's propaganda is, first, that the South is justified in its present attitude toward the Negro because of the Negro's degradation; secondly, that the prime cause of the Negro's failure to rise more quickly is his wrong education in the past; and, thirdly, that his future rise depends primarily on his own efforts. Each of these propositions is a dangerous half-truth. The supplementary truths must never be lost sight of: first, slavery and race-prejudice are potent if not sufficient causes of the Negro's position; second, industrial and common-school training were necessarily slow in planting because they had to await the black teachers trained by higher institutions,—it being extremely doubtful if any essentially different development was possible, and certainly a Tuskegee was unthinkable before 1880; and, third, while it is a great truth to say that the Negro must strive and strive mightily to help himself, it is equally true that unless his striving be not simply seconded, but rather aroused and encouraged, by the initiative of the richer and wiser environing group, he cannot hope for great success.

25   In his failure to realize and impress this last point, Mr. Washington is especially to be criticized. His doctrine has tended to make the whites, North and South, shift the burden of the Negro problem to the Negro's shoulders and stand aside as critical and rather pessimistic spectators; when in fact the burden belongs to the nation, and the hands of none of us are clean if we bend not our energies to righting these great wrongs.

The South ought to be led, by candid and honest criticism, to assert her better self and do her full duty to the race she has cruelly wronged and is still wronging. The North—her co-partner in guilt—cannot salve her conscience by plastering it with gold. We cannot settle this problem by diplomacy and suaveness, by "policy" alone. If worse come to worst, can the moral fiber of this country survive the slow throttling and murder of nine millions of men?

The black men of America have a duty to perform, a duty stern and delicate,—a forward movement to oppose a part of the work of their greatest leader. So far as Mr. Washington preaches Thrift, Patience, and Industrial Training for the masses, we must hold up his hands and strive with him, rejoicing in his honors and glorying in the strength of this Joshua called of God and of man to lead the headless host. But so far as Mr. Washington apologizes for injustice, North or South, does not rightly value the privilege and duty of voting, belittles the emasculating effects of caste distinctions, and opposes the higher training and ambition of our brighter minds,—so far as he, the South, or the Nation, does this,—we must unceasingly and firmly oppose them. By every civilized and peaceful method we must strive for the rights which the world accords to men, clinging unwaveringly to those great words which the sons of the Fathers would fain forget: "We hold these truths to be self-evident: That all men are created equal; that they are endowed by their Creator with certain unalienable rights; that among these are life, liberty, and the pursuit of happiness."

Jane Addams

Why Women Should Vote, 1910

Jane Addams (1860–1935).

Published in the January 1910 **Ladies Home Journal,** *this article by* **Jane Addams,** *U.S. social reformer and Nobel laureate, reached out to middle-class women on the issue of suffrage. Arguing that a more complex world required women to expand their horizons beyond their homes and consider their responsibilities to society, Addams brought the issue of suffrage to the nonpolitical housewives of America. Written ten years before the* **Nineteenth Amendment** *guaranteed women the right to vote, Addam's argument is a rather conservative one—**claiming that women's values and character brought into public issues will only tend to clean up society**—as opposed to the then more radical notion that women should vote because it is their right as citizens.*

For many generations it has been believed that woman's place is within the walls of her home, and it is indeed impossible to imagine the time when her duty there shall be ended or to forecast any social change which shall release her from that paramount obligation.

This paper is an attempt to show that many women today are failing to discharge their duties to their own households properly simply because they do not perceive that as society grows more complicated it is necessary that woman shall extend her sense of responsibility to many things outside of her own home if she would continue to preserve the home in its entirety. One could illustrate in many ways. A woman's simplest duty, one would say, is to keep her house clean and wholesome and to feed her children properly. Yet if she lives in a tenement house, as so many of my neighbors do, she cannot fulfill these simple obligations by her own efforts because she is utterly dependent upon the city administration for the conditions which render decent living possible. Her basement will not be dry, her stairways will not be fireproof, her house will not be provided with sufficient windows to give light and air, nor will it be equipped with sanitary plumbing, unless the Public Works Department sends inspectors who constantly insist that these elementary decencies be provided. Women who live in the country sweep their own dooryards and may either feed the refuse of the table to a flock of chickens or allow it innocently to decay in the open air and sunshine. In a crowded city quarter, however, if the street is not cleaned by the city authorities no amount of private sweeping will keep the tenement free from grime; if the garbage is not properly collected and destroyed a tenement-house mother may see her children sicken and die of diseases from which she alone is powerless to shield them, although her tenderness and devotion are unbounded. She cannot even secure untainted meat for her household, she cannot provide fresh fruit, unless the meat has been inspected by city officials, and the decayed fruit, which is so often placed upon sale in the tenement districts, has been destroyed in the interests of public health. In short, if woman would keep on with her old business of caring for her house and rearing her children she will have to have some conscience in regard to public affairs lying quite outside of her immediate household. The individual conscience and devotion are no longer effective.

Chicago one spring had a spreading contagion of scarlet fever just at the time the school nurses had been discontinued because business men had pronounced them too expensive. If the women who sent their children to the schools had been sufficiently public-spirited and had been provided with an implement through which to express that public spirit they would have insisted that the schools be supplied with nurses in order that their own children might be protected from contagion. In other words, if women would effectively continue their old avocations they must take part in the slow upbuilding of that code of legislation which is alone sufficient to protect the home from the dangers incident to modern life. One might instance the many deaths of children from contagious diseases; the germs of which had been carried in tailored clothing. Country doctors testify as to the outbreak of scarlet fever in remote neighborhoods each autumn, after the children have begun to wear the winter overcoats and cloaks which have been sent from infected city sweatshops. That their mothers mend their stockings and guard them from "taking cold" is not a sufficient protection when the tailoring of the family is done in a distant city under conditions which the mother cannot possibly control. The sanitary regulation of sweat-shops by city officials is all that can be depended upon to prevent such needless destruction. Who shall say that women are not concerned in the enactment and enforcement of such legislation if they would preserve their homes?

Even women who take no part in public affairs in order that they may give themselves entirely to their own families, sometimes going so far as to despise those other women who are endeavoring to secure protective legislation, may illustrate this point. The Hull-House neighborhood was at one time suffering from a typhoid epidemic. A careful investigation was made by which we were able to establish a very close connection between the typhoid and a mode of plumbing which made it most probable that the infection had been carried by flies. Among the people who been exposed to the infection was a widow who had lived in the ward for a number of years, in a comfortable little house which she owned. Although the Italian immigrants were closing in all around her she was not willing to sell her property and to move away until she had finished the education of her children. In the mean time she held herself quite aloof from her Italian neighbors and could never be drawn into any of the public efforts to protect them by securing a better code of tenement-house sanitation. Her two daughters were sent to an Eastern college; one June, when one of them had graduated and the other still had two years before she took her degree, they came to the spotless little house and to their self-sacrificing mother for the summer's holiday. They both fell ill, not because their own home was not clean, not because their mother was not devoted, but because next door to them and also in the rear were wretched tenements, and because the mother's utmost efforts could not keep the infection out of her own house. One daughter died and one recovered but was an invalid for two years following. This is, perhaps, a fair illustration of the futility of the individual conscience when woman insists upon isolating her family from the rest of the community and its interests. The result is sure to be a pitiful failure.

One of the interesting experiences in the Chicago campaign for inducing the members   5
of the Charter Convention to recommend municipal franchise for women in the provisions of the new charter was the unexpected enthusiasm and help which came from large groups of foreign-born women. The Scandinavian women represented in many Lutheran Church societies said quite simply that in the old country they had had the municipal franchise upon the same basis as men since the seventeenth century; all the women formerly living under the British Government, in England, Australia or Canada, pointed out that Chicago women were asking now for what the British women had long had. But the most unexpected response came from the foreign colonies in which women had never heard such problems discussed and took the prospect of the municipal ballot as a simple device—which it is—to aid them in their daily struggle with adverse city conditions. The Italian women said that the men engaged in railroad construction were away all summer and did not know anything about their household difficulties. Some of them came to Hull-House one day to talk over the possibility of a public wash-house. They do not like to wash in their own tenements, they have never seen a washing-tub until they came to America, and find it very difficult to use it in the restricted space of their little kitchens and to hang the clothes within the house to dry. They say that in the Italian villages the women all go to the streams together; in the town they go to the public washhouse; and washing, instead of being lonely and disagreeable, is made pleasant by cheerful conversation. It is asking a great deal of these women to change suddenly all their habits of living, and their contention that the tenement-house kitchen is too small for laundry-work is well taken. If women in Chicago knew the needs of the Italian colony they would realize that any change bringing cleanliness and fresh clothing into the Italian household would be a very sensible and hygienic measure. It is, perhaps, asking a great deal that the members of the City Council should understand this, but surely a comprehension of the needs of these women and efforts toward ameliorating their lot might be regarded as matters of municipal obligation on the part of voting women.

The same thing is true of the Jewish women in their desire for covered markets which have always been a municipal provision in Russia and Poland. The vegetables piled high upon the wagons standing in the open markets of Chicago become covered with dust and soot. It seems to these women a violation of the most rudimentary decencies and they sometimes say quite simply: " If women had anything to say about it they would change all that."

. . . The duty of a woman toward the schools which her children attend is so obvious that it is not necessary to dwell upon it. But even this simple obligation cannot be effectively carried out without some form of social organization as the mothers' school clubs and mothers' congresses testify, and to which the most conservative women belong because they feel the need of wider reading and discussion concerning the many problems of childhood. It is, therefore, perhaps natural that the public should have been more willing to accord a vote to women in school matters than in any other, and yet women have never been members of a Board of Education in sufficient numbers to influence largely actual school curriculi. If they had been kindergartens, domestic science courses and school playgrounds would be far more numerous than they are. More than one woman has been convinced of the need of the ballot by the futility of her efforts in persuading a businessman that young children need nurture in something besides the three r's. Perhaps, too, only women realize the influence which the school might exert upon the home if a proper adaptation to actual needs were considered. An Italian girl who has had lessons in cooking at the public school will help her mother to connect the entire family with American food and household habits. That the mother has never baked bread in Italy—only mixed it in her own house and then taken it out to the village oven—makes it all the more necessary that her daughter should understand the complication of a cooking-stove. The same thing is true of the girl who learns to sew in the public school, and more than anything else, perhaps, of the girl who receives the first simple instruction in the care of little children, that skillful care which every tenement-house baby requires if he is to be pulled through his second summer. The only time, to my knowledge, that lessons in the care of children were given in the public schools of Chicago was one summer when the vacation schools were being managed by a volunteer body of women. The instruction was eagerly received by the Italian girls, who had been "little mothers" to younger children ever since they could remember.

As a result of this teaching I recall a young girl who carefully explained to her Italian mother that the reason the babies in Italy were so healthy and the babies in Chicago were so sickly was not, as her mother had always firmly insisted, because her babies in Italy had goat's milk and her babies in America had cow's milk, but because the milk in Italy was clean and the milk in Chicago was dirty . . . . She also informed her mother that the "City Hall wanted to fix up the milk so that it couldn't make the baby sick, but that they hadn't quite enough votes for it yet." The Italian mother believed what her child had been taught in the big school; it seemed to her quite as natural that the city should be concerned in providing pure milk for her younger children as it should provide big schools and teachers for her older children. She reached this naive conclusion because she had never heard those arguments which make it seem reasonable that a woman should be given the school franchise but no other.

But women are also beginning to realize that children need attention outside of school hours; that much of the petty vice in cities is merely the love of pleasure gone wrong, the overrestrained boy or girl seeking improper recreation and excitement. It is obvious that a little study of the needs of children, a sympathetic understanding of the conditions under which they go astray, might save hundreds of them. Women traditionally have had an opportunity to observe the plays of children and the needs of youth, and yet in Chicago, at least, they had done singularly little in this vexed problem of juvenile delinquency until they helped to inaugurate the juvenile Court movement a dozen years ago. The juvenile Court Committee, made up largely of women, paid the salaries of the probation officers connected with the court for the first six years of its existence, and after the salaries were cared for by the county the same organization turned itself into a juvenile Protective League, and through a score of paid officers are doing valiant service in minimizing some of the dangers of city life which boys and girls encounter . . . .

10   The more extensively the modern city endeavors on the one hand to control and on the other hand to provide recreational facilities for its young people the more necessary it

is that women should assist in their direction and extension. After all, a care for wholesome and innocent amusement is what women have for many years assumed. When the reaction comes on the part of taxpayers women's votes may be necessary to keep the city to its beneficent obligations toward its own young people.

. . . Ever since steam power has been applied to the processes of weaving and spinning woman's traditional work has been carried on largely outside of the home. The clothing and household linen are not only spun and woven, but also usually sewed, by machinery; the preparation of many foods has also passed into the factory and necessarily a certain number of women have been obliged to follow their work there, although it is doubtful, in spite of the large numbers of factory girls, whether women now are doing as large a proportion of the world's work as they used to do. Because many thousands of those working in factories and shops are girls between the ages of fourteen and twenty-two there is a necessity that older women should be interested in the conditions of industry. The very fact that these girls are not going to remain in industry permanently makes it more important that some one should see to it that they shall not be incapacitated for their future family life because they work for exhausting hours and under unsanitary conditions.

If woman's sense of obligation had enlarged as the industrial conditions changed she might naturally and almost imperceptibly have inaugurated the movements for social amelioration in the line of factory legislation and shop sanitation. That she has not done so is doubtless due to the fact that her conscience is slow to recognize any obligation outside of her own family circle, and because she was so absorbed in her own household that she failed to see what the conditions outside actually were. It would be interesting to know how far the consciousness that she had no vote and could not change matters operated in this direction. After all, we see only those things to which our attention has been drawn, we feel responsibility for those things which are brought to us as matters of responsibility. If conscientious women were convinced that it was a civic duty to be informed in regard to these grave industrial affairs, and then to express the conclusions which they had reached by depositing a piece of paper in a ballot box, one cannot imagine that they would shirk simply because the action ran counter to old traditions.

To those of my readers who would admit that although woman has no right to shirk her old obligations, that all of these measures could be secured more easily through her influence upon the men of her family than through the direct use of the ballot; I should like to tell a little story. I have a friend in Chicago who is the mother of four sons and the grandmother of twelve grandsons who are voters. She is a woman of wealth, of secured social position, of sterling character and clear intelligence, and may, therefore, quite fairly be cited as a "woman of influence" . . . . I happened to call at her house on the day that Mr. McKinley was elected President against Mr. Bryan for the first time. I found my friend much disturbed. She said somewhat bitterly that she had at last discovered what the much-vaunted influence of woman was worth; that she had implored each one of her sons and grandsons, had entered into endless arguments and moral appeals to induce one of them to represent her convictions by voting for Bryan! That, although sincerely devoted to her, each one had assured her that his convictions forced him to vote the Republican ticket . . . . I contended that a woman had no right to persuade a man to vote against his own convictions; that I respected the men of her family for following their own judgment regardless of the appeal which the honored head of the house had made to their chivalric devotion. To this she replied that she would agree with that point of view when a woman had the same opportunity as a man to register her convictions by vote. I believed then as I do now, that nothing is gained when independence of judgment is assailed by "influence," sentimental or otherwise, and that we test advancing civilization somewhat by our power to respect differences and by our tolerance of another's honest conviction.

This is, perhaps, the attitude of many busy women who would be glad to use the ballot to further public measures in which they are interested and for which they have been working for years. It offends the taste of such a woman to be obliged to use "indirect influence" when she is accustomed to well-bred, open action in other affairs, and she very much resents the time spent in persuading a voter to take her point of view, and possibly to give up his own, quite as honest and valuable as hers, although different because resulting from a totally different experience. Public-spirited women who wish to use the ballot, as I know them, do not wish to do the work of men nor to take over men's affairs. They simply want an opportunity to do their own work and to take care of those affairs which naturally and historically belong to women, but which are constantly being overlooked and slighted in our political institutions . . . . To turn the administration of our civic affairs wholly over to men may mean that the American city will continue to push forward in its commercial and industrial development, and continue to lag behind in those things which make a city healthful and beautiful. After all, woman's traditional function has been to make her dwelling-place both clean and fair. Is that dreariness in city life, that lack of domesticity which the humblest farm dwelling presents, due to a withdrawal of one of the naturally cooperating forces? If women have in any sense been responsible for the gentler side of life which softens and blurs some of its harsher conditions, may they not have a duty to perform in our American cities?

15   In closing, may I recapitulate that if woman would fulfill her traditional responsibility to her own children; if she would educate and protect from danger factory children who must find their recreation on the street; if she would bring the cultural forces to bear upon our materialistic civilization; and if she would do it all with the dignity and directness fitting one who carries on her immemorial duties, then she must bring herself to the use of the ballot—that latest implement for self government. May we not fairly say that American women need this implement in order to preserve the home?

The Indian Citizenship Act of 1924

*Approved by the Sixty-eighth Congress on June 2, 1924, the Indian Citizenship Act was just one in a long line of steps by the U.S. government to try **to further integrate the Native Americans living in the United States into American culture.** Almost two thirds of American Indians were already citizens—including military veterans of WWI—and this act extended citizenship to all native peoples, yet it did not appreciably improve their standard of living or status as wards of the state.*

CHAP. 233.—An Act to authorize the Secretary of the Interior to issue certificates of citizenship to Indians.

Be it enacted by the Senate and House of Representatives of the United States of America in Congress assembled, That all non-citizen Indians born within the territorial limits of the United States be, and they are hereby, declared to be citizens of the United States: Provided, That the granting of such citizenship shall not in any manner impair or otherwise affect the right of any Indian to tribal or other property.

Franklin D. Roosevelt

The Four Freedoms, January 6, 1941

Franklin D. Roosevelt (1882–1945).

*The only man to be elected four times (1933–1945), thirty-second president **Franklin D. Roosevelt** came to office during the Great Depression, the country's biggest domestic crisis since the Civil War. He offered the country a "New Deal" to counter the economic downslide, and as he gave his **State of the Union address,** the world was at war. At this point, the United States was not yet actively involved in hostilities. Roosevelt chose this occasion to speak on the threat to American security, but his closing words put the speech into national memory. He pointed toward the day when the world would be founded on **four freedoms: freedom of speech and worship and freedom from want and fear.***

Mr. Speaker, members of the 77th Congress:

I address you, the members of this new Congress, at a moment unprecedented in the history of the union. I use the word "unprecedented" because at no previous time has American security been as seriously threatened from without as it is today. Since the permanent formation of our government under the Constitution in 1789, most of the periods of crisis in our history have related to our domestic affairs. And, fortunately, only one of these—the four-year war between the States—ever threatened our national unity. Today, thank God, 130,000,000 Americans in forty-eight States have forgotten points of the compass in our national unity.

It is true that prior to 1914 the United States often has been disturbed by events in other continents. We have even engaged in two wars with European nations and in a number of undeclared wars in the West Indies, in the Mediterranean and in the Pacific, for the maintenance of American rights and for the Principles of peaceful commerce. But in no case has a serious threat been raised against our national safety or our continued independence. What I seek to convey is the historic truth that the United States as a nation has at all times maintained opposition—clear, definite opposition—to any attempt to lock us in behind an ancient Chinese wall while the procession of civilization went past. Today, thinking of our children and of their children, we oppose enforced isolation for ourselves or for any other part of the Americas.

That determination of ours, extending over all these years, was proved, for example, in the early days during the quarter century of wars following the French Revolution. While the Napoleonic struggle did threaten interests of the United States because of the French foothold in the West Indies and in Louisiana, and while we engaged in the War of 1812 to vindicate our right to peaceful trade, it is nevertheless clear that neither France nor Great Britain nor any other nation was aiming at domination of the whole world.

5   And in like fashion, from 1815 to 1914—ninety-nine years—no single war in Europe or in Asia constituted a real threat against our future or against the future of any other American nation. Except in the Maximilian interlude in Mexico, no foreign power sought to establish itself in this hemisphere. And the strength of the British fleet in the Atlantic has been a friendly strength; it is still a friendly strength. Even when the World War broke out in 1941 it seemed to contain only small threat of danger to our own American future. But as time went on, as we remember, the American people began to visualize what the downfall of democratic nations might mean to our own democracy.

We need not overemphasize imperfections in the peace of Versailles. We need not harp on failure of the democracies to deal with problems of world reconstruction. We should remember that the peace of 1919 was far less unjust than the kind of pacification which began even before Munich, and which is being carried on under the new order of tyranny that seeks to spread over every continent today. The American people have unalterably set their faces against that tyranny. I suppose that every realist knows that the democratic way of life is at this moment being directly assailed in every part of the world— assailed either by arms or by secret spreading of poisonous propaganda by those who seek to destroy unity and promote discord in nations that are still at peace.

During sixteen long months this assault has blotted out the whole pattern of democratic life in an appalling number of independent nations, great and small. And the assailants are still on the march, threatening other nations, great and small. Therefore, as your President, performing my constitutional duty to "give to the Congress information of the state of the union," I find it unhappily necessary to report that the future and the safety of our country and of our democracy are overwhelmingly involved in events far beyond our borders.

Armed defense of democratic existence is now being gallantly waged in four continents. If that defense fails, all the population and all the resources of Europe and Asia, Africa and Australia will be dominated by conquerors. And let us remember that the total of those populations in those four continents, the total of those populations and their resources greatly exceeds the sum total of the population and the resources of the whole of the Western Hemisphere—yes, many times over.

In times like these it is immature—and, incidentally, untrue—for anybody to brag that an unprepared America, single-handed and with one hand tied behind its back, can hold off the whole world. No realistic American can expect from a dictator's peace international generosity, or return of true independence, or world disarmament, or freedom of expression, or freedom of religion—or even good business. Such a peace would bring no security for us or for our neighbors. Those who would give up essential liberty to purchase a little temporary safety deserve neither liberty nor safety.

10   As a nation we may take pride in the fact that we are soft-hearted; but we cannot afford to be soft-headed. We must always be wary of those who with sounding brass and a tinkling cymbal preach the ism of appeasement. We must especially beware of that small group of selfish men who would clip the wings of the American eagle in order to feather

their own nests. I have recently pointed out how quickly the tempo of modern warfare could bring into our very midst the physical attack which we must eventually expect if the dictator nation win this war.

There is much loose talk of our immunity from immediate and direct invasion from across the seas. Obviously, as long as the British Navy retains its power, no such danger exists. Even if there were no British Navy, it is not probable that any enemy would be stupid enough to attack us by landing troops in the United States from across thousands of miles of ocean, until it had acquired strategic bases from which to operate. But we learn much from the lessons of the past years in Europe—particularly the lesson of Norway, whose essential seaports were captured by treachery and surprise built up over a series of years.

The first phase of the invasion of this hemisphere would not be the landing of regular troops. The necessary strategic points would be occupied by secret agents and by their dupes—and great numbers of them are already here and in Latin America. As long as the aggressor nations maintain the offensive they, not we, will choose the time and the place and the method of their attack. And that is why the future of all the American Republics is today in serious danger. That is why this annual message to the Congress is unique in our history. That is why every member of the executive branch of the government and every member of the Congress face great responsibility—great accountability.

The need of the moment is that our actions and our policy should be devoted primarily—almost exclusively—to meeting this foreign peril. For all our domestic problems are now a part of the great emergency. Just as our national policy in internal affairs has been based upon a decent respect for the rights and the dignity of all of our fellow men within our gates, so our national policy in foreign affairs has been based on a decent respect for the rights and the dignity of all nations, large and small. And the justice of morality must and will win in the end.

Our national policy is this: First, by an impressive expression of the public will and without regard to partisanship, we are committed to all-inclusive national defense. Second, by an impressive expression of the public will and without regard to partisanship, we are committed to full support of all those resolute people everywhere who are resisting aggression and are thereby keeping war away from our hemisphere. By this support we express our determination that the democratic cause shall prevail, and we strengthen the defense and the security of our own nation. Third, by an impressive expression of the public will and without regard to partisanship, we are committed to the proposition that principle of morality and considerations for our own security will never permit us to acquiesce in a peace dictated by aggressors and sponsored by appeasers. We know that enduring peace cannot be bought at the cost of other people's freedom. In the recent national election there was no substantial difference between the two great parties in respect to that national policy. No issue was fought out on the line before the American electorate. And today it is abundantly evident that American citizens everywhere are demanding and supporting speedy and complete action in recognition of obvious danger.

Therefore, the immediate need is a swift and driving increase in our armament production. Leaders of industry and labor have responded to our summons. Goals of speed have been set. In some cases these goals are being reached ahead of time. In some cases we are on schedule; in other cases there are slight but not serious delays. And in some cases—and, I am sorry to say, very important cases—we are all concerned

15

by the slowness of the accomplishment of our plans. The Army and Navy, however, have made substantial progress during the past year. Actual experience is improving and speeding up our methods of production with every passing day. And today's best is not good enough for tomorrow.

I am not satisfied with the progress thus far made. The men in charge of the program represent the best in training, in ability and in patriotism. They are not satisfied with the progress thus far made. None of us will be satisfied until the job is done. No matter whether the original goal was set too high or too low, our objective is quicker and better results. To give you two illustrations: We are behind schedule in turning out finished airplanes. We are working day and night to solve the innumerable problems and to catch up. We are ahead of schedule in building warships, but we are working to get even further ahead of that schedule. To change a whole nation from a basis of peacetime production of implements of peace to a basis of wartime production of implements of war is no small task. The greatest difficulty comes at the beginning of the program, when new tools, new plant facilities, new assembly lines, new shipways must first be constructed before the actual material begins to flow steadily and speedily from them.

The Congress of course, must rightly keep itself informed at all times of the progress of the program. However, there is certain information, as the Congress itself will readily recognize, which, in the interests of our own security and those of the nations that we are supporting, must of needs be kept in confidence. New circumstances are constantly begetting new needs for our safety. I shall ask this Congress for greatly increased new appropriations and authorizations to carry on what we have begun.

I also ask this Congress for authority and for funds sufficient to manufacture additional munitions and war supplies of many kinds, to be turned over to those nations which are now in actual war with aggressor nations. Our most useful and immediate role is to act as an arsenal for them as well as for ourselves. They do not need manpower, but they do need billions of dollars' worth of the weapons of defense. The time is near when they will not be able to pay for them all in ready cash. We cannot, and we will not, tell them that they must surrender merely because of present inability to pay for the weapons which we know they must have.

I do not recommend that we make them a loan of dollars with which to pay for these weapons—a loan to be repaid in dollars. I recommend that we make it possible for those nations to continue to obtain war materials in the United States, fitting their orders into our own program. And nearly all of their material would, if the time ever came, be useful in our own defense. Taking counsel of expert military and naval authorities, considering what is best for our own security, we are free to decide how much should be kept here and how much should be sent abroad to our friends who, by their determined and heroic resistance, are giving us time in which to make ready our own defense.

20   For what we send abroad we shall be repaid, repaid within a reasonable time following the close of hostilities, repaid in similar materials, or at our option in other goods of many kinds which they can produce and which we need. Let us say to the democracies: "We Americans are vitally concerned in your defense of freedom. We are putting forth our energies, our resources and our organizing powers to give you the strength to regain and maintain a free world. We shall send you in ever-increasing numbers, ships, planes, tanks, guns. That is our purpose and our pledge."

In fulfillment of this purpose we will not be intimidated by the threats of dictators that they will regard as a breach of international law or as an act of war our aid to the democracies which dare to resist their aggression. Such aid is not an act of war, even if a dictator should unilaterally proclaim it so to be. And when the dictators—if the dictators—are ready to make war upon us, they will not wait for an act of war on our part. They did not wait for Norway or Belgium or the Netherlands to commit an act of war. Their only interest is in a new one-way international law which lacks mutuality in its observance and therefore becomes an instrument of oppression. The happiness of future generations of Americans may well depend on how effective and how immediate we can make our aid felt. No one can tell the exact character of the emergency situations that we may be called upon to meet. The nation's hands must not be tied when the nation's life is in danger.

Yes, and we must prepare, all of us prepare, to make the sacrifices that the emergency—almost as serious as war itself—demands. Whatever stands in the way of speed and efficiency in defense, in defense preparations at any time, must give way to the national need. A free nation has the right to expect full cooperation from all groups. A free nation has the right to look to the leaders of business, of labor and of agriculture to take the lead in stimulating effort, not among other groups but within their own groups.

The best way of dealing with the few slackers or trouble-makers in our midst is, first, to shame them by patriotic example, and if that fails, to use the sovereignty of government to save government. As men do not live by bread alone, they do not fight by armaments alone. Those who man our defenses and those behind them who build our defenses must have the stamina and the courage which come from unshakeable belief in the manner of life which they are defending. The mighty action that we are calling for cannot be based on a disregard of all the things worth fighting for.

The nation takes great satisfaction and much strength from the things which have been done to make its people conscious of their individual stake in the preservation of democratic life in America. Those things have toughened the fiber of our people, have renewed their faith and strengthened their devotion to the institutions we make ready to protect. Certainly this is no time for any of us to stop thinking about the social and economic problems which are the root cause of the social revolution which is today a supreme factor in the world. For there is nothing mysterious about the foundations of a healthy and strong democracy.

The basic things expected by our people of their political and economic systems are simple. They are: Equality of opportunity for youth and for others. Jobs for those who can work. Security for those who need it. The ending of special privilege for the few. The preservation of civil liberties for all. The enjoyment of the fruits of scientific progress in a wider and constantly rising standard of living. These are the simple, the basic things that must never be lost sight of in the turmoil and unbelievable complexity of our modern world. The inner and abiding strength of our economic and political systems is dependent upon the degree to which they fulfill these expectations.

Many subjects connected with our social economy call for immediate improvement. As examples: We should bring more citizens under the coverage of old-age pensions and unemployment insurance. We should widen the opportunities for adequate medical care. We should plan a better system by which persons deserving or needing gainful employment may obtain it. I have called for personal sacrifice, and I am assured of the willingness of almost all Americans to respond to that call. A part of the sacrifice means the payment of more money in taxes. In my budget message I will recommend that a greater portion of this great defense program be paid for from taxation than we are paying for today. No person should try, or be allowed to get rich out of the program, and the principle of tax payments in accordance with ability to pay should be constantly before our eyes to guide our legislation.

If the congress maintains these principles the voters, putting patriotism ahead of pocketbooks, will give you their applause. In the future days which we seek to make secure, we look forward to a world founded upon four essential human freedoms.

The first is freedom of speech and expression—everywhere in the world.

The second is freedom of every person to worship God in his own way—everywhere in the world.

30

The third is freedom from want, which, translated into world terms, means economic understandings which will secure to every nation a healthy peacetime life for its inhabitants—everywhere in the world.

The fourth is freedom from fear, which, translated into world terms, means a world-wide reduction of armaments to such a point and in such a thorough fashion that no nation will be in a position to commit an act of physical aggression against any neighbor—anywhere in the world.

That is no vision of a distant millennium. It is a definite basis for a kind of world attainable in our own time and generation. That kind of world is the very antithesis of the so-called "new order" of tyranny which the dictators seek to create with the crash of a bomb. To that new order we oppose the greater conception—the moral order. A good society is able to face schemes of world domination and foreign revolutions alike without fear. Since the beginning of our American history we have been engaged in change, in a perpetual, peaceful revolution, a revolution which goes on steadily, quietly, adjusting itself to changing conditions without the concentration camp or the quicklime in the ditch. The world order which we seek is the cooperation of free countries, working together in a friendly, civilized society.

This nation has placed its destiny in the hands, heads and hearts of its millions of free men and women, and its faith in freedom under the guidance of God. Freedom means the supremacy of human rights everywhere. Our support goes to those who struggle to gain those rights and keep them. Our strength is our unity of purpose.

To that high concept there can be no end save victory.

Franklin D. Roosevelt

Pearl Harbor Speech, December 8, 1941

The day after Pearl Harbor was bombed by the Japanese navy, Franklin Roosevelt addressed the full Congress (and the entire United States via radio broadcast) **asking for a declaration of war against Japan.** *Thus America entered the* **Second World War**—*a worldwide struggle against the Axis (Germany, Japan, and Italy) that would* **propel America out of the Depression and onto the world stage as a great superpower in the twentieth and twenty-first centuries.** *Although a strong advocate for England and France in their struggle against Germany, Roosevelt made no mention of Nazi Germany in his speech; Germany, however, would subsequently declare war on* *the United States as a result of treaties with Japan. For many years rumors persisted that Roosevelt, who felt America should join the war as soon as possible, had military intelligence that warned of the coming attack on Pearl Harbor, but no hard evidence has ever been produced to support the claim that the attack was anything but a terrible surprise.*

Yesterday, Dec. 7, 1941—a date which will live in infamy—the United States of America was suddenly and deliberately attacked by naval and air forces of the Empire of Japan.

The United States was at peace with that nation and, at the solicitation of Japan, was still in conversation with the government and its emperor looking toward the maintenance of peace in the Pacific. Indeed, one hour after Japanese air squadrons had commenced bombing in Oahu, the Japanese ambassador to the United States and his colleagues delivered to the Secretary of State a formal reply to a recent American message. While this reply stated that it seemed useless to continue the existing diplomatic negotiations, it contained no threat or hint of war or armed attack. It will be recorded that the distance of Hawaii from Japan makes it obvious that the attack was deliberately planned many days or even weeks ago. During the intervening time, the Japanese government has deliberately sought to deceive the United States by false statements and expressions of hope for continued peace.

The attack yesterday on the Hawaiian Islands has caused severe damage to American naval and military forces. Very many American lives have been lost. In addition, American ships have been reported torpedoed on the high seas between San Francisco and Honolulu. Yesterday, the Japanese government also launched an attack against Malaya.

Last night, Japanese forces attacked Hong Kong.

Last night, Japanese forces attacked Guam. 5

Last night, Japanese forces attacked the Philippine Islands.

Last night, the Japanese attacked Wake Island.

This morning, the Japanese attacked Midway Island.

Japan has, therefore, undertaken a surprise offensive extending throughout the Pacific area. The facts of yesterday speak for themselves. The people of the United States have already formed their opinions and well understand the implications to the very life and safety of our nation.

As commander in chief of the Army and Navy, I have directed that all measures be 10 taken for our defense. Always will we remember the character of the onslaught against us. No matter how long it may take us to overcome this premeditated invasion, the American people in their righteous might will win through to absolute victory.

I believe I interpret the will of the Congress and of the people when I assert that we will not only defend ourselves to the uttermost, but will make very certain that this form of treachery shall never endanger us again.

Hostilities exist. There is no blinking at the fact that our people, our territory and our interests are in grave danger. With confidence in our armed forces—with the unbounding determination of our people—we will gain the inevitable triumph—so help us God.

I ask that the Congress declare that since the unprovoked and dastardly attack by Japan on Sunday, Dec. 7, a state of war has existed between the United States and the Japanese empire.

Executive Order 9981

Harry S. Truman (1884–1972).

*Issued nearly a decade before what we commonly think of as the beginning of the modern **civil rights movement**, President Truman's executive order bypassed both houses of Congress and integrated the armed forces. African Americans had served in the military since colonial times—beginning with Crispus Attucks, who was killed by British soldiers in the Boston Massacre in 1770, but they were usually relegated to all-black units trained for service (such as cooks and mechanics), not combat. Truman's executive order **mandated that all soldiers** (regardless of race, color, religion, or national origin) **would train, fight, and, perhaps, die together.** Because Congress passed the Selective Service Act of 1948 ("the draft") to support troop levels in peace, the Korean War, and the Vietnam War, millions of young men (and later women) who lived in a segregated society would serve in an integrated military.*

The White House
July 26, 1948

Whereas it is essential that there be maintained in the armed services of the United States the highest standards of democracy, with equality of treatment and opportunity for all those who served in our country's defense:

Now, therefore, by virtue of the authority invested in me as President of the United States, and as Commander in Chief of the armed services, it is hereby ordered as follows:

1. It is hereby declared to be the policy of the President that there shall be equality of treatment and opportunity for all persons in the armed services without regard to race, color, religion or national origin. This policy shall be put into effect as rapidly as possible, having due regard to the time required to effectuate any necessary changes without impairing efficiency or morale.
2. There shall be created in the National Military Establishment an advisory committee to be known as the President's Committee on Equality of Treatment and Opportunity in the Armed Services, which shall be composed of seven members to be designated by the President.
3. The Committee is authorized on behalf of the President to examine into the rules, procedures and practices of the armed services in order to determine in what respect such rules, procedures and practices may be altered or improved with a view to

carrying out the policy of this order. The Committee shall confer and advise with the Secretary of Defense, the Secretary of the Army, the Secretary of the Navy, and Secretary of the Air Force, and shall make such recommendations to the President and to said Secretaries as in the judgment of the Committee will effectuate the policy hereof.

4. All executive departments and agencies of the Federal Government are authorized and directed to cooperate with the Committee in its work, and to furnish the Committee such information or the services of such persons as the Committee may require in the performance of its duties.

5. When requested by the Committee to do so, persons in the armed services or in any of the executive departments and agencies of the Federal Government shall testify before the Committee and shall make available for use of the Committee such documents and other information as the Committee may require.

6. The Committee shall continue to exist until such time as the President shall terminate its existence by Executive Order.

Supreme Court of the United States
Brown v. Board of Education (1954)

Argued December 9, 1952; Reargued December 8, 1953; Decided May 17, 1954

The case known as **Brown v. Board of Education** *actually encompasses cases presented from Kansas, South Carolina, Virginia, and Delaware.* **Brown** *overturned the doctrine of "separate but equal," which had been declared constitutional by* **Plessy v. Ferguson** *in 1896.* **Thurgood Marshall,** *who would one day be named the first African American on the Supreme Court, successfully argued the case.* **Chief Justice Earl Warren** *understood the historical ramifications of the case, about which he declared that* **"separate but equal" had no place in public education,** *and that, in fact,* **"separate educational facilities are inherently unequal."** *Warren knew that a divided court would not make a strong enough statement for such an important and life-altering case, so he lobbied and won a unanimous decision for* **Brown.**

Appeal from the United States District Court for the District of Kansas*

Syllabus

Segregation of white and Negro children in the public schools of a State solely on the basis of race, pursuant to state laws permitting or requiring such segregation, denies to Negro children the equal protection of the laws guaranteed by the Fourteenth Amendment—even though the physical facilities and other "tangible" factors of white and Negro schools may be equal.

(a) The history of the Fourteenth Amendment is inconclusive as to its intended effect on public education.

(b) The question presented in these cases must be determined not on the basis of conditions existing when the Fourteenth Amendment was adopted, but in the light of the full development of public education and its present place in American life throughout the Nation.

(c) Where a State has undertaken to provide an opportunity for an education in its public schools, such an opportunity is a right which must be made available to all on equal terms.

(d) Segregation of children in public schools solely on the basis of race deprives children of the minority group of equal educational opportunities, even though the physical facilities and other "tangible" factors may be equal.

(e) The "separate but equal" doctrine adopted in Plessy v. Ferguson, 163 U.S. 537, has no place in the field of public education.

(f) The cases are restored to the docket for further argument on specified questions relating to the forms of the decrees.

Opinion

MR. CHIEF JUSTICE WARREN delivered the opinion of the Court.

These cases come to us from the States of Kansas, South Carolina, Virginia, and Delaware. They are premised on different facts and different local conditions, but a common legal question justifies their consideration together in this consolidated opinion.

In each of the cases, minors of the Negro race, through their legal representatives, seek the aid of the courts in obtaining admission to the public schools of their community on a nonsegregated basis. In each instance, they had been denied admission to schools attended by white children under laws requiring or permitting segregation according to race. This segregation was alleged to deprive the plaintiffs of the equal protection of the laws under the Fourteenth Amendment. In each of the cases other than the Delaware case, a three-judge federal district court denied relief to the plaintiffs on the so-called "separate but equal" doctrine announced by this Court in Plessy v. Ferguson, 163 U.S. 537. Under that doctrine, equality of treatment is accorded when the races are provided substantially equal facilities, even though these facilities be separate. In the Delaware case, the Supreme Court of Delaware adhered to that doctrine, but ordered that the plaintiffs be admitted to the white schools because of their superiority to the Negro schools.

The plaintiffs contend that segregated public schools are not "equal" and cannot be made "equal," and that hence they are deprived of the equal protection of the laws. Because of the obvious importance of the question presented, the Court took jurisdiction. Argument was heard in the 1952 Term, and reargument was heard this Term on certain questions propounded by the Court.

Reargument was largely devoted to the circumstances surrounding the adoption of the Fourteenth Amendment in 1868. It covered exhaustively consideration of the Amendment in Congress, ratification by the states, then-existing practices in racial segregation, and the views of proponents and opponents of the Amendment. This discussion and our own investigation convince us that, although these sources cast some light, it is not enough to resolve the problem with which we are faced. At best, they are inconclusive. The most avid proponents of the post-War Amendments undoubtedly intended them to remove all legal distinctions among "all persons born or naturalized in the United States." Their opponents, just as certainly, were antagonistic to both the letter and the spirit of the Amendments and wished them to have the most limited effect. What others in Congress and the state legislatures had in mind cannot be determined with any degree of certainty.

An additional reason for the inconclusive nature of the Amendment's history with respect to segregated schools is the status of public education at that time. In the South, the movement toward free common schools, supported by general taxation, had not yet taken hold. Education of white children was largely in the hands of private groups. Education of Negroes was almost nonexistent, and practically all of the race were illiterate. In fact, any education of Negroes was forbidden by law in some states. Today, in contrast, many Negroes have achieved outstanding success in the arts and sciences, as well as in the business and professional world. It is true that public school education at the time of the Amendment had advanced further in the North, but the effect of the Amendment on Northern States was generally ignored in the congressional debates. Even in the North, the conditions of public education did not approximate those existing today. The curriculum was usually rudimentary; ungraded schools were common in rural areas; the school term was but three months a year in many states, and compulsory school attendance was virtually unknown. As a consequence, it is not surprising that there should be so little in the history of the Fourteenth Amendment relating to its intended effect on public education.

In the first cases in this Court construing the Fourteenth Amendment, decided shortly after its adoption, the Court interpreted it as proscribing all state-imposed discriminations against the Negro race. The doctrine of "separate but equal" did not make its appearance in this Court until 1896 in the case of *Plessy v. Ferguson*, supra, involving not education but transportation. American courts have since labored with the doctrine for over half a century. In this Court, there have been six cases involving the "separate but equal" doctrine in the field of public education. In *Cumming v. County Board of Education*, 175 U.S. 528, and *Gong Lum v. Rice*, 275 U.S. 78, the validity of the doctrine itself was not challenged. In more recent cases, all on the graduate school level, inequality was found in that specific benefits enjoyed by white students were denied to Negro students of the same educational qualifications. Missouri ex rel. *Gaines v. Canada*, 305 U.S. 337; *Sipuel v. Oklahoma*, 332 U.S. 631; *Sweatt v. Painter*, 339 U.S. 629; *McLaurin v. Oklahoma State Regents*, 339 U.S. 637. In none of these cases was it necessary to reexamine the doctrine to grant relief to the Negro plaintiff. And in *Sweatt v. Painter*, supra, the Court expressly reserved decision on the question whether *Plessy v. Ferguson* should be held inapplicable to public education.

In the instant cases, that question is directly presented. Here, unlike *Sweatt v. Painter*, there are findings below that the Negro and white schools involved have been equalized, or are being equalized, with respect to buildings, curricula, qualifications and salaries of teachers, and other "tangible" factors. Our decision, therefore, cannot turn on merely a comparison of these tangible factors in the Negro and white schools involved in each of the cases. We must look instead to the effect of segregation itself on public education.

In approaching this problem, we cannot turn the clock back to 1868, when the Amendment was adopted, or even to 1896, when *Plessy v. Ferguson* was written. We must consider public education in the light of its full development and its present place in American life throughout the Nation. Only in this way can it be determined if segregation in public schools deprives these plaintiffs of the equal protection of the laws.

Today, education is perhaps the most important function of state and local governments. Compulsory school attendance laws and the great expenditures for

10

education both demonstrate our recognition of the importance of education to our democratic society. It is required in the performance of our most basic public responsibilities, even service in the armed forces. It is the very foundation of good citizenship. Today it is a principal instrument in awakening the child to cultural values, in preparing him for later professional training, and in helping him to adjust normally to his environment. In these days, it is doubtful that any child may reasonably be expected to succeed in life if he is denied the opportunity of an education. Such an opportunity, where the state has undertaken to provide it, is a right which must be made available to all on equal terms.

We come then to the question presented: Does segregation of children in public schools solely on the basis of race, even though the physical facilities and other "tangible" factors may be equal, deprive the children of the minority group of equal educational opportunities? We believe that it does.

In *Sweatt v. Painter*, supra, in finding that a segregated law school for Negroes could not provide them equal educational opportunities, this Court relied in large part on "those qualities which are incapable of objective measurement but which make for greatness in a law school." In *McLaurin v. Oklahoma State Regents*, supra, the Court, in requiring that a Negro admitted to a white graduate school be treated like all other students, again resorted to intangible considerations: ". . . his ability to study, to engage in discussions and exchange views with other students, and, in general, to learn his profession." Such considerations apply with added force to children in grade and high schools. To separate them from others of similar age and qualifications solely because of their race generates a feeling of inferiority as to their status in the community that may affect their hearts and minds in a way unlikely ever to be undone. The effect of this separation on their educational opportunities was well stated by a finding in the Kansas case by a court which nevertheless felt compelled to rule against the Negro plaintiffs:

Segregation of white and colored children in public schools has a detrimental effect upon the colored children. The impact is greater when it has the sanction of the law, for the policy of separating the races is usually interpreted as denoting the inferiority of the negro group. A sense of inferiority affects the motivation of a child to learn. Segregation with the sanction of law, therefore, has a tendency to [retard] the educational and mental development of negro children and to deprive them of some of the benefits they would receive in a racial[ly] integrated school system.

Whatever may have been the extent of psychological knowledge at the time of *Plessy v. Ferguson*, this finding is amply supported by modern authority. Any language in *Plessy v. Ferguson* contrary to this finding is rejected.

15   We conclude that, in the field of public education, the doctrine of "separate but equal" has no place. Separate educational facilities are inherently unequal. Therefore, we hold that the plaintiffs and others similarly situated for whom the actions have been brought are, by reason of the segregation complained of, deprived of the equal protection of the laws guaranteed by the Fourteenth Amendment. This disposition makes unnecessary any discussion whether such segregation also violates the Due Process Clause of the Fourteenth Amendment.

Because these are class actions, because of the wide applicability of this decision, and because of the great variety of local conditions, the formulation of decrees in these cases presents problems of considerable complexity. On reargument, the consideration of appropriate relief was necessarily subordinated to the primary question—the constitutionality of segregation in public education. We have now announced that such segregation is a denial of the equal protection of the laws. In order that we may have the full assistance of the parties in formulating decrees, the cases will be restored to the docket, and the parties are requested to present further argument on Questions 4 and 5 previously propounded by the Court for the reargument this Term The Attorney General of the United States is again invited to participate. The Attorneys General of the states requiring or permitting segregation in public education will also be permitted to appear as amici curiae upon request to do so by September 15, 1954, and submission of briefs by October 1, 1954.

It is so ordered.

Dwight D. Eisenhower

Farewell Address, January 17, 1961

Dwight D. Eisenhower (1890–1969).

Sometimes compared with George Washington's Farewell Address (which encouraged international trade and discouraged international military alliances), **Eisenhower's Farewell Address** *comes on* **the eve of his leaving office and our involvement in Vietnam.** *A West Point graduate, war hero, and life-long soldier, Eisenhower sees a threat to America from the arms industry that grew out of World War II and the cold war, even as he says America is dependent upon the same industry for its protection. His address is* **something of a warning,** *and in hindsight,* **many have turned to it as a prediction we might have heeded before entering into a** **full-blown conflict with Vietnam**—*which would cost America over 58,000 lives and fail to contain communism.*

Good evening, my fellow Americans.

First, I should like to express my gratitude to the radio and television networks for the opportunities they have given me over the years to bring reports and messages to our nation. My special thanks go to them for the opportunity of addressing you this evening.

Three days from now, after a half century in the service of our country, I shall lay down the responsibilities of office as, in traditional and solemn ceremony, the authority of the Presidency is vested in my successor.

This evening I come to you with a message of leave-taking and farewell, and to share a few final thoughts with you, my countrymen. Like every other citizen, I wish the new President, and all who will labor with him, Godspeed. I pray that the coming years will be blessed with peace and prosperity for all.

5   Our people expect their President and the Congress to find essential agreement on issues of great moment, the wise resolution of which will better shape the future of the nation. My own relations with the Congress, which began on a remote and tenuous basis when, long ago, a member of the Senate appointed me to West Point, have since ranged to the intimate during the war and immediate post-war period, and finally to the mutually interdependent during these past eight years. In this final relationship, the Congress and the Administration have, on most vital issues, cooperated well, to serve the nation good, rather than mere partisanship, and so have assured that the business of the nation should go forward. So, my official relationship with Congress ends in a feeling—on my part—of gratitude that we have been able to do so much together.

We now stand ten years past the midpoint of a century that has witnessed four major wars among great nations. Three of these involved our own country. Despite these holocausts, America is today the strongest, the most influential, and most productive nation in the world. Understandably proud of this pre-eminence, we yet realize that America's leadership and prestige depend, not merely upon our unmatched material progress, riches and military strength, but on how we use our power in the interests of world peace and human betterment.

Throughout America's adventure in free government, our basic purposes have been to keep the peace, to foster progress in human achievement, and to enhance liberty, dignity and integrity among peoples and among nations. To strive for less would be unworthy of a free and religious people. Any failure traceable to arrogance or our lack of comprehension or readiness to sacrifice would inflict upon us grievous hurt, both at home and abroad.

Progress toward these noble goals is persistently threatened by the conflict now engulfing the world. It commands our whole attention, absorbs our very beings. We face a hostile ideology global in scope, atheistic in character, ruthless in purpose, and insidious in method. Unhappily, the danger it poses promises to be of indefinite duration. To meet it successfully, there is called for, not so much the emotional and transitory sacrifices of crisis, but rather those which enable us to carry forward steadily, surely, and without complaint the burdens of a prolonged and complex struggle with liberty the stake. Only thus shall we remain, despite every provocation, on our charted course toward permanent peace and human betterment.

Crises there will continue to be. In meeting them, whether foreign or domestic, great or small, there is a recurring temptation to feel that some spectacular and costly action could become the miraculous solution to all current difficulties. A huge increase in newer elements of our defenses; development of unrealistic programs to cure every ill in agriculture; a dramatic expansion in basic and applied research—these and many other possibilities, each possibly promising in itself, may be suggested as the only way to the road we wish to travel.

10   But each proposal must be weighed in the light of a broader consideration: the need to maintain balance in and among national programs, balance between the private and the public economy, balance between the cost and hoped for advantages, balance between the clearly necessary and the comfortably desirable, balance between our essential requirements as a nation and the duties imposed by the nation upon the individual, balance between actions of the moment and the national welfare of the future. Good judgment seeks balance and progress. Lack of it eventually finds imbalance and frustration. The record of many decades stands as proof that our people and their

Government have, in the main, understood these truths and have responded to them well, in the face of threat and stress.

But threats, new in kind or degree, constantly arise. Of these, I mention two only.

A vital element in keeping the peace is our military establishment. Our arms must be mighty, ready for instant action, so that no potential aggressor may be tempted to risk his own destruction. Our military organization today bears little relation to that known by any of my predecessors in peacetime, or, indeed, by the fighting men of World War II or Korea.

Until the latest of our world conflicts, the United States had no armaments industry. American makers of plowshares could, with time and as required, make swords as well. But now we can no longer risk emergency improvisation of national defense. We have been compelled to create a permanent armaments industry of vast proportions. Added to this, three and a half million men and women are directly engaged in the defense establishment. We annually spend on military security alone more than the net income of all United States corporations.

Now this conjunction of an immense military establishment and a large arms industry is new in the American experience. The total influence—economic, political, even spiritual—is felt in every city, every Statehouse, every office of the Federal government. We recognize the imperative need for this development. Yet we must not fail to comprehend its grave implications. Our toil, resources, and livelihood are all involved. So is the very structure of our society.

In the councils of government, we must guard against the acquisition of unwarranted influence, whether sought or unsought, by the military-industrial complex. The potential for the disastrous rise of misplaced power exists and will persist. We must never let the weight of this combination endanger our liberties or democratic processes. We should take nothing for granted. Only an alert and knowledgeable citizenry can compel the proper meshing of the huge industrial and military machinery of defense with our peaceful methods and goals, so that security and liberty may prosper together.

Akin to, and largely responsible for the sweeping changes in our industrial-military posture, has been the technological revolution during recent decades. In this revolution, research has become central, it also becomes more formalized, complex, and costly. A steadily increasing share is conducted for, by, or at the direction of, the Federal government.

Today, the solitary inventor, tinkering in his shop, has been overshadowed by task forces of scientists in laboratories and testing fields. In the same fashion, the free university, historically the fountainhead of free ideas and scientific discovery, has experienced a revolution in the conduct of research. Partly because of the huge costs involved, a government contract becomes virtually a substitute for intellectual curiosity. For every old blackboard there are now hundreds of new electronic computers. The prospect of domination of the nation's scholars by Federal employment, project allocations, and the power of money is ever present—and is gravely to be regarded.

Yet, in holding scientific research and discovery in respect, as we should, we must also be alert to the equal and opposite danger that public policy could itself become the captive of a scientific-technological elite.

It is the task of statesmanship to mold, to balance, and to integrate these and other forces, new and old, within the principles of our democratic system—ever aiming toward the supreme goals of our free society.

20   Another factor in maintaining balance involves the element of time. As we peer into society's future, we—you and I, and our government—must avoid the impulse to live only for today, plundering for our own ease and convenience the precious resources of tomorrow. We cannot mortgage the material assets of our grandchildren without risking the loss also of their political and spiritual heritage. We want democracy to survive for all generations to come, not to become the insolvent phantom of tomorrow.

     During the long lane of the history yet to be written, America knows that this world of ours, ever growing smaller, must avoid becoming a community of dreadful fear and hate, and be, instead, a proud confederation of mutual trust and respect. Such a confederation must be one of equals. The weakest must come to the conference table with the same confidence as do we, protected as we are by our moral, economic, and military strength. That table, though scarred by many past frustrations, cannot be abandoned for the certain agony of the battlefield.

     Disarmament, with mutual honor and confidence, is a continuing imperative. Together we must learn how to compose differences, not with arms, but with intellect and decent purpose. Because this need is so sharp and apparent, I confess that I lay down my official responsibilities in this field with a definite sense of disappointment. As one who has witnessed the horror and the lingering sadness of war, as one who knows that another war could utterly destroy this civilization which has been so slowly and painfully built over thousands of years, I wish I could say tonight that a lasting peace is in sight.

     Happily, I *can* say that war has been avoided. Steady progress toward our ultimate goal has been made. But so much remains to be done. As a private citizen, I shall never cease to do what little I can to help the world advance along that road.

     So, in this my last good night to you as your President, I thank you for the many opportunities you have given me for public service in war and in peace. I trust that in that service you find some things worthy. As for the rest of it, I know you will find ways to improve performance in the future.

25   You and I, my fellow citizens, need to be strong in our faith that all nations, under God, will reach the goal of peace with justice. May we be ever unswerving in devotion to principle, confident but humble with power, diligent in pursuit of the Nations' great goals.

     To all the peoples of the world, I once more give expression to America's prayerful and continuing aspiration: We pray that peoples of all faiths, all races, all nations, may have their great human needs satisfied; that those now denied opportunity shall come to enjoy it to the full; that all who yearn for freedom may experience its few spiritual blessings. Those who have freedom will understand, also, its heavy responsibilities; that all who are insensitive to the needs of others will learn charity; and that the scourges of poverty, disease and ignorance will be made to disappear from the earth; and that, in the goodness of time, all peoples will come to live together in a peace guaranteed by the binding force of mutual respect and love.

     Now, on Friday noon, I am to become a private citizen. I am proud to do so. I look forward to it.

     Thank you, and good night.

John F. Kennedy

Inaugural Address, January 20, 1961

John F. Kennedy (1917–1963).

The youngest man ever elected to the presidency, Kennedy used this Inaugural Address to introduce the nation to the idea that a young, vigorous generation had come to power in an administration that was going **to ask American citizens to both fight Communism and serve their fellow man at home and abroad.** *The contrast he drew between himself and Eisenhower was dramatic and deliberate and served to galvanize a nation of young people who would join the Peace Corps. Famous for its language and energy,* **this speech took on greater meaning after President Kennedy was assassinated** *on November 22, 1963, leaving much of the work of his administration undone in Vietnam, civil rights, and the fight against poverty in America.*

Vice President Johnson, Mr. Speaker, Mr. Chief Justice, President Eisenhower, Vice President Nixon, President Truman, Reverend Clergy, fellow citizens:

We observe today not a victory of party but a celebration of freedom—symbolizing an end as well as a beginning—signifying renewal as well as change. For I have sworn before you and Almighty God the same solemn oath our forbears prescribed nearly a century and three-quarters ago.

The world is very different now. For man holds in his mortal hands the power to abolish all forms of human poverty and all forms of human life. And yet the same revolutionary beliefs for which our forebears fought are still at issue around the globe—the belief that the rights of man come not from the generosity of the state but from the hand of God.

We dare not forget today that we are the heirs of that first revolution. Let the word go forth from this time and place, to friend and foe alike, that the torch has been passed to a new generation of Americans—born in this century, tempered by war, disciplined by a hard and bitter peace, proud of our ancient heritage—and unwilling to witness or permit the slow undoing of those human rights to which this nation has always been committed, and to which we are committed today at home and around the world.

Let every nation know, whether it wishes us well or ill, that we shall pay any price, bear any burden, meet any hardship, support any friend, oppose any foe to assure the survival and the success of liberty.

This much we pledge—and more.

To those old allies whose cultural and spiritual origins we share, we pledge the loyalty of faithful friends. United there is little we cannot do in a host of cooperative ventures.

5

Divided there is little we can do—for we dare not meet a powerful challenge at odds and split asunder.

To those new states whom we welcome to the ranks of the free, we pledge our word that one form of colonial control shall not have passed away merely to be replaced by a far more iron tyranny. We shall not always expect to find them supporting our view. But we shall always hope to find them strongly supporting their own freedom—and to remember that, in the past, those who foolishly sought power by riding the back of the tiger ended up inside.

To those people in the huts and villages of half the globe struggling to break the bonds of mass misery, we pledge our best efforts to help them help themselves, for whatever period is required—not because the communists may be doing it, not because we seek their votes, but because it is right. If a free society cannot help the many who are poor, it cannot save the few who are rich.

10 To our sister republics south of our border, we offer a special pledge—to convert our good words into good deeds—in a new alliance for progress—to assist free men and free governments in casting off the chains of poverty. But this peaceful revolution of hope cannot become the prey of hostile powers. Let all our neighbors know that we shall join with them to oppose aggression or subversion anywhere in the Americas. And let every other power know that this Hemisphere intends to remain the master of its own house.

To that world assembly of sovereign states, the United Nations, our last best hope in an age where the instruments of war have far outpaced the instruments of peace, we renew our pledge of support—to prevent it from becoming merely a forum for invective—to strengthen its shield of the new and the weak—and to enlarge the area in which its writ may run.

Finally, to those nations who would make themselves our adversary, we offer not a pledge but a request: that both sides begin anew the quest for peace, before the dark powers of destruction unleashed by science engulf all humanity in planned or accidental self-destruction.

We dare not tempt them with weakness. For only when our arms are sufficient beyond doubt can we be certain beyond doubt that they will never be employed.

But neither can two great and powerful groups of nations take comfort from our present course—both sides overburdened by the cost of modern weapons, both rightly alarmed by the steady spread of the deadly atom, yet both racing to alter that uncertain balance of terror that stays the hand of mankind's final war.

15 So let us begin anew—remembering on both sides that civility is not a sign of weakness, and sincerity is always subject to proof. Let us never negotiate out of fear. But let us never fear to negotiate.

Let both sides explore what problems unite us instead of belaboring those problems which divide us.

Let both sides, for the first time, formulate serious and precise proposals for the inspection and control of arms—and bring the absolute power to destroy other nations under the absolute control of all nations.

Let both sides seek to invoke the wonders of science instead of its terrors. Together let us explore the stars, conquer the deserts, eradicate disease, tap the ocean depths and encourage the arts and commerce.

Let both sides unite to heed in all corners of the earth the command of Isaiah—to "undo the heavy burdens . . . (and) let the oppressed go free."

And if a beachhead of cooperation may push back the jungle of suspicion, let both   20
sides join in creating a new endeavor, not a new balance of power, but a new world of
law, where the strong are just and the weak secure and the peace preserved.

All this will not be finished in the first one hundred days. Nor will it be finished in the
first one thousand days, nor in the life of this Administration, nor even perhaps in our lifetime on this planet. But let us begin.

In your hands, my fellow citizens, more than mine, will rest the final success or failure of our course. Since this country was founded, each generation of Americans has been
summoned to give testimony to its national loyalty. The graves of young Americans who
answered the call to service surround the globe.

Now the trumpet summons us again—not as a call to bear arms, though arms we
need—not as a call to battle, though embattled we are—but a call to bear the burden of a
long twilight struggle, year in and year out, "rejoicing in hope, patient in tribulation"—
a struggle against the common enemies of man: tyranny, poverty, disease and war itself.

Can we forge against these enemies a grand and global alliance, North and South,
East and West, that can assure a more fruitful life for all mankind? Will you join in that
historic effort?

In the long history of the world, only a few generations have been granted the role of   25
defending freedom in its hour of maximum danger. I do not shrink from this responsibility—
I welcome it. I do not believe that any of us would exchange places with any other people
or any other generation. The energy, the faith, the devotion which we bring to this
endeavor will light our country and all who serve it—and the glow from that fire can truly
light the world.

And so, my fellow Americans: ask not what your country can do for you—ask what you
can do for your country.

My fellow citizens of the world: ask not what America will do for you, but what
together we can do for the freedom of man.

Finally, whether you are citizens of America or citizens of the world, ask of us here the
same high standards of strength and sacrifice which we ask of you. With a good conscience
our only sure reward, with history the final judge of our deeds, let us go forth to lead the
land we love, asking His blessing and His help, but knowing that here on earth God's work
must truly be our own.

Martin Luther King, Jr.

Letter from a Birmingham Jail, April 16, 1963

Birmingham, Alabama, in 1963 is often referred to as the **epicenter of the civil rights movement.** In early April, **Martin Luther King, Jr.** was invited to Birmingham by organizer **Rev. Fred Shuttlesworth** to participate in an event called **Project C,** for confrontation. Protesters were being arrested daily, and King was slated to have his turn in jail on Good
Friday, April 12. He told his aids: "Look, I don't know what to do. I just know that something
has got to change in Birmingham. I don't know whether I can raise money to get people out
of jail. I do know that I can go into jail with them." King was arrested and put in solitary con-
finement. While he was there, he read a letter in the newspaper **from eight white
clergymen, encouraging him to withdraw his support from the demonstrators,** and

Martin Luther King, Jr. (1929–1968).

work toward peace in the courts, not in the streets. The clergymen were appealing to his "common sense." King's well known **letter was written in response to the clergymen's request.** He wrote it on the sides of the newspaper, and whatever scraps of paper he could pull together in prison. In this eloquently definitive response, King explains why **the time has come for nonviolent action— demonstrations, going to jail when arrested; the patient waiting for the white man to correct injustice no longer was common sense.**

MY DEAR FELLOW CLERGYMEN:

While confined here in the Birmingham city jail, I came across your recent statement calling my present activities "unwise and untimely." Seldom do I pause to answer criticism of my work and ideas. If I sought to answer all the criticisms that cross my desk, my secretaries would have little time for anything other than such correspondence in the course of the day, and I would have no time for constructive work. But since I feel that you are men of genuine good will and that your criticisms are sincerely set forth, I want to try to answer your statements in what I hope will be patient and reasonable terms.

I think I should indicate why I am here in Birmingham, since you have been influenced by the view which argues against "outsiders coming in." I have the honor of serving as president of the Southern Christian Leadership Conference, an organization operating in every southern state, with headquarters in Atlanta, Georgia. We have some eighty-five affiliated organizations across the South, and one of them is the Alabama Christian Movement for Human Rights. Frequently we share staff, educational and financial resources with our affiliates. Several months ago the affiliate here in Birmingham asked us to be on call to engage in a nonviolent direct-action program if such were deemed necessary. We readily consented, and when the hour came we lived up to our promise. So I, along with several members of my staff, am here because I was invited here. I am here because I have organizational ties here.

But more basically, I am in Birmingham because injustice is here. Just as the prophets of the eighth century B.C. left their villages and carried their "thus saith the Lord" far beyond the boundaries of their home towns, and just as the Apostle Paul left his village of Tarsus and carried the gospel of Jesus Christ to the far corners of the Greco-Roman world, so am I compelled to carry the gospel of freedom beyond my own home town. Like Paul, I must constantly respond to the Macedonian call for aid.

5   Moreover, I am cognizant of the interrelatedness of all communities and states. I cannot sit idly by in Atlanta and not be concerned about what happens in Birmingham.

Injustice anywhere is a threat to justice everywhere. We are caught in an inescapable network of mutuality, tied in a single garment of destiny. Whatever affects one directly, affects all indirectly. Never again can we afford to live with the narrow, provincial "outside agitator" idea. Anyone who lives inside the United States can never be considered an outsider anywhere within its bounds.

You deplore the demonstrations taking place In Birmingham. But your statement, I am sorry to say, fails to express a similar concern for the conditions that brought about the demonstrations. I am sure that none of you would want to rest content with the superficial kind of social analysis that deals merely with effects and does not grapple with underlying causes. It is unfortunate that demonstrations are taking place in Birmingham, but it is even more unfortunate that the city's white power structure left the Negro community with no alternative.

In any nonviolent campaign there are four basic steps: collection of the facts to determine whether injustices exist; negotiation; self-purification; and direct action. We have gone through these steps in Birmingham. There can be no gainsaying the fact that racial injustice engulfs this community. Birmingham is probably the most thoroughly segregated city in the United States. Its ugly record of brutality is widely known. Negroes have experienced grossly unjust treatment in the courts. There have been more unsolved bombings of Negro homes and churches in Birmingham than in any other city in the nation. These are the hard, brutal facts of the case. On the basis of these conditions, Negro leaders sought to negotiate with the city fathers. But the latter consistently refused to engage in good-faith negotiation.

Then, last September, came the opportunity to talk with leaders of Birmingham's economic community. In the course of the negotiations, certain promises were made by the merchants—for example, to remove the stores humiliating racial signs. On the basis of these promises, the Reverend Fred Shuttlesworth and the leaders of the Alabama Christian Movement for Human Rights agreed to a moratorium on all demonstrations. As the weeks and months went by, we realized that we were the victims of a broken promise. A few signs, briefly removed, returned; the others remained.

As in so many past experiences, our hopes had been blasted, and the shadow of deep disappointment settled upon us. We had no alternative except to prepare for direct action, whereby we would present our very bodies as a means of laying our case before the conscience of the local and the national community. Mindful of the difficulties involved, we decided to undertake a process of self-purification. We began a series of workshops on nonviolence, and we repeatedly asked ourselves: "Are you able to accept blows without retaliating?" "Are you able to endure the ordeal of jail?" We decided to schedule our direct-action program for the Easter season, realizing that except for Christmas, this is the main shopping period of the year. Knowing that a strong economic withdrawal program would be the by-product of direct action, we felt that this would be the best time to bring pressure to bear on the merchants for the needed change.

Then it occurred to us that Birmingham's mayoralty election was coming up in March, 10 and we speedily decided to postpone action until after election day. When we discovered that the Commissioner of Public Safety, Eugene "Bull" Connor, had piled up enough votes to be in the run-off we decided again to postpone action until the day after the run-off so that the demonstrations could not be used to cloud the issues. Like many others, we waited to see Mr. Connor defeated, and to this end we endured postponement after post-ponement. Having aided in this community need, we felt that our direct-action program could be delayed no longer.

You may well ask: "Why direct action? Why sit-ins, marches and so forth? Isn't negotiation a better path?" You are quite right in calling for negotiation. Indeed, this is the very purpose of direct action. Nonviolent direct action seeks to create such a crisis and foster such a tension that a community which has constantly refused to negotiate is forced to confront the issue. It seeks so to dramatize the issue that it can no longer be ignored. My citing the creation of tension as part of the work of the nonviolent-resister may sound rather shocking. But I must confess that I am not afraid of the word "tension." I have earnestly opposed violent tension, but there is a type of constructive, nonviolent tension which is necessary for growth. Just as Socrates felt that it was necessary to create a ten-sion in the mind so that individuals could rise from the bondage of myths and half-truths to the unfettered realm of creative analysis and objective appraisal, we must see the need for nonviolent gadflies to create the kind of tension in society that will help men rise from the dark depths of prejudice and racism to the majestic heights of understanding and brotherhood.

The purpose of our direct-action program is to create a situation so crisis-packed that it will inevitably open the door to negotiation. I therefore concur with you in your call for negotiation. Too long has our beloved Southland been bogged down in a tragic effort to live in monologue rather than dialogue.

One of the basic points in your statement is that the action that I and my associates have taken in Birmingham is untimely. Some have asked: "Why didn't you give the new city administration time to act?" The only answer that I can give to this query is that the new Birmingham administration must be prodded about as much as the outgoing one, before it will act. We are sadly mistaken if we feel that the election of Albert Boutwell as mayor will bring the millennium to Birmingham. While Mr. Boutwell is a much more gentle person than Mr. Connor, they are both segregationists, dedicated to maintenance of the status quo. I have hope that Mr. Boutwell will be rea-sonable enough to see the futility of massive resistance to desegregation. But he will not see this without pressure from devotees of civil rights. My friends, I must say to you that we have not made a single gain in civil rights without determined legal and nonvi-olent pressure. Lamentably, it is an historical fact that privileged groups seldom give up their privileges voluntarily. Individuals may see the moral light and voluntarily give up their unjust posture; but, as Reinhold Niebuhr has reminded us, groups tend to be more immoral than individuals.

We know through painful experience that freedom is never voluntarily given by the oppressor; it must be demanded by the oppressed. Frankly, I have yet to engage in a direct-action campaign that was "well timed" in the view of those who have not suffered unduly from the disease of segregation. For years now I have heard the word "Wait!" It rings in the ear of every Negro with piercing familiarity. This "Wait" has almost always meant 'Never.' We must come to see, with one of our distinguished jurists, that "justice too long delayed is justice denied."

15   We have waited for more than 340 years for our constitutional and God-given rights. The nations of Asia and Africa are moving with jetlike speed toward gaining political

independence, but we stiff creep at horse-and-buggy pace toward gaining a cup of coffee at a lunch counter. Perhaps it is easy for those who have never felt the stinging dark of segregation to say, "Wait." But when you have seen vicious mobs lynch your mothers and fathers at will and drown your sisters and brothers at whim; when you have seen hate-filled policemen curse, kick and even kill your black brothers and sisters; when you see the vast majority of your twenty million Negro brothers smothering in an airtight cage of poverty in the midst of an affluent society; when you suddenly find your tongue twisted and your speech stammering as you seek to explain to your six-year-old daughter why she can't go to the public amusement park that has just been advertised on television, and see tears welling up in her eyes when she is told that Funtown is closed to colored children, and see ominous clouds of inferiority beginning to form in her little mental sky, and see her beginning to distort her personality by developing an unconscious bitterness toward white people; when you have to concoct an answer for a five-year-old son who is asking: "Daddy, why do white people treat colored people so mean?"; when you take a cross-country drive and find it necessary to sleep night after night in the uncomfortable corners of your automobile because no motel will accept you; when you are humiliated day in and day out by nagging signs reading "white" and "colored"; when your first name becomes "nigger," your middle name becomes "boy" (however old you are) and your last name becomes "John," and your wife and mother are never given the respected title "Mrs."; when you are harried by day and haunted by night by the fact that you are a Negro, living constantly at tiptoe stance, never quite knowing what to expect next, and are plagued with inner fears and outer resentments; when you are forever fighting a degenerating sense of "nobodiness" then you will understand why we find it difficult to wait. There comes a time when the cup of endurance runs over, and men are no longer willing to be plunged into the abyss of despair. I hope, sirs, you can understand our legitimate and unavoidable impatience.

You express a great deal of anxiety over our willingness to break laws. This is certainly a legitimate concern. Since we so diligently urge people to obey the Supreme Court's decision of 1954 outlawing segregation in the public schools, at first glance it may seem rather paradoxical for us consciously to break laws. One may ask: "How can you advocate breaking some laws and obeying others?" The answer lies in the fact that there are two types of laws: just and unjust. I would be the first to advocate obeying just laws. One has not only a legal but a moral responsibility to obey just laws. Conversely, one has a moral responsibility to disobey unjust laws. I would agree with St. Augustine that "an unjust law is no law at all."

Now, what is the difference between the two? How does one determine whether a law is just or unjust? A just law is a man-made code that squares with the moral law or the law of God. An unjust law is a code that is out of harmony with the moral law. To put it in the terms of St. Thomas Aquinas: An unjust law is a human law that is not rooted in eternal law and natural law. Any law that uplifts human personality is just. Any law that degrades human personality is unjust. All segregation statutes are unjust because segregation distorts the soul and damages the personality. It gives the segregator a false sense of superiority and the segregated a false sense of inferiority. Segregation, to use the terminology of the Jewish philosopher Martin Buber, substitutes an "I-it" relationship for an "I-thou" relationship and ends up relegating persons to the status of things. Hence segregation is not only politically, economically and sociologically unsound, it is morally wrong and sinful. Paul Tillich has said that sin is separation. Is not segregation an existential expression of man's tragic separation, his awful estrangement, his terrible sinfulness? Thus it is that I can urge men to obey the 1954 decision of the Supreme Court, for it is morally right; and I can urge them to disobey segregation ordinances, for they are morally wrong.

Let us consider a more concrete example of just and unjust laws. An unjust law is a code that a numerical or power majority group compels a minority group to obey but does not make binding on itself. This is difference made legal. By the same token, a just law is a code that a majority compels a minority to follow and that it is willing to follow itself. This is sameness made legal.

Let me give another explanation. A law is unjust if it is inflicted on a minority that, as a result of being denied the right to vote, had no part in enacting or devising the law. Who can say that the legislature of Alabama which set up that state's segregation laws was democratically elected? Throughout Alabama all sorts of devious methods are used to prevent Negroes from becoming registered voters, and there are some counties in which, even though Negroes constitute a majority of the population, not a single Negro is registered. Can any law enacted under such circumstances be considered democratically structured?

20   Sometimes a law is just on its face and unjust in its application. For instance, I have been arrested on a charge of parading without a permit. Now, there is nothing wrong in having an ordinance which requires a permit for a parade. But such an ordinance becomes unjust when it is used to maintain segregation and to deny citizens the First Amendment privilege of peaceful assembly and protest.

I hope you are able to see the distinction I am trying to point out. In no sense do I advocate evading or defying the law, as would the rabid segregationist. That would lead to anarchy. One who breaks an unjust law must do so openly, lovingly, and with a willingness to accept the penalty. I submit that an individual who breaks a law that conscience tells him is unjust and who willingly accepts the penalty of imprisonment in order to arouse the conscience of the community over its injustice, is in reality expressing the highest respect for law.

Of course, there is nothing new about this kind of civil disobedience. It was evidenced sublimely in the refusal of Shadrach, Meshach and Abednego to obey the laws of Nebuchadnezzar, on the ground that a higher moral law was at stake. It was practiced superbly by the early Christians, who were willing to face hungry lions and the excruciating pain of chopping blocks rather than submit to certain unjust laws of the Roman Empire. To a degree, academic freedom is a reality today because Socrates practiced civil disobedience. In our own nation, the Boston Tea Party represented a massive act of civil disobedience.

We should never forget that everything Adolf Hitler did in Germany was "legal" and everything the Hungarian freedom fighters did in Hungary was "illegal." It was "illegal" to aid and comfort a Jew in Hitler's Germany. Even so, I am sure that, had I lived in Germany at the time, I would have aided and comforted my Jewish brothers. If today I lived in a Communist country where certain principles dear to the Christian faith are suppressed, I would openly advocate disobeying that country's antireligious laws.

I must make two honest confessions to you, my Christian and Jewish brothers. First, I must confess that over the past few years I have been gravely disappointed with the white moderate. I have almost reached the regrettable conclusion that the Negro's great stumbling block in his stride toward freedom is not the White Citizen's Counciler or the Ku Klux Klanner, but the white moderate, who is more devoted to "order" than to justice; who prefers a negative peace which is the absence of tension to a positive peace which is the presence of justice; who constantly says: "I agree with you in the goal you seek, but I cannot agree with your methods of direct action"; who paternalistically believes he can set the timetable for another man's freedom; who lives by a mythical concept of time and who constantly advises the Negro to wait for a "more convenient season." Shallow understanding from people of good will is more frustrating than absolute misunderstanding from people of ill will. Lukewarm acceptance is much more bewildering than outright rejection.

I had hoped that the white moderate would understand that law and order exist for the purpose of establishing justice and that when they fail in this purpose they become the dangerously structured dams that block the flow of social progress. I had hoped that the white moderate would understand that the present tension in the South is a necessary phase of the transition from an obnoxious negative peace, in which the Negro passively accepted his unjust plight, to a substantive and positive peace, in which all men will respect the dignity and worth of human personality. Actually, we who engage in nonviolent direct action are not the creators of tension. We merely bring to the surface the hidden tension that is already alive. We bring it out in the open, where it can be seen and dealt with. Like a boil that can never be cured so long as it is covered up but must be opened with all its ugliness to the natural medicines of air and light, injustice must be exposed, with all the tension its exposure creates, to the light of human conscience and the air of national opinion before it can be cured.

In your statement you assert that our actions, even though peaceful, must be condemned because they precipitate violence. But is this a logical assertion? Isn't this like condemning a robbed man because his possession of money precipitated the evil act of robbery? Isn't this like condemning Socrates because his unswerving commitment to truth and his philosophical inquiries precipitated the act by the misguided populace in which they made him drink hemlock? Isn't this like condemning Jesus because his unique God-consciousness and never-ceasing devotion to God's will precipitated the evil act of crucifixion? We must come to see that, as the federal courts have consistently affirmed, it is wrong to urge an individual to cease his efforts to gain his basic constitutional rights because the quest may precipitate violence. Society must protect the robbed and punish the robber.

I had also hoped that the white moderate would reject the myth concerning time in relation to the struggle for freedom. I have just received a letter from a white brother in Texas. He writes: "And Christians know that the colored people will receive equal rights eventually, but it is possible that you are in too great a religious hurry. It has taken Christianity almost two thousand years to accomplish what it has. The teachings of Christ take time to come to earth." Such an attitude stems from a tragic misconception of time, from the strangely rational notion that there is something in the very flow of time that will inevitably cure all ills. Actually, time itself is neutral; it can be used either destructively or constructively. More and more I feel that the people of ill will have used time much more effectively than have the people of good will. We will have to repent in this generation not merely for the hateful words and actions of the bad people but for the appalling silence of the good people. Human progress never rolls in on wheels of inevitability; it comes through the tireless efforts of men willing to be co-workers with God, and without this hard work, time itself becomes an ally of the forces of social stagnation. We must use time creatively, in the knowledge that the time is always ripe to do right. Now is the time to make real the promise of democracy and transform our pending national elegy into a creative psalm of brotherhood. Now is the time to lift our national policy from the quicksand of racial injustice to the solid rock of human dignity.

You speak of our activity in Birmingham as extreme. At first I was rather disappointed that fellow clergymen would see my nonviolent efforts as those of an extremist. I began thinking about the fact that I stand in the middle of two opposing forces in the Negro community. One is a force of complacency, made up in part of Negroes who, as a result of long years of oppression, are so drained of self-respect and a sense of "somebodiness" that they have adjusted to segregation; and in part of a few middle class Negroes who, because of a degree of academic and economic security and because in some ways they profit by segregation, have become insensitive to the problems of the masses. The other force is one of bitterness and hatred, and it comes perilously close to advocating violence. It is expressed in the various black nationalist groups that are springing up across the nation, the largest and best-known being Elijah Muhammad's Muslim movement. Nourished by the Negro's frustration over the continued existence of racial discrimination, this movement is made up of people who have lost faith in America, who have absolutely repudiated Christianity, and who have concluded that the white man is an incorrigible "devil."

I have tried to stand between these two forces, saying that we need emulate neither the "do-nothingism" of the complacent nor the hatred and despair of the black nationalist. For there is the more excellent way of love and nonviolent protest. I am grateful to God that, through the influence of the Negro church, the way of nonviolence became an integral part of our struggle.

30   If this philosophy had not emerged, by now many streets of the South would, I am convinced, be flowing with blood. And I am further convinced that if our white brothers dismiss as "rabble-rousers" and "outside agitators" those of us who employ nonviolent direct action, and if they refuse to support our nonviolent efforts, millions of Negroes will, out of frustration and despair, seek solace and security in black-nationalist ideologies a development that would inevitably lead to a frightening racial nightmare.

Oppressed people cannot remain oppressed forever. The yearning for freedom eventually manifests itself, and that is what has happened to the American Negro. Something within has reminded him of his birthright of freedom, and something without has reminded him that it can be gained. Consciously or unconsciously, he has been caught up by the Zeitgeist, and with his black brothers of Africa and his brown and yellow brothers of Asia, South America and the Caribbean, the United States Negro is moving with a sense of great urgency toward the promised land of racial justice. If one recognizes this vital urge that has engulfed the Negro community, one should readily understand why public demonstrations are taking place. The Negro has many pent-up resentments and latent frustrations, and he must release them. So let him march; let him make prayer pilgrimages to the city hall; let him go on freedom rides—and try to understand why he must do so. If his repressed emotions are not released in nonviolent ways, they will seek expression through violence; this is not a threat but a fact of history. So I have not said to my people: "Get rid of your discontent." Rather, I have tried to say that this normal and healthy discontent can be channeled into the creative outlet of nonviolent direct action. And now this approach is being termed extremist.

But though I was initially disappointed at being categorized as an extremist, as I continued to think about the matter I gradually gained a measure of satisfaction from the label. Was not Jesus an extremist for love: "Love your enemies, bless them that curse you, do good to them that hate you, and pray for them which despitefully use you, and persecute you." Was not Amos an extremist for justice: "Let justice roll down like waters and righteousness like an ever-flowing stream." Was not Paul an extremist for the Christian gospel: "I bear in my body the marks of the Lord Jesus." Was not Martin Luther an extremist: "Here I stand; I cannot do otherwise, so help me God." And John Bunyan: "I will stay in jail to the end of my days before I make a butchery of my conscience." And Abraham Lincoln: "This nation cannot survive half slave and half free." And Thomas Jefferson: "We hold these truths to be self-evident, that all men are created equal . . ." So the question is not whether we will be extremists, but what kind of extremists we will be. Will we be extremists for hate or for love? Will we be extremists for the preservation of injustice or for the extension of justice? In that dramatic scene on Calvary's hill three men were crucified. We must never forget that all three were crucified for the same crime—the crime of extremism. Two were extremists for immorality, and thus fell below their environment. The other, Jesus Christ, was an extremist for love, truth and goodness, and thereby rose above his environment. Perhaps the South, the nation and the world are in dire need of creative extremists.

I had hoped that the white moderate would see this need. Perhaps I was too optimistic; perhaps I expected too much. I suppose I should have realized that few members of the oppressor race can understand the deep groans and passionate yearnings of the oppressed race, and still fewer have the vision to see that injustice must be rooted out by strong, persistent and determined action. I am thankful, however, that some of our white brothers in the South have grasped the meaning of this social revolution and committed themselves to it. They are still too few in quantity, but they are big in quality. Some—such as Ralph McGill, Lillian Smith, Harry Golden, James McBride Dabbs, Ann Braden and Sarah Patton Boyle—have written about our struggle in eloquent and prophetic terms. Others have marched with us down nameless streets of the South. They have languished in filthy, roach-infested jails, suffering the abuse and brutality of policemen who view them as "dirty nigger lovers." Unlike so many of their moderate brothers and sisters, they have recognized the urgency of the moment and sensed the need for powerful "action" antidotes to combat the disease of segregation.

Let me take note of my other major disappointment. I have been so greatly disappointed with the white church and its leadership. Of course, there are some notable exceptions. I am not unmindful of the fact that each of you has taken some significant stands on this issue. I commend you, Reverend Stallings, for your Christian stand on this past Sunday, in welcoming Negroes to your worship service on a non segregated basis.

I commend the Catholic leaders of this state for integrating Spring Hill College several years ago.

35   But despite these notable exceptions, I must honestly reiterate that I have been disappointed with the church. I do not say this as one of those negative critics who can always find something wrong with the church. I say this as a minister of the gospel, who loves the church; who was nurtured in its bosom; who has been sustained by its spiritual blessings and who will remain true to it as long as the cord of life shall lengthen.

When I was suddenly catapulted into the leadership of the bus protest in Montgomery, Alabama, a few years ago, I felt we would be supported by the white church. I felt that the white ministers, priests and rabbis of the South would be among our strongest allies. Instead, some have been outright opponents, refusing to understand the freedom movement and misrepresenting its leaders; all too many others have been more cautious than courageous and have remained silent behind the anesthetizing security of stained-glass windows.

In spite of my shattered dreams, I came to Birmingham with the hope that the white religious leadership of this community would see the justice of our cause and, with deep moral concern, would serve as the channel through which our just grievances could reach the power structure. I had hoped that each of you would understand. But again I have been disappointed.

I have heard numerous southern religious leaders admonish their worshipers to comply with a desegregation decision because it is the law, but I have longed to hear white ministers declare: "Follow this decree because integration is morally right and because the Negro is your brother." In the midst of blatant injustices inflicted upon the Negro, I have watched white churchmen stand on the sideline and mouth pious irrelevancies and sanctimonious trivialities. In the midst of a mighty struggle to rid our nation of racial and economic injustice, I have heard many ministers say: "Those are social issues, with which the gospel has no real concern." And I have watched many churches commit themselves to a completely other worldly religion which makes a strange, un-Biblical distinction between body and soul, between the sacred and the secular.

I have traveled the length and breadth of Alabama, Mississippi and all the other southern states. On sweltering summer days and crisp autumn mornings I have looked at the South's beautiful churches with their lofty spires pointing heavenward. I have beheld the impressive outlines of her massive religious-education buildings. Over and over I have found myself asking: "What kind of people worship here? Who is their God? Where were their voices when the lips of Governor Barnett dripped with words of interposition and nullification? Where were they when Governor Wallace gave a clarion call for defiance and hatred? Where were their voices of support when bruised and weary Negro men and women decided to rise from the dark dungeons of complacency to the bright hills of creative protest?"

40   Yes, these questions are still in my mind. In deep disappointment I have wept over the laxity of the church. But be assured that my tears have been tears of love. There can be no deep disappointment where there is not deep love. Yes, I love the church. How could I do otherwise? I am in the rather unique position of being the son, the grandson and the great-grandson of preachers. Yes, I see the church as the body of Christ. But, oh!

How we have blemished and scarred that body through social neglect and through fear of being nonconformists.

There was a time when the church was very powerful—in the time when the early Christians rejoiced at being deemed worthy to suffer for what they believed. In those days the church was not merely a thermometer that recorded the ideas and principles of popular opinion; it was a thermostat that transformed the mores of society. Whenever the early Christians entered a town, the people in power became disturbed and immediately sought to convict the Christians for being "disturbers of the peace" and "outside agitators." But the Christians pressed on, in the conviction that they were "a colony of heaven," called to obey God rather than man. Small in number, they were big in commitment. They were too God-intoxicated to be "astronomically intimidated." By their effort and example they brought an end to such ancient evils as infanticide and gladiatorial contests.

Things are different now. So often the contemporary church is a weak, ineffectual voice with an uncertain sound. So often it is an archdefender of the status quo. Par from being disturbed by the presence of the church, the power structure of the average community is consoled by the church's silent and often even vocal sanction of things as they are.

But the judgment of God is upon the church as never before. If today's church does not recapture the sacrificial spirit of the early church, it will lose its authenticity, forfeit the loyalty of millions, and be dismissed as an irrelevant social club with no meaning for the twentieth century. Every day I meet young people whose disappointment with the church has turned into outright disgust.

Perhaps I have once again been too optimistic. Is organized religion too inextricably bound to the status quo to save our nation and the world? Perhaps I must turn my faith to the inner spiritual church, the church within the church, as the true ekklesia and the hope of the world. But again I am thankful to God that some noble souls from the ranks of organized religion have broken loose from the paralyzing chains of conformity and joined us as active partners in the struggle for freedom, They have left their secure congregations and walked the streets of Albany, Georgia, with us. They have gone down the highways of the South on tortuous rides for freedom. Yes, they have gone to jail with us. Some have been dismissed from their churches, have lost the support of their bishops and fellow ministers. But they have acted in the faith that right defeated is stronger than evil triumphant. Their witness has been the spiritual salt that has preserved the true meaning of the gospel in these troubled times. They have carved a tunnel of hope through the dark mountain of disappointment.

I hope the church as a whole will meet the challenge of this decisive hour. But even if the church does not come to the aid of justice, I have no despair about the future. I have no fear about the outcome of our struggle in Birmingham, even if our motives are at present misunderstood. We will reach the goal of freedom in Birmingham, ham and all over the nation, because the goal of America is freedom. Abused and scorned though we may be, our destiny is tied up with America's destiny. Before the pilgrims landed at Plymouth, we were here. Before the pen of Jefferson etched the majestic words of the Declaration of Independence across the pages of history, we were here. For more than two centuries our forebears labored in this country without wages; they made cotton king; they built the homes of their masters while suffering gross injustice and shameful humiliation—and yet out of a bottomless vitality they continued to thrive and develop. If the inexpressible cruelties of slavery could not stop us, the opposition we now face will surely fail. We will win our freedom because the sacred heritage of our nation and the eternal will of God are embodied in our echoing demands.

Before closing I feel impelled to mention one other point in your statement that has troubled me profoundly. You warmly commended the Birmingham police force for keeping "order" and "preventing violence." I doubt that you would have so warmly commended the police force if you had seen its dogs sinking their teeth into unarmed, nonviolent Negroes. I doubt that you would so quickly commend the policemen if you were to observe their ugly and inhumane treatment of Negroes here in the city jail; if you were to watch them push and curse old Negro women and young Negro girls; if you were to see them slap and kick old Negro men and young boys; if you were to observe them, as they did on two occasions, refuse to give us food because we wanted to sing our grace together. I cannot join you in your praise of the Birmingham police department.

It is true that the police have exercised a degree of discipline in handing the demonstrators. In this sense they have conducted themselves rather "nonviolently" in pubic. But for what purpose? To preserve the evil system of segregation. Over the past few years I have consistently preached that nonviolence demands that the means we use must be as pure as the ends we seek. I have tried to make clear that it is wrong to use immoral means to attain moral ends. But now I must affirm that it is just as wrong, or perhaps even more so, to use moral means to preserve immoral ends. Perhaps Mr. Connor and his policemen have been rather nonviolent in public, as was Chief Pritchett in Albany, Georgia but they have used the moral means of nonviolence to maintain the immoral end of racial injustice. As T. S. Eliot has said: "The last temptation is the greatest treason: To do the right deed for the wrong reason."

I wish you had commended the Negro sit-inners and demonstrators of Birmingham for their sublime courage, their willingness to suffer and their amazing discipline in the midst of great provocation. One day the South will recognize its real heroes. They will be the James Merediths, with the noble sense of purpose that enables them to face jeering and hostile mobs, and with the agonizing loneliness that characterizes the life of the pioneer. They will be old, oppressed, battered Negro women, symbolized in a seventy-two-year-old woman in Montgomery, Alabama, who rose up with a sense of dignity and with her people decided not to ride segregated buses, and who responded with ungrammatical profundity to one who inquired about her weariness: "My feets is tired, but my soul is at rest." They will be the young high school and college students, the young ministers of the gospel and a host of their elders, courageously and nonviolently sitting in at lunch counters and willingly going to jail for conscience' sake. One day the South will know that when these disinherited children of God sat down at lunch counters, they were in reality standing up for what is best in the American dream and for the most sacred values in our Judeo-Christian heritage, thereby bringing our nation back to those great wells of democracy which were dug deep by the founding fathers in their formulation of the Constitution and the Declaration of Independence.

Never before have I written so long a letter. I'm afraid it is much too long to take your precious time. I can assure you that it would have been much shorter if I had been writing from a comfortable desk, but what else can one do when he is alone in a narrow jail cell, other than write long letters, think long thoughts and pray long prayers?

If I have said anything in this letter that overstates the truth and indicates an unreasonable impatience, I beg you to forgive me. If I have said anything that understates the truth and indicates my having a patience that allows me to settle for anything less than brotherhood, I beg God to forgive me.

I hope this letter finds you strong in the faith. I also hope that circumstances will soon make it possible for me to meet each of you, not as an integrationist or a civil rights leader but as a fellow clergyman and a Christian brother. Let us all hope that the dark clouds of racial prejudice will soon pass away and the deep fog of misunderstanding will be lifted from our fear-drenched communities, and in some not too distant tomorrow the radiant stars of love and brotherhood will shine over our great nation with all their scintillating beauty.

Yours for the cause of Peace and Brotherhood,
MARTIN LUTHER KING, JR.

Martin Luther King, Jr.

"I Have a Dream" Speech, August 28, 1963

*On the one-hundredth anniversary of the signing of the Emancipation Proclamation, over 250,000 people gathered in the shadow of Lincoln's Memorial on the mall in Washington, D.C., to **demonstrate for full citizenship in America's democracy.** The idea for the **March on Washington** came from long-time civil rights activist **A. Philip Randolph.** The National Association for the Advancement of Colored People (NAACP), the Congress of Racial Equality (CORE), the Southern Christian Leadership Conference (SCLC), Student Nonviolent Coordinating Committee (SNCC), and the Urban League agreed to work together to call attention to the need for civil rights legislation. **Martin Luther King, Jr.** departed from his prepared comments when he was encouraged by the crowd to talk about his dream, a speech that King had delivered on a number of earlier occasions. When he responded to the request, he stole the moment and the day, delivering his finest oratorical effort, and **arguably the most powerful and eloquent speech of the twentieth century.** King passed his dream onto his listeners that day, **a dream for freedom for all the people**—black and white, Jews and Gentiles, Protestants and Catholics.*

I am happy to join with you today in what will go down in history as the greatest demonstration for freedom in the history of our nation.

Five score years ago, a great American, in whose symbolic shadow we stand today, signed the Emancipation Proclamation. This momentous decree came as a great beacon light of hope to millions of Negro slaves, who had been seared in the flames of withering injustice. It came as a joyous daybreak to end the long night of their captivity. But one hundred years later, the Negro still is not free. One hundred years later, the life of the Negro is still sadly crippled by the manacles of segregation and the chains of discrimination.

One hundred years later, the Negro lives on a lonely island of poverty in the midst of a vast ocean of material prosperity. One hundred years later, the Negro is still languished in the corners of American society and finds himself an exile in his own land. So we've come here today to dramatize a shameful condition.

In a sense we have come to our nation's capital to cash a check. When the architects of our republic wrote the magnificent words of the Constitution and the Declaration of Independence, they were signing a promissory note to which every American was to fall heir. This note was a promise that all men, yes, black men as well as white men, would be guaranteed the inalienable rights of life, liberty and the pursuit of happiness.

5   It is obvious today that America has defaulted on this promissory note insofar as her citizens of color are concerned. Instead of honoring this sacred obligation, America has given the Negro people a bad check, a check which has come back marked "insufficient funds."

But we refuse to believe that the bank of justice is bankrupt. We refuse to believe that there are insufficient funds in the great vaults of opportunity of this nation. So we have come to cash this check, a check that will give us upon demand the riches of freedom and the security of justice.

We have also come to this hallowed spot to remind America of the fierce urgency of Now. This is no time to engage in the luxury of cooling off or to take the tranquilizing drug of gradualism. Now is the time to make real the promises of democracy. Now is the time to rise from the dark and desolate valley of segregation to the sunlit path of racial justice. Now is the time to lift our nation from the quicksands of racial injustice to the solid rock of brotherhood. Now is the time to make justice a reality for all of God's children.

It would be fatal for the nation to overlook the urgency of the moment. This sweltering summer of the Negro's legitimate discontent will not pass until there is an invigorating autumn of freedom and equality. Nineteen sixty-three is not an end but a beginning. Those who hope that the Negro needed to blow off steam and will now be content will have a rude awakening if the nation returns to business as usual.

There will be neither rest nor tranquility in America until the Negro is granted his citizenship rights. The whirlwinds of revolt will continue to shake the foundations of our nation until the bright day of justice emerges.

10   But there is something that I must say to my people who stand on the warm threshold which leads into the palace of justice. In the process of gaining our rightful place we must not be guilty of wrongful deeds. Let us not seek to satisfy our thirst for freedom by drinking from the cup of bitterness and hatred. We must ever conduct our struggle on the high plane of dignity and discipline. We must not allow our creative protest to degenerate into physical violence. Again and again we must rise to the majestic heights of meeting physical force with soul force.

The marvelous new militancy which has engulfed the Negro community must not lead us to a distrust of all white people, for many of our white brothers, as evidenced by their presence here today, have come to realize that their destiny is tied up with our destiny. They have come to realize that their freedom is inextricably bound to our freedom. We cannot walk alone.

And as we walk, we must make the pledge that we shall always march ahead. We cannot turn back. There are those who are asking the devotees of civil rights, "When will you be satisfied?" We can never be satisfied as long as the Negro is the victim of the unspeakable horrors of police brutality. We can never be satisfied as long as our bodies, heavy with the fatigue of travel, cannot gain lodging in the motels of the highways and the hotels of the cities. We cannot be satisfied as long as a Negro in Mississippi cannot vote and a Negro in New York believes he has nothing for which to vote. No, no, we are not satisfied and we will not be satisfied until justice rolls down like waters and righteousness like a mighty stream.

I am not unmindful that some of you have come here out of great trials and tribulations. Some of you have come fresh from narrow jail cells. Some of you have come from areas where your quest for freedom left you battered by the storms of persecutions and staggered by the winds of police brutality. You have been the veterans of creative suffering. Continue to work with the faith that unearned suffering is redemptive. Go back to Mississippi, go back to Alabama, go back to South Carolina, go back to Georgia, go back to Louisiana, go back to the slums and ghettos of our northern cities, knowing that somehow this situation can and will be changed. Let us not wallow in the valley of despair. I say to you today, my friends, so even though we face the difficulties of today and tomorrow. I still have a dream. It is a dream deeply rooted in the American dream.

I have a dream that one day this nation will rise up and live out the true meaning of its creed; we hold these truths to be self-evident that all men are created equal.

I have a dream,   15

that one day on the red hills of Georgia the sons of former slaves and the sons of former slave owners will be able to sit down together at the table of brotherhood.

I have a dream,

that one day even the state of Mississippi, a state sweltering with the heat of injustice, sweltering with the heat of oppression, will be transformed into an oasis of freedom and justice.

I have a dream,

that my four little children will one day live in a nation where they will not be judged   20
by the color of their skin but by the content of their character.

I have a dream today!

I have a dream that one day, down in Alabama, with its vicious racists, with its governor having his lips dripping with the words of interposition and nullification; one day right down in Alabama little black boys and black girls will be able to join hands with little white boys and white girls as sisters and brothers. I have a dream today!

I have a dream that one day every valley shall be exalted, and every hill and mountain shall be made low, the rough places will be made plain and the crooked places will be made straight and the glory of the Lord shall be revealed and all flesh shall see it together.

This is our hope. This is the faith that I will go back to the South with. With this faith we will be able to hew out of the mountain of despair a stone of hope. With this faith we will be able to transform the jangling discords of our nation into a beautiful symphony of brotherhood. With this faith we will be able to work together, to pray together, to struggle together, to go to jail together, to stand up for freedom together, knowing that we will be free one day. This will be the day, this will be the day when all of God's children will be able to sing with new meaning "My country 'tis of thee, sweet land of liberty, of thee I sing. Land where my fathers died, land of the Pilgrim's pride, from every mountainside, let freedom ring!" And if America is to be a great nation, this must become true.

And so let freedom ring   25

from the prodigious hilltops of New Hampshire.

Let freedom ring from the mighty mountains of New York.

Let freedom ring from the heightening Alleghenies of Pennsylvania.

Let freedom ring from the snow-capped Rockies of Colorado.

Let freedom ring from the curvaceous slopes of California.   30

But not only that.

Let freedom ring from Stone Mountain of Georgia.

Let freedom ring from Lookout Mountain of Tennessee.

Let freedom ring from every hill and molehill of Mississippi, from every mountainside, let freedom ring! And when this happens, when we allow freedom to ring, when we let it ring from every village and every hamlet, from every state and every city, we will be able to speed up that day when all of God's children, black men and white men, Jews and Gentiles, Protestants and Catholics, will be able to join hands and sing in the words of the old Negro spiritual, "Free at last, free at last. Thank God Almighty, we are free at last."

Lyndon B. Johnson

"Great Society" Speech, May 22, 1964

Lyndon B. Johnson (1908–1973).

*President **Lyndon B. Johnson** chose the commencement speech to the University of Michigan's Class of 1964 to define his ideas about the Great Society. Inheriting the presidency after the assassination of John F. Kennedy, Johnson made war on poverty and an end to racial discrimination top priorities in his domestic efforts. In this speech, he **defined the Great Society as "a challenge constantly renewed," and set forth the building of this society in the city, the countryside, and the classroom.** Cities were crumbling from within, the natural beauty of the country was being eroded through pollution, and classrooms were falling short on delivering the educational needs to America's youth. He chose to deliver the challenge to the graduates of a major university, asking that this vision become a reality through their efforts.*

President Hatcher, Governor Romney, Senators McNamara and Hart, Congressmen Meader and Staebler, and other members of the fine Michigan delegation, members of the graduating class, my fellow Americans:—

It is a great pleasure to be here today. This university has been coeducational since 1870, but I do not believe it was on the basis of your accomplishments that a Detroit high school girl said, "In choosing a college, you first have to decide whether you want a coeducational school or an educational school."

Well, we can find both here at Michigan, although perhaps at different hours. I came out here today very anxious to meet the Michigan student whose father told a friend of mine that his son's education had been a real value. It stopped his mother from bragging about him.

I have come today from the turmoil of your Capital to the tranquility of your campus to speak about the future of your country.

The purpose of protecting the life of our Nation and preserving the liberty of our citizens   5
is to pursue the happiness of our people. Our success in that pursuit is the test of our success as a Nation.

For a century we labored to settle and to subdue a continent. For half a century we called upon unbounded invention and untiring industry to create an order of plenty for all of our people.

The challenge of the next half century is whether we have the wisdom to use that wealth to enrich and elevate our national life, and to advance the quality of our American civilization.

Your imagination, your initiative, and your indignation will determine whether we build a society where progress is the servant of our needs, or a society where old values and new visions are buried under unbridled growth. For in your time we have the opportunity to move not only toward the rich society and the powerful society, but upward to the Great Society.

The Great Society rests on abundance and liberty for all. It demands an end to poverty and racial injustice, to which we are totally committed in our time. But that is just the beginning.

The Great Society is a place where every child can find knowledge to enrich his mind   10
and to enlarge his talents. It is a place where leisure is a welcome chance to build and reflect, not a feared cause of boredom and restlessness. It is a place where the city of man serves not only the needs of the body and the demands of commerce but the desire for beauty and the hunger for community.

It is a place where man can renew contact with nature. It is a place which honors creation for its own sake and for what it adds to the understanding of the race. It is a place where men are more concerned with the quality of their goals than the quantity of their goods.

But most of all, the Great Society is not a safe harbor, a resting place, a final objective, a finished work. It is a challenge constantly renewed, beckoning us toward a destiny where the meaning of our lives matches the marvelous products of our labor.

So I want to talk to you today about three places where we begin to build the Great Society—in our cities, in our countryside, and in our classrooms.

Many of you will live to see the day, perhaps 50 years from now, when there will be 400 million Americans—four-fifths of them in urban areas. In the remainder of this century urban population will double, city land will double, and we will have to build homes, highways, and facilities equal to all those built since this country was first settled. So in the next 40 years we must rebuild the entire urban United States.

Aristotle said: "Men come together in cities in order to live, but they remain together   15
in order to live the good life." It is harder and harder to live the good life in American cities today. The catalog of ills is long: there is the decay of the centers and the despoiling of the suburbs. There is not enough housing for our people or transportation for our traffic. Open land is vanishing and old landmarks are violated.

Worst of all, expansion is eroding the precious and time honored values of community with neighbors and communion with nature. The loss of these values breeds loneliness and boredom and indifference.

Our society will never be great until our cities are great. Today the frontier of imagination and innovation is inside those cities and not beyond their borders. New experiments are already going on. It will be the task of your generation to make the American city a place where future generations will come, not only to live but to live the good life.

I understand that if I stayed here tonight I would see that Michigan students are really doing their best to live the good life.

This is the place where the Peace Corps was started. It is inspiring to see how all of you, while you are in this country, are trying so hard to live at the level of the people.

20   A second place where we begin to build the Great Society is in our countryside. We have always prided ourselves on being not only America the strong and America the free, but America the beautiful. Today that beauty is in danger. The water we drink, the food we eat, the very air that we breathe, are threatened with pollution. Our parks are overcrowded, our seashores overburdened. Green fields and dense forests are disappearing.

A few years ago we were greatly concerned about the "Ugly American." Today we must act to prevent an ugly America.

For once the battle is lost, once our natural splendor is destroyed, it can never be recaptured. And once man can no longer walk with beauty or wonder at nature his spirit will wither and his sustenance be wasted.

A third place to build the Great Society is in the classrooms of America. There your children's lives will be shaped. Our society will not be great until every young mind is set free to scan the farthest reaches of thought and imagination. We are still far from that goal.

Today, 8 million adult Americans, more than the entire population of Michigan, have not finished 5 years of school. Nearly 20 million have not finished 8 years of school. Nearly 54 million—more than one-quarter of all America—have not even finished high school.

25   Each year more than 100,000 high school graduates, with proved ability, do not enter college because they cannot afford it. And if we cannot educate today's youth, what will we do in 1970 when elementary school enrollment will be 5 million greater than 1960? And high school enrollment will rise by 5 million. College enrollment will increase by more than 3 million.

In many places, classrooms are overcrowded and curricula are outdated. Most of our qualified teachers are underpaid, and many of our paid teachers are unqualified. So we must give every child a place to sit and a teacher to learn from. Poverty must not be a bar to learning, and learning must offer an escape from poverty.

But more classrooms and more teachers are not enough. We must seek an educational system which grows in excellence as it grows in size. This means better training for our teachers. It means preparing youth to enjoy their hours of leisure as well as their hours of labor. It means exploring new techniques of teaching, to find new ways to stimulate the love of learning and the capacity for creation.

These are three of the central issues of the Great Society. While our Government has many programs directed at those issues, I do not pretend that we have the full answer to those problems.

But I do promise this: We are going to assemble the best thought and the broadest knowledge from all over the world to find those answers for America. I intend to establish working groups to prepare a series of White House conferences and meetings—on the cities, on natural beauty, on the quality of education, and on other emerging challenges.

And from these meetings and from this inspiration and from these studies we will begin to set our course toward the Great Society.

The solution to these problems does not rest on a massive program in Washington,   30
nor can it rely solely on the strained resources of local authority. They require us to create new concepts of cooperation, a creative federalism, between the National Capital and the leaders of local communities.

Woodrow Wilson once wrote: "Every man sent out from his university should be a man of his Nation as well as a man of his time."

Within your lifetime powerful forces, already loosed, will take us toward a way of life beyond the realm of our experience, almost beyond the bounds of our imagination.

For better or for worse, your generation has been appointed by history to deal with those problems and to lead America toward a new age. You have the chance never before afforded to any people in any age. You can help build a society where the demands of morality, and the needs of the spirit, can be realized in the life of the Nation.

So, will you join in the battle to give every citizen the full equality which God enjoins and the law requires, whatever his belief, or race, or the color of his skin? Will you join in the battle to give every citizen an escape from the crushing weight of poverty?

Will you join in the battle to make it possible for all nations to live in enduring peace—   35
as neighbors and not as mortal enemies?

Will you join in the battle to build the Great Society, to prove that our material progress is only the foundation on which we will build a richer life of mind and spirit?

There are those timid souls who say this battle cannot be won; that we are con-demned to a soulless wealth. I do not agree. We have the power to shape the civilization that we want. But we need your will, your labor, your hearts, if we are to build that kind of society.

Those who came to this land sought to build more than just a new country.

They sought a new world. So I have come here today to your campus to say that you can make their vision our reality. So let us from this moment begin our work so that in the future men will look back and say: It was then, after a long and weary way, that man turned the exploits of his genius to the full enrichment of his life.

Thank you. Goodbye.   40

Malcolm X

"The Ballot or the Bullet" Speech, April 3, 1964, Cory Methodist Church in Cleveland, Ohio

*Malcolm X, also known as El-Hajj Malik El-Shabazz, was a civil rights advocate and member of the Nation of Islam—a black Muslim organization. He was famous for **his provocative declaration that blacks should strive to achieve equality "by any means necessary," which stood in direct opposition to Martin Luther King's strategy of nonviolence.** Speeches such as this, advocating black economic and political power and alluding to the possibility of violence, served to motivate black Americans who were look-ing to be empowered and to frighten whites who feared the implied violence. Malcolm X often characterized white Americans as devils or evil, but after a trip to Mecca near the end of his life, where he saw a more international face of Islam as he worshipped with Muslims*

Malcolm X (1925–1965).

of all colors, he seemed to moderate his stance toward white Americans. Malcolm X was assassinated in 1965, most likely by members of the Nation of Islam.

1. Mr. Moderator, Brother Lomax, brothers and sisters, friends and enemies: I just can't believe everyone in here is a friend and I don't want to leave anybody out. The question tonight, as I understand it, is "The Negro Revolt, and Where Do We Go From Here?" or "What Next?" In my little humble way of understanding it, it points toward either the ballot or the bullet.

2. Before we try and explain what is meant by the ballot or the bullet, I would like to clarify something concerning myself. I'm still a Muslim, my religion is still Islam. That's my personal belief. Just as Adam Clayton Powell is a Christian minister who heads the Abyssinian Baptist Church in New York, but at the same time takes part in the political struggles to try and bring about rights to the black people in this country; and Dr. Martin Luther King is a Christian minister down in Atlanta, Georgia, who heads another organization fighting for the civil rights of black people in this country; and Rev. Galamison, I guess you've heard of him, is another Christian minister in New York who has been deeply involved in the school boycotts to eliminate segregated education; well, I myself am a minister, not a Christian minister, but a Muslim minister; and I believe in action on all fronts by whatever means necessary.

3. Although I'm still a Muslim, I'm not here tonight to discuss my religion. I'm not here to try and change your religion. I'm not here to argue or discuss anything that we differ about, because it's time for us to submerge our differences and realize that it is best for us to first see that we have the same problem, a common problem, a problem that will make you catch hell whether you're a Baptist, or a Methodist, or a Muslim, or a nationalist. Whether you're educated or illiterate, whether you live on the boulevard or in the alley, you're going to catch hell just like I am. We're all in the same boat and we all are going to catch the same hell from the same man. He just happens to be a white man. All of us have suffered here, in this country, political oppression at the hands of the white man, economic exploitation at the hands of the white man, and social degradation at the hands of the white man.

4. Now in speaking like this, it doesn't mean that we're anti-white, but it does mean we're anti-exploitation, we're anti-degradation, we're anti-oppression. And if the white man doesn't want us to be anti-him, let him stop oppressing and exploiting and degrading us. Whether we are Christians or Muslims or nationalists or agnostics or atheists, we must first learn to forget our differences. If we have differences, let us differ in the closet; when we come out in front, let us not have anything to argue about until we get finished arguing with the man. If the late President Kennedy could get

together with Khrushchev and exchange some wheat, we certainly have more in common with each other than Kennedy and Khrushchev had with each other.

5. If we don't do something real soon, I think you'll have to agree that we're going to be forced either to use the ballot or the bullet. It's one or the other in 1964. It isn't that time is running out—time has run out! 1964 threatens to be the most explosive year America has ever witnessed. The most explosive year. Why? It's also a political year. It's the year when all of the white politicians will be back in the so-called Negro community jiving you and me for some votes. The year when all of the white political crooks will be right back in your and my community with their false promises, building up our hopes for a letdown, with their trickery and their treachery, with their false promises which they don't intend to keep. As they nourish these dissatisfactions, it can only lead to one thing, an explosion; and now we have the type of black man on the scene in America today—I'm sorry, Brother Lomax—who just doesn't intend to turn the other cheek any longer.

6. Don't let anybody tell you anything about the odds are against you. If they draft you, they send you to Korea and make you face 800 million Chinese. If you can be brave over there, you can be brave right here. These odds aren't as great as those odds. And if you fight here, you will at least know what you're fighting for.

7. I'm not a politician, not even a student of politics; in fact, I'm not a student of much of anything. I'm not a Democrat, I'm not a Republican, and I don't even consider myself an American. If you and I were Americans, there'd be no problem. Those Hunkies that just got off the boat, they're already Americans; Polacks are already Americans; the Italian refugees are already Americans. Everything that came out of Europe, every blue-eyed thing, is already an American. And as long as you and I have been over here, we aren't Americans yet.

8. Well, I am one who doesn't believe in deluding myself. I'm not going to sit at your table and watch you eat, with nothing on my plate, and call myself a diner. Sitting at the table doesn't make you a diner, unless you eat some of what's on that plate. Being here in America doesn't make you an American. Being born here in America doesn't make you an American. Why, if birth made you American, you wouldn't need any legislation, you wouldn't need any amendments to the Constitution, you wouldn't be faced with civil-rights filibustering in Washington, D.C., right now. They don't have to pass civil-rights legislation to make a Polack an American.

9. No, I'm not an American. I'm one of the 22 million black people who are the victims of Americanism. One of the 22 million black people who are the victims of democracy, nothing but disguised hypocrisy. So, I'm not standing here speaking to you as an American, or a patriot, or a flag-saluter, or a flag-waver—no, not I. I'm speaking as a victim of this American system. And I see America through the eyes of the victim. I don't see any American dream; I see an American nightmare.

10. These 22 million victims are waking up. Their eyes are coming open. They're beginning to see what they used to only look at. They're becoming politically mature. They are realizing that there are new political trends from coast to coast. As they see these new political trends, it's possible for them to see that every time there's an election the races are so close that they have to have a recount. They had to recount in Massachusetts to see who was going to be governor, it was so close. It was the same way in Rhode Island, in Minnesota, and in many other parts of the country. And the same with Kennedy and

Nixon when they ran for president. It was so close they had to count all over again. Well, what does this mean? It means that when white people are evenly divided, and black people have a bloc of votes of their own, it is left up to them to determine who's going to sit in the White House and who's going to be in the dog house.

11. It was the black man's vote that put the present administration in Washington, D.C. Your vote, your dumb vote, your ignorant vote, your wasted vote put in an administration in Washington, D.C., that has seen fit to pass every kind of legislation imaginable, saving you until last, then filibustering on top of that. And your and my leaders have the audacity to run around clapping their hands and talk about how much progress we're making. And what a good president we have. If he wasn't good in Texas, he sure can't be good in Washington, D.C. Because Texas is a lynch state. It is in the same breath as Mississippi, no different; only they lynch you in Texas with a Texas accent and lynch you in Mississippi with a Mississippi accent. And these Negro leaders have the audacity to go and have some coffee in the White House with a Texan, a Southern cracker—that's all he is—and then come out and tell you and me that he's going to be better for us because, since he's from the South, he knows how to deal with the Southerners. What kind of logic is that? Let Eastland be president, he's from the South too. He should be better able to deal with them than Johnson.

12. In this present administration they have in the House of Representatives 257 Democrats to only 177 Republicans. They control two-thirds of the House vote. Why can't they pass something that will help you and me? In the Senate, there are 67 senators who are of the Democratic Party. Only 33 of them are Republicans. Why, the Democrats have got the government sewed up, and you're the one who sewed it up for them. And what have they given you for it? Four years in office, and just now getting around to some civil-rights legislation. Just now, after everything else is gone, out of the way, they're going to sit down now and play with you all summer long—the same old giant con game that they call filibuster. All those are in cahoots together. Don't you ever think they're not in cahoots together, for the man that is heading the civil-rights filibuster is a man from Georgia named Richard Russell. When Johnson became president, the first man he asked for when he got back to Washington, D.C., was "Dicky"—that's how tight they are. That's his boy, that's his pal, that's his buddy. But they're playing that old con game. One of them makes believe he's for you, and he's got it fixed where the other one is so tight against you, he never has to keep his promise.

13. So it's time in 1964 to wake up. And when you see them coming up with that kind of conspiracy, let them know your eyes are open. And let them know you got something else that's wide open too. It's got to be the ballot or the bullet. The ballot or the bullet. If you're afraid to use an expression like that, you should get on out of the country, you should get back in the cotton patch, you should get back in the alley. They get all the Negro vote, and after they get it, the Negro gets nothing in return. All they did when they got to Washington was give a few big Negroes big jobs. Those big Negroes didn't need big jobs, they already had jobs. That's camouflage, that's trickery, that's treachery, window-dressing. I'm not trying to knock out the Democrats for the Republicans, we'll get to them in a minute. But it is true—you put the Democrats first and the Democrats put you last.

14. Look at it the way it is. What alibis do they use, since they control Congress and the Senate? What alibi do they use when you and I ask, "Well, when are you going to keep

your promise?" They blame the Dixiecrats. What is a Dixiecrat? A Democrat. A Dixiecrat is nothing but a Democrat in disguise. The titular head of the Democrats is also the head of the Dixiecrats, because the Dixiecrats are a part of the Democratic Party. The Democrats have never kicked the Dixiecrats out of the party. The Dixiecrats bolted themselves once, but the Democrats didn't put them out. Imagine, these lowdown Southern segregationists put the Northern Democrats down. But the Northern Democrats have never put the Dixiecrats down. No, look at that thing the way it is. They have got a con game going on, a political con game, and you and I are in the middle. It's time for you and me to wake up and start looking at it like it is, and trying to understand it like it is; and then we can deal with it like it is.

15. The Dixiecrats in Washington, D.C., control the key committees that run the government. The only reason the Dixiecrats control these committees is because they have seniority. The only reason they have seniority is because they come from states where Negroes can't vote. This is not even a government that's based on democracy. It is not a government that is made up of representatives of the people. Half of the people in the South can't even vote. Eastland is not even supposed to be in Washington. Half of the senators and congressmen who occupy these key positions in Washington, D.C., are there illegally, are there unconstitutionally.

16. I was in Washington, D.C., a week ago Thursday, when they were debating whether or not they should let the bill come onto the floor. And in the back of the room where the Senate meets, there's a huge map of the United States, and on that map it shows the location of Negroes throughout the country. And it shows that the Southern section of the country, the states that are most heavily concentrated with Negroes, are the ones that have senators and congressmen standing up filibustering and doing all other kinds of trickery to keep the Negro from being able to vote. This is pitiful. But it's not pitiful for us any longer; it's actually pitiful for the white man, because soon now, as the Negro awakens a little more and sees the vise that he's in, sees the bag that he's in, sees the real game that he's in, then the Negro's going to develop a new tactic.

17. These senators and congressmen actually violate the constitutional amendments that guarantee the people of that particular state or county the right to vote. And the Constitution itself has within it the machinery to expel any representative from a state where the voting rights of the people are violated. You don't even need new legislation. Any person in Congress right now, who is there from a state or a district where the voting rights of the people are violated, that particular person should be expelled from Congress. And when you expel him, you've removed one of the obstacles in the path of any real meaningful legislation in this country. In fact, when you expel them, you don't need new legislation, because they will be replaced by black representatives from counties and districts where the black man is in the majority, not in the minority.

18. If the black man in these Southern states had his full voting rights, the key Dixiecrats in Washington, D. C., which means the key Democrats in Washington, D.C., would lose their seats. The Democratic Party itself would lose its power. It would cease to be powerful as a party. When you see the amount of power that would be lost by the Democratic Party if it were to lose the Dixiecrat wing, or branch, or element, you can see where it's against the interests of the Democrats to give voting rights to Negroes

in states where the Democrats have been in complete power and authority ever since the Civil War. You just can't belong to that Party without analyzing it.

19. I say again, I'm not anti-Democrat, I'm not anti Republican, I'm not anti-anything. I'm just questioning their sincerity, and some of the strategy that they've been using on our people by promising them promises that they don't intend to keep. When you keep the Democrats in power, you're keeping the Dixiecrats in power. I doubt that my good Brother Lomax will deny that. A vote for a Democrat is a vote for a Dixiecrat. That's why, in 1964, it's time now for you and me to become more politically mature and realize what the ballot is for; what we're supposed to get when we cast a ballot; and that if we don't cast a ballot, it's going to end up in a situation where we're going to have to cast a bullet. It's either a ballot or a bullet.

20. In the North, they do it a different way. They have a system that's known as gerrymandering, whatever that means. It means when Negroes become too heavily concentrated in a certain area, and begin to gain too much political power, the white man comes along and changes the district lines. You may say, "Why do you keep saying white man?" Because it's the white man who does it. I haven't ever seen any Negro changing any lines. They don't let him get near the line. It's the white man who does this. And usually, it's the white man who grins at you the most, and pats you on the back, and is supposed to be your friend. He may be friendly, but he's not your friend.

21. So, what I'm trying to impress upon you, in essence, is this: You and I in America are faced not with a segregationist conspiracy, we're faced with a government conspiracy. Everyone who's filibustering is a senator—that's the government. Everyone who's finagling in Washington, D.C., is a congressman—that's the government. You don't have anybody putting blocks in your path but people who are a part of the government. The same government that you go abroad to fight for and die for is the government that is in a conspiracy to deprive you of your voting rights, deprive you of your economic opportunities, deprive you of decent housing, deprive you of decent education. You don't need to go to the employer alone, it is the government itself, the government of America, that is responsible for the oppression and exploitation and degradation of black people in this country. And you should drop it in their lap. This government has failed the Negro. This so-called democracy has failed the Negro. And all these white liberals have definitely failed the Negro.

22. So, where do we go from here? First, we need some friends. We need some new allies. The entire civil-rights struggle needs a new interpretation, a broader interpretation. We need to look at this civil-rights thing from another angle—from the inside as well as from the outside. To those of us whose philosophy is black nationalism, the only way you can get involved in the civil-rights struggle is give it a new interpretation. That old interpretation excluded us. It kept us out. So, we're giving a new interpretation to the civil-rights struggle, an interpretation that will enable us to come into it, take part in it. And these handkerchief-heads who have been dillydallying and pussy footing and compromising—we don't intend to let them pussyfoot and dillydally and compromise any longer.

23. How can you thank a man for giving you what's already yours? How then can you thank him for giving you only part of what's already yours? You haven't even made progress, if what's being given to you, you should have had already. That's not progress. And I love my Brother Lomax, the way he pointed out we're right back

where we were in 1954. We're not even as far up as we were in 1954. We're behind where we were in 1954. There's more segregation now than there was in 1954. There's more racial animosity, more racial hatred, more racial violence today in 1964, than there was in 1954. Where is the progress?

24. And now you're facing a situation where the young Negro's coming up. They don't want to hear that "turn the-other-cheek" stuff, no. In Jacksonville, those were teenagers, they were throwing Molotov cocktails. Negroes have never done that before. But it shows you there's a new deal coming in. There's new thinking coming in. There's new strategy coming in. It'll be Molotov cocktails this month, hand grenades next month, and something else next month. It'll be ballots, or it'll be bullets. It'll be liberty, or it will be death. The only difference about this kind of death—it'll be reciprocal. You know what is meant by "reciprocal"? That's one of Brother Lomax's words, I stole it from him. I don't usually deal with those big words because I don't usually deal with big people. I deal with small people. I find you can get a whole lot of small people and whip hell out of a whole lot of big people. They haven't got anything to lose, and they've got every thing to gain. And they'll let you know in a minute: "It takes two to tango; when I go, you go."

25. The black nationalists, those whose philosophy is black nationalism, in bringing about this new interpretation of the entire meaning of civil rights, look upon it as meaning, as Brother Lomax has pointed out, equality of opportunity. Well, we're justified in seeking civil rights, if it means equality of opportunity, because all we're doing there is trying to collect for our investment. Our mothers and fathers invested sweat and blood. Three hundred and ten years we worked in this country without a dime in return—I mean without a dime in return. You let the white man walk around here talking about how rich this country is, but you never stop to think how it got rich so quick. It got rich because you made it rich.

26. You take the people who are in this audience right now. They're poor, we're all poor as individuals. Our weekly salary individually amounts to hardly anything. But if you take the salary of everyone in here collectively it'll fill up a whole lot of baskets. It's a lot of wealth. If you can collect the wages of just these people right here for a year, you'll be rich—richer than rich. When you look at it like that, think how rich Uncle Sam had to become, not with this handful, but millions of black people. Your and my mother and father, who didn't work an eight-hour shift, but worked from "can't see" in the morning until "can't see" at night, and worked for nothing, making the white man rich, making Uncle Sam rich.

27. This is our investment. This is our contribution—our blood. Not only did we give of our free labor, we gave of our blood. Every time he had a call to arms, we were the first ones in uniform. We died on every battlefield the white man had. We have made a greater sacrifice than anybody who's standing up in America today. We have made a greater contribution and have collected less. Civil rights, for those of us whose philosophy is black nationalism, means: "Give it to us now. Don't wait for next year. Give it to us yesterday, and that's not fast enough."

28. I might stop right here to point out one thing. When ever you're going after something that belongs to you, anyone who's depriving you of the right to have it is a criminal. Understand that. Whenever you are going after something that is yours, you are within your legal rights to lay claim to it. And anyone who puts forth any effort to deprive you

of that which is yours, is breaking the law, is a criminal. And this was pointed out by the Supreme Court decision. It outlawed segregation. Which means segregation is against the law. Which means a segregationist is breaking the law. A segregationist is a criminal. You can't label him as anything other than that. And when you demonstrate against segregation, the law is on your side. The Supreme Court is on your side.

29. Now, who is it that opposes you in carrying out the law? The police department itself. With police dogs and clubs. Whenever you demonstrate against segregation, whether it is segregated education, segregated housing, or anything else, the law is on your side, and anyone who stands in the way is not the law any longer. They are breaking the law, they are not representatives of the law. Any time you demonstrate against segregation and a man has the audacity to put a police dog on you, kill that dog, kill him, I'm telling you, kill that dog. I say it, if they put me in jail tomorrow, kill that dog. Then you'll put a stop to it. Now, if these white people in here don't want to see that kind of action, get down and tell the mayor to tell the police department to pull the dogs in. That's all you have to do. If you don't do it, someone else will.

30. If you don't take this kind of stand, your little children will grow up and look at you and think "shame." If you don't take an uncompromising stand—I don't mean go out and get violent; but at the same time you should never be nonviolent unless you run into some nonviolence. I'm nonviolent with those who are nonviolent with me. But when you drop that violence on me, then you've made me go insane, and I'm not responsible for what I do. And that's the way every Negro should get. Any time you know you're within the law, within your legal rights, within your moral rights, in accord with justice, then die for what you believe in. But don't die alone. Let your dying be reciprocal. This is what is meant by equality. What's good for the goose is good for the gander.

31. When we begin to get in this area, we need new friends, we need new allies. We need to expand the civil-rights struggle to a higher level—to the level of human rights. Whenever you are in a civil-rights struggle, whether you know it or not, you are confining yourself to the jurisdiction of Uncle Sam. No one from the outside world can speak out in your behalf as long as your struggle is a civil-rights struggle. Civil rights comes within the domestic affairs of this country. All of our African brothers and our Asian brothers and our Latin-American brothers cannot open their mouths and interfere in the domestic affairs of the United States. And as long as it's civil rights, this comes under the jurisdiction of Uncle Sam.

32. But the United Nations has what's known as the charter of human rights, it has a committee that deals in human rights. You may wonder why all of the atrocities that have been committed in Africa and in Hungary and in Asia and in Latin America are brought before the UN, and the Negro problem is never brought before the UN. This is part of the conspiracy. This old, tricky, blue eyed liberal who is supposed to be your and my friend, supposed to be in our corner, supposed to be subsidizing our struggle, and supposed to be acting in the capacity of an adviser, never tells you anything about human rights. They keep you wrapped up in civil rights. And you spend so much time barking up the civil-rights tree, you don't even know there's a human-rights tree on the same floor.

33. When you expand the civil-rights struggle to the level of human rights, you can then take the case of the black man in this country before the nations in the UN. You can

take it before the General Assembly. You can take Uncle Sam before a world court. But the only level you can do it on is the level of human rights. Civil rights keeps you under his restrictions, under his jurisdiction. Civil rights keeps you in his pocket. Civil rights means you're asking Uncle Sam to treat you right. Human rights are some thing you were born with. Human rights are your God given rights. Human rights are the rights that are recognized by all nations of this earth. And any time any one violates your human rights, you can take them to the world court. Uncle Sam's hands are dripping with blood, dripping with the blood of the black man in this country. He's the earth's number-one hypocrite. He has the audacity—yes, he has—imagine him posing as the leader of the free world. The free world! And you over here singing "We Shall Overcome." Expand the civil-rights struggle to the level of human rights, take it into the United Nations, where our African brothers can throw their weight on our side, where our Asian brothers can throw their weight on our side, where our Latin-American brothers can throw their weight on our side, and where 800 million Chinamen are sitting there waiting to throw their weight on our side.

34. Let the world know how bloody his hands are. Let the world know the hypocrisy that's practiced over here. Let it be the ballot or the bullet. Let him know that it must be the ballot or the bullet.

35. When you take your case to Washington, D.C., you're taking it to the criminal who's responsible; it's like running from the wolf to the fox. They're all in cahoots together. They all work political chicanery and make you look like a chump before the eyes of the world. Here you are walking around in America, getting ready to be drafted and sent abroad, like a tin soldier, and when you get over there, people ask you what are you fighting for, and you have to stick your tongue in your cheek. No, take Uncle Sam to court, take him before the world.

36. By ballot I only mean freedom. Don't you know—I disagree with Lomax on this issue—that the ballot is more important than the dollar? Can I prove it? Yes. Look in the UN. There are poor nations in the UN; yet those poor nations can get together with their voting power and keep the rich nations from making a move. They have one nation—one vote, everyone has an equal vote. And when those brothers from Asia, and Africa and the darker parts of this earth get together, their voting power is sufficient to hold Sam in check. Or Russia in check. Or some other section of the earth in check. So, the ballot is most important.

37. Right now, in this country, if you and I, 22 million African-Americans—that's what we are—Africans who are in America. You're nothing but Africans. Nothing but Africans. In fact, you'd get farther calling yourself African instead of Negro. Africans don't catch hell. You're the only one catching hell. They don't have to pass civil-rights bills for Africans. An African can go anywhere he wants right now. All you've got to do is tie your head up. That's right, go anywhere you want. Just stop being a Negro. Change your name to Hoogagagooba. That'll show you how silly the white man is. You're dealing with a silly man. A friend of mine who's very dark put a turban on his head and went into a restaurant in Atlanta before they called themselves desegregated. He went into a white restaurant, he sat down, they served him, and he said, "What would happen if a Negro came in here? And there he's sitting, black as night, but because he had his head wrapped up the waitress looked back at him and says, "Why, there wouldn't no nigger dare come in here."

38. So, you're dealing with a man whose bias and prejudice are making him lose his mind, his intelligence, every day. He's frightened. He looks around and sees what's taking place on this earth, and he sees that the pendulum of time is swinging in your direction. The dark people are waking up. They're losing their fear of the white man. No place where he's fighting right now is he winning. Everywhere he's fighting, he's fighting someone your and my complexion. And they're beating him. He can't win any more. He's won his last battle. He failed to win the Korean War. He couldn't win it. He had to sign a truce. That's a loss. Any time Uncle Sam, with all his machinery for warfare, is held to a draw by some rice eaters, he's lost the battle. He had to sign a truce. America's not supposed to sign a truce. She's supposed to be bad. But she's not bad any more. She's bad as long as she can use her hydrogen bomb, but she can't use hers for fear Russia might use hers. Russia can't use hers, for fear that Sam might use his. So, both of them are weapon less. They can't use the weapon because each's weapon nullifies the other's. So the only place where action can take place is on the ground. And the white man can't win another war fighting on the ground. Those days are over. The black man knows it, the brown man knows it, the red man knows it, and the yellow man knows it. So they engage him in guerrilla warfare. That's not his style. You've got to have heart to be a guerrilla warrior, and he hasn't got any heart. I'm telling you now.

39. I just want to give you a little briefing on guerrilla warfare because, before you know it, before you know it . . . . It takes heart to be a guerrilla warrior because you're on your own. In conventional warfare you have tanks and a whole lot of other people with you to back you up, planes over your head and all that kind of stuff. But a guerrilla is on his own. All you have is a rifle, some sneakers and a bowl of rice, and that's all you need—and a lot of heart. The Japanese on some of those islands in the Pacific, when the American soldiers landed, one Japanese sometimes could hold the whole army off. He'd just wait until the sun went down, and when the sun went down they were all equal. He would take his little blade and slip from bush to bush, and from American to American. The white soldiers couldn't cope with that. Whenever you see a white soldier that fought in the Pacific, he has the shakes, he has a nervous condition, because they scared him to death.

40. The same thing happened to the French up in French Indochina. People who just a few years previously were rice farmers got together and ran the heavily-mechanized French army out of Indochina. You don't need it—modern warfare today won't work. This is the day of the guerrilla. They did the same thing in Algeria. Algerians, who were nothing but Bedouins, took a knife and sneaked off to the hills, and de Gaulle and all of his highfalutin' war machinery couldn't defeat those guerrillas. Nowhere on this earth does the white man win in a guerrilla warfare. It's not his speed. Just as guerrilla warfare is prevailing in Asia and in parts of Africa and in parts of Latin America, you've got to be mighty naive, or you've got to play the black man cheap, if you don't think some day he's going to wake up and find that it's got to be the ballot or the bullet.

41. I would like to say, in closing, a few things concerning the Muslim Mosque, Inc., which we established recently in New York City. It's true we're Muslims and our religion is Islam, but we don't mix our religion with our politics and our economics and our social and civil activities—not any more. We keep our religion in our mosque. After our religious services are over, then as Muslims we become involved in political action,

economic action and social and civic action. We become involved with anybody, any where, any time and in any manner that's designed to eliminate the evils, the political, economic and social evils that are afflicting the people of our community.

42. The political philosophy of black nationalism means that the black man should control the politics and the politicians in his own community; no more. The black man in the black community has to be re-educated into the science of politics so he will know what politics is supposed to bring him in return. Don't be throwing out any ballots. A ballot is like a bullet. You don't throw your ballots until you see a target, and if that target is not within your reach, keep your ballot in your pocket. The political philosophy of black nationalism is being taught in the Christian church. It's being taught in the NAACP. It's being taught in CORE meetings. It's being taught in SNCC Student Nonviolent we should control the economy of our community. Why should white people be running all the stores in our community? Why should white people be running the banks of our community? Why should the economy of our community be in the hands of the white man? Why? If a black man can't move his store into a white community, you tell me why a white man should move his store into a black community. The philosophy of black nationalism involves a re-education program in the black community in regards to economics. Our people have to be made to see that any time you take your dollar out of your community and spend it in a community where you don't live, the community where you live will get poorer and poorer, and the community where you spend your money will get richer and richer. Then you wonder why where you live is always a ghetto or a slum area. And where you and I are concerned, not only do we lose it when we spend it out of the community, but the white man has got all our stores in the community tied up; so that though we spend it in the community, at sundown the man who runs the store takes it over across town somewhere. He's got us in a vise.

43. So the economic philosophy of black nationalism means in every church, in every civic organization, in every fraternal order, it's time now for our people to become conscious of the importance of controlling the economy of our community. If we own the stores, if we operate the businesses, if we try and establish some industry in our own community, then we're developing to the position where we are creating employment for our own kind. Once you gain control of the economy of your own community, then you don't have to picket and boycott and beg some cracker downtown for a job in his business.

44. The social philosophy of black nationalism only means that we have to get together and remove the evils, the vices, alcoholism, drug addiction, and other evils that are destroying the moral fiber of our community. We our selves have to lift the level of our community, the standard of our community to a higher level, make our own society beautiful so that we will be satisfied in our own social circles and won't be running around here trying to knock our way into a social circle where we're not wanted.

45. So I say, in spreading a gospel such as black nationalism, it is not designed to make the black man re-evaluate the white man—you know him already—but to make the black man re-evaluate himself. Don't change the white man's mind—you can't change his mind, and that whole thing about appealing to the moral conscience of America—America's conscience is bankrupt. She lost all conscience a long time ago. Uncle Sam has no conscience. They don't know what morals are. They don't try and eliminate an

evil because it's evil, or because it's illegal, or because it's immoral; they eliminate it only when it threatens their existence. So you're wasting your time appealing to the moral conscience of a bankrupt man like Uncle Sam. If he had a conscience, he'd straighten this thing out with no more pressure being put upon him. So it is not necessary to change the white man's mind. We have to change our own mind. You can't change his mind about us. We've got to change our own minds about each other. We have to see each other with new eyes. We have to see each other as brothers and sisters. We have to come together with warmth so we can develop unity and harmony that's necessary to get this problem solved our selves. How can we do this? How can we avoid jealousy? How can we avoid the suspicion and the divisions that exist in the community? I'll tell you how.

46. I have watched how Billy Graham comes into a city, spreading what he calls the gospel of Christ, which is only white nationalism. That's what he is. Billy Graham is a white nationalist; I'm a black nationalist. But since it's the natural tendency for leaders to be jealous and look upon a powerful figure like Graham with suspicion and envy, how is it possible for him to come into a city and get all the cooperation of the church leaders? Don't think because they're church leaders that they don't have weaknesses that make them envious and jealous—no, everybody's got it. It's not an accident that when they want to choose a cardinal as Pope over there in Rome, they get in a closet so you can't hear them cussing and fighting and carrying on.

47. Billy Graham comes in preaching the gospel of Christ, he evangelizes the gospel, he stirs everybody up, but he never tries to start a church. If he came in trying to start a church, all the churches would be against him. So, he just comes in talking about Christ and tells everybody who gets Christ to go to any church where Christ is; and in this way the church cooperates with him. So we're going to take a page from his book. Our gospel is black nationalism. We're not trying to threaten the existence of any organization, but we're spreading the gospel of black nationalism. Anywhere there's a church that is also preaching and practicing the gospel of black nationalism, join that church. If the NAACP is preaching and practicing the gospel of black nationalism, join the NAACP. If CORE is spreading and practicing the gospel of black nationalism, join CORE. Join any organization that has a gospel that's for the uplift of the black man. And when you get into it and see them pussyfooting or compromising, pull out of it because that's not black nationalism. We'll find another one.

48. And in this manner, the organizations will increase in number and in quantity and in quality, and by August, it is then our intention to have a black nationalist convention which will consist of delegates from all over the country who are interested in the political, economic and social philosophy of black nationalism. After these delegates convene, we will hold a seminar, we will hold discussions, we will listen to everyone. We want to hear new ideas and new solutions and new answers. And at that time, if we see fit then to form a black nationalist party, we'll form a black nationalist party. If it's necessary to form a black nationalist army, we'll form a black nationalist army. It'll be the ballot or the bullet. It'll be liberty or it'll be death.

49. It's time for you and me to stop sitting in this country, letting some cracker senators, Northern crackers and Southern crackers, sit there in Washington, D.C., and come to a conclusion in their mind that you and I are supposed to have civil rights. There's no white man going to tell me anything about my rights. Brothers and sisters, always

remember, if it doesn't take senators and congressmen and presidential proclamations to give freedom to the white man, it is not necessary for legislation or proclamation or Supreme Court decisions to give freedom to the black man. You let that white man know, if this is a country of freedom, let it be a country of freedom; and if it's not a country of freedom, change it.

50. We will work with anybody, anywhere, at any time, who is genuinely interested in tackling the problem head-on, nonviolently as long as the enemy is nonviolent, but violent when the enemy gets violent. We'll work with you on the voter-registration drive, we'll work with you on rent strikes, we'll work with you on school boycotts—I don't believe in any kind of integration; I'm not even worried about it because I know you're not going to get it anyway; you're not going to get it because you're afraid to die; you've got to be ready to die if you try and force yourself on the white man, because he'll get just as violent as those crackers in Mississippi, right here in Cleveland. But we will still work with you on the school boycotts because we're against a segregated school system. A segregated school system produces children who, when they graduate, graduate with crippled minds. But this does not mean that a school is segregated because it's all black. A segregated school means a school that is controlled by people who have no real interest in it whatsoever.

51. Let me explain what I mean. A segregated district or community is a community in which people live, but outsiders control the politics and the economy of that community. They never refer to the white section as a segregated community. It's the all-Negro section that's a segregated community. Why? The white man controls his own school, his own bank, his own economy, his own politics, his own everything, his own community—but he also controls yours. When you're under someone else's control, you're segregated. They'll always give you the lowest or the worst that there is to offer, but it doesn't mean you're segregated just because you have your own. You've got to control your own. Just like the white man has control of his, you need to control yours.

52. You know the best way to get rid of segregation? The white man is more afraid of separation than he is of integration. Segregation means that he puts you away from him, but not far enough for you to be out of his jurisdiction; separation means you're gone. And the white man will integrate faster than he'll let you separate. So we will work with you against the segregated school system because it's criminal, because it is absolutely destructive, in every way imaginable, to the minds of the children who have to be exposed to that type of crippling education. Last but not least, I must say this concerning the great controversy over rifles and shotguns. The only thing that I've ever said is that in areas where the government has proven itself either unwilling or unable to defend the lives and the property of Negroes, it's time for Negroes to defend themselves. Article number two of the constitutional amendments provides you and me the right to own a rifle or a shotgun. It is constitutionally legal to own a shotgun or a rifle. This doesn't mean you're going to get a rifle and form battalions and go out looking for white folks, although you'd be within your rights—I mean, you'd be justified; but that would be illegal and we don't do anything illegal. If the white man doesn't want the black man buying rifles and shotguns, then let the government do its job. That's all. And don't let the white man come to you and ask you what you think about what Malcolm says—why, you old Uncle Tom. He would never ask you if he thought you were going to say, "Amen!" No, he is making a Tom out of you. So, this doesn't

mean forming rifle clubs and going out looking for people, but it is time, in 1964, if you are a man, to let that man know. If he's not going to do his job in running the government and providing you and me with the protection that our taxes are supposed to be for, since he spends all those billions for his defense budget, he certainly can't begrudge you and me spending $12 or $15 for a single-shot, or double-action. I hope you understand. Don't go out shooting people, but any time, brothers and sisters, and especially the men in this audience—some of you wearing Congressional Medals of Honor, with shoulders this wide, chests this big, muscles that big—any time you and I sit around and read where they bomb a church and murder in cold blood, not some grownups, but four little girls while they were praying to the same god the white man taught them to pray to, and you and I see the government go down and can't find who did it. Why, this man—he can find Eichmann hiding down in Argentina somewhere. Let two or three American soldiers, who are minding somebody else's business way over in South Vietnam, get killed, and he'll send battleships, sticking his nose in their business. He wanted to send troops down to Cuba and make them have what he calls free elections—this old cracker who doesn't have free elections in his own country. No, if you never see me another time in your life, if I die in the morning, I'll die saying one thing: the ballot or the bullet, the ballot or the bullet.

53. If a Negro in 1964 has to sit around and wait for some cracker senator to filibuster when it comes to the rights of black people, why, you and I should hang our heads in shame. You talk about a march on Washington in 1963, you haven't seen anything. There's some more going down in '64. And this time they're not going like they went last year. They're not going singing "We Shall Overcome." They're not going with white friends. They're not going with placards already painted for them. They're not going with round-trip tickets. They're going with one way tickets.

54. And if they don't want that non-nonviolent army going down there, tell them to bring the filibuster to a halt. The black nationalists aren't going to wait. Lyndon B. Johnson is the head of the Democratic Party. If he's for civil rights, let him go into the Senate next week and declare himself. Let him go in there right now and declare himself. Let him go in there and denounce the Southern branch of his party. Let him go in there right now and take a moral stand—right now, not later. Tell him, don't wait until election time. If he waits too long, brothers and sisters, he will be responsible for letting a condition develop in this country which will create a climate that will bring seeds up out of the ground with vegetation on the end of them looking like something these people never dreamed of. In 1964, it's the ballot or the bullet. Thank you.

Civil Rights Act of 1964

*This legislation was signed by **President Lyndon B. Johnson,** but it was **begun by President John F. Kennedy**—and left unfinished at the time of his assassination. The passage was difficult, with the House holding on to it in committee and then the Senate filibustering in hopes of defeat. Johnson called on the floor leadership in the Senate of Hubert Humphrey (D-Minnesota) and Everett Dirksen (R-Illinois) to break the filibuster and get the legislation passed. In honor of Kennedy and with Johnson working in the background, the act finally passed; it has been called the **most sweeping civil rights*** *legislation since Reconstruction. In all, the law consists of eleven titles; among them, they spell out the details on voting rights, discrimination in places of public accommodation, desegregation of public facilities, desegregation of public schools, nondiscrimination in federally assisted programs, and equal employment opportunities.*

To enforce the constitutional right to vote, to confer jurisdiction upon the district courts of the United States to provide injunctive relief against discrimination in public accommodations, to authorize the Attorney General to institute suits to protect constitutional rights in public facilities and public education, to extend the Commission on Civil Rights, to prevent discrimination in federally assisted programs, to establish a Commission on Equal Employment Opportunity, and for other purposes.

Be it enacted by the Senate and House of Representatives of the United States of America in Congress assembled, That this Act may be cited as the "Civil Rights Act of 1964."

Approved: July 2, 1964.

*The **heart of the Civil Rights Act deals with public accommodations,** a legal assurance that there will be no discrimination against any person in places that house, feed, entertain, or conduct business.*

Title II

Sec. 201. (a) All persons shall be entitled to the full and equal enjoyment of the goods, services, facilities, privileges, advantages, and accommodations of any place of public accommodation, as defined in this section, without discrimination or segregation on the ground of race, color, religion, or national origin.

(b) Each of the following establishments which serves the public is a place of public accommodation within the meaning of this title if its operations affect commerce, or if discrimination or segregation by it is supported by State action:

1. any inn, hotel, motel, or other establishment which provides lodging to transient guests, other than an establishment located within a building which contains not more than five rooms for rent or hire and which is actually occupied by the proprietor of such establishment as his residence;

2. any restaurant, cafeteria, lunchroom, lunch counter, soda fountain, or other facility principally engaged in selling food for consumption on the premises, including, but not limited to, any such facility located on the premises of any retail establishment; or any gasoline station;

3. any motion picture house, theater, concert hall, sports arena, stadium or other place of exhibition or entertainment; and

4. any establishment (A) (i) which is physically located within the premises of any establishment otherwise covered by this subsection, or (ii) within the premises of which is physically located any such covered establishment, and (b) which holds itself out as serving patrons of such covered establishment.

(c) The operations of an establishment affect commerce within the meaning of this title if (1) it is one of the establishments described in paragraph (1) of subsection (b);

(2) in the case of an establishment described in paragraph (2) of subsection (b), it serves or offers to serve interstate travelers or a substantial portion of the food which it serves, or gasoline or other products which it sells, has moved in commerce; (3) in the case of an establishment described in paragraph (3) of subsection (b), it customarily presents films, performances, athletic teams, exhibitions, or other sources of entertainment which move in commerce; and (4) in the case of an establishment described in paragraph (4) of subsection (b), it is physically located within the premises of, or there is physically located within its premises, an establishment the operations of which affect commerce within the meaning of this subsection. For purposes of this section, "commerce" means travel, trade, traffic, commerce, transportation, or communication among the several States, or between the District of Columbia and any State, or between any foreign country or any territory or possession and any State or the District of Columbia, or between points in the same State but through any other State or the District of Columbia or a foreign country.

(d)   Discrimination or segregation by an establishment is supported by State action within the meaning of this title if such discrimination or segregation (1) is carried on under color of any law, statute, ordinance, or regulation; or (2) is carried on under color of any custom or usage required or enforced by officials of the State or political subdivision thereof; or (3) is required by action of the State or political subdivision thereof . . .

(e) The provisions of this title shall not apply to a private club or other establishment not in facts open to the public, except to the extent that the facilities of such establishment are made available to the customers or patrons of an establishment within the scope of subsection (b).

Sec 202. All persons shall be entitled to be free, at any establishment or place, from discrimination or segregation of any kind on the ground of race, color, religion, or national origin, if such discrimination or segregation is or purports to be required by any law, statute, ordinance, regulation, rule, or order of a State or any agency or political subdivision thereof.

Sec. 203. No person shall (a) withhold, deny, or attempt to withhold or deny, or deprive or attempt to deprive, any person of any right or privilege secured by section 201 or 202, or (b) intimidate, threaten, or coerce, or attempt to intimidate, threaten, or coerce any person with purpose of interfering with any right or privilege secured by section 201 or 202, or (c) punish or attempt to punish any person for exercising or attempting to exercise any right or privilege secured by section 201 or 202.

National Organization for Women

Statement of Purpose (1966)

*In the summer of 1966, at the **Third National Conference of the Commission of the Status of Women** (a commission established by President Kennedy to consider the rights of women), twenty-eight women decided to break away and form their own group—which became the **National Organization for Women,** or NOW. **Betty Friedan,** author of*

The Feminine Mystique *(a 1963 book often credited with starting the modern women's movement) served as the first president of NOW. By the fall of 1966, NOW was beginning to organize at its first conference, where this Statement of Purpose was adopted. NOW's early focus was on enforcing laws that already existed to protect women, such as Title VII of the Civil Rights Act of 1964, which prohibited discrimination in employment. **NOW would go on to call for new laws to be passed, supporting affordable child care, gay rights, and a woman's right to have a safe, legal abortion.** Their struggle for the Equal Rights Amendment, however, would end in defeat.*

(Adopted at the organizing conference in Washington, D.C., October 29, 1966)

We, men and women, who hereby constitute ourselves as the National Organization for Women, believe that the time has come for a new movement toward true equality for all women in America, and toward a fully equal partnership of the sexes, as part of the world-wide revolution of human rights now taking place within and beyond our national borders.

The purpose of NOW is to take action to bring women into full participation in the mainstream of American society now, exercising all the privileges and responsibilities thereof in truly equal partnership with men.

We believe the time has come to move beyond the abstract argument, discussion and symposia over the status and special nature of women which has raged in America in recent years; the time has come to confront, with concrete action, the conditions that now prevent women from enjoying the equality of opportunity and freedom of which is their right, as individual Americans, and as human beings.

NOW is dedicated to the proposition that women, first and foremost, are human beings, who, like all other people in our society, must have the chance to develop their fullest human potential. We believe that women can achieve such equality only by accepting to the full the challenges and responsibilities they share with all other people in our society, as part of the decision-making mainstream of American political, economic and social life.

We organize to initiate or support action, nationally, or in any part of this nation, by individuals or organizations, to break through the silken curtain of prejudice and discrimination against women in government, industry, the professions, the churches, the political parties, the judiciary, the labor unions, in education, science, medicine, law, religion and every other field of importance in American society. Enormous changes taking place in our society make it both possible and urgently necessary to advance the unfinished revolution of women toward true equality, now. With a life span lengthened to nearly 75 years it is no longer either necessary or possible for women to devote the greater part of their lives to child-rearing; yet childbearing and rearing which continues to be a most important part of most women's lives-still is used to justify barring women from equal professional and economic participation and advance.

Today's technology has reduced most of the productive chores which women once performed in the home and in mass-production industries based upon routine unskilled labor. This same technology has virtually eliminated the quality of muscular strength as a criterion for filling most jobs, while intensifying American industry's need for creative intelligence. In view of this new industrial revolution created by automation in the mid-twentieth century, women can and must participate in old and new fields of society in full equality—or become permanent outsiders.

Despite all the talk about the status of American women in recent years, the actual position of women in the United States has declined, and is declining, to an alarming degree throughout the 1950's and '60s. Although 46.4% of all American women between the ages of 18 and 65 now work outside the home, the overwhelming majority—75%— are in routine clerical, sales, or factory jobs, or they are household workers, cleaning women, hospital attendants. About two-thirds of Negro women workers are in the lowest paid service occupations. Working women are becoming increasingly—not less— concentrated on the bottom of the job ladder. As a consequence full-time women work- ers today earn on the average only 60% of what men earn, and that wage gap has been increasing over the past twenty-five years in every major industry group. In 1964, of all women with a yearly income, 89% earned under $5,000 a year; half of all full-time year round women workers earned less than $3,690; only 1.4% of full-time year round women workers had an annual income of $10,000 or more.

Further, with higher education increasingly essential in today's society, too few women are entering and finishing college or going on to graduate or professional school. Today, women earn only one in three of the B.A.'s and M.A.'s granted, and one in ten of the Ph.D.s.

In all the professions considered of importance to society, and in the executive ranks of industry and government, women are losing ground. Where they are present it is only a token handful. Women comprise less than 1% of federal judges; less than 4% of all lawyers; 7% of doctors. Yet women represent 51% of the U.S. population. And, increas- ingly men are replacing women in the top positions in secondary and elementary schools, in social work, and in libraries—once thought to be women's fields.

10   Official pronouncements of the advance in the status of women hide not only the reality of this dangerous decline, but the fact that nothing is being done to stop it. The excellent reports of the President's Commission on the Status of Women and of the State Commissions have not been fully implemented. Such Commissions have power only to advise. They have no power to enforce their recommendations; nor have they the free- dom to organize American women and men to press for action on them. The reports of these commissions have, however created a basis upon which it is now possible to build.

Discrimination in employment on the basis of sex is now prohibited by federal law, in Title VII of the Civil Rights Act of 1964. But although nearly one-third of the cases brought before the Equal Employment Opportunity Commission during the first year dealt with sex discrimination and the proportion is increasing dramatically, the Commission has not made clear its intention to enforce the law with the same seriousness on behalf of women as of other victims of discrimination. Many of these cases were Negro women, who are the vic- tims of the double discrimination of race and sex. Until now, too few women's organiza- tions and official spokesmen have been willing to speak out against these dangers facing women. Too many women have been restrained by the fear of being called "feminist."

There is no civil rights movement to speak for women, as there has been for Negroes and other victims of discrimination. The National Organization for Women must therefore begin to speak.

WE BELIEVE that the power of American law, and the protection guaranteed by the U. S. Constitution to the civil rights of all individuals, must be effectively applied and enforced to isolate and remove patterns of sex discrimination, to ensure equality of oppor- tunity in employment and education, and equality of civil and political rights and respon- sibilities on behalf of women, as well as for Negroes and other deprived groups.

We realize that women's problems are linked to many broader questions of social justice; their solution will require concerted action by many groups. Therefore, convinced that human rights for all are indivisible, we expect to give active support to the common cause of equal rights for all those who suffer discrimination and deprivation, and we call upon other organizations committed to such goals to support our efforts toward equality for women.

WE DO NOT ACCEPT the token appointment of a few women to high-level positions in government and industry as a substitute for a serious continuing effort to recruit and advance women according to their individual abilities. To this end, we urge American government and industry to mobilize the same resources of ingenuity and command with which they have solved problems of far greater difficulty than those now impeding the progress of women.

WE BELIEVE that this nation has a capacity at least as great as other nations, to innovate new social institutions which will enable women to enjoy true equality of opportunity and responsibility in society, without conflict with their responsibilities as mothers and homemakers. In such innovations, America does not lead the Western world, but lags by decades behind many European countries. We do not accept the traditional assumption that a woman has to choose between marriage and motherhood, on the one hand, and serious participation in industry or the professions on the other. We question the present expectation that all normal women will retire from job or profession for 10 or 15 years, to devote their full time to raising children, only to reenter the job market at a relatively minor level. This in itself, is a deterrent to the aspirations of women, to their acceptance into management or professional training courses, and to the very possibility of equality of opportunity or real choice, for all but a few women. Above all, we reject the assumption that these problems are the unique responsibility of each individual woman, rather than a basic social dilemma which society must solve. True equality of opportunity and freedom of choice for women requires such practical, and possible innovations as a nationwide network of child-care center which will make it unnecessary for women to retire completely from society until their children are grown, and national programs to provide retraining for women who have chosen to care for their own children full-time.

WE BELIEVE that it is as essential for every girl to be educated to her full potential of human ability as it is for every boy—with the knowledge that such education is the key to effective participation in today's economy and that, for a girl as for boy, education can only be serious where there is expectation that it be used in society. We believe that American educators are capable of devising means of imparting such expectations to girl students. Moreover, we consider the decline in the proportion of women receiving higher and professional education to be evidence of discrimination. This discrimination may take the form of quotas against the admission of women to colleges, and professional schools; lack of encouragement by parents, counselors and educators; denial of loans or fellowships; or the traditional or arbitrary procedures in graduate and professional training geared in terms of men, which inadvertently discriminate against women. We believe that the same serious attention must be given to high school dropouts who are girls as to boys.

WE REJECT the current assumptions that a man must carry the sole burden of supporting himself, his wife, and family, and that a woman is automatically entitled to lifelong support by a man upon her marriage, or that marriage, home and family are primarily woman's world and responsibility—hers to dominate—his to support. We believe that a true partnership between the sexes demands a different concept of marriage an equitable sharing of the responsibilities of home and children and of the economic burdens of their support. We believe that proper recognition should be given to the economic and social value of homemaking and child-care. To these ends we will seek to open a reexamination of laws and mores governing marriage and divorce, for we believe that the current state of "half-equality" between the sexes discriminates against both men and women, and is the cause of much unnecessary hostility between the sexes.

WE BELIEVE that women must now exercise their political rights and responsibility as American citizens. They must refuse to be segregated on the basis of sex into separate-and-not-equal ladies auxiliaries in the political parties, and they must demand representation according to their numbers in the regularly constituted part committees—at local, state, and national levels—and in the informal power structure, participating fully in the selection of candidates and political decision-making, and running for office themselves.

20   IN THE INTERESTS OF THE HUMAN DIGNITY OF WOMEN, we will protest, and endeavor to change, the false image of women now prevalent in the mass media, and in the texts, ceremonies, laws, and practices of our major social institutions. Such images perpetuate contempt for women by society and by women for themselves. We are similarly opposed to all policies and practices—in church, state, college, factory, or office—which, in the guise of protectiveness, not only deny opportunities but also foster in women self-denigration, dependence, and evasion of responsibility, undermine their confidence in their own abilities and foster contempt for women.

NOW WILL HOLD ITSELF INDEPENDENT OF ANY POLITICAL PARTY in order to mobilize the political power of all women and men intent on our goals. We will strive to ensure that no party, candidate, president, senator, governor, congressman, or any public official who betrays or ignores the principle of full equality between the sexes is elected or appointed to office. If it is necessary to mobilize the votes of men and women who believe in our cause, in order to win for women the final right to be fully free and equal human beings, we so commit ourselves.

WE BELIEVE THAT women will do most to create a new image of women by acting now, and by speaking out in behalf of their own equality, freedom, and human dignity—not in pleas for special privilege, nor in enmity toward men, who are also victims of the current, half-equality between the sexes—but in an active, self-respecting partnership with men. By so doing, women will develop confidence in their own ability to determine actively, in partnership with men, the conditions of their life, their choices, their future and their society.

Supreme Court of the United States

Roe v. Wade

Argued December 13, 1971; Reargued October 11, 1972; Decided January 22, 1973

*A **single woman (Roe) in Texas** wanted to **terminate her pregnancy**, but the law in Texas at the time permitted abortions only to save the life of the pregnant woman. The case made its way to the Supreme Court asking this question: **Does the Constitution permit a woman's right to terminate her pregnancy by abortion?** Abortion, the court held, fell within the woman's right to privacy, which is protected by the Fourteenth Amendment. A woman would have autonomy over her pregnancy during the first* *trimester; after the first three months, the process of terminating a pregnancy remains mired in different state laws. The subject of abortion—pro-life, pro-choice, pro-child— remains a politically hot issue, and the name of the case—***Roe v. Wade***—has become a synonym for "the right to choose an abortion."*

Appeal from the United States District Court for the Northern District of Texas

Syllabus:

A pregnant single woman (Roe) brought a class action challenging the constitutionality of the Texas criminal abortion laws, which proscribe procuring or attempting an abortion except on medical advice for the purpose of saving the mother's life. A licensed physician (Hallford), who had two state abortion prosecutions pending against him, was permitted to intervene. A childless married couple (the Does), the wife not being pregnant, separately attacked the laws, basing alleged injury on the future possibilities of contraceptive failure, pregnancy, unpreparedness for parenthood, and impairment of the wife's health. A three-judge District Court, which consolidated the actions, held that Roe and Hallford, and members of their classes, had standing to sue and presented justiciable controversies. Ruling that declaratory, though not injunctive, relief was warranted, the court declared the abortion statutes void as vague and overbroadly infringing those plaintiffs' Ninth and Fourteenth Amendment rights. The court ruled the Does' complaint not justiciable. Appellants directly appealed to this Court on the injunctive rulings, and appellee cross-appealed from the District Court's grant of declaratory relief to Roe and Hallford.

Held:

1. While 28 U.S.C. § 1253 authorizes no direct appeal to this Court from the grant or denial of declaratory relief alone, review is not foreclosed when the case is properly before the Court on appeal from specific denial of injunctive relief and the arguments as to both injunctive and declaratory relief are necessarily identical.

   1. Roe has standing to sue; the Does and Hallford do not.
   2. Contrary to appellee's contention, the natural termination of Roe's pregnancy did not moot her suit. Litigation involving pregnancy, which is "capable of repetition, yet evading review," is an exception to the usual federal rule that an actual controversy must exist at review stages, and not simply when the action is initiated.
   3. The District Court correctly refused injunctive, but erred in granting declaratory, relief to Hallford, who alleged no federally protected right not assertable as a defense against the good faith state prosecutions pending against him. *Samuels v. Mackell*, 401 U.S. 66.
   4. The Does' complaint, based as it is on contingencies, any one or more of which may not occur, is too speculative to present an actual case or controversy.

2. State criminal abortion laws, like those involved here, that except from criminality only a life-saving procedure on the mother's behalf without regard to the stage of her pregnancy and other interests involved violate the Due Process Clause of the Fourteenth Amendment, which protects against state action the right to privacy,

including a woman's qualified right to terminate her pregnancy. Though the State cannot override that right, it has legitimate interests in protecting both the pregnant woman's health and the potentiality of human life, each of which interests grows and reaches a "compelling" point at various stages of the woman's approach to term.

1. For the stage prior to approximately the end of the first trimester, the abortion decision and its effectuation must be left to the medical judgment of the pregnant woman's attending physician.
2. For the stage subsequent to approximately the end of the first trimester, the State, in promoting its interest in the health of the mother, may, if it chooses, regulate the abortion procedure in ways that are reasonably related to maternal health.
3. For the stage subsequent to viability the State, in promoting its interest in the potentiality of human life, may, if it chooses, regulate, and even proscribe, abortion except where necessary, in appropriate medical judgment, for the preservation of the life or health of the mother.

3. The State may define the term "physician" to mean only a physician currently licensed by the State, and may proscribe any abortion by a person who is not a physician as so defined.
4. It is unnecessary to decide the injunctive relief issue, since the Texas authorities will doubtless fully recognize the Court's ruling that the Texas criminal abortion statutes are unconstitutional.

Resignation Speech, August 8, 1974

Richard M. Nixon

Richard M. Nixon (1913–1994).

The thirty-seventh president of the United States is the first and only one to be forced to resign the highest office in the land. **Richard Nixon's trouble began with a break-in at the Democratic National Committee's offices in the Watergate complex in Washington, D.C., on June 17, 1972.** *Soon thereafter links were made between the Oval Office and the burglars. Though Nixon won reelection, his second term was clouded with hints of scandal.* **Impeachment proceedings** *were under way in the House Judiciary Committee (see Barbara Jordan's speech in Chapter 3). From across the nation, people were calling for Nixon's resignation. When it appeared he no* *longer had the support in Congress and that an impeachment trial would have sent him from the office in disgrace, he chose what many consider the lesser of two evils— to resign, holding on to whatever dignity he could muster. His speech reflects on **the positive aspects of his presidency**—his opening the doors with the People's Republic of China, his work to end the war in Vietnam—but nowhere does he apologize for his connections with Watergate. The focus here is on issues of peace in a global setting, not the scandal that drove him from office.*

Good evening.

This is the 37th time I have spoken to you from this office, where so many decisions have been made that shaped the history of this Nation. Each time I have done so to discuss with you some matter that I believe affected the national interest.

In all the decisions I have made in my public life, I have always tried to do what was best for the Nation. Throughout the long and difficult period of Watergate, I have felt it was my duty to persevere, to make every possible effort to complete the term of office to which you elected me.

In the past few days, however, it has become evident to me that I no longer have a strong enough political base in the Congress to justify continuing that effort. As long as there was such a base, I felt strongly that it was necessary to see the constitutional process through to its conclusion, that to do otherwise would be unfaithful to the spirit of that deliberately difficult process and a dangerously destabilizing precedent for the future.

But with the disappearance of that base, I now believe that the constitutional purpose   5
has been served, and there is no longer a need for the process to be prolonged.

I would have preferred to carry through to the finish whatever the personal agony it would have involved, and my family unanimously urged me to do so. But the interest of the Nation must always come before any personal considerations.

From the discussions I have had with Congressional and other leaders, I have concluded that because of the Watergate matter I might not have the support of the Congress that I would consider necessary to back the very difficult decisions and carry out the duties of this office in the way the interests of the Nation would require.

I have never been a quitter. To leave office before my term is completed is abhorrent to every instinct in my body. But as President, I must put the interest of America first. America needs a full-time President and a full-time Congress, particularly at this time with problems we face at home and abroad.

To continue to fight through the months ahead for my personal vindication would almost totally absorb the time and attention of both the President and the Congress in a period when our entire focus should be on the great issues of peace abroad and prosperity without inflation at home.

Therefore, I shall resign the Presidency effective at noon tomorrow. Vice President   10
Ford will be sworn in as President at that hour in this office.

As I recall the high hopes for America with which we began this second term, I feel a great sadness that I will not be here in this office working on your behalf to achieve those hopes in the next 2½ years. But in turning over direction of the Government to Vice President Ford, I know, as I told the Nation when I nominated him for that office 10 months ago, that the leadership of America will be in good hands.

In passing this office to the Vice President, I also do so with the profound sense of the weight of responsibility that will fall on his shoulders tomorrow and, therefore, of the understanding, the patience, the cooperation he will need from all Americans.

As he assumes that responsibility, he will deserve the help and the support of all of us. As we look to the future, the first essential is to begin healing the wounds of this Nation, to put the bitterness and divisions of the recent past behind us, and to rediscover those shared ideals that lie at the heart of our strength and unity as a great and as a free people.

By taking this action, I hope that I will have hastened the start of that process of healing which is so desperately needed in America.

15   I regret deeply any injuries that may have been done in the course of the events that led to this decision. I would say only that if some of my judgments were wrong, and some were wrong, they were made in what I believed at the time to be the best interest of the Nation.

To those who have stood with me during these past difficult months, to my family, my friends, to many others who joined in supporting my cause because they believed it was right, I will be eternally grateful for your support.

And to those who have not felt able to give me your support, let me say I leave with no bitterness toward those who have opposed me, because all of us, in the final analysis, have been concerned with the good of the country, however our judgments might differ.

So, let us all now join together in affirming that common commitment and in helping our new President succeed for the benefit of all Americans.

I shall leave this office with regret at not completing my term, but with gratitude for the privilege of serving as your President for the past 5½ years. These years have been a momentous time in the history of our Nation and the world. They have been a time of achievement in which we can all be proud, achievements that represent the shared efforts of the Administration, the Congress, and the people.

20   But the challenges ahead are equally great, and they, too, will require the support and the efforts of the Congress and the people working in cooperation with the new Administration.

We have ended America's longest war, but in the work of securing a lasting peace in the world, the goals ahead are even more far-reaching and more difficult. We must complete a structure of peace so that it will be said of this generation, our generation of Americans, by the people of all nations, not only that we ended one war but that we prevented future wars.

We have unlocked the doors that for a quarter of a century stood between the United States and the People's Republic of China.

We must now ensure that the one quarter of the world's people who live in the People's Republic of China will be and remain not our enemies but our friends.

In the Middle East, 100 million people in the Arab countries, many of whom have considered us their enemy for nearly 20 years, now look on us as their friends. We must continue to build on that friendship so that peace can settle at last over the Middle East and so that the cradle of civilization will not become its grave.

25   Together with the Soviet Union we have made the crucial breakthroughs that have begun the process of limiting nuclear arms. But we must set as our goal not just limiting but reducing and finally destroying these terrible weapons so that they cannot destroy civilization and so that the threat of nuclear war will no longer hang over the world and the people.

We have opened the new relation with the Soviet Union. We must continue to develop and expand that new relationship so that the two strongest nations of the world will live together in cooperation rather than confrontation.

Around the world, in Asia, in Africa, in Latin America, in the Middle East, there are millions of people who live in terrible poverty, even starvation. We must keep as our goal turning away from production for war and expanding production for peace so that people everywhere on this earth can at last look forward in their children's time, if not in our own time, to having the necessities for a decent life.

Here in America, we are fortunate that most of our people have not only the blessings of liberty but also the means to live full and good and, by the world's standards, even abundant lives. We must press on, however, toward a goal of not only more and better jobs but of full opportunity for every American and of what we are striving so hard right now to achieve, prosperity without inflation.

For more than a quarter of a century in public life I have shared in the turbulent history of this era. I have fought for what I believed in. I have tried to the best of my ability to discharge those duties and meet those responsibilities that were entrusted to me.

Sometimes I have succeeded and sometimes I have failed, but always I have taken   30
heart from what Theodore Roosevelt once said about the man in the arena, "whose face is marred by dust and sweat and blood, who strives valiantly, who errs and comes short again and again because there is not effort without error and shortcoming, but who does actually strive to do the deed, who knows the great enthusiasms, the great devotions, who spends himself in a worthy cause, who at the best knows in the end the triumphs of high achievements and who at the worst, if he fails, at least fails while daring greatly."

I pledge to you tonight that as long as I have a breath of life in my body, I shall continue in that spirit. I shall continue to work for the great causes to which I have been dedicated throughout my years as a Congressman, a Senator, a Vice President, and President, the cause of peace not just for America but among all nations, prosperity, justice, and opportunity for all of our people.

There is one cause above all to which I have been devoted and to which I shall always be devoted for as long as I live.

When I first took the oath of office as President 5 ½ years ago, I made this sacred commitment, to "consecrate my office, my energies, and all the wisdom I can summon to the cause of peace among nations."

I have done my very best in all the days since to be true to that pledge. As a result of these efforts, I am confident that the world is a safer place today, not only for the people of America but for the people of all nations, and that all of our children have a better chance than before of living in peace rather than dying in war.

This, more than anything, is what I hoped to achieve when I sought the Presidency.   35
This, more than anything, is what I hope will be my legacy to you, to our country, as I leave the Presidency.

To have served in this office is to have felt a very personal sense of kinship with each and every American. In leaving it, I do so with this prayer: May God's grace be with you in all the days ahead.

Ronald W. Reagan

Official Announcement for Candidacy for President of the United States, November 13, 1979

Ronald W. Reagan (1912–2004).

In this, one of his most famous speeches, Ronald Reagan defined his vision for a new, more prosperous and more powerful America. Alluding to the 1630 speech of **John Winthrop,** *who declared of that small settlement that was to become America, "We shall be a city upon a hill," Reagan began his eight-year remaking of America in the shape of his own vision.* **Reagan urged a return to a past—where America had more international power and prestige, fewer regulations at home, and thrived in a culture of entrepreneurship, self-sufficiency, and responsibility.** *He is credited with bringing down the Soviet Union. His eight years in office changed forever the way we viewed big government and is still held as a golden age of conservatism by many who support his policies.*

Good evening. I am here tonight to announce my intention to seek the Republican nomination for President of the United States.

I'm sure that each of us has seen our country from a number of viewpoints depending on where we've lived and what we've done. For me it has been as a boy growing up in several small towns in Illinois. As a young man in Iowa trying to get a start in the years of the Great Depression and later in California for most of my adult life.

I've seen America from the stadium press box as a sportscaster, as an actor, officer of my labor union, soldier, officeholder and as both a Democrat and Republican. I've lived in America where those who often had too little to eat outnumbered those who had enough. There have been four wars in my lifetime and I've seen our country face financial ruin in the Depression. I have also seen the great strength of this nation as it pulled itself up from that ruin to become the dominant force in the world.

To me our country is a living, breathing presence, unimpressed by what others say is impossible, proud of its own success, generous, yes and naive, sometimes wrong, never mean and always impatient to provide a better life for its people in a framework of a basic fairness and freedom.

5   Someone once said that the difference between an American and any other kind of person is that an American lives in anticipation of the future because he knows it will be a great place. Other people fear the future as just a repetition of past failures. There's a lot of truth in that. If there is one thing we are sure of it is that history need not be relived;

that nothing is impossible, and that man is capable of improving his circumstances beyond what we are told is fact.

There are those in our land today, however, who would have us believe that the United States, like other great civilizations of the past, has reached the zenith of its power; that we are weak and fearful, reduced to bickering with each other and no longer possessed of the will to cope with our problems.

Much of this talk has come from leaders who claim that our problems are too difficult to handle. We are supposed to meekly accept their failures as the most which humanly can be done. They tell us we must learn to live with less, and teach our children that their lives will be less full and prosperous than ours have been; that the America of the coming years will be a place where—because of our past excesses—it will be impossible to dream and make those dreams come true.

I don't believe that. And, I don't believe you do either. That is why I am seeking the presidency. I cannot and will not stand by and see this great country destroy itself. Our leaders attempt to blame their failures on circumstances beyond their control, on false estimates by unknown, unidentifiable experts who rewrite modern history in an attempt to convince us our high standard of living, the result of thrift and hard work, is somehow selfish extravagance which we must renounce as we join in sharing scarcity. I don't agree that our nation must resign itself to inevitable decline, yielding its proud position to other hands. I am totally unwilling to see this country fail in its obligation to itself and to the other free peoples of the world.

The crisis we face is not the result of any failure of the American spirit; it is failure of our leaders to establish rational goals and give our people something to order their lives by. If I am elected, I shall regard my election as proof that the people of the United States have decided to set a new agenda and have recognized that the human spirit thrives best when goals are set and progress can be measured in their achievement.

During the next year I shall discuss in detail a wide variety of problems which a new 10 administration must address. Tonight I shall mention only a few.

No problem that we face today can compare with the need to restore the health of the American economy and the strength of the American dollar. Double-digit inflation has robbed you and your family of the ability to plan. It has destroyed the confidence to buy and it threatens the very structure of family life itself as more and more wives are forced to work in order to help meet the ever-increasing cost of living. At the same time, the lack of real growth in the economy has introduced the justifiable fear in the minds of working men and women who are already overextended that soon there will be fewer jobs and no money to pay for even the necessities of life. And tragically as the cost of living keeps going up, the standard of living which has been our great pride keeps going down.

The people have not created this disaster in our economy; the federal government has. It has overspent, overestimated, and over-regulated. It has failed to deliver services within the revenues it should be allowed to raise from taxes. In the 34 years since the end of World War II, it has spent $448 billion more than it has collected in taxes—$448 billion of printing-press money, which has made every dollar you earn worth less and less. At the same time, the federal government has cynically told us that high taxes on business will in some way "solve" the problem and allow the average taxpayer to pay less. Well, business is not a taxpayer; it is a tax collector. Business has to pass its tax burden on to the customer as part of the cost of doing business. You and I pay taxes imposed on business every time we go to the store. Only people pay taxes and it is political demagoguery or economic illiteracy to try and tell us otherwise.

The key to restoring the health of the economy lies in cutting taxes. At the same time, we need to get the waste out of federal spending. This does not mean sacrificing essential services, nor do we need to destroy the system of benefits which flow to the poor, elderly, the sick and the handicapped. We have long since committed ourselves, as a people, to help those among us who cannot take care of themselves. But the federal government has proven to be the costliest and most inefficient provider of such help we could possibly have.

We must put an end to the arrogance of a federal establishment which accepts no blame for our condition, cannot be relied upon to give us a fair estimate of our situation and utterly refuses to live within its means. I will not accept the supposed "wisdom" which has it that the federal bureaucracy has become so powerful that it can no longer be changed or controlled by any administration. As President I would use every power at my command to make the federal establishment respond to the will and the collective wishes of the people.

15   We must force the entire federal bureaucracy to live in the real world of reduced spending, streamlined function and accountability to the people it serves. We must review the function of the federal government to determine which of those are the proper province of levels of government closer to the people.

The 10th article of the Bill of Rights is explicit in pointing out that the federal government should do only those things specifically called for in the Constitution. All others shall remain with the states or the people. We haven't been observing that 10th article of late. The federal government has taken on functions it was never intended to perform and which it does not perform well. There should be a planned, orderly transfer of such functions to states and communities and a transfer with them of the sources of taxation to pay for them.

The savings in administrative overhead would be considerable and certainly there would be increased efficiency and less bureaucracy.

By reducing federal tax rates where they discourage individual initiative—especially personal income tax rates—we can restore incentives, invite greater economic growth and at the same time help give us better government instead of bigger government. Proposals such as the Kemp-Roth bill would bring about this kind of realistic reductions in tax rates.

In short, a punitive tax system must be replaced by one that restores incentive for the worker and for industry; a system that rewards initiative and effort and encourages thrift.

20   All these things are possible; none of them will be easy. But the choice is clear. We can go on letting the country slip over the brink to financial ruin with the disaster that it means for the individual or we can find the will to work together to restore confidence in ourselves and to regain the confidence of the world. I have lived through one Depression. I carry with me the memory of a Christmas Eve when my brother and I and our parents exchanged our modest gifts—there was no lighted tree as there has been on Christmases past. I remember watching my father open what he thought was a greeting from his employer. We all watched and yes, we were hoping it was a bonus check. It was notice that he no longer had a job. And in those days the government ran the radio announcements telling workers not to leave home looking for jobs—there were no jobs. I'll carry with me always the memory of my father sitting there holding that envelope, unable to look at us. I cannot and will not stand by while inflation and joblessness destroy the dignity of our people.

Another serious problem which must be discussed tonight is our energy situation. Our country was built on cheap energy. Today, energy is not cheap and we face the prospect that some forms of energy may soon not be available at all.

Last summer you probably spent hours sitting in gasoline lines. This winter, some will be without heat and everyone will be paying much more simply to keep home and family warm. If you ever had any doubt of the government's inability to provide for the needs of the people, just look at the utter fiasco we now call "the energy crisis." Not one straight answer nor any realistic hope of relief has come from the present administration in almost three years of federal treatment of the problem. As gas lines grew, the administration again panicked and now has proposed to put the country on a wartime footing; but for this "war" there is no victory in sight. And, as always, when the federal bureaucracy fails, all it can suggest is more of the same. This time it's another bureau to untangle the mess by the ones we already have.

But, this just won't work. Solving the energy crisis will not be easy, but it can be done. First we must decide that "less" is not enough. Next, we must remove government obstacles to energy production. And, we must make use of those technological advantages we still possess.

It is no program simply to say "use less energy." Of course waste must be eliminated and efficiently promoted, but for the government simply to tell people to conserve is not an energy policy. At best it means we will run out of energy a little more slowly. But a day will come when the lights will dim and the wheels of industry will turn more slowly and finally stop. As President I will not endorse any course which has this as its principal objective.

We need more energy and that means diversifying our sources of supply away from the OPEC countries. Yes, it means more efficient automobiles. But it also means more exploration and development of oil and natural gas here in our own country. The only way to free ourselves from the monopoly pricing power of OPEC is to be less dependent on outside sources of fuel.

25

The answer, obvious to anyone except those in the administration it seems, is more domestic production of oil and gas. We must also have wider use of nuclear power within strict safety rules, of course. There must be more spending by the energy industries on research and development of substitutes for fossil fuels.

In years to come solar energy may provide much of the answer but for the next two or three decades we must do such things as master the chemistry of coal. Putting the market system to work for these objectives is an essential first step for their achievement. Additional multi-billion-dollar federal bureaus and programs are not the answer.

In recent weeks there has been much talk about "excess" oil company profits. I don't believe we've been given all the information we need to make a judgment about this. We should have that information. Government exists to protect us from each other. It is not government's function to allocate fuel or impose unnecessary restrictions on the marketplace. It is government's function to determine whether we are being unfairly exploited and if so to take immediate and appropriate action. As President I would do exactly that.

On the foreign front, the decade of the 1980s will place severe pressures upon the United States and its allies. We can expect to be tested in ways calculated to try our patience, to confound our resolve and to erode our belief in ourselves. During a time when the Soviet Union may enjoy nuclear superiority over this country, we must never waiver in our commitment to our allies nor accept any negotiation which is not clearly in the national interest. We must judge carefully. Though we should leave no initiative untried in our pursuit of peace, we must be clear voiced in our resolve to resist any unpeaceful act wherever it may occur. Negotiation with the Soviet Union must never become appeasement.

30   For the most of the last 40 years, we have been preoccupied with the global struggle—the competition—with the Soviet Union and with our responsibilities to our allies. But too often in recent times we have just drifted along with events, responding as if we thought of ourselves as a nation in decline. To our allies we seem to appear to be a nation unable to make decisions in its own interests, let alone in the common interest. Since the Second World War we have spent large amounts of money and much of our time protecting and defending freedom all over the world. We must continue this, for if we do not accept the responsibilities of leadership, who will? And if no one will, how will we survive?

The 1970s have taught us the foolhardiness of not having a long-range diplomatic strategy of our own. The world has become a place where, in order to survive, our country needs more than just allies—it needs real friends. Yet, in recent times we often seem not to have recognized who our friends are. This must change. It is now time to take stock of our own house and to resupply its strength.

Part of that process involves taking stock of our relationship with Puerto Rico. I favor statehood for Puerto Rico and if the people of Puerto Rico vote for statehood in their coming referendum I would, as President, initiate the enabling legislation to make this a reality.

We live on a continent whose three countries possess the assets to make it the strongest, most prosperous and self-sufficient area on Earth. Within the borders of this North American continent are the food, resources, technology and undeveloped territory which, properly managed, could dramatically improve the quality of life of all its inhabitants.

It is no accident that this unmatched potential for progress and prosperity exists in three countries with such long-standing heritages of free government. A developing closeness among Canada, Mexico and the United States—a North American accord—would permit achievement of that potential in each country beyond that which I believe any of them—strong as they are—could accomplish in the absence of such cooperation. In fact, the key to our own future security may lie in both Mexico and Canada becoming much stronger countries than they are today.

35   No one can say at this point precisely what form future cooperation among our three countries will take. But if I am elected President, I would be willing to invite each of our neighbors to send a special representative to our government to sit in on high level planning sessions with us, as partners, mutually concerned about the future of our continent. First, I would immediately seek the views and ideas of Canadian and Mexican leaders on this issue, and work tirelessly with them to develop closer ties among our peoples. It is time we stopped thinking of our nearest neighbors as foreigners.

By developing methods of working closely together, we will lay the foundations for future cooperation on a broader and more significant scale. We will put to rest any doubts of those cynical enough to believe that the United States would seek to dominate any relationship among our three countries, or foolish enough to think that the governments and peoples of Canada and Mexico would ever permit such domination to occur. I for one, am confident that we can show the world by example that the nations of North America are ready, within the context of an unswerving commitment to freedom, to see new forms of accommodation to meet a changing world. A developing closeness between the United States, Canada and Mexico would serve notice on friends and foe alike that we were prepared for a long haul, looking outward again and confident of our future; that together we are going to create jobs, to generate new fortunes of wealth for many and provide a legacy for the children of each of our countries. Two hundred years ago, we taught the world that a new form of government, created out of the genius of man to cope with his circumstances, could succeed in bringing a measure of quality to human life previously thought impossible.

Now let us work toward the goal of using the assets of this continent, its resources, technology, and foodstuffs in the most efficient ways possible for the common good of all its people. It may take the next 100 years but we can dare to dream that at some future date a map of the world might show the North American continent as one in which the people's commerce of its three strong countries flow more freely across their present borders than they do today.

In recent months leaders in our government have told us that, we, the people, have lost confidence in ourselves, that we must regain our spirit and our will to achieve our national goals. Well, it is true there is a lack of confidence, an unease with things the way they are. But the confidence we have lost is confidence in our government's policies. Our unease can almost be called bewilderment at how our defense strength has deteriorated. The great productivity of our industry is now surpassed by virtually all the major nations who compete with us for world markets. And, our currency is no longer the stable measure of value it once was.

But there remains the greatness of our people, our capacity for dreaming up fantastic deeds and bringing them off to the surprise of an unbelieving world. When Washington's men were freezing at Valley Forge, Tom Paine told his fellow Americans: "We have it in our power to begin the world over again," we still have that power.

We—today's living Americans—have in our lifetime fought harder, paid a higher price for freedom and done more to advance the dignity of man than any people who have ever lived on this Earth. The citizens of this great nation want leadership—yes—but not a "man on a white horse" demanding obedience to his commands. They want someone who believes they can "begin the world over again." A leader who will unleash their great strength and remove the roadblocks government has put in their way. I want to do that more than anything I've ever wanted. And it's something that I believe with God's help I can do.

I believe this nation hungers for a spiritual revival; hungers to once again see honor placed above political expediency; to see government once again the protector of our liberties, not the distributor of gifts and privilege. Government should uphold and not undermine those institutions which are custodians of the very values upon which civilization is founded—religion, education and, above all, family. Government cannot be clergyman, teacher and patriot. It is our servant, beholden to us.

We who are privileged to be Americans have had a rendezvous with destiny since the moment in 1630 when John Winthrop, standing on the deck of the tiny Arbella off the coast of Massachusetts, told the little band of Pilgrims, "We shall be a city upon a hill. The eyes of all people are upon us so that if we shall deal falsely with our God in this work we have undertaken and so cause Him to withdraw His present help from us, we shall be made a story and a byword throughout the world."

A troubled and afflicted mankind looks to us, pleading for us to keep our rendezvous with destiny; that we will uphold the principles of self-reliance, self-discipline, morality, and—above all—responsible liberty for every individual that we will become that shining city on a hill.

I believe that you and I together can keep this rendezvous with destiny.

45   Thank you and good night.

George H. W. Bush

Inaugural Address, January 20, 1989

George H. W. Bush (1924–).

The forty-first president of the United States was the first sitting vice president to win the presidency since Martin Van Buren in 1836. **George H. W. Bush's** *campaign pitch was filled with repeated references to* **"a thousand points of light,"** *and he returns to that image in his Inaugural Address: "I have spoken of a thousand points of light, of all the community organizations that are spread like stars throughout the Nation, doing good." And doing good is the leitmotif of his speech. Few things are controversial here at the dawn of the last decade of the last century in a time of peace and prosperity for many. Bush calls for a kindler, gentler nation, one that sees freedom as right, and that is willing to invest in a new engagement in doing good for others. He is also aware of divisiveness in the country and that both sides of the aisle—the Democrats and the Republicans—will have to come together so that the country can move forward. The speech serves as a* **reminder of what America can be when it chooses to operate in the best spirit of its high ideals.**

Mr. Chief Justice, Mr. President, Vice President Quayle, Senator Mitchell, Speaker Wright, Senator Dole, Congressman Michel, and fellow citizens, neighbors, and friends:

There is a man here who has earned a lasting place in our hearts and in our history. President Reagan, on behalf of our Nation, I thank you for the wonderful things that you have done for America.

I have just repeated word for word the oath taken by George Washington 200 years ago, and the Bible on which I placed my hand is the Bible on which he placed his. It is right that the memory of Washington be with us today, not only because this is our Bicentennial Inauguration, but because Washington remains the Father of our Country. And he would, I think, be gladdened by this day; for today is the concrete expression of a stunning fact: our continuity these 200 years since our government began.

We meet on democracy's front porch, a good place to talk as neighbors and as friends. For this is a day when our nation is made whole, when our differences, for a moment, are suspended.

And my first act as President is a prayer. I ask you to bow your heads: 5

Heavenly Father, we bow our heads and thank You for Your love. Accept our thanks for the peace that yields this day and the shared faith that makes its continuance likely. Make us strong to do Your work, willing to heed and hear Your will, and write on our hearts these words: "Use power to help people." For we are given power not to advance our own purposes, nor to make a great show in the world, nor a name. There is but one just use of power, and it is to serve people. Help us to remember it, Lord. Amen.

I come before you and assume the Presidency at a moment rich with promise. We live in a peaceful, prosperous time, but we can make it better. For a new breeze is blowing, and a world refreshed by freedom seems reborn; for in man's heart, if not in fact, the day of the dictator is over. The totalitarian era is passing, its old ideas blown away like leaves from an ancient, lifeless tree. A new breeze is blowing, and a nation refreshed by freedom stands ready to push on. There is new ground to be broken, and new action to be taken. There are times when the future seems thick as a fog; you sit and wait, hoping the mists will lift and reveal the right path. But this is a time when the future seems a door you can walk right through into a room called tomorrow.

Great nations of the world are moving toward democracy through the door to freedom. Men and women of the world move toward free markets through the door to prosperity. The people of the world agitate for free expression and free thought through the door to the moral and intellectual satisfactions that only liberty allows.

We know what works: Freedom works. We know what's right: Freedom is right. We know how to secure a more just and prosperous life for man on Earth: through free markets, free speech, free elections, and the exercise of free will unhampered by the state.

For the first time in this century, for the first time in perhaps all history, man does not 10 have to invent a system by which to live. We don't have to talk late into the night about which form of government is better. We don't have to wrest justice from the kings. We only have to summon it from within ourselves. We must act on what we know. I take as my guide the hope of a saint: In crucial things, unity; in important things, diversity; in all things, generosity.

America today is a proud, free nation, decent and civil, a place we cannot help but love. We know in our hearts, not loudly and proudly, but as a simple fact, that this country has meaning beyond what we see, and that our strength is a force for good. But have we changed as a nation even in our time? Are we enthralled with material things, less appreciative of the nobility of work and sacrifice?

My friends, we are not the sum of our possessions. They are not the measure of our lives. In our hearts we know what matters. We cannot hope only to leave our children a bigger car, a bigger bank account. We must hope to give them a sense of what it means to be a loyal friend, a loving parent, a citizen who leaves his home, his neighborhood and town better than he found it. What do we want the men and women who work with us to say when we are no longer there? That we were more driven to succeed than anyone around us? Or that we stopped to ask if a sick child had gotten better, and stayed a moment there to trade a word of friendship?

No President, no government, can teach us to remember what is best in what we are. But if the man you have chosen to lead this government can help make a difference; if he can celebrate the quieter, deeper successes that are made not of gold and silk, but of better hearts and finer souls; if he can do these things, then he must.

America is never wholly herself unless she is engaged in high moral principle. We as a people have such a purpose today. It is to make kinder the face of the Nation and gentler the face of the world. My friends, we have work to do. There are the homeless, lost and roaming. There are the children who have nothing, no love, no normalcy. There are those who cannot free themselves of enslavement to whatever addiction—drugs, welfare, the demoralization that rules the slums. There is crime to be conquered, the rough crime of the streets. There are young women to be helped who are about to become mothers of children they can't care for and might not love. They need our care, our guidance, and our education, though we bless them for choosing life.

15   The old solution, the old way, was to think that public money alone could end these problems. But we have learned that is not so. And in any case, our funds are low. We have a deficit to bring down. We have more will than wallet; but will is what we need. We will make the hard choices, looking at what we have and perhaps allocating it differently, making our decisions based on honest need and prudent safety. And then we will do the wisest thing of all: We will turn to the only resource we have that in times of need always grows—the goodness and the courage of the American people.

I am speaking of a new engagement in the lives of others, a new activism, hands-on and involved, that gets the job done. We must bring in the generations, harnessing the unused talent of the elderly and the unfocused energy of the young. For not only leadership is passed from generation to generation, but so is stewardship. And the generation born after the Second World War has come of age.

I have spoken of a thousand points of light, of all the community organizations that are spread like stars throughout the Nation, doing good. We will work hand in hand, encouraging, sometimes leading, sometimes being led, rewarding. We will work on this in the White House, in the Cabinet agencies. I will go to the people and the programs that are the brighter points of light, and I will ask every member of my government to become involved. The old ideas are new again because they are not old, they are timeless: duty, sacrifice, commitment, and a patriotism that finds its expression in taking part and pitching in.

We need a new engagement, too, between the Executive and the Congress. The challenges before us will be thrashed out with the House and the Senate. We must bring the Federal budget into balance. And we must ensure that America stands before the world united, strong, at peace, and fiscally sound. But, of course, things may be difficult. We need compromise; we have had dissension. We need harmony; we have had a chorus of discordant voices.

For Congress, too, has changed in our time. There has grown a certain divisiveness. We have seen the hard looks and heard the statements in which not each other's ideas are challenged, but each other's motives. And our great parties have too often been far apart and untrusting of each other. It has been this way since Vietnam. That war cleaves us still. But, friends, that war began in earnest a quarter of a century ago; and surely the statute of limitations has been reached. This is a fact: The final lesson of Vietnam is that no great nation can long afford to be sundered by a memory. A new breeze is blowing, and the old bipartisanship must be made new again.

20   To my friends—and yes, I do mean friends—in the loyal opposition—and yes, I mean loyal: I put out my hand. I am putting out my hand to you, Mr. Speaker. I am putting out my hand to you Mr. Majority Leader. For this is the thing: This is the age of the offered hand. We can't turn back clocks, and I don't want to. But when our fathers were young,

Mr. Speaker, our differences ended at the water's edge. And we don't wish to turn back time, but when our mothers were young, Mr. Majority Leader, the Congress and the Executive were capable of working together to produce a budget on which this nation could live. Let us negotiate soon and hard. But in the end, let us produce. The American people await action. They didn't send us here to bicker. They ask us to rise above the merely partisan. "In crucial things, unity"—and this, my friends, is crucial.

To the world, too, we offer new engagement and a renewed vow: We will stay strong to protect the peace. The "offered hand" is a reluctant fist; but once made, strong, and can be used with great effect. There are today Americans who are held against their will in foreign lands, and Americans who are unaccounted for. Assistance can be shown here, and will be long remembered. Good will begets good will. Good faith can be a spiral that endlessly moves on.

Great nations like great men must keep their word. When America says something, America means it, whether a treaty or an agreement or a vow made on marble steps. We will always try to speak clearly, for candor is a compliment, but subtlety, too, is good and has its place. While keeping our alliances and friendships around the world strong, ever strong, we will continue the new closeness with the Soviet Union, consistent both with our security and with progress. One might say that our new relationship in part reflects the triumph of hope and strength over experience. But hope is good, and so are strength and vigilance.

Here today are tens of thousands of our citizens who feel the understandable satisfaction of those who have taken part in democracy and seen their hopes fulfilled. But my thoughts have been turning the past few days to those who would be watching at home to an older fellow who will throw a salute by himself when the flag goes by, and the women who will tell her sons the words of the battle hymns. I don't mean this to be sentimental. I mean that on days like this, we remember that we are all part of a continuum, inescapably connected by the ties that bind.

Our children are watching in schools throughout our great land. And to them I say, thank you for watching democracy's big day. For democracy belongs to us all, and freedom is like a beautiful kite that can go higher and higher with the breeze. And to all I say: No matter what your circumstances or where you are, you are part of this day, you are part of the life of our great nation.

A President is neither prince nor pope, and I don't seek a window on men's souls. In fact, I yearn for a greater tolerance, an easy-goingness about each other's attitudes and way of life.

There are few clear areas in which we as a society must rise up united and express our intolerance. The most obvious now is drugs. And when that first cocaine was smuggled in on a ship, it may as well have been a deadly bacteria, so much has it hurt the body, the soul of our country. And there is much to be done and to be said, but take my word for it: This scourge will stop.

And so, there is much to do; and tomorrow the work begins. I do not mistrust the future; I do not fear what is ahead. For our problems are large, but our heart is larger. Our challenges are great, but our will is greater. And if our flaws are endless, God's love is truly boundless.

Some see leadership as high drama, and the sound of trumpets calling, and sometimes it is that. But I see history as a book with many pages, and each day we fill a page with acts of hopefulness and meaning. The new breeze blows, a page turns, the story unfolds.

And so today a chapter begins, a small and stately story of unity, diversity, and generosity—shared, and written, together.

Thank you. God bless you and God bless the United States of America.

Oklahoma City Bombing Speech, April 23, 1995

On **April 19, 1995,** at what would have been the beginning of a work day in the **Alfred P. Murrah Federal Building in Oklahoma City,** a bomb exploded, killing 168 people, 19 of them children. Timothy McVeigh was executed on June 11, 2001, for their collective deaths. President Clinton paid a visit to the site four days after the bombing, when the city and the country were still in the throes of dealing with the devastation. Though president, Clinton's words come from a fellow American, who with his wife by his side, demonstrates that he first knows what it is to be human—to experience loss, to lean on faith and friends. Clinton's references here are to the Bible and to other Americans who have experienced loss. **His words are reassuring to people in the midst of grief,**

William Jefferson Clinton (1946–).

letting them know that all of America will stand beside them in their time of need.

Thank you very much. Governor Keating and Mrs. Keating, Reverend Graham, to the families of those who have been lost and wounded, to the people of Oklahoma City, who have endured so much, and the people of this wonderful state, to all of you who are here as our fellow Americans.

I am honored to be here today to represent the American people. But I have to tell you that Hillary and I also come as parents, as husband and wife, as people who were your neighbors for some of the best years of our lives.

Today our nation joins with you in grief. We mourn with you. We share your hope against hope that some may still survive. We thank all those who have worked so heroically to save lives and to solve this crime—those here in Oklahoma and those who are all across this great land, and many who left their own lives to come here to work hand in hand with you.

We pledge to do all we can to help you heal the injured, to rebuild this city, and to bring to justice those who did this evil.

5   This terrible sin took the lives of our American family, innocent children in that building, only because their parents were trying to be good parents as well as good workers; citizens in the building going about their daily business; and many there who served

the rest of us—who worked to help the elderly and the disabled, who worked to support our farmers and our veterans, who worked to enforce our laws and to protect us. Let us say clearly, they served us well, and we are grateful.

But for so many of you they were also neighbors and friends. You saw them at church or the PTA meetings, at the civic clubs, at the ball park. You know them in ways that all the rest of America could not. And to all the members of the families here present who have suffered loss, though we share your grief, your pain is unimaginable, and we know that. We cannot undo it. That is God's work.

Our words seem small beside the loss you have endured. But I found a few I wanted to share today. I've received a lot of letters in these last terrible days. One stood out because it came from a young widow and a mother of three whose own husband was murdered with over 200 other Americans when Pan Am 103 was shot down. Here is what that woman said I should say to you today:

The anger you feel is valid, but you must not allow yourselves to be consumed by it. The hurt you feel must not be allowed to turn into hate, but instead into the search for justice. The loss you feel must not paralyze your own lives. Instead, you must try to pay tribute to your loved ones by continuing to do all the things they left undone, thus ensuring they did not die in vain.

Wise words from one who also knows.

You have lost too much, but you have not lost everything. And you have certainly not   10 lost America, for we will stand with you for as many tomorrows as it takes.

If ever we needed evidence of that, I could only recall the words of Governor and Mrs. Keating. If anybody thinks that Americans are mostly mean and selfish, they ought to come to Oklahoma. (Applause.) If anybody thinks Americans have lost the capacity for love and caring and courage, they ought to come to Oklahoma.

To all my fellow Americans beyond this hall, I say, one thing we owe those who have sacrificed is the duty to purge ourselves of the dark forces which gave rise to this evil. They are forces that threaten our common peace, our freedom, our way of life.

Let us teach our children that the God of comfort is also the God of righteousness. Those who trouble their own house will inherit the wind. Justice will prevail.

Let us let our own children know that we will stand against the forces of fear. When there is talk of hatred, let us stand up and talk against it. When there is talk of violence, let us stand up and talk against it. In the face of death, let us honor life. As St. Paul admonished us, let us not be overcome by evil, but overcome evil with good.

Yesterday Hillary and I had the privilege of speaking with some children of other   15 federal employees—children like those who were lost here. And one little girl said something we will never forget. She said, we should all plant a tree in memory of the children. So this morning before we got on the plane to come here, at the White House, we planted that tree in honor of the children of Oklahoma.

It was a dogwood with its wonderful spring flower and its deep, enduring roots. It embodies the lesson of the Psalms—that the life of a good person is like a tree whose leaf does not wither.

My fellow Americans, a tree takes a long time to grow, and wounds take a long time to heal. But we must begin. Those who are lost now belong to God. Some day we will be with them. But until that happens, their legacy must be our lives.

Thank you all, and God bless you.

George W. Bush

Address to the Nation after 9/11, September 20, 2001

George W. Bush (1946–).

Often compared to Franklin Roosevelt's Pearl Harbor Speech, **George Bush's address after September 11, 2001, served to inform, comfort, and unite the country in a time of great national crisis.** *Speaking to Congress, the American people, and the entire world, President Bush thanked the world for its support and called upon other nations to be part of the struggle against terrorism. While many people had heard the name* **Osama bin Laden** *before, this speech marked the first time most Americans heard that a group known as* **Al Qaeda** *was behind the hijackings that resulted in the deaths of over three thousand people. This speech was also a turning point where an otherwise unfocused administration found meaning and purpose that would carry it forward into war and a second term.* **This speech marked the beginning of an international focus on fundamental Islamic terrorist groups, and would lead to the invasion of Afghanistan and later Iraq.**

Mr. Speaker, Mr. President Pro Tempore, members of Congress, and fellow Americans:

In the normal course of events, Presidents come to this chamber to report on the state of the Union. Tonight, no such report is needed. It has already been delivered by the American people.

We have seen it in the courage of passengers, who rushed terrorists to save others on the ground—passengers like an exceptional man named Todd Beamer. And would you please help me to welcome his wife, Lisa Beamer, here tonight.

We have seen the state of our Union in the endurance of rescuers, working past exhaustion. We have seen the unfurling of flags, the lighting of candles, the giving of blood, the saying of prayers—in English, Hebrew, and Arabic. We have seen the decency of a loving and giving people who have made the grief of strangers their own.

5 My fellow citizens, for the last nine days, the entire world has seen for itself the state of our Union—and it is strong.

Tonight we are a country awakened to danger and called to defend freedom. Our grief has turned to anger, and anger to resolution. Whether we bring our enemies to justice, or bring justice to our enemies, justice will be done.

I thank the Congress for its leadership at such an important time. All of America was touched on the evening of the tragedy to see Republicans and Democrats joined together on the steps of this Capitol, singing "God Bless America." And you did more than sing; you acted, by delivering $40 billion to rebuild our communities and meet the needs of our military.

Speaker Hastert, Minority Leader Gephardt, Majority Leader Daschle and Senator Lott, I thank you for your friendship, for your leadership and for your service to our country.

And on behalf of the American people, I thank the world for its outpouring of support. America will never forget the sounds of our National Anthem playing at Buckingham Palace, on the streets of Paris, and at Berlin's Brandenburg Gate.

We will not forget South Korean children gathering to pray outside our embassy in 10 Seoul, or the prayers of sympathy offered at a mosque in Cairo. We will not forget moments of silence and days of mourning in Australia and Africa and Latin America.

Nor will we forget the citizens of 80 other nations who died with our own: dozens of Pakistanis; more than 130 Israelis; more than 250 citizens of India; men and women from El Salvador, Iran, Mexico and Japan; and hundreds of British citizens. America has no truer friend than Great Britain. Once again, we are joined together in a great cause—so honored the British Prime Minister has crossed an ocean to show his unity of purpose with America. Thank you for coming, friend.

On September the 11th, enemies of freedom committed an act of war against our country. Americans have known wars—but for the past 136 years, they have been wars on foreign soil, except for one Sunday in 1941. Americans have known the casualties of war—but not at the center of a great city on a peaceful morning. Americans have known surprise attacks—but never before on thousands of civilians. All of this was brought upon us in a single day—and night fell on a different world, a world where freedom itself is under attack.

Americans have many questions tonight. Americans are asking: Who attacked our country? The evidence we have gathered all points to a collection of loosely affiliated terrorist organizations known as al Qaeda. They are the same murderers indicted for bombing American embassies in Tanzania and Kenya, and responsible for bombing the USS Cole.

Al Qaeda is to terror what the mafia is to crime. But its goal is not making money; its goal is remaking the world—and imposing its radical beliefs on people everywhere.

The terrorists practice a fringe form of Islamic extremism that has been rejected by 15 Muslim scholars and the vast majority of Muslim clerics—a fringe movement that perverts the peaceful teachings of Islam. The terrorists' directive commands them to kill Christians and Jews, to kill all Americans, and make no distinction among military and civilians, including women and children.

This group and its leader—a person named Osama bin Laden—are linked to many other organizations in different countries, including the Egyptian Islamic Jihad and the Islamic Movement of Uzbekistan. There are thousands of these terrorists in more than 60 countries. They are recruited from their own nations and neighborhoods and brought to camps in places like Afghanistan, where they are trained in the tactics of terror. They are sent back to their homes or sent to hide in countries around the world to plot evil and destruction.

The leadership of al Qaeda has great influence in Afghanistan and supports the Taliban regime in controlling most of that country. In Afghanistan, we see al Qaeda's vision for the world.

Afghanistan's people have been brutalized—many are starving and many have fled. Women are not allowed to attend school. You can be jailed for owning a television. Religion can be practiced only as their leaders dictate. A man can be jailed in Afghanistan if his beard is not long enough.

The United States respects the people of Afghanistan—after all, we are currently its largest source of humanitarian aid—but we condemn the Taliban regime. It is not only repressing its own people, it is threatening people everywhere by sponsoring and sheltering and supplying terrorists. By aiding and abetting murder, the Taliban regime is committing murder.

20 And tonight, the United States of America makes the following demands on the Taliban: Deliver to United States authorities all the leaders of al Qaeda who hide in your land. Release all foreign nationals, including American citizens, you have unjustly imprisoned. Protect foreign journalists, diplomats and aid workers in your country. Close immediately and permanently every terrorist training camp in Afghanistan, and hand over every terrorist, and every person in their support structure, to appropriate authorities. Give the United States full access to terrorist training camps, so we can make sure they are no longer operating.

These demands are not open to negotiation or discussion. The Taliban must act, and act immediately. They will hand over the terrorists, or they will share in their fate.

I also want to speak tonight directly to Muslims throughout the world. We respect your faith. It's practiced freely by many millions of Americans, and by millions more in countries that America counts as friends. Its teachings are good and peaceful, and those who commit evil in the name of Allah blaspheme the name of Allah. The terrorists are traitors to their own faith, trying, in effect, to hijack Islam itself. The enemy of America is not our many Muslim friends; it is not our many Arab friends. Our enemy is a radical network of terrorists, and every government that supports them.

Our war on terror begins with al Qaeda, but it does not end there. It will not end until every terrorist group of global reach has been found, stopped and defeated.

Americans are asking, why do they hate us? They hate what we see right here in this chamber—a democratically elected government. Their leaders are self-appointed. They hate our freedoms—our freedom of religion, our freedom of speech, our freedom to vote and assemble and disagree with each other.

25 They want to overthrow existing governments in many Muslim countries, such as Egypt, Saudi Arabia, and Jordan. They want to drive Israel out of the Middle East. They want to drive Christians and Jews out of vast regions of Asia and Africa.

These terrorists kill not merely to end lives, but to disrupt and end a way of life. With every atrocity, they hope that America grows fearful, retreating from the world and forsaking our friends. They stand against us, because we stand in their way.

We are not deceived by their pretenses to piety. We have seen their kind before. They are the heirs of all the murderous ideologies of the 20th century. By sacrificing human life to serve their radical visions—by abandoning every value except the will to power—they follow in the path of fascism, and Nazism, and totalitarianism. And they will follow that path all the way, to where it ends: in history's unmarked grave of discarded lies.

Americans are asking: How will we fight and win this war? We will direct every resource at our command—every means of diplomacy, every tool of intelligence, every instrument of law enforcement, every financial influence, and every necessary weapon of war—to the disruption and to the defeat of the global terror network.

This war will not be like the war against Iraq a decade ago, with a decisive liberation of territory and a swift conclusion. It will not look like the air war above Kosovo two years ago, where no ground troops were used and not a single American was lost in combat.

Our response involves far more than instant retaliation and isolated strikes. Americans should not expect one battle, but a lengthy campaign, unlike any other we have ever seen. It may include dramatic strikes, visible on TV, and covert operations, secret even in success. We will starve terrorists of funding, turn them one against another, drive them from place to place, until there is no refuge or no rest. And we will pursue nations that provide aid or safe haven to terrorism. Every nation, in every region, now has a decision to make. Either you are with us, or you are with the terrorists. (Applause.) From this day forward, any nation that continues to harbor or support terrorism will be regarded by the United States as a hostile regime. 30

Our nation has been put on notice: We are not immune from attack. We will take defensive measures against terrorism to protect Americans. Today, dozens of federal departments and agencies, as well as state and local governments, have responsibilities affecting homeland security. These efforts must be coordinated at the highest level. So tonight I announce the creation of a Cabinet-level position reporting directly to me—the Office of Homeland Security.

And tonight I also announce a distinguished American to lead this effort, to strengthen American security: a military veteran, an effective governor, a true patriot, a trusted friend—Pennsylvania's Tom Ridge. He will lead, oversee and coordinate a comprehensive national strategy to safeguard our country against terrorism, and respond to any attacks that may come.

These measures are essential. But the only way to defeat terrorism as a threat to our way of life is to stop it, eliminate it, and destroy it where it grows.

Many will be involved in this effort, from FBI agents to intelligence operatives to the reservists we have called to active duty. All deserve our thanks, and all have our prayers. And tonight, a few miles from the damaged Pentagon, I have a message for our military: Be ready. I've called the Armed Forces to alert, and there is a reason. The hour is coming when America will act, and you will make us proud.

This is not, however, just America's fight. And what is at stake is not just America's freedom. This is the world's fight. This is civilization's fight. This is the fight of all who believe in progress and pluralism, tolerance and freedom. 35

We ask every nation to join us. We will ask, and we will need, the help of police forces, intelligence services, and banking systems around the world. The United States is grateful that many nations and many international organizations have already responded—with sympathy and with support. Nations from Latin America, to Asia, to Africa, to Europe, to the Islamic world. Perhaps the NATO Charter reflects best the attitude of the world: An attack on one is an attack on all.

The civilized world is rallying to America's side. They understand that if this terror goes unpunished, their own cities, their own citizens may be next. Terror, unanswered, can not only bring down buildings, it can threaten the stability of legitimate governments. And you know what—we're not going to allow it.

Americans are asking: What is expected of us? I ask you to live your lives, and hug your children. I know many citizens have fears tonight, and I ask you to be calm and resolute, even in the face of a continuing threat.

I ask you to uphold the values of America, and remember why so many have come here. We are in a fight for our principles, and our first responsibility is to live by them. No one should be singled out for unfair treatment or unkind words because of their ethnic background or religious faith.

40   I ask you to continue to support the victims of this tragedy with your contributions. Those who want to give can go to a central source of information, libertyunites.org, to find the names of groups providing direct help in New York, Pennsylvania, and Virginia.

    The thousands of FBI agents who are now at work in this investigation may need your cooperation, and I ask you to give it.

    I ask for your patience, with the delays and inconveniences that may accompany tighter security; and for your patience in what will be a long struggle.

    I ask your continued participation and confidence in the American economy. Terrorists attacked a symbol of American prosperity. They did not touch its source. America is successful because of the hard work, and creativity, and enterprise of our people. These were the true strengths of our economy before September 11th, and they are our strengths today.

    And, finally, please continue praying for the victims of terror and their families, for those in uniform, and for our great country. Prayer has comforted us in sorrow, and will help strengthen us for the journey ahead.

45   Tonight I thank my fellow Americans for what you have already done and for what you will do. And ladies and gentlemen of the Congress, I thank you, their representatives, for what you have already done and for what we will do together.

    Tonight, we face new and sudden national challenges. We will come together to improve air safety, to dramatically expand the number of air marshals on domestic flights, and take new measures to prevent hijacking. We will come together to promote stability and keep our airlines flying, with direct assistance during this emergency.

    We will come together to give law enforcement the additional tools it needs to track down terror here at home. We will come together to strengthen our intelligence capabilities to know the plans of terrorists before they act, and find them before they strike.

    We will come together to take active steps that strengthen America's economy, and put our people back to work.

    Tonight we welcome two leaders who embody the extraordinary spirit of all New Yorkers: Governor George Pataki, and Mayor Rudolph Giuliani. As a symbol of America's resolve, my administration will work with Congress, and these two leaders, to show the world that we will rebuild New York City.

50   After all that has just passed—all the lives taken, and all the possibilities and hopes that died with them—it is natural to wonder if America's future is one of fear. Some speak of an age of terror. I know there are struggles ahead, and dangers to face. But this country will define our times, not be defined by them. As long as the United States of America is determined and strong, this will not be an age of terror; this will be an age of liberty, here and across the world.

    Great harm has been done to us. We have suffered great loss. And in our grief and anger we have found our mission and our moment. Freedom and fear are at war. The advance of human freedom—the great achievement of our time, and the great hope of every time—now depends on us. Our nation—this generation—will lift a dark threat of violence from our people and our future. We will rally the world to this cause by our efforts, by our courage. We will not tire, we will not falter, and we will not fail.

    It is my hope that in the months and years ahead, life will return almost to normal. We'll go back to our lives and routines, and that is good. Even grief recedes with time and grace. But our resolve must not pass. Each of us will remember what happened that day, and to whom it happened. We'll remember the moment the news came—where we were and what we were doing. Some will remember an image of a fire, or a story of rescue. Some will carry memories of a face and a voice gone forever.

And I will carry this: It is the police shield of a man named George Howard, who died at the World Trade Center trying to save others. It was given to me by his mom, Arlene, as a proud memorial to her son. This is my reminder of lives that ended, and a task that does not end.

I will not forget this wound to our country or those who inflicted it. I will not yield; I will not rest; I will not relent in waging this struggle for freedom and security for the American people.

The course of this conflict is not known, yet its outcome is certain. Freedom and fear, justice and cruelty, have always been at war, and we know that God is not neutral between them.

Fellow citizens, we'll meet violence with patient justice—assured of the rightness of our cause, and confident of the victories to come. In all that lies before us, may God grant us wisdom, and may He watch over the United States of America.

Thank you.

Preface to the 9/11 Commission Report

Written primarily **by Thomas H. Kean (chair) and Lee H. Hamilton (vice chair) of the 9/11 Commission**—*an independent, bipartisan panel—the preface to the Commission Report stated that the task of the panel was to investigate the events of September 11, 2001, and to provide an accurate and detailed report to the president, Congress, and the American people. The report itself, published in paperback form at a reduced price ($10 retail), became a best-seller across the nation. (The entire report could also be downloaded at no cost.)* **The Commission Report was the best and most detailed explanation that the government could produce of how things happened, who conspired in what manner, and what series of events led up to the tragedy, not withstanding concerns of national security.**

We present the narrative of this report and the recommendations that flow from it to the President of the United States, the United States Congress, and the American people for their consideration. Ten Commissioners—five Republicans and five Democrats chosen by elected leaders from our nation's capital at a time of great partisan division—have come together to present this report without dissent.

We have come together with a unity of purposes because our nation demands it. September 11, 2001, was a day of unprecedented shock and suffering in the history of the United States. The nation was unprepared. How did this happen, and how can we avoid such tragedy again?

To answer these questions, the Congress and the President created the National Commission on Terrorist Attacks Upon the United States (Public Law 107-306, November 27, 2002).

Our mandate was sweeping. The law directed us to investigate "facts and circumstances relating to the terrorist attacks of September 11, 2001," including those related to intelligence agencies, law enforcement agencies, diplomacy, immigration issues and border control, the flow of assets to terrorist organizations, commercial aviation, the role of congressional over-sight and resource allocation, and other areas determined relevant by the Commission.

5   In pursuing our mandate, we have reviewed more than 2.5 million pages of documents and interviewed more than 1,200 individuals in ten countries. This included nearly every senior official from the current and previous administrations who had responsibility for topics covered by our mandate.

We have sought to be independent, impartial, thorough, and nonpartisan. From the outset, we have been committed to share as much of our investigation as we can with the American people. To that end, we held 19 days of hearings and took public testimony from 160 witnesses.

Our aim has not been to assign individual blame. Our aim has been to provide the fullest possible account of the events surrounding 9/11 and to identify lessons learned.

We learned about an enemy who is sophisticated, patient, disciplined, and lethal. The enemy rallies broad support in the Arab and Muslim world by demanding redress of political grievances, but its hostility towards us and our values is limitless. Its purpose is to rid the world of religious and political pluralism, the plebiscite, and equal rights for women. It makes no distinction between military and civilian targets. *Collateral damage* is not in its lexicon.

We learned that the institutions charged with protecting our borders, civil aviation, and national security did not understand how grave this threat could be, and did not adjust their policies, plans, and practices to deter or defeat it. We learned of fault lines within our government—between foreign and domestic intelligence, and between and within agencies. We learned of pervasive problems of managing and sharing information across a large and unwieldy government that had been built in a different era to confront different dangers.

10   At the outset of our work, we said we were looking backward in order to look forward. We hope that the terrible losses chronicled in this report can create something positive—an America that is safer, stronger, and wiser. That September day, we came together as a nation. The test before us is to sustain that unity of purpose and meet the challenges now confronting us.

We need to design a balanced strategy for the long haul, to attack terrorists and prevent their ranks from swelling while at the same time protecting our country against future attacks. We have been forced to think about the way our government is organized. The massive departments and agencies that prevailed in the great struggles of the twentieth century must work together in new ways, so that all the instruments of national power can be combined. Congress needs dramatic change as well to strengthen oversight and focus accountability.

As we complete our final report, we want to begin by thanking our fellow Commissioners, whose dedication to this task has been profound. We have reasoned together over every page, and the report has benefited from this remarkable dialogue. We want to express our considerable respect for the intellect and judgment of our colleagues, as well as our great affection for them.

We want to thank the Commission staff. The dedicated professional staff, headed by Philip Zelikow, has contributed innumerable hours to the completion of this report, setting aside other important endeavors to take on this all-consuming assignment. They have conducted the exacting investigative work upon which the Commission has built. They have given good advice, and faithfully carried out our guidance. They have been superb.

We thank the Congress and the President. Executive branch agencies have searched records and produced a multitude of documents for us. We thank officials, past and present, who were generous with their time and provided us with insight. The PENTTBOM team at the FBI, the Director's Review Group at the CIA, and Inspectors General at the Department of Justice and the CIA provided great assistance. We owe a huge debt to their investigative labors, painstaking attention to detail, and readiness to share what they have learned. We have built on the work of several previous Commissions, and we thank the Congressional Joint Inquiry, whose fine work helped us get started. We thank the City of New York for assistance with documents and witnesses, and the Government Printing Office and W.W. Norton & Company for helping us get this report to the broad public.

We conclude this list of thanks by coming full circle: We thank the families of 9/11, whose persistence and dedication helped create the Commission. They have been with us each step of the way, as partners and witnesses. They know better than any of us the importance of the work we have undertaken.

We want to note what we have done, and not done. We have endeavored to provide the most complete account we can of the events of September 11, what happened and why. This final report is only a summary of what we have done, citing only a fraction of the sources we have consulted. But in an event of this scale, touching so many issues and organizations, we are conscious of our limits. We have not interviewed every knowledgeable person or found every relevant piece of paper. New information inevitably will come to light. We present this report as a foundation for a better understanding of a landmark in the history of our nation.

We have listened to scores of overwhelming personal tragedies and astounding acts of heroism and bravery. We have examined the staggering impact of the events of 9/11 on the American people, and their amazing resilience and courage as they fought back. We have admired their determination to do their best to prevent another tragedy while preparing to respond if it becomes necessary. We emerge from this investigation with enormous sympathy for the victims and their loved ones, and with enhanced respect for the American people. We recognize the formidable challenges that lie ahead.

We also approach the task of recommendations with humility. We have made a limited number of them. We decided consciously to focus on recommendations we believe to be most important, whose implementation can make the greatest difference. We came into this process with strong opinions about what would work. All of us have had to pause, reflect, and sometimes change our minds as we studied these problems and considered the views of others. We hope our report will encourage our fellow citizens to study, reflect—and act.

PART THREE

Points of Contact: A Reader about Citizenship Issues

CHAPTER 5

Point of Contact: Race

As you think back on your childhood, you will most likely remember the now late Fred Rogers. He greeted you on your television screen each weekday with a song about your neighborhood. That song always concluded with a question: "Won't you be my neighbor?" The invitation included everyone. No one was left out. Mr. Rogers's show, aimed at those two to five years old, offered your younger selves some core values, and certainly an overarching theme was one of kindness and inclusiveness. Mr. Rogers helped us all to see that our neighborhood included many different kinds of people. So let's start with that idea of inclusiveness.

In your "neighborhood" today, how many people are like you? How many share your skin color, your celebration of holidays, your food choices, your cultural identity, your religious preferences? How diverse is your neighborhood? Of people who are not of your race, how many have visited in your home, eaten at your table, shared your celebrations, and joined you in your place of worship?

Because of the U.S. Supreme Court case *Brown v. Board of Education*, each of you has had the opportunity to attend school with people who are different from you. But that does not mean that you have taken full advantage of getting to know as many people as you can who are different from you. Because we live in a global village, the more we know about those who are not like us, the richer our lives can be.

This Point of Contact will focus on and address the following three specific clusters that relate to race:

1. The Role of Race in Education
2. Crying Wolf: The Susan Smith Case
3. Being Mixed Race in America

Issues surrounding the subject of race are complicated, and the national discussion—some of which has been going on for hundreds of years—is very much in the news today. These reading selections should offer a way to enter the conversation with information you can use to develop arguments grounded in various types of evidence. Think about what kind of evidence is most likely to persuade you. Think, too, about the challenges these clusters offer our own experiment in democracy.

THE ROLE OF RACE IN EDUCATION

The fiftieth anniversary of *Brown v. Board of Education of Topeka, Kansas* (May 17, 2004) turned out to be an opportunity for the media to focus once again on the state of school desegregation in America. Reporters combed the country—returning to the geographical hot spots of over fifty years ago where African American citizens, who had finally had enough of being second-class citizens, turned to the National Association for the Advancement of Colored People (NAACP) and its legal staff to take their issues to the highest court in the land. Four places—Clarendon County, South Carolina; Prince Edward County, Virginia; Wilmington, Delaware; and Topeka, Kansas—combined to become the 1954 Supreme Court case that history would refer to as *Brown*, which declared that "separate but equal" was now unconstitutional. All public schools were to be integrated.

When the active days of the civil rights movement ended in 1968 with the death of Martin Luther King Jr., its most eloquent spokesman, affirmative action polices became the way the courts adjudicated issues of racial inequality. According to a recent, wide-ranging poll conducted by the American Association of Retired People (AARP; see Chapter 2), on the occasion of the half-century marker of *Brown*, most Americans have positive feelings about race relations, but different races answer the same questions differently. The dream King spoke about is not yet a reality.

The following selections offer a variety of information and ideas about the role of race in education. None declares what the role of race in education should be; some offer possibilities and plans for diversity, expanded beyond race. Some turn the mirror to themselves or others, declaring a racial or cultural breakdown. Together the selections should expand your understanding of the issues and help you enter the conversation.

First is a brief introductory piece from *Time* on some of the biggest surprises in education since *Brown*. Two pieces—"A New Campus Crusader" and "New Admissions System at U. of Michigan . . ."—address an important Supreme Court case challenging the affirmative action policies at Michigan. The undergraduate admissions policy, which awarded points for being a particular race, was declared unconstitutional. Professionals in the office of admissions hope that the university can use a new essay-writing component of the application process as one of several ways to define "diversity." One article looks at the importance of diversity on law review boards, for without that designation, some feel, law school graduates will be denied top opportunities in their fields. Two other selections—one from the inside and one from the outside—explore the black and Latino/Latina cultures. Also included is one student essay that offers a look at what it feels like to be the only black student in an otherwise all-white classroom.

Rebecca Winters

No Longer Separate, but Not Yet Equal

Time, May 10, 2004

No one—not the celebrating black families, not the enraged white Southerners and Midwesterners, not the curious onlookers in the Northeast and the West—would have guessed the way race relations in America would evolve a half-century later. For 50 years after the Supreme Court rules in *Brown v. Board of Education of Topeka, Kans.,* that "separate educational facilities are inherently unequal," the most integrated schools in the U.S. are in the South. The most segregated are in New York and California. The federal courts— once the preferred tool of integrationists—have become a major force in the resegregation of schools. And the formerly black-and-white issue of racial integration is more intricate— last year Latinos became the country's largest minority group.

"The promise of *Brown* was not fulfilled in the way that we envisioned it," says U.S. Secretary of Education Rod Paige, who was a student at Mississippi's all-black Jackson State University when the decision was handed down. Within the first few years after the decision, paratroopers were protecting black students entering Central High School in Little Rock, Ark., schools were shuttered entirely in Prince Edward County, Va., and white families across the South put their children into private schools. By 1971, the court had endorsed busing to overcome the residential segregation that was keeping black and white children apart. Particularly in the South, the integration drive worked, as the share of black children attending majority white schools rose from 0.1% in 1960 to a high of 44% in 1988.

But a series of court decisions in the early to mid-1990s reversed the trend. The courts found that school systems had complied with their obligations to desegregate, and many communities abandoned their busing plans. Today the share of black students in majority white schools in the South is 30%, about the same percentage as in 1970. Even in communities that are well integrated, barriers still exist within the school walls themselves. While 72% of white students graduate from high school on schedule, just over half of black and Hispanic students do. White fourth-graders are more than three times as likely to read proficiently as black fourth-graders. "The WHITE and COLORED signs did come down," says Derrick Bell, New York University law professor and author of *Silent Covenants,* a book on the unfulfilled hopes of *Brown*. "But the idea that putting black kids together with whites would solve our problems was naïve in the extreme."

Keith Naughton

A New Campus Crusader

Newsweek, December 29, 2003–January 5, 2004

Growing up in Georgia, Mary Sue Coleman was caught in the school-desegregation battle. After the Supreme Court's landmark *Brown v. Board of Education* ruling in 1954, hard-line segregationists threatened to padlock public schools before they would admit black students. So Coleman's father moved his family north to Iowa. "My parents were very scared," recalls Coleman. "They wanted to go to a place where public schools were supported."

Nearly 50 years later, Coleman is still in the thick of the fight. But this time, she's president of the University of Michigan and writing the rule book on how to foster diversity. Last June, Michigan won its own landmark case when the Supreme Court upheld its affirmative-action policy for admitting students to its law school. However, the court struck down Michigan's undergrad admissions process, which, unlike the law school, awarded extra points to minorities to give them an edge. So, U-M drafted a new undergrad application—one that many other colleges are scrutinizing as the next model for diversity. But opponents are intent on outlawing race-based college admissions. "I hope Michigan voters would see that this is something that will help our nation," she says.

What Coleman sees is the opportunity to go beyond traditional definitions of affirmative action to create a more "diverse diversity," based on students from wider socioeconomic backgrounds. She notes that poor kids are nearly as scarce on campus as minorities. Just one in five of Michigan's 25,000 undergrads comes from a family making less than $50,000 a year. Coleman is after kids with backgrounds like her father's, who grew up in Kentucky's coal country. "Our research shows that all students benefit from having different points of view in a classroom," she says. "A student from the hills of Kentucky would be quite interesting and different."

To go beyond black and white diversity, Michigan has crafted an application with an 18-page form that delves deeper into personal information, asking if your parents and grandparents went to college and if you help support your family. One of the four new essay questions challenges all students to explain how they would contribute to campus diversity. A boy from Michigan's mostly white Upper Peninsula wrote of the tolerance lessons he learned helping his sister come out as a lesbian. Says Coleman: "Those are the kinds of kids we want."

Coleman is comfortable plowing new ground. Inspired by the sputnik launch, she became a scientist and broke into the old-boys club of the lab. And she's the first woman president at Michigan. Initially, some feared she wouldn't fight for affirmative action with the zeal of her predecessor Lee Bollinger, a legal scholar. But she's driven by something more personal. "Because I'd grown up in the South," she says, "I felt like this is just so important to the nation." Now the nation will see how Coleman's life lessons will redefine diversity on campus—and in society.

5

Candace Warren

How to Survive When You're the Only Black in the Classroom

Student Essay

When I was in high school, I took an anthropology class. It was largely discussion based. There were debates on a plethora of issues: male biases in the "Man the Hunter" model of evolution, the existence or absence of moral absolutes, and various cross-cultural comparisons. These were all important and insightful discussions, however the most memorable debate, in my opinion, was on social stratification. What began as a discussion on the importance of diversity quickly escalated into a heated debate on the race problem in America. I can remember the exact comment that sparked the turn in the discussion. Someone made the statement, "Things are going really good in this country now, especially for black people. I mean, they can marry white people and go to white schools." Being

African American, I was especially irritated by this comment, and vocalized my frustration. Consequently, the class verbally attacked me for my personal views. I was told by several of my peers that my "people" have no cause for complaint because we can go to "their" white schools. Additionally, the race problem in America is purely economic; this is apparent because I have never had to deal with crosses burning in our front yard or effigies hanging from our trees. I tried to point out that although I have never experienced such blatant displays of prejudice, racism is still a major issue in this country. This was the rebuttal to my point: "Why can't you all just get over slavery?" The whole experience was extremely frustrating. However, the worst part was that the teacher didn't do anything. I was the first black student she had ever had, so she just sat politely while I defended my race and got chastised by my culturally deprived peers.

I describe my peers as "culturally deprived" because that is exactly what they were. Littleton, Colorado is an extremely homogenous area. According to the 2000 U.S. census, African Americans only comprised 3.8 percent of its total population. Many of my peers had never lived outside Littleton. In fact, for most, I was the only black person they interacted with on a regular basis. Their lack of interaction with African Americans was apparent in their arguments.

That discussion facilitated my realization of a major fault in the American educational system. The inherent flaw in our educational system is the vast inequities between the races. This problem is not just isolated to obvious acts. It is much more far reaching. Such subtle instances can prove to be detrimental, especially in an educational situation. In an educational setting, white students enjoy a number of privileges unavailable to black students. This "white advantage" can foster resentment and create disillusionment.

When you are the only black student in the class, this privilege becomes extremely obvious. For example, white students are never asked what the "white" viewpoint is. As an African American who has attended predominately white schools for all of my education, I have frequently been asked, "How do black people feel about . . ." What none of my peers or teachers realized is that it is quite difficult to speak on behalf of an entire race. Actually, it's impossible. There is no way to give the "black" opinion on any issue because, like any group of people, there are a number of different beliefs and ideals. Not all black people are democrats, like Jesse Jackson, and voted for Bill Clinton. In my entire educational career, I have never heard a teacher ask a white student how white people feel about any given issue. This is because teachers recognize that there is no one "white" opinion. Such stereotyping would be considered offensive, but is acceptable when dealing with black students. This inconsistent behavior can potentially cause black students to resent their teachers.

5   Another privilege enjoyed by white students is that teachers do not make assumptions of them based on race. There are certain expectations teachers expect you to live up to. The expectation is that black students speak with an urban "ebonic" dialect. Diverge from the expectation at all, and suddenly you are a credit to your entire race. Then there are the empty compliments like, "You speak so well." Nobody realizes what an insult this is. This lowered expectation is offensive. Surely, in most cases this is not deliberate, but this behavior is still present and still detrimental to the black student. Knowing that teachers have modified expectations of them can potentially be damaging to the black student's educational experience. It can conceivably lower the student's expectation of himself or herself, thus resulting in poor academic performance.

This system also has larger implications outside of the classroom. It can foster a feeling of self-hatred among black students. If societal expectations are consistently diminished for the black student, then he may become resentful of his race. His race becomes a source of embarrassment and shame. Society's modified expectations of him will then become his own.

The worst aspect of this system of advantage based on race is the subtlety. It is easy to deal with overt racism, but how does one deal with racism that is nearly indistinguishable? How do you survive when you're the only black in the classroom? Awareness is the first step. The realization that it is likely that this system will never change is crucial. You will be asked for the "black" viewpoint on various issues. You will have your educators and peers make assumptions about you because of your race. You will be in contact with ignorant people. These things are inevitable, so there is no sense in lamenting your ill treatment. Because we cannot find any means to change the system, we must find the means to cope with it. Recognizing the futility of fighting the system is key. Ignorance will always be ever-present in American society; therefore, it should be no surprise that it is present in American institutions like education. Nothing can be done to change the situation of blacks in an educational setting.

Although it is important to realize the ineffectiveness of attempting to change this system, it is equally important to realize the positive possibilities of the system. As a people, our greatest asset is the way we are vastly underestimated by mainstream society. It will be this discrepancy between the expected performance of blacks and the actuality that will be key in our advancement in American society.

America is only superficially based on equality. This is the innate fault of American society; therefore, it is not surprising that there are total inequalities in American institutions. These inequalities are so subtle that they often fall below public radar. This can be attributed to the fact that many whites like to think that they work hard for all of their accomplishments, that nothing is ever handed to them. This is what makes recognizing their own "white advantage" difficult for whites. It makes it difficult to separate achievements based on merit from achievements based on race. This does not, however, make them unaccountable for their "advantage." Denial of "white advantage" only further perpetuates the problem.

Ideally, all people should be treated equally in all facets of society. However, this system of advantage is our reality. As long as white students are rewarded for their race, black students will suffer the consequences because of their race. It is an unfair advantage, but is always present in society. There is no way to cause a change in the system because it is based on the inherent preconceived notions people have; there is no way of eliminating them. These are all accurate observations. However, it is important to realize that despite these apparent inequities and hindrances, blacks will continue to advance in society. This will be our greatest achievement.

Katherine S. Mangan

In Search of Diversity on Law Reviews

Chronicle of Higher Education, September 5, 2003

Amy DeVaudreuil knew she had her work cut out for her when she was named diversity editor of the *California Law Review,* the flagship law journal of the University of California at Berkeley. Over the past four years, the highly selective journal has had only six black or Hispanic students among the 180 it has chosen.

But Ms. DeVaudreuil, who is white, says she was unprepared for the battle that followed—and that prompted her and two other editors to resign from the publication in protest last year.

"The journal liked the idea of having a diversity editor—it looked good on the masthead," says Ms. DeVaudreuil, who graduated in May. "But when it came to actually talking about diversity and trying to do something about it, people were very resistant to change."

The journal's members voted this year to eliminate the position of diversity editor, an indication, perhaps, of how weary they were of debating a question that has confounded their peers around the country: How can law reviews increase the number of minority students on their staffs without compromising the applicants' anonymity or the journal's academic standards?

5   While many law schools have, through affirmative action and aggressive recruiting, made modest gains in their minority-students enrollments over the past decade, relatively few minority students are making it onto law-review boards—positions that serve as springboards to judicial clerkships and other top jobs.

"Once you move out of the most elite schools, if you don't have law review on your resume, many firms won't even look at you," says Maraleen Shields, who was the first black student accepted by the University of Pittsburgh School of Law's law review in 13 years when she was named to the review two years ago.

She and Ms. DeVaudreuil agree that having a diverse staff serves a broader purpose. Says Ms. Shields, "The law review should represent the entire law school, and the more perspectives and viewpoints you have, the better product you'll be able to offer."

But others argue just as passionately that membership in the law review is, above all, an honor that should be reserved for those who have distinguished themselves academically.

"One of the strengths of the law review is its focus on scholarship, and the way that's measured in law school is through grades and writing," says Shawn R. Johnson, who graduated in May from the Vanderbilt University Law School.

10   He thinks it would be a bad idea to reserve slots on the journal for members of minority groups or to even consider a person's race as a factor in admission. Grades, he argues, are an objective, easily quantifiable indicator of merit that puts everyone on an equal footing.

"There's a lot of value in having diverse views, but we have to make sure the competition is fair to everyone," he says.

Weighing Diversity

While some law reviews have adopted affirmative-action plans, students are usually selected based on a combination of their grades and their performance in a writing and editing competition held at the end of their first year. A typical editing test might require a student to clean up a portion of a legal article, replete with botched footnotes and legal citations.

Law reviews vary in how much weight they put on grades and writing. Some automatically accept students whose first-year grades place them at the top of the class, and some require a minimum class rank in order to try out for the writing portion. Many others judge all applicants on both grades and writing. The *California Law Review* selects students based solely on a writing and editing competition, as well as a personal statement, and doesn't factor in grades at all.

All law reviews remove the names from applications and replace them with numbers before the applications are assessed by student editors, who make the final selections without knowing the applicants' identities or, in most cases, their races.

Because black and Hispanic students, on average, have lower first-year grades, many   15
don't fare well in that portion of the contest. That became painfully obvious at Vanderbilt
last year when no black or Hispanic editors were named to any of Vanderbilt's three
student journals, even though the student body is about 14 percent black and 6 percent
Hispanic.

Last year, all three journals conducted a joint competition, which included a 20-page
writing assignment that students had 17 days to complete. The *Vanderbilt Law Review*
selected 5 of the 30 students based solely on their performance in the writing competition, with the other 25 chosen by giving equal weight to their first-year grades and their
writing scores.

Still, not a single black or Hispanic student was selected for the prestigious *Vanderbilt
Law Review* this summer.

"When a law school is able to get an influx, or even a critical mass, of minority students, but none of these students ends up showing up in law review, that reinforces the
perception that these students aren't as qualified," says Ms. Shields.

The law school's dean, Kent D. Syverud, says he has been reluctant to intervene in
the workings of a student-run publication, but that he considers the lack of minority representation on any of the journals "one of the biggest challenges I've faced as dean."

"Serving on a law journal is one of the most valuable learning experiences a student   20
can have during law school, and his opportunity appeared to be unavailable to a large proportion of our students," he says. "That created a crisis that became an opportunity to
re-evaluate our selection criteria."

After months of debate, the editors of the *Vanderbilt Law Review* rejected the idea of
creating an affirmative-action policy.

By allowing five students to qualify on the basis of their writing, they hoped to attract
more minority candidates. But even the writing contests, which take place just as students
are recovering from final exams and are about to head off to summer jobs, can seem particularly daunting for black and Hispanic students who look at their law reviews' masthead
and imagine a sea of white faces.

"When you look at the statistics, it's easy to become discouraged and figure you don't
have much chance of making it," says Sisera Dowdy, the outgoing president of Vanderbilt's
Black Law Students Association.

Even though Ms. Dowdy tried out, unsuccessfully, for the law review, she believes that
"a lot of students figure it's not worth the effort."

Paul Helms, departing editor in chief of the *Vanderbilt Law Review*, would like to see   25
faculty members and administrators step in and start a discussion about the appropriate
role for the law review. Should it be primarily an honor society that rewards students who
have the highest grades, or should it be viewed as an educational tool that reflects the
diversity of students at the law school?

"We're so busy ranking people by their grades that we don't take the time to consider
the educational purpose of the law review," says Mr. Helms, who graduated this year.
"Students learn from having a diversity of viewpoints."

Pressing for Change

Some law reviews allow students to write a personal statement as part of their application that, without identifying them, gives the journal staff an idea of how the applicant
might bring a different perspective to the publication.

"We value any diversity they bring to the table, whether it's work experience, upbringing, race, whatever," says Jenny Tran, managing editor of the *University of Pennsylvania Law Review*, which adopted a new policy aimed at increasing diversity that was applied to the students selected this summer. Applicants are required to submit personal statements of up to two pages.

Although the selection criteria vary from year to year, generally about 40 percent of the new editors at Penn are chosen based primarily on their writing, and the remaining 20 percent based on a composite score that includes their personal statement.

30   When Penn's *Journal of International Economic Law* instituted a more explicit affirmative-action policy in 1996, however, a second-year student resigned from the staff, saying the policy amounted to discrimination against white students.

But it was the lack of an explicit affirmative-action plan that prompted three editors of Berkeley's premier law journal to quit last year. They argued that the journal wasn't doing enough to boost the numbers of minority students, who over the past four years made up 10 to 13 percent of the law school's student body but only 3 percent of the journal's staff members.

In an article that appeared in the July issue of the *California Law Review* Ms. DeVaudreuil lambasted the publication for perpetuating what she calls its "history of institutional racism."

Ms. DeVaudreuil quit the journal in November after an internal newsletter was distributed to the staff that she believes belittled her efforts to diversify the group. The newsletter, which the authors said was meant to be humorous, drew attention to the fact that the journal's diversity editor was white and that she hadn't delivered a report the day it was due. The newsletter, which also poked fun at other editors, included a cartoon of Ms. DeVaudreuil botching simple office tasks.

The newsletter resulted in one of the authors being suspended from the publication's staff and another demoted. It also led to a bitter split between those who felt that Ms. DeVaudreuil and her allies were being overly sensitive and too pushy in their demands and those who agreed with her that diversity efforts were being ignored.

35   In addition to Ms. DeVaudreuil, two Asian-American students, Donna Maeda and Janet Tung, who also pushed for greater diversity, quit in the aftermath of the newsletter controversy.

Ms. Maeda, who took a three-year leave from her job as an associate professor of religious studies at Occidental College to get her law degree, says she was fed up with the journal's inaction on the diversity issue. "Anyone who pushed for more diversity was seen as having a political agenda or trying to take over," she says.

No one knows that better than Gabriela A. Gallegos, last year's editor in chief of the *California Law Review.*

Ms. Gallegos, the first Hispanic editor of the law review in its 91-year history, says she ran for the position on a promise to help create a more diverse journal. And while she believes most staff members support that goal in theory, getting them to acknowledge that diversity was a serious issue that deserved immediate attention was another matter.

"It's hard to talk about these issues that are very important to you in a room full of white people," she says, adding that her critics on the staff repeatedly referred to her efforts to promote the work of Ms. DeVaudreuil and other diversity supporters as a "coup."

Complex Factors

But some students say the problem is more complex than white people feeling   40
threatened by policies that appear to give an edge to minority applicants. They say that
some promising minority students are being siphoned off by some of the school's nine
other, less-competitive journals, which select their editors earlier in the academic year.

The journals include the *African-American Law and Policy Report* and the *Berkeley La
Raza Law Journal*, which focuses on legal issues facing Hispanics.

In addition, this year's editor in chief of the *California Law Review*, Jean Galbraith,
points out that there have been fewer minority students in the law school since the passage of **Proposition 209**, the 1996 California law that banned the use of affirmative
action by colleges.

"Berkeley's hands are particularly tied by Proposition 209," she says. She is seeking
legal advice on whether the law review, as a non-profit entity, is bound by that measure's
restrictions.

The journal's editors have also compared notes with their counterparts at other law
schools to see how they are dealing with the problem. One of the more aggressive campaigns to diversify is being mounted by the *New York University Law Review*. It explicitly
spells out its commitment to diversity on its Web page, which states that "grades and writing scores alone do not fully indicate an individual's achievements or ability to contribute
effectively to the journal."

Of the approximately 42 students invited to participate in NYU's law review, the first   45
32 or so are chosen based on their grades and writing scores. The remaining 10 to 12 are
selected through the publication's affirmative-action plan, which is open to any remaining
applicants who score in the top 50 percent based on their grades and writing. Personal
statements submitted by the applicants are also considered.

Matthew W. Howard, who will enter his third year at NYU this fall, is one of seven black
students on its law journal. Mr. Howard, an articles editor who also serves on the diversity
committee, says the journal's policy of actively seeking diverse candidates appears to be
working: "Many students who may have felt that they didn't have a chance of getting on
the law review are throwing their hats in the ring."

Diane Carman

Tough Love on Culture, Progress

The *Denver Post*, May 18, 2004

As I listened to Lawrence Harrison, I felt all the familiar symptoms of growing unease.
My face got tense, hands clenched. I squirmed uncomfortably in my chair.

I wasn't alone. A current of psychic distress charged the room, which was populated
in a veritable cross-cultural gumbo of Denver demographics. Our assumptions were being
challenged, politely but ruthlessly, and it wasn't pleasant.

Harrison, who directed the U.S. Agency for International Development in Latin
America in the 1980s and is at the Academy for International and Area Studies at Harvard,
made the case Monday that the reason so many Latino immigrants drop out of high school
and earn lower incomes in the United States is their culture.

Put simply, it's their own fault.

5   Or at least the fault of their parents.

For generations, they've been programmed in values that inhibit their advancement. As a result, economic, political and professional success is the exception for Latinos, Harrison argued, and always will be unless they change.

He's written books on the subject and he circulated a long list of characteristics that define "progress-prone" and "progress-resistant" cultures.

Suffice it to say, he's accustomed to leaving a room with only polite applause after he finishes a presentation.

Still, his message sticks with you.

10   Over lunch at the University of Denver, he presented a stark contrast between cultures—some might call them stereotypes—to demonstrate why Anglo-Saxon Protestant, Asian and Jewish cultures produce doctors, lawyers, CEOs and political leaders in large numbers while the Latino culture doesn't.

There's the matter of time, for example. The progress-prone cultures focus on the future. They make plans and value punctuality, he said. The progress-resistant cultures value the present and the past more highly, which discourages planning, saving and being on time.

He cites attitudes about fertility as well, with the progress-prone believing that the number of children in a family should be limited to its capacity to rear and educate them, and the progress-resistant more likely to believe that children no matter what are an economic asset, a blessing and a gift from God.

The values taught by the Latino family and church—that poverty is a virtue, that girls don't need education because their highest goal should be to marry and have children, and that boys should join the workforce as soon as they are able—ensure that they will remain at the margins of society for generations. Education, entrepreneurship, devotion to work and a belief that one can shape his own destiny are the keys to success, he said.

But **Horatio Alger** is still a myth, and a cynical one at that.

15   So even if there is merit to Harrison's body of work—and there surely is—many of us in the room found ourselves identifying with all those Latinos who were insulted by the characteristics of the progress-resistant.

We were the ones who might actually exemplify the best of the values of the progress-prone but still feel shut out.

As Ginger Maloney, dean of education at DU, noted, the revolution of the women's movement created enormous change in the culture, emphasizing education, birth control, hard work and professional experience, but women continue to earn far less than men.

"Indeed, culture does matter," she said, "but you're blaming the wrong culture here."

Those who control the culture of power also control the access. The statistics tell the story.

20   The average salaries of Latino men with college degrees are $15,000 less than those of white male college grads. The average salaries for Latinas and white women with college degrees are $20,000 less.

Culture matters, sure. So does intelligence, courage, motivation, stamina, hard work and leadership ability.

Unfortunately, for too many in the U.S., that's still not enough.

Peter Schmidt

New Admissions System at U. of Michigan to Seek Diversity through Essays

Chronicle of Higher Education, September 5, 2003

Detroit, Michigan—March 1, 2003—Thousands marched in Detroit in support of the University of Michigan's affirmative action programs. A challenge to the university's affirmative action policies was before the Supreme Court at the time of the demonstration.

The University of Michigan at Ann Arbor announced last week that it had devised a new, essay-driven undergraduate-admissions process to replace the point-based system that the U.S. Supreme Court struck down in a key affirmative-action ruling in June.

University officials said that the new admissions policy would maintain diversity on the campus while complying with the Supreme Court's requirement that colleges treat applicants as individuals, and not automatically give some an edge based on their ethnicity or race.

"Our fundamental values haven't changed," said the university's president, Mary Sue Coleman. "We believe that in order to create a dynamic learning environment for all our students, we must bring together students who are highly qualified academically and who represent a wide range of backgrounds and experiences."

The university's announcement was greeted skeptically by the Center for Individual Rights, a Washington-based advocacy group that helped represent the plaintiffs in the legal battle against Michigan's race-conscious admissions policies.

"It is certainly too soon to say whether the legal fight over the university's race-based admissions system has ended," said Curt A. Levey, the center's director of legal and public affairs. "The devil is in the details," he said, and "we will be watching to see how they implement what is on paper."

The center's president, Terence Pell, said that "if, under any new system, race ends up trumping most other admissions factors, then the new system will be just as illegal as the systems the court struck down."

Enrollments to Be Watched

Several leaders of student groups on the campus said they feared that young applicants might have difficulty writing essays that adequately reflected the impact of their race or ethnicity on their lives, and minority enrollments would decline as a result.

Ricardo Valle, a senior who is a spokesman for a student group called La Voz Latina, said that, before college, "I did not know what diversity was or how to interpret my experiences as a Latino youth."

Officials at Michigan said they planned to monitor enrollments carefully to make sure that minority representation on the campus did not decline.

10   The revised admissions process is a response to two Supreme Court decisions in lawsuits filed against Michigan by rejected white applicants: *Grutter v. Bollinger,* involving the law school, and *Gratz v. Bollinger*, involving Michigan's chief undergraduate college. The court upheld the law school's admissions policy in a 5-to-4 ruling in June, but struck down the undergraduate admissions policy in a 6-to-3 decision handed down the same day.

In *Grutter*, the majority said that the law school had a compelling interest in enrolling a racially diverse student body because of the educational benefits that diversity provides. The majority said that the law school's race-conscious admissions policy was an acceptable means of achieving that diversity because it considered race as just one of several factors in evaluating each individual.

What doomed the undergraduate admissions policy before the court in *Gratz* was Michigan's reliance on a point system that awarded each black, Hispanic, and American Indian applicant a 20-point bonus on its 150-point scale. To put that bonus in context, 20 points is the difference between what applicants would receive for a 4.0 and a 3.0 grade-point average.

Writing for the *Gratz* majority, Chief Justice William H. Rehnquist said that the policy was too formulaic and mechanistic, and treated whole groups of applicants differently based solely on their race. Because the policy was not "narrowly tailored" to achieving educational diversity, he said, it violated the Constitution's equal-protection clause and Title VI of the Civil Rights Act of 1964, which prohibits racial discrimination by any institution, public or private, that receives federal funds.

"The central teaching of the cases was that race needed to be evaluated flexibly," said Marvin Krislov, Michigan's general counsel. "That is exactly what we are doing."

15   University officials said that they had used the law school's admissions policy as a road map for determining what sort of undergraduate policy might pass muster at the court, while also consulting faculty members, other colleges, and organizations such as the College Board.

Careful Readings

The university's revised application form calls for each applicant to submit one 500-word essay and two 250-word essays. For one of the 250-word essays, students are asked to respond to either of two questions dealing with diversity. The first says, "At the University of Michigan, we are committed to building an academically superb and widely diverse educational community. What would you as an individual bring to our campus community?" The second says, "Describe an experience you've had where cultural diversity—or a lack thereof—has made a difference to you."

The new application also asks students to provide information about the educational backgrounds of their parents, grandparents, and siblings, and gives them the option of reporting their family's household income. Applicants are asked to have their high-school counselor or principal fill out a form that solicits comment on "any socio-economic, personal, or educational circumstance that may have affected this student's achievement, either positively or negatively."

As before, applicants must submit their high-school grades and standardized-test scores. Paul N. Courant, Michigan's provost and executive vice president for academic affairs, said academic factors—including the competitiveness and quality of the curriculum at each applicant's high school—will continue to be the most important criteria for evaluating students.

Under the new system, each application will be reviewed by a trained application reader—in many cases, a former educator—and by a professional admissions counselor familiar with a particular region. The readers and counselors will be precluded from knowing each other's recommendations, which will be accepted by an assistant admissions director if they agree. If they disagree and the assistant director cannot resolve their differences, their views may be forwarded to a committee for a final decision.

Theodore L. Spencer, director of Michigan's office of undergraduate admissions, said   20
he was hiring 16 part-time readers and increasing his staff of full-time admissions counselors to 22 from 17, to handle the additional work associated with the new process. The system is expected to cost an additional $1.5 million to operate in its first year, but those expenses are predicted to fall over time.

The first applicants to experience the new system will be those seeking to enroll as transfer students this winter. The first large cohort affected will be applicants for admission in the fall of 2004. The university receives about 25,000 applicants annually for each freshman class of 5,200.

Ernie Suggs

Cosby: Blacks Own Enemy

Cox News Service, in *Rocky Mountain News,* November 20, 2004

ATLANTA—Bill Cosby is on fire.

But the humorist isn't laughing much these days.

Instead, he is filling auditoriums across the country in what some call a crusade to tell the truth to and about "his people."

The message: Too many young black men and women have devalued life, judgment and morals in favor of a life filled with low expectations, few options and irresponsibility.

"My biggest cry is for us to really reflect on who we are," Cosby said this week. "Who   5
are we in our manhood? Who are we in our responsibility to the black woman and the black child?"

Cosby has blasted black parents who have not taken an active role in the education and upbringing of their children. He has argued that too many black men are abusing women through violence and language, and that their priorities are so out of line that a generation of children is growing up not knowing how to read or write.

He has criticized the rap music industry for promoting images of sex, misogyny and violence, while also placing blame on consumers for rewarding the misbehavior at the cash register.

On the simplest level, Cosby would be happy if young people would just pull their pants up.

"I am not going to bite my tongue and . . . allow people to walk away," the 67-year-old entertainer said.

10   Cosby has visited Atlanta, Springfield, Mass., Newark, N.J., and Milwaukee. He has been featured on television news shows everywhere in between.

"I totally agree with him," said Mildred Cunningham, a 44-year-old claims specialist from Stone Mountain, Ga. "We expect too little from our children, young adults and parents as well. We must start demanding that our young people respect, first, themselves, each other and others in general. It's with that respect that we can then start to build our foundations for the future. His words may seem harsh, but it's reality."

Not everyone has embraced Cosby's message. Critics, many of them black Americans, have accused the multimillionaire, who has a doctorate in education from the University of Massachusetts, of being out of touch with the people he is criticizing.

Some say he is committing what may be the worst sin in the black community: airing its dirty laundry.

Cosby says he doesn't care.

15   "People who are worried about what white people hear Bill Cosby saying have their heads in the sand," he said. "Do you really think that white people—while riding on the bus, listening to our people get out of school, hearing them use profanity, watching how they address each other with 'nigger'—don't know? You think that these white people don't go back and tell their friends about the horrors of having to ride the bus?"

Cosby said he has grown tired of black people using racism as an easy excuse for past and current failures. "When did we decide that it is OK for the African-American male to become the biological father of three or four children from three or four different women and not have the wont to take on the responsibility?" Cosby asked. "The white man didn't tell us to do that."

That Cosby has suddenly become a lightning rod in a debate over black culture is both ironic, since he has always cultivated a serene fatherly image, and surprising, since nothing he has said is really new.

Cosby has donated millions of dollars to black colleges, including Atlanta's Spelman College, has been a champion of family values and respect, and has been critical of under-achievers. This has been the case from his early stand-up comic routines to his highly successful forays into television, including the "Fat Albert" cartoons, which Cosby always started with: "If you pay attention, you just might learn something." His ground-breaking "Cosby Show" of the 1980s depicted a black family unlike any seen before on TV.

Cosby's cause became very public during an NAACP-sponsored celebration of the 50th anniversary of the Supreme Court's landmark ruling outlawing school segregation.

20   In a Washington speech, he said many poor parents are more concerned about buying their children expensive shoes than buying educational tools.

He went on to chastise some blacks for their failure to speak English correctly.

Cosby was stung by the negative reaction he got from the speech, particularly from blacks, said *Milwaukee Journal Sentinel* columnist Eugene Kane.

"He figured out he is going to have to get his message out directly to the people," said Kane, who wound up coordinating Cosby's trip to Milwaukee. "He sincerely feels . . . this is a crusade."

"To not say to your children, here is where the snakes and land mines are and not being able to know what is good and what is bad, then you've got no business having a child," Cosby said.

"We have to turn the mirror around and look at ourselves," he said. "These children   25
are trying to tell us something, and we are not listening. This is about saving our children."

Writing Prompts

1. Write a three-page essay in response to the information given in the *Time* introductory piece. What differences do you think *Brown* made at your high school?
2. Using the questions that the University of Michigan has made a part of the undergraduate admissions process, write a 250-word essay showing how you contribute to diversity at your university.
3. Write a comparison-contrast essay using the Ernie Suggs column on Bill Cosby's attack on blacks and the Diane Carman column on Lawrence Harrison's attack on the Latino culture as being "progress-resistant." Consider the audiences to whom Cosby and Harrison are speaking, along with their own positions in relationship to their audiences. Do Carman and Suggs intrude into the argument or do they remain outside the fray as disinterested reporters?
4. Like Candace Warren, have you ever been the only one of your race in a situation where you were asked to speak for a group of people you did not know personally?
5. After you read carefully the selection on law review diversity, what would be your solution to this significant issue?

What Is at Stake for Citizenship?

1. In the twenty-first century, should race still be considered in a definition of "diversity"?
2. Are labels such as "progress-prone" and "progress-resistant" helpful or limiting in identifying racial cultures?
3. Should resegregation of public schools be a concern?
4. What difference does it make if the top positions on law school review boards are all white?
5. Should teachers ask minority students to speak for "their people"?

CRYING WOLF: THE SUSAN SMITH CASE

Over a decade ago, a mother of two young boys called the nation's attention to Union, South Carolina, where on the evening of October 25, 1994, she reported that a black man had carjacked her, forced her out of the car, and abducted her two sons from the backseat. For nine days, Susan Smith, and her estranged husband, David, appeared on television news shows pleading for the return of their children.

John D. Long Lake, Union, South Carolina.

A sketch of the alleged black man appeared in the local paper, was picked up by weekly news magazines, and circulated on flyers throughout a multistate area. For nine days, black men between the ages of twenty-five and forty-five were closely scrutinized, a number of them were held for questioning, and all were released.

While divers were repeating their search of the local John D. Long Lake, Union County sheriff Howard Wells was fabricating a story to get a confession from the mother herself. Two hours before the bodies of Michael, age three, and Alex, fourteen months, were brought up from the bottom of the lake, still inside the car and strapped into their seats, Susan Smith admitted there was no black man. She had driven to the lake, gotten out of the car, and aimed the car so that it would drive itself into the lake.

In July 1995, Susan Smith was found guilty and sentenced to life in prison. She will be available for parole on November 4, 2024, at age fifty-three.

The following readings about the Susan Smith case offer deeper ways to think about her choice to point the finger at a black man, about how that choice fits into a long history of making the "other" a scapegoat, and how that choice continues to affect the small southern city that must live with this horrific crime. On the occasion of the tenth anniversary of the young boys' murder, the local daily paper, the *Union Daily Times*, chose silence. However, the paper in nearby Spartanburg, South Carolina, the *Herald-Journal*, chose to run a front-page story with oversized color pictures of the children and more pictures and copy on inside pages.

The first reading, "Search Widens for Carjacking Suspect," is the first news story that appeared about the abduction of the children. Within two weeks everyone would know that almost every word that prompted the action of the news story was fictitious. The second, "Stranger in the Shadows," is a news weekly editorial, which places the activity of blaming in a broader, more historically recent context. The next, "Continuing Saga of Sex, Murder, and Racism," is an article from a liberal group, which used Smith's activities while incarcerated to comment once again on the race question. The next two pieces offer two ways to consider the extent to which Smith's action was seen as racist: "Mother's Actions Not Seen as Racially Motivated," from her hometown newspaper, and a response from *Jet*, a periodical with a focus on African American people and issues. The final news feature is by an Associated Press reporter who revisited Union a decade later, spoke with the same preacher who was interviewed at the time of the tragedy, and heard a different story about race relations.

Anna Brown

Search Widens for Carjacking Suspect

Union Daily Times (S.C.), October 26, 1994

Union County Courthouse, site of the Susan Smith Trial.

An all-points bulletin has been issued in four states for a man who forced a Union woman from her car at gunpoint Tuesday night, taking her two sons.

The carjacking occurred around 9 p.m. in the Monarch community. Susan V. Smith, 23, of Toney Road was stopped at the traffic light on S.C. 49 where it intersects with the Monarch-Santuck Highway when a black male armed with a pistol opened her passenger door and jumped into the front seat beside her, according to Union Country Sheriff Howard Wells. Mrs. Smith's two sons–Michael, 3 years old, and Alex, 14 months old–were in the back seat of her car. The man told Mrs. Smith to drive, and she headed east on Highway 49.

Several miles later, near the entrance to John D. Long Lake, the suspect ordered Mrs. Smith to stop the car–a burgundy 1990 Mazda Protege–and get out, according to Mrs. Smith's husband, David.

"He told her to stop the car in the middle of the road," said Smith. "He told her to get out, and she asked why. He said for her just to get out. She asked him if she could have the babies, and he said he didn't have time, but that he wouldn't hurt them. He pushed her out of the way, and drove off toward Lockhart."

Mrs. Smith ran to a neighboring house and called for help, Smith said.

The suspect is described as a black male, 20 to 30 years old, 5 feet 9 inches to 6 feet tall. When he got into the car, he was wearing a dark blue toboggan cap, plaid jacket, and blue jeans.

"If anyone saw a suspect matching this description in the Monarch area last night and might know his identity, please give us a call," said Wells. "By his pattern of behavior–that he didn't harm Mrs. Smith and he stated he would not harm the children–we are hopeful we will be able to locate the children unharmed."

Wells said the suspect threatened Mrs. Smith, told her to shut up and threatened to kill her, but he did not harm her physically.

Wells said his office has received assistance from all area law enforcement agencies. The State Law Enforcement Division (SLED) helicopter has been flying over the area since early this morning, looking for the vehicle, and the SLED HART (hostage rescue) team is also in Union.

"The highway patrol has been alerted, all the roads are covered," said Wells. "Officers are patrolling the back roads. There are more SLED people here than I have ever

5

10

seen in Union County, and they have given great assistance. The FBI Violent Task Force is on the way."

Authorities think he may have driven to North Carolina, SLED spokesman Hugh Munn said [that] an all-points bulletin was issued in North Carolina, South Carolina, Georgia and Tennessee.

"There's no reason to think that he would stay in state because he's close enough to North Carolina to go anywhere," Munn said.

Wells said that if Mrs. Smith's car is located, citizens should not approach it, but should notify the sheriff's office immediately, as they want to preserve it for evidence.

Mrs. Smith's four-door car has the license place GBK-167. The 3-year-old was wearing white jogging pants, a green shirt and a light blue jacket. The 14-month-old child was wearing a red and white stripped outfit and a blue and red jacket.

15   Investigators had a report that about a half-hour later a car that may match the description of Mrs. Smith's pulled into a gas station in Sharon, about halfway between Union and Charlotte, N.C.

The driver bought $10 of gas, Munn said. Investigators were checking the station's security cameras to see if they could get a good picture of the man, he said.

Smith said his wife is resting at the home of her mother and stepfather, Mr. and Mrs. Beverly Russell.

"She's doing O.K., considering," he said.

"This is an unfortunate occurrence, and we don't usually have this type of crime in Union County," Wells said. "We hope we can resolve this quickly with the children being recovered safely."

Richard Lacayo

Stranger in the Shadows

Time, November 14, 1994

Susan Smith knew what a kidnapper should look like. He should be a remorseless stranger with a gun. But the essential part of the picture—the touch she must have counted on to arouse the primal sympathies of her neighbors and to cut short any doubts—was his race. The suspect had to be a black man. Better still, a black man in a knit cap, a bit of hip-hop wardrobe that can be as menacing in some minds as a buccaneer's eye patch. Wasn't that everyone's most familiar image of the murderous criminal?

As it turns out, the murderous criminal in the saga of Michael and Alexander Smith looks like an innocuous young white woman with wisps of teased hair. But while her invention failed to save her, Smith was scheming in a long and effective tradition. For centuries men and women have denied their own deadly impulses by recasting them in the features of some unnerving outsider. Depending on the time and place, the villains might be Jews, immigrants, longhairs or blacks, whoever might do as targets for the shared anxieties of the age.

In late 20th century America, we keep ourselves supplied with useful goblins. When his wife and children were murdered in 1971, Dr. Jeffrey MacDonald, the Green Beret physician eventually convicted of the crime, insisted that the killers were Charles Manson-type hippies who had broken into their home. What better suspect in a time when, in the minds of many, the whole counterculture was a bug-eyed intruder? And in a society that began to demonize African Americans almost as long ago as it first enslaved them, blacks have endured being cast as menacing shadows at the edge of bad dreams. What has changed is that political rhetoric and pop culture are increasingly willing to exploit these shadows. When George Bush's 1988 campaign needed a name and a face for the bogey-man, it came up with Willie Horton. Some black rappers have turned the stereotype to their own profit, striking "gangsta" poses—in black knit caps. Susan Smith didn't have to use much imagination. She just had to reach for the available nightmares.

The process of demonization reached meltdown five years ago when Charles Stuart, a white furrier from a Boston suburb, claimed that a black stranger had leaped into his car as he and his wife were returning from a natural-childbirth class, forced them to drive to a remote location, then robbed and shot them both, killing her. It was Stuart, of course, who had murdered his pregnant wife, then shot himself to make his story unassailable. Stuart would eventually be unmasked and take his own life, but not before Boston police had bought the lies, rounding up scores of black men and further fouling the city's already polluted racial atmosphere.

In a pinch, whole cities can be demonized. Last spring Joseph Bales and Helene Lemay, a French-Canadian couple, found their 10-week-old daughter Muguet dead in her crib. Convinced that they might be accused of killing her, they disposed of the child's body in a wooded area 100 miles from home, then proceeded in their pickup truck to New York City, where they told police that their daughter had disappeared in Central Park. In the two-day search that followed, helicopters, bloodhounds and scuba divers scoured the park and its waterways until the couple broke down and confessed. They had thought it would be enough to say that Manhattan itself had opened its jaws and swallowed their daughter. Everyone knows the profile of a killer. It's a jagged and ominous skyline.

Susan Smith's invention of a black culprit didn't work as well as she had hoped. Her own not-quite-right account of the kidnapping, and perhaps memories of the Stuart case, kept people from rejecting the possibility that the distraught mother was a suspect herself. And though she may not have thought about or cared how her self-serving concoctions would affect race relations around Union, South Carolina, the worst was avoided. Despite the police sketch of a black suspect that papered the area, feelings never boiled over and authorities weren't goaded into harassing the black community. The ploy of the dark-faced stranger works only when those around you share your worst assumptions. And this time, in this case, enough people were prepared to recognize that the face of the killer could be hers.

5

Tom Turnipseed

Continuing Saga of Sex, Murder, and Racism: Susan Smith Is Still Scheming in Prison

Common Dreams News Center, September 14, 2000

COLUMBIA, SC—Susan Smith, who was sentenced to life in prison for murdering her two toddler sons, has admitted having sex with a prison guard at the South Carolina Department of Corrections. In 1994, Smith led the country on a wild goose chase for nine days by blaming a fictitious black man for carjacking her Mazda with her sons still in the car. The practice of unjustly blaming blacks and imprisoning them with alarming racial disparity is not fictitious. It is a real national tragedy.

There is irony in Smith being satisfied by a prison guard. Prosecutors in her highly publicized trial that devastated a small South Carolina town and horrified a nation argued that she had viewed her sons as baggage in her effort to capture her upscale extramarital lover. The newest erotic episode in the life of Susan Smith was discovered after an investigation into Smith's medical records to find if a tabloid story alleging that Smith had been beaten was true. Her medical records did not reveal a beating but that she had been treated for a sexually transmitted disease "other than HIV" and under questioning she admitted having sex with Houston Cagle, a prison guard.

Cagle, a 13-year jailer at the Women's Correctional Institution in Columbia, appeared before a judge at a bail bond hearing with his wife, Tammy. A former prison inmate, Tammy sobbingly told the judge, "I feel like I've been murdered too, just like those two little boys, she took my life from me." It has not been determined if Tammy and Houston knew each other "biblically" while she was in the big house, but documents submitted to the S.C. Senate's Corrections Committee that is holding hearings into the matter revealed that 10 instances of sexual misconduct have occurred in South Carolina prisons since January 1999.

It's interesting that Cagle might not have been the first South Carolinian to have sex with a convicted female killer. According to "Ol' Strom," a biography of Senator Strom Thurmond by Jack Bass, Randall Johnson, the driver of a state vehicle transporting a convicted female killer named Sue Logue to the prison death house in 1943, said then U.S. Army Major Thurmond got into the back seat with his friend Logue and they were "a huggin' and a kissin' the whole way." Joe Frank Logue said his Aunt Sue "was the only person ever seduced on the way to the electric chair."

5   Headline grabbing hearings about sex with Susan Smith behind bars are scintillating but scheming. Susan's racist attempt to blame a black man in a knit cap for her horrible deed is a continuing tradition that goes way back to demonizing blacks to justify enslaving them. Legislative hearings about sexual wrongdoing in prisons don't deal with the greatest wrongdoing in our criminal justice system. What will we do about the shocking racial injustices that appear in the media, but seem to go away before white folk's consciences become too troubled?

Nationally, black youth are 6 times more likely to be locked up than white youth charged with similar crimes and having similar criminal records. Black youth are far more likely to be arrested, detained and sentenced than white youth according to state and federal juvenile justice officials. In South Carolina, blacks make up 36% of the juvenile population but comprised 54% of juveniles referred to prosecutors and 62% of youths committed to facilities or programs in 1999. From 1985 to 1994, blacks accounted for 80% of the cases of juveniles that prosecutors requested be tried as adults.

Human Rights Watch reports that blacks comprise only 13% of the U. S. population but are 62% of the drug offenders in our state prisons, although studies show that whites use 5 times more illegal drugs than blacks. In South Carolina, with a black population of 30%, 86% of the drug offenders in prison are blacks.

For the past 5 years, 75% of the cases in which federal prosecutors sought the death penalty the defendant was a minority and in more than half were black. For the past 10 years only 40% of murder victims were white in the Carolinas but with present death row inmates almost 70% of their murder victims were white.

Odds are if Susan Smith had been successful in "blaming the black," he wouldn't be alive to have sex in prison.

Charles L. Warner

Mother's Actions Not Seen as Racially Motivated

Union Daily Times (S.C.), November 4, 1994

Most African-American residents in Union County do not view Susan Smith's decision to blame a black man for the kidnapping of her children as a racially-motivated action, a Union minister says.

"We don't believe it and I don't believe that," Rev. A.L. Brackett, pastor of St. Paul Baptist Church, said Thursday night. "I gave a radio interview last Sunday evening and I stated then that I didn't believe it was racial. It was an isolated incident that happened. We were praying that the children would be returned safely. We were treating it as Sheriff Wells was treating it: as a carjacking. I think it was an isolated incident and I don't think it was racially motivated. I don't know why she created that image in her mind but certainly it was not racially motivated."

Brackett said that "we're trying to encourage our people not to even think that way. I've given three or four interviews and tomorrow morning I'll be giving one to CBS here because I want to point out the fact of the good relationship the black and white have here in this community."

Brackett's comments were made shortly after Wells announced that Mrs. Smith had been arrested and charged with the murder of her two sons. Mrs. Smith's car, along with what are believed to be the bodies of Michael and Alex Smith, had been found in John D. Long Lake. Following Wells' statement an individual described onlookers as an African-American male began shouting.

"Some man got loud and got sort of disorderly," Union Public Safety Director Russell Roark said. "When we arrived on the scene he quieted down and he went back into a place of business across from the county jail. There was no arrest incident. It was just a matter of quieting down this individual. 5

"I had taken the sheriff back to the helicopter and when I got back to Main Street I heard the call," he said. "By the time I got here most of the disturbance was over and they were getting him into the business across from the county jail."

Roark said he heard only part of what the man said. "He was shouting something about this incident was racial and so on, but I think the people that were with him kind of quieted him down and got him off to the side."

According to Roark there were no further incidents and he said he felt "everything will be OK now." He said his officers were on the scene to help with traffic and crowd control, adding that "everybody is orderly. I don't know how long the crowd will be here but we will stay until the majority of the crowd leaves."

Other African-Americans echoed Brackett's comments, expressing sorrow for the children and rejecting the idea that the matter was racially motivated.

"When they announced them kids were dead tonight it brought tears to my eyes," Joanne Smith said. "I am very sorry about them kids, but from the first beginning of it I knew there was something strange about it because I would not have left my kids. I have kids myself and ain't nobody can make me run off and leave them. Nobody." 10

Mrs. Smith said that she never considered the incident a racial one and had been suspicious "when she pinpointed it was a black man and she said he had black hair and he was wearing a toboggan . . . if he had a toboggan on how could she tell what color hair he had under it? That's what got me to thinking. Everybody at work with me didn't buy it, even the white people at work they did not even buy the fact that she was saying it was a black man. I hated that she had his picture everywhere, that's what I hated. Picture all over the United States for something that was untrue and she knowing where those poor little innocent kids were at. That's what I hate."

Carlisle Mayor Janie Goree said that the news of the alleged carjacking and kidnapping bothered her. "When I heard about the children being taken I was very disturbed because I do love children. I felt so sorry for the mother and the father and I kept hoping that they would be found alive and that they would be brought back home safely. As the story continued to weave I began to lose hope but I kept praying for those little children and I was hoping everything would come out all right. I've been very saddened ever since I heard about it.

Mrs. Goree said she was also "sorry for the mother. We don't know what happened to her and whatever happened I just hope and pray that God will be with her as he would anybody else. I don't see how anybody could take the life of their own children."

Mrs. Goree rejected any implication that the incident was a racial one explaining that "I think everybody was concerned and hoping and praying the children would be found. I hadn't thought in terms of it being racial; I feel like she was trying to use some kind of escape and that's what she turned to. I don't think you can hold anybody responsible for what she said but her."

15   A somewhat dissenting view was expressed by Belinda Hills who said, "I don't really believe it is totally a racial matter but the fact that when something bad happens they point their finger to somebody black and say 'That person did it' and get off because Union hides a lot of dirt by pointing its finger at black people and this is just something that comes to the surface."

Mrs. Hills added that the incident "ought to make America want to wake up and say 'What's really going on?' Every time you do something wrong are you going to point your finger at a black person and try to get off? If the media and everybody hadn't been here I think they would have locked up somebody black and he would have made a lot of time for murdering those kids if she hadn't came forth."

However, Mrs. Hills added that "my heart is sick for the kids because they didn't get a chance to live and they were just babies. I'm really saddened in my heart for the children because I just can't understand how somebody in their right mind could kill their own children."

Blacks Still Angry over White Woman Who Claimed Black Man Kidnapped Her Two Boys

Jet, November 28, 1994

It's going to take more than an apology to heal the wounds in Union, SC.

Some Blacks there are still angry with Susan Smith, 23, who claimed a Black carjacker kidnapped her young sons.

After a nine-day nationwide search and numerous prayer vigils in this town of 10,000, one third of which is Black, Smith admitted it was all a hoax and confessed to killing her two boys, Michael, 3, and Alexander, 14 months.

Michael Moorman, 24, is still dealing with his rage over Smith's false accusation of a Black man.

"It's disappointing because she blamed our race—the Black people," Moorman told JET, his voice still filled with resentment. He added, "They do Black folks wrong down here. They always sweat our neighborhoods," pointing out how Blacks are often the target of police harassment.

His views are similar to those held by a number of young Blacks in the area. During the investigation into Smith's claims, most Black men between the age of 25 and 45 became suspects.

A cloud of suspicion settled over the heads of Black men in this textile mill town, located about 28 miles South of Spartanburg, who showed any remote resemblance to the phony composite drawing police came up with based on Smith's description.

When Smith finally confessed, she told authorities the children were still strapped in their car seat when she pushed her 1990 Mazda Protege into John D. Long Lake, sending them to a watery grave.

In an effort to heal the wounds of local Blacks, many of whom had spent hours searching and praying for the safe return of the Smith boys, her father-in-law Charles Smith and older brother Scotty Vaughn apologized for her deceit.

"On behalf of my family, we want to apologize to the Black community of Union," Vaughn stated. "It's real disturbing to think that anyone would think this was ever a racial issue. We apologize to all the Black citizens in Union and everywhere."

Choking back tears, Charles Smith, the father of Susan's estranged husband David, said: "David loves each and every one of you."

The tearful apologies, however, did little to ease the pain and hurt of the Black community.

Rainbow Coalition President Jesse Jackson empathized with the hostility many Blacks harbor as a result of the case. During a recent visit to Union, where he laid a wreath for the two slain brothers at the lake where authorities say their mother drowned them, Jackson said the case indicates there are growing racial fears around the nation.

Jackson said Mrs. Smith "exploited a climate of racial hostility and fear that is much bigger than Union." Numerous residents agree the accusation reflected deeper racial wounds and that those scars are still quite painful.

As the eyes of the nation continue to focus on the tiny Southern town, Smith was taken off a suicide watch and held in prison without bail.

Prosecutors are considering seeking the death penalty for Smith, while her lawyers have indicated they may enter a plea of insanity as her defense for the heinous crime.

Union resident Anthony McMahon said he knew of at least 25 Black men who had been questioned in the case. "They were looking at us funny," McMahon was quoted as saying. "They think if you're a Black man you're always doing something."

William E. Free III, a Union business owner, said because Blacks and Whites joined the search for the children who were believed to be missing, Blacks were shocked to learn the story was fictitious.

Free's Shoe Repair Shop, located across the street from the Courthouse.

"When we found out the truth, we went through a range of emotions from hurt and anger to sympathy," Free said.

As the town tries to regroup from this miscarriage of justice, the question as to why Smith had to point the finger at a Black man is still on everyone's lips. "She had to think of a way to explain how her car was missing," said the Rev. Samuel Farr, pastor of New Bethel Baptist Church in nearby Woodruff, SC. "Even though when carjackings take place, it's not always a Black person, most of the time when you hear about carjackings, it involves a Black man. I believe her thinking was that by saying a Black person hijacked the car, her story would be more believable. I'm sorry to say that, but that's the way it is."

To ever get an answer to why Smith made up the story, the Rev. A.L. Brackett told JET, "We would have to have a psychiatrist go into her mind . . . I sort of feel it was just easier to believe it was a Black man, but she had to be sick."

Furthermore, he said, "We've learned that she had a lot of problems: her father committed suicide, she was sexually molested as a child, the breakup of her marriage, her boyfriend threw her aside. So there were a lot of things going on with Susie."

Brackett continued, "My message to the world is don't make it a Black/White issue. It was a sick, deranged mind who created a Black person to lay (the blame) on as a route to escape," he said.

Pastor at St. Paul Baptist Church in Union for more than two decades, Brackett said through it all the tragedy has been a blessing in disguise. "I have seen it bring a town and county and—hopefully—a nation closer together." He added, "I think some good has already come of it. We are relating to one another as we have never done in the last 20 years."

Amy Geier Edgar

S.C. Town Still Coping with Child Killings: Susan Smith Case

Associated Press, in The *Denver Post*, October 24, 2004

UNION, S.C. (AP)—A decade after Susan Smith strapped her sons in their car seats and let her car roll into a lake, carrying the boys to their deaths, residents are trying to move on.

But for some, the case still evokes strong emotions, even hatred toward Smith.

Prosecutor Tommy Pope, who tried Smith for the crime, said he recently started a conversation in a store with a "little old lady." She was very sweet and polite until the subject of Smith came up, then the woman began to "sound like a sailor," he said.

Memorial to Michael and Alex on the road to John D. Long Lake.

Smith's boys, 3-year-old Michael and 14-month-old Alex, disappeared Oct. 25, 1994. She told deputies they had been taken in a carjacking and cried on national television as she begged for their safe return.

Nine days later, Smith confessed, and the boys' bodies were found in the car, submerged a few feet from a boat ramp at John D. Long Lake in Union County.

Family members and many officials involved in the case remain silent. Smith, sentenced to life in prison, is not allowed to give prison interviews.

"Some people don't want to talk about it anymore," said Union resident Jimmy Dawkins, fishing at the lake on a recent afternoon. "They want it buried."

Smith was convicted in July 1995. Pope had sought the death penalty, and he considers the case a loss.

A photo of Michael and Alex—given to him during the trial by the boys' father, David Smith—still sits in his office, reminding him of why his job is important. "Too often, we lose focus on the victims all too easily," Pope said.

The case incensed the black community because Smith claimed a black man carjacked her and drove off with the children.

"It had the makings of one of the worst scenarios you could come across," said Howard Free, owner of Free's Shoe Shop, across the street from the courthouse where Smith's trial was held.

Healing grew out of a faith-based effort, said the Rev. A.L. Brackett, one of the church leaders who worked to bring calm. Blacks and whites joined for prayer vigils at churches.

The tombstone of Michael and Alexander Smith, located in the church cemetery of Bogansville United Methodist, a few miles outside of Union, South Carolina.

"Instead of dividing the races at this particular time any further . . . it brought them closer together," Brackett said. "It wasn't only whites out there looking for those kids when they thought they'd been kidnapped and taken away."

But 10 years later, he said, the sense of racial unity "wore off" and many people have returned to old habits.

Smith is up for parole on Nov. 4, 2024. Pope says he

likely won't go to the hearing but will send his standard letter opposing early release from life sentences.

"I feel strongly about the case, but I'm not vindictive toward her," he said. "I'm not like the lady at Wal-Mart. I don't wake up with hatred."

Writing Prompts

1. Write a three-page essay on the issue of using others as scapegoats, particularly when the other is of a different race. Try to answer the question of why people find the "other" so threatening. Use evidence from at least two selections.
2. Write a comparison-contrast essay using two pieces that give different positions on the race question. Pay attention to the audience for each piece as you determine your thesis.
3. The first selection is a news story, and we expect news stories to be full of facts that have a basis in truth. What happens to our trust level about the genre when we later discover the story has little or no truth?
4. Write about a time that you had some personal experience with someone you know who was used as a scapegoat? What happened and how was the issue resolved? Is a conclusion ever possible when a scapegoat is named?
5. Put yourself in Union in the fall of 1994 for the nine days when a black man was the suspect. If you were black, how would you look at others around you who were black? Would it be different from how you would look at those who were white? If you were white, how would you look at blacks—those you already knew and those you did not?

What Is at Stake for Citizenship?

1. What does such a scenario as that described in this cluster suggest about "innocent until proven guilty" in our system of justice?
2. Should American citizens have to walk on the streets of their town in fear?
3. Should we be concerned about statistical data that shows that the percentage of African Americans who are incarcerated is far higher than the percentage of whites?
4. Should false accusations be protected by the First Amendment freedom of speech clause?
5. Are we well served when we are reminded of tragic events in our national history, or is it best not to acknowledge these anniversaries?

BEING MIXED RACE IN AMERICA

Before 1970, a person's race was determined by a census taker who simply looked at the person and made an appropriate check mark on a form. On the 2000 U.S. Census, individuals, for the first time, were permitted to self-identify by selecting one or more of the following six categories:

- White
- Black, African American or Negro
- American Indian or Alaska Native
- Asian, including Asian Indian, Chinese, Filipino, Japanese, Korean, Vietnamese, and other Asian
- Native Hawaiian, Guamanian or Chamarro, Samoan and other Pacific Islander
- Some other race

This change made comparative analysis by race with earlier census data no longer possible. Over seven million people chose two or more races. According to a brief article in *Forecast* ("The Geography of Multiracials," December 17, 2001) Allison Stein Wellner determined from the data that 40 percent of multiracial Americans live in the West, 27 percent in the South. A full two-thirds of multiracial people live in ten states; the two largest multiracial communities are found in two of America's largest cities—400,000 live in New York City, 200,000 live in Los Angeles.

While statistical data is interesting, seven million people out of the total population of the United States is a small percentage. Shifting attitudes about acceptance, the complicated lives of real people, and textbook studies of what the numbers mean deliver a rich story behind the statistics of being mixed race in America today.

The selections included in this cluster begin with Randall Kennedy's essay on interracial intimacy. His argument, that as white opposition has lessened, black opposition has increased, suggests a difficult move toward common ground and hints at a future of colorism—where light-skinned people of all races will hold an advantage in society and status over those with darker skins. Three case studies of young adults with one white parent and one black parent offer insight into varied ways individuals might come to see themselves. A look at two brief memoirs suggests both the richness and the painfulness of having parents of different races—one black and white, one Chinese and white. One commentary offers background information on the activity of counting ourselves in racial terms and offers thoughtful insight about the value of doing so. The final selection looks at the challenges of the multi-colored family—through mixed-race parents and through parents who choose to adopt multiracial children.

Race is one way we identify who we are in America. W. E. B. Du Bois declared over a hundred years ago that the problem of America was a problem of color. In 1903, he had in mind a black-white issue. Today, the question of race and color is far more complex, and equally if not more challenging. These selections will help you more thoughtfully enter the conversation about being mixed race in America.

Randall Kennedy

Interracial Intimacy: White-Black Dating, Marriage, and Adoption Are on the Rise

The *Atlantic Monthly,* December 2002

Austin, Texas: Interracial couple in their mid-twenties feeding each other cake at their wedding.

Americans are already what racial purists have long feared: a people characterized by a great deal of racial admixture, or what many in the past referred to distastefully as "mongrelization." In pigmentation, width of noses, breadth of lips, texture of hair, and other telltale signs, the faces and bodies of millions of Americans bear witness to interracial sexual encounters. Some were joyful, passionate, loving affairs. Many were rapes. Others contained elements of both choice and coercion. These different kinds of interracial intimacy and sexual depredation all reached their peak in the United States during the age of slavery, and following the Civil War they decreased markedly. Since the end of the civil-rights revolution, interracial dating, interracial sex, and interracial marriage have steadily increased, as has the number of children born of interracial unions. This development has prompted commentators to speak of the "creolization" or "browning" or "beiging" of America.

Over the years legions of white-supremacist legislators, judges, prosecutors, police officers, and other officials have attempted to prohibit open romantic interracial attachments, particularly those between black men and white women. From the 1660s to the 1960s, forty-one territories, colonies, or states enacted laws–anti-**miscegenation** statutes—barring sex or marriage between blacks and whites, and many states ultimately made marriage across the color line a felony. Such laws crystallized attitudes about interracial intimacy that remain influential today, but all were invalidated by the U.S. Supreme Court in 1967, in the most aptly named case in all of American constitutional history: **Loving v. Commonwealth of Virginia.** Although white and black Americans are far more likely to date and marry within their own race than outside it, the cultural environment has changed considerably since *Loving*. Recall what happened in the spring of 2000, when George W. Bush, at a crucial moment in his primary campaign, paid a highly publicized visit to Bob Jones University, in South Carolina. During that visit he offered no criticism of the university's then existing prohibition against interracial dating. In the controversy that ensued, no nationally prominent figures defended Bob Jones's policy. Public opinion not only forced Bush to distance himself from Bob Jones but also prompted the notoriously stubborn and reactionary administration of that institution to drop its ban.

The de-stigmatization in this country of interracial intimacy is profoundly encouraging. Against the tragic backdrop of American history, it is a sign that Frederick Douglass may have been right when he prophesied, even before the abolition of slavery, that eventually "the white and colored people of this country [can] be blended into a common nationality, and enjoy together . . . the inestimable blessings of life, liberty and the pursuit of happiness."

The great but altogether predictable irony is that just as white opposition to white-black intimacy finally lessened, during the last third of the twentieth century, black opposition became vocal and aggressive. In college classrooms today, when discussions about the ethics of interracial dating and marriage arise, black students are frequently the ones most likely to voice disapproval.

Marital Integration

Despite some ongoing resistance (a subject to which I will return), the situation for people involved in interracial intimacy has never been better. For the most part, the law prohibits officials from taking race into account in licensing marriages, making child-custody decisions, and arranging adoptions. Moreover, the American public accepts interracial intimacy as it never has before. This trend will almost certainly continue; polling data and common observation indicate that young people tend to be more liberal on these matters than their elders.

In 1960 there were about 51,000 black-white married couples in the United States; in 1970 there were 65,000, in 1980 there were 121,000, in 1990 there were 213,000, and by 1998 the number had reached 330,000. In other words, in the past four decades black-white marriages increased more than sixfold. And black-white marriages are not only becoming more numerous. Previously, the new couples in mixed marriages tended to be older than other brides and grooms. They were frequently veterans of divorce, embarking on second or third marriages. In recent years, however, couples in mixed marriages seem to be marrying younger than their pioneering predecessors and seem more inclined to have children and to pursue all the other "normal" activities that married life offers.

It should be stressed that black-white marriages remain remarkably rare—fewer than one percent of the total. In 1998, when 330,000 black-white couples were married, 55,305,000 couples were married overall. Moreover, the racial isolation of blacks on the marriage market appears to be greater than that of other people of color: much larger percentages of Native Americans and Asian-Americans marry whites. According to 1990 Census data, in the age cohort twenty-five to thirty-four, 36 percent of U.S.-born Asian-American husbands and 45 percent of U.S.-born Asian-American wives had white spouses; 53 percent of Native American husbands and 54 percent of Native American wives had white spouses. Only eight percent of African-American husbands and only four percent of African-American wives had white spouses. The sociologist Nathan Glazer was correct in stating, in *The Public Interest* (September 1995), that "blacks stand out uniquely among the array of American ethnic and racial groups in the degree to which marriage remains within the group." Of course, the Native American and Asian-American populations are so much smaller than the African-American population that relatively few intermarriages make a big difference in percentage terms. But the disparity is real: it has to do not only with demographics but also with generations' worth of subjective judgments about marriage-ability, beauty, personality, comfort, compatibility, and prestige. Even now a wide array of social pressures continue to make white-black marriages more difficult and thus less frequent than other interethnic or interracial marriages.

Nevertheless, the trend toward more interracial marriage is clear, as is a growing acceptance of the phenomenon. Successful, high-profile interracial couples include the white William Cohen (a former senator from Maine and the Secretary of Defense under Bill Clinton) and the black Janet Langhart; and the white Wendy Raines and the black Franklin Raines (he is a former director of the Office of Management and Budget and the CEO of Fannie Mae). Some African-Americans whose positions make them directly dependent on black public opinion have nonetheless married whites without losing their footing. A good example is Julian Bond, the chairman of the board of directors of the National Association for the Advancement of Colored People. Though married to a white woman, Bond ascended to the chairmanship of the oldest and most influential black-advancement organization in the country in 1998, and as of this writing continues to enjoy widespread support within the NAACP.

There are other signs that black-white romance has become more widely accepted; indeed, it is quite fashionable in some contexts. One is advertising. When advertisers addressing general audiences use romance to deliver their messages, they most often depict couples of the same race. But now at least occasionally one sees interracial couples deployed as enticements to shop at Diesel or Club Monaco, or to buy furniture from Ikea, jeans from Guess, sweaters from Tommy Hilfiger, cologne from Calvin Klein, or water from Perrier.

10   Scores of interracial support groups have emerged across the country, among them Kaleidoscope, at the University of Virginia; Students of Mixed Heritage at Amherst College; Interracial Family Club, in Washington, D.C.; Half and Half, at Bryn Mawr; and Mixed Plate, at Grinnell. Although most of these organizations lack deep roots, many display a vigor and resourcefulness that suggest they will survive into the foreseeable future. They stem from and represent a community in the making. It is a community united by a demand that the larger society respect and be attentive to people who by descent or by choice fall outside conventional racial groupings: interracial couples, parents of children of a different race, and children of parents of a different race. Those within this community want it known that they are not products or agents of an alarming mongrelization, as white racists still believe; nor are they inauthentic and unstable in-betweeners, as some people of color would have it. They want security amid the established communities from which they have migrated. They want to emerge from what the writer Lise Funderburg has identified as the "racial netherworld," and they want to enjoy interaction with others without regret or fear, defensiveness or embarrassment.

"Sleeping White"

African-Americans largely fall into three camps with respect to white-black marriage. One camp, relatively small, openly champions it as a good. Its members argue that increasing rates of interracial marriage will decrease social segregation, encourage racial open-mindedness, enhance blacks' access to enriching social networks, elevate their status, and empower black women in their interactions with black men by subjecting the latter to greater competition in the marketplace for companionship.

A second camp sees interracial marriage merely as a choice that individuals should have the right to make. For example, while noting in *Race Matters* (1993) that "more and more white Americans are willing to interact sexually with black Americans on an equal basis," Cornel West maintains that he views this as "neither cause for celebration nor reason for lament." This is probably the predominant view among blacks. It allows a person simultaneously to oppose anti-miscegenation laws and to disclaim any desire to marry across racial lines. Many African-Americans are attracted to this position, because, among other things, it helps to refute a deeply annoying assumption on the part of many whites: that blacks would like nothing more than to be intimate with whites and even, if possible, to become white.

A third camp opposes interracial marriage, on the grounds that it expresses racial disloyalty, suggests disapproval of fellow blacks, undermines black culture, weakens the African-American marriage market, and feeds racist mythologies, particularly the canard that blacks lack pride of race. Such opposition has always been a powerful undercurrent. When Walter White, the executive secretary of the NAACP, divorced his black wife (the mother of their two children) and married a white woman from South Africa, in 1949, the Norfolk (Virginia) Journal and Guide spoke for many blacks when it asserted, "A prompt and official announcement that [White] will not return to his post . . . is in order." Part of the anger stemmed from apprehension that segregationists would seize upon White's marriage to substantiate the charge that what black male civil-rights activists were really after was sex with white women. Part stemmed from a widespread sense that perhaps White thought no black woman was good enough for him.

By the late 1960s, with the repudiation of anti-miscegenation and Jim Crow laws, increasing numbers of blacks felt emboldened to openly oppose mixed marriages. "We Shall Overcome" was giving way to "Black Power": improving the image of blacks in the minds of whites seemed less important than cultivating a deeper allegiance to racial solidarity. To blacks, interracial intimacy compromised that allegiance. The African-American social reformer George Wiley dedicated himself to struggles for racial justice as a leading figure in the Congress for Racial Equality (CORE) and the founder of the National Welfare Rights Organization. Yet many black activists denounced him for marrying and remaining married to a white woman. When he addressed a rally in Washington, D.C., on African Liberation Day in April of 1972, a group of black women heckled him by chanting, "Where's your white wife? Where's your white wife?" When he attempted to focus his remarks on the situation of black women, the hecklers merely took up a different chant: "Talking black and sleeping white."

Other politically active blacks married to whites—James Farmer, a founder of CORE, and Julius Hobson, a tenacious activist in Washington—faced similar pressure. Julius Lester, a longtime member of the Student Nonviolent Coordinating Committee, wrote a book with one of the most arresting titles of that flamboyant era: Look Out, Whitey! Black Power's Gon' Get Your Mama! (1968). But to many black activists, Lester's writings and ideas were decidedly less significant than his choice of a white wife. To them, his selection bespoke hypocrisy. Ridiculing Lester, one black woman wrote a letter to the editor of Ebony in which she suggested that it was foolish to regard him as a trustworthy leader. After all, she cautioned, he couldn't even "crawl out of bed" with whites. The "sleeping white" critique embarrassed a wide variety of people as distinctions between the personal and the political evaporated. At many colleges and universities black students ostracized other blacks who dated (much less married) whites. A black student who wanted to walk around "with a blonde draped on his arm" could certainly do so, a black student leader at the University of Washington told St. Clair Drake, a leading African-American sociologist. "All we say," the student continued, "is don't try to join the black studies association." Drake himself became

15

the target of this critique. When he visited his old high school in 1968, he says, the Black Student Union refused to have anything to do with him, because he was involved in an interracial relationship. Drake's classmate Charles V. Hamilton, a co-author, with Stokely Carmichael, of *Black Power: The Politics of Liberation in America* (1967), was shunned for the same reason.

In some instances black opposition to interracial intimacy played a part in destroying a marriage. A dramatic example is the breakup of Everett LeRoi Jones (now known as Amiri Baraka) and Hettie Jones. LeRoi Jones was born of middle-class black parents in Newark, New Jersey, in 1934. For two years he attended Howard University, which he detested. He served in the Air Force for a short time, and in 1957 he moved to Greenwich Village. He worked for the magazine *Record Changer* and was a co-editor, with Hettie Cohen, of *Yugen*, an avant-garde magazine that published writings by William Burroughs, Gregory Corso, Allen Ginsberg, Jack Kerouac, Charles Olson, and Jones himself. Hettie Cohen was a woman of Jewish parentage who had grown up in suburban New York and attended Mary Washington, the women's college of the University of Virginia. Jones and Cohen married in 1958. Although his parents accepted the marriage easily, her parents totally opposed it.

For a while LeRoi and Hettie Jones lived together in what she remembers as a loving relationship. But then the pressure of bohemian penury, the demands of two children, and mutual infidelities (including one in which LeRoi fathered a baby by another woman who also happened to be white) caused their marriage to falter. Other forces also emerged to doom the union: LeRoi's deep internal tensions, his ambition to become a black leader, and the growing sense in many black communities that no purported leader could be trusted who "talked black but slept white."

As the black protest movement gathered steam in the early sixties, Jones aimed at becoming an important figure in it. At the same time, his career as a writer blossomed. He wrote well-regarded poetry, social and political essays, and a significant book, *Blues People* (1963), on the history of African-American music. What made LeRoi Jones a celebrity, however, and what ensures him a niche in American literary history, is his two-act play *Dutchman*, which opened in New York City in March of 1964. In *Dutchman* a reticent, bookish middle-class black man named Clay meets a white temptress named Lula in a New York subway car. The play consists mainly of their verbal combat. Angered by Clay's refusal to dance with her, Lula shouts, "Come on, Clay. Let's rub bellies on the train . . . Forget your social-working mother for a few seconds and let's knock stomachs. Clay, you liver-lipped white man. You would-be Christian. You ain't no nigger, you're just a dirty white man." Clay responds in kind.

> "Tallulah Bankhead! . . . Don't you tell me anything! If I'm a middle-class fake white man . . . let me be . . . Let me be who I feel like being. Uncle Tom. Thomas. Whoever. It's none of your business . . . I sit here, in this buttoned-up suit, to keep myself from cutting all your throats . . . You great liberated whore! You fuck some black man, and right away you're an expert on black people. What a lotta shit that is."

But Lula has the last word, so to speak: she suddenly stabs Clay to death. Other passengers throw his body out of the subway car and depart. Alone, Lula re-occupies her seat. When another black man enters the car, she begins her lethal routine anew.

Though living in a predominantly white, bohemian environment when he wrote *Dutchman*, Jones had begun to believe that it was blacks to whom he should be addressing his art. Increasingly successful, he was also becoming increasingly radical in his condemnation of white American society. Asked by a white woman what white people could do to help the race problem, Jones replied, "You can help by dying. You are a cancer. You can help the world's people with your death." An outrageous statement coming from anyone, this comment was even more arresting coming from a man who was married to a white woman. Jones was by no means alone in living within this particular contradiction. He noted in his autobiography that at one point he and some other black intellectuals objected to the presence of white radicals on a committee they were in the process of establishing. "What was so wild," he recalled, "was that some of us were talking about how we didn't want white people on the committee but we were all hooked up to white women . . . Such were the contradictions of that period of political organization."

The more prominent Jones became, however, the more critics, both black and white, charged him with being hypocritical. The critic Stanley Kauffmann, for example, asserted that Jones constituted an exemplary figure in "the Tradition of the Fake." Stung by such charges, infatuated with black-nationalist rhetoric, inspired by the prospect of re-creating himself, and bored with a disappointing marriage, LeRoi Jones divorced Hettie Jones in 1965.

20

Throughout the black-power era substantial numbers of African-Americans loudly condemned black participation in interracial relationships (especially with whites), deeming it to be racial betrayal. A reader named Joyce Blake searingly articulated this sentiment in a letter to the editor of the *Village Voice*.

> It really hurts and baffles me and many other black sisters to see our black brothers (?) coming down the streets in their African garbs with a white woman on their arms. It is fast becoming a standard joke among the white girls that they can get our men still— African styles and all . . .
>
> It certainly seems to many black sisters that the Movement is just another sub-terfuge to aid the Negro male in procuring a white woman. If this be so, then the black sisters don't need it, for surely we have suffered enough humiliation from both white and black men in America.

A Demographic Betrayal?

Although racial solidarity has been the principal reason for black opposition to inter-marriage over the years, another reason is the perception that intermarriage by black men weakens black women in the marriage market. A reader named Lula Miles asserted this view in an August 1969 letter to the editor of *Ebony*. Responding to a white woman who had expressed bewilderment at black women's anger, Miles wrote, "Non-sister wonders why the sight of a black man with a white woman is revolting to a black woman . . . The name of the game is 'competition': Non-sister, you are trespassing!"

Another letter writer, named Miraonda J. Stevens, reinforced this point: "In the near future there aren't going to be enough nice black men around for us [black women] to marry." This "market" critique of interracial marriage has a long history. In 1929 Palestine Wells, a black columnist for the Baltimore, *Afro-American*, wrote,

> I have a sneaking suspicion that national intermarriage will make it harder to get husbands. A girl has a hard time enough getting a husband, but methinks 'twill be worse. Think how awful it would be if all the ofay girls with a secret hankering for brown skin men, could openly compete with us.

Forty-five years later an *Ebony* reader named Katrina Williams echoed Wells. "The white man is marrying the white woman," she wrote. "The black man is marrying the white woman. Who's gonna marry me?"

25   Behind her anxious question resides more than demographics: there is also the perception that large numbers of African-American men believe not only that white women are relatively more desirable but that black women are positively unattractive. Again the pages of *Ebony* offer vivid testimony. A reader named Mary A. Dowdell wrote in 1969,

> Let's just lay all phony excuses aside and get down to the true nitty, NITTY-GRITTY and tell it like it really is. Black males hate black women just because they are black. The whole so-called Civil Rights Act was really this: "I want a white woman because she's white and I not only hate but don't want a black woman because she's black." . . . The whole world knows this.

Decades later African-American hostility to interracial intimacy remained widespread and influential. Three examples are revealing. The first is the movie *Jungle Fever* (1991), which portrays an interracial affair set in New York City in the early 1990s. The director, Spike Lee, made sure the relationship was unhappy. Flipper Purify is an ambitious, college-educated black architect who lives in Harlem with his black wife and their young daughter. Angie Tucci, a young white woman, works for Purify as a secretary. Educated only through high school, she lives in Bensonhurst, Brooklyn, with her father and brothers, all of whom are outspoken racists. One evening when Flipper and Angie stay late at his office, work is superseded by erotic longing tinged with racial curiosity. He has never been sexually intimate with a white woman, and she has never been sexually intimate with a black man. They close that gap in their experience, and then stupidly confide in indiscreet friends, who carelessly reveal their secret. Angie's father throws her out of the family home after viciously beating her for "fucking a black nigger." Flipper's wife, Drew, throws him out as well. Flipper and Angie move into an apartment together, but that arrangement falls apart rather quickly under the pressure of their own guilt and uncertainty and the strong disapproval they encounter among blacks and whites alike.

The second example is Lawrence Otis Graham's 1995 essay "I Never Dated a White Girl." Educated at Princeton University and Harvard Law School, Graham sought to explain why "black middle-class kids . . . [who are] raised in integrated or mostly white neighborhoods, [and] told to befriend white neighbors, socialize and study with white classmates, join white social and professional organizations, and go to work for mostly white employers" are also told by their relatives, "Oh, and by the way, don't ever forget that you are black, and that you should never get so close to whites that you happen to fall in love with them." Graham did more than explain, however; he justified this advice in a candid polemic that might well have been titled "Why I Am Proud That I Never Dated a White Girl."

The third example is "Black Men, White Women: A Sister Relinquishes Her Anger," a 1993 essay by the novelist Bebe Moore Campbell. Describing a scene in which she and her girlfriends spied a handsome black celebrity escorting a white woman at a trendy Beverly Hills restaurant, Campbell wrote,

> In unison, we moaned, we groaned, we rolled our eyes heavenward. We gnashed our teeth in harmony and made ugly faces. We sang "Umph! Umph! Umph!" a cappella-style, then shook our heads as we lamented for the ten thousandth time the perfidy of black men and cursed trespassing white women who dared to "take our men." . . . Before lunch was over I had a headache, indigestion, and probably elevated blood pressure.

Only a small percentage of black men marry interracially; one report, published in 1999, estimated that seven percent of married black men have non-black wives. But with poverty, imprisonment, sexual orientation, and other factors limiting the number of mar-riageable black men, a substantial number of black women feel this loss of potential mates acutely. In 1992 researchers found that for every three unmarried black women in their twenties there was only one unmarried black man with earnings above the poverty level. Given these realities, black women's disparagement of interracial marriage should come as no surprise. "In a drought," Campbell wrote, "even one drop of water is missed."

Compiling a roster of prominent blacks—Clarence Thomas, Henry Louis Gates Jr., Quincy Jones, Franklin A. Thomas, John Edgar Wideman—married to or otherwise roman-tically involved with whites, Graham voiced disappointment. When a prominent black role model "turns out to be married to a white mate," he wrote, "our children say, 'Well, if it's so good to be black, why do all my role models date and marry whites?' . . . As a child growing up in the 'black is beautiful' 1970s, I remember asking these questions."

Anticipating the objection that his views amount to "reverse racism," no less an evil than anti-black bigotry, Graham wrote that his aim was neither keeping the races separate nor assigning superiority to one over the other. Rather, he wanted to develop "solutions for the loss of black mentors and role models at a time when the black community is over-run with crime, drug use, a high dropout rate, and a sense that any black who hopes to find . . . career success must necessarily disassociate himself from his people with the assistance of a white spouse." He maintained, It's not the discrete decision of any one of these individuals that makes black America stand up and take notice. It is the cumulative effect of each of these personal decisions that bespeaks a frightening pattern for an increasingly impoverished and wayward black community. The cumulative effect is that the very blacks who are potential mentors and supporters of a financially and psychologically depressed black community are increasingly deserting the black community en masse, both physically and emotionally.

The Case for Amalgamation

Although Graham's view is widespread, there are blacks who not only tolerate but applaud increasing rates of interracial intimacy. The most outspoken and distinguished African-American proponent of free trade in the marital marketplace is the Harvard sociol-ogist Orlando Patterson. Patterson makes three main claims. First, he maintains that inter-racial marriage typically gives people access to valuable new advice, know-how, and social networks. "When we marry," he writes in *Rituals of Blood: Consequences of Slavery in Two American Centuries*, "we engage in an exchange of social and cultural dowries potentially far more valuable than gold-rimmed china. The cultural capital exchanged in ethnic inter-marriage is considerably greater than that within ethnic groups."

Patterson's second claim is that removing the informal racial boundaries within the marriage market would especially benefit black women—because large numbers of white men are and will increasingly become open to marrying black women, if given a chance. He notes that if only one in five nonblack men were to court black women, the pool of potential spouses available to those women would immediately double. According to Patterson, this would be good not only because it would make marriage more accessible to black women but also because larger numbers of white (and other) suitors might well fortify black women in their dealings with black men. As Patterson sees it, by forswearing nonblack suitors, many black women have senselessly put themselves at the mercy of black men, who have declined to be as accommodating as they might be in the face of greater competition.

Patterson's third claim is that widespread intermarriage is necessary to the integration of blacks into American society. He agrees with the writer Calvin Hernton that intermarriage is "the crucial test in determining when a people have completely won their way into the mainstream of any given society." In *Ordeals of Integration* he therefore urges blacks, particularly women, to renounce their objections to interracial intimacy. Higher rates of intermarriage "will complete the process of total integration as [blacks] become to other Americans not only full members of the political and moral community, but also people whom 'we' marry," he counsels. "When that happens, the goal of integration will have been fully achieved."

35   Some may question whether higher rates of interracial marriage will do as much or signify as much as Patterson contends. The history of racially divided societies elsewhere suggests that it will not. Addressing "the uncertain legacy of miscegenation," Professor Anthony W. Marx, of Columbia University, writes that despite considerable race mixing in Brazil, and that country's formal repudiation of racism, Brazil nonetheless retains "an informal racial order that [discriminates] against 'blacks and browns.'" Contrary to optimistic projections, Brazil's multiracialism did not so much produce upward mobility for dark Brazilians as reinforce a myth of mobility. That myth has undergirded a pigmentocracy that continues to privilege whiteness. A similar outcome is possible in the United States. Various peoples of color—Latinos, Asian-Americans, Native Americans, and light-skinned African-Americans—could well intermarry with whites in increasingly large numbers and join with them in a de facto alliance against darker-skinned blacks, who might remain racial outcasts even in a more racially mixed society.

Historically, though, at least in the United States, openness to interracial marriage has been a good barometer of racial enlightenment in thought and practice. As a general rule, those persons most welcoming of interracial marriage (and other intimate interracial associations) are also those who have most determinedly embraced racial justice, a healthy respect for individualistic pluralism, and a belief in the essential oneness of humanity.

Randall Kennedy is a professor at Harvard Law School. He is the author of *Nigger* (2002) and *Interracial Intimacies: Sex, Marriage, Identity, and Adoption* (2003).

Ursula M. Brown

Three Case Studies: Matthew, Sidney, and Claudette

The Interracial Experience: Growing Up Black/White, Racially Mixed in the United States, 2001

A journey into the world of three interracial people will offer the reader a glimpse into the lives, struggles, frustrations, and joys of biracial people. Psychosocial issues that are unique to them will be highlighted. In addition, experiences that influenced their adjustment will be addressed. Their accounts will demonstrate that the path toward a racial identity in mixed-race people does not necessarily lead to blackness, as is commonly assumed, but may defy social convention. The three interracial people presented here do not represent all black/white interracial people. Rather, their dilemmas and their resolutions constitute key patterns that were repeated in the lives of the 119 people I interviewed while researching the book.

Matthew: Toward a Black Identity

Matthew was twenty-two years old when I met him. He had just graduated from college and had returned to New York City where he grew up and wanted to settle. Matthew had a medium-brown complexion, and despite having facial features and curly hair suggesting white roots, he embraced a strong black identity. Over the phone he had asked to meet me at his favorite downtown jazz club. My concerns about acoustical problems were alleviated as we entered the club and were met by the beautiful and mellow sounds of a jazz quartet. In addition, Matthew had requested a balcony seat so that we could talk comfortably. Over a hearty evening meal, Matthew shared his experiences of growing up with a white mother and a black father.

When Matthew was young, he thought he was adopted because he looked so different from his mother. She was able not only to dispel his doubts but also to encourage him not to "limit himself to one race" and to embrace both sides of his racial heritage.

His father, a jazz musician, took a different approach. He wanted Matthew to "come to grips" with the reality that the outside world would view him as black. To accomplish this goal, he made black culture and particularly jazz an intricate part of Matthew's life. He also sent Matthew to a predominately black elementary school where the principal, a black nationalist, made sure that his students became acquainted with black history, black traditions, and the "Black Power" and "Black Pride" principles. Matthew developed a strong black identity in this environment, and he liked his teachers—particularly the principal, who became an important role model for him.

However, his sense of well-being and belonging in this mostly black social milieu became disturbed when he was seen with his white mother. Being connected to her made him stand out as different, raised questions about his authenticity as a black person, and made him vulnerable to shaming, taunts, and caustic remarks. At the same time he worried about hurting his mother's feelings and losing her love if she knew about his fears, his feelings of shame, and his wishes to hide her.

The change to a mostly all-white high school brought relief to the conflicts he experienced about his mother. However, his blackness became a source of frustration and turmoil for it presented a barrier to acceptance. The message that "black is beautiful," prominent in the black elementary school he attended, was changed to blackness is inferior and you should "act white." Upset and angry about the school's prejudices and assimilation attempts, he became increasingly defiant, and as he explained, he emerged from high school a "pretty intense Black Nationalist."

Exposure to different political, historical, and cultural viewpoints in college seemed to diminish his anger toward whites. His outlook on race and racial issues began to broaden. He dated both black and white women and did not rule out interracial marriage, but his strong black identity remained intact. He explained, "No matter who I marry, I will be who I am. If it's black, I will be black. It's white, I still would be black. In every way shape or form, I will be black." Matthew seemed at peace with who he was. His black identity was in harmony with his inner self, his physical characteristics as well as social stipulations. The identification with his black father, his **phenotype,** and his socialization in a predominately black social milieu laid the foundation for a strong black identity in adulthood.

5

Sidney: Trying to Fit In

Sidney, a petite young woman with olive-toned skin, light-brown curly hair, and the facial features of a black person, was twenty-four years old when I met her. An interracial woman I had interviewed for the purpose of this study introduced us. Sidney felt that interracial people are the "forgotten" people in this country and was pleased about the study and the prospect of participating in it. We met for the interview in a neighborhood café in Boston, where she had been working part time in the computer field.

Sidney arrived at the appointed place a few minutes late. After screening the café, she steered toward me, apologized for her lateness, and settled down. Over pastry and coffee she began talking about a rather sad and lonely life that had been shaped and dominated by racism. When she was born, her white grandparents in the South disowned her mother and told friends and relatives that their daughter had died. Sidney's mother was devastated by her parents' reaction. Her pleadings to change their minds seemed to fall on deaf ears. Only after she broke off with Sidney's father and married a white man did the rift begin to mend.

Sidney felt accepted by her stepfather, a blue-collar worker who eventually adopted her. The relationship with her mother, however, deteriorated over the years because of the mother's obvious preference for a fair-skinned half brother and sister. Whether this preference was due to some personality traits of Sidney, racial bigotry the mother had internalized within a racist society, or the mother's difficulties in coping with the societal devaluation she suffered for having a racially mixed child is not evident from Sidney's account. What is clear is that the mother was uncomfortable with her daughter's black roots. Sidney recalled, "My mother did not accept me as who I was. She wanted me to be white. I was 'good' when I acted 'white,' and 'bad' when I 'acted black.'" She interpreted her mother's communication as "black is lesser than white, black is negative, and being black is unacceptable."

10   Sidney did not know whether her biological father was dead or alive. Her mother rarely spoke of him and then mostly in derogatory terms. No efforts were made to establish contact with other black relatives or friends or to acquaint her with black culture. In a predominantly white neighborhood and school, she was subjected to teasing and racial slurs pertaining to blacks or racially mixed children. Not being exposed to interracial or black role models with whom she could identify and who could counteract the negative messages she was getting about blackness, Sidney felt little connection to blacks. Her own blackness was a source of discomfort and shame. She remembered, "My association to black people was people on welfare, dark-skinned rapists, uneducated. I did not know that there were educated blacks, so I certainly did not see being black as a positive thing."

Sidney felt tormented by conflicts and confusion about who she was racially. She wanted to be white, blend in, and feel part of her family and her white neighborhood. During her adolescent years, she became increasingly withdrawn and depressed. Her sense of being different was exacerbated when her friends began dating and she failed to be asked out throughout her high school years. Attributing her lack of suitors to her own personal deficits she recalled, "I felt very ugly and I thought that there was something deeply wrong with me." She could not wait to leave home and a community where she felt out of place, unwanted, and shamed for her blackness.

College marked the beginning of a better life. She started dating, made some friends, and began to come to grips with the fact that she would never be able to pass as white. With the acceptance of this reality, she became more interested in her black roots. For a short time, she joined the black college community. However, her hopes of finding a social, intellectual, and emotional home there failed. Her unwillingness to deny her whiteness and her white cultural orientation presented a barrier to acceptance. Finally, the racial tensions between black and white college communities made membership in both an impossible challenge. She remembered, "I really tried very hard to fit in, but the black professors saw whites as the enemy and here I had white friends and this whole white family. Also, the campus was very segregated. I would try to be friends with the black kids, but to be friends with them, you could not be friends with the white kids. It was definitely an either/or." Looking for a "safer means" to become acquainted with the black side of herself, she turned to books. While her reading seemed to help her to become less biased, her identification with blacks and pride in her own blackness failed to flourish.

After Sidney graduated from college, her energies continued to be directed at becoming comfortable with herself. Ties with her family had been severed with the exception of one sister. "She is my family," Sidney explained sadly and defiantly. Her family's and community's inability to embrace her as who she was left her angry, bitter, and deeply hurt.

Claudette: Out of the Closet

Claudette, a twenty-five-year-old college graduate with light brown skin, curly dark brown hair, and expressive eyes was in the midst of preparing her wedding to a European immigrant when I first met her. She had just moved into a new apartment and had changed her job to work in an art gallery. While she seemed consumed with the changes in her life, she readily agreed to an interview when she heard the name of the family friend who had recommended that I call her. She invited me to come to her apartment, which, as she laughingly explained, was not furnished yet but had a table and chairs "enough to hold a good conversation."

Claudette greeted me graciously at the door. After inviting me into the living room and wondering if I would join her for a light supper, she served an attractively decorated platter of smoked fish, cheeses, fresh bread, and fruits. The table setting, fresh flowers, and candles and Claudette's casual but tasteful clothing suggested her sense of style. During our meal, Claudette told me about her coming wedding. The fact that she was crossing racial and cultural boundaries with her choice of mate seemed of little significance to her. Her white Jewish father and black Christian mother had married before mixed-race marriages were legalized in 1967 and apparently had weathered successfully the various storms that confronted interracial couples at that time. Things had improved since then, Claudette felt, for interracial marriages are more common, less of a novelty, and therefore more accepted. What concerned her more, she explained, was that her children would not have to go through the identity problems she had encountered. She was pleased that interracial families were beginning to organize and fight for a socially and legally recognized interracial category, which she felt would have spared her and many others like her much anguish.

Claudette remembered considerable uncertainty about who she was while growing up. Her interracial self-perceptions, which her parents seemed to foster, had changed during grade school to a mostly white identity. She was not quite sure how this happened for she attended a private elementary school that prided itself on embracing cultural diversity. Her parents, both successful professionals, tried to instill pride in both racial heritages, by exposing her to Jewish and Christian traditions. Holidays of both sides were celebrated, and both black and white relatives were an integral part of Claudette's upbringing.

15

Despite her family's efforts, the message that white is better than black, which continues to be prevalent in this white-dominated country, seemed to increasingly affect her. In an effort to undo what she perceived as a blemish, she overcompensated with high achievements in school and as a ballet dancer. She recalled: "I was very compulsive about everything, a perfectionist and an overachiever. I wanted to be the best. I drove myself awfully hard."

It was not until her adolescence that she came to terms with the fact that she was not white. The identification with her black mother, greater emotional readiness to own both parts of her racial makeup, as well as her phenotype, which clearly showed signs of her black heritage, seemed to play an important role in her acceptance of that reality. With the resolution of her racial group membership question, Claudette began to feel more comfortable with herself and looked forward to becoming more deeply acquainted with her black roots in college. However, the racial tensions there destroyed that dream. She remembered: "Blacks sat in their little corner in the dining room and whites in theirs. It was really strange." When she declined an invitation to become a member of the Black Student Organization, refused to give up her white friends, and insisted on the recognition of her dual racial background, she started to attract negative attention with the black community. The situation deteriorated further when she failed to take the black side in a racial controversy that was debated in the student newspaper. Being viewed as a traitor in the black community made life increasingly unbearable for her. She recalled being screamed at, taunted, ridiculed, and threatened with physical violence by a few militant black students. Frightened to attend classes and eat in the dining hall, she started to withdraw to the safety of her room.

After her freshman year, Claudette transferred to a college that was more receptive to racial differences. Much happier there, she completed her college education. Growing up as an interracial person in America, however, left a bitter taste in her mouth. At the end of the interview she confided: "If I had a choice, I would live in a foreign country, probably Europe or South America. My experience has been that people celebrate racial differences in these countries, while they are condemned in America."

Tamar Jacoby

An End to Counting by Race?

Commentary, June 2001

The decennial census required by the U.S. Constitution has always been entangled with questions of race. The constitutional provision that, until passage of the Fourteenth Amendment, counted a black man as only three-fifths of a person raised problems from the beginning. But race remained a part of the government's population tally even after the Civil War. Until 1970, the Census Bureau decided people's race for them: the enumerator who knocked on the door determined it, sometimes by inquiring, sometimes with a quick look. Since then, respondents have been allowed to answer the question for themselves, picking from an ever-expanding list of racial, ethnic, and national possibilities.

Still, for all these changes, the census continued to conform in one key respect to most people's understanding of what race meant. As the instructions on the form emphasized, "Fill ONE circle for the race that the person considers himself/herself to be." Race was an exclusive category—if you were one thing, you were necessarily not something else, just as you were either male or female.

But the census forms that arrived in the nation's mailboxes in March 2000 were different. It was not that the federal government had decided race and ethnicity were no longer important. Far from it: on both the short and long versions of the questionnaire, one of the first substantive items inquired, "Is this person Spanish/Hispanic/Latino?" A second question probed more directly for race but added, by way of instruction, something truly novel: "Mark one or *more*" (emphasis added). Still more surprising, some seven million Americans did just that, refusing to describe themselves as only white, black, Asian, Latino, Korean, Samoan, or one of the other categories listed.

Though the number of those who indicated more than one race was seemingly insignificant—less than 3 percent of the population—their action was nothing short of momentous, and may well herald the beginning of the end of racial classifications as we know them.

The change in the 2000 census form was no bureaucratic accident, but rather the   5
product of a long, bitter political battle. In the early 1990s, a small group of interracial families began to lobby the government on behalf of their children, who, they maintained, should be able to describe themselves as "multiracial" on the census. A grassroots parents' movement made its case on websites and in special-interest magazines, arguing that young people should not be forced to choose between the identities of their mothers and their fathers. In 1993, this group convinced the Office of Management and Budget (OMB), which determines the racial categories used by the federal government, to open an inquiry into the idea of putting a mixed-race box on the census form.

The civil-rights establishment immediately mobilized to fight back. Organizations like the NAACP, the National Urban League, and the National Council of La Raza recognized the threat such a mixed-race box would pose to the classifications that justify their existence: after all, every dark-skinned child registered in this category would shrink the government's official count of blacks or Latinos or American Indians, eventually reducing the political influence of the organizations claiming to represent these groups. For the better part of the '90s, minority activists and their allies in the federal government mounted an unstinting effort to block any change in the census form.

In 1997, the racial advocates appeared to prevail. After four years of study and angry public debate, OMB decided against allowing the Census Bureau to include the category of "multiracial" or "mixed race." Only as an afterthought did OMB announce that the census would permit respondents to check more than one racial box. And the agency eventually decided that, for official purposes, those who checked both white and a minority category would be counted simply as members of that minority.

Together, these decisions seemed to spell certain defeat for the mixed-race families. Just to make sure, in the months before the census, the civil-rights establishment spent millions of dollars on advertising urging blacks, Latinos, and American Indians to check only one box, counting themselves as one and only one race.

Nevertheless, Americans of mixed heritage were not deterred. People of every color and from every region and age group checked more than one box: 5 percent of blacks, 6 percent of Hispanics, 14 percent of Asians, 40 percent of American Indians. In New York City and other areas heavily populated by immigrants, the proportion ran as high as one in four. Most tellingly for the future, people under the age of eighteen were twice as likely as their elders to identify themselves as multiracial.

10   The significance of these figures was apparent from the moment they were released—if only, at first, in the chaos they created. The Census Bureau's racial percentages now added up to well over 100. Journalists and the social scientists they looked to for elucidation could not compare the 2000 census to the 1990 count or any that came before it. In short order, Americans found they no longer had clear-cut answers to the simplest questions about who we are as a nation.

How many blacks are there in the United States today? If one counts only the people who checked black alone, the answer is 34.7 million. But if one includes those who checked both black and something else, the number rises to 36.4 million. Are blacks still the country's largest minority group, or do Latinos now outnumber them? It depends whether one includes those extra 1.7 million: yes if one does, no if one does not.

Even more confusing is what happened to the tally of American Indians. If one counts only the people who checked American Indian alone, there are 2.5 million. But add in those whites and blacks who think they have a little Indian blood—and who, prompted by pride or whim, took the trouble to say so on their census forms—and the number jumps to an astonishing 4.1 million, an increase of nearly 65 percent.

What accounts for this shift in how Americans are choosing to identify themselves racially? At the center of it, plainly, are mixed-race couples and their children—fruit of the unprecedented rise in intermarriage in recent decades. Even excluding Latinos, who are among the most likely to marry outside their group—but whom the government does not recognize as a race—marriages between whites and non-whites grew tenfold between 1960 and 1990. Among third-generation Latinos and Asians, intermarriage rates now exceed 50 percent, and in California, more mixed-race children than black children are already being born every year.

But intermarriage is not the only factor at work. Latino immigrants, most of whom come from heavily mixed-race countries, are often baffled by the rigid racial categories they discover in the U.S., and are among the Americans most likely to identify themselves as belonging to more than one group. The Census Bureau's illogical insistence on asking a separate question about Hispanic identity—another concession to civil-rights advocates anxious to maintain their group's official numbers—reveals even more starkly than the form otherwise would just how many Latinos consider themselves multiracial. Last year, 48 percent of those who identified themselves as Hispanic also checked white, 2 percent also checked black, 6 percent checked two or more additional boxes, and 42 percent marked "other" (probably a way of suggesting that they equate their race with their ethnicity). Altogether, that makes well over half who identified themselves both as Hispanic and as members of some other group conventionally recognized as a race.

15   What is more, as demonstrated most dramatically by the tally of American Indians, many of those declaring two or more backgrounds were not the children of recent mixed marriages at all. Some had simply decided that their blended ancestry, however remote, was important enough to them to be mentioned. Still others undoubtedly saw the new options on the census in a more radical light: a chance to stage a small, private revolt against the yoke of race by declaring at last that the monolithic categories long used to define them did not capture the reality of who they were.

The response to the 2000 census is hardly the first indication in the history of America or the modern world that human reality is too varied and fluid to be shoehorned into racial categories. In the 19th century, the U.S. census classified people with both black and white ancestors as mulattos, quadroons, and octoroons; but even at a time when interracial marriage was strictly prohibited, these labels soon became odious and absurd. South African apartheid considered a man black if he could not pull a comb through his tightly curled hair. The Nazis had their tests; white Southerners in the Jim Crow era had other tests. The classifications that resulted were always arbitrary and artificial, and in almost every context—when they did not lead to genocide—they eventually collapsed of their own weight.

Nor are the results of the 2000 census the only indication that Americans are tiring of rigid racial categories. While both history and politics argue that race is an immutable characteristic, social scientists find that ordinary people often do not feel this is the case. A recent survey by researchers at the University of Michigan asked teenagers to fill out a form about race at school, then had interviewers put the same questions to them at home, usually in the presence of their parents. On the form, twice as many indicated they were multiracial as said so when they were asked in person.

Recent trends in popular culture—from white teenagers' fascination with rap to the popularity of mixed-race celebrities like Tiger Woods and Mariah Carey—make a mockery of racial categories. So do soaring rates of interracial friendship and dating. This is no fringe phenomenon: according to one recent survey, more than 60 percent of American teenagers have dated someone of another color or ethnic group. And a USA Today/CNN/Gallup poll conducted in March found that 64 percent of the public—and 75 percent of those under eighteen—thought it was "good for the country" to have more Americans "think of themselves as multiracial rather than belonging to a single race."

None of this means that race and ethnicity are dead or dying in America. Blacks, whites, Latinos, and Asians are not, in the foreseeable future, going to "melt" into one large, uniform brown race. In practice, even the children of intermarriage make ethnic choices. More often than not, they choose one side of the family over another; and often, several generations later, their descendants are still celebrating the heritage they have chosen. Nevertheless, the solidity of these categories, and their significance for individuals, are plainly changing.

For some people, race remains the most important aspect of their identity. But for others, it is more like a hobby, what sociologists call "symbolic ethnicity." For intermarried Asians and Latinos, and even for some blacks, it can be a voluntary thing. For many Americans, it is a matter not of essence but of choices—about belonging, loyalty, cultural affinity, and the relative weight they assign to ethnic identity. The syndicated columnist Clarence Page, who is black, has characterized this complexity with a vivid metaphor. Race is real enough, he suggests, but also like Jell-O: too slippery and elusive to grab by the handful.

Thanks to the 2000 census, it is likely to become only more so, causing ever-widening ripples of dismay among racial advocates and their allies in government. Consider the confusion spawned by the greatly increased number of people who identified themselves as American Indian. Officials are well aware that this count is an artifact of the new form: no one thinks the largely static Indian population really grew by 65 percent in just ten years. Nevertheless, for official purposes, even those who marked Indian and something else are to be counted as Indians. Does this mean that the federal government is now obligated to increase the services it provides for Native Americans by 65 percent—despite the fact that most of the 1.6 million "new" Indians live nowhere near a reservation and do not formally belong to any tribe? On reflection, even Washington must recognize that this would make no sense.

This may be an extreme example, but it is a taste of things to come. American government spends more than $185 billion a year on special provisions for minorities, and all sorts of public goods are handed out according to racial percentages. Legislative districts, municipal contracts, slots at prestigious universities, government jobs, antipoverty benefits—name the public benefit, and we divide it up by race.

But how can this continue if we can no longer count reliably by race—as race itself is revealed as a largely artificial or voluntary construct? The policy most clearly at risk is affirmative action. How is a city or state to set aside some proportionate number of jobs for minority contractors if it cannot determine the number of minority contractors in the population? So too with racial gerrymandering. How will a state legislature go about creating, say, a majority Latino district if it cannot specify who is Latino and who is not? And how can that be determined when some people say they are Latino in one context but not in another? What about those who are half-Latino, or one-quarter, or who merely happen to have a Spanish surname?

Nor will it be any easier to use racial accounting as a tool to detect discrimination. Though the concept of "disparate impact" has been much challenged, and rightly so, demonstrating that a particular policy has such an effect remains the most common way to allege discrimination and build a case for racial redress. But what will happen when prosecutors can no longer show disparate impact—when they can no longer compare, for example, the number of Latino drivers being stopped and arrested on the New Jersey Turnpike with the number of Latinos who use that highway? Surely we would not want the courts to resort to the same criterion used by offending state troopers—namely, whether a driver "looks" Hispanic.

25   If a new multiracial or "mestizo" order is emerging in the United States—and, in the wake of the census, more and more people are acknowledging that such a transformation is under way—a large, troubling question remains: will blacks be part of it?

For those who fear the answer is no, exhibit A is history: the long and often ugly experience of blacks in America and the consequences, psychological and other, that it continues to spawn. Prejudice may also play some part: despite an encouraging abatement of bigotry, many whites continue to view blacks in a less positive light than they view new immigrants, whatever their color or nationality. Then there is black poverty—the persistence of a small but intractable black underclass—that no notion of voluntary ethnicity seems likely to dispel. But perhaps the greatest obstacle of all is the angry, separatist attitudes so prevalent in much of black America, both poor and middle-class. That doing well in school is "acting white," that the only way to be manly is to be ruthlessly predatory, that to cooperate with "the system" is to betray one's origins: it is not difficult to see how this oppositional culture might prevent any significant softening of the hard outlines of racial identity among many blacks.

Still, troubling as these concerns are, there are also signs pointing in a different direction. It is true, for example, that blacks marry outside their group far less frequently than Latinos and Asians; but the rate at which they are doing so has grown significantly over the last generation. In 1960, fewer than 1 percent of married black men had non-black wives; today the figure is more than fifteen times higher. Even more dramatic is the number of black-white interracial births, which, according to one estimate, more than tripled in the 1990's. And given the way attitudes are shifting, particularly in places like California where the racial and immigrant mix is most pronounced, this trend can only accelerate.

Nor is this the only sign that blacks too may be on the cusp of a new and looser racial understanding. In fact, the 2000 census suggests that blacks may be among the Americans most eager for a change in that direction. Not only were blacks under eighteen far more inclined than their elders to mark more than one racial box, but young blacks were twice as likely to do so as other young people: astonishingly, nearly one in 10 of them chose this option. Equally telling in this regard is the USA Today/CNN/Gallup poll, which found that blacks approved of the new easing of racial lines no less heartily than whites did.

Certainly the black-white color line is going to be harder to cross or blur than other racial and ethnic boundaries. When it comes to race, what other people think you are often matters as much as, if not more than, what you think. And blacks who checked more than one box on the census may be ignoring the political reality of the world around them—a reality shaped as much these days by the civil-rights establishment as by lingering white prejudice. Still, by making their choices known, multiracial Americans have taken a big step toward changing that reality.

It will not do—and it helps no one—to be Pollyana-ish. Obscuring or blurring the lines among groups will hardly solve all problems of race and ethnicity. It will not tell Americans how to negotiate their differences with one another, or how far to go in developing their identities. Nor will it answer the increasingly pressing question of what ideals and purposes we share as a nation. But it might help us to do something almost as important: to separate the realm where race and ethnicity matter, and should matter, from the realm where they do not, if only because they cannot.

An age-old American formula that has long worked for white ethnics, if not for blacks, distinguishes the role race and ethnicity play in the public sphere from the part they can and should play in our private lives, at home, and in our neighborhoods. Our long-held ideals argue that the public realm must be race-neutral, while in private, race and ethnicity may be fostered, celebrated—or ignored, as individuals choose. This is hardly a foolproof formula, but in a nation composed of a multitude of groups it is a necessary one. And the beauty of it today, given the way Americans' feelings about race are changing, is that it need not be arbitrarily imposed or enforced from above.

On the contrary, as the 2000 census suggests, the line has begun to draw itself naturally. The more Americans realize that ethnic and even racial identification can be a matter of personal choice, the fuzzier such categories will grow—and, one can only hope, the harder it will be for government to traffic in them.

Beverly Yuen Thompson

Memories from a Mixed Childhood

Iris: A Journal about Women, Spring 2002

My parents tell me that at age two and a half, I ran around the house shouting "I'm an American, I'll speak English!" I rejected my mother's heritage in vicious outbursts as she told me bedtime stories about "long loy lew" and used picture flash cards with words on them I could only pronounce haltingly. I had no desire to learn a language that would set me apart from my school peers. Without speaking Chinese, my whiteness would have more validity. My mother doesn't appear ashamed when she reminds me of the story— instead she smiles and teases me in a good-natured way. My father tisks, "It's a shame you didn't learn Chinese." His face is not illuminated with pride by his "daddy's girl," the daughter who desired to become him, a white American. In those moments, I want him to explain the mystery to me: How did I learn at two-and-a-half that to speak anything other than English would make me less than "American"?

Even with my narrow views on language as a child, I always secretly delighted in my mother's linguistic ability during our trips to Seattle, where we could eat in Chinatown, despite my father's grumbling resistance. At those moments I would soak up all the names of the dim sum dishes and ask the waiter for "my daan" to my mother's beaming delight. The waiters always looked at me, turned to my mother, and asked, "Can she speak Chinese?" Shaking her head, the waiters would chastise her deficiencies in motherhood. During these moments, the potential of a bilingual existence would send a thrill of excitement through me: Oh the doors that it would open. Upon return to Spokane, these thoughts faded; there were few bilingual people in my hometown to remind me of this distant desire.

Only in Seattle's Chinatown could my mother culturally relax, surrounded by her native cuisine and language. On these trips there was not any negotiation, compromise or discussion about food selection. Her taste buds came back to life after the months, years, of consuming Americanized Chinese food on the Spokane boulevards where the only Chinese people present were the owners. She would stock up on Chinese cooking supplies, pulling me behind her through the maze of cluttered store aisles, arguing in loud, colorful Chinese, like someone preparing for a drought. My father would follow along in defeat, protesting against the women leading him around in unfamiliar territory. He verbalized his longing for his comfort food, his safe ground. He wanted to eat at McDonald's. "You can eat at McDonald's anywhere. How often do I get to have yum cha?" Indeed, this was perhaps the only place in the entire state of Washington where one could savor the delicious dim sum.

But my father understood the important role of food in cultural imperialism, even in the microcosm of our family. Rarely did my mother cook Chinese food in our home, but rather, she cooked his favorite dishes. When she would place steaming noodle soup in front of him with a ceramic Chinese spoon sticking out of the bowl, he would jump up and throw the spoon in the sink, walk over to the cabinet, pull out a thin metal spoon and chastise her, "I want my Army general spoon with the stripes, not that clunker."

5 Occasionally, my aunt would stop by with her children and fill the house with loud guttural Chinese that would scare my father off to the basement. I was impressed that my younger cousins could understand what our mothers were discussing, yet they also rejected the language and would only reply in English. My aunt was much more insistent with them. She would continue in Chinese; they would retort with English. My mother would slowly recount the conversation between herself and her sister after my aunt had left the house. My father would become enraged and shout out, "I'm going to impose a new rule: Only English spoken in this household! Your sister can tell me what she thinks to my face in English, not in her secret Chinese."

Perhaps if I had learned Chinese, my father's patriarchy within our home would have been undermined—something he would not tolerate. I imagine the power shift that would have come from my mother and me having our own secret language. My father can pity the lost opportunity, but had it not been lost, it certainly would have created tension.

The truth is, my parents rarely spent time analyzing their own racial situation. When I asked my father to be interviewed by a journalist on cross-racial relationships, he didn't know what to say except, "Well, I've never thought about your mother and me that way. I wouldn't know what to say." He never thought deeply about his racial privilege and the consequent effects on his life. Occasionally, he would admit that, because of her non-white ethnicity, my mother had it rough applying for jobs in Spokane. Yet he would never admit that he had it easy because of his race and gender. The doors to professional accomplishment were thrown wide open to him. My mother's race denied her entry into many professions where she could have succeeded. Even as my father was lulled into racial unconsciousness by the glare of his white skin, my mother's struggle was a shocking counterpoint to his theories of level playing fields. Accustomed to blaming the victim for not trying hard enough and not succeeding, he had to admit that something was awry—my mother tried harder than anyone did.

I started wondering what race I was when I had to fill out the ethnicity question on the school forms. I asked my father about this dilemma and he raised his eyebrows in hesitation and answered, "I don't know, I guess you could put one or the other." Indeed, "one or the other" was the answer that the form attempted to draw forth. But which one? Which one? How could I choose between identifying with my mother over my father, my father over my mother? I asked my mother for a solution. She would smile absently and respond, "Why, you are Amerasian." Yet Amerasian was not an option on the simplistic forms that categorize people into artificial boxes. My parents never defined me racially. They never gave me a ready made, self-descriptive term that I could wear like a badge.

So, I was ill-prepared when I was sixteen and attended summer school in Seattle, along with one hundred international students from Asia and four American white girls. It was the first time that I was around Asians almost exclusively, and I felt extremely isolated. I was terrified that they would all speak the same language and I would be left mute. The white girls looked at me as if I was a foreigner. They commented with surprise on my knowledge of baseball during an outing at a Mariners game—I had been explaining the rules to my Chinese comrades. It was the first time the white girls reconsidered their notion of me as they thought, How does she know so much about baseball? It was also the first time they talked to me. Once they realized that I was from Washington State just like them, and only spoke English, they became more sociable. But I had been confused by their reaction: Baseball had been my passion, how could the white girls make such a mistake?

When racist things happened to me outside my home, I rarely told my father who couldn't understand. Like the time when I ran into an old white woman in an elevator at the hospital and she asked, "Where are you from?" My father merely chuckled and said, "Little did she know you were born in that building. She thought you were from China!" Or the time when I was helping a visiting professor from China find housing. I spoke on the phone with the white woman who was renting the room, and explained that I was a student assisting a visiting professor. The white woman fetishized all things Chinese—she had been to China and loved it, and she loved to see how truly different those Chinese people were. When Ji Min and I arrived at the woman's door, she threw it open and exclaimed with frustration, "Well, which one of you is from China!" She spoke with such a sense of entitlement, as if she were offended by such trickery.

Often these encounters with racism were, and still are, completely intertwined with gender and sexuality. White men use my race as a sexual pick-up; they attempt to pry me open and scrutinize my level of exoticness. They feel entitled to enter my space, rest a hand on my skin, and ask personal questions about my identity. All of these incidents have

10

added up and contribute to my stockpile of ready-made verbal comebacks. It leaves me entering the world with a strong shield of defensiveness. Constantly, I am put on guard as I protect myself from all the jeers, racial comments, stereotypes, and jokes. "Is your name Me Ling?" "Oh, konitchiwa, you speak English?" "Where you from? No, I mean, where are you really from—like, where are your parents from?" "You know—what are you?" Over the last few years I have shot back angry retorts, no longer willing to be patient with racists as they attempt to pigeonhole me. If they are allowed to ask my race, I am allowed to answer in any way I choose, including with silence or anger. Why are they compelled to question my race in order to relate to me?

I am no longer willing to hide, nor to ignore or forget these comments. The questioner is often utterly shocked that I should be offended! After all, they were just curious, they didn't mean anything, they really think it's cool, and so on. Yet these questions stem from a deep-rooted obsession with race, fueled by racism and white supremacy. We cannot ignore the history of this country, and how that shapes every racial encounter. Not only are they shocked that I should be offended by their racial inquisition, but it counters their stereotyped expectations. They think I'll giggle at their question, or be flattered at the racial attention from a white man. When I respond with curt anger and disapproval to their questions, they are utterly flabbergasted. I'm not some sweet little Asian girl after all.

I initiated a serious study of mixed race issues while attending graduate school. Being in a Women's Studies program, I was encouraged to explore many aspects of identity. It was the first time I discovered books on this topic, and I was surprised. I joined mixed race groups and attended conferences in which I was among hundreds of people like me. My story was similar to so many—and this was quite a comfort. I met people who had also rejected their mother's native language, who faltered over the racial question on forms, even those with familial tensions like mine. And I met people who celebrated their dual heritage, who learned about all their cultures, and who were proud of their identity. It was the first time I began to write about myself, with a voice rooted in identity.

I realized that no matter how much I rejected my ethnic background, it would nonetheless mark my existence within this country. I learned a great deal about U.S. history from the perspective of Asian American struggles and interracial contact over the last hundred years. For example, the Supreme Court decision that ended anti-miscegenation laws occurred ten years previous to my parents' marriage. Just ten years earlier and their marriage may have been illegal! My father was largely shaped by the national events that transpired since his birth in 1926—events that created his perspectives on race and nationalism. During WWII he sat in a graduate class in the Midwest and was surprised that his Japanese teacher wasn't interned. Such historical events crafted perspectives he holds to this day.

15   Writing about my mixed race identity has contributed a great deal to my personal growth. I am grounded in a firm knowledge of my history and am no longer ashamed of my ethnic background. Now I realize the asset of speaking Chinese. Having moved to New York City I live in Chinatown—in the same apartment where my mother lived when she first came to the United States thirty years earlier.

Cantonese surrounds me as I walk down the street in my neighborhood, and I can recognize the few words that my mother taught me. Yet when the waiters speak to me in Chinese, I respond in English. If my mother were there, they would turn to her and ask, "Can she speak Chinese?" My mother would be compelled to shake her head and receive another lecture in her deficiencies. Yet the distant familiarity of the language surprises me, and perhaps it is never too late. Just last week I called my mom on the telephone to ask for a few more words to learn. I teased her that she'd be surprised to know I've passed for Chinese three times already, by responding in Cantonese to my neighbors in the building.

The Pain of a Divided Family

Scott Minerbrook

U.S. News & Word Report, December 25, 1990

No race war is worse than one inside a single family. This is one man's story of what he learned as he tried to heal his own racial wounds.

Mine is the intermingled blood of resourceful Africans, of Choctaw Indian survivors, of Scotch-Irish sharecroppers, of a stray Hollander, of a French porteur who worked the Mississippi and settled down with a Cherokee woman, a veteran of the Trail of Tears. Brave stories all, but this is America, and knowing the rules of racial conduct, I know that if my black and white relatives were gathered in a room, it would not be a happy meeting. Soon the white ones would begin calling the darker ones names, and there would be a little race war.

Because my father is black and my mother is white, to my mother's half of the family, I do not exist. In their world, the horror of a black man marrying a white woman runs fearfully deep. Every generation invents its own racial dilemmas, but the drama doesn't change. This to me is the meaning of America's racial divide.

If you are born to a family like mine, you learn race manners very early. You learn that your life will be valued and governed by rules fundamentally different from those that shape the lives of your white relatives, because your skin is darker, your lips fuller, your hair a different texture. To me, race corrupts the meaning of the word family. And if my white relatives have killed me off in their hearts, I have tried to kill them off no less in mine.

Exiled. When I was born, in 1951, interracial marriages were illegal in most states. Missouri's laws were probably unnecessary, backed as they were by an unwritten social code against "race mixing." When my parents were married in 1949, after they met as students in Chicago, she became an exile. Fearing social disgrace in the Bible-belt town of Caruthersville, her family treated her as one already dead. Always braver than her three siblings, she bore this with courage. But my understanding of family begins with the fact that may grandfather, who is still alive, stopped communicating with his daughter. I have never met him, my white cousins, nieces, nephews.

I met my grandmother, Ocieola, once—in 1967, the month the U.S. Supreme Court voided state bans on interracial marriage. When she came to our Connecticut home, I hoped the racial divide would close at last. But there were quarrels, and Ocieola left after one day. In memory, I see her cool, gray eyes, hear the lilt of her voice. In that brief meeting, Ocieola became real, my flesh and blood. But I knew that since I could never be white she would never open her life to me. She became, on a conscious level, "that racist," not "my grandmother."

About two years ago, my older brother tried to get in touch with Ocieola. To prepare for his trip, my mother sent pictures of me and my two sons—her great-grandchildren. Months passed. Finally, Ocieola returned the envelope unopened, and wrote to my brother: "Don't come. We are just too prejudiced." My brother abandoned his plans.

Nobody hates like the rejected, and Ocieola's letter tore open angry wounds. In some ways, I believe I have felt the injustice of race hate more keenly than my black friends, because of them, racism didn't reside inside the family. But racism has kept half my family from me. It turned me against myself and made me distrust white people.

I decided this war must end. I would visit Ocieola myself. "You're in for a world of pain," my mother warned. But I longed to be free of the hatred. I didn't want it to poison my own children. I would tell Ocieola, now 83, that I was willing to let go of the past. I would tell her of my family, my career, my brothers. I would bring pictures to leave by her bedside. I felt sorry for Ocieola. Her rules didn't allow her to acknowledge her own kin. She was a prisoner of race.

10   I called Ocieola and told her about my plan. She was horrified. "I want to keep things just as they are," she protested. Her daughter, my Aunt Mary, was even more pointed. "Please don't come," she pleaded. "We have to live here. Your visit would serve no purpose."

The quickest way to Caruthersville, Mo., is a plane to Memphis and then a 90-minute drive. Locked in the "boot heel" of Missouri, Caruthersville had always seemed an allegory to me, some place of my mother's invention. Driving along the interstate, I remembered my mother's warning: "They carry guns." As I drove through downtown, I saw a large mural depicting black field hands in antebellum garb, picking cotton under the watchful eyes of an overseer. And in a restaurant the local farmers watched me. "Neeger, ain't he?" said one. "Yep," said another. "Neeger, all right." I looked over and saw eight men. I decided to forgo the meal.

From a phone booth 100 yards away from Ocieola's nursing home, I called to let her know I had arrived. She seemed quite calm. "You can't come here," she said. "I don't want to see you and besides, I've got company." I felt giddy, then very tired. "I've come a long way," I said. "I'd like to see you." "I'm sorry," Ocieola said, and hung up.

At home I have a picture of Ocieola among the photographs of my elegant black Chicago relatives. The picture shows her with her children, the ones who are afraid to speak my name because of my color. Getting home, I had a powerful urge to burn that picture. So far, I have resisted. I want my children to know that these are the faces of people who are paralyzed by their hate, prisoners of the past. In making my trip, I feel I let go of much grief and rage that were poisoning me. I tell my children, these are my relatives. It would be foolish to believe you can get rid of your relatives so easily.

Reported by Ann Blackman,
Wendy Cole, Michele Donley,
Timothy Roche, Megan Rutherford,
and Jacqueline Savaiano

Multi-Colored Families: Racially Mixed Households Face Their Own Challenges

Time, May 3, 1999

From the day Karen Katz brought her infant daughter Lena home, there was a certain question she knew was coming. It finally came when Lena was four; she turned to her mother and asked, "Mommy, how come I'm not the same color as you?" Her heart stopped. Then Katz, who is white, explained to her cinnamon-skinned, Guatemalan-born daughter that they came from different countries. Over the years, Katz and her husband

Gary Richards have consciously worked to minimize the distance between themselves and their daughter: taking a trip to Mexico to surround Lena, now eight, with people who look like her and choosing to live in a polyglot Manhattan neighborhood where she blends in easily. Nonetheless, Lena sometimes seems to reject her dark skin, crying over her inability to match her parents. But recently she's begun to explain proudly to strangers her adopted status. "Which isn't to say we're home free now," says Katz. "It's an ongoing conversation."

Dialogues about difference are going on in an increasing number of American households that have been made multiracial through either intermarriage or transracial adoption. The Census Bureau estimates that there are more than 1.3 million interracial marriages. Nearly a third of the children adopted from the public foster-care system are placed with families of a different race. And in the past decade, the number of children adopted from China, for example, has jumped from less than 200 to more than 4,000. You see it even in Hollywood, where Steven Spielberg, Tom Cruise and Michelle Pfeiffer are parents of adopted nonwhite children.

And like Katz, more and more parents are wrangling with tough questions: how to handle the external aspects—the stares, comments and other public behaviors that arise when families look different—and perhaps more important, how to handle the internal— the need to affirm the family bond while helping a child craft a strong racial sense of self.

Dealing with Insensitivity

The spectrum of multiracial families is broad but embraces some common issues. For example, parents can't be as arbitrary in their choices of neighborhoods, schools, play groups or other social situations when they have a mixed household. "For a child, it's easier to blend," says Mary Durr, an executive with the Adoption Services Information Agency in Washington. She and other experts suggest searching out racially diverse communities—much as Susan Weiss, a Chicago social worker, had to do after acknowledging the negative racial remarks to which her adopted daughters, Indian-born Cathryn, 12, and Peruvian-born Amanda, 7, were subjected in the city. The family moved to a more mixed neighborhood in Oak Park, where, says Weiss, "there are so many parents and kids that don't 'match' that no one notices."

Despite such efforts to create a comforting environment, a trip to the supermarket or McDonald's can be fraught with insensitive public behavior. People stare, children taunt, strangers ask rude questions. To be constantly asked, "Are you just the baby-sitter?" or "Do they look like their father?" can be trying, say those who have endured such questioning. "Some days I want to scream out . . . 'Leave us alone. My life is none of your business!'" rages Chicago drama teacher Jennifer Viets in "The Coffee Man and the Milk Maid," a monologue about being the white mother of three biracial children. In most cases screaming is the worst response, since it sends a message of anger and tension to the child. Calm, assured answers ("We're blessed to be an adoptive family," "My husband is Chinese") disarm loaded questions and offer examples of coping behavior. "I had to model appropriate behavior and give answers I hope my children would use," says Nancy G. Brown, co-founder of Multiracial Americans of Southern California (MASC) and mother of Nicole and Rachelle, two biracial black-and-white girls. Her daughters, now teenagers, handle questions with aplomb and simple, swift replies.

Harder to handle than the public incidents are sticky situations among extended family and friends. Some cases are dire, like the grandparent who threatens to cease contact because of racial differences. But even the gray areas—family members who treat children differently or unwittingly make racist remarks—are tough. Limiting contact or forcing difficult conversations can be painful, but, says Faye Mandell, president of MASC, "parents must say, 'Treat them equally—or not at all.'"

But there are also grace notes, as in how time and communication can resolve dicey situations. At first Kim Felder, a California family recruiter for adoptions with one biological child, encountered what she perceived as resistance from her parents to her intention to adopt transracially. She and her husband Carl decided to go ahead with the adoption and limit contact with Kim's parents. The following day, her parents explained that they were reacting to the prejudice they had faced as Italian immigrants—an experience they didn't want for their daughter. "They weren't prejudiced—they wanted to protect us," says Felder. "Now they're our biggest supporters." The Felders ultimately adopted four kids of varying African-American, Hispanic and white backgrounds.

Having a child of a different or blended race also has a habit of shaking up racial orientations. "I lost my white privilege; I began to experience reactions from people," says Jennifer Viets. That can be difficult if there are unresolved issues. Filippo Santoro, 34, an Italian American, is married to Trayce, 36, an African American. But he grew up hearing blacks referred to in derogatory terms. Even now, he admits, "Trayce still says I'm a racist." These feelings make both parents more conscientious in the raising of biracial Philip, 2, and Lena, six months. "You find yourself," he says of his evolving handling of the race issue. Indeed, the experience of being part of a multiracial family invariably heightens awareness of racism and often inspires parents to take action. Katz, for example, has written two children's books, *Over the Moon*, on adoption, and *The Colors of Us*, on skin hues.

Drawing Your Own Boundaries

While some, such as Charles Byrd, editor of the webzine *Interracial Voice*, argue that race is a false construct, few deny that it nonetheless acts as a dividing line. Parenting a child who straddles that line means addressing not only the question of "Who am I?" but also "Where do I belong?"—an issue that parents must grapple with before they are swept away by the rapids of everyday family living. "The father and mother have to get together on what they're going to say so the child is not given two different spiels," says Clayton Majete, a lecturer at New York City's Baruch College who studies interracial families. He suggests waiting for the children to raise the issue and then taking the time to deal with it.

10   Until recently, conventional wisdom typically classified a mixed-race child as being of the same race as the minority parent. But that rule is being challenged as more interracial couples insist that their children be allowed to claim all sides of their heritage—an approach that experts think makes for a more settled, secure child.

It's an approach, however, that requires diligence on the part of the parents. Project RACE (Reclassify All Children Equally)—a campaign started by Ryan Graham, a biracial Florida teenager, and his mother Susan—has won changes in the ACT college-entrance-exam forms and some minor alterations in the U.S. Census form as well as on some local and state government forms. But most of society has not yet taken to the concept of biracial identity. Most government forms don't include a multiracial box, and it's usually up to the parent to make sure a child isn't compartmentalized. "I tell my kids that if somebody gives them a hard time about checking black and white, come get me, and I'll take care of it for them," says Edwin Darden, a Virginia father of two biracial kids who successfully pushed for a multiracial box on his school-district forms.

Parents may prefer that children embrace their full racial heritage, and it can be painful for, say, a white mother to see her biracial child choose to identify herself as black. But there are limits to parental influence, as well as immense pressure to choose sides. "One of the things we find is that in the teenage years, they stray from the teachings of their parents," says Darden, who has encountered this while running a local interracial-family support group. "It's too difficult to be different." Parents can offer their support and advice, but they should be ready to accept the child's decision on how to be classified.

Are You Ready

In the past 10 years the number of people willing to consider transracial adoptions has surged. In 1972 the National Association of Black Social Workers made waves when it declared itself vehemently opposed to transracial placements. Representatives of the association argued that minority children need parents like them in order to form a strong sense of identity. While that view is shared by many officials in the foster-care system, there are now laws in place forbidding officials to use race as a routine consideration. And proponents of transracial placement have research behind them. "The bottom line is that these children grow up healthy and with ties to their culture," says sociologist Rita Simon.

Still, even those who assist in such placements advise that would-be parents need to answer key questions. "How committed is one to making a child feel a part of a racial community as well as the family?" asks Gail Steinberg, co-director of Pact, a group that handles transracial adoptions. "Instead of looking with goo-goo eyes at an adorable child, prospective parents must raise their decision to an adult level."

It's wise, say experts, to review the decision with a transracial-adoption specialist or to get hold of information like Pact's "Insider's Guide to Transracial Adoption," which tracks the stages of interracial adoption and explains how racial identity differs over time and between races. The 420-page manual poses some self-probing questions: Are you the retiring type, or do you naturally like to stand out? Do you need groups, or are you fine with independence? If your "hard wire" traits lean toward the demure, then family life in a constant spotlight may not be a good idea. 15

Even if your heart is in the right place, there are practical hurdles to overcome. "Love is not enough," says Simon. "A child needs a sense of cultural identity and racial history." Which church to join, what mall to shop in, which dentist to frequent are choices to be examined through a new perspective. And they are especially important to children from disadvantaged minority backgrounds. "You must surround them with people who look like them so they know they are as good as they can be and know what they can do," says Felder.

Another helpful step for parents of foreign-born children is to include the customs, language and history of their birth land as part of the family tradition. While Katz waited to be allowed to take Lena home, she toured the girl's native village and took pictures to show her later. Families might also plan a trip to the child's birth country—or take advantage of summer camps sprouting up for multiracial families, at which kids are given the chance to learn more about their culture and experience life as a majority. "It's a very emotional experience," says Gail Walton, director of one such camp, Hands Around the World, in Wheeling, Ill.

Just as important as helping a child with his uniqueness is affirming his current family ties. Unlike biological families, in which a child can see resemblances and grasp a genealogical connection, families formed by adoption have to take special steps to make a child feel secure. This can range from reaching out to religious leaders and extended family in order to help reaffirm the adopted child's inclusion, to keeping a watchful eye out for unhelpful, if well-intended, teasing ("My little Mexican one"). Lyn and Arthur Dobrin of Westbury, N.Y., adopted an African-American child, Kori, as a sibling to their biological son Eric. They devised a game they called Categories, in which Daddy and Eric were boys, Mommy and Kori were girls; Mommy and Daddy were adults, Eric and Kori were kids. The point was to show that there are many facets to each person—and that race is only one of them.

As they tend to be for all families, the years of adolescence and early adulthood are the most difficult. Extra effort and understanding are needed to defend against derogatory remarks about a child's looks or race. In later teen years, it's not easy for a white parent to explain to his dark-skinned daughter why other white parents don't want their sons to date her. Amy and Brad Russell of Mount Vernon, Iowa, refuse to let any of their seven multi-ethnic adopted kids use race as a crutch. They also know the struggle will be lifelong. "I'm going to have six young black men in the house," Amy says. "I worry for their emotional and physical safety."

20   Yet if there is a thread that runs through the many stories about mixed-race families, it is the amazing resilience of the kids. As difficult as the questions about their identity may be, they swiftly find ways to right themselves and move on. That resilience should prove less necessary as they move into what is inexorably becoming the mainstream.

Writing Prompts

1. Write a three-page essay exploring the three camps that Kennedy identifies for African Americans' positions on interracial marriages: They see them as good, as a choice, and as negative. Base your response on his essay and the three case studies.

2. Write a comparison-contrast essay in which you look closely at the experiences of Minerbrook and Thompson. Who is the audience for both first-person accounts? What do you think is the purpose of each one, and based on your answers to audience and purpose, do you think Minerbrook's and Thompson's voices are appropriate in accomplishing their respective purposes?

3. Kennedy argues that just at a time when many white Americans are becoming more accepting of mixed races, opposition among black Americans is beginning. Do you think his argument is convincing? Analyze the evidence he uses to support his thesis.

4. Based on the information about adoptive families that are multiracial/multi-ethnic and families that are mixed race because their parents are different races, what kinds of similarities do you find in the two settings that are the most helpful to the children's success? What is most harmful to the children's success?

5. Much ado has been made about the change in the 2000 census form for claiming a racial identity. Using the material in the commentary by Jacoby, do you believe that it will always be necessary to identify our American citizenship by race? Or do you find Jacoby's conclusion convincing—that the fuzziness in the racial claims may make it harder for the government to use race in the ways it has historically done so?

What Is at Stake for Citizenship?

1. Do you think outspoken advocates for black causes who are married to white spouses—those who have been accused of "talking black and sleeping white"—should be judged harshly? In other words, should your private world intrude on your public business?
2. Should our government continue to count people by racial makeup?
3. Should a law dictate which race the government will assign to a person who declares a mixed racial heritage? What difference does it make? Who should be permitted to decide how a person's race will count?
4. Should people of one race be permitted to adopt children of another race? Should any restrictions or regulations come with the right to do so?
5. Some people claim that racial mixing/diversity is celebrated in other countries while in the United States it is more like a cross to bear. What does this opinion say about living in a land that boasts of freedom?

EXPANDING VOCABULARY

Horatio Alger Myth: Named in honor of a nineteenth-century American writer whose main characters all followed a similar pattern of development. All of them triumphed over adversity by working hard, which led to success. It is sometimes referred to as a "rags to riches" story.

Loving v. Commonwealth of Virginia: In June 1958 a black woman named Mildred Jeter and a white man named Richard Loving were married in Washington, D.C. They then moved to Virginia, where at the time the state's antimiscegenation statutes made it a felony punishable by one to five years in prison to marry outside one's race. The Lovings were indicted by a grand jury and sentenced to a year in jail. The sentence was then suspended for twenty-five years if the Lovings would move out of the state for those years. They returned to Washington, D.C., and in the early 1960s began a series of lawsuits asking if it was a violation of the Fourteenth Amendment to be denied a legal marriage to a person based solely on that person's race. Though the lower courts upheld the laws, the Supreme Court decided unanimously on June 12, 1967, that the antimiscegenation laws were unconstitutional.

Miscegenation: The mixing of races. Besides Virginia, fifteen other states until the mid-twentieth century had antimiscegenation statutes on the books. It was a felony to marry outside a person's race.

Phenotype: Living organisms are classified and described by observable features of structure, function, and behavior, so to describe someone by skin pigmentation, hair texture, or facial or body qualities is to determine a phenotype for that particular person.

Proposition 209: This initiative on the November 1996 ballot passed by 54 percent of California voters. Proposition 209 declared that the "state shall not discriminate against, or grant preferential treatment to, any individual or group on the basis of race, sex, color, ethnicity, or national origin in the operation of public employment, public education, or public contracting." The result was the elimination of affirmative action policies in California.

CHAPTER 6

Point of Contact: Immigration and the Changing Face of America

In Chapter 1, we began a discussion of America by exploring how and why different people came to this land. Native Americans, who were here prior to the first attempts to colonize the New World, have been in North America so long that their previous origins are less easily determined. Everyone else who is identified as an "American" is actually from someplace else that we can often identify, if only by continent. Some came for new opportunity and some came in chains, but all of our families had roots in foreign soil. While the United States is not entirely unique in its diversity—consider Canada, New Zealand, Australia, and much of the Caribbean—perhaps, the common argument goes, we are the most powerful country in the world because we have people from all parts of the world—a nation that includes the best of all humanity.

Such celebrations of our diversity, however, are most often directed at our past. We are proud to be a nation of and built by immigrants, and proud of our faraway beginnings, even if we have never been to the faraway places we claim. This notion of international citizenship is set deep into our psyches—ask people what they are, and they don't just say "American." They say, "I'm Irish on my mother's side, but my paternal grandmother was a Cherokee," or "I am African American," or "I am Chinese and French, and my husband's family is Sicilian." We mix and match the pieces of our personal histories into an individual modern identity. Underneath it all is the implied American citizenship—the only nationality that celebrates other nations.

We should not delude ourselves into thinking that all immigrants have been welcomed throughout American history and that only now are we having problems with the idea of new or different people. The Irish, the Chinese, enslaved Africans, Italians, Jews, and, of course, the Native Americans who were here first, to name just a few—many different peoples have been the target of our anti-immigration/ **xenophobic** sentiments. But much of our common identity is about a nation of individuals who took their differences and built a great nation of opportunity and freedom over the years. Most of us can agree upon that.

The moment the discussion turns to immigration *today,* however, all bets are off. Immigration—both legal and illegal—in the twenty-first century is a contentious issue, fraught with anger and disagreement on all sides. Suddenly those of us who are here now are Americans, and those who want to join us are suspect—will they use our resources to help them succeed or take advantage of our generosity? Are they coming here to learn about us, or will they even bother to learn English? Will they enrich our culture, or turn out to be terrorists who want to destroy our way of life? There are no easy answers. Although most of us feel that our ancestors had a right to come here in the past, whether that right should be available today is up for debate. More than any other issue, the future of immigration in America will shape the future of America itself.

This Point of Contact will focus on and address the following three specific clusters that relate to Immigration and the Changing Face of America:

1. The DREAM Act: Illegal Alien to College Student
2. Struggle at the Border: Two Nations with a Common Future
3. International Students: Turning Away from America?

THE DREAM ACT: ILLEGAL ALIEN TO COLLEGE STUDENT

Students protest for the DREAM Act at graduation.

The story is a simple one and all too common. Millions of illegal immigrants in this country are from Mexico, and many of them brought their children with them when they came over the border. These children grew up in America, learned English, played soccer, and went to the movies. They were just like the other students in their schools, except for one thing: They were breaking the law each day they stayed in America. As they grew up, the problem became more obvious. They didn't have social security numbers, so they couldn't legally work. When they tried to go to college, they were told they were not eligible for in-state tuition, or financial aid—making college nearly impossibleto afford.

There are those who feel that this situation, however tragic for the children of illegal immigrants, is the logical result of their parents living and working in America illegally. The parents who brought their children here illegally created this problem, not American laws or schools. To offer these children financial benefits that we reserve for citizens is to take tuition money away from other students who are not breaking the law. That is the truth of the situation. But equally true is the fact that these children did not willingly break immigration laws, and they had no voice in the matter of their coming here. Enter the "DREAM Act"—The Development, Relief and Education for Alien Minors Act—which attempts to offer illegal minors who have grown up in

America a chance at education, legal employment, and citizenship. Some say it is the only humane course to follow, while others say it rewards criminals for their perseverance against our immigration laws. The DREAM Act has widespread support, but it has yet to be voted upon in Congress.

Both interpretations of the aforementioned situation are true, but as you read these essays and consider all the facts, which truth would you take as your own? What do you think should be done, if anything, for the minor children of aliens living illegally in our country?

The Next Question

The Oregonian, September 30, 2004

Does the Dream Act extend the dream of a college education to immigrants or make it unattainable for some American students?

Legislation is pending before the U.S. Senate that would allow some illegal immigrants to live here while attending college and allow them to pay in-state tuition. The Development, Relief and Education for Alien Minors Act, known as the Dream Act, would give conditional residency to students if they have lived in the United States since before their 16th birthday, or for at least five years before the adoption of the bill. After six years, they could become permanent residents if they attended college or served in the military for two years. Under the bill, undocumented immigrant students who have been educated in the United States would be eligible for in-state tuition at public colleges and universities. Opponents of the measure say it would drain federal aid and steal the spots of students who are citizens or legal residents.

A handful of students from Portland Community College's Rock Creek campus were among supporters nationwide who participated in a fast last month in support of the bill. Should the Senate pass the Dream Act? Is it fair for youths who were brought to the United States as children, usually without their say and who consider this country home, to have a chance to attend college? Should they have access to legal residency? Or will this bill end up costing taxpayers money and limit the resources for legal students who are also struggling financially? Will this bill motivate more people to immigrate illegally?

Jennifer Mena

"Dream Act" Offers Hope for Immigrant Students

Los Angeles Times, September 19, 2004

On a good day, 20-year-old Elvia Flores feels she's making her family proud, studying in college to become a nurse while working nearly full-time to help pay her family's bills.

But in darker moments, Flores wonders if all the work and sacrifice is worth it.

Flores is an undocumented immigrant. And despite the nation's shortage of bilingual nurses, Flores will likely end up after graduation with little more than a low-paying restaurant job, because she lacks a Social Security number and a legal residency card.

Flores is one of about 65,000 undocumented students across the United States who graduates from high school each year, according to estimates by the Urban Institute, a non-profit economic and social policy research organization.

For them, a high school or college diploma doesn't guarantee a good job or more   5
money. Because as children they were brought into the country illegally, they face a life-time in the shadows.

And still Flores goes to school, hoping she can have a better life than her parents.

Like many others, Flores is hoping for passage of federal legislation that could help her achieve her goal. The Development, Relief and Education for Alien Minors Act, known as the Dream Act, would give conditional U.S. residency to students who entered the country five years or more before the bill's enactment and before they were 16 years old.

Residency would become permanent if, within six years of obtaining conditional resi-dency, the immigrant either graduates from a two-year college, studies for two years toward a bachelor's degree, serves in the U.S. armed forces for two years or performs 910 hours of volunteer community service.

Opponents of the measure say the bill would undermine immigration law; its sup-porters say it would benefit relatively few—but worthy—students.

Rallies in support of the Dream Act were held Saturday throughout the country.   10

On Sept. 13, college students accompanied by members of immigrant rights, civil rights, human rights, labor and religious organizations gathered at the University of South-ern California to begin a 12-day fast to draw attention to the bill. And last month, the Los Angeles Unified School District Board of Education voted to support the bill.

In Santa Ana, Flores said of the Dream Act, "It would change my whole life."

Entering Illegally

Elvia Flores' farming parents abandoned their small village in Mexico when they couldn't afford the tools and field hands to harvest their corn. In 1989, with her mother leading the way, 7-year-old Elvia and three of her siblings ducked into a tunnel beneath the U.S. border, scurried across the desert and hitched a ride to Orange County, where they rejoined her father, who had entered illegally before them.

Flores was enrolled in school, learned English by fifth grade and never thought much about her immigration status until friends in 11th grade got jobs. She couldn't, because she didn't have a Social Security card. But because colleges don't review citizenship sta-tus, Flores pursued higher education.

She graduated from high school and, in her second year of college, won a $1,000   15
scholarship from the college because of her above-average grades.

Flores' counselor knew she wanted to become a nurse, but because she didn't have a Social Security card, recommended instead that Flores pursue a Spanish language degree. Chasing a more career-oriented degree would be futile, the counselor hinted.

"That made me feel very low," said Flores. "I wondered was it worth it to keep going to school. What's the point?"

Her uncertainties worsened during her first year in college when her father, a $7.50-an-hour factory worker who earned most of the family's income, suffered a disabling stroke. The family bought food and medicine with a credit card, amassing $6,000 in debt.

To help the family, Flores bought a fake Social Security number and a bogus residency card and landed a job as a restaurant cashier.

20   "I feel guilty going to school," said Flores, tears filling her eyes. "My family needs the money and I'm studying and I don't even know if I will ever get a good job."

The 'Dream Act'

The Dream Act was introduced by Sens. Orrin Hatch (R-Utah) and Richard Durbin (D-Ill.) in July 2001 with 45 cosponsors from both parties. After delays in the wake of the Sept. 11 attacks, it has passed through the Judiciary Committee and is awaiting a full Senate vote.

Hatch aide Margarita Tapia said she expects Congress to pass the bill this year.

The Bush administration has not taken a stand on the act; Sen. John F. Kerry supports it. Congressional observers say the bill's passage could send a symbolic message without upsetting opponents of illegal immigration because it affects relatively few people and has no major fiscal effect.

Helping undocumented students is not without precedent. California legislation in 2001 exempted them from paying out-of-state tuition if they had attended three years of high school in California, graduated from a California school and gained admission to a state university or community college.

25   Josh Bernstein, federal legislative director for the National Immigration Law Center, an immigrant advocacy organization, said the Dream Act stalled in Congress because of doubts about immigrant rights in the wake of the Sept. 11 attacks, but he believes it will ultimately be approved.

"A lot of immigration issues are contentious. This one has not been. I guess it's because, how can you really be against these kids?" said Bernstein. The legislation "speaks to a value, that every individual should be treated on their own merits. . . . It corrects a flaw in immigration law, which is not to recognize the good works of these particular kids."

Sen. Jeff Sessions (R-Ala.) disagrees: "This legislation would provide an additional incentive for illegal immigration. If we were to pass this, it would be a statement to the world that we have no intention of enforcing immigration laws."

Adolfo Flores, Elvia's father, hopes the act is passed so his children can achieve more than he has. He did not advance beyond sixth grade and never earned more than $8 an hour.

"I've suffered and worked so my children can get ahead," said Adolfo Flores. "I don't want them to be like me. I can't even speak English. Why don't people who make laws see that we are just trying to work and get ahead?"

Her Family's Hope

30   Elvia Flores feels stressed. She hears her parents' admonishment to "salir adelante"— to get ahead.

She is the family's hope and role model for five younger siblings, two of whom are undocumented immigrants. A younger sister graduated from high school in June and is attending a local college with hopes of becoming an architect.

Her father encourages Flores and her sister to continue their schooling—even though he appreciates the money Flores earns to help pay family bills. When he taught Flores to drive so she could get to work and pick up her mother, both father and daughter were in tears. He feared she'd be caught driving without a license and be deported; she was scared of traffic.

It was a necessary risk, they decided, in order for Flores to earn a diploma. Flores' two older siblings, also undocumented, dropped out of college. One got married. The other became a security guard.

"I tell my children to prepare themselves for battle," said Adolfo Flores, wearing a straw hat that makes it seem he left Mexico only yesterday. "Not to fight but to prepare themselves for the challenges, to present themselves in this society, to speak for all of us, to get ahead and be more than I ever could."

The encouragement doesn't always sustain his daughter. One minute Elvia Flores is ebullient about helping others as a nurse. The next minute, she tearfully wonders whether the goal is attainable. Young adults in her neighborhood are similarly burdened. 35

Going to college is like saying a prayer, said Eric Leon, 22, an undocumented immigrant who came to the United States at age 6 and works in restaurants. "Are you doing it for nothing or will you get a big reward?" he said of seeking higher education. "You want to give up but you want to make sure you did what you could."

Flor Valente, 19, is so focused on her future that she holds a full-time job as a janitor—from 6 p.m. to 2:30 a.m.—while attending school during the day. "I'll feel guilty if I don't at least try," Valente said.

Such personal drive among undocumented high school students amazes Adriana Huezo, a higher education coordinator at Century High School in Santa Ana. She cautions students about what their future holds.

"For a good portion of our students, there is an immigration [status] issue. I tell them no one will stop you from going to college. But you may not be able to practice your chosen profession," Huezo said. "It can be very discouraging. Some of them let go of their dreams because of it."

A Typical Day

Because of her father's illness and her family's financial needs, Flores dropped three of her four classes in the spring, then enrolled in the college's summer session to make them up. She is now enrolled in two classes. 40

Most days, Flores goes to school midmorning and stays until nearly 3 p.m., doing homework and reading in the library.

There is nowhere to study at home. Eight family members share six beds in a one-bedroom apartment.

Driving an 18-year-old family compact car without a driver's license—which she cannot obtain without a Social Security number—Flores returns home from school for a snack, changes into her restaurant uniform and takes her mother to a sewing job and goes to her own job. Flores works until 11 p.m., picks up her mother, then returns home.

"One day, I have faith I will be one of those people in the cap and gown," she said. "Other days, I wonder if there's any point."

Nancy Mitchell

Students Speak out on Behalf of Their Undocumented Friends

Rocky Mountain News, February 15, 2005

Julieta Quinonez saw friends drop out of school at 15 and 16, frustrated because their illegal status meant college was not likely in their future.

She watched as another friend, a smart girl in the top 10 percent of their class at Denver's North High School, gave up her dream of becoming a doctor. Instead, the girl, an undocumented student, went straight to work.

"When I was filling out all my applications for college, some of my friends couldn't," said Quinonez, now a freshman at the University of Denver.

Monday, Quinonez and three other students at North High School called on state lawmakers to support a bill that would allow students illegally in the country to pay in-state tuition for state colleges and universities.

5   To qualify, students must have attended a private or public high school in Colorado for at least three years before graduating or obtaining a GED.

Students also would have to sign an affidavit stating they will apply to become a permanent resident as soon as they are eligible.

"Most students I talked to today were like, thank you for speaking for us," said North senior Juan Evangelista of his undocumented friends. "They are basically hanging by a thread if this doesn't pass."

State Rep. Val Vigil, D-Thornton, is sponsoring the bill for a third year. This year, he believes, it will win the approval of state lawmakers but could be vetoed by Gov. Bill Owens.

Owens' spokesman, Dan Hopkins, said the governor is concerned because a similar bill passed in Kansas has prompted lawsuits. In one case, some out-of-state students are challenging allowing undocumented students to pay in-state rates.

10   Now, undocumented students can attend college in Colorado but must pay out-of-state tuition, which can run triple the in-state rate. That's out of reach for many immigrant families, said Pat Salas, a veteran guidance counselor at Adams City High School in Commerce City.

Salas, like the North students, knows students who have dropped out of school or left the state to pursue their education elsewhere. States such as California and Texas allow in-state tuition for undocumented students.

"These kids are hungry for an education," she said, "they're hungry for a future."

The Colorado Commission on Higher Education estimates that 300 undocumented students are turned away from Colorado colleges each year. Carlos Valverde, whose family foundation assists students at two Denver high schools, said he received more than 30 scholarship applications from undocumented students in 2003, the foundation's first year.

Vigil said the chief objection to his bill seems to be that it will reward those who have broken the law. But he said many undocumented students came here as children.

15   "These kids have been here 13 or 14 or 15 years," he said. "Where do you want them to go? What do you want them to do?"

Kate Taylor

For These Top Students, Dreams Falter

The Oregonian, June 8, 2004

In spring 1993, Corina Valencia-Chavez was a McMinnville High School senior with good grades and the dream of going to college to become a neurologist.

That was before a college adviser explained what it meant to be undocumented: Without a Social Security number, she couldn't get government financial aid to pay for college.

State colleges don't require proof of citizenship or legal residency, but undocumented students pay thousands more a year in out-of-state tuition even if they graduate from Oregon high schools.

Valencia-Chavez—who has since become a legal resident and teaches at an elementary charter school—knows first hand the dilemma facing undocumented students graduating in Oregon this month.

The nonprofit Urban Institute, a national research organization, puts the number of   5
undocumented youths reaching graduation age in Oregon this year at between 800 and 1,000, of which 600 to 750 are Latino and have been living in the country for five years or more.

The Oregon University System estimates that 100 to 150 undocumented students would enroll in state colleges if they had access to student aid.

Elsewhere, benefits enacted in the past three years, California, New York, Texas, Utah, Illinois, Washington and Oklahoma have enacted state laws providing in-state tuition benefits to undocumented students. Similar legislation is pending in many more states.

In Oregon, opponents and supporters are struggling over the issue of affordable college education for undocumented students.

Providing federal aid to undocumented students would be "a slap in the face to the rule of law," said Jim Ludwick, president of Oregonians for Immigration Reform. "In fact, it's a slap in the face to legal immigrants."

Ludwick and other opponents argue that undocumented students threaten to soak up   10
federal aid and take up spaces that documented students should have.

Senate President Peter Courtney, D-Salem, sees it as a fairness issue.

In 2003, he proposed Senate Bill 10, which would have extended in-state tuition to students without legal residency. The bill passed the Senate, then died in the House.

"It was a basic fairness-for-kids bill, fairness for kids who've worked hard," Courtney said. "And it was blown to pieces. It had a very chilling effect on a lot of kids and a lot of hopes."

Lack of legal residency and enough money to pay out-of-state tuition can make the difference between a "motivated Latino or Latina high school student and one who is deterred," said Steffeni Mendoza Gray, executive director of the Oregon Council for Hispanic Advancement. "No child's dream should be thwarted."

Valencia-Chavez, who was born in Tijuana and came to the United States at age 15,   15
said she began dreaming of becoming a neurologist the day her brother Ulises had his first epileptic fit in front of her.

In high school in McMinnville, she found several teachers who supported her hard work and ambition. But they couldn't change a law that made it financially impossible for her to attend a four-year college.

At her high school graduation, she smiled for the camera in a red cap and gown, but she "felt sadness more than anything else," said Valencia-Chavez, sitting with her husband, Jorge Chavez, in their McMinnville home recently. "I'd always loved school, and I'd always been competitive. I wanted to go to a (four-year) college more than anything."

Many undocumented Latino students have the ambition and grades to attend college, teachers and counselors say, but can't because of financial obstacles. The students also fear—with the Homeland Security Act in effect—that registering at a school may put them at risk for deportation.

Gathered in a Portland-area high school office, four undocumented students talked with a reporter on the condition that their names not be used in this article. They said they are graduating with top honors and heavy hearts.

20   Three planned to attend community colleges, which have a less-formal application process and offer a more affordable education but which often don't offer the curriculum students need to reach career goals. The students consider the community colleges safer for people who are undocumented, even though the schools also must report students' information to federal immigration authorities.

Others planned to find the best jobs they could.

"I see all my friends, and they're talking about college and asking each other where they're going to go," said an 18-year-old girl, who has scrapped her plans to be a dentist and instead plans to take community college classes to become a dental assistant.

"I would like to say, 'I'm going to a four-year college like you guys are,' because I want to become a professional. I could, but it's not like I have those opportunities."

One graduating student with high grades said he's shelving his aspiration to become a teacher in favor of a computer programming career. Another graduating senior wept when she said she had agreed to live apart from her family with a relative just so she could go to school in this country, hoping that the payoff would be a career in psychology. But now she'll probably do something else.

25   Many undocumented students came to this country wrapped in baby blankets and don't consider returning to Mexico to study or work an option.

"Sometimes I think, where do I go?" said one graduating senior. "Here there are the opportunities, but I can't really have them. But in Mexico, with the economy—I wouldn't make it there either."

Finding employment now that they understand they can't get financial aid, they also understand that it may also be difficult to find employment. Ludwick, of Oregonians for Immigration Reform, said employers shouldn't hire people who are here illegally no matter how hard they've studied in school.

"We have a concept in this country that we expect everybody to obey the law, but this would reward people for evading the law," Ludwick said.

Counselors, teachers and some legislators call the students' situation a tragic waste.

30   "Right now I'm writing recommendations. Five (of the graduating Latino students at one high school) are state college material or better. But I can only push one," said Vickki Shelley, a counselor who works with many Latino students in the Tigard-Tualatin School District. "These are jewels of kids who don't have documentation."

A happy turn of events soon after graduation in 1993, Valencia-Chavez stopped crying and started planning. Her father had gained citizenship by proving that he was born in California in 1933 while his parents were doing railway work in this country.

Valencia-Chavez made an appointment with U.S. immigration services, hoping that her father's new citizenship could help her.

She began taking classes at Chemeketa Community College and got a job as a special education teaching assistant. For 2½ years, she worked with a student who was blind and autistic. She reveled in his breakthroughs and realized she was meant to be an educator.

After three years of waiting, the federal agency called her in 1996 and, in one afternoon, the world opened up.

"The part that I remember is toward the end, when (the interviewer) said 'So, what   35
are you going to do, what are your plans now that you have residency? The first thing I said was 'Oh! I am going to college! I am going to school!'"

Within months, she'd transferred to Western Oregon University.

She says now she was lucky and laments that so many other Latino graduates in Oregon will not have the same opportunities.

Valencia-Chavez, a new mother, said that legal residency has allowed her to have a life that is rewarding and full of hope. As a charter-school teacher with a bilingual curriculum, she works to inspire children from many different cultural backgrounds.

"It is the best job I could ever imagine," she said. "I only wish that same experience was available for all these other young people."

Nurith C. Aizenman and Amy Argetsinger
Virginia Order Decried by Immigrant Advocates; State Turning Colleges into Police, They Say

The *Washington Post*, November 16, 2002

A new directive from the Virginia attorney general's office that warns public colleges not to enroll illegal immigrants has placed the state squarely at odds with a national trend toward offering undocumented students greater access to higher education.

The September memo by Attorney General Jerry W. Kilgore (R), which also instructs Virginia's colleges to report to federal authorities any illegal immigrants they find on campus, drew fire yesterday from Latino and immigrant rights organizations.

At a news conference in Arlington, the groups said Kilgore's action unfairly penalizes foreign-born children for their parents' decision to come to the United States illegally and goes beyond any federal or state law by asking educators to act as police—potentially in violation of confidentiality policies.

Kilgore staff members countered by saying they are concerned that illegal immigrants could be taking seats at state schools that would otherwise go to U.S. citizens. They also said that since last year's terrorist attacks, all universities carry a greater responsibility to help the U.S. **Immigration and Naturalization Service** monitor foreign students.

"This is about differentiating between those who obey the law and those who willfully   5
break it," said the attorney general's spokesman, Tim Murtaugh.

Virginia's move comes as many states are taking a dramatically different approach, not only allowing illegal immigrants to enroll in public colleges but also granting them in-state tuition.

California, Texas and New York have passed laws to that effect in the last two years. Similar measures are either pending or being drafted in Maryland, North Carolina, Massachusetts, Minnesota and Utah.

And several bills in Congress, including one introduced by Sen. Orrin G. Hatch (R-Utah), would encourage other states to follow suit.

There is no specific federal prohibition against colleges and universities enrolling illegal immigrants. However, federal law places some restrictions on allowing such students to pay in-state tuition rates, and it prohibits them from receiving federal financial aid.

10   Efforts to open public colleges to undocumented students stem from a growing view among some lawmakers—vehemently rejected by others—that excluding the nation's estimated 8 million illegal immigrants from benefits such as health care and higher education only threatens the safety and economic well-being of the communities in which they live.

Since the Sept. 11, 2001, terrorist attacks, that approach has been offset by a competing impulse among many state and federal authorities to curtail illegal immigration.

Among other actions, more than a dozen states have cracked down on driver's license fraud, requiring applicants to provide more extensive proof of their identity and legal residency before issuing licenses.

Immigrant rights advocates contend that such steps merely victimize otherwise law-abiding drivers and endanger the public by preventing them from getting auto insurance.

Yesterday, critics offered similar arguments against Kilgore's directive.

15   Virginia's undocumented students "are the epitome of what we consider the American dream," said Tisha Tallman, regional counsel for the Mexican American Legal Defense and Educational Fund, which organized the news conference. "They've gone to high school here, they're hardworking and high-achieving."

In Maryland, Prince George's Community College President Ronald A. Williams has also argued that local communities have as much to gain from illegal immigrants attending college as the immigrants themselves. "They are going to need skills to become taxpayers who are not a burden on society," he said.

However, Steven Camarota, director of research at the Center for Immigration Studies, countered that expanding college benefits to illegal immigrants encourages more people to come to the United States illegally.

"It conveys to the world the message that America just isn't serious about its immigration laws," he said. "It's also a slap in the face to the people who play by the rules by waiting for their turn to immigrate in their home countries."

Immigrant rights advocates estimate that 50,000 illegal immigrants graduate from U.S. high schools every year. It is unclear how many go on to college. Although many college applications ask students if they are legal residents, the institutions rarely do background checks unless they are verifying a student's eligibility for federal assistance or in-state tuition.

20   Several higher education officials and immigration experts said there are few illegal immigrants at U.S. colleges. "Most of these kids face huge barriers in terms of language and their parents' lack of education, and their ability to afford out-of-state tuition," said Josh Bernstein, a senior policy analyst at the National Immigration Law Center.

Williams, of Prince George's Community College, said that every year a couple of hundred illegal immigrants come to register at the school's northern county office, which serves an area dominated by immigrants. But they walk out the door when they find out they will have to pay out-of-state tuition, which is three times as high as the in-county rate.

Many advocates also fear that Kilgore's directive will mainly end up affecting students who are legal immigrants, subjecting them to undue scrutiny and possibly even racial profiling.

Authorities at Virginia's public universities said that they believe they have been in compliance with state and federal law and that the Kilgore memo has not changed the way they deal with students.

Bill Walker, a spokesman for the College of William and Mary, said the memo would serve as "a reminder for us to maintain our standards."

Editorial Desk

Punishing the Innocent

Los Angeles Times, October 1, 2004

Regardless of one's stance on the rights of illegal immigrants, it's more than a little harsh to discriminate against their children. The parents may have made a decision to cross the border illegally; the kids had no choice but to go along for the ride.

Yet they are often condemned to permanent second-class status.

Every year, about 65,000 talented immigrant students who have grown up in the United States, graduate from high school and want to go to college find themselves barred from accessing state and federal financial assistance and in-state tuition rates available to their classmates. There's a solution, but it has been allowed to languish in Congress.

The Dream Act, which counts Republican Sen. Orrin G. Hatch of Utah among its sponsors, would repeal Section 505 of the 1996 Immigration Act, which requires any state that provides in-state tuition to undocumented immigrant students to provide the same tuition rate to out-of-state residents. In 2001, California, setting an example that should now expand nationwide, exempted undocumented students from paying out-of-state tuition if they had attended three years of high school in the state and were admitted to college.

The Dream Act would allow conditional U.S. residence to students who came to this country before age 16, had been accepted into a two- or four-year college, resided in the U.S. when the law was enacted and had lived here for at least five years.

This is a narrowly tailored measure that addresses one of the more unfortunate symptoms of the nation's dysfunctional approach to immigration matters. In a year when President Bush promised a sweeping overhaul of immigration laws, it is somewhat pathetic that he can't seem to get his troops on Capitol Hill to pass this bill before going home.

Letters to the *Times:* Deportation or Education?

Los Angeles Times, October 6, 2004

Re "Punishing the Innocent," editorial, Oct. 1: Thank you for recommending immediate approval of the Dream Act. As it relates to the plight of the millions of children of undocumented Latino immigrants residing in the U.S., these infants, children and teens never had the capacity to consent or dissent to the actions taken by their parents. Yet we hold them responsible and oppress them, based upon the immoral treatment afforded them under current U.S. immigration policy. Some of the brightest and most hard-working teens are not legal residents, brought here by their parents when they were young. They have grown up pledging their allegiance to our flag their whole lives, only to find rejection. They are unable to obtain a Social Security card and all of the privileges that go with it: the privilege to drive, work, get a loan, have a bank account and attend college.

> Bill and Jacki Dahl
> Irvine

For every illegal immigrant admitted to a state university, an American citizen will be rejected. Likely most illegal immigrants seeking in-state tuition at public universities aren't responsible for violating our laws, having been brought into this country illegally by their parents. But it also is true that in-state American citizens who will be rejected when illegal aliens join the queue are being punished for the actions of illegal alien parents.

> Michael Scott
> Glendora

I support the Dream Act. Our bright young undocumented students should live with dignity and hope, rather than fear deportation and face barriers to higher education. These young students are our future, and their positive efforts deserve to become a part of this society.

> Dae Yoon
> Los Angeles

Punishing the innocent? It's American taxpayers who are getting punished. *The Times* obviously feels that free K-12 education and other social services aren't enough. Now we're expected to give illegal immigrants a subsidized college education.

If these kids want to go to college, they should return to their own countries and do so. And the proponents of this bill have the audacity to call it the Dream Act. A nightmare is more like it. Anyone who is in this country illegally should be deported, not rewarded.

> Randle C. Sink
> Brea

Nina Bernstein

Immigrants Lost in the Din: Security vs. the Dream

The *New York Times*, September 20, 2004

Passersby glanced curiously at the few dozen young people rallying on the sidewalk outside the Interfaith Center of New York on Thursday, immigrant students wearing bright orange stickers saying "Ask Me Why I'm Fasting." But no one stopped to ask, and as student speakers addressed a handful of reporters; their words were often muffled by the roar of midday traffic in Midtown.

It was Day 2 of a five-day fast that organizers called a National Week of Action for Immigrants' Rights. There were protests in 70 cities around the country. But even in New York, where immigrant concerns have historically been the bread and butter of local politics, it was hard to draw attention to issues that seem, for many, to be stuck on the back burner this election year.

Many advocates cited a disconnect between convention rhetoric that prominently celebrated immigrant opportunity in America, and a darkening reality since Sept. 11, 2001. Time is also running out on several immigration bills languishing in Congress, including the most modest bipartisan measure, known as the Dream Act, which would give access to college aid to high-achieving teenagers in families of illegal immigrants.

Yet some also see a disconnect between the expansive legislative goals of national immigration organizations, which are busy lobbying for pathways to legal residency and citizenship, and a grass-roots panic over day-to-day shortcuts to criminalization: administrative policies and computer crackdowns that lead to the loss of driver's licenses, immigration arrests at traffic stops, and the detention and deportation of longtime residents who leave their children, United States citizens, behind.

The director of the New York Immigration Coalition, Margaret McHugh, said her trips   5
to Washington for immigration meetings were like trips to another world.

"Down there, it's about what are the components of a good legalization bill going to be," she said. "And here we're frantic, because every day we're seeing the de-legalization and the criminalization of so many immigrants."

Scores of community organizations participated in the week of vigils and symbolic hunger strikes, which are to culminate locally today with a community hearing in Harlem, and tomorrow in Washington with a day of lobbying. Among the most active participants are students like 18-year-old Alejandra, who would not give her last name for fear of deportation. Alejandra was 7 when her mother brought her to New York from their native Colombia, and she was valedictorian of her high school class in Queens in June, but she could not apply for government financial aid for college.

"These children are de facto Americans," contended Partha Banerjee, director of New Immigrant Community Empowerment, a group taking part in the sidewalk rallies. "But because of all the 9/11 problems, their hopes are being dashed on a daily basis."

Despite public enthusiasm for the speeches of Barack Obama and Arnold Schwarzenegger, it is a generation coming of age in a climate of growing hostility to immigration, say those who have supported amnesty programs for illegal immigrants.

In the last three years, they say, economic insecurity has converged with national   10
security concerns—and a new influx of immigrants—to revive the immigration backlash of the early 1990s.

"At one level," said Muzaffar A. Chishti, a senior policy analyst at the Migration Policy Institute, "everyone wants to appease immigrants—mainstream Republicans and mainstream Democrats—because they're seen as a very important voting bloc.

"But they don't want to do too much toward moving the ball forward, because they run into this problem of the rest of the country, the feeling of insecurity both on economic grounds and on security grounds," he said.

As the specter of job loss to foreigners angers parts of the Democratic base, immigration advocacy, too, may rely on symbols to stand in for substance. The National Week of Action, for example, was billed as the first anniversary of the Immigrant Workers Freedom Ride, modeled after the Freedom Rides for civil rights in the 1960s. But, Mr. Chishti said, black Democratic leaders acknowledge—only privately—that many of their native-born black constituents are increasingly resentful about illegal immigration.

Few leaders are discussing the hard issues that emerged from a study issued in July by the Center for Labor Studies at Northeastern University in Boston, which found that recently arrived immigrants accounted for all the employment growth in the United States since 2001. With little net job growth, employment of new immigrants, mostly from Mexico and Latin America, appears to be displacing some established immigrants and native-born workers, especially black men in central cities, the study's author, the economist Andrew Sum, concluded.

15   Even where there is political common ground, as on issues involving the police, local officials may not be in a position to call the shots. In a rally on the steps of City Hall on Friday, two members of the City Council and several immigrant organizations complained about Attorney General John Ashcroft's decision in 2002 to load thousands of civil immigration records into the national crime database, which the F.B.I. uses to notify law enforcement agencies about people wanted for crimes.

This, said the council members and advocates, had subverted Mayor Michael R. Bloomberg's Executive Order 41, which, in 2003, promised that no immigrant would be arrested by the police for illegal status alone.

By late last year, Garrison Courtney, a spokesman for United States Immigration and Customs Enforcement, reported that 317 non-citizens with immigration violations had been arrested in New York by the police using routine computer checks, out of a total of 5,092 nationwide.

Federal officials said adding immigration records to the database strengthened homeland security.

But several advocacy groups have challenged that reasoning. The National Council of La Raza, the New York Immigration Coalition, the American-Arab Anti-Discrimination Committee, the Latin American Workers Project and Unite, joined in 2003 in a class action lawsuit against the use of the criminal database for immigrant violations.

20   "The federal government is subverting the express will of the residents and mayor of New York," Monica Tarazi, the New York director of the American-Arab Anti-Discrimination Committee, contended at the City Hall rally.

One of the pending immigration bills that the national week of rallies was meant to oppose would require local police to enforce federal immigration laws. The police in New York and several other large cities say that would undermine local crime-fighting by making immigrants even more fearful of reporting crimes or helping an investigation. Supporters of the measure, sponsored by United States Representative Charles Norwood, Republican of Georgia, say that it is the only serious way to crack down on illegal immigration.

"Security has become so central to any position on immigration that unless you can frame your argument on security grounds, it doesn't have legs," Mr. Chishti said.

In that context, even a measure like the Dream Act, which highlights the most appealing cases, can have trouble gaining traction. Though the Democratic presidential nominee, John Kerry, has endorsed the bill, Democrats in Congress are doing little to push it to a vote, advocates and critics agree.

"It's really just amnesty du jour," said Mark Krikorian, director of the Center for Immigration Studies, which supports more restrictive immigration. "And it doesn't matter because it's not going to pass anyway."

25   That leaves the future uncertain for young people like those at the rally on Thursday. "Every day I see students, bright students, who drop out of college because they can't get a loan, because of their immigration status," Mr. Banerjee said. "What is going to happen to all these young kids, hoping that something is going to fall from the sky?"

Writing Prompts

1. The DREAM Act would set a uniform standard for all fifty states. Do we need such federal legislation, or should individual states address this issue as they please?
2. Read the editorial "Punishing the Innocent" from the *Los Angeles Times*, and the letters to the editor that follow. Write your own letter to the editor arguing for or against the DREAM Act.
3. Most members of Congress seem to support the DREAM Act, but as of early 2006 it wasn't making much progress toward passage. Write an essay arguing why members of Congress need to act on this legislation in a timely manner.
4. Write an essay in response to the following: College costs more every year. Would you support the DREAM Act if it raised your own in-state tuition $500 a year? What about $1,000?
5. Do we have different obligations to our citizens than we do to those who are here illegally? Write an essay supporting your opinion with information from at least one of the essays.

What Is at Stake for Citizenship?

1. Should minor children be held accountable when their parents break the law?
2. Is going to college a right or a privilege? Should people who are breaking the law be given the same educational opportunities as those who are law abiding?
3. Should the process of becoming a citizen be different for minors than it is for adults? Why or why not?
4. Would you change immigration law? How and why?
5. Would the DREAM Act give "special rights" to the children of illegal immigrants? Is that fair?

STRUGGLE AT THE BORDER: TWO NATIONS WITH A COMMON FUTURE

Mexico and the United States share a border that stretches approximately two thousand miles. Although these two countries have not been at war with each other since 1848, when Mexico lost most of its northern territories in the Mexican-American War, the border is heavily guarded, regularly patrolled on foot and by air, and more recently, electronically monitored. On the surface, such aggressive fortifications make no sense. Mexico is our ally and our third largest trading partner. The United States is Mexico's largest trading partner. We have signed many treaties together, including NAFTA (the North American Free Trade Agreement). Many American companies have opened factories in Mexico. Every year tens of thousands of Americans flock to Mexico's beautiful beaches. So why

Juarez, Chihauhau, Mexico; U.S.-Mexican border, facing Mexico.

would we need these guards, fences, and hi-tech monitoring devices between two peaceful allies? Illegal immigration—streams of Mexicans coming north to find a better life, that's why.

Before World War II the Mexican-American border was easily crossed in either direction. During the war Mexican men were encouraged to come north to take jobs left by Americans who were serving in the armed forces. Only in the 1950s did America begin to institute programs designed to prevent Mexicans from coming north. "Operation Wetback" (unfortunately named for the pejorative term for Mexicans who entered the United States by swimming the Rio Grande) began in 1954 and was designed to find illegal immigrants and send them back to Mexico. Over the years the border between these two peaceful trading partners has been fenced, walled, and guarded with greater and greater intensity, but nothing has stopped the constant stream of people who come north in hopes of finding work and the better life that comes with it.

Like many of the other issues in this book, illegal immigration from Mexico is not a simple situation. It is not enough to say "just keep them from coming." That's impossible, as evidenced by the following essays. And Mexican citizens play an important role in the American economy; in many cases we need what they have to offer—their expertise and job skills. So it's not an entirely one-sided situation. As you read these essays, the issues on both sides of the border will likely become more complex, as will your ideas about how to shape the relationship between Mexico and the United States.

Kevin Sullivan

An Often-Crossed Line in the Sand; Upgraded Security at U.S. Border Hasn't Deterred Illegal Immigration from Mexico

Washington Post, March 7, 2005

An ancient blue school bus pulled up at Erlinda Juarez Martinez's house one recent afternoon, and 20 poor farmers wearing jeans and baseball caps hopped off. They had traveled for days to reach this village of crumbling adobe homes, separated from the United States by nothing but a few strands of barbed wire and a dirty desert breeze.

Every hour, mud-caked buses and pickup trucks dropped off other new loads of travelers, their backpacks filled with tortillas and toilet paper, their heads filled with dreams of America. For them, Las Chepas was a locker room of illegal immigration, a place to find food, water, traveling companions and a guide.

One of the men on the porch was Jesus Alonzo Camacho, 44. He and six friends had left home in Michoacan state, where they earn about $6 a day working in the fields. "We can't support ourselves at home; we need the money from the other side," Camacho said. His only plan was to slip across the border and walk north until he found someone to give him work. "Anyone," he said. "Anywhere."

Facing Camacho and the others across a nearby ditch was an astounding high-tech spider web spun by the U.S. Border Patrol in New Mexico. Motion sensors were buried in the ground. High-resolution infrared cameras were mounted on poles, able to spot people five miles off. A man hiding in the dark would pop up larger than life on video monitors 35 miles away, so detailed that technicians could see him sneeze.

On the ground, agents in big sport-utility vehicles were armed with night-vision   5
goggles and satellite global positioning devices. Helicopters buzzed up and down the border, shining powerful spotlights. U.S. Army units preparing to head for Iraq were holding exercises here, catching illegal immigrants with precision surveillance equipment designed for war.

Every day of the year, such high-tech barricades help U.S. authorities catch more than 3,000 people along the 2,000-mile U.S.-Mexico border. Yet despite the unprecedented investment in technology and manpower, illegal immigrants are still coming in waves—and their numbers are increasing.

A decade ago, the United States began trying to fortify the border, starting with Operation Gatekeeper in 1994. Since then, U.S. officials have added more patrols, lights and walls every year, especially since the attacks of Sept. 11, 2001. Yet instead of stopping illegal immigration, those measures have just made many Mexicans already in the United States stay longer, according to Mexican officials.

U.S. officials made 1.1 million apprehensions along the border last year, a 24 percent increase over the year before. It is unclear whether the rising apprehensions signify that more people are trying to cross or that a greater percentage are being caught. But experts in both countries estimate that perhaps 500,000 or more still make it through each year.

Because it has proved impossible to jail the huge numbers of immigrants who cross the border illegally each year, Border Patrol officials are focusing on identifying and arresting those with criminal records and watching for potential terrorists.

The officials said they have caught more than 53,000 people with criminal records—   10
including about 9,000 felony offenders—since September, when a new computerized system was started to allow agents to quickly check a migrant's background against the FBI's database. The vast majority do not have criminal records, however. They are simply driven to the border and released into Mexico, where many keep crossing until they succeed.

"What we're doing is not working," Sen. John Cornyn (R-Tex.), chairman of the Senate Judiciary subcommittee on immigration and border security, said in a telephone interview. "I don't believe you can build a wall high enough or wide enough to keep out people who have no hope or opportunity where they live."

How to better manage the contentious issue of immigration will top the agenda when President Bush meets with Mexican President Vicente Fox later this month in Texas. Secretary of State Condoleezza Rice is scheduled to visit Mexico on Thursday to take up the issue.

Bush has advocated a large-scale guest worker program that would allow Mexicans to work legally in the United States for several years and then return home. Cornyn said he believed Bush and both parties in Congress were serious about trying to enact some type of temporary worker program, while at the same time strengthening border security against potential terrorists.

Mexican workers in the United States, including millions of illegal immigrants, are vital to the Mexican economy, sending a record $17 billion home last year. Mexico cannot create enough jobs for the more than 1 million young people who enter the workforce each year, making crossing the border as alluring as ever—no matter how much the United States fortifies it.

15   While many U.S. employers welcome such workers, other Americans view them as lawbreakers who take away jobs and drain school and hospital budgets. Some opponents of illegal immigration, led by James Gilchrist, a Vietnam veteran from California, are organizing a protest action next month in Arizona. Their plan is to hold a mass "community watch" involving at least 500 volunteers who will patrol the border, observe illegal immigration and report their findings to the Border Patrol.

According to the group's Web site, the United States is being "devoured and plundered by the menace of tens of millions of invading illegal aliens." Unless illegal immigration is curbed, it warns, "Future generations will inherit a tangle of rancorous, unassimilated, squabbling cultures."

About 50 yards from the tumbledown shacks of Las Chepas, Joe and Teresa Johnson stood on the U.S. side of the border one recent day, putting up a new fence. The southern edge of their cattle farm abuts the border. They said a mile of five-tiered barbed-wire fence, and all the posts, had been stolen—and not for the first time.

The Johnsons said it would cost them about $10,000 to replace the fence. They called the theft the most recent irritation caused by the fast-escalating traffic of illegal immigrants across their large ranch, which has been in the family since 1918.

"I'm just a rancher, but I know something's got to be done; it's getting worse every day," said Joe Johnson, noting that immigrants have left vast amounts of trash on his ranch and have come to his home demanding food and water.

20   Teresa Johnson said the Border Patrol does not have enough leeway to deal effectively with the immigrants, who she said include a growing number of "thugs" and gang members. "The Border Patrol should be able to use their guns," she said. And if they are threatened by the immigrants, she said, "they should shoot them, take them out."

She said she was not sure if a guest worker program, or other solutions being considered in Washington, might ease the problems on her land. "I'm so mad right now," she said, staring angrily toward Las Chepas. "I don't want any of them over here."

On a recent Tuesday evening, there were 80 newly caught immigrants in the Border Patrol's processing trailer in the tiny town of Columbus, N.M., about 20 miles east of Las Chepas. One by one, they were taken out of five holding cells in the trailer, and their fingerprints were sent by computer to the FBI.

Within minutes, an alert came back for a stocky 24-year-old man in a yellow sweat shirt. According to the FBI, he had served time in a New Jersey prison for homicide and was registered as a sex offender before being deported to Mexico. Agents said he would be charged with returning to the United States after deportation, a crime punishable by up to three years in prison.

More typical was Judith Rodriguez, 23, who said she was on her way to a $300-a-week job picking onions on a New Mexico farm. She said she had crossed over twice before to work on the same farm, and this was the first time she'd been caught.

"To keep my kids in school I need shoes, clothes, food and school supplies," said   25
Rodriguez, who said her daughters, 10 and 9, were being cared for by her mother.

Like the vast majority of the immigrants captured every day, Rodriguez shortly would
be driven to the border and sent back to Mexico. Asked if she would try to sneak across
again, she smiled. "Of course," she said. "Tomorrow."

That night, in this 40-mile stretch of border alone, 229 people were caught and taken
to the processing trailer. Two hundred were later returned to Mexico and nine were held
because they had criminal records. Agents estimated that for every immigrant they catch,
at least one or two more make it through.

"I don't let that get to me; there's nothing we can do about it," said Jack T. Jeffreys, a
Border Patrol agent guarding the border in his SUV. He compared his job to that of a police
officer writing speeding tickets. They may not stop people from speeding, he said, but that
doesn't mean police shouldn't write them.

Mexican guides known as coyotes study the Border Patrol's movements with binocu-
lars and use radios to coordinate their crossings. "They are as good at what they do as we
are at what we do," Jeffreys said.

As enforcement has increased in Arizona, California and Texas, immigrants are   30
increasingly coming to places such as Las Chepas, located in the remote desert. Except for
the big border cities of El Paso and Ciudad Juarez, which are about 90 miles to the east,
there is nothing but desert and a few small communities for 100 miles in any direction.

"You can't stop these guys, because they are desperate to make a dollar in the
United States," said Hugo Snyder, 35, a Las Chepas resident in red cowboy boots and dark
sunglasses. "And the coyotes are real wise. They just outsmart the Americans."

Jose Cruz Anduaga is an official of Grupo Beta, a unit of the Mexican national immigration agency that offers medical care and advice to immigrants. One recent day he was
riding in a bright orange pickup truck in the desert near Las Chepas when he found five
men, ages 15 to 30, sitting sadly in the dirt.

They had walked 12 hours in hopes of finding a less-guarded place to cross. They were
hoping to make it to Phoenix, more than 250 miles away. They had no map and no water.

"I feel powerless," Cruz said. "You want them to stay in their country with their family
and their people, but there's nothing we can do about their economic need. We tell them
not to go and they say, 'Are you going to give me a job?' "

A Border Patrol helicopter hovered in the distance.   35

Ruben Navarrette, Jr.

What Really Matters in the Debate on Immigration

The *San Diego Union-Tribune,* March 2, 2005

Some people wonder if Americans have the will to tackle the problem of illegal immigration. But the real question is whether they have the intellectual honesty to tackle it in a
way that will do any good.

It doesn't always seem as if they do.

For starters, there's the way in which many Americans lazily fall back on that one
word—illegal—in an attempt to short-circuit the debate.

San Diego-Tijuana border.

I see it in my e-mail. After I've written a column that anti-immigrant hard-liners think is soft on illegals, a reader will write in and ask, rhetorically: "What part of illegal don't you understand?"

Actually, as the son of a cop, I think I've got a handle on the concept. "Illegal" activity refers not only to the estimated 3 million immigrants who each year sneak into the United States without documents, but also to the millions of U.S. employers who knowingly hire them because cheap labor enhances the bottom line. Here's the part that is dishonest: Americans love to complain about one group of lawbreakers while turning a blind eye to the other.

I was hoping for more vision from the present class of White House Fellows when I addressed them recently in San Diego. The program allows young professionals to spend a year in Washington shadowing members of the Cabinet. Their trip to the West Coast gave them a chance to study the immigration issue up close.

In my speech, I insisted that it was silly for some Americans to worry that the immigrants of today are not up to snuff when compared to the immigrants of 100 years ago. That's pretty much what was being said on the cultural right: that the immigrants of the early 2000s, more than 80 percent of whom came from Latin America and Asia, have refused to blend into the mainstream and insisted on retreating into cultural enclaves. The result, according to people such as Harvard Professor Samuel Huntington, is a weakening of America's national identity.

Personally, I think that's a dumb argument that shows Huntington doesn't understand immigrants or what it means to be an American. There are any number of studies pointing out that most of today's immigrants are doing what those in the past did—assimilating, working hard, pushing their kids to succeed, learning English, having smaller families and all the rest.

In fact, I told the fellows, the Census Bureau has just released a survey of recent immigrants which contends that those who have come to the United States since 2000 were more educated than those who arrived in the late 1990s. The same study said that "second-generation" Americans—those who have at least one foreign-born parent—typically attend and graduate from college, earn higher incomes than their parents, own their own homes and otherwise live the American Dream.

Of the 6 million immigrants aged 25 or older who arrived since 2000, 34.3 percent had a bachelor's degree or higher. That's an improvement on the 32.5 percent of immigrants in the late 1990s who had a bachelor's degree or higher.

Right about then, a White House Fellow asked a question that I bet many of you are asking now: "Were these immigrants legal, or illegal?"

What does it have to do with the price of tequila in Juarez?

Not much, said Census Bureau spokesman Robert Bernstein when I called later to put to him the question that had been put to me. "We included both legal and illegal immigrants," he said. "We didn't ask the respondents whether they were here legally or not. And we didn't have separate statistics breaking them down according to the legality of their residence. We just combined them."

Some people won't like hearing that. They'll misunderstand. They'll assume that someone is saying that it doesn't matter that people are coming here illegally. But this study is about what kind of immigrants are coming, and how they behave once they get here. Their legal status isn't likely to impact the data one way or another.

Unless someone can demonstrate that the very act of migrating to the United States   15
illegally somehow makes one less likely to be educated, or less likely to assimilate and prosper, then the whole question of the immigrants' legal status is irrelevant. The fact that some people won't accept that is just another example of intellectual dishonesty—the sort that Americans will have to rid themselves of if they are ever going to address the immigration issue in a responsible and meaningful way.

Alex Pulaski

Legislation Helps Both Farmers, Laborers

The Oregonian, February 11, 2005

Mark Krautmann is a Salem nursery owner who thinks this country hasn't had the courage to admit, much less fix, its reliance on illegal immigrants.

Carlos Hernandez is a Washington County farm worker who, 14 years and two children after an illegal border crossing, obtains work with the same fake identification papers he bought in California.

In farm fields, the interests of laborers and employers often stand at odds, but both Krautmann and Hernandez see promise in federal legislation introduced Thursday: A guest-worker bill that would allow an estimated 500,000 farm laborers to cross borders legally and eventually gain permanent residency.

Krautmann hopes he can obtain a reliable supply of legal workers, and Hernandez envisions being able to easily visit family members in Mexico and eventually earn permanent residency for himself and his family.

The bill, introduced by Sen. Larry Craig, R-Idaho, mirrors legislation that stalled in the   5
past Congress over election-year politics and resentment against illegal immigration, particularly in a faltering economy and the post-Sept. 11 environment.

Opposition remains strong. Craig Nelsen, director of ProjectUSA, a Washington, D.C.-based organization that has used billboards to promote eliminating illegal immigration and reducing legal immigration, described the guest-worker proposal as "a monstrous bill" at a time when the country already is overpopulated.

"If Americans knew their representatives had signed onto this thing," he said, "they'd be outraged."

Nelsen said that for the United States to have an effective border policy it can't periodically offer to forgive illegal immigrants. The last widespread immigration amnesty was in 1986 and led to 3 million people gaining permanent residency.

Although the new bill offers no such blanket amnesty, it is targeted at undocumented farm laborers who can demonstrate having worked for at least 100 days in this country since July 2003.

10 The bill would allow them to travel freely between this country and their home country—Mexico, for most workers. It also would grant temporary resident status to spouses and minor children.

After six years, those workers who meet minimums for hours worked annually could apply for permanent residency. They could become eligible for U.S. citizenship five years after that.

For a decade, farmers have complained that hiring rules are a charade. Half or more of the country's 1.6 million agricultural workers are here illegally, according to U.S. Department of Labor estimates.

In Oregon, farm employment peaks at more than 70,000 each summer. The state's nursery and greenhouse industry alone employs about 20,000.

No one is sure how many of those workers came here illegally.

15 But Krautmann and other farm employers routinely review the identification papers they are presented, sort those that appear genuine from those that don't, and face an annual notification from the Social Security Administration that some employees' names don't match their numbers.

"The government makes me into an immigration agent," he said. "I see a lot of IDs. Some of them are clearly bad, but there (are) some nice IDs out there."

Hernandez, the Washington County fieldworker, said he would welcome the opportunity to travel freely between this country and his birthplace in southern Mexico.

Arturo Rodriguez, president of the United Farm Workers union, said Thursday that the union and other bill supporters would try to distinguish between the immigration debate and the country's fight against terrorism.

"We have to make people realize that these people are not our enemies," he said. "If it weren't for them we wouldn't eat every day."

Maria Anglin

Immigration Comic Glams up Danger

San Antonio Express-News (Texas), January 10, 2005

It's past Jan. 6—time to glare at neighbors who haven't taken down the holiday lights. It's also time for the many undocumented workers who went home for the holidays to make tracks to the United States and get back to work.

Lucky for them, the Mexican government is trying to ease the trip back by sending them off with a little light reading—a comic called the "Mexican Migrant's Guide."

Express-News staff writers Hernan Rozemberg and Dane Schiller reported on the 32-page comic in early December, when the guides were first distributed in bus stations throughout Mexico. The report quoted a Foreign Ministry spokesman as saying the guide isn't meant to encourage illegal immigration, but rather as a means to help Mexicans making the journey anyway to stay safe.

It warns of the dangers of hopping in the water wearing heavy clothes that will get heavier when wet. It advises that putting salt in drinking water might make one thirstier, but retaining water is the goal.

For those who get caught, there's a what-not-to-do list—it's better to be detained and   5
repatriated a few hours later than to get lost in the desert, the guide warns. The guide also
advises those who make it to keep a low profile. Don't attract the cops, pass on the loud
parties, and wear your seat belt.

Never mind the big law they're breaking by crossing illegally.

But until both countries get serious about the immigration issue, breaking those laws
almost seems beside the point. People are going to come across the border anyway, and
there are plenty of menial jobs waiting on this side of the border. It's silly to get worked up
over what seems to be blatant disregard for American laws since it's become a win-win
situation.

What's really offensive is how the Mexican government has glamorized crossing over
to Gringolandia.

All the immigrants in the comic book look like Superman's little brothers and sisters.
They've got that perfectly tousled jet-black hair with blue highlights and flawless porcelain
skin. They look more like Kate Beckinsale than La India Maria.

Perhaps you don't know what La India Maria looks like, but when was the last time   10
you saw news clips of undocumented immigrants who looked like Kate Beckinsale?

The comic's men are all square-jawed and cut, except for a few of the bad
guys, like the weird older one taking money from a group of immigrants filing into an
18-wheeler. The Americans are all blonde and built like Barbie with breast implants.
Hubba hubba!

Even the Rio Grande gets an extreme makeover. A group of the chiseled immigrants
are depicted crossing in crystalline water. No maquiladora-polluted shores in this book!

There's a "you have rights" section of the comic that lists what rights seized immigrants should expect. Nothing wrong with that, except that it tends to cast American law
enforcement as the bad guys.

And while there are pictures of immigrants running for the hills at the sight of agents,
there are no drawings of bodies floating in the Rio Grande, dehydrated children in the
desert or dozens of bodies being hauled away from boxcars and trucks.

Of course not. That might discourage those who risk their lives to send home the dol-   15
lars that keep Mexico's economy humming.

If we are to believe that drawings of Joe Camel are meant to lure kids to the smoke-
filled world of cigarettes, then are drawings of sexy immigrants meant to draw young
Mexicans into the world of separated families, deadly risks and, at best, low-wage jobs? Did
someone say "Sure hope so!"?

There's something wrong about a government encouraging its young people to
break laws and risk their lives. Sure, they're coming over anyway and the idea of life-
saving tips is benevolent, but there's a creepy undercurrent at work here. Mexico
shouldn't do this.

And the United States should disapprove.

The guide markets the dangerous journey as a superhero's adventure—it
amounts to an ad for illegal immigration. And an ad for crossing the border just
crosses the line.

Michael A. Fletcher

Bush Immigration Plan Meets GOP Opposition; Lawmakers Resist Temporary-Worker Proposal

Washington Post, January 2, 2005

President Bush's plan to liberalize the nation's immigration laws to allow millions of undocumented workers the opportunity for legal status appears to be on a collision course with newly aroused sentiment among House Republicans pushing for a crackdown on illegal immigration.

Bush describes his immigration proposal as one of the top goals of his second term, calling it a humane way to get a handle on the nation's mushrooming illegal immigration problem. Republican strategists, led by White House chief political adviser Karl Rove, also see the proposal as an important element in their plan to expand the party's base among the nation's fast-growing Hispanic population.

The key prong in Bush's plan is a temporary-worker program that would offer the nation's estimated 10 million illegal immigrants a chance to earn legal status that would allow them to stay in the country as long as six years. Once they register as temporary workers, they would be eligible to begin the long process of applying for citizenship or permanent residency.

"It's a compassionate way to treat people who come to our country. It recognizes the reality of the world in which we live," Bush said during a news conference last week. "There are some people—there are some jobs in America that Americans won't do and others are willing to do."

5   But an increasingly vocal group of House Republicans is threatening to undercut Bush's vision, which the president has discussed with passion but has not formally advanced since taking office in 2001. Many House Republicans oppose any effort to grant legal status to undocumented workers, saying it would have the effect of rewarding lawbreakers. Instead, they are seeking to ratchet up enforcement efforts against undocumented workers, an approach with proven voter appeal if unproven results when it comes to slowing illegal immigration.

When the new Congress commences this month, key House Republicans are promising to push legislation to complete a controversial fence along the Mexican border near San Diego, to make it tougher for immigrants to attain asylum and to prevent illegal immigrants from receiving driver's licenses. At the insistence of Judiciary Chairman F. James Sensenbrenner Jr. (R-Wis.)—and with the White House's approval—Speaker J. Dennis Hastert (R-Ill.) has promised to attach those measures "to the first must-pass legislation" that moves in the House.

Last month, House Republicans wrested a pledge from Bush to cooperate in enacting tougher immigration provisions by blocking legislation to restructure the nation's intelligence community. The intelligence bill passed only after Bush promised to "work with" House Republicans to enact those measures.

Bush's concession meant that Congress will begin the year on an anti-immigration note, which promises to continue as many of those pushing for the tough enforcement measures also are likely to oppose the president's "guest worker" plan.

"I'm no longer the only person in the caucus bringing the issue of illegal immigration to the American people," said Rep. Tom Tancredo (R-Colo.), who heads the House's

71-member Immigration Reform Caucus, which has a section on its Web site listing crimes, health problems and other problems it says are caused by illegal immigrants. "Now others appear to be willing to go to the mat on it."

How the White House plans to reconcile its stated desire for a temporary-worker program with its pledge to toughen immigration laws is unclear, although some supporters of Bush's plan say the two goals are not incompatible. Backers of a guest-worker plan argue that there is no way to effectively crack down on undocumented workers, given the ineffectiveness of the nation's immigration laws. The new program, they said, would create incentives for people to enter the country legally.

Efforts to hold employers accountable for hiring illegal immigrants have been largely frustrated by a booming industry in forged documents. Attempts to stem the tide by building a fence and beefing up patrols along the southwestern border have only shifted much of the flow of illegal immigrants east from California, often to the rugged Arizona desert. Hundreds of would-be illegal immigrants have died attempting to make the perilous journey across the southwestern border, even as an estimated 1 million illegal immigrants make it into the country each year.

Many supporters say a temporary-worker program would enhance national security by identifying who is in the country; by boosting the economy with a continuing supply of highly motivated, low-skill workers; and by helping undocumented workers avoid exploitation by granting them the protections that come with legal status. The workers, meanwhile, would be free to return to their home countries, allowing them to stay connected with their families.

"The idea is to make the system respond to the fact that we have an integrated labor market that interacts with Mexico and Central America," said Frank Sharry, executive director of the National Immigration Forum, an immigrants' rights group. "You are trying to transform it from a black market, chaotic, hard-to-control flow to a more orderly, regulated flow."

Still, tougher enforcement provisions are popular among voters, particularly in areas where residents feel overwhelmed by illegal immigrants. "If the White House and the Republican establishment think promoting amnesty is good politics, they are crazy," said Mark Krikorian, director of the Center for Immigration Studies, which opposes a guest-worker program. "It has the real potential of turning off their base."

In November, Arizona voters approved a ballot initiative requiring proof of citizenship or legal residency for people to access a wide array of government services. The measure passed despite the opposition of some of the state's most powerful elected officials.

Sen. John McCain (R-Ariz.), who opposed the ballot initiative, has argued that enforcement measures alone will not solve the illegal immigration problem. "If anyone believes that simply strengthening our borders is the answer to our nation's illegal immigration problem, they don't understand the problem," he said as the Senate passed the intelligence bill last month. "Where there's a demand, there's going to be a supply."

Bush, who often points out that he was confronted with the complicated politics surrounding illegal immigration when he was governor of Texas, outlined plans for a temporary-worker program in the early days of his presidency, but they were shelved after the Sept. 11, 2001, terrorist attacks. The president again outlined his principles for immigration 11 months ago, but the issue rarely surfaced during the campaign. The White House has put it back on the table since Bush's reelection, in which some exit polls found Bush winning more than 40 percent of the Hispanic vote.

"I fully understand the politics of immigration reform. I was the governor of Texas, right there on the front lines of border politics," Bush said. "I know what it means to have mothers and fathers come to my state and across the border of my state to work. Family values do not stop at the Rio Grande River, is what I used to tell the people of my state."

McCain, who is planning his own immigration legislation that would couple a guest-worker program and a sharp increase in the number of permanent resident slots available to unskilled workers with tougher enforcement provisions, met with Bush on the subject in the days after the election. Such a measure would likely be successful only with bipartisan support.

20   Some advocacy groups who champion comprehensive immigration changes are less concerned about the sentiment among House Republicans than they are about Bush's commitment to the issue. Although Bush talks movingly about the subject, they say, he has yet to expend any political capital to push his proposal.

"It's not the House Republicans that so far has not been coming through on immigration reform," said Ana Avendano, associate general counsel and director of the Immigrant Worker Program for the AFL-CIO. "It's been the White House."

Linda Chavez

Take off the Blinders on Illegal Immigration

The *Baltimore Sun*, December 16, 2004

Bernard Kerik might not have been the dream candidate for homeland security secretary that most of us imagined when the president first announced his nomination, but disqualifying him for the job because he hired an illegal alien should give pause to lawmakers and citizens alike.

Whether we care to admit it or not, most of us benefit from the services of illegal aliens, even if indirectly, and the law that ensnared Mr. Kerik has turned many good people into scofflaws.

There are some 12 million illegal aliens living—and working—in the United States, which makes lawbreakers of the millions of otherwise law-abiding Americans who hire illegal immigrants as nannies, housekeepers, gardeners, painters, carpenters and for other odd jobs. Is this really a good thing for the country or an effective way to control illegal immigration?

I have special reason to be concerned. My own nomination to be secretary of labor was derailed in 2001 when it became public that a decade earlier I had taken into my home and given modest financial assistance to a battered and abused woman from Guatemala, who at the time was illegally living in the United States.

5   Although the actual circumstances of my situation were different from Mr. Kerik's—and from those of Clinton Cabinet nominees felled by this policy, Zoe Baird and Kimba Wood—the underlying issue was the same. If there is an illegal alien in your past, forget about serving your country in any high-level position.

Although some news organizations have suggested that other ethical and moral lapses doomed Mr. Kerik's nomination, this does not appear to be the case.

The Washington Post reports, "White House officials said they knew in advance about other disclosures now emerging about Kerik's background, including alleged extramarital affairs and reported ties to a construction company with supposed mob connections, but had concluded that they were not disqualifying." So suspicions about mob ties don't doom a nomination but hiring an illegal alien does? Something is very wrong here.

When the Immigration Reform and Control Act (IRCA) passed Congress in 1986, there were 3 million illegal aliens living in the United States. The law was supposed to stem illegal immigration by punishing employers who hired illegal aliens, and not just big companies. Even individuals who hired someone to cut their grass or take care of their babies were suddenly turned into quasi-immigration officials. The law required all employers to check documents to make sure that prospective workers had a right to be in the United States and maintain records for five years.

So did this cumbersome and bureaucratic enforcement mechanism work to reduce illegal immigration? No. In fact, the number of illegal immigrants living here has quadrupled since the law passed. Like Prohibition, the IRCA has been a monumental failure.

Although most Americans abhor illegal immigration, according to recent polls on the subject, they would not like the consequences if we actually were able to kick out the 12 million illegal aliens currently living here. 10

Are we really prepared to pay more for everything from burgers at the local fast-food restaurant to the cost of new homes? There is no question this would happen if we eliminated those workers from our labor pool.

The only solution is to make it easier—not harder—for immigrants who want to work to come here legally. The president's much-maligned guest worker proposal is a step in the right direction. But a solution still has to be found for dealing with those illegal aliens already here. It makes no sense to kick them out in order to bring in millions of different people to fill their jobs.

A one-time fine of both illegal aliens and the employers who knowingly hire them, along with the chance for undocumented workers to legalize their status if they have not broken other laws, would seem the proper punishment. Then maybe we could quit disqualifying otherwise good candidates from serving the nation.

Yeh Ling-Ling

Bush's Unwise Immigration Proposal

The *San Diego Union-Tribune*, November 29, 2004

With the election now over, the Bush administration is resuming immigration talks with Mexico. President Bush would make a costly mistake if he believes that his re-election means strong support for his de-facto amnesty proposal. Further, if passed, his plan would seriously exacerbate major problems of concern to Americans.

A November 2003 poll by the Pew Research Center showed 76 percent of both Democrats and independents and 82 percent of Republicans wanted stricter immigration controls. CBS News' Bob Schaeffer, the moderator of the third presidential debate, indicated on that occasion that he had received more e-mails on immigration than any other subject. In addition, not only did voters in Arizona handily pass an initiative aimed at deterring illegal immigration, voters in Georgia, Idaho, Colorado and California are working to place similar measures on future ballots.

Numerous recent polls have shown that high health care costs, homeland security and the economy were among the top concerns of voters as our schools, law enforcement agencies, hospitals, and labor markets are extremely overburdened. Yet, President Bush's deceptive plan would initially grant unlimited numbers of visas to foreign workers, low-skilled and professional, who are here illegally as well as those who are living abroad, as long as they can find employers willing to hire them. Subsequently, those "temporary" workers could apply for U.S. citizenship.

In fact, more than 100,000 American programmers are still unemployed, not counting the underemployed, according to UC Davis Computer Science Professor Norman Matloff's study. This country still has millions of able-bodied welfare recipients and unemployed low-skilled workers. Even so, once naturalized, unlimited numbers of new-comers under the Bush plan could petition for their extended families to immigrate to the United States, thus adding unlimited numbers of new students, job-seekers, drivers, water and energy consumers and social service recipients to this country through births and chain migration.

5   The link between immigration and high health care costs should not be ignored. Hospitals in many states are on the verge of bankruptcy due to the health care they are required by law to provide to illegal immigrants. Based on the Center for Immigration Studies' analysis of the 2003 Current Population Survey conducted by the Census Bureau, immigrants arriving since 1998 and their U.S.-born children accounted for 95 percent of the growth of the uninsured population in this country. Millions of existing illegal migrant workers and their future family members arriving here under President Bush's plan would make health costs skyrocket.

If the president is a serious champion of moral values, he should not teach Americans the wrong values by rewarding illegals who have broken our laws with work permits and eventually U.S. citizenship. Also, if he really wants education reform to work, he should restrict his "No Child Left Behind" policy to legal resident children to further reduce immigration. Indeed, according to the Census Bureau, between 2000 and 2003, 21 percent of elementary and high school students had at least one foreign-born parent. American children are falling behind in education compared to those in Japan and many Western nations as many schools are overwhelmed with non-English-speaking students.

The president should learn a lesson from former California Gov. Gray Davis, who signed legislation giving driver's licenses and in-state tuition to illegal immigrants in the hope of boosting his popularity. Last year, the Democratic governor lost his job to Arnold Schwarzenegger, a Republican who pledged to repeal the driver's license law during the recall campaign.

Caving in to the cheap labor lobby and Mexico's pressure is politically and economically unwise. President Bush should listen to the public and immediately call for a substantial reduction in legal immigration, oppose all amnesty proposals, enforce immigration laws, and urge Congress to adopt legislation to make it illegal to grant benefits to illegal immigrants. These steps are necessary so that this country can effectively address voters' concerns, save jobs and invest in Americans and legal immigrants who are already here.

Writing Prompts

1. It has been argued that we need Mexicans to come to the United States and take the jobs we don't want to do ourselves. Write an essay in which you agree or disagree with this theory, and from it draw conclusions about what to do with Mexican illegal immigrants.
2. Has your family, or anyone you know, ever employed an illegal immigrant? Write an essay about why that would or would not be a good idea.
3. Choose an essay in this illegal immigration cluster you most disagree with. Write an essay stating the main points of that piece and argue against them to support your views.
4. Write a friendly letter to prospective illegal aliens letting them know why or why not you think they should come here.
5. Write an essay about how your family came to America. Research what the immigration laws were at the time your ancestors arrived and consider how they might differ from the laws of today.

What Is at Stake for Citizenship?

1. Should a "nation of immigrants" (as the United States has so often been called) keep out people who want to be Americans?
2. Should our relationship with Mexico and its citizens be different from our relationship with Norway or India or Japan? Should Mexicans be allowed to come to America and work in a way that other people are not?
3. What does it say about us when our regard for Mexican people is that they should only perform low-paying, unskilled, and often backbreaking labor here in America?
4. If we let too many immigrants into our country (legally or illegally), do we risk diluting our national identity with so many foreign people and cultures? What is our national identity?
5. If you knew someone was here illegally from Mexico, would you report that person to the INS? If you could do so anonymously, would that be easier? What if you had to leave your name and the person would know who called the authorities?

INTERNATIONAL STUDENTS: TURNING AWAY FROM AMERICA?

America's educational system is the envy of the world. Our colleges and universities are well funded, our faculties highly qualified, and our technology is cutting edge. For many students in different parts of the world—from western Europe to rural India—an American education is the key to opportunity, success, and prestige, and so for many years some of the finest students from across the globe have traveled here to earn undergraduate and graduate degrees. We have a lot to offer these students. But they have a lot to offer us; international students studying in America is a win-win situation—for the student and for the United States. International students bring tuition dollars and cultural diversity. They educate us about their countries when they come to learn with us, sharing their perspectives with us. And they take their often fond memories of our people and our culture back home to their own countries, where their perceptions of America may play a crucial role later in the governance of their own nations. So why would this be a problem? The simple answer is September 11. At least one of the hijackers came to this country on student visas. And in reality many of them were students; they were enrolled at flight schools learning to fly planes into buildings. Since that time, the rules and regulations governing student visas and international students have tightened. Fewer people are able to and/or interested in coming to study in America. *As you read about this problem, think about how you might come up with a solution that protects our security but keeps our colleges and universities open to international students.*

John Downes

US Envoy Tries to Reverse Decline in J1 Student Visas

The *Irish Times*, January 18, 2005

International students have to work harder to study in America, post-9/11.

In an unprecedented attempt to reverse a dramatic decline in the numbers of Irish students taking part in the J1 summer visa program, the American ambassador to Ireland is to address information seminars for students here.

Describing the decline in the program's popularity as a "hugely important issue for us," Mr. James C. Kenny said it allows students to learn that the US is not "what they just see on the front page of the headlines every day."

Under the J1 program, Irish students can legally work and live in the US for a maximum of four months over the summer.

However, last year *The Irish Times* revealed that applications for the program received by the student travel agency, USIT, had fallen from 6,500 to 2,800.

5   Mr. Kenny said he was aware that there was some anti-US sentiment among students as a result of the war in Iraq, but he believed there were a number of other factors, which contributed to the decrease in applications for the program.

These include the increased popularity of other countries such as Australia, the strong economy here—meaning students can easily find summer jobs at home—and tighter controls on entry procedures.

The J1 program has long been seen as a traditional "rites of passage" by generations of Irish students. But students have been put off by tighter security controls since the September 11th attacks.

For the first time last year, any student wanting to participate in the program was required to attend an interview in the US embassy in Dublin. This means students, from outside Dublin in particular, can be faced with significant additional travel expenses to attend the five-minute interview—which costs EUR 100 through USIT.

Participants also face mandatory fingerprinting at airports, and must agree to register with the US authorities so that they can be tracked while in the country. A restriction on final-year students enrolling on the program has also affected participation rates.

"By the end of the J1 season last year, we were pretty disappointed," Mr. Kenny said. "What we hope to do is get the numbers back up to where they were previously to 2004. I hope that we can . . . make it easier and more welcoming for people to come experience the U.S. Because I'm telling you it is a hugely important issue for us in America to be that way."

10

Mr. Kenny added that he was prepared to miss this week's presidential inauguration, which takes place on Thursday, to focus on the new J1 recruitment drive. The information seminars will be held in TCD and UCC later today and tomorrow.

He ruled out any relaxation of the new procedures, and said the focus would be on making the process more streamlined.

John Hughes

Cure for U.S.–Arab Tensions: More Student Visas

Christian Science Monitor (Boston, MA), January 12, 2005

In my holiday mail, I got a Christmas card from one of my former journalism students. It carried a photo of her gorgeous children, the proud product of an American mother and an Arab father. The parents weren't in the picture and I wondered whether it was because the Dad, an American citizen, had served in his country's military in a noble but sometimes discreet role that made it inadvisable to publicize his face.

It set me to thinking about the ways my life, and our society, have been enriched by other friends of Arab descent.

As I write, for instance, my 13-year-old son is shooting basketballs with one of his closest friends, whose family happens to be from Kuwait. Sometimes when we take the two of them on long trips, we need to stop at certain times so my son's friend can get out his prayer rug and kneel in the direction of Mecca. The father in this family was a general in the Kuwaiti Air Force during the Gulf War. The mother and children survived Iraqi occupation. Now they live in America, moving easily between Arab and American cultures. An older son was quarterback in his American high school. Older daughters are scholarship students, attired in American dress, but scrupulously observing Islamic codes.

Another good friend was the director of communications for Sudan before an oppressive government forced his departure. He is now a professor at a prestigious American university. He has written sensitively about Islam and its relationship to democracy, and about misunderstandings between Islam and the West. He talks with wry humor about the old days in Khartoum, when the rare visiting Western reporter, sometimes ill-informed and on a quick in-and-out visit, would seek him out because it was "take a Muslim to lunch" day.

5 Another academic friend of Egyptian origin and international stature runs a Middle East study center that attracts prominent guest lecturers from around the world to his American campus.

Such friends as these, who in their different ways are making significant contributions to better understanding between Americans and the Arab and Islamic world, are not always in agreement with every aspect of American policy. But discourse with them is healthy and civil. Their exposure to American culture, and American exposure to theirs, is mutually beneficial.

We need much more of this. One problem inhibiting it is the US security crackdown on visas, particularly for the thousands of international students who have traditionally and eagerly enrolled at US universities. The overall number of such students is down 2.4 percent this year, with graduate students down 6 percent. In part, there is a perception that America is less hospitable than before 9/11, but there are horror stories of bureaucratic delays in processing visas, and even the granting of reentry visas to students who have studied in the US for years.

American families are generous and kindly to international visitors and hundreds of thousands of them return to their countries with positive memories of American lifestyles, ideas, and principles. As Secretary of State Colin Powell once said: "I can think of no more valuable asset to our country than the friendship of future world leaders who have been educated here." Half the Jordanian cabinet, for example, was educated in the US.

More vigilant screening since 9/11 of potential terrorists is desirable and understandable. But as Harvard Professor Joseph Nye wrote in The New York Times, it would be tragic if "in an effort to exclude a dangerous few, we are keeping out the helpful many."

10 In the past, a key part of US public diplomacy was the encouragement of thousands of journalists, artists, budding politicians, teachers, and opinion leaders to visit America for varying periods of time, to observe it and its people firsthand. Students, especially if they pursue graduate studies, spend five or six or more years living in American communities and rarely return to their homelands unchanged by that experience.

In the hidden training camps of Al Qaeda, and the angry madrassahs of the extremist Islamic world, potential new terrorists are being given a distorted and hate-filled picture of America and what it stands for.

That needs to be offset by the real picture. It is best communicated by people-to-people contacts between human beings who have a real desire to understand and appreciate each other. And we can build more enduring relationships than "take a Muslim to lunch" day.

Chimamanda Ngozi Adichie

The Line of No Return

The *New York Times*, November 29, 2004

I watch dawn split open. The ashy darkness separates and light creeps over all of us standing in line outside the United States Embassy. For the first time, I see the blues and pinks of the buba the woman in front of me is wearing. And the hawkers and touts walking around are no longer shadows; I see their scarred faces, their calculating smiles. I have been in line since 4 a.m. Some of the people in front of me spent the night under a tent opposite the embassy.

I feel a strange kinship with them, and yet I am not particularly friendly. I do not start a conversation with anybody: perhaps because my eyes are still cloudy from lack of sleep, perhaps because I feel resentment at the inconveniences of having to be here so early. I wish I had not come back to Nigeria to renew my American student visa, I wish I had done it in England or Canada. Then I chastise myself. This is my country. The reason I did not bother to go to another country was that I knew I would be asked to return to my "home country."

I buy a Maltina from a hawker, and drink it while I listen to the people around me exchange stories, forming friendships that will dissolve with the visa line.

The touts swarm around. "I have serious connections inside the embassy, Auntie," one of them tells me. "Just 1,000 and you will enter today for sure."

I would not give him 1,000 naira even if I had it to spare. The 12,000 naira visa   5
fee is steep enough. As the sun rises, I estimate how much the embassy will make from the people in line today. They will give visas only to a fraction of these people but will take almost $100 worth of naira from each of them. Perhaps $40,000 for today. Conservatively.

When I finally get to the entrance, the Nigerian guard looks through my passport. He is upset that I travel to England often. "Why?" he asks. I want to tell him that he is working for the United States Embassy, not the British, and that his job is simply to make sure I have the right documents. But I say nothing. He puffs his shoulders and grunts with self-importance. "Passport photos?" he asks.

I hand them to him.

"Use your right hand!" he says.

I transfer my files to my left hand and then hand him the photos with my right. He notices they are the same photos I have used in my British visa. "Get back!" he says. "Go and take another picture and come back! You cannot wear the same dress in two passports!"

I stare at him. "What does it matter as long as the photo is not more than six   10
months old?"

"Are you insulting me?" he asks. "Are you insulting me, eh?"

I turn and leave. Insult means many things to us Nigerians. Our self-confidence is so fragile that anything—a challenge, a correction, a question—could well become an insult.

I come back the next day, with new photos in which I look ridiculous because the photographer—his signboard said, "Expert in American Visa Passport Photos"—stuck little balls of paper behind my ears. The Americans want to make sure your ears show, he told me. He didn't listen when I said that my ears don't need to stick out like lettuce leaves, that the Americans simply don't want your hair to cover your ears.

I am relieved to finally get into the cool embassy building, with garish paintings on the wall: an American girl holding a Nigerian flag, a Nigerian holding an American flag. The room is crowded. Preening and smirking, guards walk around, with comical jaunts to their gaits. Once in a while, they call out names and people rise eagerly, nervously, and walk to the interview booths. Babies cry. There are many children here, because the Americans do not believe you when you tell them how many children you have; they have been known to give visas to only four out of five children in one family. Next to me, a little boy, about 4 years old, is telling his father in a high voice, "We will bring a gun and shoot

Mummy today!" He points at his mother as he speaks. She ignores him, carefully going through files to make sure they have everything the Americans want.

15   The man beside me watches them, appalled. "What is happening to our children?" he asks me. "And see how the father is laughing!" He says that he is a philosophy professor and teaches at a college in Atlanta. There is a steady hum of talking around the room, but it dies down when a white woman comes in, with short hair that sticks up on her head like brush bristles. She is the director of the visa section, the philosophy professor tells me. She holds a loudspeaker to her mouth: "Raise your hands if you are here to renew a student or a work visa! Raise your hands high! I can't see! High!"

Her tone makes me feel like I am in primary school again.

"Keep the hands up! O.K., down!" She is wearing a multicolored caftan with jagged edges—the sort of thing a foreigner will wear to look African but an African will never wear. A child has walked up to her and is holding onto the caftan, looking up at her and smiling. He wants to play.

"Get this kid off me! Get this kid off me!" she says. She gestures wildly and for a moment I am afraid she will hit the child with the loudspeaker. The little boy is laughing now; he thinks it's some sort of game. There is the rumble of laughter through the room. "Oh children," someone says.

But the woman is not amused. "Who has this child?" She shakes her caftan as if to shake the child off until his mother goes and picks him up. "He just likes you," she tells the woman. The woman glares at us. "You think it's funny? O.K., I won't tell you what I wanted to tell you about the interview process. Go ahead and figure it out for yourselves."

20   She turns and walks away. The room is immediately mired in worry. "We should not have laughed," somebody says. "You know white people do not see things the way we do."

"White people don't play with children," another says. "She was angry." "Somebody should beg her not to be angry." "I hope they will still interview us." "Please, somebody should go and beg her."

The philosophy professor is incensed. "Can you imagine her talking to people in America or Europe like this?" he says. "She wouldn't dare."

I nod. I am as angry as he is—because of the collective humiliation of being in this soulless lounge, but also because of how quickly my people have forgiven her, have created different rules to excuse her unprofessional rudeness, her infantile tantrum.

I am acutely aware of the complex layers of injustice here. The first is the larger injustice of our history, the benignly brutal colonialism that spawned vile military regimes—events that made this scene possible. Then there is the injustice of this glaring power dynamic: our government cannot demand that we be treated with dignity within our own borders. And, saddest of all, the injustice that we perpetrate on ourselves by not giving ourselves any value, by accepting it when other people strip us of our dignity.

25   When it is my turn to present my case, the young American who interviews me says that she grew up in Philadelphia, where I lived for a short time during college. She has hazel eyes and is friendly and warm. She tells me that my new visa will be ready the next day. Later, when I tell my friend about this woman, I am told how lucky I was to get one of the few good ones.

As I leave the building, I hear the philosophy professor yelling at a man behind a glass screen. "How can you say I am lying?" he asks. "Why don't you call Atlanta and verify? How can you say I am lying?"

He has not been as lucky as I have been.

Olivia Winslow

Growth Reverses; Surveys: Fewer Foreign Students in U.S. Colleges

Newsday (New York), November 12, 2004, Friday

Once here, many international students do not go home to visit, fearing new immigration policies that make it harder to return.

Two surveys released this week show a declining number of international students enrolled in U.S. colleges and universities, reversing several years of growth.

The reasons for the decline, the reports suggest, may include difficulty in obtaining U.S. student visas, a perception that the country is less welcoming of foreign students, rising tuition costs and competition from other nations.

According to the Open Doors 2004, an annual survey of more than 2,300 colleges by the Institute of International Education released Wednesday, the number of international students decreased by 2.4 percent in 2003-04 to 572,509.

The drop occurred, the report said, following an increase of 0.6 percent the previous year, which in turn was preceded by five years of steady growth. The decline "is the first absolute decline in foreign enrollments since 1971-72," the report said.

A second report also released Wednesday, the fall 2004 "snapshot survey" of 480 institutions conducted by five educational organizations, found that nearly 55 percent of doctoral and research institutions reported a decline in new international graduate student enrollment.

Among undergraduate foreign student enrollment, 38 percent of the institutions surveyed reported declines, while 35 percent reported increases. Another 24 percent were unchanged.

While California hosts more international students than any other state, with 77,186, the Open Door report found that the New York City area had more foreign students—54,424—than any other metropolitan area in the country, led by Columbia University, with 5,362 foreign students, and New York University, with 5,070, which ranked second and fourth on the list. The University of Southern California had the most international students, with 6,647.

Among the colleges with more than 1,000 foreign students were three Long Island colleges: Stony Brook University, with 2,019; New York Institute of Technology, with 1,076; and Nassau Community College, with 1,049.

Nassau Community's spokesman, Reginald Tuggle, said international students have increased by 60 percent at the college between 1998–99 and 2003–04, attracted by the English Language Institute. "This gets them into an intensive academic environment to learn English so they can take courses for credit" later.

5

10 Stony Brook has seen a "slight decline" in foreign students since 2002, when it had 2,155 students, said Elizabeth Barnum, assistant dean for international services at the Graduate School. She attributed the dip in 2003 to a "bubble" of more students than expected accepting the university's offer of admission a year earlier, rather than to any obstacles posed by tighter immigration regulations.

"We had a large group of students from India at the master's level come in 2002, which was sort of a fluke," Barnum said.

There are clear benefits in having foreign students study in the United States, said Peggy Blumenthal, a vice president at the Institute of International Education. "The first, of course, is the United States gets to train future leaders of the world," exposing them to an "American way of thinking." Also, American students gain from interacting with international students, and the country benefits, she said, pointing to the $13 billion foreign students pumped into the American economy last year.

Mark Bixler

Foreign Student Ranks Decline; Stricter Security after 9/11 Cited

The *Atlanta Journal-Constitution*, November 10, 2004

The number of foreign students in the United States declined 2.4 percent last year, the first decline in more than 30 years, according to a report released today in New York.

The study cited increased security measures after the Sept. 11, 2001, terrorist attacks for the decline. It said some measures were needed but that others went too far, making it hard for foreign nationals to obtain a student visa.

"We are keeping out many legitimate people and making the country too hard to get into," said Vic Johnson, associate executive director of NAFSA: Association of International Educators in Washington.

The number of foreign students in Georgia fell 2.1 percent in the 2003-04 school year, according to the "Open Doors" report, prepared by the Institute of International Education in New York. The report estimates that 12,010 foreign students spent $248 million in Georgia in the 2003–04 school year.

5 About half the foreign students in Georgia attended Georgia Tech, Georgia State University or the University of Georgia. The leading countries of origin were India (13 percent of the total), China (12 percent), South Korea (11 percent), Japan (3 percent) and Canada (3 percent). Those countries, in order, also topped the national list of the leading countries of origin among the 572,509 foreign students in the United States.

Schools reported modest increases in enrollment from Latin America and Africa but decreases from parts of Asia and the Middle East. There were declines ranging from 9 percent to 15 percent among students from Hong Kong, Thailand, Pakistan and Indonesia and from 15 percent to 30 percent among those from Jordan, Saudi Arabia, Kuwait and the United Arab Emirates.

After the Sept. 11 attacks, Congress steamed ahead with long-delayed plans for an online system to monitor foreign students. It also ordered changes to more closely monitor foreign tourists and businesspeople.

The Institute of International Education cited several factors for the enrollment decline, including "real and perceived difficulties in obtaining student visas" as well as "rising tuition costs, vigorous recruitment efforts by other English-speaking nations and perceptions abroad that international students may no longer be welcome in the U.S."

Patricia Harrison, assistant U.S. secretary of state for education and cultural affairs, said in a statement that authorities had granted 11 percent more student visas in the first six months of 2004 than in the comparable period last year.

The fact that some students didn't use their visas "suggests that international students   10
understand the very real need we had to put in place systems to screen applicants for entry into the United States, systems that provide everyone—including foreign visitors—with a greater sense of security," she said.

Randy Furst

Caught in the Details of Immigration Law

Star Tribune (Minneapolis, MN), November 8, 2004

More than eight months after he was handcuffed and arrested, Mohammed Haider remains in prison, facing imminent deportation back to his native Bangladesh. Haider, who married an American last year, says he doesn't understand why.

"In 10 years I haven't had a single crime, not even a parking ticket," said Haider, 30, sitting in a small conference room at the state prison at Rush City.

Immigration officials say otherwise: Haider dropped out of Winona State University while in the country on a student visa a decade ago and illegally went to work.

"He violated the terms of his [student] visa," said Tim Counts, Twin Cities spokesman for U.S. Bureau of Immigration and Customs Enforcement. "He came as a student and then he continued breaking the law all of those years. All of that was illegal and . . . a consequence of that is removal from the United States."

Legal experts say that under normal circumstances, Haider would probably be free,   5
regardless of his student visa violations, because he is married to a U.S. citizen. But in a post-Sept. 11 world, immigration law is a lot less forgiving, they say.

Haider's deportation process, now under appeal, was set in motion because he failed to show up for a deportation hearing in Bloomington in August 2003.

He said he missed it because he and his wife had moved from their third-floor apartment in Roseville to a first-floor apartment but didn't file a formal change-of-address notice. And Haider's attorney was not informed of the hearing because the immigration court had not been informed that she was representing him.

So the hearing notice that was mailed to Haider was returned to authorities. And after Haider missed the hearing, a judge ordered the deportation.

"The entire process is Kafkaesque," said Demetrios Papademetriou, president of the Migration Policy Institute, a think tank in Washington, D.C., and former director of immigration policy and research at the U.S. Labor Department.

"The rules say absolutely zero tolerance. The officials themselves, even if there is still   10
any flexibility left . . . they are not going to use it, because they do not want to take chances."

Immigration authorities have lots of tools at their disposal and since Sept. 11, 2001, have been using them more aggressively, said Stephen Yale-Loehr, a professor of immigration law at Cornell University Law School. "Unfortunately, people like Mr. Haider are caught, even when it wasn't their fault—they didn't know about their deportation hearing.

"Immigration law is very complex, and the agency should exercise a little more discretion to try to help people who are not real bad guys, but rather have violated some technical procedural rules."

Counts replied, "Our job is to carry out the law. Many times immigration judges don't have much discretion when people fail to appear for their hearings. In the 1990s, Congress removed a lot of discretion from judges. People were skipping out of their immigration hearings as a way to avoid being deported."

Coming to America

Haider came to Winona State in March 1994, but his father died soon after, and other family members couldn't support him. So he quit school and went to work, sending a few hundred dollars a month back to Bangladesh to support his family, he said. The jobs included working as a manager at a drug store and in several video stores.

15   In late 2002, a federal program was introduced requiring men to register if they came from one of 30 countries—virtually all of them with significant Muslim populations—that are considered to pose a potential security risk. Bangladesh was one of those countries.

Haider, who married his girlfriend, Jami, in March 2003, turned up with his attorney and registered in April 2003. They were told they would be notified of the deportation hearing. When he did not attend the hearing, a warrant was issued. In December 2003, federal authorities suspended the annual registration system.

Meanwhile, Haider and his wife filed applications for him to gain residency status because of their marriage. They came to an interview in February so officials could review proof that their marriage was legitimate.

After the interview, Haider was taken to the Sherburne County jail. "I thought it was a mistake," Jami Haider said. "I thought for sure they just didn't know. I thought this would never happen in the United States—just because of the change of address. It doesn't make sense."

The next day, his wife received a notice that her marriage petition was approved. But the couple also learned it was irrelevant because Mohammed Haider now faced deportation.

Trying to Carry on

20   Haider was businesslike while recounting his case during an interview at the prison last month. But he briefly lost his composure when he spoke of his wife and his life behind bars.

He said Jami was using the money she earned as a secretary to pay his legal bills and help his family in Bangladesh.

"I am her husband, and I am supposed to support her," he said, his voice cracking. "I shouldn't be held. I have eight months in detention because, bottom line, I moved three floors, three flights of stairs."

He said he didn't know he had to tell immigration officials of his apartment change. "My lawyer didn't tell me, nobody told me these things," he said, although he acknowledged he had signed a document agreeing to report address changes. "I signed a paper, but I can't read these things."

Haider would probably have residency status today if he had attended his deportation hearing, said David Leopold of Cleveland, a member of the board of governors of the American Immigration Lawyers Association.

"What makes this situation heart-wrenching [is] he complied with the law," Leopold   25
said. "He was one of the people that stepped up to the plate and went in to register. Obviously the people who show up are the ones to comply with the law, so common sense tells you they are the least likely to be terrorists."

Robin Goldfaden, staff counsel for the American Civil Liberties Union's Immigrant Rights Project in Oakland, Calif., said what's happened to Haider is tragic, but not uncommon. Goldfaden said that 13,000 people received notices nationally for removal proceedings, often for fairly technical problems, as a result of the 2003 registration program.

He said the registration program has been criticized as an ineffective national security tool. "It was based on a blanket approach, singling out people based on religion, national origin and ethnicity. The whole idea that someone who is a national security threat would go to an immigration office was not very plausible."

An immigration appeals panel has upheld Haider's deportation, and his new attorney, Matthew M. Armbrecht, has appealed to the U.S. Eighth Circuit Court of Appeals. "I think the primary reason he should stay is he is married to an American citizen," Armbrecht said.

"I'm hopeful that the circuit court would apply the law as it is intended, not punish people who take reasonable steps to tell them where they are," said Dan Kesselbrenner of Boston, executive director of the National Immigration Project of the National Lawyers Guild. "It seems like they are scapegoating people over issues which have nothing to do with national security, people who have something to contribute to society."

In the meantime, immigration authorities are reluctant to stop a deportation, said   30
Papademetriou of the Migration Policy Institute.

"I find it very hard to believe that a mid-level official in Minnesota would be willing to invest any of his or her political capital to try to reverse a process that appears irreversible at this time," he said. "On the human rights end of a story, this is a hell of a thing to be happening to an individual."

Hernán Rozemberg

An Education in Red Tape

San Antonio Express-News (Texas), October 28, 2004

At the end of the spring semester two years ago, Borghan Nezami Narajabad, a graduate student from Iran, went home during the summer break to marry his fiancée.

His plan was to return to Austin in the fall to continue research for a doctorate in economics at the University of Texas. But on the first day of classes, Nezami was stuck in Iran, still waiting for the U.S. government to renew his student visa.

After nearly four months, Nezami's application passed FBI background checks. He arrived in Austin on Thanksgiving, missing nearly the entire semester.

"I'm not sure what they got out of it," said Nezami, who has to travel to Turkey or Dubai to apply for a visa because there's no U.S. embassy in Iran. "Maybe they do it to make the American people feel safer."

5   Thousands of international students in Texas and across the country are still feeling the impact of increased immigration restrictions and security measures implemented by the U.S. government following the 9-11 attacks.

One of the 19 plane hijackers entered the country with a student visa.

The U.S. State Department, which approves or rejects visa applications after they pass through immigration checks, said it has improved the process.

Most requests no longer are being tossed around among several agencies and a decision is rendered in less than a month, according to a statement released last week.

Foreign student visa applications and approvals are up from this time last year, thanks to an additional 350 officers that were dispatched to consulates, the statement said.

10   Academic leaders acknowledged the government has made some progress, but they say bureaucratic nightmares remain, driving foreign students to drop their U.S. applications and opt instead to study in other countries, such as England and Australia.

As a result, leaders lamented, U.S. institutions have developed a case of brain drain—many foreign students lead national scientific research and they educate U.S. students as teaching assistants—and are taking a financial hit from tuition dollars going elsewhere.

Foreign students pump about $12 billion yearly into the U.S. economy, according to the Institute for International Education, a global group headquartered in New York City.

After reporting hefty increases in international student enrollment into the late 1990s, leading university presidents and academic experts say the flow has now stagnated and even decreased at the graduate level.

More than 586,000 students from abroad enrolled for the 2002–2003 academic year, the last count available. That's about the same as the previous year—but experts fear a decrease is looming.

15   Marlene Johnson, who heads the Association of International Educators, said at a U.S. Senate Foreign Relations Committee hearing this month that foreign students still face extreme delays. Many are denied entry because of an unrealistic requirement of proof they won't stay in the country once they're done studying, she said.

And a $100 nonrefundable fee starting this fall, meant to pay for the government's new foreign student electronic tracking system, adds to the unwelcoming environment, Johnson said.

The main problem is that the U.S. government has not yet been able to clear many of the security-related obstacles it created since the 9-11 attacks, another witness, Theodore Kattouf, told senators.

Kattouf, a former U.S. ambassador to Syria and the United Arab Emirates, said international students take what they learn back home, bolstering the U.S. image abroad and increasing global understanding.

"It is in our national interests to get out the word that the U.S. remains a country welcoming of foreign students and other visitors," said Kattouf, now president of Amideast, an organization that recruits and helps Middle Eastern students to study here.

20   Many local colleges and universities have registered a stagnation or decline in foreign student enrollment.

The University of Texas at Austin is home to the fifth-largest foreign student population in the country, with more than 4,500. Even though enrollment actually increased a year after the attacks, it has since declined.

Because of visa delays, Ahmad El-Zaatari thought he was going to join the university's no-longer-enrolled list.

A senior from Lebanon studying mechanical engineering, he went home in 2003 to attend his sister's engagement party. He only had one semester left to graduate, so he agonized every day for nearly a year and a half over the lack of response to his visa application.

Finally back in Austin this fall, the delay has forced him to take an extra semester to complete courses needed to graduate—and he received a visit this month from the FBI to boot. Agents inquired about an English class paper he wrote in 1999 about a suicide bomber.

Still, El-Zaatari has no regrets—he prefers U.S. societal opportunities and freedoms.   25

"In this country, at least you feel like a human being," he said. "Back home, you're treated like a dog."

Perhaps it's that kind of resiliency that has led the University of Texas at San Antonio to experience an increase in foreign student enrollment—from 355 in 1999 to 809 this fall. Likely related to the recent UTSA boom, the trend stops at the graduate school, where foreign student enrollment is down.

The university isn't relying solely on the government to increase the flow. For the first time, recruiters this year are being dispatched overseas to find potential candidates, said Jane Dunham, UTSA assistant director of international programs.

At least one aspect of their life here looks much brighter now than three years ago, international students said. Once they get here, they can lead normal lives.

Immediately after the attacks, many students, especially Muslims and Arabs, felt like   30
scapegoats for public anger. Many stayed inside locked doors. Countless others rushed home.

But tolerance has returned and many people even go out of their way to make them comfortable, foreign students said.

Still, a feeling of uncertainty permeates college campuses, as threats of more terrorist attacks come and go.

"Fear has taken over this society," said El-Zaatari, the Lebanese student in Austin. "I'm afraid of other peoples' fear."

Christopher Grimes

Colleges Get a Hard Lesson in Making the US More Secure

Financial Times (London, England), April 29, 2004

When the presidents of the top U.S. universities met Tom Ridge, the homeland security secretary, last week to lobby for changing the way student visas are issued, they revealed the depth of their concern at the fall in applications from foreign students.

Applications to U.S. colleges from China, India and western Europe have dropped dramatically this year.

The decline—which included a 76 per cent drop in Chinese graduate applications this year—is raising concerns that the US could lose a longtime source of competitive advantage in research, science and engineering.

University officials put part of the blame on stringent visa requirements enacted after September 11.

5   A recent government study showed that science students faced waits averaging 67 days for security checks to be completed last year. Students in parts of India waited up to 12 weeks to be interviewed for visas.

At Michigan State University, such delays caused some visiting scholars to miss part of the academic year.

Lobbying pressure by colleges has already prompted the State Department to begin streamlining the visa application process. An electronic system for submitting security checks is expected to speed up the process.

But U.S. university officials worry that the visa issue is only part of the problem. Universities in Britain, Canada and Australia have launched aggressive recruiting efforts that have attracted increased international student applications.

International students pump about 13 billion dollars (Euros 11bn, Pounds 7bn) a year into the U.S. economy, according to the Institute of International Education, which administers the prestigious U.S. government-backed Fulbright scholarships.

10   But beyond their immediate economic impact, university officials say they benefit the U.S. in myriad other ways—including taking home positive ideas about the U.S.

Lawrence Summers, president of Harvard, last week warned Colin Powell, the secretary of state, that the decline in foreign students threatens the quality of research coming from U.S. universities.

"If the next generation of foreign leaders are educated elsewhere, we also will have lost the incalculable benefits derived from their extended exposure to our country and its democratic values," Mr. Summers wrote to Mr. Powell.

Some officials at US universities are concerned that anti-US sentiment has contributed to the falling numbers. Danielle Guichard-Ashbrook, associate dean for international students at the Massachusetts Institute of Technology, says she is concerned that the U.S. no longer seems "welcoming" to foreign students. International applications to MIT's graduate programs fell by 17 percent this year.

"Applications are down across the country. Is it because students have tried to apply but had trouble, or is it the perception that the US is not friendly? I think it's more of the latter," she says.

15   The extent of the problem was highlighted by a recent study by the Council of Graduate Schools. The survey showed that graduate applications from international students fell 32 percent over the last year. The worst declines were from China and India, followed by the Middle East, Korea and western Europe.

Though alarming to U.S. university officials, these figures are unlikely to translate into big falls in enrollment in the next academic year because universities are still oversubscribed, albeit less so than they have been in previous years.

Peter Briggs, director of Michigan state's office for international students and scholars, says he is pleased with the quality of applicants for the 2004–2005 academic year.

"What we don't know is whether this is the beginning of a longer trend line, where competition from the UK, Australia and Canada is going to be more attractive because the US has sent out unwelcoming signals," he says.

Regardless of the cause, university officials say they are concerned about the consequences of falling applications—particularly at a time when the U.S. needs to promote a positive image abroad.

Writing Prompts

1. In "Cure for U.S.–Arab Tensions: More Student Visas," John Hughes argues that the way to better our relations with the Arab world is to have more Arabs come to America as students. The implication is that more international students equals fewer terrorists. Write an essay in which you agree or disagree with Hughes's idea.
2. Write a letter to a prospective international student highlighting all of the wonderful things your campus has to offer. Think of yourself as marketing your American school to someone from another country.
3. How is the issue of attracting international students in a post-9/11 world different from the DREAM Act for illegal immigrants? Write an essay in which you compare/contrast the issues in these two separate clusters.
4. Imagine that it was possible for every college student around the world to spend a semester abroad, studying in another country. Write an essay arguing for or against such a system, offering evidence from the essays in this cluster. Would you want to be part of such a system?
5. If you were going to study abroad, how might you introduce your hosts to the United States? Write an essay exploring some elements of American culture and society you think the rest of the world should know about.

What Is at Stake for Citizenship?

1. If we don't have international students who want to come to America to study, how will we introduce our culture and our values to the rest of the world in a positive way?
2. How might it change your college experience to have (or not have) international students in class with you?
3. Are student visas just an easy way for terrorists to infiltrate our society? Does that mean we should keep those people more likely to be terrorists (based on their age, sex, and country of origin) out of America completely? What do you think of that sort of profiling?
4. Should we care what the rest of the world thinks of us? We are, after all, the only superpower on the planet.
5. Assuming that we could separate legitimate students from terrorists, should we make it easier or harder to come to the United States to study? Why?

EXPANDING VOCABULARY

Immigration and Naturalization Service (INS): Once a part of the Department of Justice, the INS regulated deportation, rejection, and admission of aliens. The creation of the Department of Homeland Security divided the INS into the Bureau of Citizenship and Immigration Services and the Bureau of Border Security.

Xenophobia: From the Greek *xenos* (stranger or foreigner) and *phobos* (fear), it literally means to fear strangers. In the twentieth century this meaning was expanded to include a fear of difference or hostility toward foreigners. Often linked to racism and nationalism, xenophobia is at times the driving force behind efforts to end multiculturalism.

CHAPTER

Point of Contact:
Religion in Public Space

On the back of our currency are the words "In God We Trust." When we pledge our allegiance to the flag of the United States, we proclaim that we are "one nation under God." Many early Europeans who came to America did so in search of religious freedom. Our Constitution assures "no law respecting an establishment of religion, or prohibiting the free exercise thereof." This freedom is listed before that of speech, press, peaceable assembly, and the right to petition the government over grievances. When our president takes the oath of office every four years in a public inauguration, he has placed one hand on the Bible and asserted "so help me God." We are a people who historically have attached God to our shared civic life.

What happens, though, when one view of God begins to dominate our public space? A majority of people may make a lot of noise and command a great deal of attention, and their views may drown out the minority voice. In this Point of Contact, three clusters will address the following paths into thinking, talking, and writing about Religion in Public Space:

1. Bible Clubs and Public Schools
2. The Ten Commandments Judge in Alabama
3. United Church of Christ's Advertising Campaign: Controversy and Censorship

These clusters offer varying perspectives on the encroachment of religion into public space. At what point should we be concerned about the erosion of the wall that separates church and state? *How do these readings help you to enter a conversation that is ongoing in the daily news?*

BIBLE CLUBS AND PUBLIC SCHOOLS

In 1984, Congress passed the **Equal Access Law** permitting public secondary schools that receive federal aid and already have at least one student-led, extracurricular club to open their doors to any and all groups. The details of the law are relatively simple: Attendance must be voluntary, and the club must be student initiated and student led. School employees, government officials, or adult persons from the community may not be involved. The clubs must not be disruptive. Teachers or other school officials have the right to monitor the activities to ensure that school property is not harmed. According to some religious websites, Bible clubs in 1980 numbered around 100; by 1995, there were over 15,000. The Equal Access Law is the main reason that the growth in Bible clubs has been so substantial.

Since the Equal Access Law was passed, the courts have remained fairly active in resolving differences between school officials and members of various Bible clubs. Over the last few years, the courts have been sympathetic to the rights of the students in these clubs. While some people worry about the collapse of the wall between church and state, others rejoice in a wider perspective of freedom of speech.

Among the voices collected here are examples of the diversity of the challenges to communities across the United States. First, a principal in Mississippi granted a Bible club permission to use school time to sponsor a "happening," which turned into an all-day revival. The majority of people in the community appeared to support the event. A student in Louisiana sued the school system and won when she was denied permission to start a Bible club during lunch. The Supreme Court supported the establishment of a Bible club in an elementary school in New York. In Massachusetts, students who were barred from passing out peppermint candy canes with religious messages during school hours sued and won the right to do so. The separation of the school curriculum and Bible club activities on school premises is becoming less clear; the dividing line is becoming harder to define. *After reading the selections, at what place do you enter the conversation?*

Todd Starnes

Revival at Public School Stirs 100 Students to Conversion; Fellowship of Christian Athletes Presentation Continues for Hours

Christianity Today, May 9, 2000

What started as a special presentation by the Pearl River Central High School's **Fellowship of Christian Athletes** turned into a full-fledged revival that has transformed the Carriere, Mississippi school and left school administrators astounded.

"It was the most incredible thing I've seen in all my years as an educator," said Pearl River principal Lolita Lee. "The meeting couldn't be stopped. You could tell something spiritual was happening in the lives of those students."

The revival started during a special program sponsored by the Carriere, Miss., school's FCA and attended by nearly 90 percent of the school's 670 students. The program was originally scheduled for one hour, but when the bell rang, Lee said there were more than 100 students standing in line to pray and make spiritual decisions.

So Lee did something that she said probably doesn't happen in normal public school settings—she let the service continue. And continue it did for more than four hours. Through three class periods and lunch, students wept, prayed, sang and made amends with one another.

"It was heart-stopping," said Lee, a member of Lees Chapel No. 1 Baptist Church. "When I realized how many students needed to pray, I went ahead and let the program continue."

5

Following a hastily arranged telephone call to the school superintendent, Lee went back to the gymnasium where the revival was taking place. "Who was I to say to these students, 'Hey, you aren't important. Go back to class.'"

And nearly one month later, Lee said the results of the revival are manifested in the hallways of Pearl River Central High. "I've had teachers and staff tell me how much better the students are," she said. "This has been a wonderful thing for our kids."

The spiritual awakening all started a month earlier when a group of FCA leaders met with their faculty sponsor to discuss plans for the remainder of the school year.

"Everyone was writing down goals and plans when suddenly a teacher suggested we reach our school for Christ," said Cary-Anne Dell, a member of the FCA's leadership team. "That's pretty much how it all got started and the Lord took it from there."

The plan involved an in-school rally during which FCA members would perform skits and share testimonies about what it means to be a Christian.

10

The 18-year-old Dell, who is a member of Pine Grove Baptist Church, said the FCA members shared their plans with churches throughout the area. "We had people praying for us all over south Mississippi," Dell said. "It was incredible to see how all those prayers were answered."

Tim Tolleson, youth pastor at First Baptist Church in nearby Picayune, Miss., said his entire church was involved in praying for the rally. One of his youth, 16-year-old Ben Helger, was also a member of the FCA leadership team.

"Ben spoke during our Sunday night worship service and in the course of his speech he told us about plans for the rally," Tolleson said. "Our church is known as a praying church and we took up the challenge to lift up those kids."

One prayer involved a sound system. The acoustics in the school's gymnasium were terrible, Dell said. "We didn't have a sound system so we started praying. The next day, two churches called the school and offered to provide one."

Since the entire event was student-led and student-organized, Lee said the club didn't have to seek permission from the school board. "In other words, they had my blessing," Lee said.

15

A team of 16 students wrote skits and prepared the rally—all except for the closing. "We just decided that the Lord was going to figure out the closing," Dell said.

On the day of the event, the entire school was invited to participate. At first, Lee said she was skeptical of the meeting. "You know how it is with kids wanting to get out of class," she said. She said 90 percent of the school's population turned out for the meeting.

Midway through the skits, Lee said it was obvious the spirit of the Lord was moving. "I even had tears in my eyes," said the veteran educator.

"You should have seen God working," Dell said. "It was so awesome. I had the chance to lead someone to the Lord right there in the gym."

20   At one point, Lee said she counted 120 students lined up to share testimonies and be counseled. "And keep in mind," Lee added, "this was entirely student-led. Our staff only observed."

For Dell, who will spend a good portion of her summer as a missionary to Haiti with Teen Mania Ministries, the experience was unforgettable. "It is so wonderful to be chosen by God to do his work," she said.

Lee, too, is grateful for the revival service. "Our hallways are filled with students who say how their lives have been changed," Lee said.

Tolleson said the atmosphere at Pearl Central has always been a bit different. "The students and faculty are more open to spiritual things," he said. "So to be honest, I wasn't surprised to see how God moved.

"The FCA had prayed so much and they had so many church families praying for them. This was truly wonderful," he added.

25   David Smale, a spokesman for the Fellowship of Christian Athletes headquarters in Kansas City, Mo., said he was quite pleased to hear the news. "It's actually great news," he said. "And to be honest, it's very unusual in a public school to have something like that."

As for Lee, she said she hasn't suffered any repercussions by allowing the revival to span the course of a school day. "So far, so good," she said. And even if there are, Lee said looking back, she would do the same thing again.

Bruce Nolan

Christian Groups Rejoice in Fervor at Public School

The *Times Union* (Albany, NY), May 28, 2000

Carriere, Miss.—Football jocks wept in the gym. Teenagers took the microphone, haltingly confessing their personal demons and begging for friends' prayers. Students in corridors wept on one another's shoulders.

In an unusual outbreak of fervor being applauded by conservative Christians nationwide, the regular class schedule at Pearl River Central High School broke down one day last month as teachers and administrators at first watched, then joined students in expressions of faith, personal testimonies and prayer in a student Bible club meeting that lasted four hours.

Since that day, news of the so-called "Pearl River Revival" or "Pearl River Happening" has been spreading on Christian radio and Web sites, where it is being noted approvingly as a supernatural event—and a welcome example of a public school's hospitality to Christianity.

Meanwhile, hundreds of congratulatory e-mails have formed a pile 4 inches thick on the desk of Principal Lolita Lee, who suspended classes April 12, the day a late-morning program by Pearl River's Christian students mushroomed into a daylong, schoolwide camp meeting.

5   Some letters, such as one from the conservative **American Family Association** in St. Louis, include a touch of defiance, promising money or other help if Lee or the county school system comes under fire for her decision.

But there is no criticism yet, largely because the event is still not widely known outside conservative circles, and because students, faculty and families in heavily evangelical Pearl River County overwhelmingly approve of what occurred that day, Lee said.

"In the first couple of weeks I must've had 30 or 40 calls from parents, and they were all just real glad that it had happened," she said.

"I think this was a message from God that we need to put God back in our schools," said Judy Mitchell, one of the Bible club's faculty supervisors. "That's how I understood it, and that's become my goal."

But the high school's official hospitality to the class-time event, including teachers' own participation, apparently violated the state of Mississippi's duty to act as "a neutral, honest broker" among all faiths, said Charles Haynes, a constitutional scholar at the **Freedom Forum First Amendment Center** in Arlington, Va., and a consultant generally regarded as a friend of educators' attempts to integrate faith into school life.

"The First Amendment does not keep religion out of schools," Haynes said. "But it   10 says religion can come in only in a way that protects the rights of all the kids, protects them from the government either denigrating or promoting a particular religion."

I grant you, there are times of great emotion when a principal cannot just bring out a gong, as it were, and gong a show to an end without it being hurtful or damaging to young people. That may be the case in times of great stress, if young people gather and begin to pray after a shooting, for instance. I sympathize with that.

"But even then they have to set some kind of limit, and more important, this school I think should not have put itself in that position in the first place."

The Pearl River phenomenon began when the school let a student group, the Fellowship of Christian Athletes, sponsor a 90-minute program for other students during the last class before lunch that day, Lee said.

That in itself was not unusual, Lee said. Similar arrangements have been made for blood drives or student fund-raisers.

Students who wanted to attend were excused from class. "About 90 percent" of Pearl   15 River's 640 students gathered in the school's gym to watch a series of skits promoting Christian life, prepared by the fellowship's members.

"We didn't know what the closing would be, so we left that to God, and he totally took over," said Cary-Anne Dell, a senior and one of the event's organizers. "God was like, 'This can't end.'"

In short order, students began to open up with sometimes intense, emotional confessions in a process that began to feed on itself, Dell and others said.

"I said to myself, 'The Spirit is filling these kids, and I'm going to let it continue. I don't want it to stop,'" said Lee, who had been sitting in the front row.

The line of students waiting to talk quickly grew to 30 or more, she said. Several administrators and teachers, starting with Lee, took the microphone to offer their own testimonies, several participants said.

"Everybody was crying, hugging and kissing," said Jaquaila Jefferson, a 14-year-old   20 freshman.

Lee announced the arrival of the lunch hour, but few people left, said Don Davis, one of the club's supervisors. A little later, Lee placed a call to her supervisor, county school Superintendent Zeno Carter. "But I wasn't calling to ask permission to let it continue," she said. "I wanted him to come see this."

Students grouped and regrouped to pray among themselves in the gym and nearby corridors, participants said.

The club had arranged for youth ministers from two local churches to be on hand to talk to students, "but nobody needed them," Dell said. "It was all kids coming up to other kids and asking, 'Will you pray with me?'"

"We don't have an official number, but something like 15 or 20 came up on faith," as a sign of personal conversion, Davis said. "I guess hundreds gave testimonies and rededicated their lives to Christ. It just kept ballooning and ballooning."

25 "The only reason we stopped is because the buses came at 3:15 p.m., and we still had kids waiting to speak," he said.

Amid all the applause, there have been one or two reservations, among them an unidentified Pearl River teacher who told Lee she may have broken the law.

If so, Lee said she is unsure how, given that the session was student-led and voluntary.

"If the **ACLU (American Civil Liberties Union)** wants to come, go ahead, but the most they can make us do is make up a day," she said. "The students have told us if that's what it means, it's fine by them."

Since the event, she said she also has learned that one teacher and perhaps two students at the school are Jewish, but none has complained, "and I'm not even sure whether they were there."

30 But protecting minority faiths from state-approved religious activity is what the Constitution requires, "and that's a good thing for religion," Haynes said.

Cecilia Student Sues after School Denies Bible Club

State Times/Morning Advocate (Baton Rouge, La.) March 3, 2001

Lafayette—The sophomore class president at a St. Martin Parish high school sued the school system in federal court Friday because she was not allowed to start a lunchtime Bible club and Fellowship of Christian Athletes.

The lawsuit against the St. Martin Parish School Board contends that a school that allows any club not directly related to course work to use the school must also allow religious clubs to do so.

Attorney Mathew D. Staver filed the lawsuit two days after the U.S. Supreme Court heard arguments in a New York State case that makes the same claim.

Louisiana is among 11 states that filed briefs supporting the contention that a student's right to free speech is violated when all religious clubs are barred from after-hours use of school buildings.

5 Opponents say the clubs amount to using schools as churches.

St. Martin Parish School Superintendent Roland J. Chevalier said he could not comment because he had not seen the lawsuit or been told about it.

Dominique Begnaud, 15, is a member of several school teams and several student clubs at Cecilia High School.

She asked Principal Malcolm Calais in the fall for permission to start a Bible club and Fellowship of Christian Athletes. Her letter said the Bible club would meet in the gym or a classroom on Wednesdays during lunch. It gave no time for fellowship meetings.

The St. Martin Parish School Board responded that allowing any religious clubs would violate the constitution's separation of church and state. Its letter said Begnaud should hold such meetings at her church or home, according to the lawsuit.

That stand violates the 1984 Equal Access Act, Staver said in a news release. He said   10
the law forbids public schools from discriminating against any club because of religious or political content.

"Equal access means equal treatment," he said. "If school administrators can't understand the simple message of equal access, you wonder how they can teach children anything." The Equal Access Act would cover an after-school club, but not one that meets during school hours, said Joe Cook, executive director of the American Civil Liberties Union's Louisiana chapter.

"If you allow one noncurriculum club, you've got to allow these others," he said.

However, he said, the group would have to be entirely student-led and student-run and could not have any adult members or any regular adult speakers or faculty sponsors.

Begnaud's letter said her group would prefer to have a parent or church member lead the group but that a student would lead it if necessary.

The FCA "is sponsored by a teacher from the school," she wrote.   15

The Wall between Church and State

Editorial, *Buffalo News* (New York), June 16, 2001

The Supreme Court has decided that 6-year-old kids can easily see the difference between groups who use elementary school buildings for after-school religious proselytizing and school endorsements of religious practices. It's hard to even imagine an "amen" to that.

The high court's 6-3 ruling in favor of a Bible club, of course, is aimed not at the kids but at the adults who determine how public school property is used. The decision merely extends earlier rulings that said denying religious groups the same after-hours access other types of organizations have had to public high school and university facilities is discrimination and a denial of the constitutional right to free speech.

But it's the children who are at the heart of this ruling, which gives a green light to religious groups of all types to use school facilities that are already open, after school, to other community uses.

Although the majority deemed otherwise, citing a requirement for parental permission to participate, it is simply unreasonable to expect children 6 to 12 years old to draw a definite distinction between a classroom teacher's authority on one side of the school bell and a preacher's exhortations half an hour later—or to distinguish between teaching character and values from a religious point of view, Justice Clarence Thomas' description, from outright worship and evangelizing. The court description, as dissenting Justice David H. Souter rightly noted, "ignores reality."

According to University at Buffalo constitutional law expert Lee A. Albert, the distinc-   5
tion between children and older students has been noted in other Supreme Court rulings, including those on school prayer. But, he added, "the wall of separation is less today than it was a decade ago."

The Supreme Court's case involved the **Good News Club** run by the Rev. Stephen D. Fournier's church in the Milford Central School, which doubles as the main community center in a small town between Albany and Syracuse. The club is part of a national movement sponsored by **Child Evangelism Fellowship** to "evangelize boys and girls with the Gospel of the Lord Jesus Christ." But Fournier recognizes his victory—which he describes as a victory against discrimination—could open the school door to a range of other groups, including some with which he would disagree. Rights are rights, he argues with some justification.

And the ruling does not mandate that schools be opened to such activities. Religious groups must only be allowed in if other outside groups have access to the facilities. While simply closing down after-school activities would be a real blow in such small hamlets as Milford or in impoverished urban neighborhoods that need "lighted schoolhouse" programs, school boards might find a reasonable if inconvenient compromise by banning outside uses until an hour or more after the school day ends.

But the slow erosion of the traditional wall between church and state is troubling nonetheless. So is the thought of tasking the very young to recognize the differences between lessons in the same classroom separated only by minutes. Moreover, the court's ruling ignores the real risk that children and families who choose not to participate in religious after-school programs could be made to feel like outsiders in their own schools.

There is a place for religion and a place for public education, but that place is not always the same.

Dave Condren

Staff Problems Keeping Church Groups from Elementary Schools

Buffalo News (New York), June 19, 2001

The U.S. Supreme Court recently opened the doors of public elementary schools to Bible clubs, but it does not appear that anyone in Western New York is poised to rush through them—at least not yet.

The obstacle is a practical one.

"We are not prepared to go into elementary schools. We are not waiting with a team of people to do something like this. Hardly a church in Western New York has enough staff to start clubs in elementary schools," said Rev. Jim Walton, youth pastor at Randall Memorial Baptist Church in Williamsville.

The high court ruled two weeks ago in a case involving the Good News Club, a Christian organization for children ages 6 to 12, that sought to establish an after-school Bible study at Milford Central School, a district between Albany and Syracuse.

5   The school district, which had opened its doors to such groups as 4-H Club and scouts, denied access to the Good News Club, saying that doing so might be seen as an endorsement of religion.

The court disagreed, finding that the religious organization was entitled to the same freedom-of-speech protection as other groups and extending that right to elementary schools. Religion clubs earlier won court authorization to meet in high schools and colleges.

In Western New York, about 50 Bible clubs meet in high schools and middle schools. But the people most closely associated with them say it is unlikely that there will be a rush to establish new ones in elementary schools.

"Churches not having the staff is the issue," said Mike Chorey, director of Buffalo-Western New York **Youth for Christ,** a nondenominational group that supports the Bible clubs, known as First Priority Clubs.

Chorey said the clubs, all of which are student-led, are sponsored or supported by local churches that provide guidance through youth pastors. Those pastors usually are hired to work with junior high and senior high youngsters.

Youth for Christ, which provides materials and training to the local churches and students leaders, is not authorized by its charter to work in elementary schools, Chorey noted.

"Now with elementary schools available, I think the church would be remiss if it did not reach out to more students," he added. "The question is when."

Randall provides support to a Bible Club at Williamsville South High School.

"A lot of youth pastors are seeing a need to get God into the lives of kids at an earlier age," said the Rev. Jason Protzman, youth minister at Love Joy Gospel Church in Lancaster.

"We'll certainly look into it but we don't have a full-time children's pastor to lead it," he said.

The Rev. Daniel Manns, youth pastor at Resurrection Life Fellowship in Cheektowaga, said his church would be interested in starting an elementary school club "if a church member stepped up and said 'I want to do that sort of thing.'"

Resurrection will sponsor a club in Depew High School in September.

The Rev. Gene Coplin Jr., who runs Project Learning and Earning Experiences in Buffalo public schools, said he would start Bible clubs in the elementary schools if pupils and parents indicated an interest.

The Rev. Barry W. Lynn, executive director of Americans United for Separation of Church and State, fears there will be too much reaching out.

The ruling means "aggressive fundamentalist evangelists have a new way to proselytize school kids," Lynn said.

"I don't think the issue is proselytizing. I think the issue is the need to save kids," said Chorey. "I see this as a time for the church to reach out and really help young people."

Gregory Baylor, who wrote a supporting court brief for Child Evangelism Fellowship, the national organization that sponsors the Good News Clubs, said the decision means the Good News Club has to be treated like any other community organization.

There also is an assumption that elementary school Bible clubs could be led by adults, if other after-school groups have adult leadership, he said.

Baylor said attorneys assumed that "after school" means the time when mandated classes end for the day.

That point was an issue for the Good News Club in the Milford case because its leaders wanted to meet immediately after classes to attract the most children.

However, David D. White, a Williamsville attorney, predicted that more litigation may be necessary to determine the precise meaning of "after school."

"I'm sure some creative school board member will suggest that time for after-school meetings be provided at 7 p.m.," said White, one of the lawyers who represented students at Buffalo's McKinley High in a successful lawsuit to start an after-school Bible club there in 1990.

John McElhenny

Federal Rule Aids Student Lawsuit; Bible Club Fights Ban on Messages

Boston Globe, March 2, 2003

A new federal regulation strengthening protections for prayer in public schools will buttress a lawsuit brought by six Westfield students suspended for distributing candy canes with religious messages, the students' lawyers said.

The regulation also threatens local school districts with a loss of federal money if they prevent students from praying in school, and requires local school officials to prove to the state that they are not denying students the right to pray in school.

Students may pray with fellow students during the school day on the same terms and conditions that they may engage in other conversation or speech, said the new US Department of Education regulation, which was issued Feb. 7.

The stated purpose of this guidance is to clarify the extent to which prayer in public schools is legally protected.

5   Local public schools have until March 15 to prove to the state in writing that they have no policy that keeps students from praying, according to the regulation. After that, state education officials have until April 15 to give the US Department of Education a list of schools that haven't filed or are in violation.

Schools found in violation will be ineligible for federal funds distributed under the **No Child Left Behind Act,** US Secretary of Education Rod Paige said. Last year, Massachusetts schools received $114 million in new federal money from the act.

In the Westfield Operation Candy Cane case, lawyers for the students praised the new regulation, and said they would submit it in court papers in support of their lawsuit.

The students, who are members of the school's Bible Club, are asking the US District Court in Springfield to throw out their one-day suspensions, allow them to distribute religious materials in school, and declare the school's actions unconstitutional.

The case has drawn national attention.

10   "They clearly are discriminating against these students because of the religious content of their literature," said Mathew Staver, lead counsel for the students and president of the **Liberty Counsel,** a Florida-based group affiliated with the Rev. Jerry Falwell, the conservative Protestant leader.

"These guidelines buttress our case and confirm its validity," said Staver.

William Newman, director of the Western Massachusetts office of the ACLU, who also has supported the students, agreed that the new guideline strengthens the students' case.

Thomas McDowell, the Westfield superintendent of schools, has said the issue has nothing to do with the students' religious views. He said they were prohibited from passing out the candy canes because students are not allowed to distribute anything on school grounds that is unrelated to the curriculum.

McDowell and the high school principal, Thomas W. Daley, did not return repeated phone calls, and Daley's lawyer, Terrence M. Dunphy, declined to comment.

15   Like other states, Massachusetts benefited financially from the federal No Child Left Behind Act of 2001, which pumped billions of dollars into schools across the country. Last year, Massachusetts received $826 million in federal education funds, including the

$114 million increase from the No Child Left Behind Act, said Heidi Perlman, spokeswoman for the state Department of Education.

But the new guideline shows that the federal money comes with strings attached, and now Westfield, like other districts around the state, will have to prove that it doesn't discriminate against prayer in its schools.

Westfield received more than $2.5 million in federal education funds last year, including about $450,000 in No Child Left Behind funding, Perlman said.

Education Commissioner David Driscoll has sent an e-mail to the state's superintendents, notifying them of the new guideline and the March 15 deadline for proving their compliance.

The Westfield controversy originated in December when the students, in what they called Operation Candy Cane, passed out 450 pieces of candy in hallways and at lunch despite school officials' stated opposition and threats of suspension.

The candy canes contained notes declaring that the J shape stood for Jesus and that   20
the red and white stripes symbolized Christ's blood and purity.

The students were told on Jan. 2 that they would have to serve one-day in-school suspensions. Less than two weeks later, they sued in federal court, saying school officials had violated their free speech rights.

The suspensions were put off until the conclusion of the legal proceedings. The US Department of Justice and the Massachusetts ACLU filed legal briefs in support of the students last week, and on Tuesday, US District Judge Frank H. Freedman took the case under advisement. No date was set for a decision.

"We feel this is something God wants us to do," said Sharon Sitler, 17, a Westfield High School senior and one of the Bible Club members taking part in the lawsuit.

"We want the Bible Club to be able to do this every year without being rebels against the administration."

Matthew D. Staver
Federal Court Upholds Student Right to Dispense Candy Canes

Junto Society for Legal Issues, Liberty Counsel, March 18, 2003

WESTFIELD, MASS—Yesterday, federal district court Judge Frank Freedman issued an injunction against the Westfield Public Schools, prohibiting the school from disciplining six students who distributed candy canes with a religious message to their fellow students. The students, all members of the L.I.F.E. Bible Club at Westfield High School, are represented by Matthew D. Staver, President and General Counsel of Liberty Counsel, and Erik W. Stanley, Litigation Counsel for Liberty Counsel. Liberty Counsel is a civil liberties legal defense and education organization based in Orlando, Florida.

In December of 2002, the student members of the Bible Club decided to pass out candy canes with an attached folded card which contained the story of the candy cane as well as Bible verses. The attached message talked about the Bible Club meetings, contained a scripture verse, and then told the story of a candy cane maker who wanted to invent a candy that was a witness to Christ. The distribution of the candy canes and the attached literature was to occur one day prior to the Christmas break on December 19, 2002. Some of the students who are members of the Bible Club approached the principal to request permission to distribute the candy canes during non-class time. The principal refused the request, indicating that the Christian message contained in the literature may be "offensive" to other students. He then consulted with the superintendent, Thomas McDowell, and he too agreed that other students could be offended by the Christian message. He denied the request. Believing that God called them to share the Gospel message, these students distributed about 450 candy canes to their fellow classmates during non-class time. After the seven students returned from Christmas break on January 2, 2003, they were summoned to the principal's office and told that they would be suspended for distributing their literature. Members of the Bible Club the previous school year made a similar request to distribute candy canes with the same message. At that time, the school principal denied the request but finally agreed that the only message which could be contained on the candy canes was "Happy Holidays." However, this time, the students believed that it was wrong to compromise the Christian message and felt compelled to share their faith in Christ.

The students filed a federal lawsuit against the school claiming that the school's denial of their request to distribute religious literature violated their right to free speech. The students asked the Court to issue an injunction against the school to prohibit the school from disciplining the students and to prohibit the school from enforcing its unconstitutional literature distribution policies.

In his decision, Judge Freedman found that the school's actions in disciplining the students for distributing the religious candy canes violated the students' First Amendment rights. The Judge also found that the school's literature distribution policies were likely to be found unconstitutional. The opinion clearly identified the distribution of the candy canes as private student speech which was governed by the Free Speech Clause and rejected the school's argument that allowing the students to distribute the religious literature would violate the Establishment Clause.

5   Mat Staver, President and General Counsel of Liberty Counsel, stated, "This case strikes a mighty blow for student free speech. The Judge made it abundantly clear that the Free Speech Clause clearly protects a student's right to hand a religious message to a fellow student. In my opinion, this is the best and most well-reasoned legal decision in print on the issue of student literature distribution." Staver continued, "The Supreme Court, in 1969, clearly held that students do not shed their constitutional rights when they enter the schoolhouse gates. This case reaffirms that principle and is a powerful reminder to school officials throughout the nation that the First Amendment is alive and well and should not be ignored. This decision is a masterpiece that will become a classic and frequently cited case defending the rights of student free speech on public school campuses." Erik Stanley, Litigation Counsel for Liberty Counsel stated, "We are extremely pleased with the Injunction entered in this case. The Court, in a well-reasoned opinion, very clearly explained the rights of public school students to distribute religious literature." Stanley concluded, "Students should be aware of their rights and not be intimidated by unconstitutional school policies that violate their rights."

Writing Prompts

1. Write a three-page paper arguing for or against the Supreme Court's decision to permit Bible clubs in elementary schools. Consider Justice David Souter's position that the Court's ruling "ignores reality." Do you agree?
2. Write a letter to the principal of Pearl River Central High School giving your position on the revival that happened during school hours.
3. If you have personal knowledge of or experience with a Bible club during your high school days, what position would that group have taken on the candy cane distribution?
4. According to McElhenny, federal funds from the No Child Left Behind Act have strings attached. Should schools have to provide a written declaration that explains that students will not be denied the right to pray at school?
5. Compare the message and the voice in the two pieces about the candy cane case.

What Is at Stake for Citizenship?

1. Do the majority of students who supported the activity at Pearl River Central High have any responsibility for the rights of the silent minority?
2. Should elementary school-aged children be expected to know the difference between their school activities and a Bible club's activities after school hours?
3. Should students be able to make their own decisions about how they spend time during their lunch hour?
4. Should students be permitted to give away religious tokens during a school day?
5. Is there a difference between someone handing or offering you something and your being invited to take something out of a common box? Should students have the right to hand out religious messages to other students and teachers?

THE TEN COMMANDMENTS JUDGE IN ALABAMA

At the beginning of 2004, a city council member in Winston-Salem, North Carolina, placed a one-ton granite monument etched with the Ten Commandments in front of city hall. Later that year, a judge in Alabama began wearing a judicial robe embroidered with the Ten Commandments. Both events were inspired by Judge Roy Moore of Alabama, who has been in the news since the early days of the twenty-first century, especially for the two and a half ton Ten Commandments monument he placed in the rotunda of the Alabama Supreme Court building in the summer of 2001. Since then, Judge Moore has been ordered to remove the monument, and when he failed to comply, he was ousted as chief justice of the Alabama Supreme Court. But Judge Moore has not gone away quietly. Meanwhile, the monument, known as "Roy's Rock," has been touring the nation.

Part of the architectural design of the Supreme Court of the United States in Washington, D.C., includes sculptures of Moses and the Ten Commandments, but many historians interpret Moses as one in a line of the world's historical lawgivers. His presence at the highest court in the country, then, is not a religious statement but rather an historical one. How you choose to interpret Moses and the Ten Commandments in Washington will likely influence your thoughts about Moore's activities in Alabama.

The commentary included in this cluster follows a chronological progression. The first piece offers some background information on how Moore rose to Alabama's highest judiciary seat. Following are responses in other newspaper accounts after the installation of the large monument in the rotunda. Even when Moore's own Supreme Court justice peers ruled that he must remove the monument, he chose, instead, to resist. Ultimately, this resistance was at the heart of his own removal from the bench. However, many citizens believe Moore was within his rights to display the monument. He gave the rock to a Houston-based group, **American Veterans Standing for God and Country,** who, since July 2004, has taken the monument on a tour of America that has included over a hundred stops at various gatherings. *After reading the following pieces, how would you enter the conversation?*

Stan Bailey

Moore: Will Seek Blessings of God

The *Birmingham News,* January 16, 2001

Ten Commandments monument.

MONTGOMERY—Roy Moore became Alabama's 28th chief justice on Monday with a promise to seek God's blessings and promote understanding of the U.S. Constitution.

A standing-room-only crowd packed the domed chamber and balcony of the Alabama Supreme Court and gave Moore a lengthy standing ovation after he took the oath of office.

Moore, whose refusal to remove a hand-carved plaque of the Ten Commandments from his Gadsden courtroom made national headlines and propelled his election to the state's top court job, said his first official act as chief justice would be to acknowledge God.

Before a crowd of dignitaries that included two former governors and two former chief justices, Moore quoted from George Washington's 1789 address to Congress in which he sought God's blessing on the nation.

"We need today, as they did then, God's blessings," Moore said.   5

Judges are bound by the Constitution as the supreme law of the land, Moore said, but he said the Constitution doesn't prohibit the acknowledgment of God.

"I hope that in my tenure as chief justice, I will bring back an understanding of that Constitution, which remains law," Moore said. "I ask that you join with me to secure the blessings of liberty," Moore said, "and that once again we'll be one nation, under God, with liberty and justice for all."

Perry O. Hooper Sr., the white-haired retiring chief justice, administered the oath to his successor. He praised Moore for his courage during his military service and his legal battle over the Ten Commandments.

"That shows the courage you have," said Hooper, the state's first Republican chief justice in a century.

Gov. Don Siegelman wasn't present for the ceremony, but former governors Guy Hunt   10 and John Patterson attended, along with former U.S. Sen. and Alabama Chief Justice Howell Heflin and former chief justice Sonny Hornsby.

During his formal remarks, Moore made no mention of the Ten Commandments plaque, but he has said he will defer to other members of the Supreme Court on whether to hang it in the chamber.

"In due time we'll let you know about that," Moore said after the ceremony. He said he brought the plaque with him to Montgomery but hasn't unpacked it yet.

Barry Lynn, executive director of **Americans United for Separation of Church and State,** which has criticized Moore's display of the Ten Commandments in his Gadsden courtroom, said his group has no objection to placing the plaque in Moore's private office. But he said Moore risks another suit if he places it in the Supreme Court chamber. "He would again be in defiance of the Constitution of the United States. I hope he would not be foolish enough to disgrace the oath he took," Lynn said.

Paul Greenberg

Dueling Symbols

Arkansas Democrat-Gazette, August 12, 2001

At least since the time of another Fighting Judge—George C. Wallace—the state of Alabama has provided a perfect backdrop for the duel of symbols that regularly takes the place of political dialogue in American life.

Now it's the chief justice of Alabama's Supreme Court, Roy Moore, who has set the stage for a constitutional confrontation, and Alabama is welcome to it. Here in Arkansas, we're just getting over the one Orval Faubus staged in 1957.

Chief Justice Moore first made national headlines and case law when he was plain Judge Moore, and posted a plaque of the Ten Commandments in his Northern Alabama courtroom.

Now elected to the state's highest court, probably on the strength of that display, he's gone Cecil B. DeMille on us. Talk about an epic production: One night last week, the chief justice directed the installation of a 5,280-pound granite monument to the Ten Commandments right in the middle of the rotunda of the Alabama Supreme Court. It sits there like an indoor boulder. That'll show 'em.

5   Just who Them are is a shifting but well understood category in these latitudes. Atheists. Communists. Civil Libertarians. Pointy-headed Intellectuals. All those who believe in a strict separation of church and state. Or just any favorite infidel you'd like to throw into the mix on cultural, racial, political or ethnic grounds. (For those who keep up with fashion in these matters, Hispanics seem to have replaced black folks as the scape-goat du jour in these latitudes.) In short, the Other. Them.

As in, "Just let 'em come try and move that rock!" Can't you just hear a young, throaty-voiced George Corley Wallace Jr. yelling that line for the umpteenth time at the end of a long day on the stump? It's enough to bring back the old days. Days only a newspaper-man desperate for good copy might miss.

This rock with the Ten Commandments engraved on it also includes quotations from various Great Americans pointing out the religious basis of the Constitution and the American system in general. The additional quotes may be necessary to keep the rock-in-the-rotunda constitutionally kosher. Since the real Supreme Court has ruled that stand-alone religious displays on public property may infringe on the First Amendment, but may pass legal muster as part of an historical or cultural exhibit.

That is, religious art is okay if it's sufficiently secularized. Which is how those most intent on imposing their own religious symbols wind up desacralizing them.

Now along comes a judge and plants a rock. Think of Moses coming down the mountain bearing the tablets of the law and, on the reverse side, a variety of endorse-ments from the leading politicians of the era. Just to give the Commandments a little moral weight. Call it sacrilege. There's a lot of it going around these days, but most of it is unconscious, respectable sacrilege. Chief Justice Moore, bless his heart, doubtless thinks of his rock as some kind of testament to piety rather than hubris.

10   Men live by symbols, a justice of the U.S. Supreme Court famously said. He did not need to point out that men also die for symbols. For one man's object of veneration is another's act of provocation. Which is why the species keeps engaging in that paradox, reli-gious wars.

This spectacle in Montgomery is the architectural equivalent of Protestant Orangemen staging their annual parade through Catholic Belfast. Chief Justice Moore has just fired a shot across the Other's bow. And the Other will respond in kind. The legal briefs should soon be crossing each other in the mail. Happily, in this part of the world we deploy legal precedents instead of pipe bombs. (Which is another benefit of separating church and state.)

One state representative, Alvin Holmes from Montgomery, is striking back. He says he's hired an artist to prepare his own, separate-but-equal display of Martin Luther King's "I Have a Dream" speech for the rotunda. And if anybody tries to stop him, he says, he'll go to federal court. Nothing like adding racial to religious tensions. Can the culture wars have come back? Or did they ever go away? And how long before the rotunda is full of competing icons and their worshippers? Welcome to religious witness in America, 2001. Which isn't always easy to tell from just another political, cultural, and ethnic donnybrook.

One of the most illuminating little books about the American system is Daniel Boorstin's *The Genius of American Politics.* And one of the most illuminating chapters in it is entitled, "The Mingling of Religious and Political Thought." Which is not to be confused with the mingling of church and state. Some of our most religious thinkers, like Roger Williams, have also been our most ardent separationists. Perhaps the most illuminating sentence in that chapter is this one: "Intellectually speaking, 'religions' are unimportant in American life; but Religion is of enormous importance."

A tolerant, civil, non-denominational kind of Religion in General unites us, creating an atmosphere of mutual respect. For religious ideas are implicit in the American system. (See the Declaration of Independence and Lincoln's Second Inaugural.) But once those ideas become explicit dogma, a mandatory creed, a religious test, they no longer unite but divide.

An empty public square is a useful thing. It allows us to stay apart together. Start fill- 15
ing it up with granite monuments and counter-monuments, and our attentions are diverted, our loyalties split. Our public spaces become like a Roman pantheon full of com-peting gods. And we turn on one another, sneaking our favorite symbol into the forum under cover of night, and daring Them to remove it. What ought to elevate and unite us divides us, and reduces faith to a rhetorical contest. To quote Finley Peter Dunne's amiable Irish barkeep, Mr. Dooley: "Rayligion's a quare thing. Be itself, rayligion's all right. But sprin-kle a little pollytics into it, and dinnymite is bran flour compared with it. Alone it prepares a man fir a better life. Combined with pollytics, it hurries him to it."

For space and light, for enough room both to come together and avoid trampling one another, it's hard to beat a big, beautiful, spacious, and uncluttered rotunda. In the ancient Temple, they say, the mysterious Holy of Holies contained no symbols at all.

Paul Greenberg, editorial page editor of the *Arkansas Democrat-Gazette,* has won the Pulitzer Prize for editorial writing.

Lee McAuliffe Rambo

The Ten Commandments: Halt Judge's High-Handed Campaign to Push Religion

The *Atlanta Journal-Constitution,* July 24, 2003

It's a monument to ignorance and it has to go.

For the second time in as many years, a federal court has ordered Alabama Chief Jus-tice Roy Moore to remove a two-ton display of the Ten Commandments from the rotunda of the state Judicial Building in Montgomery. The 11th Circuit Court of Appeals recently upheld a ruling that the exhibit violates the constitutional separation of church and state.

Widely known as the "Ten Commandments Judge," Moore vowed to take his crusade to the Supreme Court.

"We must defend our rights and preserve our Constitution," he said. "For the federal courts to adopt the agenda of the ACLU [American Civil Liberties Union] and to remove the knowledge of God and morality from our lives is wrong."

Recent months have seen several legal contests over the public display of the Ten 5
Commandments, but none so theatrical as this. Moore has been a hero of the religious right since 1995, when he hung a carving of the Commandments behind his bench at the

state courthouse in Gadsden. The ACLU threatened suit and Moore rode the ensuring publicity to election as chief justice in 2000.

Since installing the shrine—at his own expense, in the middle of the night and without the knowledge of his colleagues—Moore has gained the support of TV evangelist D. James Kennedy and Alabama Attorney General William Pryor, whom President Bush recently nominated to the 11th Circuit Court of Appeals.

Thank goodness the current judges were unmoved by the Decalogue Demagogue. In a 50-page ruling, the panel scoffed at Moore's high-handed effort to promote his own religion.

"If we adopted his position," they wrote, "the chief justice would be free to adorn the walls of the Alabama Supreme Court's courtroom with sectarian religious murals and decidedly religious quotations painted above the bench. Every government building could be topped with a cross, a menorah or a statue of Buddha, depending on the views of the officials with authority over the premises."

Rather than draft another brief at taxpayers' expense, Moore would be wise to do a little research in moral philosophy. He might be surprised to learn that his view of morality is a minority opinion that is widely regarded as immature.

10   Moore and his supporters believe that religion alone fosters morality, that God issues moral directives that one ignores at one's peril. This stage of moral development, exemplified by very young children, focuses on taboos, obedience and penalties.

This deity is a judge; it's easy to understand why Moore would identify with him. No doubt the jurist was emulating his god when he installed the monument. As he told the *Los Angeles Times,* "I'm the highest legal authority in the state and I wanted it here."

Here's the objection: This notion makes God's power the basis for what is right, and "might makes right" is a fallacy that virtually all ethical systems (and kindergarten teachers) seek to correct. According to this code, your God can order the destruction of Marietta and since there is no independent measure for evaluating that command—it's goodbye, Big Chicken.

What's more, the idea that morality depends on religion is contradicted by the vast numbers of nonreligious people who behave morally—many to an admirable degree.

Socrates is considered the founder of ethics and one of the most upright people who ever lived. Yet, there is no evidence that he believed in a god who issued decrees. Both Augustine and Aquinas held that human reason alone, without the aid of faith, was an adequate guide to knowing right from wrong.

15   Today, ethicists hold that folks both religious and secular can achieve the highest level of morality, doing what is right because it is intrinsically good.

Megh Duwadi

High Court Refuses to Hear Ten Commandments Case

Houston Chronicle, Washington Bureau, November 4, 2003

WASHINGTON—The Supreme Court on Monday declined to hear the appeals of an Alabama judge seeking to reinstall a 5,280-pound monument of the Ten Commandments in his courthouse.

Without providing additional analysis, the court said it will not hear two appeals by Alabama Chief Justice Roy Moore, now on suspension for ignoring a federal judge's order in August to remove from the state supreme court building a massive granite monument inscribed with the commandments.

As Alabama's top judge, Moore argued that his authority superseded that of a lower federal court. He also called for a new judicial standard to replace the court's current test of church-state separation.

Moore has drawn fire from civil liberties groups for flouting the Constitution's church-state separation, but he maintained there was nothing wrong with displaying the monument in the rotunda of the Alabama state Judicial Building.

The biblical depiction shows "God as the source of the community morality so essential to a self-governing society," Moore argued in a court petition to re-install the slab. 5

Moore, a Republican who dubbed himself "the Ten Commandments judge" in a successful 2000 campaign for Alabama chief justice, said the display was in fact constitutional and does not break the First Amendment's clause barring the establishment of a government-sanctioned religion.

The Ten Commandments promote moral rectitude as much as they promote religion, Moore said, noting that "the U.S. has no problem taking up other moral issues, like sodomy . . . and murder."

A federal judge disagreed, mandating in August that the monument be taken down. Moore refused, filing a quickly rejected motion to the Supreme Court for a stay preventing its removal, but his fellow justices on the state supreme court bench complied. After two years of prominent display, the monument was removed on Aug. 27. It remains stashed in a courthouse closet, far from public sight.

Lawyers representing the three Alabama lawyers who sued Moore in 2001 hailed Monday's decision as a victory for the government staying out of religious affairs.

"It is time for Moore to face facts: he's on the wrong side of the Constitution," said the Rev. Barry Lynn, executive director of Americans United for Separation of Church and State. "Religious symbols belong in our homes and houses of worship, not our courthouses." 10

Richard Cohen, general counsel for the **Southern Poverty Law Center,** said the next step is for Moore to resign from office. The once-obscure Alabama judge faces charges of judicial ethics violations. A hearing has been set for Nov. 12.

The Supreme Court's unanimous refusal to hear the Alabama chief justice's appeals is "just a reflection" of the extreme nature of his views, Cohen said.

But Moore, a favorite of fundamentalist Christian groups and a longtime supporter of public displays of the Ten Commandments, said he isn't backing down just yet.

"We've got to understand where our morality comes from," he said Monday on a FOX News Channel broadcast from Prattville, Ala. "It comes from God."

Cal Thomas

Tough Questions in Alabama

Chattanooga Times Free Press, August 27, 2003

Logicians say it is impossible to hold two conflicting thoughts simultaneously. But I do when it comes to the Ten Commandments case in Alabama and the ongoing debate about the relationship between church and state.

Alabama Chief Justice Roy Moore issued a statement Aug. 14, challenging an order by federal U.S. District Judge Myron Thompson. Thompson ordered the removal of a stone depiction of the Ten Commandments from the rotunda of the Alabama Judicial Building. Moore refused to obey the order and appealed the ruling to the U.S. Supreme Court, which rejected the appeal, allowing the order to stand.

Moore is right about the history of the country and the religious language that runs through the public pronouncements and documents of the Founders (though not all who used it believed in a personal God). He is also right when he says, "The entire justice system (of Alabama) is established in the Alabama Constitution,' . . . invoking the favor and guidance of Almighty God.'" And Moore is correct again when he says, "Under the 10th Amendment to the U.S. Constitution, federal courts have absolutely no power, authority or jurisdiction to tell the state of Alabama that we cannot acknowledge God as the source of our justice system."

In recent years, the federal courts—egged on by groups like the ACLU and Americans United for the Separation of Church and State—have regularly targeted religious expression for removal from public life. Two of the more outrageous rulings have come from the 9th Circuit Court of Appeals, which found the "under God "clause in the Pledge of Allegiance unconstitutional, and the 4th Circuit Court, which ordered an end to a 20-second ecumenical dinner blessing that has been recited at Virginia Military Institute throughout its 162-year history.

5   The building blocks of our nation and culture are being dismantled by judges who are unaccountable to "we the people." Can a nation expect the kind of moral purpose it requires of its soldiers if they are sent into battle to defend the stock market or earthly philosophies?

I am offended many times a day by what I see on the streets, in the media and by the rulings of some courts. But I am told that in a pluralistic society I must tolerate those who hold other views. Why, then, must others not similarly accommodate my views?

The conflicting thought is that nowhere in Scripture is the secular state expected to acknowledge God. The state is an instrument of God, which Paul tells us we are to obey for our own good (Romans 13:1-5). There are verses about nations being "blessed whose God is the Lord" (Psalm 33:12). But there is no expectation or command for the state to be an instrument in spreading God's message to humankind. That is clearly the job of those who follow Him. In fact, when the state takes upon itself the work of spreading God's message (or is asked to do so by God's followers), it often does a poor job.

Does the presence of the Ten Commandments in a courthouse, or a creche on public property in December, or a cross on state property, advance or detract from the message these symbols are supposed to communicate? Will an irreligious people who worship their personal golden calves of pleasure and affluence be more likely to "seek first the Kingdom of God and His righteousness" (Matthew 6:33) if they see such displays, or be lulled into a false security that God is somehow pleased or tolerant of the increasingly secular outlook of His creation?

If the ultimate question is how best for God's followers to interest more people in Him and His message, then the ultimate answer ought to come from internal, not external, things. Loving your enemies, praying for those who persecute you, feeding the hungry, clothing the naked, visiting those in prison and caring for widows and orphans make up the "strategy" laid down by the Founding Father of the Christian faith. Could it be that too many have forsaken the harder but more effective work in favor of exterior symbols that, like crosses worn as jewelry, tell the observer nothing about one's heart?

It's a conflict, not only between church and state, but between God and man. 10

Natalie Hopkinson

Beliefs Carved in Stone; Christians, Atheists Gather at Ten Commandments Rock

Washington Post, October 23, 2004

"Roy's Rock" on tour.

Everyone wants a piece of the rock. So much so, that they nearly come to blows over it.

The Canadian "abortion survivor" circling on roller blades wants to snap it with his digital camera. The Bible-clutching Native Americans from Oregon want to chant Scripture over it. The Christian flagmaker wants to drop to her knees, weep, rub her fingers over its inscriptions. Even the atheists want a piece of "Roy's Rock."

For two years, the gray granite Ten Commandments monument stood in an Alabama courthouse, a 2½-ton slab inscribed with biblical verse and words from the Founding Fathers. But since a federal court ordered it removed last year, and former Alabama chief justice Roy Moore was fired for his refusal, it has crossed a sacred, mythical threshold that has ignited the faithful.

"It's more than just a bunch of rock now," says Dan Karasik, a 27-year-old messianic Jew from Philadelphia, as yesterday's America for Jesus Rally was projected onto big-screen televisions behind him. "It represents what is happening in the country. They are trying to remove God from the foundation of this country."

"It's a piece of history now," says 20-year-old John Russell, flanked by his young wife, 5
Jennifer. "It's good [that it is here] because they are not allowing it to be forgotten."

In late July, Moore gave the Ten Commandments monument to the Houston-based American Veterans Standing for God and Country, part of the American Veterans in Domestic Defense, who have taken his rock—perched atop a flatbed truck—on a road trip to churches, revivals, schools and festivals. It came to the Mall for an event organized by Bishop John Gimenez, pastor of the Rock Church in Virginia Beach. Hundreds came to the Mall for the rally.

Folks steadily stream past the monument because they want to study it up close, unclouded by the lenses of TV cameras and unsullied by the snickers of "liberal-media" types. They want to touch it, feel it, take in the cool breeze sailing past it, step over the golden fall leaves dropping around it, snap pictures of loved ones smiling beside it.

Shelly Eley and her friend Peggy Zuckero, up from Petersburg, Va., stand on the truck and caress the lectern-size granite for the second time. The first time, they say, they both wept. This time, their eyes are dry as they step down. "I was just so overcome," Eley says.

"John Kerry!" a cyclist screams out.

10   "Dubya!" Eley screams at the man's back.

On a small portable CD player, country singer Darren Pearson is singing a Ten Commandments song commissioned for the tour. Nearby, a lonely white sign is painted with red letters reading "Elect Jesus Christ Head of Your Life: Paid for by His Precious Blood." Behind a row of portable potties, two young boys wrestle in the grass. A woman hoists a massive wooden cross spray-painted "Jesus Died 4 U."

Marshall Tall Eagle, a 67-year-old member of the Apache tribe is wearing head-to-foot regalia covered in colorful ribbons. He is a devoted Christian who came to pray. Tall Eagle spots a man approaching holding a sign reading "God Is Just Pretend," and wearing a gray baseball cap proclaiming himself "UNSAVED."

"What does that hat say?" Tall Eagle demands of Ron Hertzel. Hertzel is a 62-year-old retiree from Altoona, Pa., who came to see the monument along with about a dozen other atheists and humanists to protest The Rock.

Terse words are exchanged. A crowd begins to form. U.S. Park Police begin to drift over. A handful of similar arguments are breaking out between believers and nonbelievers in front of Roy's Rock.

15   "You are a product of my religion!"

"No, I'm a product of reason!"

"It started 'Under God.'"

"It's a personal matter!"

"Thomas Jefferson said . . . "

20   "That's my hero!"

Minutes later, Tall Eagle and Hertzel are still going at it. Hertzel tosses his "UNSAVED" hat at Tall Eagle, who grabs it and throws it across the grass. The atheists and Christians retreat back to their respective corners.

"Don't shake hands with any of these people, or they'll try to pray for you," says Ron Stauffer, another atheist from Altoona, brushing off his hands and scowling as if he just stepped in something.

Hertzel, who is still without his "UNSAVED" hat, asks, "Where were you when I needed you?"

Marcia Eldreth steps down from the flatbed truck. She's wearing a brown suede cowboy hat and matching vest. In the spring of 2003, she got a vision from God: an eagle carrying a banner in his beak with the words "Take heed that no man deceive you." She drew up the vision on a large white flag that she called "the United States National Christian Flag." "It's the battle and victory flag to reclaim this land for Christ," says Eldreth, a former laborer from Cecil County, Md. "He will be back soon, just as sure as Christ came the first time."

25   On the truck, her U.S. National Christian Flag waves in the brisk air. About a dozen believers are on top of the truck. There are a handful of Native American Christians. Another dozen are part of Line of Judah, a team of musicians sounding deep calls on the horns of African antelopes. Several also wear prayer shawls inscribed with Hebrew. They read a few Scriptures. Then the horns ring out their version of the watchman's warning, calling on the world to repent.

Writing Prompts

1. Greenberg makes a comparison between Moore's actions and the events that happened in his state of Arkansas in 1957. Greenberg is referring to the integration of Central High School in Little Rock, Governor Faubus's challenge to the Constitution, and President Dwight Eisenhower's subsequent defense of the Constitution when he called in the 101st Airborne troopers to protect the nine integrating black students. After you research the Central High School integration online (look for "Little Rock Nine"), do you believe Greenberg is correct in making a connection with that event and Moore's stand in support of his Ten Commandments monument?
2. Rambo calls the rock a "monument to ignorance." Is this appropriate language? Is the argument supported with ample evidence?
3. The Supreme Court refused to hear an appeal about the removal of the monument. Do you agree with that decision?
4. Use Thomas to support an argument that religious language does have a place in the public arena. How and where do you think the line should be drawn?
5. Are you aware of religious displays in the public space of your hometown? If so, do you think they should or should not be there? Use evidence from the readings to support your thinking.

What Is at Stake for Citizenship?

1. Moore's monument has inspired other elected officials to appropriate the Ten Commandments to make a statement in public space. What effect does the display of the biblical laws in places where you least expect to find them have on you?
2. Is it possible to see images or language associated with religious doctrine in public space without making a connection to a particular religious persuasion?
3. Do you think size, shape, weight, decoration, and presentation all help determine the religious seriousness of the statement?
4. After you reread the First Amendment of the Constitution, do you believe Moore has a viable case for his position?
5. Why does the presence of the Ten Commandments rock cause people to become enraged with each other?

UNITED CHURCH OF CHRIST'S ADVERTISING CAMPAIGN: CONTROVERSY AND CENSORSHIP

The United Church of Christ (UCC) is a relatively small Protestant denomination that came into being in 1957, the result of a merger between the Congregational Christian Church and the Evangelical and Reformed Church. According to the church's website, the UCC emphasizes the four main words from their previous incarnations to characterize themselves: Christian, Reformed, Congregational, and Evangelical. UCC membership is about 1.3 million, but unlike other larger denominations, the UCC does not enjoy wide name recognition. The church takes some pride in being the first mostly white mainstream denomination to ordain a black man, a woman, and a white gay man as ministers.

The church sponsored a recent survey that showed that a large number of people had stopped attending worship services because of feeling not welcomed and not wanted. The UCC decided to launch a television advertising campaign that would introduce themselves to those who had felt the sting of being left out.

The campaign gathered momentum and gained millions of dollars of free media attention during the Christmas season of 2004 when two major networks—CBS and NBC—decided not to run the ads because they found them "too controversial." The thirty-second spot is described several times below among the selections offered. *After reading about the ad, decide what you would have the networks do.*

In the pieces below, the various authors' perspectives and biases are made clear either within the piece or in remarks about the author at the end of the account. All come from newspaper accounts of the campaign. While local UCC pastors ground their support for inclusiveness in biblical texts, others suggest that the ad may be more complicated than what first meets the eye. Does the ad suggest that only the UCC offers open doors to all people while other mainline Protestant denominations do not? Does the ad offer an opportunity for even more denominations to enter a nuanced discussion? Should television networks accept any religious advertisement? Is the networks' "controversial" label suggesting that their interpretation is limited to the inclusion of gays in worship service? *When religion enters public space and the sacred comes into the secular world, how would you enter the conversation?*

Deb Price

A Progressive Church Serves God by Welcoming Differences

Asheville Citizen-Times, December 23, 2004

Three years ago, the message on a postcard in a Los Angeles shop grabbed Ron Buford's attention: "Never place a period where God has placed a comma."

Cigar-twirling comedian George Burns had found that instruction in papers his wife and sidekick, Gracie Allen, left for him when she died.

For Buford, the simple rule was a powerful wakeup call literally. It jolted him awake at 3 a.m. Suddenly, the public relations manager for the United Church of Christ (UCC), a denomination whose roots go back to the Pilgrims, found himself reciting words from the final sermon before the Mayflower sailed for America: "Oh God, grant yet more light and truth to break forth from your word."

Inspired by his progressive denomination's belief that God's message for all mankind is continually unfolding, Buford distilled that 17th-century prayer and Gracie Allen's TV-age guidance down to their bumper sticker-sized essence: "God is still speaking."

The United Church of Christ quickly embraced that good news slogan as a godsend 5
for its work in the world: Sharing God's inclusive love by rolling out a welcome mat for all
people—no exceptions.

Now, through miraculously good timing, the UCC's message of comfort,
acceptance and welcome has aired as ads on national TV at the very moment that countless millions of Americans felt traumatized by November's election results and body-
slammed by religious groups that equate voting Republican with being a good Christian.

The ad shows a fierce-looking bouncer picking who can come into a church—driving
home the point that God's house ought not be treated like an exclusive club. Then, the
UCC assures viewers, "Jesus didn't turn people away. Neither do we."

UCC spokesman Robert Chase says, "We view the Bible as a living document. And
the history of our church is a reflection of that." Believing God calls the church to bring
Christian teachings to bear on social injustices, the UCC battled to an end slavery. And it
was the first mainstream, predominantly white denomination to ordain a black minister, a
woman and a gay man.

Now, UCC is delighted that its controversial ad—two TV networks rejected it for being 10
gay-friendly—is bringing alienated Christians back into pews just in time to celebrate the joy
of Christmas.

Before creating the ad, the UCC conducted focus groups to find out why so many
people of faith had stopped going to any church. Again and again, ex-churchgoers painfully
described how they'd been made to feel unwelcome.

They wore the wrong clothes. They were of a different racial or ethnic background.
They didn't have much money. They were single moms, disabled, emotionally needy or
gay. They list went on and on.

"It was very alarming and disturbing to me as a lifelong religious professional to witness the profound hurt and sense of rejection that people in those focus groups
expressed," the Rev. Chase recalls.

So, UCC, which had been searching for a way to introduce itself to Americans unfamiliar with its progressive outlook, seized on the theme of hospitality, echoing Jesus'
extravagant welcome to all. And a hand-holding gay couple was among the would-be churchgoers that UCC's ad depicted as being rejected elsewhere.

"Folks try to make (the UCC TV ad) a gay issue. But it's also about racial justice, the poor and people with disabilities," Chase explains. "That's what captivates people; they read themselves into the script, 'God is still speaking.' "

Thanks to the millions of dollars' worth of free 15
publicity generated by the networks' rejection of UCC's all-inclusive message, believers who had no church home are discovering that a UCC congregation is a place where they can feel welcome.

If you're old enough to have rediscovered a belief in miracles, then it's not hard to have faith that God is indeed still speaking. Gracie Allen was right.

"Never place a period
where God has placed a comma"
| Gracie Allen |

God is still speaking,

U C C . O R G

UNITED CHURCH
OF CHRIST

Deb Price is the co-author of *Courting Justice: Gay Men and Lesbians v. the Supreme Court* (Basic Books). Her column is distributed by Gannett News Service and syndicated by Creators Syndicate. Write to Price at GNS Features, 7950 Jones Branch Drive, McLean, VA 22107

Leonard Pitts

Sleaze, Yes; God's Love, No

Charlotte Observer, December 13, 2004

Let me put my bias right up front so nobody can miss it: I am a member of the United Church of Christ. I joined the UCC—a little-known denomination out of Cleveland—about five years ago. It was the first church I'd ever seen that seemed to take seriously the idea that inclusion is a Christian value. It was also the first that actively sought to resolve divisions of culture, class, race, and sexual orientation.

So you can imagine how I feel about the news that CBS and NBC have rejected a new UCC commercial celebrating just that characteristic: I am appalled. Frankly, I'd feel that way even if I didn't have a personal connection.

The ad in question is part of a campaign called "God is still speaking," which is meant to highlight the church's vision of a deity who still is as opposed to one who once was. The campaign was commissioned in response to marketing research indicating that most people have never heard of the United Church of Christ, though it reports more than 1.3 million members in 6,000 congregations nationwide.

Barb Powell, a UCC spokeswoman, says the same research found that many people who opt out of church do so because they've had bad experiences that left them "angry or alienated." She says the ad was directed specifically to them.

5   It shows two bouncers working a rope line in front of a church. They turn away a gay couple and what appears to be a Hispanic man and a black girl. A *white family* is allowed to pass. The text onscreen says, "Jesus didn't turn people away. Neither do we." A narrator closes the ad, speaking over a montage of old people, white people, black people, Hispanic people, lesbian people, human people.

"The United Church of Christ," he says. "No matter who you are or where you are on life's journey, you're welcome here."

According to the UCC, this is the message two broadcast networks deemed too "controversial" to air. I called CBS for comment and was read a prepared statement that said in its entirety, "The network has a longstanding policy of not accepting advocacy advertising." I'm still waiting to hear back from NBC.

Meantime, if you want to see the ad for yourself, the UCC says it's running on TV Land, Nick at Night, BET and several other networks that had no problem airing it.

But you won't find it on NBC or CBS. Am I the only one who's flummoxed by that?

10   I mean, work with me here. The maggot eaters of "Fear Factor" are evidently OK to broadcast. Janet Jackson's nipple somehow makes it to the air. Two half-naked vixens can even wrestle in a pool, arguing over whether their beer tastes great or is less filling. But a commercial that says only that God's love includes us all is too controversial to show?

Unbelievable.

And yes, I know where this is coming from. Gay bashing under the guise of religious conservatism is on the rise. The thought of gay men and lesbians being able to solemnize their relationships in ceremonies that carry legal weight has some people walking the floors at night. Those folks would not be happy with an ad showing gays become welcomed anywhere, much less in church. But even understanding that, it is shocking to see two major broadcast networks act with such gutless hypocrisy.

For the record, the UCC ad is accurate in its portrayal of church exclusion. Blacks and Hispanics were once widely unwelcome at worship houses outside their own communities. Gay men and lesbians still are.

Thankfully, the ad is also accurate in its portrayal of a love larger than human bigotry.

Or as Powell told me, "We as a denomination strive to be like Jesus and welcome all   15 people." I consider that a goal worth seeking.

Apparently the networks do not.

Leonard Pitts is a *Miami Herald* columnist: lpitts@herald.com

Who Is Beyond God's Reach?

Nancy Ellett Allison and Nathan King

Charlotte Observer, December 13, 2004

As pastors of two local United Church of Christ congregations, we've been delighted our tiny, money-strapped denomination has the vision and imagination to develop a television commercial proclaiming Christ's welcome to all. Now we're astounded that these commercials have been rejected by some of the TV networks as "too controversial."

The commercial features two "bouncers" standing guard outside a church, choosing which persons are allowed in to offer their worship to God and denying entry to many. The scene is broken by a black screen which proclaims, "Jesus didn't turn people away. Neither do we."

Though the disabled, people of color, senior adults and traditional families are all shown as welcomed in the closing scene, apparently the sight of one young woman's arm across the shoulder of another's is too much for the executives who air "Will and Grace" and "Saturday Night Live."

A church body visibly throws open its doors to all people and CBS responds with rejection.

It is alarming that, in a nation that increasingly scapegoats people in minority com-   5 munities, it has become impossible for the inclusive and welcoming voice of Jesus to be heard on NBC and CBS. Many non-churchgoers believe the institutional church does exclude them because of race, age, gender, economic circumstance or sexual orientation.

No one is beyond God's reach and blessing.

In Leviticus and Deuteronomy, eunuchs, those who were sexually different, were forbidden entrance to the temple. God-fearing foreigners were only allowed into the outer courts. Limits were placed on women, the lame, the blind, those with communicable diseases.

Isaiah, the prophet we love to quote at Christmastime, stands against the Levitical code and proclaims a different vision of God's extravagant welcome: "For thus says the

Lord: To the eunuchs who keep my Sabbaths, who choose the things that please me and hold fast my covenant, I will give, in my house and within my walls, a monument and a name better than sons and daughters; I will give them an everlasting name that shall not be cut off. And the foreigners who join themselves to the Lord, to minister to him, to love the name of the Lord, and to be his servants, all who keep the Sabbath, and do not profane it, and hold fast my covenant—these I will bring to my holy mountain, and make them joyful in my house of prayer; their burnt offerings and their sacrifices will be accepted on my altar; for my house shall be called a house of prayer for all peoples."

Jesus strode into the temple quoting Isaiah: "The Spirit of the Lord is upon me, because he has anointed me to bring good news to the poor. He has sent me to proclaim release to the captives and recovery of sight to the blind, to let the oppressed go free, to proclaim the year of the Lord's favor" (Luke 4:15-19).

10   Many churches today cling to the clear mandates of the Levitical codes because they provide a certainty that comforts. But always, alongside this certainty, the Bible has proclaimed an alternative vision of a radical inclusion.

Who are our outcasts today? Who is beyond God's reach? Every human has felt less-than-acceptable at some point in their life journey: too dumb, too ugly, too wrong-sized or wrong-colored, too poor, too rich, too liberal, too intellectual, too skeptical, too judgmental, too crippled, too ill, too bizarre, too desperate, too depleted, too laughable, too vulnerable. All who seek to honor God, to work for God's justice in this world, are welcome to kneel in prayer within many of God's holiest sanctuaries.

Search for that place. Find a family of faith where you, with all your limits, will be welcomed and blessed as God's beloved child. God has a way of reaching beyond all barriers to set the oppressed free. We are outcasts, one and all, united in the Christ born among us in a stable.

At our churches, we welcome everyone, including NBC and CBS, to the table of Christ's feast.

Allison is pastor of Holy Covenant UCC, 3501 West W.T. Harris Blvd, Charlotte, NC 28269. King is pastor of Trinity UCC, 38 Church Street NE, Concord, NC 28025.

Joseph Loconte

Houses of Worship: Exclusion and Embrace

Wall Street Journal, December 3, 2004

Leaders of the United Church of Christ are incensed that two TV networks, CBS and NBC, are refusing to air a commercial celebrating the denomination's "all-inclusive welcome," not least toward gays and lesbians. Network executives call the ad "too controversial," while church leaders cry censorship. Both sides are missing an opportunity to elevate the debate about gay marriage.

The 30-second ad shows a beefy bouncer working a rope line outside a church. He's keeping various people out: Latinos, African-Americans and gay couples. Words flash across the screen: "Jesus didn't turn people away. Neither do we." The scene shifts to the inside of a UCC church, with an obviously diverse and happy congregation. Two women embrace in the final scene.

UCC officials are explicit about the ad's discrimination theme. "In the 1960s, the issue was the mixing of races. Today the issue appears to be sexual orientation," says Ron Buford, coordinator for the UCC campaign. "In both cases, it's about exclusion." In other words, according to UCC logic, churches that uphold traditional marriage are on par with the racists of the Jim Crow South. Call it faith-based bigotry.

That kind of slur was apparently too much for NBC, whose spokeswoman said that the network objected not to the portrayal of same-sex couples in church but to the insinuation that other faith traditions routinely discriminate. Both CBS and NBC also have policies banning "advocacy" ads and cite the current debate over the federal marriage amendment. The ad has been accepted by other broadcast and cable networks, however, including ABC Family, BET, Fox, TNT and Nick@Nite.

Nevertheless, the UCC smells censorship—and worse. "By refusing to air the United 5
Church of Christ's paid commercial, CBS and NBC are stifling religious expression," says UCC spokeswoman Gloria Tristani. Such decisions, she says, put freedom of speech "in jeopardy." That's overheated. Media outlets have a First Amendment right to reject messages they find too controversial, misleading or inflammatory.

Still, the two networks might want to rethink their decision and air the ads—as long as they offer equal time to competing views. The problem with media coverage of the debate over homosexuality is that it's so intellectually deficient: The most extreme voices get most of the air time. The "traditional" view, when it's heard, usually amounts to a red-faced minister quoting from Leviticus to explain why "God hates gays." Paid TV spots would give churches and other religious groups a chance to craft their messages carefully, free of the caricatures that drive network coverage of religion.

Giving advertising time to religious viewpoints would also help counter the impulse to stigmatize traditional religious ideals. It's a growing problem: At a gathering of pro-gay activists in Geneva earlier this year, I heard a United Nations official compare the agenda of traditional marriage groups to the Nazi campaign against homosexuals. Everyone in the room nodded in agreement.

Indeed, the UCC ad symbolizes the mischief created by the partnership between liberal religion and "progressive" causes. Sometimes that alliance has been a constructive force, as in the civil-rights movement. But too often it has fueled ideas that undermine the family, religious liberty and civil society—from the eugenics movement of the 1920s to the Marxist "liberation" groups of the 1960s and '70s. In their attempt to make the gospel "relevant" to contemporary culture, progressive churches have appeared irrelevant to more and more Americans.

Hence the UCC ad, part of a $1.7 million campaign to boost the visibility of the church. Over the past 15 years, membership has declined 23 percent to barely 1.3 million churchgoers. Ted Pulton of Gotham Inc., an advertising agency advising the UCC campaign, describes the church's name recognition as "negligible at best."

The ad campaign could increase brand recognition, but will that translate into a larger 10
market share? Will the denomination's embrace of gay marriage embolden the faithful and expand the flock? A warning from William Inge, dean of St. Paul's Cathedral, comes to mind: "He who marries the spirit of the age will soon find himself a widower."

Peter Steinfels

In Rejecting a Church's Ad, Two Networks Provide Fodder for a Different Debate

New York Times, December 18, 2004

CBS and NBC could not have done the United Church of Christ a bigger favor than when they decided against running an advertisement for the church on their networks.

Last spring, tests of the 30-second spot, heralding the church's welcoming atmosphere, were broadcast in local markets on a number of stations, including CBS and NBC affiliates. They produced no raging controversy.

Now, thanks to the two networks' rejection, and the inevitable cries of censorship, far more people know about the advertisement's message.

Anyone who cannot catch the paid commercial on Fox or over cable stations where it occasionally runs can see it at a special church Web site, www.stillspeaking.com. The spot features two nightclub-style bouncers outside a church who let in well-dressed, seemingly affluent white people for the service while turning away two dark-skinned young people, a man in a wheelchair and two men—look carefully!—holding hands.

5   The point then comes on the screen: "Jesus didn't turn away people. Neither do we." A narrator explains that for the United Church of Christ, commonly referred to as the UCC, "no matter who you are, or where you are on life's journey, you are welcome here."

Given television's almost infinitely malleable standards of acceptability, it is indeed astonishing that a three-second specter of a (presumably) gay couple should have incited the two networks' concerns that the advertisement was too controversial or constituted "issue advocacy." (ABC, because it does not broadcast any religious commercials at all, was a bystander to the brouhaha.)

But whether the networks should or should not have broadcast the advertisement is distinct from other questions about its substance. They are, in fact, interesting questions, and not to be answered in 30 seconds of air time.

Here is an advertisement whose message has been hailed as one of openness, welcome and compassion. But rather than "proclaiming love and acceptance of all people," as one supporter put it, does the commercial actually misrepresent other churches? Does it misrepresent the 1.3-million-member United Church of Christ? And, most interestingly, does it misrepresent Jesus?

Diane Knippers, a leader of the evangelical Association for Church Renewal and frequent critic of liberal churches like the UCC, complained that the advertisement "insinuates that the typical American church turns away ethnic minorities, the disabled and homosexuals whereas the UCC is uniquely welcoming of all persons."

10   "The facts," Ms. Knippers said, "do not bear out this false picture."

The attractive Web site mentioned above also tries to parry the criticism. Among frequently asked questions about the advertising campaign, it includes: "Are you saying the UCC is better than other churches?"

"No," comes the answer. "Each denomination witnesses to the Gospel in its own distinctive way."

Somehow that seems a bit evasive. The UCC believes not only that it is distinctive, especially in regard to homosexuality (for three decades the church has left to local congregations the decisions about accepting openly gay people to serve in the clergy), but also that this distinctiveness is "better."

The United Church of Christ is clearly committed to racial and economic diversity and accommodating the disabled. But so are a lot of other churches. And a lot of them, including many with very conservative doctrinal profiles, do at least as well, if not better, in practice.

"We're not as racially and ethnically diverse as we would like to be," acknowledged the Rev. Robert Chase, the denomination's director of communications, who devoted a generous chunk of his time this week to talk over these questions.   15

Two radio advertisements the church will soon begin broadcasting only underscore the problem. One parodies a Christmas carol with lines like "O come, some of ye faithful, powerful and privileged," and then announces that "God invites all the faithful; so do we— the United Church of Christ." The other satirizes high-fashion worshipers, and then proclaims: "God doesn't care what you wear to church. Neither do we."

Worthy sentiments unquestionably, but is the UCC's track record vis-a-vis the not so powerful or well dressed really any better than that of other churches, including churches that hold to traditional moral strictures about sex? The UCC's admirable aspiration to inclusiveness does seem to be bought at the expense of indulging a few stereotypes about other churches.

But the most interesting thing about the television advertisement may be its view of Jesus. Did Jesus turn anyone away? Well, yes and no. Jesus scandalized many around him by associating with outcasts and sinners. On the other hand, he drew sharp lines between sheep and goats, demanded extraordinary sacrifices and issued harsh judgments.

Calling the television spot "masterful propaganda," R. Albert Mohler Jr., president of the Southern Baptist Theological Seminary, in Louisville, Ky., argued that "Jesus Christ did indeed come to seek and to save the lost, but as he said to the woman caught in adultery, 'Go and sin no more'; he did not invite persons to stay in sinful lifestyles."

In response, Mr. Chase noted that the sharp lines Jesus drew were hardly ever about   20
sex but consistently challenged the existing assumptions and power structures of his society. He called the priests and scribes hypocrites, respected the despised Samaritans, warned that the rich had less chance of entering the kingdom of God than camels of passing through the eye of a needle, and so on.

Yet the discussion need not end there, either. What might Jesus' parable about the Pharisee whose prayer celebrates his own distinctive merits versus the publican who declares his sinfulness suggest about the advertisement? Somewhere along the line, Mr. Chase spoke of "the problem of getting into a nuanced theological conversation."

Precisely. That, in fact, is exactly what is needed. Instead of shying away from a blink of religious controversy, instead of pretending to represent religion by inviting the Rev. Jerry Falwell and the Rev. Al Sharpton into a Sunday morning talk show, what the networks should risk is "getting into a nuanced theological conversation." That, as they like to say, would really be pushing the envelope.

Tim Feran

Networks Air Dirty Laundry, Not Church Ad

The *Columbus (Ohio) Dispatch*, December 13, 2004

And the angel said unto them, Fear not: for, behold, I bring you good tidings of great joy, which shall be to all people.

Well, maybe not to all people—maybe just those who enjoy watching two hours of prime-time programming devoted to a 12-year-old interview with Princess Diana.

The tidings of great joy, on the other hand, might not be shared by the folks at the United Church of Christ, who wanted to buy ad time on network television to spread a 2,000-year-old message from a certain fellow whose birthday many of us celebrate this month.

Salacious details of a dead British princess' sad marriage? Sure thing. NBC was more than happy to air two nights of programming about something that many critics likened to Desperate Royal Housewives.

5   But let's not get carried away, eh?

We can't have an ad, or so NBC and CBS say, that shows two bouncers stationed outside a church, refusing to admit various people based on their race, age or sexual orientation. The message: "Jesus didn't turn people away. Neither do we."

NBC has a "long-standing policy against accepting ads dealing with issues of public controversy. The controversy stems from the ad saying other churches aren't open to all people for a variety of reasons."

And CBS explains that, because of "the fact the executive branch has recently proposed a constitutional amendment to define marriage as a union between a man and a woman, this spot is unacceptable for broadcast on the (CBS and UPN) networks."

To be fair, this is hardly the first time that the networks have been wary of programming with an overtly religious message.

10   CBS went ahead and aired *A Charlie Brown Christmas* to great acclaim, way back in 1965.

Perhaps the difference between now and then is that the United Church of Christ commercial features live actors and the Peanuts show employed cartoon characters.

Maybe the United Church of Christ erred: The ad could have shown muscle-bound bouncers blocking Pigpen from entering the church because he's filthy, Peppermint Patty because she squeezed Lucy on the shoulder and Charlie Brown because he's a loser.

The producers wouldn't even have to film a new ending for the ad. They could just go back to the finale of *A Charlie Brown Christmas* and have Linus quote from the King James Bible again.

Good grief.

Writing Prompts

1. Price, Pitts, and the two pastors, Allison and King, make abundantly clear their positions and feelings about the networks' choice not to run the ads. Write a three-page paper in which you argue that knowing their biases makes their stand more persuasive.
2. Using what you know from *A Charlie Brown Christmas,* do you agree with Feran's use of that now-classic seasonal television show to shed more light on the UCC advertisement controversy? Do you believe the comparison is appropriate?
3. Write a two-page paper in which you use information from these selections to support CBS's and NBC's decision not to air the ad.
4. Several writers suggest that the networks banned the ad primarily because of the exclusion of the gay couple from the church. What evidence in the selections supports this line of reasoning?
5. Write a letter to CBS or NBC in which you either agree or disagree with their position. Use evidence from the selections as well as from your own experience and observations.

What Is at Stake for Citizenship?

1. In the twenty-first century, how should we define the word "controversial"?
2. Is banning controversial subject content censorship or a right?
3. Should religious institutions be permitted to show any kinds of advertisements on television if they are paying the requested fees?
4. Should the same restrictions that govern television programming be applied to paid television advertising?
5. How does the First Amendment apply to both the networks' decision and the UCC's advertising request?

EXPANDING VOCABULARY

American Civil Liberties Union (ACLU): On the organization's website, it states: "The ACLU is our nation's guardian of liberty. We work daily in courts, legislatures, and communities to defend and preserve the individual rights and liberties guaranteed to every person in this country by the Constitution and laws of the United States. Our job is to conserve America's original civic values: the Constitution and the Bill of Rights." ACLU was founded in 1920.

American Family Association (AFA): On the organization's website, it states: "The American Family Association represents and stands for traditional family values, focusing primarily on the influence of television and other media—including pornography—on our society. AFA believes that the entertainment industry, through its various products, has played a major role in the decline of those values on which our country was founded and which keep a society and its families strong and healthy." AFA was founded in 1977.

Americans United for Separation of Church and State (AU): On the organization's website, it states: "Americans United for Separation of Church and State was founded in 1947 by a broad coalition of religious, educational, and civic leaders. At that time, proposals were pending in the U.S. Congress to extend government aid to private religious schools. Many Americans opposed this idea, insisting that government support for religious education would violate church–state separation. The decision was made to form a national organization to promote this point of view and defend the separation principle. The organization worked to educate members of Congress, as well as state and local lawmakers, about the importance of maintaining church-state separation."

American Veterans Standing for God and Country: A part of the American Veterans in Domestic Defense, this subgroup took control of the tour for Roy Moore's Ten Commandments' rock. Dates and places for the tour are not posted after March 2005.

Child Evangelism Fellowship (CEF): According to their organization's website, its purpose is "to evangelize boys and girls with the Gospel of the Lord Jesus Christ and to establish (disciple) them in the Word of God and in a local church for Christian living." CEF was founded in 1937.

Equal Access Law: Passed in 1984, this law applies to public high schools that receive federal funding and already have at least one student-led non-curriculum club that meets outside of class time. The rules dictate that attendance at the club is voluntary and student-initiated. The club should not be sponsored or attended by any school employee, not disruptive to the community, and not open to persons from the community. While originally backed by conservative Christian groups for the purpose of Bible Clubs, the law has become popular with gay/lesbian/bisexual support groups and atheist and Goth clubs.

Fellowship of Christian Athletes (FCA): On the organization's website, it states: "Since 1954, the Fellowship of Christian Athletes has been challenging coaches and athletes on the professional, college, high school, junior high, and youth levels to use the powerful medium of athletics to impact the world for Jesus Christ. FCA is the largest Christian sports organization in America. FCA focuses on serving local communities by equipping, empowering, and encouraging people to make a difference for Christ."

Freedom Forum First Amendment Center: Founded in 1991, the Forum is a nonpartisan foundation dedicated to free speech, free press, and free spirit for all people. The foundation focuses on three priorities: the "Newseum," the First Amendment and newsroom diversity.

Good News Club: Under the auspices of the Child Evangelism Fellowship, this club, according to the CEF website, is for "boys and girls ages 5 through 12 to gather with their friends to sing interesting visualized songs. They enjoy playing games that help them memorize a verse from God's Word. Through the missionary time they learn of children around the world who are following Jesus. The visualized Bible story applies God's Word to what is happening in their lives. They play review games that help them remember what was taught. An opportunity to receive Jesus Christ as Savior is given. Activities that help them grow in Christ are presented."

Liberty Counsel: On the organization's website, it states: "Liberty Counsel is a nonprofit litigation, education, and policy organization dedicated to advancing religious freedom, the sanctity of human life, and the traditional family. Established in 1989, Liberty Counsel is a national organization headquartered in Orlando, Florida, with branch offices in

Virginia and hundreds of affiliate attorneys in all 50 states." The legal team has close ties with Jerry Falwell and the conservative religious right.

No Child Left Behind Act (NCLB): Passed into law in 2002, this act affects public education from kindergarten through high school. It is built on four principles: accountability for results, more choices for parents, greater local control and flexibility, and an emphasis on doing what works based on scientific research.

Southern Poverty Law Center: On the organization's website, it states: "Today, the Center is internationally known for its tolerance education programs, its legal victories against white supremacists, and its tracking of hate groups." The Center was founded in 1971 in Montgomery, Alabama, as a small civil rights law firm.

Youth for Christ (YFC): On the organization's website, it states that YFC communicates a "life-changing message of Jesus Christ to young people." Founded in the mid-1940s, Billy Graham was its first full-time worker. It has grown into an international organization, presenting mass rallies to introduce young people to Christian principles.

CHAPTER 8

Point of Contact:
Sexuality and Identity

As we move into the twenty-first century, many of the choices, changes, and challenges that face U.S. citizens revolve around issues of sex, gender, and sexuality. Who we are, what we do with our lives, and how we relate to both men and women are all greatly influenced by our sex, our sexual identity, and our sexual interests.

But these topics are surrounded by controversy. Some would argue that we live in a free and open society where options, education, and acceptance make the world better for us all; we need to escape the hang-ups and stereotypes of the past. Others would argue that we are being overwhelmed with inappropriate sexual imagery and sexuality at every turn—in movies, music, television, advertising, even video games—and that we have lost the clarity we once had on gender roles. These people believe that we must return to our previous values or risk the destruction of our culture and morality.

The issues of sexuality and identity today raise many questions. These questions are more easily asked than answered, and answers are not always black and white. *What do you think? Are we corrupted by the amount of sexuality and blurred boundaries in our culture, or liberated by the freedom now available to all citizens? Or is there a position somewhere between those two polar opposites you would like to argue for?*

The question is not whether the roles for men and women have changed over the last few decades—they have. Look around you. In the last few years, jobs, roles, divorce law, fashions, and social movements have all played a part in the ways our lives as men and women have changed and continue to change. The questions (and differences) arise when citizens with differing ideas come together to start talking about what all these changes mean.

Sex, sexuality, and gender roles are at the heart of what are known as the **culture wars**, and at the heart of this battle is who determines what the core values of our nation are going to be, both today and in the future. It's **progressives** versus **conservatives**—and the fight centers on the nature and amount of change in American lives, values, and communities in the last twenty years. Should we march forward into the changes brought on by our modern world? Or should we hold the line, preserving the traditional America that made us great? Nothing less than the future of our society is at stake. But how might we enter such a heated discussion? As a beginning, there are many important questions, and answers, to consider. Is there a right time for young people to become sexually active? Why does virginity matter today? What should we teach in public schools about young people having, or not having, sex? Or is sex education better left to parents? What does it mean to be a man? What does it mean to be a woman? Are those gender roles carved in stone? What does it mean to be straight or gay? Should gays be allowed to marry? What about **civil unions**? Or is the whole issue a matter of social progress, a sin, or just another issue for Americans to argue over?

As we explore this Point of Contact, Sexuality and Identity, think about the questions these issues might raise for you. You may not have thought about such topics as **sex education,** changing **gender roles,** or **gay marriage**, but many people have. For each of these topics you will find a collection of essays, with each essay taking a specific position or perspective. Be aware that each author will likely take a specific position and argue for a certain outcome. Likewise, as you begin thinking and reading and talking about these issues, you will begin to form your own opinions and take a position in the national debate.

This Point of Contact will focus on and address the following three specific questions that relate to sexuality and identity:

1. Sex Education or Teaching Abstinence: Both, Either, or Neither?
2. Gender and Gender Roles: New Lives for Men and Women
3. Gay Marriage: New Questions for an Old Institution

SEX EDUCATION OR TEACHING ABSTINENCE: BOTH, EITHER, OR NEITHER?

Vines High School Abstinence Club.

Ideally, public schools are safe, supportive places that provide an intellectually stimulating environment for America's children. Ideally, students can be in school and free of conflict and politics as they learn and grow. But in reality, public schools (and public school policy) can be as controversial and divisive as an election. People don't check their opinions at the schoolhouse door; instead, it seems that public schools are a catalyst for conflict. Students, parents, taxpayers, civic leaders—all have opinions about how their schools should be. Fifty years ago the number one issue in American schools was racial segregation. Folks either wanted to integrate the schools to further equality or to maintain the separation of black and white students to further segregation. Today the issues that get the most press and cause the most conflict are **creationism** versus **evolution** and sex education. While the question of whether to teach Darwin's theory of evolution or Christian-based creationism may spark people's interest, it cannot compare to the intense conflict between those who have differing views on sexual education. Evolution, however much it may conflict with some religious teachings, does not evoke terror in the hearts of parents the way a pregnant daughter or a son with a **sexually transmitted disease** (STD) does.

The question today is not whether to teach sex education but rather what constitutes sexual education and how should it be taught to get the best results. There are many positions, but most people take one of three general positions:

- Those who wish to teach **abstinence**.
- Those who wish to teach abstinence along with other sexual information.
- Those who wish to teach information on sex, birth control, and STDs without mention of abstinence.

People who wish to teach abstinence exclusively—meaning that the primary goal of the curriculum is to encourage students to abstain from or avoid sexual contact before marriage—note that students can't get **HIV/AIDS** (or any other sexually transmitted disease) or get pregnant if they are not having sex. Others want to offer information both on having sex (think condoms and AIDS) and abstinence, offering students all possible choices and leaving it up to the students to determine their actions. They want students to make a fully informed choice. Finally, there are those who want to offer information about sex and **contraception** without presenting abstinence before marriage as a viable choice; their view is that educated, informed young people make good choices when (not if) they choose to be sexually active, and that abstinence only is unrealistic.

The following collection of essays presents many differing views, ideas, and political opinions. It is safe to say that everyone writing cares about young people and wants students to be healthy and happy and safe, no matter where he or she stands on the issues of teen sexuality and sex education. Nevertheless, opinions differ on how to best reach that health, happiness and safety. *As you read, you might want to consider what sort of sexual education was offered in your school, and how well you feel the information offered you fit your own circumstances, experiences, and behaviors.*

Priscilla Pardini

The History of Sexuality Education

Rethinking Schools Online—Let's Talk About Sex

The 1960s saw the beginning of the current wave of controversy over sex ed in U.S. schools. But as early as 1912, the National Education Association called for teacher training programs in sexuality education.

In 1940, the U.S. Public Health Service strongly advocated sexuality education in the schools, labeling it an "urgent need." In 1953, the American School Health Association launched a nationwide program in family life education. Two years later, the American Medical Association, in conjunction with the NEA, published five pamphlets that were commonly referred to as "the sex education series" for schools.

Support for sexuality education among public health officials and educators did not sway opponents, however. And for the last 30 years, battles have raged between conservatives and health advocates over the merits—and format—of sexuality education in public schools.

The first wave of organized opposition, from the late 1960s to the early 1980s, took the form of attacks aimed at barring any form of sex ed in school. Sex education programs were described by the Christian Crusade and other conservative groups as "smut" and "raw sex." The John Birch Society termed the effort to teach about sexuality "a filthy Communist plot." Phyllis Schlafly, leader of the far-right Eagle Forum, argued that sexuality education resulted in an increase in sexual activity among teens.

Efforts to curtail sex ed enjoyed only limited success, however. Sex education programs in public schools proliferated, in large part due to newly emerging evidence that such programs didn't promote sex but in fact helped delay sexual activity and reduce teen pregnancy rates.

By 1983, sexuality education was being taught within the context of more comprehensive family life education programs or human growth and development courses. Such an approach emphasized not only reproduction, but also the importance of self-esteem, responsibility, and decision making. The new courses covered not only contraception, but also topics such as family finances and parenting skills.

In the mid 1980s, the AIDS epidemic irrevocably changed sexuality education. In 1986, U.S. Surgeon General C. Everett Koop issued a report calling for comprehensive AIDS and sexuality education in public schools, beginning as early as the third grade. "There is now no doubt that we need sex education in schools and that it [should] include information on heterosexual and homosexual relationships," Koop wrote in his report. "The need is critical and the price of neglect is high."

But if Koop's report helped promote sexuality education, it also forced the Religious Right to rethink its opposition strategies. Even the most conservative of sex-ed opponents now found it difficult to justify a total ban on the topic. Instead, the Right responded with a new tactic: fear-based, abstinence-only sexuality education.

Joel Mowbray

Abstinence Works: The Evidence

National Review Online, April 11, 2002

A battle is brewing on Capitol Hill between two rather similar-sounding concepts, abstinence-only and abstinence-plus education, but the differences couldn't be greater—or more shocking. Despite the "abstinence" in the name, parents would be appalled to see the sexually explicit material peddled to kids in abstinence-plus programs.

Under current federal law, there are two basic approaches, abstinence-only and comprehensive sex education, and the latter receives far more cash. This issue is much larger than just money going to schools, as funds go to outside groups as part of a whole host of federal programs, including welfare and education block grants.

President Bush's campaign pledge, on which he is trying to make good, would bring abstinence, which focuses heavily on marriage and the value of waiting, and traditional sex ed, which emphasizes safe sex when "hooking up," into funding parity. But there's a big hurdle to clear in the interim. Leftist groups like Planned Parenthood are scheming to change the federal government's insistence for abstinence-only to the mislabeled abstinence-plus programs.

To get a glimpse of the practical implications of this debate, look no further than a new report released by Physicians Consortium, a socially conservative group representing 2,000 doctors. The Centers for Disease Control (CDC) already monitors state- and locally-funded sex-ed courses and promotes ones it finds particularly effective to middle and high schools in an official initiative called "Programs that Work."

5   In one exercise, students are encouraged to pursue various alternatives to sexual intercourse. So far, so good. But the recommended activities? Body massage, bathing together, "sensuous feeding," joint masturbation, and watching "erotic movies." Of course, when teens engage in these not-quite PG-13 activities, they'll no doubt be satisfied and exclaim, "Wow—thank goodness I have no need to have sex now!"

Taking the prize for sheer absurdity, however, is a priceless exercise called the "Condom Race." Students are divided into two teams, and every child is handed a condom. Forming two lines, each student has to put condoms on and remove them from his or her team's designated "cucumber or dildo." The team that finishes first, wins.

Perhaps the most disturbing element of both these programs is the target demographic: 9 to 15 year olds. Rather than condemning these courses as purveyors of promiscuity to young children, the CDC lauds them as model examples for others to emulate.

If abstinence-plus becomes the law of the land at the federal level, outlandish and offensive "abstinence" programs would replace abstinence-only ones that have logged significant success in recent years. Given that three million teenagers contract sexually transmitted diseases every year, reducing sexual activity—not just making it "safer"—is imperative. A recent report from the Heritage Foundation's Robert Rector compiles ten separate scientific evaluations of abstinence programs throughout the country, and each course analyzed has made significant strides in keeping kids out of compromising positions.

Promoting abstinence works both in the classroom and through a public-relations campaign. Abstinence by Choice, which operates in 20 schools in and around Little Rock, Arkansas, has had a measurable impact on the lives of the 4,000 7th-9th graders it reaches each year. Sexual-activity rates among boys plunged 30 percent, and the rate for girls plummeted 40 percent.

10   *Not Me, Not Now* is a community-wide campaign that targets 9 to 14 year olds in Monroe County, New York, which includes the city of Rochester. The abstinence program spreads its message through billboards, paid TV and radio ads, an interactive website, posters in schools, educational materials for parents, and sessions in school and community settings. *Not Me, Not Now* is effective, achieving 95-percent awareness among its target demographic, slashing the sexual-activity rate of 15-year-olds in the county by over 30 percent, and reducing the pregnancy rate among 15 to 17-year-olds by nearly 25 percent.

Sometimes something as simple as a commitment to abstinence can yield results. Rector's analysis of several comprehensive studies found that virginity-pledge programs show progress. In one study, the level of sexual activity among teens who had taken a formal pledge of virginity was one-fourth that of their peers who had taken no such pledge. Obviously students who would be willing to take such a pledge in the first place have a natural inclination toward chaste behavior, but a 75 percent reduction is awfully compelling.

Abstinence programs work for the simple reason that kids can keep their hormones in check. Though they may seem like it at times, teenagers don't lack human willpower. Kids can, and often do, take a message of responsibility to heart.

When the slugfest starts soon over the type of abstinence education funded at the federal level, don't be fooled by the term "abstinence-plus." More than half of all federal dollars already go to programs that push comprehensive sex ed, including all sorts of information about safe sex and condoms. Given that funding disparity, money devoted to abstinence should actually promote abstinence. It's that simple.

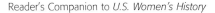

Sex Education

Wendy Stock

Reader's Companion to *U.S. Women's History*

A teacher demonstrates how to put on a condom.

Sexuality education ideally would encompass sexual knowledge, beliefs, attitudes, values, and behaviors. Included would be anatomy, physiology, and biochemistry of the sexual response system, gender roles, identity and personality, and thoughts, feelings, behaviors, and relationships. In addition, moral and ethical concerns, group and cultural diversity, and social change would be addressed. Unfortunately, sexuality education classes in the United States fall far from this ideal. In 1992 Debra Haffner found that less than 10 percent of U.S. children "receive comprehensive sexuality education from kindergarten through adulthood." Although most students are exposed to some type of sexuality education before they complete high school, they usually study only biology, reproduction, and virology. Sexuality education classes often focus on disaster prevention. In elementary grades, sexual abuse is presented; HIV/AIDS is introduced by junior high school; and in high schools, date rape is addressed. Although these areas are all crucial and essential components of sexuality education, omission of more positive aspects of sexuality conveys a powerful message that sex is dangerous. Most programs in the United States promote abstinence from sexual behaviors without offering equal attention to a presentation of safe sex. The official curriculum focuses on heterosexual reproductive sexuality, excluding discussion of gender politics, sexual violence, and pleasure.

Parallel to the "official curriculum" in sexuality education in the typical U.S. high school exists the "hidden curriculum," which teaches teenagers that popularity requires one to be attractive, physically fit, able-bodied, and heterosexual to conform to gender-role expectations and to dress according to school norms. For males, social status depends on "scoring" the sexual conquests of females; for females, social status requires a sexually attractive appearance based on highly unrealistic standards, paired with denial of desire and sexual agency. The double standard continues to exert great influence on the sexuality of adolescents and remains largely unaddressed and uncontested by standard sexuality curricula. Sexuality educators in James Sears's 1992 *Sexuality and the Curriculum: The Politics and Practices of Sexuality Education* critique sexuality education as "an instrument of social control, often reinforcing patriarchal, anti-sexual norms." Although politically conservative forces have lost the battle to prevent sexuality education, opposition groups promote the teaching of moral absolutes, sexual abstinence, and witholding information in an attempt to prevent adolescents' sexual behavior.

According to Sears, the abortion controversy, AIDS, and teenage pregnancy have resulted in the mandating of sexuality education in twenty-two states, compared to three in 1980. Two-thirds of the nation's largest school districts require sex education. What the classes include, however, varies considerably. For example, South Carolina prohibits teaching about abortion or homosexuality, and in Utah it is a misdemeanor for school personnel to discuss condoms with students without parental consent. Only three states (New Jersey, New York, and Wisconsin) and Washington, D.C., have a program on sex education and AIDS education. The most common sexuality-related topics covered in schools are anatomy and physiology (e.g., changes at puberty, physical differences), sexually transmitted diseases, and sexual decision making with particular emphasis on abstinence. Topics least discussed are homosexuality, gynecologic examinations, birth control, abortion, and masturbation and other safer sex practices.

Treatment of sexuality in the curriculum does not meet students' needs and concerns. Given that a substantial number of youth are sexually active before they encounter sexuality education, it is clear that the timing of sexuality education is generally too late to have an impact on adolescents' decisions to engage in sexual activities. However, adolescent females who have had exposure to sexuality education are more likely to seek birth-control services when available. Unfortunately, this holds only for white women; for African Americans and Latinas, studies find no relationship between sexuality instruction and contraceptive behavior. This may indicate that even at best, the sexuality curriculum fails to help many students of color.

5 In addition to inappropriate timing of sexuality education, a gap exists between topics of interest to adolescents and content of such courses. One Chicago-based survey found that teens were most concerned about birth control, abortion, and how to handle sexual feelings while 75 percent of sexuality teachers believed that students should be taught not to have sex. Given a social context in which the former U.S. Surgeon General, Dr. Joycelyn Elders, was dismissed for acknowledging the normalcy of masturbation, it is not surprising that sexuality educators may feel constrained in their choice of material.

The dominant sexuality conveyed in curriculum materials, according to Sears, presents sexuality as a "natural human drive to be held in abeyance through self-control, self-management, and postponement of sexual gratification." As a result, these curricula are poorly timed in presentation and prove irrelevant and damaging by omission of crucial information. Michelle Fine argues that the naming of desire, pleasure, or sexual entitlement, particularly for females, barely exists in the formal agenda of public schooling on sexuality. When spoken, it is tagged with reminders of "consequences." Fine cites the approved discourses on adolescent female sexuality as discourses of victimization, disease, and morality. She suggests that the missing discourse of desire may result in girls' failure to know themselves as the subjects of their own sexuality.

Deborah Tolman notes, "If girls could conceive of themselves as sexual subjects, they could then potentially make decisions about their sexual behavior and experience that would be healthy for them." The importance of social context has also been acknowledged by some sexuality educators, suggesting that having just more sexuality education, or earlier is not enough, and that sexuality education will be more effective when accompanied by efforts to improve social conditions, decrease poverty, and train people in life skills.

Debra W. Haffner, *Sex Education in 2000: A Call to Action* (New York: Sex Information and Education Council of the U.S., 1990); James Sears, ed., *Sexuality and the Curriculum: The Politics and Practice of Sexuality Education* (New York: Teachers College Press, Columbia University, 1992); Deborah Tolman, "Adolescent Girls, Women and Sexuality: Discerning Dilemmas of Desire," *Women and Therapy, Women, Girls, and Psychotherapy: Reframing Resistance,* 11, no. 3/4 (1991): 55-70.

Paul M. Weyrich

The Value of Abstinence Education

Free Congress Foundation, 2004

The idea that we've got to take the good with the bad isn't acceptable. Especially not when the bad news is that the latest available statistics show there are still over 850,000 teen pregnancies a year—the highest rate in the industrialized world. The good news is that the teen pregnancy rate has been declining for a decade just isn't good enough. But there's one more piece of good news: We have a President who thinks that rate is unacceptable and he is willing to put his reputation on the line to fight the bad news.

President Bush made that clear when he said: "Each year, about three million teenagers contract sexually transmitted diseases that can harm them, or kill them, or prevent them from ever becoming parents. In my budget, I propose a grassroots campaign to help inform families about these medical risks . . . Abstinence for young people is the only certain way to avoid sexually transmitted diseases. Decisions children make now can affect their health and character for the rest of their lives. All of us—parents, schools, government—must work together to counter the negative influence of the culture, and to send the right messages to our children."

This program will come with a price tag. President Bush is proposing doubling spending on abstinence only programs from $135 million to over $270 million in his proposed FY 2005 budget. Many conservatives, myself included, have been sounding alarms about soaring spending by the Federal Government. Rightfully so. But this effort deserves a break and here's why. The Institute of Medicine estimates that the overall costs of Sexually Transmitted Diseases—excluding AIDS—presently exceeds $10 billion a year. Often the money to treat the STDs is paid for directly or indirectly by the Federal Government. Then, there are the cases where teens become pregnant. Who do you think picks up the tab for the birth and the raising of children born out of wedlock? Paying the cost of an effective abstinence only program can help save the Federal government plenty of money.

Indeed, this is more than a dollars and cents issue. Our nation has already been paying a heavy price for the upheaval caused by the sexual revolution and all the problems it brought us in its wake. The ultimate cost is borne by our society in terms of damaged relationships, and premature deaths. The most vicious of these "costs" is the cycle of babies born to teen parents barely able to support themselves. The children are raised in single parent households and the cycle continues when those youngsters fall prey to the same bad choices made by their own parents.

5   President Bush's willingness to use his bully pulpit to emphasize the importance of "abstinence only" to teens and parents can help our nation to regain a sound perspective toward sex and marriage. It's important to note that the President's plan calls for a thorough review of all Federal programs and the messages they are sending to teens and parents about sex and marriage. There is a desire within the Administration to ensure that the message being sent by the Federal Government is consistent and emphasizes the importance of abstinence until marriage. This review would even include the "politically correct" AIDS programs that push the misleadingly labeled "safe sex" message that say it's okay to have promiscuous sex as long as condoms are used. This only inspires risk-taking, often with tragic consequences.

The cornerstone of the plan calls for improving communication between parents and children. That has been the missing link. No doubt, in many cases the parents raised with the mores of the 1960s and 1970s, believe incorrectly that their children do not want their input on sex and marriage. In fact, the exact opposite is true. A recent survey by the National Campaign to Prevent Teen Pregnancy (NCTPTP), not a pro-abstinence only group, confirms what other surveys have found: Teens are very much interested in receiving guidance from their parents on the big decisions in their lives. The NCTPTP survey showed nearly 90 percent of teens felt that way. When parents shirk their responsibility to provide guidance, it is like refusing to throw a life ring to a struggling swimmer. Unfortunately, many churches and faith-based groups are not coming to the rescue either. President Bush's "abstinence only" initiative will work to bridge the generation gap. Sifting the curricula and teaching methods of proven programs, "abstinence only" programs such as "True Love Waits" to discover what really works, the Department of Health & Human Services will distill its findings into a set of "best practices" on how parents and community and religious leaders can best inform teens about the adverse consequences of premarital sex and why it is important to wait until marriage. Down the road, the administration appears intent on developing targeted communications campaigns to further promote abstinence only.

This effort by the administration is a continuation of the effort started in the 1996 welfare reform bill to encourage "abstinence only." The Clinton administration had to be pushed by the Congress to sign it. President Bush, however, is not only personally committed to the program but intends to speak out on it during the coming year. That can start to make a huge difference and, if given the opportunity this November, he will be able to continue his work on this vital issue for the next four years.

Conservatives need to support this initiative, but we also need to make sure that it stays true to its intentions. If careful oversight is not provided, the Federal bureaucrats will hijack this program and impose their own agenda. However, this is an effort well worth doing and conservatives who care about making sure this program works can ensure it works right.

Parents can make a real difference in their children's lives, and a President committed to an abstinence agenda can help to sway national opinion on this issue. There will always be cynics. For too long, this nation has held itself in thrall of the dead-end belief that "just do it" was a message worth emulating. Now, even liberals are starting to recognize the terrible price we have paid for devaluing marriage and sending the message that premarital sex is inevitable.

It's time we as a nation come to our senses once more about the value of the human person, sex and marriage. 10

Paul M. Weyrich is Chairman and CEO of the Free Congress Foundation.

Ceci Connolly

Some Abstinence Programs Mislead Teens, Report Says

Washington Post, December 2, 2004

Many American youngsters participating in federally funded abstinence-only programs have been taught over the past three years that abortion can lead to sterility and suicide, that half the gay male teenagers in the United States have tested positive for the AIDS virus, and that touching a person's genitals "can result in pregnancy," a congressional staff analysis has found. Those and other assertions are examples of the "false, misleading, or distorted information" in the programs' teaching materials, said the analysis, released yesterday, which reviewed the curricula of more than a dozen projects aimed at preventing teenage pregnancy and sexually transmitted disease.

In providing nearly $170 million next year to fund groups that teach abstinence only, the Bush administration, with backing from the Republican Congress, is investing heavily in a just-say-no strategy for teenagers and sex. But youngsters taking the courses frequently receive medically inaccurate or misleading information, often in direct contradiction to the findings of government scientists, said the report, by Rep. Henry A. Waxman (D-Calif.), a critic of the administration who has long argued for comprehensive sex education.

Several million children ages 9 to 18 have participated in the more than 100 federal abstinence programs since the efforts began in 1999. Waxman's staff reviewed the 13 most commonly used curricula—those used by at least five programs apiece.

The report concluded that two of the curricula were accurate but the 11 others, used by 69 organizations in 25 states, contain unproved claims, subjective conclusions or outright falsehoods regarding reproductive health, gender traits and when life begins. In some cases, Waxman said in an interview, the factual issues were limited to occasional misinterpretations of publicly available data; in others, the materials pervasively presented subjective opinions as scientific fact.

Among the misconceptions cited by Waxman's investigators: 5

- A 43-day-old fetus is a "thinking person."
- HIV, the virus that causes AIDS, can be spread via sweat and tears.
- Condoms fail to prevent HIV transmission as often as 31 percent of the time in heterosexual intercourse.

One curriculum, called "Me, My World, My Future," teaches that women who have an abortion "are more prone to suicide" and that as many as 10 percent of them become sterile. This contradicts the 2001 edition of a standard obstetrics textbook that says fertility is not affected by elective abortion, the Waxman report said.

"I have no objection talking about abstinence as a surefire way to prevent unwanted pregnancy and sexually transmitted diseases," Waxman said. "I don't think we ought to lie to our children about science. Something is seriously wrong when federal tax dollars are being used to mislead kids about basic health facts."

When used properly and consistently, condoms fail to prevent pregnancy and sexually transmitted diseases (STDs) less than 3 percent of the time, federal researchers say, and it is not known how many gay teenagers are HIV-positive. The assertion regarding gay teenagers may be a misinterpretation of data from the Centers for Disease Control and Prevention that found that 59 percent of HIV-infected males ages 13 to 19 contracted the virus through homosexual relations.

Joe S. McIlhaney Jr., who runs the Medical Institute for Sexual Health, which developed much of the material that was surveyed, said he is "saddened" that Waxman chose to "blast" well-intentioned abstinence educators when there is much the two sides could agree on.

10   McIlhaney acknowledged that his group, which publishes "Sexual Health Today" instruction manuals, made a mistake in describing the relationship between a rare type of infection caused by chlamydia bacteria and heart failure. Chlamydia also causes a common type of sexually transmitted infection, but that is not linked to heart disease. But McIlhaney said Waxman misinterpreted a slide that warns young people about the possibility of pregnancy without intercourse. McIlhaney said the slide accurately describes a real, though small, risk of pregnancy in mutual masturbation.

Congress first allocated money for abstinence-only programs in 1999, setting aside $80 million in grants, which go to a variety of religious, civic and medical organizations. To be eligible, groups must limit discussion of contraception to failure rates.

President Bush has enthusiastically backed the movement, proposing to spend $270 million on abstinence projects in 2005. Congress reduced that to about $168 million, bringing total abstinence funding to nearly $900 million over five years. It does not appear that the abstinence-only curricula are being taught in the Washington area.

Waxman and other liberal sex-education proponents argue that adolescents who take abstinence-only programs are ill-equipped to protect themselves if they become sexually active. According to the latest CDC data, 61 percent of graduating high school seniors have had sex. Supporters of the abstinence approach, also called abstinence until marriage, counter that teaching young people about "safer sex" is an invitation to have sex.

Alma Golden, deputy assistant secretary for population affairs in the Department of Health and Human Services, said in a statement that Waxman's report is a political document that does a "disservice to our children." Speaking as a pediatrician, Golden said, she knows "abstaining from sex is the most effective means of preventing the sexual transmission of HIV, STDs and preventing pregnancy."

15   Nonpartisan researchers have been unable to document measurable benefits of the abstinence-only model. Columbia University researchers found that although teenagers who take "virginity pledges" may wait longer to initiate sexual activity, 88 percent eventually have premarital sex.

Bill Smith, vice president of public policy at the Sexuality Information and Education Council of the United States, a comprehensive sex education group that also receives federal funding, said the Waxman report underscored the need for closer monitoring of what he called the "shame-based, fear-based, medically inaccurate messages" being disseminated with tax money. He said the danger of abstinence education lies in the omission of useful medical information. Some course materials cited in Waxman's report present as scientific fact notions about a man's need for "admiration" and "sexual fulfillment" compared with a woman's need for "financial support." One book in the "Choosing Best" series tells the story of a knight who married a village maiden instead of the princess because the princess offered so many tips on slaying the local dragon.

"Moral of the story," notes the popular text: "Occasional suggestions and assistance may be alright, but too much of it will lessen a man's confidence or even turn him away from his princess."

Priscilla Pardini

Two Approaches to Sexuality Education

Rethinking Schools Online, Winter 2002/2003

"So, what would make you decide to take a risk—drink that beer, smoke that doobie, drive without a seatbelt, have sex?" Paul Zettel, a health teacher at Milwaukee's Riverside High School, asks his 34 tenth grade students. The students sit up straight. Hands wave in the air.

"To have fun or have an adventure," answers one.

"To do what my friends were doing," says another.

"To see what it was like," volunteers a third.

Clearly, Zettel has a lot of work to do.   5

Within a few weeks, Zettel will have moved beyond teaching decision-making skills to lessons on personal wellness, mental health, risky behaviors and sexuality. The sexuality unit includes information on relationships, human reproduction, teen pregnancy, contraception, abortion, and homosexuality. To be sure, he'll encourage his students to abstain from sex—he describes the curriculum as "abstinence-based"—but he also covers contraception, sexual harassment and sexual assault, sexually transmitted diseases, and HIV.

Zettel is passionate about what he does and about the importance of comprehensive sexuality education. His one-semester class is based on Milwaukee Public Schools' human growth and development curriculum. "If I don't give them all the facts, they're more likely to make unhealthy choices," he says.

Meanwhile, Pat Kirby's message, as she welcomes 30 seventh-grade girls to a Best Friends class at Lincoln Center Middle School of the Arts, isn't all that different from Zettel's. One of the first things her students are going to be learning, she tells them, is "to make good decisions."

And when Kirby polls her students on why they've volunteered to be in Best Friends, their answers are as painfully revealing and every bit as honest as those of Zettel's students:

"I don't know."   10

"To get out of class."

"Because my friend is in it."

"To get the necklace."

Kirby, urging some of the girls to "rethink that answer," goes on to explain what else they can expect from the program. "We're going to be talking about what it means to be a best friend, how to respect yourselves and how to take responsibility for your behavior," she says. "And about abstinence—saying 'No' to drugs, sex, alcohol, and violence."

15   Kirby's students are quiet and shy—she has to work hard to draw much of a response from them. That is, until they hear the word "sex," which unleashes a chorus of little girl giggles. But if Kirby starts out much like Zettel, with lessons on the importance of making good decisions, her scope is much more narrow. Girls who sign up for the program sign pledges vowing to abstain from sexual activity. And the only time Kirby mentions contraception is to talk about failure rates.

Best Friends (as well as its companion programs, Diamond Girls for high school girls and Best Men for adolescent boys) is a youth development program that focuses on the value of abstinence from sex, drugs, and alcohol. All three programs are run by the national Best Friends Foundation, which was founded in 1987 by Elayne Bennett, wife of former U.S. Secretary of Education William Bennett. In MPS, the programs are meant to be used as supplements to the district's human growth and development curriculum. Participants attend monthly classes during the school day and are matched up with mentors who can act as positive role models. Peer support is a strong component of all three programs. A total of 940 girls in fifth through 12th grades at 13 MPS schools and 550 boys in fifth grade through eighth grade at 10 schools are involved in the programs this year. According to district and state officials, funding comes from a combination of federal abstinence-only funds and private grants.

Kyle Witty, who coordinates the Best Men program, said it aimed to boost boys' self-respect and teach them to respect women. Witty said the program helped underscore the message that issues of teen sexuality should not be seen as solely the responsibility of girls. "Unfortunately, our society still has that 'boys will be boys' attitude," he said. "But [sex] is just as much, if not more, the responsibility of boys."

Although Best Friends has never been evaluated independently, officials claim that less than one percent of participants become pregnant and that 75 percent say they want to wait until marriage to have sex. The program was honored in 1997 as one of the nation's most effective programs by the National Campaign to Prevent Teen Pregnancy.

"We do see progress," said Kirby. "They grow up a lot and their attitudes change. We're able to convince many that abstinence is their very best option A lot of them, I believe, are waiting."

20   Yet, Kirby—an alcohol, drug abuse and HIV/AIDS counselor—said she hopes the girls in Best Friends were also learning about contraception. "They probably should know," she said. "Some are bound to have intercourse and at least would be able to protect themselves."

Bob Helmeniak, who oversees sex education for MPS, said the two approaches being used by Zettel and Kirby exemplify the range of sexuality education being offered in MPS. He said the district's comprehensive human growth and development curriculum, adopted in 1982 and revised in 1995, is currently being revised again. "The curriculum is there," said Helmeniak. "How the schools go about using it is up to them."

Writing Prompts

1. Write a three-page essay on the issue of sex education in which you clearly state your opinion and back it up with evidence from two of the essays.
2. Contact your local school board and find out what their policy is on sex education. Then write a one-page letter to your local newspaper in which you outline the school district's policy and either agree or disagree with it.
3. Write a two-page essay beginning with a brief anecdote about your own experiences in sex education class. Then, using evidence from at least two of the essays, critique whatever sex education you had (or didn't have) in school and either (a) argue for a different, better way to address this issue or (b) argue why the sex education methods used in your school were a success.
4. Write a three-page essay comparing/contrasting two of the essays without revealing your own position—your job is to show both sides without taking a side yourself.
5. From the essays you disagree with, choose the one that has the strongest or most convincing argument. Taking into account the first four chapters of this textbook where you read about successful writing strategies, write a two-page analysis of the author's argument and discuss the ways the author is most successful making his or her point, even though you don't agree with it.

What Is at Stake for Citizenship?

1. Should religion be a reason to limit information given to teens (in public schools) about sex? Isn't our value system already based on religion, even with the separation of church and state?
2. Which is more important, freedom or responsibility? Does your answer change when the discussion is about minors instead of adults?
3. Whose business is it—the parents' or the teen's—if a teenager wants to have sex? Does a young person have the right to information about sex and sexually transmitted diseases and access to condoms, even if the parent doesn't want that information shared? Is it censorship?
4. Is information about and access to birth control a civil right? Does one gender (male or female) have more right to this information? Is one gender more responsible for sex and more in need of either abstinence or sex education classes?
5. Do students who want something more or something different from the sex education they are getting have a right to demand change?

GENDER AND GENDER ROLES: NEW LIVES FOR MEN AND WOMEN

The images are perfectly preserved for us in the television shows of the 1950s—like *Leave It to Beaver, Father Knows Best,* and *Ozzie and Harriet*—all full of men in gray flannel suits coming home from work to find a lovely dinner cooked by their wives, while women in dresses and pearls stayed at home raising children in the suburbs. Dad saw his children when he wasn't working or golfing on the weekend. There was no such thing as "quality time" with the children. There was no need for the term "stay-at-home mom"—where else would she be staying? Boys played with trucks and girls played with dolls. A son expressed an interest in being a doctor, a fireman, or an astronaut, while a daughter could aspire to being a teacher, a nurse, or a secretary while she passed the time before marriage and motherhood. He was expected to work for the rest of his life; she was not expected to hold a job after she married. Men made more money than women because a man was presumed to have a family to feed. Many women dropped out of college to marry, figuring they wouldn't need the degree to be a wife. Certainly these are generalities, but they also served as clear cultural expectations. These values were prevalent across the cultural institutions and in the media and advertising of the 1950s. Men were men and women were women. Life wasn't fair but it was clear.

Now it seems so much is less than clear. The lives of American men and women have changed drastically over the last generation—some say for better, and some say for worse. Where once the lives of men and women were clearly defined and delineated, those boundaries are blurred in the twenty-first century. That change has occurred is obvious, but the causes—the social, political, and familial catalysts that propelled such change—are less clear.

As we begin our discussion of these changes in American society, we might start with the **Civil Rights Act of 1964**, which guaranteed women many rights they had never before enjoyed. Or we might start with traditional marriage; it has changed considerably over the last thirty years. Some say the changes in marriage began in the **women's movement** of the 1970s, which made divorce, including **no-fault divorce**, easier and led to more job opportunities and financial independence for women. Today roughly half of all marriages fail; the failure rate for second marriages is even higher. It is safe to say that no one is happy with these high divorce rates, and even safer to say that no one can agree on what to do about them. And along with all of these changes comes a lack of certainty about what the meaning of a man's or a woman's life might be. The following essays explore just a few of the issues surrounding men's and women's changing roles. Some essays offer stories of how modern couples found new ways of doing things, while others tell the stories of those who want to embrace the practices of the past, finding value in tradition. Still others tell stories of individuals who find themselves in roles or jobs that would never have been an option for their parents or grandparents. *As you read, consider how many different ways our lives can be shaped, and think about what shape you want your life to take, given all the choices of today. Even more importantly, ask yourself if we have really changed at all.*

Anne Woods Fisher

The Stay-at-Home Dad

Christianity Today, Fall 2000

Eric and Jody courted during graduate school, they assumed that when the time came to raise a family, Eric would work and Jody would stay home with the kids. Six years later, things looked different. "I liked my job, but Jody loved hers," says Eric. "Jody made lots more money than I ever could have. It became clear to each of us that she should work and I should stay home. We came to this decision through a lot of prayer and by discussing it with our church friends ad nauseum."

Three children later, Eric is passionate about being a stay-at-home dad. "My staying home and Jody engaged in her career works well for us. We each think we have the better end of the deal. I love kids, and she loves her job and our kids. I haven't traded away a gloomy future so my wife can work; I traded up. I worked for 12 years as an engineer; it was a good experience and I miss my colleagues. But I will have a more significant impact on the world by being home."

Eric and Jody aren't unusual. Estimates today place the number of stay-at-home dads in the United States at nearly two million—a number that has quadrupled since 1986 and is now the fastest growing family type. The exact number is difficult to determine because many fathers who devote themselves full-time to the job of parenting also have part-time jobs, work from home, or are between jobs.

Based on survey results by researcher Bob Frank, these families share common characteristics: they see themselves as equal partners in parenting, and they put childcare first—above traditional roles. They choose this arrangement not out of necessity, but of practicality: the husband's personality may be a better fit for raising kids full-time or he can interrupt his career more easily or work out of the home. In most cases, the wife's career provides greater benefits and career potential than the husband's.

Such was the case with Sue and Dave Jenks of Palo Alto, California. Sue worked at a technology firm, Dave was self-employed as an architectural draftsman, and they juggled childcare for their two children. "It became clear that one of us needed to stay home," says Dave. "I was trying to work late at night, but I wasn't doing too great a job at either taking care of the kids or starting my business. I was wiped out all of the time; so I suggested that I stay home. Sue had an established career with benefits and was in a marketable position. We wanted one of us to be home with the kids, and we both feel relieved of the stress of using day care. One thing I hope my kids will catch on to is how committed we are. We'll do whatever it takes to raise them in the best way."

5

Not Mr. Mom

Mr. Mom, a hit movie in the early eighties, depicts a freshly unemployed Michael Keaton struggling to adapt to being a full-time dad. He tries to be a substitute mom, and it isn't until the end of the movie that he gets it—he can still be a dad.

Fathers and mothers do not parent alike, writes Dr. Bob Frank in *Equal Balanced Parenting* (Golden). Agrees Eric: "My parents have noticed that I am not mothering the children, I'm fathering them."

In fact, studies are finding that children who have increased time with their fathers have numerous advantages chiefly because of the way a father interacts. One study from the Center for Successful Fathering in Austin, Texas, cites that when a father is an active participant in parenting, children benefit with higher grades, greater ambition, fewer anxiety disorders, and a reduced risk of delinquency or teen pregnancy. Another study found children with an actively involved father score higher on verbal skills and academic achievement.

Not Mrs. Dad

Working moms tend to blend both the "breadwinner" role with more traditional mothering activities such as helping with dinner, bathing the children, and putting them to bed. Fathers do most of the same household activities as stay-at-home moms, but still assume traditional responsibility for maintenance tasks such as yard work and fixing appliances. Peter Baylies, founder of the newsletter *At-Home Dad*, splits household chores with his schoolteacher wife. "We share cooking every other week. Dad may still be changing the oil in the car but he's doing diapers too. Mom still isn't changing the oil, however," he notes.

Effects on a Marriage

10   What impact does role reversal have on a marriage? Marital contentment with these reversed roles has much to do with why the couple chose this arrangement. If both partners choose their role, it can enhance love and commitment, eliminate stresses of juggling daycare, and foster a supportive bond. But if a couple has fallen into this arrangement by default (such as getting laid off), or the father does not establish a primary emotional bond with his children and takes less power in parent-child matters, the adjustment period can be quite difficult. In those situations, husbands run the risk of becoming secondary factors in a marriage, writes Daniel Colodner in *Full-Time Dads* magazine.

Eric and Jody claim this arrangement works beautifully for them. "It's proven to be a rocket booster—it was precisely the right thing for our marriage," says Eric. "Jody is happier at her job now, knowing I'm with the kids. I love watching her blossom. Being a full-time dad has only strengthened our marriage."

Such is the experience of Carol and Robert Hamrin, founder and president of Great Dads: Seminars for Fathers, who reversed roles in 1983. "The underlying theme for Carol and me in this area is that we are equal partners, under God's guidance, in our marriage and in our parenting. Together we seek God's guidance on what we should do career-wise, ministry-wise, and parenting-wise. He has never failed us. God is our Head, and under him we submit to one another and respect one another. As a married couple, God has a single purpose for us; we are to seek him. In practical terms, this meant making the appropriate sacrifices on the career front as God led us along the way. It has made our marriage strong and filled with joy for 30 years."

But Dave and Sue Jenks admit this arrangement isn't for everybody. "Every thought I have about our situation is fully two-sided," admits Sue. "I like our marriage even more because we are doing something original, creative, and atypical; and because we are doing something original, creative, and atypical, it's kind of lonely. I respect David even more because he has the strength of character and capability to play this role, but I'd like to test my mettle on the home front too. I'm proud and impressed that I'm financially supporting a family of four, but I feel overwhelmed and sometimes exhausted at the very notion. I love representing a productive, contributing woman in the workplace to my kids; yet I haven't learned to cook and don't have that and other 'domestic' skills to impart to my kids."

Dave shares Sue's ambivalence. "I think this changes a marriage and throws you for a while," he says. "If you've been brought up in a more traditional home, as I was, reversing things takes a lot of getting used to. It's hard not to value your contribution by money; money is just easier to measure. I feel as if I'm in a support role to Sue—so she can make money to take care of us all."

Transitioning into these roles can take time. Even Eric, enthusiastic about his role, admits to a sense of loss at first.

Peter Baylies notes that it took him a year to adjust to the new routine. "There's an adjustment period—no paycheck, no affirmation, and you're facing the hardest job you'll ever have. Parenting is a job you can never leave." Loneliness, isolation, and recreating an identity not based on achievement are the main drawbacks, says Peter. "Dads tend to try to solve problems on their own, they do not reach out for support the way mothers do—that's why some at-home dads are isolated."

Mixed reactions from acquaintances, relatives, and friends gets tiresome, says Dave. Eric finds that if a stranger makes a careless remark, he takes it in stride. If it were a remark by someone in his church group, he would take it to heart. "But our church has been incredible. We would be an incomplete story to not include the support we've received from our church," he says.

Eric's church has been especially helpful in defining his new role. "I believe I have a duty to lead," he says. "And I do lead this family. Based on my Bible study, sermons, and conversations in my men's group, however, I don't think there's a duty to provide exclusive to the husband."

Still, swimming against cultural norms will prove difficult to many stay-at-home dads. Stay-at-home dads should remember, however, as Dan Kindlon and Michael Thompson write in *Raising Cain* (Ballantine Books), "There are many ways to become a man; there are many ways to be brave, to be a good father, to be loving and strong and successful. We need to praise the artist and the entertainer, the missionary and the athlete, the soldier and the male nurse, the storeowner and the round-the-world sailor, the teacher and the CEO. There are many ways to make a contribution in this life."

Encouraging each other can make all the difference. "It's very important to both be and have a supportive partner. The two of you really need each other to make it work. Jody misses the kids and longs for more time with them," says Eric. "So I try to take care of the home front so she can come home and be 100 percent with the kids."

"In addition," advises Eric, "you have to make time for each other. For at least one 24-hour period a month, we try to get away just the two of us. We make a real effort to plan time for just us, to remind ourselves of why we fell in love in the first place."

The Payoffs

All stay-at-home dads report an amazing, powerful bond with their children. "There's no better way to really understand your children than to spend a lot of time with them," insists Peter. "Our kids are not at daycare but at home, being raised by the one or two people on the planet who love them the most."

Eric readily agrees. "We did not want to subcontract out our parenting. We felt we could only do two out of three things well—her work, my work, or raising our children.

Maybe others can juggle all three priorities. We couldn't, and we didn't want to compromise with our kids."

And all of these families insist their kids have profited by the arrangement. "I love showing our kids that they're a huge priority to us," says Sue Jenks. "We're providing 'here-and-now' benefits for them versus more financial savings for their futures. I love showing them that we'll structure things however we need to in order to 'walk that talk'".

Ms. Top Cop

Peg Tyre

Newsweek, April 12, 2004

President Bush acknowledges female officers.

When Boston's Mayor Thomas Menino swore in his city's 38th police commissioner in early February, he followed tradition. As bagpipes played, the new top cop took an oath to serve and received a gold-plated badge. Menino's choice for the job, however, was anything but traditional. For the first time in the department's 374-year history, the chief of the Boston Police Department is a woman. Menino says Kathleen O'Toole, 49, a former beat cop turned lawyer who ran her own international consulting firm, was the right person for the job. "Gender," he says, "simply wasn't a factor."

O'Toole is the newest member of a growing sorority. In the past year women have been appointed top cop in three other cities: Detroit, Milwaukee, and San Francisco. Criminal-justice scholars say these appointments could signal a major turning point in the struggle to break what has often seemed to be a bulletproof glass ceiling. In 1985, Penny Harrington became the first woman to run a major urban force when she was appointed chief in Portland, Ore. Few followed her path. Out of 18,000 departments in the country, only about 200—mostly small-town forces and campus police departments—are currently headed by women. But with women now running some of the biggest departments in the country, "it's reached critical mass," says Dorothy Schulz, a professor at John Jay College of Criminal Justice, who is writing a book about women chiefs.

That doesn't mean women are taking over policing. They now account for fewer than 15 percent of the 880,000 sworn law enforcement officers in the country. But what is changing is the definition of a good cop. Big-city forces used to run on a paramilitary model, which relied upon top-down leadership and prized physical training. These days, police officers are expected to be more service providers than soldiers. The emphasis on community policing encourages beat cops to focus on crime prevention and requires commanders to develop strong ties to neighborhood leaders. Education counts more too. In 1979, when O'Toole joined the Boston force, she was afraid to tell her bosses that she was in law school. "I didn't exactly hide it," she says, "but I didn't volunteer it either." But now, most departments require two years of college for beat cops and expect supervisors to have even more. That favors female recruits, who generally are more educated than their male counterparts.

This shift puts more women on the fast track to top jobs. Instead of giving the chief's badge to the "toughest guy in the valley," says Schulz, Mayors are looking for sophisticated CEOs who can oversee large budgets, negotiate thorny management problems and set sound department-wide policy. Modern chiefs are expected to be proficient at marketing and public relations too. "'In many ways the job has become more complex," says New York City Police Commissioner Ray Kelly, who himself recently appointed a woman chief to lead the 1,700 officers assigned to public housing. "It's become brains over brawn."

Which doesn't mean women chiefs aren't tough when they need to be. Detroit's   5
Chief Ella Bully-Cummings, 46, sounded more like Dirty Harry in February when she announced new initiatives aimed at reducing a spiking homicide rate. "We know who you are," she warned. "We know where you are. And we're coming to get you." Acting San Francisco Police Chief Heather Fong has an advanced degree in social work, but it was her reputation as a stern disciplinarian that got her the job. She was brought in to clean house after the last police chief resigned in scandal. "There will always be people who say, 'She can't do it because she's not as physically strong,'" says Fong. "But when there's a tough decision to be made, I can make it." That's the kind of strength a modern police force needs.

Alisa Weinstein

Single Father from the Start

Denver Post, October 26, 2003

Dan Stuart's wife, Caroline, was four months pregnant when doctors diagnosed her cancer. Two years earlier, she won a bout with melanoma, but the diseases returned, and this time it metastasized throughout her brain, lungs, and liver. Cancer treatments might damage the baby's brain, the doctors said, so the Stuarts decided to delay chemotherapy until after their son's birth.

In the 28th week of Caroline Stuart's pregnancy—the first week of the final trimester when the baby's lungs are almost fully developed—doctors decided to take the baby. Stuart's condition was worsening quickly, and they feared her body might not hold up much longer.

On July 9, James Daniel Stuart was delivered by caesarean section 12 weeks premature. He weighed a little more than two pounds and measured 14 inches—roughly the length of his father's forearm.

Two days later, 42-year-old Caroline Stuart went for her first radiation treatment. Afterward, weak and discouraged, she told her husband she wanted to halt treatment.

"We met with a team of three doctors, and they said, in the big picture, this might   5
extend her life, but not for long," says Stuart. "And with that big picture, we kind of got the word that there's nothing they could do but keep Caroline comfortable."

For Stuart, a soft-spoken 53-year-old cartographer, reality began to sink in: His wife would not be there to help him raise their son. On July 19, 10 days after James Daniel's birth, Caroline Stuart died.

Stuart, with his soft shape, close-shaven beard and glasses, fits the image of the cuddly, fatherly type. But when it comes to babies, he is a novice.

During one of Stuart's regular visits to his new son at Swedish Medical Center's neonatal intensive care unit, a nurse had to explain the right way to diaper a baby (elastic firmly around baby's tiny, pink legs) so that what goes inside the diaper doesn't leak out—all over his shirt.

"Dan's never been around a baby before," says Joan Gould Johnson, Caroline Stuart's mother. "He looks at it as standing on the edge of a precipice. It's like you just learned to ski and you're standing at the top of a black diamond."

10   Gould Johnson accompanied Stuart to Baby Safe class at Swedish. They learned infant CPR and other safety basics. But knowing the basics doesn't necessarily assuage the emotional insecurities that accompany any first-time father, not to mention one who is going it alone. Although Stuart is ecstatic about being a dad, he worried about falling short. What if he didn't understand his son's cries? What if he couldn't tell what the baby needed?

In the early 20th century, it wasn't uncommon for women to die in childbirth and leave a husband to care for their infant alone. According to the National Center for Health Statistics, in 1930, nearly 700 of every 100,000 women in the United States died after giving birth. But as the maternal mortality rate has declined—it was down to eight in every 100,000 in the mid-1990s—the idea of fathers being left to raise babies faded from everyday consciousness.

But mothers still die and abandon their newborns. According to a March 2000 *Current Population Survey,* nearly 200,000 men are facing single fatherhood with an infant. And parenting experts say that these single fathers face a unique set of issues.

Men are often seen as not sensitive enough to meet a child's needs, and in the case of widowers, prematurely pushed into dating by well-intentioned friends and family who think that the child needs a nurturing female. There's also the likelihood that, when a single dad is out with his kids, he'll keep running into the question "So, you got stuck with the babysitting duties today, too?"

"There is this perception lingering out there in society that a child can't survive without a mother, and that's loony," says Armin Brott, author of *The Single Father: A Dad's Guide to Parenting Without a Partner.* All the studies I've looked at have shown that men are just as compassionate."

15   Still, single fathers tend to come under more scrutiny as they learn the ropes, says Brott.

Dan Stuart is balancing his own expectations with those of his wife's close-knit family, many of who live in or near Denver. And compounding matters, they are all still grieving the loss of a sister, daughter, wife and mother despite their admiration for her accomplishment.

"She gave her life for that baby, you know that?" says Caroline Stuart's father, Hal Gould. "I don't know any more than that, except I know she had the option to take treatment . . . which would've probably terminated the baby, and she chose not to do that."

From the moment the Stuarts decided to have a baby, they knew they might face complications. Caroline Stuart had gone through early menopause at 39, so the couple decided to pursue in-vitro fertilization. To be on the safe side, the couple sought approval for the pregnancy from an oncologist at the University of Colorado Health Sciences Center who had seen Stuart concerning her previous bout with cancer. He told them to go ahead.

After that the pieces fell into place. Caroline's sister-in-law offered to donate her eggs and then in January 2003, on the third attempt to implant a fertilized egg into Caroline Stuart's womb, the procedure succeeded. Dan Stuart still remembers the day his wife called him at work and gave him the good news by singing the words to a 1965 Herman's Hermits song, "Can't You Hear My Heart Beat."

"Caroline's a real character," says Stuart. "I get this phone call, 'Baby, baby, I can hear your heart beat,'" Stuart sings, re-enacting the moment. "And I thought, 'Whoa'. I knew immediately."

In April, Caroline Stuart felt a stubborn pain under her arm. "After a couple of weeks, her mother noticed a little lump under her armpit, so we went to a doctor," remembers Stuart.

Caroline Stuart underwent a biopsy, but it wasn't until weeks later that doctors told them that the cancer had returned. "We just thought everything was going to be fine," says Stuart. "She didn't look sick."

Stuart is not dwelling on questions about whether pregnancy made his wife's cancer more aggressive of if something else could have been done to save her. He is thinking of James Daniel now, as is his wife's family, all of whom have pledged to help.

"We can rally around James with the same love that we rallied around Caroline," says Tom Wells, who is married to Caroline Stuart's sister, Julie Wells. "In the past, babies were raised by entire families."

There has also been an outpouring of help and support from the Stuart's church, Trinity Methodist in Denver. Stuart and his wife met at a Trinity singles event, and until she died, Caroline Stuart worked there as a part-time wedding coordinator.

Friends from the church cleaned their Littleton home, gave rides to Caroline Stuart's 17-year-old son, Max Thompson, and even performed a bedside baptism—complete with live music by the choir director and her husband—in Caroline Stuart's hospital room.

After Caroline Stuart died, friends cooked dinners for Stuart and Thompson, and when Stuart visited his mother for four days, they took turns visiting James Daniel in the intensive care unit. Right before the baby's Sept. 23 homecoming, the church's youth coordinator organized a baby shower for Stuart and Thompson.

While the community will help Stuart make the transition to single fatherhood, Brott warns that the amount of time others can offer may ebb and flow over time. He advised single fathers to attend single-sex support groups (men find it easier to open up when there are no women around). The groups also help fathers feel less alien in our mommy-centric world.

"The most common question I get is, 'Am I the only one who . . .?'" says Brott. "That sort of feeling of being alone or being on the margins is hard to deal with."

Brott's website, MrDad.com, contains links to support organizations and online resources for fathers. The Florida-based, stay-at-home-dads network Slowlane.com links dads to other dads and contains articles like "Stay-at-Home Dad's: Fantasy vs. Reality."

Stuart hasn't ruled out the possibility of finding a support group. But for now the new father—who is on family leave from work and planning an early retirement in December—is getting used to routine feedings, visits to the pediatrician and of course, changing diapers.

Things have gone well since James Daniel came home nearly a month ago. Stuart is managing to fit in a decent amount of sleep and has even managed to entertain family for dinner, something he and Caroline loved doing together. As for James Daniel, he is getting stronger each day. He now weighs 7 pounds and has grown to 20 inches.

Stuart's confidence as a dad is growing too, giving him time to relax and enjoy the little moments with his new son—like his first smile. "When he was ready for his bottle, I put a little napkin on him," says Stuart. "He kind of knew that that meant the bottle was coming, and he gave a little smile. That was neat."

Vanessa Juarez

Out of Bounds

Newsweek, March 8, 2004

When Violet Palmer is wearing her daytime Nike gear, ponytail and infectious smile, she reminds you of Sandra Bullock or Julia Roberts, a pal you'd like to hang out with. But once the curtain goes up, she's all business. Palmer's curtain is a basketball tip-off, her stage is the court and her craft is to make sure the 10 giants stampeding around her aren't out of bounds. She keeps them in line with a stern poker face and an encyclopedic knowledge of the rules.

As the lone female ref not only in the NBA but in virtually every men's pro league, the 39-year-old Palmer is used to her contradictory world. Reffing is tough. You've got to keep track of every movement these really big, really fast guys make as they drive to the hoop. Players yell. Coaches snap. Fans talk trash. And they were all louder than usual seven seasons ago when Palmer, who grew up playing ball with her brother in their Compton, Calif., driveway, became the first woman to officiate an NBA game. There were grumbles, even from coach Phil Jackson, who wasn't convinced she was the best person for the job. Two games later Dee Kanter became the second woman on the court, but she was dismissed in 2002 after reportedly dismal postseason reviews (she's now with the WNBA). Palmer is the sole survivor.

Palmer, who as a kid would tell her parents she wanted to be a doctor, didn't choose this career for its glory. She certainly doesn't get paid as much as the players do, and during games she doesn't get a substitute to come in for her when she's tired. What keeps her going is that she gets to stick around a game she loves (she once played for Cal Poly Pomona) without going insane. "Oh, my God, the kids needed so much attention," says Palmer of her two seasons of high-school basketball she coached. "I had migraines. I was just so tense and stressed out. I said, 'This ain't for me.'" The worst part of this job is traveling 23 days a month, says Palmer, who's single and based in Los Angeles.

Most pro referees get their start the way Palmer did—at the bottom. In seven years she went from recreation leagues, to high school, college, the WNBA, and, finally, the NBA (it takes at least a decade for most to get to the pros). When the league invited her to train to be a ref in 1994, Palmer thought it was a joke. The offer was real, but it didn't mean Palmer would work regular-season games. She still had to go through the league's developmental program, where trainees officiate in what amounts to an NBA minor league during the summer.

In October 1997, three summers later, Palmer made "the show" in a game that pitted the Vancouver Grizzlies against the Dallas Mavericks. "I will never ever, ever forget the moment I put that jacket on and walked onto that floor," she says. "I was like, 'wow, you're telling me I'm going to do this every single night!' I was more than nervous, I was going to pee in my pants." She didn't take her critics personally. "I said, 'You know what, this is just because it's different, because I'm a woman, and they just don't know any better'," says Palmer. Her philosophy: "If I prove myself, credibility will follow." And it did.

Men pray at a Promise Keepers rally.

The Promise Keepers is a group of men who espouse Christian values and urge their members to take back their traditional male role as head of household and leader in the home. Their all-male membership has large rallies in sports stadiums around the country, and after some financial setbacks in the 1990s, they are once again growing and reaching out to men who want to lead more traditional, responsible lives as husbands and fathers. They are also controversial, attacked by other Christian groups that don't care for their brand of religion and by women's groups who object to what they feel is a reassertion of **patriarchy**. In the wake of the women's movement, Promise Keepers, like the Million Man March, is part of what has been called the men's movement and seeks to empower men to lead better, more responsible, and often more traditional lives.

Fact Sheet–Promise Keepers

Promise Keepers Mission

Promise Keepers is dedicated to igniting and uniting men to be passionate followers of Jesus Christ through the effective communication of the 7 Promises. Through stadium and arena conferences, radio programming, Internet, print and multi-media resources, and outreach to local churches, Promise Keepers encourages men to live godly lives and to keep seven basic promises of commitment to God, their families, and others, in the context of the local church. Promise Keepers seeks to unite Christian men of all races, denominations, ages, cultures, and socio-economic groups, and believes that men need accountable relationships with other men. Those relationships, along with prayer, Bible study and active church membership help men in their daily life with God, their families and their communities.

Organization and Staff

Promise Keepers is a Colorado nonprofit, section 501(c)(3) tax-exempt Christ-centered religious corporation that is governed by a nine-member board of directors and operated under the daily direction of President Thomas S. Fortson. Vice Presidents include Executive Vice President Raleigh B. Washington, Vice President of Development Brian W. Blomberg, and Vice President of Creative Services Harold D. Velasquez. The Ministry was established in 1990 and is headquartered in Denver, Colorado.

Financial Integrity

Promise Keepers is dedicated to maintaining financial integrity and makes its annual financial statements available to anyone requesting them. Promise Keepers is a member of the Evangelical Council for Financial Accountability (ECFA) and complies with its standards and guidelines, including submission to an annual financial audit, which is conducted by Capin Crouse & Co. Promise Keepers is also committed to being a faithful steward of all of its resources, which requires planning and careful spending. Finally, consistent with its commitment to supporting the mission of the local church, Promise Keepers encourages men to give to their local church before making any contribution to the ministry.

Beginnings

On March 20, 1990, the head football coach for the University of Colorado, **Bill McCartney**, and his friend Dave Wardell, Ph.D., were on a three-hour car ride to a Fellowship of Christian Athletes (FCA) meeting, when they first discussed the idea of filling a stadium with Christian men. Later that year, 72 men began to fast and pray about the concept of thousands of men coming together for the purpose of Christian discipleship. In July 1991, 4,200 men gathered for the first Promise Keepers conference at the University of Colorado basketball arena. Promise Keepers marks its tenth anniversary in the year 2000, having reached more than 3.5 million men through 98 stadium and arena conferences.

Stand in the Gap: A Sacred Assembly

5   On Saturday, October 4, 1997, Promise Keepers convened a massive gathering on the National Mall in Washington, D.C. Hundreds of thousands of men participated in Stand in the Gap: A Sacred Assembly of Men, a day of personal repentance and prayer. Since the 1600s North American churches have called together sacred assemblies in time of spiritual crisis. Twelve instances are recorded in the Old Testament when the nation of Israel was called to gather for days of fasting, prayer, confession and repentance of sin because the nation had wandered away from Almighty God. Stand in the Gap was patterned after such sacred assemblies.

Clergy Conferences

Promise Keepers motivates and encourages laymen to actively support the mission of their church and to pray for their pastor(s). Since 1992, Promise Keepers men's conferences have often been preceded by special sessions for clergy. In 1996, Promise Keepers hosted the world's largest gathering of Christian clergy for a worship and teaching conference in Atlanta's Georgia Dome. Over 39,000 clergy attended that event. In early 1998, Promise Keepers hosted nine regional clergy conferences, which were attended by more than 30,000 ministers. In February 2003, Promise Keepers hosted a gathering of 10,000 pastors at Bank One Ballpark in Phoenix, Ariz.

Global Ministries

Promise Keepers has a growing international ministry with activity in more than 30 countries on every continent. In 1999, stadium events were held in South Africa, Puerto Rico and Monterrey, Mexico, while the new millennium will see conferences in Costa Rica and Ghana. Meanwhile, Promise Keepers continues to receive inquiries about developing men's ministries from countries around the globe. Indicative of the worldwide nature of the Christian men's movement, more than 100,000 men have attended men's events directly related to Promise Keepers in countries outside the United States.

Volunteers

Each year Promise Keepers places great dependence on thousands of men and women who volunteer in their local communities across the country, where the organization hosts men's conferences. On average, each conference requires more than 800 local volunteers, half of whom are women.

Seven Promises—Promise Keepers Homepage
http://www.promisekeepers.org

1. A Promise Keeper is committed to honoring Jesus Christ through worship, prayer and obedience to God's Word in the power of the Holy Spirit.
2. A Promise Keeper is committed to pursuing vital relationships with a few other men, understanding that he needs brothers to help him keep his promises.
3. A Promise Keeper is committed to practicing spiritual, moral, ethical, and sexual purity.
4. A Promise Keeper is committed to building strong marriages and families through love, protection and biblical values.
5. A Promise Keeper is committed to supporting the mission of his church by honoring and praying for his pastor, and by actively giving his time and resources.
6. A Promise Keeper is committed to reaching beyond any racial and denominational barriers to demonstrate the power of biblical unity.
7. A Promise Keeper is committed to influencing his world, being obedient to the Great Commandment (see Mark 12:30-31) and the Great Commission (see Matthew 28:19-20).

Mark 12:30-31
Love the Lord your God with all your heart and
with all your soul and with all your mind and
with all your strength. The second is this: Love
your neighbor as yourself. (NIV)

Matthew 28:19-20
Therefore go and make disciples of all nations,
baptizing them in the name of the Father and of
the Son and of the Holy Spirit, and teaching
them to obey everything I have commanded you.
And surely I am with you always, to the very end
of the age. (NIV)

Cate Terwilliger

Father Superior

The *Colorado Springs Independent*, June 26–July 2, 1996

I am sitting in a sweltering sea of 50,000 bodies, part of the growing rank-and-file army of Christian soldiers that is Promise Keepers. We are young, old, able-bodied, disabled, straight and—no doubt—gay. All variations on every category of male, except me.

Mile High Stadium is a perfect venue for Promise Keepers, the Bible-based men's group founded six years ago by then-University of Colorado football coach Bill McCartney. Like other sports stadiums at which PK rallies are held, it has a welcoming beer-and-hot-dogs-with-the-guys feeling, a distinct and familiar comfort given the emotional uncertainty of the soul work we've signed on for.

At this moment, my anxieties are more secular than profound, rooted in the Ace bandage binding my breasts, the hint of mascara thickening my eyebrows and the ball cap pulled low over newly shorn hair. I'm uncertain what to do if my cover as a taciturn but regular guy fails to conceal my biological womanhood.

But nobody's paying any attention to me, and I begin to relax. My Christian brothers have more important things on their minds: getting right with God, with each other, their families. They want to be what PK literature describes—men of integrity—and in this quest they are willing to touch each other in love, to pray and cry together, to kneel on the cement and stretch hands of praise toward a capricious sky. They are willing, in the absence of women, to become more womanly, while never forgetting they are men and warriors of God.

5   I am willing, during my brief sojourn in the alien kingdoms of masculinity and Christendom, to forget I am a woman, to see through these men's eyes and hear with their ears. To witness this bright, ascending star of evangelical Christianity without becoming blind to its shadow, where I, as a woman, must live.

A Many-colored Army

The theme of this year's conferences is "Break Down the Walls," a broad call for unity across denominational and racial lines. "Coach Mac" wastes no time indicting our mostly white gathering, which has greeted him with a standing ovation and thundering applause.

"Where are the men of color? Why are there not more of them here?" he asks as my fellow Promise Keepers fall silent. "We need to recognize that there is a spirit of white racial superiority. It's defined as insensitivity to the pain of people of color."

Most of Coach Mac's multiracial vision is clustered near the stage, where a bright, bold banner depicting a lantern-jawed, dark-skinned man, eyes upward, hands clenched in prayer, is unfurled as a backdrop. Other minority men, mostly blacks and Hispanics, will be on and near the stage this weekend, wearing the shirts and logos that identify them as PK staff and speakers.

By contrast, most of us communing in the stadium seats are white. It's time for us to get down on our knees and wash the feet of our minority brothers, Coach Mac says. He tells us how important it is that Promise Keepers present a multiracial front at a million-man prayer march planned for next year.

10   "I want you to make a bona fide effort to bring someone of a different color to Washington, D.C.," he says, bringing us to our feet in a pledge. "When we have that kind

of intentionality, that kind of sensitivity, we can stand together as the church of Jesus Christ and make a statement."

Then, he asks anyone who's willing to go a step farther and have "a bona fide relationship" with a minority brother to continue standing. Not a man among us makes a move to be seated; instead, we stand ramrod straight and square our shoulders.

"Almighty God's watching, men!" McCartney booms. "He's going to hold us to it." We cheer wildly—for Coach Mac, for each other, for the possibility of this many-colored army of men for Christ.

Racial Harmony, PK-style

Unlike most Christian Right organizations, PK has delivered on its pledge to cross color lines. Pastors and priests at February's clergy conference in Atlanta came from more than 70 American Indian tribes, as well as black, Hispanic, Asian, and other minority congregations. The ministry recently pledged $1 million to help rebuild black churches authorities suspect are being torched by racists.

But a long-time watchdog of the Right quickly casts a pall over this colorblind display of brotherly love. Chip Berlet, a senior analyst with Political Research Associates, tells me the call to racial unity is best understood as the coping strategy of a historically privileged class—white men—under fire not only from women, but from a growing minority population that wants a piece of the pie.

"Ask yourself the musical question," he says. "If people who traditionally have had greater access to power and riches in the U.S. had to make a decision between holding the race line and holding the gender line, guess which one they chose?"   15

In Promise Keepers' football stadium world, the answer is obvious. The cost to minority men answering the call is less apparent but immense, according to Berlet.

"The price that people of color pay to Promise Keepers . . . is to adopt an overwhelmingly Eurocentric view of Christianity which is at odds with the black church's traditional values," he tells me. "So really, the price you pay for being in the boys' club is to give up your ethnic heritage."

National Baptist Convention President Henry Lyons has condemned Promise Keepers' recruitment of blacks as "an attempt to put us back on the plantation." Indeed, one of the common effects of racial harmony PK-style is to forgive—after the remorseful prayers of white Promise Keepers—certain quibbling historical injustices.

"At one time this land was 100 percent ours, and today our people have only 6 percent left," an unofficial spokesman for more than 600 American Indian pastors said at the clergy conference. "But I forgive the white man. Because if the white man had never come, we never would have come to know Jesus . . . We forgive you."

'These Girls' God Has Given Us

Beach balls bounce wildly among us; we cheer the progress of Styrofoam gliders   20 launched high in the air, held aloft, it seems, as much by good will as by strong updrafts that foretell the coming storm.

We are playful with each other, and soft; when we make our way to our seats, we say, "Excuse me, brother," and "Thank you, brother." The night before, 2,500 of us had answered an altar call to make or renew a commitment to Christ. I watched one long-haired man in a black leather Harley Davidson vest pick his way down the steps to the stadium floor, legs trembling. Afterward, red-eyed Promise Keepers prayed intently in tight circles, arms around each other's shoulders, heads bowed.

Now, we are ready to hear Bishop Phillip Porter, a beefy black man with receding silver hair. Porter, a Denver minister and the father of eight, has been married 38 years and is here to teach us how to "go all out in love" for our wives. He cites 1 Peter 3:7, which commands men to honor women as "the weaker vessel," and Ephesians 5:23: "For the husband is the head of the wife as Christ is the head of the Church, his body, and is himself its savior."

"The husband is called head of the family, head of the wife. God created it that way," Porter says. "That means for the working out of the marriage, the husband has been given authority in every area. . . . Husbands must take their positions, or confusion will reign and many blessings will be cut off from the family."

Such authority comes with grave responsibility, Porter reminds us. "The husband must want what's best for his wife," he says; he should be respectful of her, and listen to her. "If you do this, you will not only be happy, but your wife will be satisfied. She'll be satisfied that you considered her before the decision was made."

25   He exhorts us to faithfulness, support, and self-sacrifice for "these girls" God has given us; as our love helps relieve the pressures in their lives, Porter explains, "they can devote themselves to our attention and the attention of our children. . . .

"God's on your side; that girl's on your side," he declares. "Go for it men—love those wives!"

'Phallic Kinds of Guys'

My brothers are on their feet, cheering wildly. I am thinking of the women at home, praying for their Promise Keepers, and women at this stadium, too—not inside with us, but working along the periphery, volunteering as ticket-checkers, lunch-servers, support crew. Helpmates.

I'm remembering what Berlet told me earlier: "What we're talking about is a theocratic world view in which God talks to men, they tell their wives what's up, and together they own their children and have dominion over the earth."

My fellow Promise Keepers are pledged to a vision of beneficent but absolute male authority. In *Seven Promises of a Promise Keeper,* published by Focus on the Family, Dallas pastor Tony Evans helps husbands regain the power they've relinquished: "The first thing you do is sit down with your wife and say something like this: 'Honey, I've made a terrible mistake. I've given you my role. I gave up leading this family, and I forced you to take my place. Now I must reclaim that role.'

30   "Don't misunderstand me," Evans continues. "I'm not suggesting that you *ask* for your role back, I'm urging you to *take it back*. If you simply ask for it, your wife is likely to [refuse]."

This retro *Father Knows Best* vision holds little appeal for feminists. "You cannot say to one whole group of people, because of their gender, that they are God-ordained to be in charge," says Rosemary Dempsey, action vice president for the National Organization for Women. "Whenever you give that kind of authority, even if you pepper it with benevolence, that absolute authority will be abused."

Dempsey tells me she's concerned about mainstream media portrayals of Promise Keepers, written mostly by male journalists. "A lot of people . . . have reported Promise

Keepers as nothing more than a great group of guys who get together and hug each other, and never talk about their primary message, which is one of male supremacy."

Indeed, when Promise Keepers in 1993 handed out 50,000 hard-cover copies of a book explaining how manhood defines a person's relationship with God, it triggered little scrutiny.

"Possessing a penis places unique requirements upon men before God in how they are to worship Him," Robert Hicks wrote in *The Masculine Journey*. "We are called to worship God as phallic kinds of guys, not some sort of androgynous, neutered non-males, or the feminized males so popular in feminist-enlightened churches."

Anointing the Next Generation

I am feeling less a part of the brotherhood by the time Dennis Rainey, director of a   35
Christian family ministry in Arkansas, takes the pulpit to tell us how to be better fathers.

"It's up to us, as the protectors and providers for our families, to rescue our children from a culture that would drown them in tolerance and lack of absolutes," he says.

Rainey offers as an example his insistence on interviewing his teenage daughter's prospective dates. "I want you to keep your hands off my daughter—totally," he tells these boys. This, he tells us, makes his daughter beam, "because her daddy is protecting her."

This "protection" sounds suspiciously like ownership to me, particularly because Rainey fails to mention a parallel safeguard for his sons. The double standard becomes clearer in another anecdote: After his young daughter tells him she wants to be a gymnastics instructor when she grows up, Rainey tempers his encouragement with a reminder that, should she have children, God would want her to stay home to raise them.

"I am sick and tired of career being exalted over motherhood," Rainey thunders. "It's time to exalt the high and holy privilege of being a mother. It may not be politically correct, but it is Biblically correct."

At this, my brothers erupt in cheers. Beneath my ball cap and Ace bandage and   40
smudge-proof eyebrows, I am separated from them now by a vast expanse: the one wall they are building up, not breaking down.

We are caught up then, suddenly, in a fluid spectacle as 4,500 young men—sons of these Promise Keepers—march into Mile High Stadium from nearby McNichols Arena, where they have completed a youth breakout session. We have been asked to stand in reverent silence as these young men, many of whom wave small crosses, file into the stadium, crowding the floor.

When cheers and foot stomping finally erupt, they roll through the stadium in a wave, and keep rolling, loud and proud and, to me, chilling—not because these men are cheering their sons, but because their daughters are absent. I sense for the first time the destructive potential of this brotherly separatist movement, in which men's emotions are so readily available and their passions so easily inflamed.

It seems harmless only if you overlook Promise Keepers' use of the language of war, its belief that it has the corner on Biblical truth, and its stated intention to "rebuild the land," as illustrated by banners depicting muscular, dark- and light-skinned forearms wielding Bibles and pickaxes. McCartney himself has directed these men to "take the nation for Jesus Christ."

"What you are about to hear is God's word to the men of this nation," he said in 1993. "We are going to war. . . . We have divine power; that is our weapon. We will not compromise. Wherever truth is at risk, in the schools or the legislature, we are going to contend for it. We will win."

45   Standing in Mile High among these cheering and chanting men, I recall an excerpt from a scathing critique of Promise Keepers posted on the World Wide Web by Indiana-based Biblical Discernment Ministries, which describes PK as "one of the most ungodly and misleading movements in the annals of Christian history." Ironically, the criticism is ferociously right wing: BDM believes PK is soft on gays, weak in its declaration of absolute male authority and willing to overlook doctrinal differences that should separate denominations.

It also believes the movement has ominous similarities to Nazism. "The large mass rallies, the exaltation of emotion over reason, the lack of doctrinal integrity, the taking of oaths, the focus on fatherland and fatherhood . . . bears a disconcerting similarity to an era which gave rise to one of the most dreadful armies in history," BDM says.

It's too far a stretch, no doubt. But I consider it anyway as 50,000 fervent Promise Keepers drop to their knees a minute later, their prayers for righteousness and strength and leadership and integrity anointing the next generation of leaders—men, and only men, like themselves.

David G. Hackett

Promise Keepers and the Culture Wars

Religion in the News, Summer 1998

The first stories about Promise Keepers were enthusiastic. Newspapers in the West pointed excitedly to what the *Dallas Morning News* called the "spirited success" of this new "Christian men's movement," focusing on the novelty and strangeness of 50,000 white, middle-aged men gathering in a Colorado football stadium to find their way back to God and their responsibilities as husbands and fathers.

The earliest commentators discussed the significance of the organizers' choice of a football environment as the best vehicle for engaging and raising men's consciousness. Surrounded by thousands of like-minded souls in the comfort of a familiar sports arena, men could open up emotionally to their failings and promise to atone. They noted how the movement tapped the athletic and military metaphors of Christian spirituality. Saint Paul in his letters talks about running the race, fighting the good fight, and putting on the armor of God.

As the Promise Keepers' membership swelled (from 4,200 in 1991 to 230,000 in 1994), journalists waxed optimistic. "Men's religious organization has a promising future" ran the headline on a column by *Houston Chronicle* religion writer Richard Vara. "Men across the nation flock to McCartney's evangelical banner" declared *Rocky Mountain News* staff writer Michael Romano. An editorial in the *Dallas Morning News* described a Dallas rally as "an impressive commitment to rebuilding American families in these socially complex times."

But by 1996 (an election year) commentators began to worry that Promise Keepers was a Trojan horse for the religious right. Steve Rabey in *The Christian Century* reported that Protestant denominations were concerned over competition from what appeared to be a new "para-church" organization. Some Lutherans, Presbyterians, and Catholics, Rabey found, criticized the movement for failing to come to grips with hard theological differences.

Time reported that 59 religious liberals, including the dean of the Vanderbilt University Divinity School and the president of New York Theological Seminary, had issued a warning about the potential dangers of Promise Keepers to the nation's churches. For their part, members of Promise Keepers stated repeatedly that their primary concern was returning men to their own—mostly Baptist—churches to take up their family responsibilities.

When East Coast publications and national broadcasts took up the story, a chorus of criticism centering on right-wing domination of the movement all but drowned out the positive note struck by the Western media. Thomas B. Edsall in the *Washington Post* described the Promise Keepers as opposed to all the "major aspects of liberal society." In an October, 1996 *Nation* cover story, Joe Conason, Alfred Ross, and Lee Cokorinos pronounced the movement "one of the most sophisticated creations of the religious right" and asserted that it represented a "third wave" of politically active religious conservatism "following the demise of the Rev. Jerry Falwell's Moral Majority and the compromises of Pat Robertson's Christian Coalition with secular Republicanism."

Full-fledged culture war had been declared by the time National Organization of Women (NOW) president Patricia Ireland, joined by other less ubiquitous feminist critics, spent one television news show after another linking the movement's founder, Bill McCartney, with the "same old pantheon of political extremists." Evidence offered was the early support of James Dobson's "Focus on the Family" and Bill Bright's "Campus Crusade for Christ," as well as McCartney's known opposition to abortion and gay-rights legislation in Colorado. Also cited were McCartney's talk of returning the country to Christ and rally speaker Tony Evans's demand that men "take back" their leadership role in the family. Writing in *The Progressive*, Suzanne Pharr claimed that it "does not matter that a right wing agenda is not overt in the formative stages of this movement; when the leaders are ready to move their men in response to their agenda, they will have thousands disciplined to obey and command."

Significantly, this "here come the lunatics" coverage moderated and became increasingly sympathetic as time progressed and reporters met Promise Keepers and observed the movement's rallies. Donna Minkowitz, a Jewish lesbian who infiltrated a rally dressed as a man to write an article for *Ms. Magazine*, found herself being genuinely moved by the sincerity of the men she encountered. As the men poured into Washington for the October 4-5, 1997 rally, they conducted themselves so well, said one CNN correspondent, "You can't help but be moved." Interviews of career-oriented and supportive Promise Keepers' wives suggested that their relationships were far more egalitarian in practice than the rhetoric of men "taking charge" implied.

The absence of politics in the Washington rally speeches reinforced the shift in attitude, as did the rally's emphasis on racial reconciliation—palpably present in scenes of black and white men hugging each other. Had any of the speakers ridiculed liberals or presented fundamentalists' nonnegotiable principles of faith, this positive perspective would likely not have lasted long. But by the end of the Washington weekend both national and regional coverage had begun to defuse the "Unwarranted Anxiety Over Promise Keepers' Moral Reawakening," as the *Chicago Tribune* headlined a column by former Reagan administration official Linda Chavez.

10   Such positive appraisals were followed by a backlash against the earlier liberal perspective, but this only reinforced the media-generated theme of culture war. Liberals were now accused of a double standard that kept them from recognizing the positive aspects of the movement. "By any normal expectation," wrote John Leo in *U.S. News and World Report*, "NOW would express at least some guarded praise" for programs that urged men to be emotionally vulnerable, honest, and respectful of their wives and families. (NOW didn't budge.) Similarly, Jim Sleeper on *All Things Considered* argued that white liberals were unwilling to face the possibility that "the civil rights movement's beloved community of black and white together has found a new, more conservative home." What Sleeper called the "biggest demonstration of racial reconciliation" since the sixties was not applauded but dismissed by liberals because, as Jesse Jackson said on CNN, these actions were "not really affecting public policy."

Not all the media attention to the Washington rally was so overly politicized. The *Washington Post* performed a signal service by surveying 882 randomly selected participants. Most turned out to be white middle-class Baptists who didn't like Bill Clinton or feminism, but were neither politically active nor interested in having Promise Keepers form a political action committee and contribute money to candidates who support Christian values. In a *New York Times* op-ed piece, University of Chicago professor Martin Marty pleaded for readers to pay attention to the movement's religious motivations. A *Chicago Tribune* reporter, citing a hot-off-the-press study by Marie Griffith of Northwestern University, suggested that secular feminists habitually misrepresent conservative women as fearful dupes of male oppressors by neglecting the real world of evangelical women and children.

But by and large, a failure to understand Promise Keepers in its evangelical Protestant context led the news media to miss the movement's real significance and prospects. In the evangelical Protestant world, Promise Keepers stands apart in its commitment to racial reconciliation—something reporters barely noticed. Though the membership is 80 percent white, the leadership is 35 percent African, Hispanic, and Asian American. The Promise Keepers' "Sixth Promise" is to reach "beyond any racial and denominational barriers to demonstrate the power of biblical unity." This is closer to the spirit of true ecumenism than many evangelicals have been prepared to come.

Promise Keepers is best understood within the long tradition of American revivalism. Appearing on the *MacNeil/Lehrer News Hour*, movement leader Paul Edwards asserted that theirs was a "revival movement," part of "the history of a tradition of going after the heart . . . rather than a reform movement." This statement squares with historians' judgments that America's great revival leaders, from George Whitefield in the 1740s First Great Awakening to Charles Finney in the early 1800s Second Great Awakening to Billy Graham today, have all been devoted to personal, spiritual transformation rather than political change.

Not that revivals have lacked for unintended political consequences. To evangelicals, nineteenth-century abolitionism and women's rights as well as the more recent efforts of the "born again" to address concerns regarding family, gender, and sexuality are finally not political but religious crusades to save souls. The overt movement of religion into politics has always been controversial, and evangelical leaders have, like Billy Graham, for the most part steered clear of organized politics. Certainly, Promise Keepers has political implications. But that is not the same as saying that its efforts are generated by a political agenda.

An awareness of the history of revivalism would likewise have allowed journalists to   15
anticipate the possibility that Promise Keepers will be short lived—with the result that the
organization's recent funding crisis would have come as less of a surprise. Efforts to lure
men back into churches by emphasizing the masculinity of Christianity have been going
on with indifferent success ever since the early nineteenth-century Industrial Revolution.
Like the "Muscular Christian" movements of the late nineteenth and early twentieth centuries, Promise Keepers relies on Saint Paul's masculine rhetoric, but softens it with a
dose of latter-day emotional sensitivity. The movement's literature emphasizes relationships between team members rather than winning; partners rather than dominant
"heads" in marriage; the principled and concerned board member vs. the hard-driving
executive. All of this suggests a conscious seeking for images and relationships that por-
tray strength as a nonviolent, noncompetitive value. Possible long-term consequences of
the movement could be dissemination of these messages through small groups and
church curriculums.

Analyzing Promise Keepers primarily through a politicized culture-wars lens has, in
short, given the news media a constricted and inaccurate view of the men's movement in
today's evangelical churches. Within the Pauline tradition of male leadership, which is
embedded in the basic vocabulary and mental framework of the evangelical churches,
conservative Protestant women are not men's obedient servants. They are complementary
partners with men in a common effort to follow Christ. As for the Promise Keepers' commitment to racial reconciliation, it has not been shown to be a political ploy. On the contrary,
all indications are that it is a sincere effort to create a world where there is neither black
nor white in Christ Jesus. To date, Promise Keepers remains a largely non-political effort of
evangelical churchmen to change their ways and keep their promises to their wives and
family. It may become a political organization, but anyone who seeks to make it such—and
there are those who would love to do so—stands to undermine the deepest commitments
that bring these men together.

CBS News

Staying at Home

Look around these days, and you'll find women in positions of real power: a woman
at the helm of the National Security Council, two Supreme Court justices, and female
board members of every Fortune 100 company.

It's just as it was supposed to be 40 years after women got in the front door.

But look for the women of the next generation—the ones everyone assumed would
follow in droves behind them, and you're likely to find many of them walking right back
out and staying at home.

Lisa Beattie Frelinghuysen was on her way to the very top of the legal profession.
At Stanford Law School, she was president of the law review. She went to work for a top
law firm, and she clerked at the Supreme Court for Ruth Bader Ginsburg.

But after she had her first baby seven years ago, she left, and never went back.   5
Correspondent Lesley Stahl reports.

"I know myself, and I know that when I'm working at something, I work hard. When
I was at the law review, I was working until midnight every night. And my husband started

a surgical residency where he was completely unavailable," recalls Frelinghuysen. "I was afraid that if I was working, there would be no parent there with the children. And I wanted to experience getting to know my children, being there in a consistent way."

She's hardly alone. Every Wednesday morning, a church in suburban Maryland is filled with professional women who have chosen to step out of the full-time work force to spend time raising children. They have organized a lecture series for intellectual stimulation.

Tori Hall, a former analyst with the Congressional Budget Office, and Sheilah Eisel, once a top sales representative for Oracle, come each week. They, along with Ann Geldzahler, a Yale graduate and lawyer, are all stay-at-home moms.

"The bottom line was, it was an emotional decision not an intellectual one," says Hall. "It doesn't make sense to give up a great job that pays a lot of money and has a lot of satisfaction for myself, just to walk away from that."

10   "I think about it for a little, and then I think I just, I love what I'm doing for right now. I do," says Geldzahler.

"I would say the first six months there were days that I had serious doubts, did I make the right decision," says Eisel. "Now, there's like bumps in the road but I'm very glad that I'm staying at home."

Could it really be that this generation of women, the first to achieve success without having to fight for it, is now walking away, willingly, and without regrets? Census bureau statistics show a 15 percent increase in the number of stay-at-home moms in less than 10 years.

Linda Hirshman is a lawyer, philosophy professor, and author. She didn't believe it, until she started researching the high-powered couples who announced their weddings in *The New York Times* in 1996.

"The first man I called answered the phone, and I told him what I was doing, and I said, 'Where's your wife?' And he said 'She's at home in Brooklyn taking care of our daughter.' And it turns out, so are all but 15 percent of the women I interviewed," says Hirshman. "Eighty-five percent of the women in my sample are staying home either full-time or part-time." She's still in the early stages of her research, but the trend has been documented by other studies. And she's convinced it's going to be the 1950s all over again.

15   Why does it matter?

"These are the women that would have gone into the jobs that run our world. These were the women who would eventually have become senators, governors. These women would have been in the pipeline to be CEOs of Fortune 500 companies," says Hirshman.

Frelinghuysen, Amy Cunningham Atkinson and Andrea Hagan are just the potential leaders she's talking about. Atkinson went to Yale and had a great job as a television producer. Hagan became managing director at a top Wall Street investment bank after Harvard Business School, where the subject of working moms came up.

"There were panel discussions about work and lifestyle issues, which as a 26-year-old, didn't mean a lot to me," recalls Hagan. "Until I had my own child did I realize what a juggling act it was going to be."

Do any of them wake up and say, "I'm June Cleaver. I'm living in the '50s?"

20   "I don't think we are. I think that's wrong," says Atkinson. "I worked for 20 years after college. And so my experience in leaving to have children is different than hers. I think

I would feel differently about my choice to stay at home for a few years if I didn't have that experience behind me."

She says she's also different from many in Stahl's generation, who were determined to stick it out no matter what. These women say they don't feel they have anything to prove. They have been successful, and if they want to take some time out to be with their kids, why shouldn't they?

"I think there's a lot of focus on what I'm sacrificing by staying home. And what's hard to articulate is how much I get back," says Hall. "I do it really—a lot of it is for me. I enjoy seeing and being with my children."

Hirshman fought her way into the workforce, stayed there despite years of male colleagues refusing to eat lunch with her—and raised a daughter, too. She's not an impartial observer. There aren't two sides in the way she sees things.

"The women that I have interviewed are completely dependent upon the goodwill of their wealthy income-producing husbands," says Hirshman. "They chose dependence." But isn't it their right to choose? "It's different to talk about their right than what's the right decision," says Hirshman. "As Mark Twain said, 'A man who chooses not to read is just as ignorant as a man who cannot read.'"

"These women are choosing lives in which they do not use their capacity for very   25
complicated work," adds Hirshman. "They are choosing lives in which they do not use their capacity to deal with very powerful other adults in the world, which takes a lot of skill. I think there are better lives and worse lives."

"I think the women's rights movement was very much about giving women choices and respecting the many choices that women make," says Frelinghuysen.

Adds Hall: "I think there's some people with preconceived notions that because I'm at home with my children all day, I must be preparing husband-delight casserole in a cocktail dress. . . . The mothers groups get together and talk about Iraq policy."

Hirshman believes that women who remain in the workplace are going to be hurt by the ones who are leaving, that there'll be a backlash. Graduate schools will stop accepting women, and companies will stop hiring them. Well, first off, that would be illegal. And second, it's not as if men stay in their jobs forever; they leave all the time.

Harvard Business School did a survey and found that just 38 percent of its female graduates in their child-raising years were in the workplace full-time. But Kim Clark, dean of the business school, told *60 Minutes* the last thing he wants to do is to stop admitting women. He says companies are going to have to change.

"I've had some friends say, 'It's driving us crazy. Why are they leaving,'" says Stahl.   30
"I've heard that from businessmen. They're frustrated. They are investing in these women for years."

"They're asking the wrong question," says Clark. "The right question is, how do we change to keep this talent active and involved with us?"

One of his goals as dean is to convince the business world it's in their interest to come up with creative solutions to keep women in—as Eisel's company tried to do.

"They said, 'Come on back. Work part time—three days a week,'" says Eisel. "This is perfect! And it actually worked out incredibly well for about three months." She was supposed to work 30 hours a week, but Eisel says it ended up being more like 40 hours on a slow week, to 50 to 60 hours. She says it really wasn't the part-time situation she had envisioned.

"I couldn't say, 'OK, this is a $3 million deal. I have a mommy-and-me play date right now with the music class. So sorry, can't come,'" says Eisel, laughing.

35   She says that working part-time also prevented her from getting top accounts: "I had great accounts, and then I had a very frank conversation with my manager who said, 'How am I going to give you the top accounts? You're here three days a week.' And I think part of it was I am there three days a week, but I can handle it."

But could she really handle it? "I couldn't handle many top accounts. But if I had one top account," says Eisel, who adds that the option was never tried.

"A lot of companies are simply cutting people off. And when they go part time, the part-time stuff is peripheral," says Clark. "It's not fulfilling, satisfying. It's not worth it. But I know from my own experience, you can create meaningful, high content, part time jobs."

Clark points to Angela Crispi, an employee of his who worked part-time for five years. "We changed her job. We lopped a piece of it off, and restructured a couple of other people, and we created this job. . . . And we kept her."

And they promoted her. She now runs the business school full-time, overseeing 1,000 employees. But what's a company to do about the women who told us they wouldn't take even the greatest part-time offer? Clark has an answer for that, too. Let them go, and bring them back later. But can companies guarantee these employees a job when they get back, even after an extended period of time?

40   "It all depends on the relationship we have with them during that period of time," says Clark. "Maybe we create a part-time thing where they're connected and so they continue to learn. It all depends on how we structure it."

Hall and Eisel say they will eventually return to the workplace. "I joke sometimes that this is my retirement now and then I'll be working till the end of my days," says Hall.

Several of the women Stahl spoke to said that a 40-year full-speed-ahead career with no breaks is something that only an all-male world would have dreamed up anyway—and that it's in everyone's interest to make some room for detours along the way.

"I think that there's a possibility that I won't achieve what I might have achieved if I never left the workforce," says Frelinghuysen. "It's sad. But it's OK, because I have three wonderful babies that I love. I do think that you make choices, and with some of those choices, although they may be wonderful choices, something takes a hit."

"What changes if you're out of the workforce for a couple of years? You haven't lost your brain power," says Hagan. "You haven't lost your organizational abilities. Maybe you've gained some new ones managing at home . . . . I think people need to be just more open-minded."

45   "This is a new thing, that women are leaving the work place," adds Atkinson, who left her job as a producer at *60 Minutes*. "I think that women like us, who have choices . . . hopefully, we'll be able to make changes. Hopefully, employers will see that this is happening and that we don't want to lose these great women. Let's make some changes so that women can work differently."

Writing Prompts

1. Write a three-page essay on the issue of the roles of men and women today clearly stating your opinion on how things should be and backing it up with evidence from two of the essays.
2. Find an article in a newspaper or periodical that focuses on an individual in a nontraditional role in the last year or so. Now imagine that you are an early twenty-second-century American college student. Write a two-page essay in which you briefly summarize the article and then analyze it as an historical document from the past. In your role as a person living a hundred years from now, imagine what Americans of the future will think of our concept of gender roles.
3. Write a three-page essay in which you consider whether there is such a thing as a traditional man or a modern woman. Draw upon your own experiences and ideas and at least one of the essays you have read here.
4. Write a three-page essay comparing/contrasting two of the essays without revealing your own position—your job is to show both sides without taking a side yourself.
5. Look at several of the essays in this section and consider for what audience they have been written. Then write a two-page essay in which you compare and consider the intended audiences for two or three of these essays. Are you ever among the intended audience, or are these authors not talking to you?

What Is at Stake for Citizenship?

1. Are men and women different? If so, should they be different under the law?
2. If we had a military draft, do you think men and women should both be drafted?
3. The Equal Rights Amendment (to the Constitution) failed to pass in 1982, but every year the ERA is presented to Congress for a vote. Do you think we still need an amendment to the Constitution that guarantees equal rights for women, or are things already equal?
4. Who seems to have more rights in American society, men or women?
5. Are there limits to what a man or a woman might accomplish today? Do you think there should be?

GAY MARRIAGE: NEW QUESTIONS FOR AN OLD INSTITUTION

Gay marriage—ten years ago you would not have heard many people talking about it, but now the topic is up for national debate. Should gays and lesbians have the right to marriage? Is marriage a right for all—even same-sex couples? Or is gay marriage a threat to traditional marriage as we know it? Before we enter into this discussion and read the authors here who are weighing in on the subject, perhaps a little background would help.

The **Gay Rights Movement** began in 1969 with a riot; having been harassed and abused by generations of New York City police, gay men rioted in the streets to protest a raid on a gay bar called Stonewall. The Stonewall Riot marks the beginning of political activism on the part of gays to fight discrimination in such areas as housing, health care, employment, and child custody. This activism sparked the beginning of a society-wide reconsideration of gays and lesbians in America and over the next thirty-five years offered the opportunity for many gays to "come out of the closet" and be recognized as valuable members of society. The AIDS crisis, now so prevalent in many populations around the globe, ravaged American gay men in the 1980s and 1990s. Although terrible discrimination resulted from AIDS, the gay community only became more active, more political, and more vocal in the American political scene. Much has changed over the last thirty-five years when it comes to gays in America. No one at the Stonewall Riot was claiming the right to gay marriage; the issue at hand was police abuse and the violence of homophobia. Today, with more gay people "out" than ever before, the issues we all face are far more subtle. At the heart of the gay marriage debate is the question whether or not a gay relationship is the same as a straight relationship. How you answer that question largely determines how you feel about gay marriage.

In 1989, Denmark became the first nation to recognize same-sex unions. The issue came to the United States in 1996 when a Hawaii Supreme Court ruling overturned a previous state law banning gay marriage. This was the beginning of the national debate, much of which centered on the fear that one state (like Hawaii) might legalize gay marriage and the rest of the states would be forced to go along, recognizing out-of-state marriages for gays the way they do for heterosexuals. Later in 1996, the House and Senate both passed the Defense of Marriage Act—which denied federal recognition of same-sex marriage and allowed individual states not to recognize gay marriages. It was signed into law by Bill Clinton, and some thirty-eight states quickly adopted similar legislation. But in 2000, Vermont became the first state to create "civil unions" for same-sex couples—a new legal status giving gay and lesbian couples the same rights as heterosexual couples. While America debated same-sex marriage, the rest of the world was also addressing this issue. In April 2000, the Netherlands offered all Dutch citizens the right to marry and adopt children regardless of sexual orientation. By 2002, Norway, Sweden, Iceland, Germany, France, and Switzerland had all passed similar laws that allow gays to marry.

In May 2003, conservative legislators introduced the **Federal Marriage Amendment**—a proposal to amend the U.S. Constitution to define marriage as between a man and a woman. Yet the courts continue to fan the flames in this debate. In June 2003, in a surprising ruling, the Supreme Court struck down a Texas law prohibiting same-sex sodomy. By removing the criminality of private consensual sexual acts, the Court shifted the legal landscape for same-sex couples, thus opening the door to gay marriage. By July 2003, the Canadian Supreme Court had found a law defining traditional marriage unconstitutional, and the provinces of Ontario and British Columbia began allowing same-sex couples to marry.

Then in February 2004, everything changed. Newly elected San Francisco mayor Gavin Newsom announced that he would allow same-sex couples to apply for marriage licenses and be married in San Francisco. The crowds of people wanting to be married made headline news, and pictures of same-sex couples filled the television screens and magazines. Nearly four thousand same-sex couples were married before the practice was stopped. (These marriages were later nullified by the state supreme court.) In March 2004, based on the legal definition of marriage in Oregon, which does not specify gender, officials in Multnomah County—Portland, Oregon—announced that they would begin issuing same-sex marriage licenses. By the time a judge stopped the practice in April, nearly three thousand couples had been married.

In November 2003, however, the Massachusetts Supreme Court ruled that banning gay marriage was legally untenable and ordered the state to address the issue. In February 2004, the court was even more decisive, paving the way for gay marriage to begin in spring 2004. To date, Massachusetts is the only state in the union that offers legal marriage to resident same-sex couples.

In July 2004, Congress voted on the Federal Marriage Amendment. Although supported by President George W. Bush and many conservative members of the House and Senate, the measure did not pass a procedural vote, thus avoiding a full vote where a two-thirds majority (of both the House and Senate) would be required to send an amendment to the states. The amendment did not have enough votes, but both supporters and opponents said this was only the beginning of the struggle. In the 2004 election, eleven more states passed laws or state constitutional amendments defining marriage as being between a man and a woman.

So where does this leave us? Not where we started. The nation is in conflict over this issue. Vermont allows "civil unions," and Massachusetts allows gay marriage for state residents, while forty-nine states have passed laws defining marriage to be between a man and a woman. In November 2004, the U.S. Supreme Court declined to hear arguments against the Massachusetts gay marriage law, which gave new life to the national movement for a constitutional amendment against gay marriage. The argument is as old as our nation itself—federalism or states' rights—and nothing is decided yet. *So now, as you consider the history of this issue and read the following essays, you can begin to think about how you might enter the public debate over gay marriage.*

The Goodrich couple, lead plaintiffs in the Massachusetts case, are the first to register at Boston City Hall to marry.

The Case for Gay Marriage

The *Economist,* February 28, 2004

So at last it is official: George Bush is in favour of unequal rights, big-government intrusiveness and federal power rather than devolution to the states. That is the implication of his announcement this week that he will support efforts to pass a constitutional amendment in America banning gay marriage. Some have sought to explain this action away simply as cynical politics, an effort to motivate his core conservative supporters to turn out to vote for him in November or to put his likely "Massachusetts liberal" opponent, John Kerry, in an awkward spot. Yet to call for a constitutional amendment is such a difficult, drastic and draconian move that cynicism is too weak an explanation. No, it must be worse than that: Mr. Bush must actually believe in what he is doing.

Mr. Bush says that he is acting to protect "the most fundamental institution of civilisation" from what he sees as "activist judges" who in Massachusetts early this month confirmed an earlier ruling that banning gay marriage is contrary to their state constitution. The city of San Francisco, gay capital of America, has been issuing thousands of marriage licences to homosexual couples, in apparent contradiction to state and even federal laws. It can only be a matter of time before this issue arrives at the federal Supreme CourtAnd those "activist judges," who, by the way, gave Mr. Bush his job in 2000, might well take the same view of the federal constitution as their Massachusetts equivalents did of their state code: that the constitution demands equality of treatment. Last June, in *Lawrence v Texas*, they ruled that state anti-sodomy laws violated the constitutional right of adults to choose how to conduct their private lives with regard to sex, saying further that "the Court's obligation is to define the liberty of all, not to mandate its own moral code." That obligation could well lead the justices to uphold the right of gays to marry.

Let Them Wed

That idea remains shocking to many people. So far, only two countries—Belgium and the Netherlands—have given full legal status to same-sex unions, though Canada has backed the idea in principle and others have conferred almost-equal rights on such partnerships. The sight of homosexual men and women having wedding days just like those enjoyed for thousands of years by heterosexuals is unsettling, just as, for some people, is the sight of them holding hands or kissing. When *The Economist* first argued in favour of legalising gay marriage eight years ago ("Let them wed", January 6, 1996) it shocked many of our readers, though fewer than it would have shocked eight years earlier and more than it will shock today. That is why we argued that such a radical change should not be pushed along precipitously. But nor should it be blocked precipitously.

The case for allowing gays to marry begins with equality, pure and simple. Why should one set of loving, consenting adults be denied a right that other such adults have and which, if exercised, will do no damage to anyone else? Not just because they have always lacked that right in the past, for sure: until the late 1960s, in some American states it was illegal for black adults to marry white ones, but precious few would defend that ban now on grounds that it was "traditional." Another argument is rooted in semantics: marriage is the union of a man and a woman, and so cannot be extended to same-sex couples. They may live together and love one another, but cannot, on this argument, be "married." But that is to dodge the real question—why not?—and to obscure the real nature of marriage, which is a binding commitment, at once legal, social and personal, between two people to take on special obligations to one another. If homosexuals want to make such marital commitments to one another, and to society, then why should they be prevented from doing so while other adults, equivalent in all other ways, are allowed to do so? **Civil unions are not enough.**

The reason, according to Mr. Bush, is that this would damage an important social institution. Yet the reverse is surely true. Gays want to marry precisely because they see marriage as important: they want the symbolism that marriage brings, the extra sense of obligation and commitment, as well as the social recognition. Allowing gays to marry would, if anything, add to social stability, for it would increase the number of couples that take on real, rather than simply passing, commitments. The weakening of marriage has been heterosexuals' doing, not gays', for it is their infidelity, divorce rates and single-parent families that have wrought social damage.

But marriage is about children, say some: to which the answer is, it often is, but not always, and permitting gay marriage would not alter that. Or it is a religious act, say others: to which the answer is, yes, you may believe that, but if so it is no business of the state to impose a religious choice. Indeed, in America the constitution expressly bans the involvement of the state in religious matters, so it would be especially outrageous if the constitution were now to be used for religious ends.

The importance of marriage for society's general health and stability also explains why the commonly mooted alternative to gay marriage—a so-called civil union—is not enough. Vermont has created this notion, of a legally registered contract between a couple that cannot, however, be called a "marriage." Some European countries, by legislating for equal legal rights for gay partnerships, have moved in the same direction (Britain is contemplating just such a move, and even the opposition Conservative leader, Michael Howard, says he would support it). Some gays think it would be better to limit their ambitions to that, rather than seeking full social equality, for fear of provoking a backlash—of the sort perhaps epitomised by Mr. Bush this week.

Yet that would be both wrong in principle and damaging for society. Marriage, as it is commonly viewed in society, is more than just a legal contract. Moreover, to establish something short of real marriage for some adults would tend to undermine the notion for all. Why shouldn't everyone, in time, downgrade to civil unions? Now that really would threaten a fundamental institution of civilisation.

Kathleen Parker

Upsetting the Natural Order

Denver Post, November 25, 2003

Following the gay marriage debate—and now the Massachusetts court ruling legalizing gay marriage—feels like being lost in a house of mirrors. Everywhere you turn, there's a dead end, a wall, a shattering of logic, a splintering of instinct.

On one hand, it seems obvious that marriage is between a man and a woman—the basic biological unit, society's foundation, civilization's keystone. On the other hand, what's wrong with allowing people of the same sex to live together under the same civil protections permitted heterosexual couples? The questions are further complicated by the fact that most of us know and/or love someone who is gay. We have gay children, gay friends, gay uncles and cousins. Some have gay fathers and lesbian mothers. Who wants to deny them respect and happiness? And so we sit back quietly and watch the reordering of society for fear of hurting a loved one's feelings or offending a coworker or losing the affection of entire blocks of people.

I figure I'm a fairly typical middle-of-the-road heterosexual married woman when I say: I love gays and well, the whole gay thing.

I love all my gay friends and relatives, not to mention my hairdresser; I love what gays do to urban neighborhoods; I love gay humor, gay style, and whatshisname in "My Best Friend's Wedding." I was what we used to call a "fag hag" when you could still use the term affectionately without fear of offending. Thanks to my very best friendship with my gay first cousin, I've had many a gay time as a token belle in the heart of San Francisco's Castro district.

5   In other words, no one who knows me would call me a homophobe. Nevertheless, I'm certain that society needn't be restructured in order to accommodate my gay friends.

Leaving God out of the question, it is irrefutable that Nature had a well-ordered design. Male plus female equals offspring. Gay unions may occur "naturally" in that one does not consciously elect to Be Gay, but such unions fall short of any design that matches Nature's intentions. It also seems clear that our moral codes and institutions were created primarily to protect that design in the interest of the species and civilization.

Thus marriage—for all its flaws and miseries—has evolved to promote, support, and nurture that basic necessary unit. If the state goes out of its way to make marriage attractive, it is because marriage is so difficult and, in many ways, unnatural. It is far more natural for humans, animals that we are, to enjoy gratification whenever and wherever than it is to settle for decades into a system of monogamy.

That many fail, however, is no justification for eliminating the goal of the nuclear, male-female, monogamous family, which has worked well, if not perfectly, for most of civilized memory.

One might argue logically for extending certain benefits to same-sex couples, but marriage isn't necessary to that end. Surely next-of-kin issues for corporate and death benefits can be managed outside of marriage. Moreover, marriage isn't only about civil rights.

10   Marriage is mostly the institutionalization of an ideal that we honor in observation of a higher natural order.

The fact that some households already include children isn't sufficiently compelling to redefine marriage, either. To extend marriage rights to gays on that basis presupposes that raising children in homosexual households is just as good as raising children in heterosexual homes with two parents.

Surely no one needs a scientific study or, God forbid, a poll, to "prove" what is written in our human DNA: that sons and daughters need the qualities of both their parents, mother and father. That said, it is unlikely that a few thousand married homosexuals will topple civilization, as some have warned.

But this is not an insignificant social experiment to be tittered over in Cappuccino bars. Making homosexual unions equal heterosexual unions—the superior natural order of which cannot be disputed—is not just a small step for equality. It is a gargantuan leap from a natural order that has served mankind throughout civilized human society.

We should look long and hard before we leap.

Andrew Sullivan

Beware the Straight Backlash

Time, August 11, 2003

Can someone please tell me which country I'm living in? Last week I sat down and watched a popular new television phenomenon. *Queer Eye for the Straight Guy* turned out to be a hilarious reality show in which five New York City homosexuals fix a hapless straight guy's home, hair, clothes and culture in order to win the heart of his female love interest. Here was a wonderful example of straight men and gay men communicating, laughing and getting along. And the gay guys were all about affirming the straight guy's relationship. At one point the straight guy actually choked up in gratitude. It was poignant and affirming—for both gays and straights.

The same day the Republican leadership of the Senate put out a report decrying the terrible possibility that gay people might actually one day have the right to marry the person they love. So alarmed were the Senators that some states might grant marriage rights to gays that they proposed amending the very Constitution of the United States to forbid gay marriage (or any legal gay relationship) anywhere, anytime, anyhow. The next day, in a press conference, President Bush came close to endorsing the move. If the high courts in Massachusetts or New Jersey decide that their state constitutions demand equality in marriage (something that most observers believe could happen very soon), the reactionary movement for an anti-gay constitutional amendment could acquire an awful momentum.

How to describe this emotional whiplash? Every day, if you're a gay person, you see amazing advances and terrifying setbacks. Wal-Mart set rules last month to protect its gay employees from discrimination—about as mainstream an endorsement as you can get. Canada just legalized gay marriage, and the U.S. Supreme Court just struck down sodomy laws across the land, legitimizing the fact that homosexual is something you are, not something you do. Polls in Massachusetts and New Jersey show majorities in favor of equal marriage rights.

And now the Vatican comes out and announces that granting legal recognition to gay spouses will destroy the family and society. The church argues that gay love is not even "remotely analogous" to heterosexual love. The Anglican Church asks a celibate, newly elected bishop in England to give up his post simply because he is gay. Even the leading Democratic candidates refuse to support equality in marriage. Senator John Kerry, who has no biological children with his current (second) wife, says marriage should be reserved for procreation, and, with few exceptions, the others toe the line too. And a new poll shows a drop in support for gay rights in the wake of the Supreme Court's decision against sodomy laws. Another cyclical backlash against gays—with echoes of the Anita Bryant campaign in the 1970s—looks quite possible.

If, like me, you're gay and politically conservative, the whiplash is even more intense. 5
As a Catholic, I love my church. But I must come to terms with its hierarchy's hatred of the very core of my being. I admire this President deeply, but I have to acknowledge that he believes my relationship is a threat to his. In the coming weeks, it will be hard not to dread the prospect of this second-class status becoming enshrined in the Constitution. Whatever bridges gays and straights have built between them could be burned in a conflagration of bitterness and anger. This year could be for gays what 1968 was for African Americans: the moment hope turns into rage.

Many say they are not hostile toward gay people; they just don't think gays should be regarded as equal to heterosexuals under the law or that gay love is as valid as straight. How am I or any homosexual supposed to respond to that? How much more personal an issue can you get?

It seems as if heterosexuals are willing to tolerate homosexuals, but only from a position of power. They have few qualms about providing legal protections, decrying hate crimes, watching gay TV shows, even having a relative bring her female spouse to Thanksgiving dinner. Yet arguing that the lesbian couple is legally or morally indistinguishable from a straight couple is where many draw the line. That's why marriage is such a fundamental issue. Allowing gay marriage is not saying We Will Tolerate You. It's saying We Are You. This, it seems, we have a hard time doing.

I'll know we've changed when we see a show called *Straight Eye for the Gay Guy.* In it a group of heterosexual men prep a gay man for the night he asks his boyfriend to marry him. When the boyfriend says yes, the straight guys cheer, and the gay guy chokes up. That will be the day gay people are no longer ornaments or accessories or objects of either derision or compassion. That will be the day gay people will finally have the description we have been seeking for so long: human beings.

Cal Thomas

Should Gays Be Allowed to Marry?
NO: It's an Affront to Tradition

Denver Post, November 23, 2003

It is not as if the ruling by the Massachusetts Supreme Judicial Court permitting the "marriage" of same sex couples came as a surprise. If Massachusetts doesn't care about the sexual practices of some of its politicians, why should it care about what some of its lesser citizens do?

The 4-3 ruling, which orders the state legislature to write a law permitting arrangements similar to what the Vermont Supreme Court approved in 1999 when it allowed "civil unions" the same benefits as marriage, is further evidence that G.K. Chesterton's warning has come true: "The danger when men stop believing in God is not that they'll believe in nothing, but that they'll believe in anything."

Marriage was not invented by the postal service as a convenient way to deliver the mail. It was established by God as the best arrangement for fallen humanity to organize and protect itself and create and rear children. Even secular sociologists have produced studies showing children need a mother and a father in the home.

The first mention of marriage is in Genesis 2:24 ". . . a man will leave his father and mother and be united to his wife, and they will become one flesh." The Massachusetts Supreme Court ruling, which will be used by gay rights groups to lobby for striking down all laws limiting marriage to heterosexuals, is just the latest example of a society that has abandoned any and all authority outside of itself.

5   History, logic, theology, and even the dictionary have defined marriage as "the mutual relation of husband and wife; wedlock; the institution whereby men and women are joined in a special kind of social and legal dependence for the purpose of founding and

maintaining a family" (Merriam-Webster); or "a legally accepted relationship between a woman and a man in which they live as husband and wife" (Cambridge).

These classic examples are being updated to reflect the mood of the times. The online Encarta dictionary defines marriage as a "legal relationship between spouses; a legally recognized relationship, established by a civil or religious ceremony, between two people who intend to live together as sexual and domestic partners." That's a big difference.

What is happening in our culture is an unraveling of all we once considered normal. Anyone who now appeals to virtue, values, ethics, or (heaven forbid!) religious faith is labeled an enemy of progress, an intolerant bigot, a homophobe and a "Neanderthal." There is no debate and no discussion. By definition, anyone who opposed "progress" in casting off the chains of religious restrictions on human behavior—which were once considered necessary for the promotion of the general welfare—is a fundamentalist fool, part of the past that brought us witch trials, slavery, and back-alley abortions.

But the problem is deeper than the courts. Some of the people who most loudly proclaim the standards by which they want all of us to live have difficulty themselves living up to those standards. A culture is made up of people, but if large numbers of them no longer "hunger and thirst after righteousness" (to invoke a biblical metaphor), neither will their government.

The constitutional way out of this in Massachusetts and in Washington is an amendment that defines marriage as between a man and a woman. Whether sufficient numbers of politicians have the courage to vote for such an amendment in the face of stiff opposition from gay rights advocates and much of the media will soon be determined.

What is most disturbing about this latest affront to tradition and biblical wisdom is that those who would undermine the old have nothing new to offer in its place. It is like morally corrupt ancient Israel when there was no king "and everyone did what was right in his own eyes" (Judges 21:25).   10

Is that the way we should live? Do we get to vote? Not if the courts play God. Voters can decide in the next election if they want to continue in this direction, or pull the country back from the precipice. Marriage defined should be the social-issue centerpiece of the coming campaign.

Richard Cohen

Should Gays Be Allowed to Marry?
YES: They May Rescue the Institution

Denver Post, November 23, 2003

If Tom DeLay had half a brain (if pigs had wings), he would have cheered the news that Massachusetts may legalize gay marriage. The institution for which the majority leader has such concern, traditional marriage, is both wobbly and wheezing—the butt of cynical jokes, a gold mine for divorce lawyers and, even for the non-initiated, the triumph of hope over experience. Gays, bless 'em, may wind up saving marriage.

In ways that DeLay and his conservative cohorts seem not to recognize, marriage itself is on the rocks. Twenty percent of all first marriages don't make it past five years, and after a mere decade, one-third of all marriage are kaput. Married couples, once dominant in both life and sitcom TV, have gone from 80 percent of all households in the 1950s to 50 percent today. If you peek into the average home, the chances of finding a married couple with kids are just one in four. DeLay, don't delay, marriage needs help.

Now along come gay couples to rescue marriage from social and economic irrelevance, casting a queer eye on a straight institution.

They seek it for pecuniary reasons—issues such as estate taxes, etc.—but also because they seem to be among the last romantics. (No shotgun marriages here.) The odd thing about the opposition to gay marriage is that if the opponents were not so blinded by bigotry and fear, they would see that homosexuals provide the last best argument for marriage: love and commitment.

5   There is scant reason for marriage anymore, which is why it has become a dicey proposition—and why 86 million adults are unmarried.

Women don't need men to support them or defend them from saber-toothed tigers—and they can, I have read, even have babies on their own.

Men, of course, still need women, if only to bear children and to remind them that they are incommunicative. (Is a gay marriage between two men a zone of total silence?) But single guys can adopt kids, and sex is readily available almost anywhere, or so I am told by various city magazines. Once sex was a rare commodity, but Paris Hilton alone has apparently changed all that.

There is an analogy here . . . I think. Just as gays are renowned for moving into urban areas that others have fled, for refurbishing whole neighborhoods and making them attractive, so they might rehabilitate and renew marriage. Of all people, they need it the least. They have already shattered convention with their lifestyles, demolished our comfy and parochial notions of sexual categories—heterosexual male, heterosexual female and nothing else. But when it comes to marriage of all things, some of them want to veer toward the traditional. They want commitment and love—a universal truth in a manner that Jane Austen never envisaged.

The dour Republican Party, with DeLay and others promising a constitutional amendment banning gay marriage (can Elizabeth Taylor be included too?), is once again willing to stand athwart history, yelling "Stop!" In the short term, it will work since little in politics has the power of bigotry—certainly not reason. The many GOP politicians who have gay children will have to stifle all their kids have taught them and fall behind DeLay in his backward march toward a vanished world. Some, though, may succumb to knowledge and empathy and suggest—softly, of course—that love and commitment are universals and not confined to a single category of sexual preference.

10   Gay marriage will not and cannot weaken the institution of marriage. A heterosexual is not somehow less married because a homosexual has tied the knot. On the contrary, the institution will be strengthened, bolstered by the very people who for conservatives represent everything loathsome about modernity. Gays are not attacking marriage. They want to practice it.

"Love. Of course, love. Flames for a year, ashes for 30." So says the Prince in Giuseppe di Lampedusa's classic novel, "The Leopard." This cynical observation, attributed to a 19th century man by a 20th century writer, is hardly out of date. Love is as much a recipe for failure as it is for success, and yet we cling to it because it ennobles us. Love is our emotional opposable thumb, what differentiates us from lower animals, and why we vow—sometimes over and over again—a lifetime's commitment, marriage. If gays can do it and maybe do it better, then Tom DeLay could do us all a real public service by just stepping aside.

A whole lot of wonderful people want to come down the aisle.

Robert P. George

One Man, One Woman

Wall Street Journal, November 28, 2003

Last week, in its ruling in *Goodridge v. Department of Public Health*, the Supreme Judicial Court of Massachusetts by a vote of 4-3 struck down that state's marriage law as "failing to meet the rational basis test for either due process or equal protection." The court gave the Legislature 180 days to revise the law in line with the judges' redefinition of marriage as "the voluntary union of two persons as spouses, to the exclusion of all others." If the Legislature fails within that time frame to direct Massachusetts public officials to issue marriage licenses to same-sex couples, the court will do it for them.

The ruling has major flaws. First, the judges invented a right of "same-sex marriage" found nowhere in the text, logic or historical understanding of the state constitution. In so doing, they usurped the authority of the people's elected representatives. Second, they ignored the philosophical and social reasons that have, for millennia, provided the "rational basis" for understanding marriage as the covenantal commitment of a man and a woman. Chief among these are the nature of marriage as a "one-flesh union" of sexually complementary spouses, and its value in ensuring that most children are reared with a biological mother and father bound to each other in a covenant shaped by moral obligations of fidelity and exclusivity.

Third, having radically redefined marriage to remove the requirement of sexual complementarity that links marriage as an institution to procreation and helps to provide its intelligible moral structure, the judges failed to provide any "rational basis" for their declaration that marriage should be closed ("to the exclusion of all others"), even if spouses happen to prefer an "open" marriage; nor did they offer any reason for treating marriage as intrinsically limited to two persons. These are the Achilles' heel of the movement for "same-sex marriage." No advocate has been able to identify a principled moral basis for the requirements of fidelity and exclusivity in marriage as they wish to redefine the institution.

What next? Following the lead of Hawaii and Alaska, whose courts tried to impose "same-sex marriage" on those states a few years ago, the citizens of Massachusetts could amend their constitution to define marriage as union of man and woman. The trouble is that in a state so liberal, an amendment to overturn *Goodridge* may not be politically feasible. In any event, it will be a long, hard slog; and an amendment could not go into effect until 2006, by then there will be hundreds of Massachusetts "same-sex marriages." And in the meantime, the movement to redefine marriage will initiate litigation throughout the country seeking recognition of Massachusetts "same-sex marriages."

The U.S. Constitution requires states to give "full faith and credit" to the "public acts, records, and judicial proceedings of every other state." Activists will invoke this principle to demand that West Virginia, for example, recognize Massachusetts marriages—even those that could not lawfully have been contracted in West Virginia. In this way, they will try to use a one-vote victory in Massachusetts to redefine marriage for the entire nation. In the end, the matter will go to the Supreme Court. That's good news for the redefiners. In *Lawrence v. Texas*, the justices struck down a state law prohibiting homosexual sodomy in a ruling so broad as to, in the words of dissenting Justice Antonin Scalia, "dismantle the structure of constitutional law that has permitted a distinction to be made between heterosexual and homosexual unions, insofar as formal recognition in marriage is concerned."

Having in mind the combination of the Massachusetts court's decision in *Goodridge* and the Supreme Court's ruling in *Lawrence*, President Bush has vowed to do "whatever is legally necessary to defend the sanctity of marriage" as the union of one man and one woman. What is necessary? Anyone who is alert to the signals being sent by the Supreme Court knows that a federal legislative approach, such as a beefed up Defense of Marriage Act, is doomed. A majority of justices have made clear that they share the view, common in elite circles, that traditional standards of sexual morality are outmoded, and distinctions of any kind between heterosexual and homosexual conduct are rooted in animus and amount to bigotry. They will strike down any legislative act by which Congress seeks to preserve the traditional understanding of marriage or uphold the authority of states to do so. That leaves but one option: amending the Constitution. The process is daunting, and it requires votes of two-thirds of both houses of Congress followed by ratification by three-quarters (i.e., 38) of the states. Is there any hope that an amendment could succeed?

Yes. The best evidence is that no serious Democratic presidential contender is willing to support "same-sex marriage." Messrs. Kerry, Lieberman, Gephardt, Clark, Edwards—even Dean—say they favor "civil unions," but oppose redefining marriage to include same-sex partners. They know that most Americans understand marriage as the union of a man and a woman and want this understanding preserved in their law. To do "whatever is necessary" to preserve it, President Bush will have to lead the fight for a federal marriage amendment. Supporters agree that it should define marriage as the union of a man and a woman. There are differences of opinion, however, on whether an amendment should forbid states from enacting civil unions or domestic partnerships. To forbid such arrangements, some contend, would be to trample on principles of federalism. To fail to forbid them, others reply, would be to protect marriage in name, but not in substance. An amendment that did not prohibit civil unions or domestic partnerships would be merely symbolic.

It is important to protect the substance of marriage, but a sound amendment need not, however, forbid states from enacting certain forms of domestic partnership. It need only ensure that laws do not treat nonmarital sexual relationships as if they were marital by making such relationships the basis for allocating benefits. An amendment protecting the substance of marriage would ensure that neither the federal government nor the states may predicate benefits, privileges, rights or immunities on the existence, recognition or presumption of nonmarital sexual relationships. In other words, domestic partnerships, if states elect to have them, should be nondiscriminatory and inclusive. They should be available to people based on needs, not on sex. The law certainly should not discriminate in favor of those unmarried people who are in sexual relationships over those with the same needs who, though committed to caring for each other, are not sexual partners. Widowed sisters living together and looking after each other, or an unmarried adult son taking care of his elderly father, may have the need for domestic partner benefits such as hospital visitation privileges and insurance rights.

A constitutionally sound domestic partnership law would not discriminate against such people by excluding them from eligibility simply because their relationships are not sexual—just as a nondiscriminatory and inclusive law would not undermine marriage by treating unmarried sexual partners as if they were married.

(Mr. George is professor of jurisprudence at Princeton.)

David Crary

Fresh Look at Nuptials Urged: Gays' Push Spurs Wider Scrutiny

The Associated Press,
Denver Post, November 22, 2004

New York—"Protection of marriage" is now the watchword for many activists fighting to prevent gays and lesbians from marrying. Some conservatives, however, say marriage in America began unraveling long before the latest gay-rights push, and they are pleading for a fresh, soul-searching look at the institution.

"When you talk about protecting marriage, you need to talk about divorce," said Bryce Christensen, a Southern Utah University professor who writes frequently about family issues. While Christensen doesn't oppose the campaign to enact state and federal bans on gay marriage, he worries it's distracting from immediate threats to marriage's place in society.

"If those initiatives are part of a broader effort to reaffirm lifetime fidelity in marriage, they're worthwhile," he said. "If they're isolated—if we don't address cohabitation and casual divorce and deliberate childlessness—then I think they're futile and will be brushed aside."

Gay-rights supporters often argued during their recent losing battles against gay-marriage bans in 11 states that if marriage in America was in fact troubled, it was heterosexuals—not gays—who bore the blame.

"That was the best argument same-sex marriage advocates had: 'Where were you   5
when no-fault divorce went through?'" said Allan Carlson, a conservative scholar who runs a family-studies center in Rockford, Ill.

"Any thoughtful defender of marriage has to say, 'You're right. We were asleep at the switch in the '60s and '70s.'" Carlson hopes the same-sex marriage debate will encourage a broader national conversation.

"For the first time in about 50 years we are honestly looking at the state of marriage in America, and what we have allowed to happen to it," he said. "I hope the conservative side will do a little soul-searching and look for ways to rebuild traditional marriage into something stronger."

Carlson decries no-fault divorce, where neither spouse is held responsible for the breakup, but acknowledges that its demise is not imminent. He proposes more modest steps: tax revisions benefiting married couples, a more positive portrayal of marriage in textbooks, policies aiding young college graduates so they can afford to marry sooner.

In several of the states that approved gay-marriage bans on Nov. 2, initiatives are underway to bolster heterosexual marriage. A bill pending in Michigan's legislature would encourage premarital education; Arkansas Gov. Mike Huckabee and his wife have invited 1,000 couples to join them in a Valentine's Day covenant marriage ceremony in which they would voluntarily reduce their options for a quick divorce.

Stephanie Coontz, a professor at Evergreen State College in Olympia, Wash., and   10
author of a new history of marriage, said passing anti-gay amendments in hopes of returning marriage to some bygone traditional status is futile.

"Heterosexuals changed marriage, not gays and lesbians," she said. "None of these measures is going to change the fact that marriage no longer plays the same central economic and political role that it used to. . . . People see it as more optional."

Writing Prompts

1. Write a three-page essay on the issue of gay marriage in which you clearly state your opinion and back it up with evidence from two of the essays.
2. Write a letter to your congressional representative or senator in which you explain your position on gay marriage and attempt to convince him or her to take the same position.
3. Summarize (one sentence per paragraph) the arguments from two essays— the one you agreed with the most and the one you agreed with the least. Do you see any common ground in these two opposing arguments?
4. Write a three-page essay in which you compare/contrast two of the essays without revealing your own position. Your job is to show both sides without taking a side yourself.
5. Of the essays you disagree with, choose the one that has the strongest or most convincing argument. Taking into account the first four chapters of this text-book where you read about successful writing strategies, write a two-page analysis of the author's argument and discuss the ways the author is most successful making his or her point.

What Is at Stake for Citizenship?

1. What's the difference between "equal rights" and what some call "special rights" for gays and lesbians?
2. Is the right to marry protected under the Constitution? Should it be?
3. How would you define "sexual discrimination," and does it apply to gay marriage?
4. Does the expansion of rights to one group threaten the rights of another group?
5. Is a constitutional ban on gay marriage a traditional use of the Constitution or an inappropriate use of that great document?

EXPANDING VOCABULARY

Abstinence: Abstinence is the practice of avoidance. In the context of sexual education, abstinence programs teach young people that the best choice they can make is to abstain from or avoid sex completely before marriage. Abstinence-only programs teach abstinence as the only option, as its supporters believe that to encourage young people to abstain from sexual activity, and then to provide information about sex and contraception, is a contradiction that will only confuse them. Abstinence programs are common in schools and are often supported by local religious communities.

Civil Rights Act of 1964: Coming near the end of the civil rights movement, this law is often best known for outlawing racial discrimination. But it also had a profound impact on the lives of women by outlawing sexual discrimination in the work place and inadvertently setting the stage for the women's movement.

Civil Union: A civil union is a civic (as opposed to religious) recognition of a long-term, same-sex relationship. Vermont is the only state in the union to allow civil unions—a legal status that mirrors marriage by offering participants all the benefits of marriage without being legally wed. A controversial idea, civil unions are praised by those who hope to gain legal recognition of same-sex relationships and condemned by those opposed to homosexuality as a step toward gay marriage.

Conservatives: A conservative outlook values the status quo, continuity, and order and often incorporates religious or traditional values into its view of the world. Political conservatives support a legislative agenda that seeks balance, conservation, and preservation of the existing social and economic orders. Values like hard work, patriotism, and personal responsibility are often part of the conservative cause.

Contraception: Contraception literally means "against conception." Also known as birth control, contraception is the practice of or means by which fertile adults engage in sexual activity without it resulting in pregnancy. Common means of contraception in the United States include the birth control pill, condoms, the diaphragm, spermicidal foam or jelly, and the IUD (intrauterine device). Success rates vary among methods. Perhaps the most controversial form of contraception is the "morning after pill," a high dose of hormones taken directly after unprotected sex (and often prescribed after sexual assault) to prevent a possible pregnancy. Contraception is at the heart of the sex education battle, caught between those who want contraception information to be part of sex education to prevent pregnancy and those who believe that teaching contraception encourages teens to have sex.

Creationism: A general term used by those who attribute the creation of all life and matter—people, animals, the earth, the stars—to God's divine hand. Those who subscribe to these beliefs are often called "creationists," and they most often endeavor to take evolution out of public school science classrooms and replace it with biblical accounts of God's creation of the world in six days. Unlike scientists who consider geology and paleontology to determine the age of the earth, creationists have, in recent debates, declared the earth to be approximately six thousand years old as determined by religious texts.

Culture Wars: A term used to describe the conflicts between liberals and conservatives about the nature of American culture and society. The term often refers to legislative and community battles over issues such as abortion, gay rights, sex education, affirmative action, divorce, school prayer, and women's rights.

Evolution: Evolution is the theory, first postulated by Charles Darwin in *Origin of Species* (1859), that addresses the changes in a biological population over time. At its heart is "natural selection," the process by which successful biological traits are passed on to future generations while less successful traits are not. Darwin's belief that humans may have evolved from other primates (like apes) goes against the Christian view that man was created in the image of God, and is the source of great strife in many public school systems.

Federal Marriage Amendment: This is a proposed amendment to the U.S. Constitution that would legally define marriage as only between and man and a woman. The Resolution (HJ Res 56) was introduced before the House of Representatives on May 21, 2003. (It is currently in committee and has not yet been debated by the full House.) For such a proposed amendment to become part of the Constitution, the resolution calling for the amendment must pass both houses of Congress with a two-thirds majority. The president is not part of the process and does not sign this resolution. Instead, it must be ratified by a three-fourths majority of the state legislatures. If this happens, the amendment becomes part of the U.S. Constitution. Congress typically establishes a seven-year time frame in which the ratifications must occur.

Gay marriage: One of the hottest topics of the twenty-first century, a gay marriage is one that extends the state of matrimony to a same-sex couple. While the cities of San Francisco, California, and Portland, Oregon, briefly offered such marriages to gay and lesbian couples in 2004, those marriages were legally declared null and void. Only the state of Massachusetts has legalized gay marriage, but the long-term legal status of those couples is yet to be seen.

Gay rights movement: Born in the Stonewall Riots of 1969, the gay rights movement is active on the local and national level in support of antidiscrimination ordinances protecting gays in employment and housing, AIDS research, adoption and custody rights for gay parents, and most recently, gay marriage. Proponents of gay rights have found their greatest success in support of employment and partner benefit issues, but in 2004 voters across the country soundly rejected the concept of gay marriage.

Gender roles: The subject of study by sociologists, gender roles comprise a loosely agreed-on set of conventions that define and typify one sex or the other. Associations with gender can be harmless, like dressing a baby boy in blue and dressing a baby girl in pink, or damaging, such as limiting a woman's choice of careers or a man's ability to express emotion. Gender roles have become much more elastic over the last several decades as both sexes have expanded what they can do in the world, but our basic gender-based assumptions about things such as clothing, hair, work, hobbies, and parenting still persist.

HIV/AIDS: AIDS and HIV are not the same thing. You get AIDS by being infected with HIV. HIV is the human immunodeficiency virus; you contract it through intimate contact with someone who has the virus in his or her system, someone who is said to be "HIV-positive." The three most common ways to become infected are: (a) having sex with someone who is infected; (b) sharing needles (for drug use usually) with an infected person; or (c) being born to a woman who is infected. Before tests for the virus were developed, blood transfusions were also a common means of infection and people (including many hemophiliacs) were infected and died of AIDS. Today our blood banks are considered safe, but such certainty is not always possible in less-developed countries. This virus drastically weakens the body's ability to fight countless opportunistic infections. If your immune system is seriously damaged, you may develop AIDS. AIDS is acquired immune deficiency syndrome, which is often fatal. In the 1980s and 1990s, AIDS amounted to a death sentence. While recent drug treatments have proven very successful at extending life of those infected, HIV/AIDS is still the most serious sexually transmitted disease we have yet faced and continues to devastate non-Western countries with less access to the latest drug treatments.

McCartney, Bill (1940–): Former head coach of the University of Colorado football team and founder of Promise Keepers.

No-fault divorce: A no-fault divorce is a divorce where no one is blamed for the breakup. In such a divorce the suing spouse must simply state a reason that places no blame; such reasons include "irreconcilable differences" or "incompatibility"—legal terms to describe the fact that the couple no longer gets along. Although all fifty states allow divorce where no one is at fault, some states require a minimum period of legal separation. Before no-fault divorce, one spouse was required to find fault with the behavior of the other and use it as grounds to divorce. Charges such as cruelty, abandonment, and adultery were common in divorce proceedings that required fault to be named.

Patriarchy: From *pater,* the Latin word for father, patriarchy is rule by the father or elder male. Under such a system wives (and by association daughters) were thought to be the property of the husband/father, and a patriarchal society is one in which women have few rights and little access to positions of influence or power. Our laws against domestic violence today are a direct rejection of this centuries-old construct of familial power. Patriarchy can be cultural but is often also religious—for instance the Catholic Church ordains only male priests and Islam has no female religious scholars or leaders in its mosques or religious schools.

Progressives: Also known as liberals, progressives work for change that constitutes social, economic, or religious progress. They seek innovation, difference, and an upset of the status quo. They wish the current social and economic classes to be transformed, not preserved, and see opportunity to improve the country as the only viable options for our future. Progressives, no matter what the era, will risk upheaval to bring about change.

Sex education: The general practice by which information about health, sexuality, gender, physical and psychological changes, sexual assault, contraception, abstinence, pregnancy, sexual intercourse, and STDs is taught in schools. There are many different views on and approaches to what constitutes an appropriate and healthy sex education curriculum.

Sexually transmitted disease (STD): Once known as "venereal diseases" (from Venus, goddess of love) sexually transmitted diseases include more than two dozen infectious diseases that are passed between people engaged in sexual activity. STDs, including herpes, syphilis, gonorrhea, chlamydia, and AIDS, are among the most common infections known, and while some diseases may be treated with antibiotics, others are untreatable and can (in the case of AIDS) lead to death. People with multiple sexual partners, or who are having unprotected sex (sex without a latex condom) are the most vulnerable to contracting an STD.

Women's movement: Just as the women's suffrage movement of the nineteenth century grew out of the abolition movement, the modern women's movement (also known as the women's liberation movement) evolved partly out of the civil rights movement and the antiwar movement of the 1960s. The early years of the movement brought the terms "women's libber," "bra-burner," and the now controversial "feminist" into the American consciousness, but beyond the names were real accomplishments in changing laws and attitudes about what women could do and be. Dedicated to bringing equal rights to American women, the women's movement continues into the twenty-first century calling for better pay for women, greater access to child care, more affordable health care (including family planning and abortion), and continuing support from law enforcement for women who are the victims of domestic abuse and sexual assault.

CHAPTER 9

Point of Contact:
Terrorism and National Security

The south tower is hit by Flight 175.

September 11, 2001. If you are old enough to be in college and reading this textbook, then you are old enough to remember where you were on that day. On the morning of September 11, 2001, nineteen radical Islamic terrorists affiliated with **Al Qaeda** and its leader, **Osama Bin Laden**, hijacked four airplanes full of passengers and flew them into the two towers of the **World Trade Center** in New York City, the **Pentagon** in Washington, D.C., and a field in rural Pennsylvania. The World Trade Center was chosen as a symbol of America's financial might around the world, and the Pentagon is the headquarters of America's great military forces. These were carefully selected targets of symbolic and actual value, where a direct hit could cause great loss of life, property, and technology.

But the field in Pennsylvania was not part of the terrorists' plan. The fourth plane the terrorists hijacked, United Flight 93, was late taking off. That brief delay enabled passengers to hear via cell phone of the other hijacked planes being flown into buildings. Believing they had no choice but to fight back, the passengers and cabin crew of Flight 93 rushed the cockpit in an attempt to overpower the hijackers. Widely believed to have had either the White House or the Capitol as its intended target, this fourth plane, full of jet fuel and innocent lives, crashed instead in a field near Shanksville, Pennsylvania.

In all, more than three thousand people, including hundreds of rescue workers, firefighters and police officers, lost their lives in a deadly terrorist attack that was almost immediately compared to the attack on **Pearl Harbor** in 1941.

In less time than it takes for you to read a few essays in this Point of Contact, we went from being a nation at peace to being a nation at war with a worldwide radical terrorist organization. This conflict would lead American forces around the world in pursuit of Al Qaeda, which was already known to have been associated with the 1993 attempt to detonate a bomb in the garage under the World Trade Center, the 1996 attack on a U.S. military base in Saudi Arabia, the 1998 bombings of U.S. embassies in Tanzania and Kenya, and the 2000 attack on the *USS Cole*. Our search for the terrorists responsible for this latest horrible attack upon America would lead to our invasion of Afghanistan, where Osama bin Laden was believed to be hiding, and the removal of the oppressive Taliban regime from power. We would also invade Iraq, capture Saddam Hussein, and then find ourselves in a difficult occupation lasting far longer than most had thought and costing many more American lives than the actual invasion.

Throughout this long and complicated war on terror (as it has become known), the only constant is change. The way we thought about our safety, as individuals and as a nation, changed. Our relationships with other nations and longtime allies were altered. Our military is strained in this new, global conflict to cover all the battlefields, which has brought rumors of another **military draft**. We have, as a largely Judeo-Christian nation, become far more aware of Islam than ever before, seeing (and in many cases reaching out to) our Muslim fellow citizens and neighbors in a new way. American Muslims found themselves suddenly visible, sometimes in very uncomfortable ways. And of course the way we travel has been changed forever; it won't be too many years until most of us forget that there once was a time where we could go through airport security without taking off our shoes, which we do because of the **shoe bomber, Richard Reid**.

Our focus in this Point of Contact, however, is somewhat different. We will not be discussing the war in Iraq, Islamic fundamentalism, or anything else that stretches across the globe. Our subjects will be much closer to home. One of the primary questions we continue to ask ourselves in the wake of 9/11 is, how does this terrible event alter our lives and our rights as Americans? For instance, does free speech still apply when we speak of the events of that terrible day? Or must we say only certain things, take only certain positions on what happened and who is to blame? Is this a time of crisis too dire for us to criticize our government or its policies? What about the **Patriot Act**—designed to help intelligence services and law enforcement track down suspected terrorists? Are we giving up some rights in the process? And what about the new technologies that have come into our space—public and private—to keep track of what we do and where we go? Cameras surround us. Do we have a right to cry foul at this near-constant surveillance and be rid of them? Or should we just be grateful that someone is watching, that someone is paying attention and trying to keep us all safe?

The question is not if we were all changed on September 11, 2001, but rather how we were changed and what we think about those changes. As you read these essays and think about the authors' many different opinions, keep in mind that you are part of a unique generation: young people who came of age in the era of 9/11. Your lives will be greatly defined by that terrible day and our many responses to it.

This Point of Contact will focus on and address the following three specific clusters that relate to terrorism and national security:

1. Free Speech and 9/11: The Case of Ward Churchill
2. A New Rule of Law: The Patriot Act
3. One Nation Under Surveillance: Camera, IDs, and Recognition Software in Public Places

FREE SPEECH AND 9/11: THE CASE OF WARD CHURCHILL

Just a few words, if carefully chosen, can make a profound difference in the world. Consider, for instance, the First Amendment to the Constitution—fewer than fifty words that are at the heart of what it means to be an American. "Congress shall make no law respecting an establishment of religion, or prohibiting the free exercise thereof; or abridging the freedom of speech, or of the press, or the right of the people peaceably to assemble, and to petition the Government for a redress of grievances." Ratified in 1791 along with nine other amendments collectively known as the Bill of Rights, the First Amendment guarantees the right to believe and say and print what we wish; it allows us to assemble with like-minded people, and to petition the government if we feel we have been wronged. The exceptions are few and well known: One cannot libel or slander or yell "fire!" in a crowded theater; we have developed definitions of obscenity, pornography, and verbal sexual harassment. In these cases the government may respond afterwards, yet speech is almost completely protected against prior restraint—meaning the government can't stop you from speaking before you speak or write something, it can only respond. We are so used to these rights that it is difficult for us today to understand how important they are. But these few words added to the Constitution established a clearing in which democracy, individual rights, and intellectual freedom have thrived for nearly 230 years.

Just a few words, if carefully chosen, can make a profound difference in the world. Consider, for instance, the case of Ward Churchill. In response to the terrorist attacks on September 11, 2001, Ward Churchill, professor of ethnic studies at the University of Colorado, sat down to write an essay in which he declared the events of 9/11 to be the logical end of America's imperial power exercised ruthlessly around the globe, and he declared the victims of the terrorists to have been culpable in their own deaths. Fashioned somewhere between a declaration and a rant, Churchill's essay was outrageous, offensive, and provocative—a sweeping indictment of America sure to stir up trouble. And no one noticed. It just sat there for three years until Professor Churchill was invited to speak at Hamilton College; suddenly the whole country knew about Ward Churchill and his essay.

College and university professors can earn something called **tenure**. Tenure was designed to encourage research and scholarship on all topics and in all directions, not just those that were socially acceptable or politically correct at any given time. Having tenure means that scholarly research—what is said and published and studied—is protected, and a tenured faculty member can pursue any line of study without fear of losing his or her position. Tenure is intended to support intellectual freedom and promote the open exchange of ideas. While freedom of speech means you won't get thrown in jail for what you say, tenure means you won't lose your job for what you write. Ward Churchill has tenure.

In the following essays, you will be able to consider this issue of free speech about 9/11, beginning with Churchill's infamous essay. You will see various opinions as to whether Churchill should be fired (as the governor of Colorado proposed), whether he should be punished, celebrated, or ignored for the essay, or whether tenure is even a good idea. One of the more interesting aspects of this freedom-of-speech case is how Ward Churchill is being vilified for so many other things—for questionable scholarship, for not having a Ph.D., for claiming to be a Native American, for embarrassing the University of Colorado, and for misrepresenting his military service. Such attacks seem to suggest that while freedom of speech is a great American idea, Churchill's critics believe that he doesn't deserve such a right. Perhaps Ward Churchill's case offers us an opportunity to understand the sentiment widely attributed to Voltaire: I disapprove of what you say but I will defend to the death your right to say it.

*The title of Churchill's essay alludes to a controversial comment **Malcolm X** made about the assassination of President Kennedy. Consider that while Churchill provides that information, he does not mention that Malcolm X's comment—widely thought to have been harsh and inappropriate in a time of national crisis— contributed to his being asked to leave the **Nation of Islam**. In other words, Malcolm X got fired for what he said.*

As you read, think about what it might be like for you if Professor Churchill was coming to speak at your college or university, and what, if anything, you would do or say in response to his essay.

Ward Churchill

"Some People Push Back:" On the Justice of Roosting Chickens

Ward Churchill.

When queried by reporters concerning his views on the assassination of John F. Kennedy in November 1963, Malcolm X famously—and quite charitably, all things considered—replied that it was merely a case of "chickens coming home to roost."

On the morning of September 11, 2001, a few more chickens—along with some half-million dead Iraqi children—came home to roost in a very big way at the twin towers of New York's World Trade Center. Well, actually, a few of them seem to have nestled in at the Pentagon as well.

The Iraqi youngsters, all of them under 12, died as a predictable—in fact, widely predicted—result of the 1991 US "surgical" bombing of their country's water purification and sewage facilities, as well as other "infrastructural" targets upon which Iraq's civilian population depends for its very survival.

If the nature of the bombing were not already bad enough—and it should be noted that this sort of "aerial warfare" constitutes a Class I Crime Against Humanity, entailing myriad gross violations of international law, as well as every conceivable standard of "civilized" behavior—the death toll has been steadily ratcheted up by US-imposed sanctions for a full decade now. Enforced all the while by a massive military presence and periodic bombing raids, the embargo has greatly impaired the victims' ability to import the nutrients, medicines and other materials necessary to saving the lives of even their toddlers.

5   All told, Iraq has a population of about 18 million. The 500,000 kids lost to date thus represent something on the order of 25 percent of their age group. Indisputably, the rest have suffered—are still suffering—a combination of physical debilitation and psychological trauma severe enough to prevent their ever fully recovering. In effect, an entire generation has been obliterated.

The reason for this holocaust was/is rather simple, and stated quite straightforwardly by President George Bush, the 41st "freedom-loving" father of the freedom-lover currently filling the Oval Office, George the 43rd: "The world must learn that what we say, goes," intoned George the Elder to the enthusiastic applause of freedom-loving Americans everywhere.

How Old George conveyed his message was certainly no mystery to the US public. One need only recall the 24-hour-per-day dissemination of bombardment videos on every available TV channel, and the exceedingly high ratings of these telecasts, to gain a sense of how much they knew.

In trying to affix a meaning to such things, we would do well to remember the wave of elation that swept America at reports of what was happening along the so-called Highway of Death: perhaps 100,000 "towel-heads" and "camel jockeys"—or was it "sand niggers" that week?—in full retreat, routed and effectively defenseless, many of them conscripted civilian laborers, slaughtered in a single day by jets firing the most hyper-lethal types of ordinance.

It was a performance worthy of the nazis during the early months of their drive into Russia. And it should be borne in mind that Good Germans gleefully cheered that butchery, too. Indeed, support for Hitler suffered no serious erosion among Germany's "innocent civilians" until the defeat at Stalingrad in 1943.

10   There may be a real utility to reflecting further, this time upon the fact that it was pious Americans who led the way in assigning the onus of collective guilt to the German people as a whole, not for things they as individuals had done, but for what they had allowed—nay, empowered—heir leaders and their soldiers to do in their name.

If the principle was valid then, it remains so now, as applicable to Good Americans as it was the Good Germans. And the price exacted from the Germans for the faultiness of their moral fiber was truly ghastly.

Returning now to the children, and to the effects of the post-Gulf War embargo—continued full force by Bush the Elder's successors in the Clinton administration as a gesture of its "resolve" to finalize what George himself had dubbed the "New World Order" of American military/economic domination—it should be noted that not one but two high

United Nations officials attempting to coordinate delivery of humanitarian aid to Iraq resigned in succession as protests against US policy.

One of them, former U.N. Assistant Secretary General Denis Halladay, repeatedly denounced what was happening as "a systematic program . . . of deliberate genocide." His statements appeared in the *New York Times* and other papers during the fall of 1998, so it can hardly be contended that the American public was "unaware" of them.

Shortly thereafter, Secretary of State Madeline Albright openly confirmed Halladay's assessment. Asked during the widely-viewed TV program *Meet the Press* to respond to his "allegations," she calmly announced that she'd decided it was "worth the price" to see that U.S. objectives were achieved.

The Politics of a Perpetrator Population

As a whole, the American public greeted these revelations with yawns   15

There were, after all, far more pressing things than the unrelenting misery/death of a few hundred thousand Iraqi tikes to be concerned with. Getting "Jeremy" and "Ellington" to their weekly soccer game, for instance, or seeing to it that little "Tiffany" and "Ashley" had just the right roll-neck sweaters to go with their new cords. And, to be sure, there was the yuppie holy war against ashtrays—for "our kids," no less—as an all-absorbing point of political focus.

In fairness, it must be admitted that there was an infinitesimally small segment of the body politic who expressed opposition to what was/is being done to the children of Iraq. It must also be conceded, however, that those involved by-and-large contented themselves with signing petitions and conducting candle-lit prayer vigils, bearing "moral witness" as vast legions of brown-skinned five-year-olds sat shivering in the dark, wide-eyed in horror, whimpering as they expired in the most agonizing ways imaginable.

Be it said as well, and this is really the crux of it, that the "resistance" expended the bulk of its time and energy harnessed to the systemically-useful task of trying to ensure, as "a principle of moral virtue" that nobody went further than waving signs as a means of "challenging" the patently exterminatory pursuit of Pax Americana. So pure of principle were these "dissidents," in fact, that they began literally to supplant the police in protecting corporations profiting by the carnage against suffering such retaliatory "violence" as having their windows broken by persons less "enlightened"—or perhaps more outraged—than the self-anointed "peacekeepers."

Property before people, it seems—or at least the equation of property to people—is a value by no means restricted to America's boardrooms. And the sanctimony with which such putrid sentiments are enunciated turns out to be nauseatingly similar, whether mouthed by the CEO of Standard Oil or any of the swarm of comfort zone "pacifists" queuing up to condemn the black block after it ever so slightly disturbed the functioning of business-as-usual in Seattle.

Small wonder, all-in-all, that people elsewhere in the world—the Mideast, for instance—   20
began to wonder where, exactly, aside from the streets of the US itself, one was to find the peace America's purportedly oppositional peacekeepers claimed they were keeping.

The answer, surely, was plain enough to anyone unblinded by the kind of delusions engendered by sheer vanity and self-absorption.

So, too, were the implications in terms of anything changing, out there, in America's free-fire zones.

Tellingly, it was at precisely this point—with the genocide in Iraq officially admitted and a public response demonstrating beyond a shadow of a doubt that there were virtually no Americans, including most of those professing otherwise, doing anything tangible to stop it—that the combat teams which eventually commandeered the aircraft used on September 11 began to infiltrate the United States.

Meet the "Terrorists"

Of the men who came, there are a few things demanding to be said in the face of the unending torrent of disinformational drivel unleashed by George Junior and the corporate "news" media immediately following their successful operation on September 11.

25
They did not, for starters, "initiate" a war with the US, much less commit "the first acts of war of the new millennium."

A good case could be made that the war in which they were combatants has been waged more-or-less continuously by the "Christian West"—now proudly emblematized by the United States—against the "Islamic East" since the time of the First Crusade, about 1,000 years ago. More recently, one could argue that the war began when Lyndon Johnson first lent significant support to Israel's dispossession/displacement of Palestinians during the 1960s, or when George the Elder ordered "Desert Shield" in 1990, or at any of several points in between. Any way you slice it, however, if what the combat teams did to the WTC and the Pentagon can be understood as acts of war— and they can—then the same is true of every US "overflight" of Iraqi territory since day one. The first acts of war during the current millennium thus occurred on its very first day, and were carried out by U.S. aviators acting under orders from their then-commander-in-chief, Bill Clinton. The most that can honestly be said of those involved on September 11 is that they finally responded in kind to some of what this country has dispensed to their people as a matter of course. That they waited so long to do so is, notwithstanding the 1993 action at the WTC, more than anything a testament to their patience and restraint.

They did not license themselves to "target innocent civilians."

There is simply no argument to be made that the Pentagon personnel killed on September 11 fill that bill. The building and those inside comprised military targets, pure and simple. As to those in the World Trade Center . . . Well, really. Let's get a grip here, shall we? True enough, they were civilians of a sort. But innocent? Gimme a break.

They formed a technocratic corps at the very heart of America's global financial empire—the "mighty engine of profit" to which the military dimension of U.S. policy has always been enslaved—and they did so both willingly and knowingly. Recourse to "ignorance"—a derivative, after all, of the word "ignore"—counts as less than an excuse among this relatively well-educated elite. To the extent that any of them were unaware of the costs and consequences to others of what they were involved in—and in many cases excelling at—it was because of their absolute refusal to see. More likely, it was because they were too busy braying, incessantly and self-importantly, into their cell phones, arranging power lunches and stock transactions, each of which translated, conveniently out of sight, mind and smelling distance, into the starved and rotting flesh of infants. If there was a better, more effective, or in fact any other way of visiting some penalty befitting their participation upon the little Eichmanns inhabiting the sterile sanctuary of the twin towers, I'd really be interested in hearing about it.

The men who flew the missions against the WTC and Pentagon were not "cowards." 30

That distinction properly belongs to the "firm-jawed lads" who delighted in flying stealth aircraft through the undefended airspace of Baghdad, dropping payload after payload of bombs on anyone unfortunate enough to be below—including tens of thousands of genuinely innocent civilians—while themselves incurring all the risk one might expect during a visit to the local video arcade. Still more, the word describes all those "fighting men and women" who sat at computer consoles aboard ships in the Persian Gulf, enjoying air-conditioned comfort while launching cruise missiles into neighborhoods filled with random human beings. Whatever else can be said of them, the men who struck on September 11 manifested the courage of their convictions, willingly expending their own lives in attaining their objectives.

Nor were they "fanatics" devoted to "Islamic fundamentalism."

One might rightly describe their actions as "desperate." Feelings of desperation, however, are a perfectly reasonable—one is tempted to say "normal"—emotional response among persons confronted by the mass murder of their children, particularly when it appears that nobody else really gives a damn (ask a Jewish survivor about this one, or, even more poignantly, for all the attention paid them, a Gypsy). That desperate circumstances generate desperate responses is no mysterious or irrational principle, of the sort motivating fanatics. Less is it one peculiar to Islam. Indeed, even the FBI's investigative reports on the combat teams' activities during the months leading up to September 11 make it clear that the members were not fundamentalist Muslims. Rather, it's pretty obvious at this point that they were secular activists—soldiers, really—who, while undoubtedly enjoying cordial relations with the clerics of their countries, were motivated far more by the grisly realities of the U.S. war against them than by a set of religious beliefs.

And still less were they/their acts "insane."

Insanity is a condition readily associable with the very American idea that one—or 35 one's country—holds what amounts to a "divine right" to commit genocide, and thus to forever do so with impunity. The term might also be reasonably applied to anyone suffering genocide without attempting in some material way to bring the process to a halt. Sanity itself, in this frame of reference, might be defined by a willingness to try and destroy the perpetrators and/or the sources of their ability to commit their crimes. (Shall we now discuss the US "strategic bombing campaign" against Germany during World War II, and the mental health of those involved in it?)

Which takes us to official characterizations of the combat teams as an embodiment of "evil."

Evil—for those inclined to embrace the banality of such a concept—was perfectly incarnated in that malignant toad known as Madeline Albright, squatting in her studio chair like Jaba the Hutt, blandly spewing the news that she'd imposed a collective death sentence upon the unoffending youth of Iraq. Evil was to be heard in that great American hero "Stormin' Norman" Schwartzkopf's utterly dehumanizing dismissal of their systematic torture and annihilation as mere "collateral damage." Evil, moreover, is a term appropriate to describing the mentality of a public that finds such perspectives and the policies attending them acceptable, or even momentarily tolerable.

Had it not been for these evils, the counterattacks of September 11 would never have occurred. And unless "the world is rid of such evil," to lift a line from George Junior, September 11 may well end up looking like a lark. There is no reason, after all, to believe that the teams deployed in the assaults on the WTC and the Pentagon were the only such, that the others are composed of "Arabic-looking individuals"—America's indiscriminately lethal arrogance and psychotic sense of self-entitlement have long since given the great majority of the world's peoples ample cause to be at war with it—or that they are in any way dependent upon the seizure of civilian airliners to complete their missions.

To the contrary, there is every reason to expect that there are many other teams in place, tasked to employ altogether different tactics in executing operational plans at least as well-crafted as those evident on September 11, and very well equipped for their jobs. This is to say that, since the assaults on the WTC and Pentagon were acts of war—no "terrorist incidents"—they must be understood as components in a much broader strategy designed to achieve specific results. From this, it can only be adduced that there are plenty of other components ready to go, and that they will be used, should this become necessary in the eyes of the strategists. It also seems a safe bet that each component is calibrated to inflict damage at a level incrementally higher than the one before (during the 1960s, the Johnson administration employed a similar policy against Vietnam, referred to as "escalation").

40   Since implementation of the overall plan began with the WTC/Pentagon assaults, it takes no rocket scientist to decipher what is likely to happen next, should the U.S. attempt a response of the inexcusable variety to which it has long entitled itself.

About Those Boys (and Girls) in the Bureau

There's another matter begging for comment at this point. The idea that the FBI's "counterterrorism task forces" can do a thing to prevent what will happen is yet another dimension of America's delusional pathology. The fact is that, for all its publicly-financed "image-building" exercises, the Bureau has never shown the least aptitude for anything of the sort.

Oh, yeah, FBI counterintelligence personnel have proven quite adept at framing anarchists, communists and Black Panthers, sometimes murdering them in their beds or the electric chair. The Bureau's SWAT units have displayed their ability to combat child abuse in Waco by burning babies alive, and its vaunted Crime Lab has been shown to pad its "crime-fighting' statistics by fabricating evidence against many an alleged car thief. But actual "heavy-duty bad guys" of the sort at issue now?

This isn't a Bruce Willis/Chuck Norris/Sly Stallone movie, after all. And J. Edgar Hoover doesn't get to approve either the script or the casting.

The number of spies, saboteurs and bona fide terrorists apprehended, or even detected by the FBI in the course of its long and slimy history could be counted on one's fingers and toes. On occasion, its agents have even turned out to be the spies, and, in many instances, the terrorists as well.

45   To be fair once again, if the Bureau functions as at best a carnival of clowns where its "domestic security responsibilities" are concerned, this is because—regardless of official hype—it has none. It is now, as it's always been, the national political police force, an instrument created and perfected to ensure that all Americans, not just the consenting mass, are "free" to do exactly as they're told.

The FBI and "cooperating agencies" can be thus relied upon to set about "protecting freedom" by destroying whatever rights and liberties were left to U.S. citizens before September 11 (in fact, they've already received authorization to begin). Sheeplike, the great majority of Americans can also be counted upon to bleat their approval, at least in the short run, believing as they always do that the nasty implications of what they're doing will pertain only to others.

Oh Yeah, and "The Company," Too

A possibly even sicker joke is the notion, suddenly in vogue, that the CIA will be able to pinpoint "terrorist threats," "rooting out their infrastructure" where it exists and/or "terminating" it before it can materialize, if only it's allowed to beef up its "human intelligence gathering capacity" in an unrestrained manner (including full-bore operations inside the US, of course).

Yeah. Right.

Since America has a collective attention-span of about 15 minutes, a little refresher seems in order: "The Company" had something like a quarter-million people serving as "intelligence assets" by feeding it information in Vietnam in 1968, and it couldn't even predict the Tet Offensive. God knows how many spies it was fielding against the USSR at the height of Ronald Reagan's version of the Cold War, and it was still caught flatfooted by the collapse of the Soviet Union.

As to destroying "terrorist infrastructures," one would do well to remember Operation Phoenix, another product of its open season in Vietnam. In that one, the CIA enlisted elite US units like the Navy Seals and Army Special Forces, as well as those of friendly countries—the south Vietnamese Rangers, for example, and Australian SAS—to run around "neutralizing" folks targeted by The Company's legion of snitches as "guerrillas" (as those now known as "terrorists" were then called).

Sound familiar?

Upwards of 40,000 people—mostly bystanders, as it turns out—were murdered by Phoenix hit teams before the guerrillas, stronger than ever, ran the US and its collaborators out of their country altogether.

And these are the guys who are gonna save the day, if unleashed to do their thing in North America?

The net impact of all this "counterterrorism" activity upon the combat teams' ability to do what they came to do, of course, will be nil. Instead, it's likely to make it easier for them to operate (it's worked that way in places like Northern Ireland). And, since denying Americans the luxury of reaping the benefits of genocide in comfort was self-evidently a key objective of the WTC/Pentagon assaults, it can be stated unequivocally that a more overt display of the police state mentality already pervading this country simply confirms the magnitude of their victory.

On Matters of Proportion and Intent

As things stand, including the 1993 detonation at the WTC, "Arab terrorists" have responded to the massive and sustained American terror bombing of Iraq with a total of four assaults by explosives inside the US. That's about 1% of the 50,000 bombs the Pentagon announced were rained on Baghdad alone during the Gulf War (add in Oklahoma City and you'll get something nearer an actual 1%). They've managed in the process to kill about 5,000 Americans, or roughly 1% of the dead Iraqi children (the percentage is far smaller if you factor in the killing of adult Iraqi civilians, not to mention troops butchered as/after they'd surrendered and/or after the "war-ending" ceasefire had been announced).

In terms undoubtedly more meaningful to the property/profit-minded American mainstream, they've knocked down a half-dozen buildings—albeit some very well-chosen ones—as opposed to the "strategic devastation" visited upon the whole of Iraq, and punched a $100 billion hole in the earnings outlook of major corporate shareholders, as opposed to the U.S. obliteration of Iraq's entire economy.

With that, they've given Americans a tiny dose of their own medicine.

This might be seen as merely a matter of "vengeance" or "retribution," and, unquestionably, America has earned it, even if it were to add up only to something so ultimately petty.

The problem is that vengeance is usually framed in terms of "getting even," a concept which is plainly inapplicable in this instance. As the above data indicate, it would require another 49,996 detonations killing 495,000 more Americans, for the "terrorists" to "break even" for the bombing of Baghdad/extermination of Iraqi children alone. And that's to achieve "real number" parity. To attain an actual proportional parity of damage—the US is about 15 times as large as Iraq in terms of population, even more in terms of territory—they would, at a minimum, have to blow up about 300,000 more buildings and kill something on the order of 7.5 million people.

60   Were this the intent of those who've entered the US to wage war against it, it would remain no less true that America and Americans were only receiving the bill for what they'd already done.

Payback, as they say, can be a real motherfucker (ask the Germans).

There is, however, no reason to believe that retributive parity is necessarily an item on the agenda of those who planned the WTC/Pentagon operation. If it were, given the virtual certainty that they possessed the capacity to have inflicted far more damage than they did, there would be a lot more American bodies lying about right now.

Hence, it can be concluded that ravings carried by the "news" media since September 11 have contained at least one grain of truth: The peoples of the Mideast "aren't like" Americans, not least because they don't "value life" in the same way. By this, it should be understood that Middle-Easterners, unlike Americans, have no history of exterminating others purely for profit, or on the basis of racial animus. Thus, we can appreciate the fact that they value life—all lives, not just their own—far more highly than do their U.S. counterparts.

The Makings of a Humanitarian Strategy

In sum one can discern a certain optimism—it might even be called humanitarianism—imbedded in the thinking of those who presided over the very limited actions conducted on September 11.

65   Their logic seems to have devolved upon the notion that the American people have condoned what has been/is being done in their name—indeed, are to a significant extent actively complicit in it—mainly because they have no idea what it feels like to be on the receiving end.

Now they do.

That was the "medicinal" aspect of the attacks.

To all appearances, the idea is now to give the tonic a little time to take effect, jolting Americans into the realization that the sort of pain they're now experiencing first-hand is no different from—or the least bit more excruciating than—that which they've been so cavalier in causing others, and thus to respond appropriately.

More bluntly, the hope was—and maybe still is—that Americans, stripped of their presumed immunity from incurring any real consequences for their behavior, would comprehend and act upon a formulation as uncomplicated as "stop killing our kids, if you want your own to be safe."

70   Either way, it's a kind of "reality therapy" approach, designed to afford the American people a chance to finally "do the right thing" on their own, without further coaxing.

Were the opportunity acted upon in some reasonably good faith fashion—a sufficiently large number of Americans rising up and doing whatever is necessary to force an immediate lifting of the sanctions on Iraq, for instance, or maybe hanging a few of America's abundant supply of major war criminals (Henry Kissinger comes quickly to mind, as do Madeline Albright, Colin Powell, Bill Clinton and George the Elder)—there is every reason to expect that military operations against the US on its domestic front would be immediately suspended.

Whether they would remain so would of course be contingent upon follow-up. By that, it may be assumed that American acceptance of onsite inspections by international observers to verify destruction of its weapons of mass destruction (as well as dismantlement of all facilities in which more might be manufactured), Nuremberg-style trials in which a few thousand US military/corporate personnel could be properly adjudicated and punished for their Crimes Against Humanity, and payment of reparations to the array of nations/peoples whose assets the US has plundered over the years, would suffice.

Since they've shown no sign of being unreasonable or vindictive, it may even be anticipated that, after a suitable period of adjustment and reeducation (mainly to allow them to acquire the skills necessary to living within their means), those restored to control over their own destinies by the gallant sacrifices of the combat teams the WTC and Pentagon will eventually (re)admit Americans to the global circle of civilized societies. Stranger things have happened.

In the Alternative

Unfortunately, noble as they may have been, such humanitarian aspirations were always doomed to remain unfulfilled. For it to have been otherwise, a far higher quality of character and intellect would have to prevail among average Americans than is actually the case.

Perhaps the strategists underestimated the impact a couple of generations-worth of   75
media indoctrination can produce in terms of demolishing the capacity of human beings to form coherent thoughts. Maybe they forgot to factor in the mind-numbing effects of the indoctrination passed off as education in the US.

Then, again, it's entirely possible they were aware that a decisive majority of American adults have been reduced by this point to a level much closer to the kind of immediate self-gratification entailed in Pavlovian stimulus/response patterns than anything accessible by appeals to higher logic, and still felt morally obliged to offer the dolts an option to quit while they were ahead.

What the hell? It was worth a try.

But it's becoming increasingly apparent that the dosage of medicine administered was entirely insufficient to accomplish its purpose.

Although there are undoubtedly exceptions, Americans for the most part still don't get it.

Already, they've desecrated the temporary tomb of those killed in the WTC, staging a   80
veritable pep rally atop the mangled remains of those they profess to honor, treating the whole affair as if it were some bizarre breed of contact sport. And, of course, there are the inevitable pom-poms shaped like American flags, the school colors worn as little red-white-and-blue ribbons affixed to labels, sportscasters in the form of "counterterrorism experts" drooling mindless color commentary during the pregame warm-up.

Refusing the realization that the world has suddenly shifted its axis, and that they are therefore no longer "in charge," they have by-and-large reverted instantly to type, working themselves into their usual bloodlust on the now obsolete premise that the bloodletting will "naturally" occur elsewhere and to someone else.

"Patriotism," a wise man once observed, "is the last refuge of scoundrels."

And the braided, he might have added.

Braided Scoundrel-in-Chief, George Junior, lacking even the sense to be careful what he wished for, has teamed up with a gaggle of fundamentalist Christian clerics like Billy Graham to proclaim a "New Crusade" called "Infinite Justice" aimed at "ridding the world of evil."

85   One could easily make light of such rhetoric, remarking upon how unseemly it is for a son to threaten his father in such fashion—or a president to so publicly contemplate the murder/suicide of himself and his cabinet—but the matter is deadly serious.

They are preparing once again to sally forth for the purpose of roasting brown-skinned children by the scores of thousands. Already, the B-1 bombers and the aircraft carriers and the missile frigates are en route, the airborne divisions are gearing up to go.

To where? Afghanistan?

The Sudan?

Iraq, again (or still)?

90   How about Grenada (that was fun)?

Any of them or all. It doesn't matter.

The desire to pummel the helpless runs rabid as ever.

Only, this time it's different.

The time the helpless aren't, or at least are not so helpless as they were.

95   This time, somewhere, perhaps in an Afghani mountain cave, possibly in a Brooklyn basement, maybe another locale altogether—but somewhere, all the same—there's a grim-visaged (wo)man wearing a Clint Eastwood smile.

"Go ahead, punks," s/he's saying, "Make my day."

And when they do, when they launch these airstrikes abroad—or may a little later; it will be at a time conforming to the "terrorists'" own schedule, and at a place of their choosing—the next more intensive dose of medicine administered here "at home."

Of what will it consist this time? Anthrax? Mustard gas? Sarin? A tactical nuclear device? That, too, is their choice to make.

100   Looking back, it will seem to future generations inexplicable why Americans were unable on their own, and in time to save themselves, to accept a rule of nature so basic that it could be mouthed by an actor, Lawrence Fishburn, in a movie, *The Cotton Club*.

"You've got to learn, " the line went, "that when you push people around, some people push back."

As they should.

As they must.

And as they undoubtedly will.

105   There is justice in such symmetry.

Addendum

The preceding was a "first take" reading, more a stream-of-consciousness interpretive reaction to the September 11 counterattack than a finished piece on the topic. Hence, I'll readily admit that I've been far less than thorough, and quite likely wrong about a number of things.

For instance, it may not have been (only) the ghosts of Iraqi children who made their appearance that day. It could as easily have been some or all of their butchered Palestinian cousins.

Or maybe it was some or all of the at least 3.2 million Indochinese who perished as a result of America's sustained and genocidal assault on Southeast Asia (1959-1975), not to mention the millions more who've died because of the sanctions imposed thereafter.

Perhaps there were a few of the Korean civilians massacred by US troops at places like No Gun Ri during the early '50s, or the hundreds of thousands of Japanese civilians ruthlessly incinerated in the ghastly fire raids of World War II (only at Dresden did America bomb Germany in a similar manner).

And, of course, it could have been those vaporized in the militarily pointless nuclear   110
bombings of Hiroshima and Nagasaki.

There are others, as well, a vast and silent queue of faceless victims, stretching from the million-odd Filipinos slaughtered during America's "Indian War" in their islands at the beginning of the twentieth century, through the real Indians, America's own, massacred wholesale at places like Horseshoe Bend and the Bad Axe, Sand Creek and Wounded Knee, the Washita, Bear River, and the Marias.

Was it those who expired along the Cherokee Trail of Tears of the Long Walk of the Navajo?

Those murdered by smallpox at Fort Clark in 1836?

Starved to death in the concentration camp at Bosque Redondo during the 1860s?

Maybe those native people claimed for scalp bounty in all 48 of the continental US   115
states? Or the Raritans whose severed heads were kicked for sport along the streets of what was then called New Amsterdam, at the very site where the WTC once stood?

One hears, too, the whispers of those lost on the Middle Passage, and of those whose very flesh was sold in the slave market outside the human kennel from whence Wall Street takes its name.

And of coolie laborers, imported by the gross-dozen to lay the tracks of empire across scorching desert sands, none of them allotted "a Chinaman's chance" of surviving.

The list is too long, too awful to go on.

No matter what its eventual fate, America will have gotten off very, very cheap.

The full measure of its guilt can never be fully balanced or atoned for.   120

Ward Churchill is professor of American Indian Studies with the Department of Ethnic Studies, University of Colorado at Boulder.

Scott Smallwood

Anatomy of a Free-Speech Firestorm: How a Professor's 3-Year-Old Essay Sparked a National Controversy

The *Chronicle of Higher Education*, February 10, 2005

Hours after the terrorist attacks of September 11, 2001, Ward Churchill compared the victims to the Nazis. A professor of ethnic studies at the University of Colorado at Boulder, he wrote in an essay that those killed at the World Trade Center were not innocent civilians but "little Eichmanns."

The analogy is so outrageous, one thinks, that surely he immediately got into trouble. Surely it prompted angry letters and calls for him to be fired. But it didn't.

Instead, for years the comparison just sat there quietly. Mr. Churchill, by contrast, rarely stays still. He has spoken on more than 40 college campuses since the 2001 attacks.

He traveled to elite liberal-arts colleges like Williams and Swarthmore, to big public universities like Arizona State and Michigan State, and to prestigious private universities like Brown and Syracuse. He spoke at community colleges in New York and Utah. Generally, he spoke about genocide and American Indian issues, but some speeches focused on foreign policy. Yet other than a brief mention in *The Burlington Free Press* during a December 2001 visit to the University of Vermont, the essay never made the news.

5   Then this winter, as he was about to speak at Hamilton College, the "little Eichmanns" time bomb went off, sparking hundreds of stories, denunciations of Mr. Churchill by governors and legislators, canceled speeches, and an investigation by Colorado administrators into his work that may threaten his tenured job.

So why now?

The answer lies in the power of Bill O'Reilly, Weblogs, and the families of September 11 victims. But before all that, the seeds of this controversy were sown not with Nazi references in an online essay but with a 1981 armored-car robbery that Mr. Churchill had nothing to do with.

Once Bitten, Twice Shy

On October 20, 1981, robbers connected with the Black Liberation Army and the Weather Underground struck a Brinks armored car while it sat outside a bank near Nyack, N.Y. One guard was killed, another wounded. Two police officers were later killed at a roadblock when robbers jumped from the back of a U-Haul truck, firing automatic rifles.

Susan Rosenberg, a 1970s leftist radical, was indicted as an accessory to the robbery, but remained free until she was arrested in New Jersey in 1984 on charges of possessing 740 pounds of explosives. She was sentenced to 58 years in prison, but the charges in the Brinks case were dropped.

10   Then in 2001, just before leaving office, President Bill Clinton granted her clemency, and she was released from prison. Now a prisoner-rights activist and writer, Ms. Rosenberg was hired in the fall by the Kirkland Project for the Study of Gender, Society, and Culture to teach a one-month course on writing memoirs at Hamilton College, in Clinton, N.Y.

That appointment created a public-relations mess for Hamilton, drawing protests from professors and negative editorials in newspapers. Ms. Rosenberg then backed out, citing "the atmosphere of such organized right-wing intimidation from a small group of students and faculty."

The Rosenberg debacle raised the antennae of Theodore Eismeier, a government professor at Hamilton. So when the Kirkland Project sent a message on December 14 highlighting its spring schedule, which included a February 3 speech by Mr. Churchill on prison issues, he checked out the Colorado professor.

After a little Internet searching, Mr. Eismeier discovered "Some People Push Back: On the Justice of Roosting Chickens," the essay in which Mr. Churchill made his now-infamous "little Eichmanns" comment. Mr. Eismeier says he immediately sent the essay and "other troubling writings" to college administrators, urging them to cancel the event.

The storm clouds were gathering.

Three days later, on Friday, December 17, Joan Hinde Stewart, the college's president,   15
met with Nancy S. Rabinowitz, director of the Kirkland Project, to discuss Mr. Churchill. The
following Monday, the president and David C. Paris, vice president for academic affairs, met
with Ms. Rabinowitz and members of the project's executive committee.

"They were saying this is going to be as bad as Susan Rosenberg," Ms. Rabinowitz
says. "And I said, Let's take a strong stand for freedom of speech." According to Ms.
Rabinowitz, the president told her to fold Mr. Churchill's speech into a planned panel discussion and change the focus to his offensive positions.

Then in January, Mr. Eismeier and three other Hamilton professors wrote two opinion
pieces about Ms. Rosenberg and Mr. Churchill. He sent them to the campus newspaper,
The Hamilton Spectator, along with a copy of "Some People Push Back."

In the essay, Mr. Churchill argues that those killed at the World Trade Center were not
truly innocent. "Let's get a grip here, shall we? True enough, they were civilians of a sort. But
innocent? Gimme a break." He adds: "If there was a better, more effective, or in fact any other
way of visiting some penalty befitting their participation upon the little Eichmanns inhabiting
the sterile sanctuary of the twin towers, I'd really be interested in hearing about it."

On January 21, the campus newspaper reported that Mr. Churchill was coming to the
campus and highlighted some of his more controversial statements. Mr. Eismeier was
quoted as saying that the event would not create a useful discussion. "It seems akin to
inviting a representative of the KKK to speak and then asking a member of the NAACP to
respond," he said.

Five days later, the news was picked up by *The Post-Standard,* a newspaper in nearby   20
Syracuse, N.Y. The pressure on Hamilton would only grow over the next seven days.
Administrators had been wrong: It wasn't going to be as bad as Susan Rosenberg. It was
going to be a lot worse.

Faster Than a Speeding Blog

In the Internet age, that report in the Syracuse newspaper quickly reached far beyond
upstate New York. A link to the article was posted on Little Green Footballs, a widely read
conservative Weblog, at 9:40 a.m., Eastern time.

Eleven minutes later a reader posted a comment, saying Mr. Churchill deserved to be
shot in the face. And then just before 10 a.m., a different reader provided the professor's
e-mail address. Before 11 a.m., another reader announced that she had just called the
Colorado governor and had written letters to *The Denver Post* and the *Rocky Mountain
News.* She followed up a few minutes later with contact information for the newspapers
so that others could do the same.

Linking to a simple article from Syracuse had unleashed the power of hundreds of
individuals, all using Google to add little bits of information. Within hours, 500 comments about the matter had been posted on Little Green Footballs alone. Readers
linked to old news releases about squabbles between Mr. Churchill and the American
Indian Movement. They linked to Hamilton news releases about alumni who were killed
in the attacks. Someone requested the name of a September 11 widow from Colorado
who might have political clout.

The blogs reached beyond the water cooler. Many readers wanted to do something—
even if it was just sending a message of protest or making a phone call. Over the next
week or so, Hamilton would receive 8,000 e-mail messages about Mr. Churchill.

25   Two days later, on January 28, as the story continued to gather momentum, readers of Freerepublic.com, another conservative Weblog, continued to talk about Mr. Churchill. One poster suggested calling Hamilton to tell officials that he would not contribute any money if they allowed Mr. Churchill to speak on the campus. Another poster replied: "Screw that! I say we cost them money. Their 1-800 admissions # should never stop ringing."

That night, the Churchill saga became a prime-time event when Bill O'Reilly led off his talk show on the Fox News Channel, *The O'Reilly Factor,* by calling Mr. Churchill "insane" and saying that Hamilton had no justification for giving him a public forum.

Mr. O'Reilly interviewed Matthew Coppo, a Hamilton sophomore whose father was killed in the World Trade Center attacks. Mr. Coppo's personal story, some now say, helped the Hamilton event get the publicity that the dozens of other speeches by Mr. Churchill never got.

The closest thing Mr. O'Reilly could find to a defender of Mr. Churchill was Philip A. Klinkner, an associate professor of government at Hamilton. Only one problem: Mr. Klinkner was one of the professors who had told the Kirkland Project that Mr. Churchill should not speak.

"Going on *O'Reilly* is a kamikaze mission," Mr. Klinkner acknowledges. "I went on to defend a principle. Colleges, if they choose to be a marketplace of ideas, have to be willing to bring in people who say pretty repugnant things." Nevertheless, he adds, "If I want to have someone come to class to talk about problems with the Treaty of Versailles, I don't have to bring in a Nazi."

30   Mr. O'Reilly ended the segment about Mr. Churchill with advice for his viewers. "I don't want anybody doing anything crazy to Hamilton College," he said. "I don't want any threats going in there. I don't want any of that. Feel free to wire or e-mail the college with your complaints. And you alumni at Hamilton, do not give them a nickel if that man appears."

Vige Barrie, a spokeswoman for Hamilton, was in the president's office as the program was shown. "When the segment stopped," she says, "the phone just started ringing."

Anywhere but Here

In the end, Hamilton canceled the event after receiving "credible threats of violence" against Mr. Churchill and college officials, including one call from a man who said he was going to bring a gun to the speech. Ms. Barrie says the police are still investigating several of the threats.

But canceling the speech will not undo the weeks of negative publicity. At Hamilton, Ms. Barrie says, some students are going to work with college officials on improving the college's image. "We want to be known for more than just Ward Churchill," she says.

And other presidents and alumni offices must be asking, Could this have happened elsewhere? Maybe at Wheaton College, in Massachusetts, where Mr. Churchill was supposed to speak in March. Or at Eastern Washington University, where he was scheduled to appear in April. Both events have been canceled.

35   The situation at Hamilton was ripe to explode into a bigger story, says Mr. Klinkner, citing the Susan Rosenberg case, the college's upstate New York location, and the student whose father perished in the attacks. And Ms. Rabinowitz, the Hamilton professor of comparative literature who invited Mr. Churchill, says the college was simply in the sights of conservative talk shows and Weblogs after the Rosenberg affair.

The controversy certainly never came up at the dozens of other institutions where Mr. Churchill has appeared since he wrote his essay.

Randall Fuller, an assistant professor of English at Drury University, in Springfield, Mo., says faculty members have been following the flap because Mr. Churchill spoke there in March 2004 without any incident. In fact, Mr. Fuller says, Mr. Churchill sparked the "most stimulating and engaged discussion" of the 18 speakers invited to the campus to commemorate the Lewis and Clark expedition. "We knew that he was a *provocateur,* and that's what we liked about him," he says.

Sharon L. Dobkin, a psychology professor at Monroe Community College, in Rochester, N.Y., invited Mr. Churchill to speak about genocide in November 2002. The college's New York location did not prompt a stir back then. She says she had not heard of the "Some People Push Back" essay at the time, but she was not surprised by it. "I think he's deliberately inflammatory," she says. "Either you love Ward Churchill or you hate him."

Not the Floor-Sweepers

Mr. Churchill's speaking engagements may dry up now, as other colleges back away from his fiery rhetoric. But he has other things to worry about —most immediately, his job. Regents in Colorado are pushing for his firing, and the interim chancellor of his campus has announced an investigation into his work to determine whether he "may have overstepped his bounds."

That investigation could be the first step toward dismissing him. Vandals have spray-painted swastikas on his pickup truck, and he has received more than 100 death threats. And now a Lamar University sociologist is charging that some of Mr. Churchill's research is fraudulent.

40

In a speech on Tuesday in Boulder, Mr. Churchill said that he would not retract his statements and that he would fight to keep his job. His essay was sparked, he said, by hearing someone call the attack "senseless." He added: "How can they positively know that? Do they really believe this operation had no purpose?"

He also told the crowd that he did not mean that everyone in the World Trade Center was a "little Eichmann." The janitors and passers-by were not the people at the heart of the "mighty engine of profit" that he derided.

Back at Hamilton, the issue has moved beyond simply Mr. Churchill's words. Mr. Klinkner says the controversy proves that academe cannot think of itself as separate from the rest of society. "You can forget about the notion of the ivory tower and that we can keep all these things in-house. Any piece of information that exists will get out. I don't think that's a bad thing," he says. "This was not good for Hamilton, but we need to acknowledge that we can no longer say, 'No, we're going to play by our own rules.'"

For Ms. Rabinowitz, director of the Kirkland Project, the question is whether the incident will make colleges reluctant to invite controversial speakers: "How many people can stomach what we've been through?"

Kirk Johnson

Incendiary in Academia May Now Find Himself Burned

The *New York Times*, February 11, 2005

Prof. Ward L. Churchill has made a career at the University of Colorado out of pushing people's buttons, colleagues and students say, clearly relishing his stance as radical provocateur and in-your-face critic.

Whether it is getting arrested by the Denver police for trying to disrupt Columbus Day, which Professor Churchill has described as a "celebration of genocide" because of the deaths of Indians that resulted from European colonization, or ruffling feathers in the faculty lounge, hyperbole and bombast have always been ready tools in the Churchill kit bag, people here say.

Now many of the offended are pushing back. The storm of controversy that has blown up around Professor Churchill over his essay about the Sept. 11 attacks, with its reference to the Nazi Adolf Eichmann—the "technocrats" at the World Trade Center were "little Eichmanns," Professor Churchill said—has turned the professor into a talking point and a political punch line. On conservative talk radio, on campuses across the country, and especially here in Boulder, debate about Professor Churchill means debate about freedom of speech, the solemnity of Sept. 11 and the supposed liberal bias of academia.

Many people here say that the professor—with his scholarly record under investigation by the university and with Gov. Bill Owens, a Republican, calling for his dismissal—has become a symbol of academic expression under fire. Others worry that subjects like Sept. 11 have become "sacred," and cordoned off from unpopular analysis. Some say that the vitriolic debate itself is the message and that people have been transformed into mirror images of the man they love or loathe—little Churchills, as it were, who are just as entrenched, over-the-top and, apparently, eager to offend as he himself.

5   "Two sides are being presented without a lot of people listening," said Joe Flasher, 24, a graduate student in astrophysics. "You already have your opinion, right. So it's one person saying what they think and then the other person saying the complete opposite. It seems very polarized. But I guess it is the ultimate exercise in free speech."

Student organizations like College Democrats and College Republicans have skirmished over Professor Churchill, a member of the ethnic studies department. The Democratic group began a petition this week saying, "The attacks on Professor Ward Churchill are attacks on the academic freedom of the university." The Republicans, in calling for his dismissal, said that alumni should freeze donations and that parents should send their children elsewhere until political balance is brought to the professorial ranks.

"It's probably in their best interest to get rid of guys like that, but why hide what this place really is: a bunch of lunatic leftists," said Matthew Schuldt, senior vice chairman of College Republicans.

The undercurrent of the debate, faculty members and students say, is anxiety about how the outside world regards the university. A football recruiting scandal and several alcohol-related deaths among students over the last year created waves of bad publicity for the institution. Now some people fear that everyone will think the university is full of people like Professor Churchill, whose essay, which drew little attention at its publication after the attacks, gained notoriety when he was scheduled to speak at Hamilton College in upstate New York last week. It suggests little emotion about the deaths of thousands of people on Sept. 11 and a cold logic of foreign policy analysis salted with terms that seemed calculated to enrage rather than enlighten.

"If he had just been a little more thoughtful, nothing would have happened," Uriel Nauenberg, a professor of physics and the former chairman of the Boulder Faculty Assembly, said. "He did not have to say these things in the manner that he did."

10   Nonetheless, Professor Nauenberg said he did not believe that Professor Churchill should be forced out because of the essay, though he added that he personally found the expressions in the essay obnoxious.

Professor Churchill, 57, a Vietnam War veteran who became a lecturer at the university in 1978 and was granted tenure in 1991, has claimed affiliations over the years with many vociferous left-wing groups, including the Black Panthers, Students for a Democratic Society and the American Indian Movement. He said in an interview that winning people's attention often meant not being nice. The United States' foreign and domestic policies, he said, are brutal, and the words to describe that can be painful.

"I don't believe in the theory that we get to treat people like dogs, but you have to talk to us in a polite way," he said.

Faculty members say that an objection to his writing style or opinions, however outrageous or unpopular, is not enough to justify firing him. The 30-day review of his "writings, speeches, tape recordings and other works," that was announced last week by the university's governing body, the Board of Regents, must find evidence of outright academic dishonesty, said R.L. Widmann, a professor of English and the chairwoman of the Academic Affairs Committee of the Boulder Faculty Assembly.

"'I published a falsehood and I knew it to be untrue'—that's what they'd have to find," Professor Widmann said.

But the passions have led to some dishonesty. University officials said on Monday, for instance, that they were canceling a speech by Professor Churchill because of security concerns. The student organizers of the speech had received death threats because of their support for the professor, university officials said, and safety could not be guaranteed.   15

The students, whose names were not released, admitted on Tuesday that the death threats were embellished.

"They said, 'We were just being political,'" Ron Stump, the vice chancellor for student affairs, said. "We expressed our disappointment."

The speech came off without incident—and without any apologies from Professor Churchill.

Many students interviewed on campus in recent days said they feared that the lines being drawn around Professor Churchill were also creating boundaries about what could be freely and safely talked about in the United States.

"I think it's no longer about free speech—it's turned into this kind of thing that we can't   20
talk about Sept 11, that it's kind of become a sacred issue," said Erin Langer, 22, a senior humanities major from Naperville, Ill. "People forget we're in a university setting, and the way ideas are challenged is by looking at an extreme view. The fact that he is so extreme challenges people to think more."

John C. Ensslin

Free Speech Can Cost Profs; Outspoken Faculty Have Paid Price in Loss of Jobs, Tenure

Rocky Mountain News, February 12, 2005

The Holocaust. Blacks. Jews. Profanity. Grades. Premarital sex.

All are topics that have landed outspoken professors at public universities in hot water.

The controversy over University of Colorado professor Ward Churchill's views of the Sept. 11 terrorist attacks is hardly the first time a faculty member's words have sparked a rancorous debate over tenure and academic freedom.

The American Association of University Professors has tracked a long history of such cases.

5 Some resulted in a professor being dismissed or let go at the end of a contract. These often end up in litigation.

"It's only in the last few decades that faculty members have been turning more and more to the courts," said Jonathan Knight, who chairs the AAUP's program on academic freedom and tenure.

There's no pattern to the cases or their outcomes, he said. And a review of court rulings in such disputes reveals mixed results.

For example, in 2000, one panel of judges in the 10th Circuit Court of Appeals upheld the dismissal of a New Mexico Highlands University professor after she advocated a no-confidence vote against four state regents.

Yet a different 10th Circuit panel ruled in 1996 that an Eastern Wyoming College professor had the right to urge a no-confidence vote against the college president.

10 The controversy over Churchill's remarks is one of several that have occurred since the Sept. 11 attacks.

"In the aftermath of 9/11, there have been a number of professors who said things that subjected them to intense pressure," Knight said. "But the institutions stood firm."

Some university administrators criticized what these faculty members said, but took no action against them.

For example, an assistant professor at Columbia University came under fire when at an anti-war teach-in he wished out loud for "a million Mogadishus," referring to the battle in Somalia in which 18 American soldiers were killed.

Columbia President Lee Bollinger posted a statement on the university's Web site, stating that he normally does not comment on faculty remarks because of academic freedom.

15 "However, this one crosses the line and I really feel the need to say something."

At City University of New York, professors Michael Levin and Leonard Jeffries both remain as tenured faculty after enduring two very different controversies.

In 1991, Levin wrote an essay in an Australian journal that stated: "The average black is significantly less intelligent than the average white."

The CUNY president started an investigation. Levin responded by filing suit. The courts agreed that Levin's First Amendment rights to free speech had been abridged.

"It's not the Middle Ages—you don't get burned at the stake," Levin said this week. "But if you're an academic, it's not that easy getting a job once you've been fired."

20 Jeffries had been chairman of the CUNY black studies department in 1991 when he gave a speech in Albany in which he made derogatory remarks about Jews. CUNY stripped him of his chairmanship, but not his job as professor.

Jeffries sued and initially won a $400,000 judgment, but it was later overturned.

Some academic controversies seem dated today.

For example, in March 1960, a biology professor at the University of Illinois at Urbana wrote a letter to the campus paper advocating for premarital sex.

"A mutually satisfactory sexual experience would eliminate the need for many hours of frustrating petting and lead to much happier and longer lasting marriages," Leo Koch wrote.

25 The university let him go at the end of his contract that year. Despite protests by other faculty, Koch never got his job back, Knight said.

Jim Spencer

Whom Does Churchill Work For?

Denver Post, February 11, 2005

The final exam in Witch Hunt 101 at the University of Colorado boils down to a single essay question:

Whom does Ward Churchill work for?

Churchill made his position clear in a campus speech to 1,000 mostly adoring students Tuesday night.

Speaking with what my friend Ray Schoch of Loveland likes to call a "junior high sneer," Churchill proclaimed to his faithful, "I do not work for the taxpayers of Colorado. I do not work for Bill Owens. I work for you."

Later in the evening, when a student asked Churchill if he would abide by results of   5
a student vote on his continued employment, he wouldn't agree.

Apparently, he works for CU students only in a metaphorical sense.

That's the way he says he referred to some civilian victims of the Sept. 11 terrorist attacks as "little Eichmanns" in an essay that has him in hot water.

Churchill continues to milk his newfound celebrity. On Tuesday, bodyguards from the American Indian Movement of Colorado escorted him. As Churchill spoke, a Native American whomped a drum to punctuate the professor's points.

The atmosphere evoked death threats and rim shots—Malcolm X meets Henny Youngman.

Still, Churchill was right about the taxpayers, Gov. Bill Owens and the CU Board of Regents,   10
to whom Churchill claimed not to answer, "at least not in the sense that they think I do."

State budget cuts to higher education have left a shell of a public university system. CU gets only 7 percent of its budget from state tax funds.

Also, Owens didn't hire Churchill. He can't fire him. As he calls for Churchill's job and tries to end tenure for college faculty, the governor looks like the kind of demagogue he and the regents enabled Churchill to become.

As for the regents, their job is not to micro-manage individual teachers, even controversial ones like Churchill. Unless, of course, they want to lose better and brighter professors who will flee their special brand of McCarthyism.

But that still doesn't answer the exam question faced by CU administrators as they conduct their 30-day witch hunt of Churchill's writings and background.

The inquisitors should remember a couple of things: 15

First, they can't fire Churchill for their own mistakes. Only 5 percent of CU's professors receive tenure without a terminal degree. Churchill is among them.

In 1991, CU officials granted Churchill an appointment as a tenured professor in communications with nothing more than a master's. In 1997, CU transferred that tenure to ethnic studies.

University officials judged Churchill's scholarship competent then. They also ignored his 9/11 essay for three years, until politicians started meddling.

Second, Churchill's claim to Indian blood may be tenuous, but as Indian activist Russell Means said: With or without Native American blood, "we have ascertained that Ward Churchill is a full-blooded Indian leader."

20 Some of the rest of us have ascertained that he is also a hypocrite.

That's not a firing offense. It's not a cause for censure or even investigation. It is merely a reality check about who subsidizes Churchill's radical beliefs.

CU officials say roughly 15 percent of Churchill's $92,000-a-year salary—$13,800 comes from state tax dollars. The remaining 85 percent—$78,200—comes from tuition. But about 74 percent of that tuition—$57,868—comes from out-of-state students, CU says.

Ward Churchill gets paid plenty by the rich parents of kids from the country's major metropolitan areas who can afford CU's hefty nonresident bills.

He owes his professional existence to the very "technicians of empire" he likened to "little Eichmanns."

25 So when Churchill contends—as he did Tuesday night—that he does not work for Bill Owens or the CU regents, he's telling the truth.

Just not the whole truth.

The system he so despises has not kept him down. It has propped him up.

Dave Curtin and Howard Pankratz

Governor Renews Call for CU Regents to Dismiss Churchill

Denver Post, February 10, 2005

Gov. Bill Owens on Wednesday renewed his call that University of Colorado professor Ward Churchill be fired, arguing that Churchill doesn't deserve to teach at the university. Churchill also managed to irritate at least two members of the Board of Regents, who are reviewing whether he should keep his job, when he spoke Tuesday night in Boulder.

Churchill implored the board Tuesday to "do its job, and I'll do mine."

The regents voted last week to authorize a 30-day investigation of Churchill's writings and speeches to determine whether they are cause for dismissal.

"I believe we are doing our job. And part of our job is to protect free-speech rights," said Regent Michael Carrigan. Carrigan said he didn't attend the speech but heard excerpts.

5 "I disagree with the content, but I support his right to say it," Carrigan said. "It speaks volumes that the University of Colorado is a place for open discourse and debate as we saw Tuesday, and the Glenn Miller Ballroom should not only be available to those who the governor approves."

Churchill, who was met with sustained applause from hundreds of supporters Tuesday night, noted that he works for the students, not the governor.

"Bill Owens, do you get it now?" Churchill asked as he was given a standing ovation.

Owens said Wednesday that he will stay out of the regents' review but warned what could happen if they keep Churchill.

"I think if the university should choose to take no action and basically accede to the view that anything a professor wants to say at any time is allowable, I think there will be ramifications from alums, donors and those from the community at large," he said.

10 He said there are grounds spelled out by CU for termination that include professional incompetence, neglect of duty and insubordination.

"I think there are a number of things that call into question his competence and his integrity," Owens said. "I think competence and integrity can be shown in what he said about Sept. 11. . . . I believe it is not incumbent upon the University of Colorado to subsidize someone who calls for more 9/11s."

Churchill infuriated families of World Trade Center victims when his essay comparing them to Nazi Adolf Eichmann came to light. He later clarified his comments, saying the term "little Eichmanns" he used to describe the victims didn't include food-service workers, janitors, children, firefighters or passers-by.

Churchill, in comments in April in *Satya* magazine, called for the United States to be put "out of existence" and said more "9/11s are necessary."

Regent Peter Steinhauer said the regents are rigorously adhering to protocol in their review.

"We're following the procedures to the nth degree even though so many want him removed immediately and others want him exonerated," Steinhauer said. Steinhauer hotly disputed Churchill's claim that he works for the students but not for CU.   15

"He works for the university because we pay his check," Steinhauer said. "He gets a check that's signed by the president and the secretary of the university."

Reggie Rivers

Can't Governor Be Offensive, Too?

Denver Post, February 11, 2005

For anyone who truly believes in the First Amendment's guarantee of freedom of speech, it's difficult to urge severe penalties against University of Colorado professor Ward Churchill just because his words are provocative.

There are many debates about whether the freedom of speech should extend to movies, paintings, novels, profanity, pornography, etc., but I've never heard any First Amendment defender argue that dissenting political speech should not be protected.

We may disagree with Churchill's words, but they are profoundly political. That means they represent exactly the type of speech that was supposed to be protected by the First Amendment.

In a letter to college Republicans at CU, Gov. Bill Owens wrote, "No one wants to infringe on Mr. Churchill's right to express himself. But we are not compelled to accept his pro-terrorist views at state taxpayer subsidy nor under the banner of the University of Colorado."

This week, the governor said, "We've always said that the First Amendment is not absolute. You don't have the right to shout 'Fire!' in a crowded theater."   5

But what if there is a fire? Can you shout then?

In the world of political speech, people often have to shout to be heard when they believe there's a fire. If you're the president, a governor, a mayor or someone else in a position of power, you have no trouble expressing yourself. Your position does the shouting for you. But if you're a regular citizen, you might have to stake out an outrageous position to get people to notice your message.

Would we be talking about Churchill if he had made the same arguments about U.S. foreign policy in innocuous terms? No. In fact, it took 3½ years for anyone to notice that he was shouting. The only way he could expose people to his core argument was to wrap it in inflammatory and outrageous statements.

But the governor and countless others continue to profess their commitment to the First Amendment, while taking the position that the taxpayers should not have to underwrite the salary of someone who says offensive things. Four House Republicans have suggested that if the regents don't fire Churchill, they'll try to strike $100,000 from CU's funding so that taxpayers would no longer be paying Churchill's salary.

10 This line of argument is especially ironic given that the governor and the legislators are subsidized by taxpayers, and they themselves often make highly offensive statements.

Imagine how odd it would sound if Colorado Democrats argued that it was not appropriate for Owens to be offensive while earning a taxpayer salary. Or if a Democrat introduced a bill that would remove the exact amount of Owens' salary from the state budget.

Owens wants to carve out an exception for Churchill because the professor is advocating murder against Americans. But in the eyes of their opponents, politicians, judges, police chiefs, district attorneys, professors and others on the public dole advocate murder every time they take a position on abortion, the death penalty, police shootings, assisted suicide, war and other life-and-death issues.

Supporters of the war in Iraq often proclaim that freedom isn't free, and they're right. This is the price. We must defend the rights of people who make offensive statements if we want to protect our freedom to speak.

The craziest part of this whole controversy is that if we, God forbid, suffer another terrorist attack, a lot of Americans will blame Churchill for his advocacy rather than President Bush for his policies.

David Harsanyi

CU Hiding behind Tenure

Denver Post, February 1, 2005

If you're unfamiliar with Ward Churchill, consider yourself lucky.

He's a professional revolutionary and America-hating activist who, when not agitating, chairs the Ethnic Studies Department at University of Colorado at Boulder.

While Churchill has made a career of trying to deny Denverites their First Amendment rights, last week we found out that it wasn't personal, just a widespread contempt for freedom.

You should understand, when I say "America-hating," I don't mean to suggest it in a flippant, love-it-or-leave-it, knee-jerk, right-wing sort of way.

5 I think it's fair to state that a majority of reasonable Americans find Churchill's contention—that the Sept. 11, 2001, terrorist attacks were justified and the victims weren't innocent but rather Nazis—reprehensible.

At least, I hope so.

His right to make these vile remarks—masked in the guise of intellectual discourse—are guaranteed.

No one wants to take that away.

The problem is, as with all tenured professors, Churchill doesn't have to answer for his actions.

10 That brings us to a delicate matter: How do we balance the need to protect diversity and academic freedom with the need to protect impressionable students from hate-filled ideologues?

"Call me an old-fashioned guy," U.S. Rep. Bob Beauprez says. "But I was raised by an old-fashioned guy who didn't mind calling right right and wrong wrong. This guy (Churchill) was clearly way out of line, way out of touch."

If we all, or most of us, agree that wrong is wrong in this case, what are our options?

"I will defend his right to free speech," Beauprez says of Churchill. "But speech has consequences. This guy is just leveraging political correctness against academic freedom for his own betterment. Most people, if they go overboard in this way, would not have kept their jobs."

What would my career prospects be if I suggested a group of murdered civilians, "little Eichmanns," deserved to be slaughtered? I'm fairly certain my next public statement would be: "Would you like fries with that?"

Churchill, on the other hand, is teaching your kids.   15

Fortunately, I have the perfect karmic solution: the market—a concept Churchill detests more than any other.

Wouldn't it be heartening to see all the little Eichmanns who scraped and saved to send Johnny and Alice to CU start calling, sending letters and applying some concentrated pressure.

Sure, guys such as Churchill hover cheerfully above the result-based reality that gives parents and students little precious extra time for activism. But Beauprez believes it's the right way to go.

"Parents and students can put enough public pressure on this guy. Most people, after a certain amount of pressure, get the message," he says.

Churchill won't. But others might.   20

CU president Betsy Hoffman? She saw fit to suspend football coach Gary Barnett for disparaging remarks about the kicking abilities of a female player.

Does accusing Sept. 11 victims of being Nazi technocrats qualify for some similar punishment?

How about Phil DiStefano, CU's interim chancellor? Though he "may find Churchill's views offensive," he "also must support" his right "to hold and express his views."

Are you as tired as I am of these spineless, cookie-cutter statements? We all know Churchill has a right to free speech. What rights do students, parents or CU have? Any?

Maybe one day we'll see a release with some backbone. If I may: 25

"Though Ward Churchill has the right as an American citizen to express himself, even in a morally indigestible and intellectually vacant manner, his comments have embarrassed CU and are out of touch with even the most liberal definition of mainstream thought.

"Consequently, we ask that Mr. Churchill do the honorable thing and step down."

The Freedom to Discuss; Americans Can Question Ideas, but the Right to Debate Them Should Always Be Protected

The Buffalo News, February 7, 2005

At Harvard, the university president is under attack for something he said about women.

At Hamilton College, near Utica, the school's administration is under attack for inviting to a panel discussion a controversial speaker who has said some outrageous things about the Sept. 11 terror attacks.

At Canisius College, right here in Buffalo, Hillary Clinton is under attack for what she has said about abortion.

The three controversies intersect on the sacred American ground of free speech. If colleges and universities cannot be havens for the exchange of ideas, then we have a problem.

5   Summers, Harvard's foot-in-mouth president, kicked off the series of squabbles by suggesting that perhaps the reason few women go into science and engineering was because they don't have the aptitude for it that men do. The ensuing uproar was both predictable and unfortunate.

It was predictable because Summers entered sensitive territory in about as clumsy a way as possible. It was unfortunate because no one disputes that men and women process information in different ways. That's not an issue of equality but of biology. Could that be one of the reasons that more men than woman gravitate to science and engineering?

It may not be the case, because many other variables come into play, but it's at least worth wondering about. At Harvard, unfortunately, they're more interested in preserving the myth that being equal means being identical. Between Summers' ham-fisted theorizing and his critics' dogmatic inflexibility, we'll be lucky ever to explore how the differences in our hard-wiring influence our lives.

Closer to home, Hamilton College invited Indian activist Ward Churchill to sit on a panel discussion. Churchill is a controversial professor who has infamously compared the victims of 9/11 to Nazis and said they deserved to die. Again, the outcry was instantaneous and understandable. One might wonder why college officials invited such a fringe figure to speak. Freedom of the press does not require a newspaper to publish pornography, after all. A right is not a compulsion.

Then again, the topic of the discussion was "The Limits of Dissent," a subject about which Churchill probably had some hard-earned ideas. And if he is nothing more than an obnoxious kook, it's better to know what your kooks are thinking than not. Churchill's appearance was eventually canceled. Reason: death threats against the speaker and college officials. So much for debate.

10   Here in Buffalo, pro-life activists were incensed that Clinton, who is pro-choice, would be invited to speak at a Catholic college. The subject was the college's "Corporal Works of Mercy" lecture series on government's role in caring for the sick, a topic that, like abortion, is intimately linked to Catholic teaching about life.

But the senator was not coming to talk about abortion and, as college Vice President John Hurley wisely observed, "We don't think that having Sen. Clinton here constitutes an endorsement of every position she holds . . . or will hold in the future." If only the protesters had such common sense.

Abortion is a divisive issue, but if either side is going to refuse to hear from the other—on any matter at all—then democratic government cannot work.

Critics can, and should, challenge the Harvard president's ideas about gender, the professor's hallucinations about terrorism and the senator's support for abortion rights. But we should all worry when the effort is not to open up the debate, but to shut down the discussion.

We ought to be about something better than that.

Writing Prompts

1. Imagine you are a student at the University of Colorado at Boulder. Write a letter to the editor of the school paper arguing for or against Ward Churchill's right to say what he did.
2. In a three-page essay, using Churchill's essay for supporting quotations, discuss the language and tone of his essay and explore why you think so many people find his writing offensive.
3. Write a three-page essay where you define what you feel are the appropriate standards of and limitations to free speech. On your own terms and based on your own beliefs and values, define free speech for the rest of us.
4. Choose two essays that disagree about what should happen to Churchill. Summarize for your reader the thesis of each, and then draw your own conclusions.
5. Can you think of a time you voiced your opinions and it got you into a conflict? Do you have opinions you feel would not be welcome if you freely stated them? What are those opinions you feel you cannot express, and why do you think others are not open to them?

What Is at Stake for Citizenship?

1. Are there certain times in history when freedom of speech is not the most important thing to protect?
2. If almost everyone agrees that Ward Churchill has the freedom to speak his mind, why is everyone so upset that he spoke his mind?
3. Does free speech work better as an ideal than a fact? Should we all have the right to say and write what we feel without losing our jobs? Or is that too high a standard to keep?
4. How would you define treason? Is Churchill's essay treason? If so, what should be done about it?
5. Do citizens of the United States have an obligation to be loyal? Would you say that Ward Churchill is a good American?

A NEW RULE OF LAW: THE PATRIOT ACT

The major piece of legislation that came out of the terrorist attacks of 9/11 is the USA Patriot Act, which was intended to make it easier for government and law enforcement agencies to investigate possible terrorists, to cooperate and share information with each other, and to expand the ways information is gathered. "USA Patriot" is an acronym for "Uniting and Strengthening America by Providing Appropriate Tools to Intercept and Obstruct Terrorism." The act also allowed the government to detain noncitizens for unlimited amounts of time and keep legal proceedings relating to terror investigations secret. The USA Patriot Act was passed with very little opposition in either the House or the Senate, so strong was the desire among lawmakers to do something that would keep us from experiencing another attack like that of 9/11.

Almost immediately after the 9/11 attacks, when we were all casting about for something concrete to do in response to this horrible event, the question was asked: Would you give up some of your rights and freedom to get more safety? "Of course!" was the answer of many Americans. "We will do whatever needs to be done. We're innocent, so we don't need to worry about the subtleties of the law. People made sacrifices in World War II, so we can make sacrifices in the war against terror. We will go through more security at the airport, if it keeps hijackers with box cutters off the planes. We will park farther away from important buildings, if that helps keep a car bomb from destroying the building. We will do whatever it takes to keep America safe."

The question is where do these sacrifices end? Where do they stop being sacrifices and start being a loss of civil rights? People have differing opinions, as you will see in the essays that follow. Is the Patriot Act keeping us safe or allowing our own government to spy on us? As you read these varying responses to the Patriot Act, consider how you might respond if asked for your opinion about the balance between safety and civil rights.

Phillip Swann

Is Your Television Watching You?

Television Week, March 3, 2003

Could the federal government find out what you're watching on TV? Even if you're not the subject of a criminal investigation?

If you're a satellite TV or TiVo owner, the answer is yes, according to legal experts and industry officials.

Under the USA Patriot Act, passed a month after the 9/11 terrorist attack, the feds can force a non-cable TV operator to disclose every show you have watched. The government just has to say that the request is related to a terrorism investigation, said Jay Stanley, a technology expert for the American Civil Liberties Union.

Under Section 215 of the Act, you don't even have to be the target of the investigation. Plus, your TV provider is prohibited from informing you that the feds have requested your personal information.

5 "The language is very broad," Mr. Stanley said. "It allows the FBI to force a company to turn over the records of their customers. They don't even need a reasonable suspicion of criminal behavior."

David Sobel, general counsel for the Electronic Privacy Information Center, a Washington think tank, said the Cable Act of 1984 gives cable operators greater protection against the Patriot Act. Cable companies do not have to release an individual's records unless the feds show that the person is the target of a criminal investigation. Even then, the individual must be notified of the request, which he can then challenge in court.

"The Patriot Act does not override the Cable Act," Mr. Sobel said.

You couldn't blame the satellite TV industry for feeling a little vulnerable these days. DirecTV, for instance, collects a large amount of individual data, such as program package orders, pay-per-view orders and even online purchases via the DirecTV-Link interactive shopping service. The Justice Department could ask DirecTV to disclose whether you sub-scribe to *Playboy* or purchased Viagra if it would help an investigation.

But Andy Wright, president of the Satellite Broadcasting Communications Association, the industry's trade group, said he does not believe the feds will make frivolous requests.

"They still have to issue a subpoena to get the data," he said. "Even in today's envi-   10
ronment, I can't imagine a judge would approve a subpoena that is not warranted."

However, the ACLU's Mr. Stanley said the Patriot Act is different because the govern-ment can get the order from the special Foreign Intelligence Surveillance Act court rather than a judicial court.

"It's not like a subpoena. The standards are much weaker than [in] a criminal case," Mr. Stanley said.

But Mr. Wright contended that satellite TV viewers should not be concerned that they will be subjected to improper searches. The satellite chief added he's not sure the federal government needs to give dish owners the same protection as cable viewers.

"I would have to study that more before supporting that," Mr. Wright said.

Anxious Times

The Patriot Act, which Attorney General John Ashcroft said is crucial to fighting   15
terrorism in the United States, has scared many civil libertarians. However, the possibility that the feds could use the law to learn about your viewing habits has been overlooked until now.

The invasion of privacy might be well intentioned and perhaps even necessary. How-ever, there's also the danger that an overzealous team of agents will abuse the law. In the spirit of the early patriots, all Americans need to remain vigilant.

John Jerney

Is Big Brother Watching You While You Surf?

The *Daily Yomiuri* (Tokyo), January 25, 2005

We tend to think that our Web browsing is mostly anonymous and private, but just how much of our online activity is being monitored by the U.S. government? And under what circumstances?

It turns out that it is impossible to tell, not because it is technically too difficult to determine but because the government refuses to tell us.

Concerned about this potential loss of civil liberties, the Electronic Frontier Foundation (EFF) recently filed a Freedom of Information Act request with various agencies in the Jus-tice Department, including the Federal Bureau of Investigation, to try to shed some light on the subject.

The goal is to get access to documents to determine whether the government has been using the Patriot Act to monitor online reading activities of users without their knowl-edge or consent, and without a search warrant.

The Patriot Act, as you might recall, was passed quickly and without much public   5
discussion shortly after Sept. 11, 2001. The act expanded several key powers of the gov-ernment, enabling it to cast a wider net in both physical and electronic surveillance.

The specific area of concern in this case is Section 216, which enables the government to perform surveillance in criminal investigations using pen registers or trap and trace devices, more commonly referred to as pen-traps.

Pen-traps record the numbers you dial on a telephone, but do not capture the resulting phone conversations. In the context of the Internet, the Patriot Act enables authorities to use pen-traps to gather e-mail addresses as well as the IP addresses of communicating systems. In fact, the U.S. Justice Department has publicly stated that these activities are within their interpretation of the Patriot Act.

What remains unclear, however, is how the Justice Department treats Web URLs.

At first glance, URLs, or Uniform Resource Locators, clearly represent addresses of Web sites. The issue quickly becomes cloudy, though, when you consider that URLs often also contain references to specific content on the Web.

10   For example, an address such as www.motherjones.com/what could go wrong.html by itself gives some indication of the type of content, especially since *Mother Jones* is a political publication. Even the high-level address www.motherjones.com conveys general information about the type of information the reader is about to consume.

Privacy advocates therefore argue that by recording URLs, authorities gain access not only to contact information, but also to varying degrees of the content of the communication. The question they ask is whether we want to give government the unstated authority to collect this type of information without reader consent.

In submitting the Freedom of Information Act request, the EFF is trying to determine whether the U.S. Department of Justice has been using pen-traps to monitor Web browsing activities, and if so, to what extent.

Specifically, the EFF is requesting access to all records (including blank forms) prepared or collected by the Justice Department, the FBI, and Attorney's Office regarding the use of pen-trap devices to monitor electronic communications or Internet-based wire communications (i.e. Voice-over-Internet-Protocol communications).

The idea is to use the acquired information, if and when it is released, to determine exactly where the Department of Justice draws the line between address information and content. The request also seeks all policy directives and guidance issued to government employees to monitor electronic communication.

15   The request further seeks to gather documents related to all cases of over-collection, where agencies acknowledge that content was captured in addition to address details using pen-trap devices. Any documents that describe how this information was used are also being sought.

The EFF, in making the Freedom of Information Act request, is seeking primarily to create greater transparency in how the government exercises its considerable powers when related to privacy and the Fourth Amendment, which protects against unreasonable search and seizure.

The issue is all the more important because pen traps are comparatively easy for authorities to acquire since they only need to certify relevance to an investigation, not demonstrate probable cause. This places a much lower burden on the government, opening the potential for abuse without proper oversight.

Governments and law enforcement agencies need the ability to be able to conduct criminal investigations. However, the standards and procedures for conducting these investigations must be transparent, documented, interpreted, publicly accepted and completed with oversight and protection for civil liberties.

These conditions are no less relevant in the world of the Internet and World Wide Web. People have a reasonable expectation of privacy when surfing the Web. As the request explains, the Justice Department "has refused to answer the public's very simple question: 'Can the government see what I'm reading on the Web without having to show probable cause?'"

This question is all the more relevant today as key provisions of the Patriot Act are being considered for extension.   20

The EFF's Freedom of Information Act request states: "The refusal of the Department of Justice to publicly state its interpretation of Patriot Act provisions regarding electronic surveillance has left the public crucially uninformed about how the executive branch is using the expanded surveillance authority granted by Congress in the wake of 9/11."

The issue of Web URLs may seem like a comparatively trivial matter in the overall struggle between government powers and the preservation of privacy and civil liberties. But simple manifestations are often at the heart of greater issues, in this case whether the government should be allowed to refuse to state the basis on which it conducts criminal and noncriminal investigations.

The government is required to respond to the Freedom of Information Act request within 20 business days. The EFF has already stated that litigation is an option should the Department of Justice fail to respond.

As the Patriot Act comes under new scrutiny following its first three years, the government's actions will be closely watched.

Salim Muwakkil

Forgotten Freedoms

In These Times, January 7, 2002

Protest against the USA Patriot Act.

Citizens of the United States, be advised that the federal government can now examine your medical, educational and financial history, all without your knowledge and without even presenting evidence of a crime.

Police now can obtain court orders to conduct so-called sneak-and-peak searches of your homes and offices and remove or alter your possessions without your knowledge. Internet service providers and telephone companies can be compelled to turn over your customer information, including the phone numbers you've called and Internet sites you've surfed—all, again, without a court order, if the FBI claims the records are relevant to a "terrorism investigation." A secret court can permit roving wiretaps of any telephone or computer you might possibly use; reading your e-mail is allowed, even before you open it.

These are just some of the provisions of the USA PATRIOT Act of 2001—the bill's title is an acronym for "Uniting and Strengthening America by Providing Appropriate Tools Required to Intercept and Obstruct Terrorism"—which President George W. Bush signed into law on October 26. In passing the legislation, Senate Majority Leader Thomas Daschle said Congress was "able to find what I think is the appropriate balance between protecting civil liberties, privacy, and ensuring that law enforcement has the tools to do what it must."

The fears provoked by the kamikaze hijackings and the anthrax incidents that followed explain why many legislators have been less protective of civil liberties. Those progressive legislators who supported the legislation said the unique and deadly circumstances of the 9/11 attacks already had predisposed them to support strong action, and many noted that a sunset provision would allow the bill's most controversial surveillance sections to expire in 2005. But the Bill of Rights was designed to offer a judicial sanctuary from political passions. If progressive legislators don't make that clear, who will?

5   The events of 9/11 make it plain that the United States has enemies willing to die for their cause, and it would be impractical, even foolish, to deny the need for increased national vigilance. Ratcheting up our security is necessary, if only to enhance citizens' sense of well-being. And, according to a *Newsweek* poll reported in the publication's December 10 edition, "86 percent think the administration has not gone too far in restricting civil liberties in its response to terrorism."

The import of the USA PATRIOT Act was presaged by the Clinton administration's anti-terrorism bill of 1996, which broadened the government's investigative and prosecutorial powers. And even before that, the Foreign Intelligence Surveillance Act of 1978 allowed the wiretapping of non-citizens by approval of a secret court with secret evidence. But this new legislation ups the ante considerably. "This new legislation goes far beyond any powers conceivably necessary to fight terrorism in the United States," says Laura Murphy of the American Civil Liberties Union. "The long-term impact on basic freedoms in this legislation cannot be justified."

Leading the charge in the wake of 9/11 is Attorney General John Ashcroft, who, for starters, launched a nationwide dragnet that rounded up more than 1,000 foreign nationals and detained most of them on minor immigration charges. Many have since been released after officials found they had no connection to terrorism. As of December 6, 603 foreign nationals remain in custody. On Halloween, Ashcroft issued an order allowing federal authorities to monitor communications between federal prisoners and their lawyers without first obtaining a judicial warrant. He argued that this new power is necessary to prevent terrorist attacks planned under cover of lawyer-client privilege.

The administration's power grab is so audacious that it has prompted a new alliance between the civil-liberties left and the libertarian right. *New York Times* columnist William Safire characterized Bush's strategy as "a sudden seizure of power by the executive branch, bypassing all constitutional checks and balances." The ACLU, joined by 16 other civil rights and human rights groups, filed suit on December 5, charging the Justice Department with violating the Constitution and federal law through its detention policies.

Mining public fears for all the right-wing treasures he can get, Ashcroft also has proposed relaxing restrictions on the FBI's spying on religious and political organizations. The guidelines Ashcroft has targeted were imposed on the FBI in the '70s after the death of J. Edgar Hoover and revelations about the COINTELPRO program—which included disclosures of the agency's surveillance and harassment of Martin Luther King Jr. In Chicago, activists recently commemorated another poignant signpost of COINTELPRO infamy: the police assassination of Black Panther leaders Fred Hampton and Mark Clark on December 4, 1969. COINTELPRO ultimately was condemned as "little more than a sophisticated vigilante action" by the Congress and shut down.

But under Section 802 of the USA PATRIOT Act, a person commits the crime of "domestic terrorism" if he engages in activity "that involves acts dangerous to human life that violate the laws of the U.S. or any state and appear to be intended: to intimidate or coerce a civilian population; to influence the policy of a government by intimidation or coercion; or to affect the conduct of a government by mass destruction, assassination or kidnapping." This definition of terrorism could allow the feds to go after environmental, civil rights or anti-globalization groups, among others, for their dissenting views or direct-action protests.

Right-wing extremism is always fertilized by external threats. At its most notorious extreme, Adolph Hitler's Nazi Party rose like a rocket after the 1933 Reichstag fire convinced the German people that the Bolsheviks were out to get them. At the Nuremberg Trials, Hitler's second-in-command, Hermann Goering, aptly explained the process: "The people can always be brought to do the bidding of the leaders. That is easy. All you have to do is tell them they are being attacked, and denounce the pacifists for lack of patriotism and exposing the country to danger."

This eerily familiar formula is so effective that it has become enshrined in U.S. traditions, even if it violates strictures of the Constitution. During times of war, the chief executive has implemented many extra-constitutional edicts: Abraham Lincoln unilaterally suspended *habeas corpus* during the Civil War; the infamous, anti-Communist Palmer Raids of 1920 arrested thousands of people without warrants or due process; Franklin D. Roosevelt ordered the internment of more than 100,000 Japanese-Americans in squalid camps. In retrospect, these excessive actions invariably have been condemned as historical blemishes.

But today's policy-makers seem oblivious to the lessons of history as they implement actions that echo—and amplify—those past excesses. Roosevelt also ordered a special military tribunal for eight accused Nazi spies, six of whom were later executed. The Supreme Court upheld Roosevelt's tribunal as it has most other questionable actions of wartime presidents. And the Bush administration has used the top court's 8-0 decision in 1942 as a precedent to bolster the president's own proposed military tribunals. Bush has assumed unchecked power as commander-in-chief to detain and try any non-citizen he suspects of committing terrorist acts or helping international terrorists. These suspects can be secretly arrested, tried, convicted and executed even if prosecutors failed to prove their case beyond a reasonable doubt.

Like the Bush administration's war, the future of our civil liberties is fuzzy and indeterminate. Since this is a war on the tactic of "terrorism" rather than on a tangible enemy, there is no entity to offer a formal surrender. The "war"—and the concomitant wartime powers and prerogatives—can be extended indefinitely; only the Bush administration has the power to declare the war's end.

Soon after 9/11, Bush said the people who perpetuated the terrorist murders hate America because of "our freedoms." After a few more executive orders and congressional capitulations, they won't have much left to hate.

Kate O'Beirne

Congress's Patriotic Act: This Is a Law That Defends America and, Yes, Preserves Civil Liberties, Dammit

National Review, September 15, 2003

Sign announcing an "elevated" threat level.

Who says you can't argue with success? In the past two years, terrorist cells in Buffalo, Detroit, Seattle, and Portland, Ore., have been dismantled; criminal charges have been brought against 225 suspected terrorists; and 132 of those suspects have been convicted. Terrorists haven't carried out another attack here because the domestic war on terrorism, aimed at prevention, has worked. Yet in July, 113 Republicans voted with a large House majority against a provision in the USA Patriot Act that federal officials see as playing a crucial role in disrupting terrorist plots. Lawmakers' ignorance of the law, the ACLU's effective disinformation campaign, a hostile media, and hysterical, partisan attacks from the presidential campaign trail now have the administration playing defense, despite its remarkablysuccessful offense against terrorism.

Prompted by the recent vote, Attorney General John Ashcroft has embarked on a tour of 18 cities to make the case for the Patriot Act to the public. Ashcroft reminds his audiences that the law, passed in the Senate by a 98-to-1 vote (and in the House by 357 to 66) six weeks after the September 11 attacks, updated the ability of federal law enforcement to confront the threat of terrorism in three central ways. It removed the legal barriers that prevented law-enforcement and intelligence agencies from sharing information and coordinating activities—barriers that Congress criticized in its report on what went wrong before 9/11. It brought surveillance laws from the era of the rotary phone into the age of cell phones and Internet communications. And it extended the authority that federal investigators use against the mafia and drug dealers to cover terrorists.

Where Congress overwhelmingly saw commonsense provisions clearly justified to protect American lives, hysterical critics are seeing a power grab by a would-be totalitarian state. According to a *Los Angeles Times* story, the Patriot Act amounts to "the legislative equivalent of a blank check." *The Cleveland Plain Dealer* spots the "seedstock of a police state." In an alarming *Newsday* op-ed, Sam Dash, the former chief counsel to the Senate Watergate Committee, warns of a presidential abuse of power that rivals the "horror" committed by Richard Nixon. Dash is now a law professor at Georgetown—but, like most of the Patriot Act alarmists, he doesn't cite a single provision of the objectionable law to bolster his case.

Democratic presidential candidates are no more specific. In his "first five seconds as president," Dick Gephardt would fire Ashcroft. Sen. Edwards gets standing ovations for declaring, "We cannot allow people like John Ashcroft to take away our rights and our freedoms." John Kerry vows that when he's president, "there will be no John Ashcroft trampling on the Bill of Rights." Each one of them voted for the Patriot Act; but Howard Dean, a former governor, routinely assails the law itself for eroding "the rights of average Americans," and calls for its repeal.

Even when the media criticize a specific part of the new law, they usually get it wrong. In May, a major *Time* magazine story was subtitled, "Can Attorney General John Ashcroft fight terrorism on our shores without injuring our freedoms?" The demonstrable answer is yes. But the article was riddled with mistakes that led to a different conclusion. For example, the authors asserted, "If you are suspected of terrorist links, law enforcement can access your records, conduct wiretaps and electronic surveillance, search and seize private property and make secret arrests—all without a warrant." In fact, federal authorities can't do any of those things without obtaining a court order.

In July, when Reps. C. L. "Butch" Otter (R., Idaho) and Dennis Kucinich (D., Ohio) argued for their amendment to prohibit funding for delayed-notification warrants, the discussion on the House floor was equally ignorant. If lawmakers don't want to be bothered understanding the law, they could at least try watching *The Sopranos* to learn how federal investigators lawfully operate. Section 213, the Patriot Act provision that the Otter amendment would de-fund, allows federal investigators to ask a court for permission to temporarily delay notifying a suspect that a court-issued search warrant has been executed. Sens. Patrick Leahy (D., Vt.) and Orrin Hatch (R., Utah) sponsored the provision, which permits delayed notification when there is a risk of flight, injury to an individual, intimidation of witnesses, destruction of evidence, or the serious jeopardizing of an investigation. In 1979, the Supreme Court called an argument that the practice is unconstitutional "frivolous." Without the ability to postpone notice of a warrant, investigators would be unable to install a wiretap in a terrorist's apartment without first informing the suspect.

The Justice Department is required to provide Congress with details on the implementation of the Patriot Act twice a year. In a 60-page report this May, the department explained that in the past two years, delayed-notice warrants under Section 213 had been sought (and approved) by courts just 47 times. This wasn't mentioned during the House's hasty consideration of the Otter amendment. Instead, Rep. Otter ludicrously claimed that Section 213 permits the CIA to operate domestically. Rep. Kucinich ignored the federal courts that have upheld the constitutionality of delaying notification of a warrant, and rested his own constitutional objection on the "common law." The amendment has not yet passed the Senate, but the administration is threatening a veto if it does.

A Republican congressional aide explains that over 100 House Republicans were not so much relying on Dennis Kucinich's legal opinions as they were reflecting what they are hearing from their constituents back home. The aide reports that his office is receiving copies of news articles about the Patriot Act from Republican constituents concerned about the alleged assaults on civil liberties. Another GOP aide notes that constituents vehemently opposed to the war in Iraq also strenuously object to the Patriot Act; voting for the amendment "gives members some cover."

Former assistant attorney general Viet Dinh, who began crafting the Patriot Act within days of 9/11, has been publicly engaging its critics over their wildly exaggerated case. In a recent debate, when Dinh had successfully defended the act's provisions, his opponent finally allowed that the alarming problem "is not within the Patriot Act, but the milieu of fear you've created." That would be a small milieu. According to a recent poll, 91 percent of the public says that the Act hasn't affected their own civil liberties.

10   Critics of the Patriot Act would rather rely on hypothetical questions, such as that cited recently in USA Today. According to Gallup, only 33 percent of Americans favor the government's taking all steps necessary to prevent terrorism "even if it means that your basic civil liberties would be violated." The two-thirds that would oppose eroding civil liberties includes Attorney General John Ashcroft.

Reid J. Epstein

University Warns Students of Patriot Act Disclosures; Government Can Get Medical Records

Milwaukee Journal Sentinel, December 18, 2004

Whitewater—In an unusual disclosure, the University of Wisconsin-Whitewater's student health center is telling patients that, because of the USA Patriot Act, if government officials ask for their medical records, they'll get to see them, and the patients will never know.

While the move to include Patriot Act language in the privacy policy is similar to policies at other hospitals, invoking the 2001 anti-terrorism legislation as its reason is a new wrinkle, said an expert on information controls.

The provision, added this summer, is included in a dense seven-page policy the school's University Health and Counseling Services distributes to students to comply with the Health Insurance Privacy and Accountability Act, or HIPAA.

The new policy reads: "In accordance with the Patriot Act, we may disclose your health information to authorized federal officials who are conducting national security and intelligence activities or providing protective services to the president or other important officials. By law we cannot reveal when we have disclosed such information to the government."

5   Charles Davis, a journalism professor at the University of Missouri who has studied HIPAA and teaches a class on information controls, said he has read privacy statements from hospitals across the country and has never seen a specific reference to the Patriot Act.

"I honestly have never heard that one," he said. "I didn't know there was anything in the Patriot Act specifically pertaining to medical data."

Anuj Desai, a law professor at the University of Wisconsin-Madison, said the Patriot Act allows the government access to all sorts of records without the target's knowledge. Before the Patriot Act's passage, he said, government agents could use the courts to acquire medical records about someone deemed to be a danger.

"The government could always go to a court and get the court to approve a warrant," Desai said. "Warrants can be secret. Prior to the Patriot Act, the government could do this anyway if the records were about the object of the investigation."

He said it appears that the campus health center is trying to subtly express its opposition to the Patriot Act, which has been decried by some civil libertarians and librarians.

"We could have similar such warnings everywhere we walk," Desai said. "To their   10
credit, if everybody started doing this, people would probably be much more alarmed."

No Political Statement

The executive director of the Whitewater campus health center, John Macek, said he
has no professional opinion about the Patriot Act and that no one should read anything
political into the center's new privacy statement.

He said he also hasn't had any calls from government agents seeking information.

"If something is law, then we want to follow what the law is," Macek said. "I don't
worry the least about the Patriot Act. I do exciting things like gardening. I hardly worry about
any kind of investigation, period."

Students interviewed at UW-Whitewater, where the student newspaper, the *Royal
Purple*, first reported on the Patriot Act provision, said they were either unaware or uncon-
cerned about the possibility of federal agents poking around their medical records.

Matthew Bayley, a 22-year-old senior from Waterford, said he assumes the Patriot Act   15
allows the government to access any records it wants.

"If it applies at the university health center, it's going to be everywhere else, too,"
Bayley said. "They're just telling people about it."

U.S. Sen. Russ Feingold (D-Wis.), who in 2001 was the only senator to vote against
the Patriot Act, has said the law fails to properly balance terrorism and privacy concerns.

If Congress extends the Patriot Act, which expires at the end of 2006, it should "adopt
a reasonable modification to strengthen the role of the courts in approving requests for
access in foreign intelligence investigations, to library, medical, and other records containing sensitive, personal information," Feingold said in a prepared statement.

At Waukesha Memorial Hospital, the privacy policy dictates that administrators may
disclose medical records to the government without telling the patient for national security
and intelligence reasons, according to Lyn Lord, the privacy officer for ProHealth Care.

The ProHealth Care policy, Lord said, invokes a law older than the Patriot Act, the   20
National Security Act of 1947. She said she does not know of any instance of federal
agents asking for records.

"The government hasn't called yet," she said. "Let's hope that doesn't have to happen."

Charlie Brennan and Karen Abbott

Did Civil Liberties Fall with the Twin Towers? Ramifications of the Patriot Act Still Being Argued

Rocky Mountain News, September 11, 2004

The worst terrorist strike on American soil in the nation's history also triggered wide-
ranging changes to citizens' civil liberties in ways that, three years later, remain the subject
of keen debate.

In a report issued this week, on the eve of the third anniversary of the Sept. 11, 2001,
attacks, the national organization Human Rights First said some steps taken by the government were "sensible and appropriate" while others represent a "disturbing erosion" of
civil liberties.

"Perhaps the most disturbing change (during the past three years) has been the suggestion by some senior government officials that it is unpatriotic to challenge the administration's approach to national security," the report said.

Cathryn Hazouri, executive director of the Colorado American Civil Liberties Union, said, "I do think that since 9/11, Americans have lost a lot of privacy. And they have lost a lot of the liberties that make us different from all the other countries in the world."

5   But U.S. Attorney John Suthers, whose first day in office was one week before the Sept. 11 attacks, believes the government has been measured in its response and that steps that have been taken—most notably the Patriot Act—haven't compromised civil liberties.

"For all the rhetoric that has been generated about the Patriot Act, even people who are searching desperately are having difficulty coming forward with anyone who has lost a constitutional liberty due to the Patriot Act," Suthers said.

The Patriot Act was rapidly passed by Congress in the wake of the terrorist attacks of 2001 and was signed into law by President Bush on Oct. 26, 2001.

Many of its provisions had been drafted under the Clinton administration but had gone nowhere under Bush's predecessor.

In the radically changed post-Sept. 11 political climate, the complex law passed easily.

10   Human Rights First and the ACLU focus on several specific provisions as particularly troubling.

The most controversial is Section 215, which allows the FBI to petition the Foreign Intelligence Surveillance Act Court for a warrant permitting access to documents such as an individual's library and bookstore records in the course of an investigation involving international terrorism.

Reaction to that provision helped prompt 336 communities in 41 states to pass resolutions—which lack the force of law—opposing some aspect of the law, according to the ACLU.

In Colorado, those doing so—according to a compilation by the ACLU—include Denver, Boulder, Fort Collins, Carbondale, Ward, Dacono, Durango, Telluride, Ridgway, Crestone and San Miguel County.

Suthers, in a speech he has given frequently in recent months, said Section 215 has been mischaracterized.

15   "In fact, the word library or bookstore is never mentioned in the Patriot Act," Suthers said. "Section 215 is a general business-records provision.

"You can't take these things out of context," Suthers added. "Prior to 1978, the government could go get this stuff without any court rulings whatsoever—and, of course, that's what they did in the '60s."

In the 1960s and earlier, people were investigated and harassed for being Communists. Today, Suthers said, "It's not enough just to be a Communist. The government would have to believe you've got designs of blowing up the Tabor Center on behalf of al-Qaida."

Civil libertarians are alarmed at the increase in applications approved for domestic counterintelligence searches and surveillance operations, as provided for under parameters expanded by the Patriot Act.

According to Human Rights First, in 2003—the last year for which figures are available—the Federal Intelligence Surveillance Court approved a record 1,724 applications for searches or surveillance, turning down just four.

20   The previous year, the same court approved 1,228.

"The probable-cause standard is not all that high" for obtaining such surveillance warrants," said Ari Cover, senior associate in the U.S. Law and Security Program for Human Rights First. "They're virtually rubber-stamped."

Suthers, however, believes that safeguards are in place to prevent abuses.

"There's a unit within the Justice Department (that) reviews all FISA applications before they're submitted to the court and whose job it is to make sure that it is being properly utilized," Suthers said.

A common theme of civil libertarians concerned about the post-Sept. 11 environment in the United States is the subject of detentions, in the United States and abroad.

A report on the subject issued in June by The Constitution Project, based at the Georgetown University Public Policy Institute in Washington, D.C., says that on Nov. 5, 2001, the government announced that 1,182 people had been detained in connection with its Sept. 11 investigation.

"After that date," the Constitution Project says, "the Justice Department stopped issuing an official tally."

The Constitution Project does not begin to try to count those detained by U.S. authorities abroad—in Afghanistan, Iraq, or elsewhere—but points to the 600-plus people detained as "enemy combatants" at Guantanamo Bay, Cuba.

Cover said what American authorities may be doing to foreign citizens, on foreign soil, is as disturbing to him as anything that might be taking place in the United States.

"Secret facilities and hiding people is an invitation for abuse and torture," Cover said. "They've made it the administration's policy to contravene existing law and treat other human beings despicably."

Suthers, however, said that American conduct in its current war on terror stands in stark contrast to abuses such as the mass internment of Japanese-Americans during World War II.

"Everybody that we arrested, everybody that we have detained, has had a legitimate law violation of some sort," Suthers said.

Key provisions of the Patriot Act are due to sunset in December 2005, but Bush is already campaigning for an extension, saying in a recent Pennsylvania campaign appearance, "It's a law that is making America safer."

Nevertheless, Boulder City Council member Will Toor says the stance taken against some aspects of the Patriot Act by his municipality and others around the country is important—and he hopes it makes a difference.

"Once you have an erosion of civil liberties for a portion of the population," Toor said, "I think it becomes inevitable that that erosion of civil liberties will be applied to a larger portion of the population."

Eleanor J. Bader

Thought Police: Big Brother May Be Watching What You Read

In These Times, November 25, 2002, Institute for Public Affairs

Within days of September 11, the police and FBI were besieged with tips informing them that several suspects—including one who fit Mohammed Atta's description—had used public libraries in Hollywood Beach and Delray Beach, Florida, to surf the Internet. Shortly thereafter, a federal grand jury ordered library staff to submit all user records to law enforcement.

The order began a pattern of government requests for information about citizens' reading material that has increased dramatically since last October's passage of the USA Patriot Act, which amended 15 federal statutes, including laws governing criminal procedure, computer fraud, foreign intelligence, wiretapping, immigration and privacy. The act gives the government a host of new powers, including the ability to scrutinize what a person reads or purchases.

According to a University of Illinois study of 1,020 libraries conducted during the first two months of 2002, government sources asked 85 university and public libraries—8.3 percent of those queried—for information on patrons following the attacks. More detail is unknown since divulging specific information violates provisions of the legislation.

"The act grants the executive branch unprecedented, and largely unchecked, surveillance powers," says attorney Nancy Chang, author of *Silencing Political Dissent,* "including the enhanced ability to track e-mail and Internet usage, obtain sensitive personal records from third parties, monitor financial transactions and conduct nationwide roving wiretaps."

5   In fact, a court can now allow a wiretap to follow a suspect wherever he or she goes, including a public library or bookstore. That's right: Booksellers can also be targeted. What's more, the government is no longer required to demonstrate "probable cause" when requesting records. "FBI and police used to have to show probable cause that a person had committed a crime when requesting materials," says Chris Finan, president of the American Booksellers Foundation for Free Expression (ABFFE).

"Now, under Section 215 of the Patriot Act," Finan continues, "it is possible for them to investigate a person who is not suspected of criminal activity, but who may have some connection to a person [who is]. Worse . . . there is a gag provision barring bookstores or libraries from telling anyone—including the suspect—about the investigation. Violators of the gag order can go to jail."

Members of Congress, as well as librarians, booksellers, and ordinary citizens have expressed outrage and concern over the Orwellian reach of the law. On June 12, the House Judiciary Committee sent a 12-page letter to the Justice Department requesting hard data on the number of subpoenas issued to booksellers and libraries since last October. Two months later, on August 19, Assistant Attorney General Daniel J. Bryant responded. The figures are "confidential," he wrote, and will only be shared with the House Intelligence Committee. The Judiciary Committee told Bryant the response was unsatisfactory. Finan reports that everyone is "waiting to see what the committee will do next."

Meanwhile, the ABFFE has joined a coalition of booksellers and libraries to denounce Section 215. They have also signed onto a Freedom of Information Act request for information on both the number and content of subpoenas issued. To date, there has been no response to their entreaty; though such responses are required by law, they can often take months or even years to complete.

But community activists, librarians and publishers have joined forces to publicize the threat that the act poses to free speech, privacy and civil liberties. The American Library Association, a national alliance of library staff, issued a statement in early 2002 affirming their position: "Librarians do not police what library users read or access in the library. Libraries ensure the freedom to read, to view, to speak, and to participate."

10   Though the ALA has agreed to cooperate with federal requests within the framework of state law, it has warned local branches not to create or retain unnecessary records, and trained staff to read subpoenas carefully before providing unnecessary information.

Despite this modicum of defiance, everyone agrees that Section 215 has begun to exact a toll. "Right after 9/11, Americans seemed eager to learn more about the world," says Larry Siems, director of International Programs at the PEN American Center. "They were reading, buying and checking out books on Islam. . . . But the administration's over-all approach discourages people from seeking information. It is counterproductive. We end up with a society that is more isolated, less able to respond to the rest of the world."

In addition, he states, the Constitution guarantees that Americans have the right to read books, write books, and express their opinions. Even when the ideas expressed are unpopular—even when they're downright unpatriotic or seditious—the government should not be in the business of prohibiting them. Indeed, he cautions, a distinction between acts and ideas is imperative.

Finan and Chang agree, and they are doing their best to ensure that the Patriot Act fades away in October 2005, when it is set to expire. "At the very least," Finan concludes, "we want changes in sections like 215, to exempt libraries and bookstores from scrutiny."

Edward Epstein

GOP Makes Time for Patriot Act Vote; Leaders Successfully Beat Back Challenge by Extending Roll Call

The *San Francisco Chronicle*, July 9, 2004

Republican House leaders, in an intense last-minute effort, pressured almost a dozen Republicans to switch their votes and save a controversial provision of the USA Patriot Act that allows the FBI to monitor people's reading, e-mail and Internet habits at public libraries.

The effort, including more than doubling the usual time for the roll call vote, generated outrage from those trying to change the library provision, who argued the House leadership again manipulated the rules to help President Bush's re-election effort.

The intense debate also provided a glimpse of the sharp battle expected in Congress next year, when the overall Patriot Act must be renewed or lapse.

Rep. Bernie Sanders of Vermont, the House's only independent and the former Socialist mayor of Burlington, had proposed an amendment to change the library provision. The White House had gone to special lengths to lobby against Sanders' amendment, announcing that Bush would veto any bill containing it. The Justice Department also sent a letter to House leaders saying that as recently as last winter and spring, FBI surveillance found a member of what was described as an al Qaeda affiliate group using a public library computer to e-mail his colleagues.

Supporters of Sanders' measure said the library section of the Patriot Act gives the federal government unprecedented and unconstitutional powers to snoop on law-abiding Americans. They said his measure would have curbed those powers, but still allow the FBI access to library records—with the approval of a judge or grand jury as in a typical criminal case.

After some heated debate, Sanders' measure—an amendment to a $43.5 billion Commerce, Justice and State departments appropriations bill—gathered a winning 219-201 margin in the 435-member House as the time limit was reached for the scheduled 15-minute vote.

5

But the vote was continued for another 23 minutes, prompting Democrats to chant "shame, shame," until the final outcome was announced.

As the vote dragged on, House Majority Leader Rep. Tom DeLay, R-Texas, buttonholed GOP members to switch their votes.

His counterpart, House Minority Leader Rep. Nancy Pelosi, D-San Francisco, raised a point of order, asking mockingly how long Republicans intended to delay the end of the vote.

10   In the end, Sanders' proposal failed on a tie vote, 210-210. One member, Rep. Zoe Lofgren, D-San Jose, voted present, and 14 were absent. Eighteen Republicans ultimately voted for the bill, down from the initial 29, according to the unofficial tally kept during the voting by C-SPAN.

Among the 11 Republicans who switched from yes to no were Reps. Zach Wamp of Tennessee, Tom Davis of Virginia, Jack Kingston of Georgia and Marilyn Musgrave of Colorado, according to a list provided by Pelosi's office.

One Democrat, Rep. Brad Sherman of Sherman Oaks (Los Angeles County), switched from a "no" to a "yes" vote.

"You win some, and some get stolen," Rep. C.L. "Butch" Otter, R-Idaho, a sponsor with Sanders of the provision and one of Congress' more conservative members, told the Associated Press.

The GOP leadership tactic infuriated Democrats, who are still smarting from October's vote to approve the Medicare prescription drug benefit. That roll call was held open for more then three hours until votes were rounded up for passage.

15   As he did then, House Minority Whip Rep. Steny Hoyer, D-Md., read 1987 comments from then-Rep. Dick Cheney, R-Wyo., after Democrats then in the majority held open a roll call. Cheney called the maneuver "the most heavy-handed, arrogant abuse of power in the 10 years I've been here."

Sanders, who generally votes with Democrats, was furious.

"I resent on behalf of the American people that the Republican leadership rigged the game. At the end of 15 minutes, we won, and it wasn't even close," he said.

Pelosi, who has made what she calls Republican heavy-handedness an issue in her effort to win back a Democratic majority, said the delayed vote proves her point.

"Today on the House floor, Republican leaders once again undermined democracy, this time so that the Bush administration can threaten our civil liberties. How thoroughly un-American," she said in a statement.

20   The debate over Section 215 of the Patriot Act, a sweeping law that Congress passed quickly in the days following the Sept. 11, 2001, terrorist attacks, is likely to be repeated next year when the overall bill is up for renewal.

Opponents of the library section have drawn support from librarians and 332 local government bodies, including the San Francisco Board of Supervisors and the Oakland City Council, and prompted a national petition drive by bookstores.

The American Civil Liberties Union has sued to overturn the provision.

Proponents say that abolishing the provision would create a haven for terrorists in public libraries, where they could go to freely e-mail co-conspirators or research how to build weapons of mass destruction free from surveillance by the FBI.

"While we fight terrorism, we must do it in a way that does not undermine the basic constitutional rights of the American people," Sanders said.

"This is not an ideological issue," he added, pointing out that his co-sponsors included   25
some of the House's most conservative members, such as Otter and Rep. Ron Paul of
Texas, who was the Libertarian Party's presidential nominee in 1988.

"You never have to sacrifice liberty to preserve it," Paul told the House, saying that
Section 215, which gives the FBI access to "books, records, papers, documents and other
items" when the agency gets a warrant from a special secret federal anti-terrorism court,
violated the Fourth Amendment's protections against unreasonable searches.

But the act's defenders said the provision is needed. "Should terrorists be able to use
taxpayer-funded library facilities without fear they will be investigated by the FBI?" asked
Rep. Howard Coble, R-N.C.

Rep. Christopher Shays, R-Conn., said the proposal denied the reality of the war on
terrorism. "I have 70 constituents who lost their lives on Sept. 11. . . . I'm not sure we're
remembering them today," he said.

Sanders said his amendment would allow the FBI to use traditional warrants or subpoenas issued by a judge or grand jury to get library or bookstore records.

Lofgren, who has been a co-sponsor of Sanders' Freedom to Read Act, which he first   30
introduced in 2002, said she voted present because his latest proposal went beyond his
earlier plan. She said the amendment would have made it impossible to track anonymous
users of library computers who launch cyber attacks.

She also said she wanted committee hearings on the legislation.

Even if Sanders' measure had prevailed, it faced long odds for passage. The House
has altered several Patriot Act provisions, but its changes have died in the Senate.

Writing Prompts

1. Having read all of these essays, both for and against the Patriot Act, write a three-page essay in which you define "the problem" of fighting terrorism (taking into account the opinions of both sides) and offer your "solution."
2. Choose two essays, one in support of and one opposing the Patriot Act. Using what you know about argumentation, in a two- to three-page essay, analyze the argument each makes and determine which author makes a stronger case, regardless of which you personally agree with.
3. Reread an essay that you absolutely disagree with, then write an essay documenting the major points of the argument and refuting them with your own evidence and opinions.
4. Write a paragraph that summarizes what the USA Patriot Act allows. Be detailed, accurate, and objective. Now, in two or three pages, write an essay discussing the strengths and weaknesses of the legislation.
5. President Bush says we are at war with the terrorists. Do some research on how laws and rights are changed during a time of war and write a three-page essay putting the USA Patriot Act into some sort of historical context.

What Is at Stake for Citizenship?

1. Are civil rights just for the guilty or those who need protection in the justice system?
2. If Muhammad Atta (leader of the 9/11 hijackers) used the public library while in the United States, does that mean the rest of us should let the government know what we are reading? Does the government have a right to know what we are reading?
3. Does wartime change civil rights? Should it?
4. Should average Americans have more civil rights than suspected terrorists?
5. Should American citizens have more rights than people who are living in the United States but are not citizens?

ONE NATION UNDER SURVEILLANCE: CAMERAS, IDS, AND RECOGNITION SOFTWARE IN PUBLIC PLACES

It began simply enough and with good intentions. Cameras were put in public places to deter and record criminal activity. Banks, casinos, and grocery stores (places with high cash flow) had cameras watching employees and customers alike. Security cameras provided a sense of safety; ideally, no one would break the law if the crime were going to be caught on film. Places with high-end merchandise hid their cameras; minimarts wanted the camera right out where everyone could see it. Then there were cameras in the department store and even in the changing rooms (so you didn't steal anything), and at ATMs and tollbooths on the turnpike. They were at intersections, so we didn't run the red. They were in subway stations to keep us from jumping the turnstile. Now there are cameras at work so we don't steal, or goof off, or commit industrial espionage. There are cameras at school and on the street and in places we wouldn't even think of looking. There are cameras everywhere now, and the question is . . . we are not doing anything wrong or illegal, should we care?

Obviously, cameras that record and document our movements are about losing privacy. ID cards and face-recognition software are about losing anonymity—the right to remain anonymous when you are out in public. Some people feel that requiring a national ID card, used each time we board public transportation or enter a sensitive building, and keeping a record of our movements are the wave of the future . . . the way to keep track of who should be somewhere and who should not. Others see it as one more means of controlling people's lives and gathering information about innocent people.

To take things one step further, computer software has become widely available that very quickly can compare elements of our faces to those of thousands of criminals. The use of face-recognition software with all those cameras can set up a trolling expedition anywhere in town, and in some towns local law enforcement has already begun using it. Get caught in the glare of such a lens and it's your own private lineup, just like on television.

It sounds strange, but isn't that what we want? Didn't we want cops with cameras and computers looking everywhere at everyone, looking for dangerous people like the 9/11 terrorists? Isn't this what we meant when we said we didn't want to be afraid anymore? That we didn't want to be scared that someone who didn't know us wanted to kill us? So what are we complaining about?

In the following essays, you will read about various communities that have chosen to install cameras in different situations that are now routinely under surveillance. Few people seem bothered by all the electronic eyes now trained upon us. Think about how you feel, knowing how often you may be "watched" throughout your day. Some of the authors argue that this influx of cameras in our lives is not just about security but instead related to a larger, systemic shift in our culture. Do you think this might be so?

Julian Guthrie and Diana Walsh

Security Cameras Abound after 9/11

The *San Francisco Chronicle*, June 10, 2003

A security camera in New York City.

The unblinking eye has recorded images of terrorists withdrawing cash from ATMs, kids calmly shooting classmates at Columbine and a mother smacking her young daughter in an Indiana parking lot. On Friday, the abductor of a 9-year-old San Jose girl was caught on surveillance tape.

Surveillance cameras, which have been in banks and commercial buildings since the 1960s and record the ordinary with the extraordinary, have proliferated since the Sept. 11, 2001, terrorist attacks, showing up in taxis, buses, stores, intersections, monuments and, now, quiet suburban neighborhoods.

In the case of the 9-year-old girl, who was kidnapped from her family's home Friday and found alive in East Palo Alto late Sunday, a neighbor's high-tech surveillance system caught grainy images of the suspect and his car.

But the ubiquity of the unblinking eye—whether in urban or suburban areas—raises questions about how to balance normal expectations of privacy with concerns for public security, experts say.

"There are always going to be times when you're glad a video camera was there," said Ann Brick, an attorney with American Civil Liberties Union in San Francisco. "But do we really expect to be caught on camera when we go to pick up the paper in our

5

bathrobe and slippers? We are getting into a situation where we are living in a fishbowl."

She added, "I don't think people really have a sense to what degree their every movement is falling under the watchful eye of a camera. It's an important issue for all of us."

The videotape showing the abductor and his car was handed over to police by Karen Kamfolt, who lives down the street from the victim's home. Kamfolt's security system includes several surveillance cameras that record the round-the-clock comings and goings of the neighborhood.

The $3,000 system was installed five years ago by Bobby Ozier, Kamfolt's godson, who owns Residential Solutions, a security firm in San Jose.

"I always planned for the unexpected," Ozier said. "I don't trust anybody. This is a terrible time we live in."

10   The security industry conservatively estimates that even before Sept. 11, there were at least 2 million surveillance cameras in the United States.

The proliferation of cameras, made possible by cheaper and better technology, has pitted security experts and consumers against privacy advocates.

"The studies that have been done are largely inconclusive as to whether cameras are a deterrent to crime," said Marc Rotenberg, executive director of the Electronic Privacy Information Center, a nonprofit advocacy group in Washington, D.C. "Our focus and concern is really on the use of video cameras by the government."

However, he added, "Private citizens use cameras in ways that are considered an invasion of privacy. We could easily become a nation of snoops."

Former San Francisco police chief Dick Hongisto, who runs a private security company that provides electronic surveillance, believes the use of personal protection systems will continue to increase.

15   "I believe they can do a lot to deter crime and solve crime," Hongisto said. "We're at a point where if you have a laptop, you can be away from home and monitor your home. It wasn't long ago that if you wanted to have a camera system, it would all be hard-wired. You'd have to run cables around. But we now have wireless cameras and infrared cameras and all types of high-tech, low-cost equipment."

Lt. John Loftus, head of the San Francisco Police Department's robbery division, said videotapes had become the first piece of evidence used in tracking robberies.

"There's been video surveillance in banks and in some larger commercial establishments for many years, but it's much more pervasive today," said Loftus. "It may make people nervous, but I don't know if their fears are justified. It's a tremendous help to us."

San Jose deputy police Chief Rob Davis was equally positive, calling the videotape taken by Kamfolt's system "a gift to us."

On Monday, several local alarm companies were planning to offer the family of the young kidnap victim a free home security system, and a national alarm company was going door-to-door selling surveillance and security systems.

20   The offer left some neighbors cold.

"I think it's immoral to capitalize on everyone's fear," said Kumar Malavey, who lives two doors down from the girl's family. "It's tacky at this time."

But one company was undeterred.

"We offered them a free home security system," said Rhino Security Services employee Ben Fortner. "As soon as we heard about the case, we knew there would be a camera at someone's house. We feel that everyone should have a home security system."

Susan Murray

"Queer Eye" for Big Brother

The Washington Post, January 28, 2004

When Congress passed the Patriot Act in October 2001, civil libertarians soundly criticized several provisions of the legislation, including its expansion of the government's surveillance authority. But while opponents of the law directed their outrage toward Washington, across the nation resistance to governmental intrusion was slowly being sapped by an unlikely source: reality television.

By reality TV, I don't mean C-SPAN's coverage of Congress. Rather, it's programs such as "Survivor" and "Joe Millionaire" (which scores of Americans watch for dating tips and a soap opera-like fantasy) that soften us up to accept increasing levels of governmental surveillance and that chip away at our belief in the sanctity of privacy. Strange as it sounds, "Queer Eye for the Straight Guy" may be doing some of John D. Ashcroft's dirty work.

As most of us are well aware by now, surveillance cameras are everywhere. In fact, the American Civil Liberties Union found that as early as 1998, about 2,400 cameras were recording New Yorkers in a multitude of parks, stores and other public places. Recent estimates say the number of cameras has reached 7,200. In addition, the Total Information Awareness program, the brainchild of John Poindexter, once national security adviser to President Ronald Reagan, promised to protect Americans by electronically tracking their every movement. Although Congress eventually scaled back the project's reach, its initial goals and its logo (an eye fixed on the globe) are chilling. Even more frightening, the U.S. government has begun scanning fingerprints and taking photographs of arriving foreigners.

We don't immediately think of reality television—with its ever-present cameras and microphones—in relation to the larger context of government surveillance. Perhaps this is because, in a post-Sept. 11 era, the recording and watching of others—and ourselves—has become a component of our everyday lives.

But reality TV does play a crucial role in mitigating our resistance to such surveillance tactics. More and more of these programs rely on the willingness of "ordinary" folk to live their lives in front of cameras. These people choose to have sex, get married, give birth, compete for prizes, work, fight, weep and brush their teeth in front of millions. We, as audience members, witness this openness to surveillance, normalize it and, in turn, open ourselves up to such a possibility.

Some of us have a desire to become reality TV celebrities; others set up a blog or a webcam. Many of the rest of us just allow video cameras and computers to follow our every movement through city streets, stores, subway stations, schools and apartment buildings. Most of us don't protest or even think about such everyday tracking. We may even take it a step further by engaging in a policing or monitoring of our own behavior—whether or not we know cameras are present—as we grow conscious of the fact that even the tiniest detail of an individual's life can be considered so socially significant as to warrant recording or broadcasting.

Certainly most of us want to believe that we would never actually choose to go on a reality program ourselves. Yet our collective fascination with the genre validates the decision of those who choose to do so. We long to watch people in both ordinary and extraordinary circumstances so we can compare their lives and decisions to our own

5

while simultaneously feeling the power that comes with being an observer. But we must realize that by participating in the process, we are entering into a tacit agreement to redefine our relationship to privacy. We can't all be watchers without eventually subjecting ourselves to being watched—just as we can't expect that the surveillance techniques protected by the Patriot Act will negatively affect only those who pose a genuine threat to us.

At a time when the government is asking us to open our lives to scrutiny in the name of national security, we should be aware of all the ways in which we've already exposed ourselves to observation. This is not to say that we can't watch and enjoy reality programming. We just need to be more thoughtful about the implications of doing so.

Robyn E. Blumner

Cards Spell End of Privacy

St. Petersburg Times (Florida), October 17, 2004

It's coming. In one form or another a national ID card is coming, and I for one am deeply concerned.

The idea of creating a hard-to-counterfeit identity card has been kicking around for quite a while. Originally, it was proposed as a way to defeat illegal immigration and identity theft. But since the Sept. 11 attacks, the issue has taken on a new sense of urgency. Every Sept. 11 hijacker except one was able to acquire identity documents, such as a Social Security number or driver's license, that allowed them to more easily navigate American society. They rented apartments, opened bank accounts and boarded airplanes with documents that were both legally and fraudulently obtained.

"Fraud in identification documents is no longer just a problem of theft," the 9/11 Commission report said. "At many entry points . . . sources of identification are the last opportunity to ensure that people are who they say they are and to check whether they are terrorists."

The commission recommended that the federal government set national standards "for the issuance of birth certificates and sources of identification, such as drivers' licenses."

5   In case you didn't hear it, a shoe just dropped.

Standardizing drivers' licenses will turn them into de facto national ID cards. Just as our Social Security numbers have morphed from a narrow use into general identifiers, once Americans are carrying around a uniform driver's license that is connected to a central database, it will be used, undoubtedly, as a form of internal passport.

Maybe at first, showing a driver's license will be required only when boarding an airplane, but soon, inevitably, it will have to be presented and scanned when entering all forms of public transportation—then government buildings, then public events. Our right to travel anonymously—to ride a train, enter a public library or go to a political rally—without the government knowing who we are or making a record of it, will disappear.

Who needs neighbor spying on neighbor like the East German Stasi or John Ashcroft's Operation TIPS program when our own identity papers will keep track of our movements? Security measures should not destroy our liberty and privacy in the process, but that is what's coming.

Both houses of Congress have passed legislation implementing some or part of the 9/11 Commission's recommendations. And although the House and Senate have passed wildly divergent versions, both legislative proposals would standardize drivers' licenses.

The Senate would grant the secretary of the Department of Homeland Security the discretion to determine what documents had to be presented to obtain a driver's license and what data would be included in the license. This could include embedded biometrics, such as a fingerprint or iris scan. Although states wouldn't be forced to go along, the secretary could require that only federally approved licenses be accepted at airports—a condition that would leave states little option but to comply.

The House would go further and require states to link their driver's license information to a central database. In addition, the legislation calls on the secretary to create "an integrated network of screening points that includes the nation's border security system, transportation system and critical infrastructure facilities." In other words, entrants should be screened at any building or public transportation node where there is potential for a terror attack.

Here is the death of anonymity coming to pass. Just as private businesses have expropriated the Social Security number for their own internal record keeping, expect them to piggyback on this too. Landlords will scan your driver's license before renting an apartment, and private security will use it to know who is entering the building. With today's computing power and data storage capacities, every scanning would be indefinitely stored and instantly retrievable.

And with all this intrusion, would we really be safer?

No. The terrorists would find a way around it.

Ultimately every identity document, no matter how ostensibly tamperproof, can be altered or forged. Also, Department of Motor Vehicle employees are not immune to bribes. Very likely a black market in drivers' licenses would arise. There is no foolproof system and terrorists will be particularly motivated to defeat whatever is put in place.

Rather than erect a huge national system to identify and track law-abiding Americans, it makes far more sense to continue to thoroughly check all passengers at airports for weapons and bombs, and use our homeland security resources to investigate real terrorist leads. For example, before the government makes us get our irises scanned, how about translating the thousands of terrorist-related intercepts that are sitting backlogged at the FBI? First things first, don't you think?

Mark F. Bonner

Parish Gets Money for Street Cameras; ACLU's Concerns Fail to Dissuade Sheriff

Times-Picayune (New Orleans), July 24, 2004

With grant money in hand, the St. Bernard Parish Sheriff's Office is going forward with its plan to install surveillance cameras at various points along the parish line to photograph motorists' faces and license plates as they leave and enter.

The cameras, which have drawn opposition from the American Civil Liberties Union, are expected to be in place by October, Sheriff Jack Stephens said this week.

The precise locations of the cameras are still being debated, but they probably will be placed at access points on Judge Perez Drive, St. Claude Avenue, Paris Road and the Chalmette ferry platform, according to Stephens.

The money is coming from a $328,000 Homeland Security grant that parish government received July 1. From that, the Sheriff's Office is getting $112,000, according to Larry Ingargiola, managing director of the parish's Office of Homeland Security and Emergency Preparedness.

5   In January, after Stephens announced his plans to install the cameras, the ACLU wrote a letter to him saying the installation of such equipment would be a violation of a citizen's privacy by setting up "a spy network without any public debate or input."

This week, Joe Cook, executive director of the ACLU in Louisiana, said that installing surveillance cameras in hopes of catching criminals is a "reckless gamble of privacy rights that wastes tax dollars."

"They don't work. They are expensive to put in and expensive to maintain," he said.

Cook cited examples, from Oakland, Calif., to London, where law enforcement agencies tried to use the cameras, but concluded their resources would be better used by placing more officers on the street.

But in Louisiana, authorities in New Orleans and Shreveport already are using public surveillance cameras.

10   "We are becoming a surveillance society," Cook said. "It chills people's conduct, changing the way they act—it's paranoia."

Stephens said he has paid attention to what Cook and the ACLU have been saying, but he doesn't think they have presented a persuasive legal argument to stop it.

The sheriff said the cameras would not be used to watch people coming in and out of the parish unless there was an event that would prompt them to look at it, such as a crime.

The images will be recorded and stored for 30 days and then erased, he said. If there is a crime or a possible terrorist attack, the images from that specific time period will be studied.

While the sheriff's plans to install cameras at parish entrances and exits has drawn some harsh criticism, the St. Bernard Port, Harbor and Terminal District has erected its own camera surveillance system with little fanfare.

15   Three months ago, the port set up about 40 surveillance cameras around its 300-acre complex using a Homeland Security grant of $380,000, according to Robert Scafidel, the executive director of the port. The money received by the port was part of the $400 million the federal agency allotted to protect the nation's shipping ports and terminals.

Scafidel said the cameras are necessary to protect the terminal "in post-9/11" America. He also said the port contributed $150,000 of its own money to finish financing the camera installation.

"It's cost-effective and efficient for surveillance," Scafidel said. "It covers a huge gambit of crime as well as terrorism."

The ACLU does draw a distinction to areas such as the port that are potentially at risk for a terrorism attack, but the line is thin.

Cook said port officials' camera usage "could possibly be justified if they can show it is a possible terrorism target and they won't abuse it. But, in general, surveillance in public areas is a bad idea."

Jay Rey

Privacy at a Premium/Think You're Alone? Think Again.
Security Cameras Are Popping up Everywhere

Buffalo News (New York), August 3, 2004

Psst.

If you feel you're being watched, you probably are.

Did you spot that camera perched atop the pole?

How about the camera tucked near the ceiling tiles?

No way you caught the one hidden in the smoke detector.   5

While it may sound like paranoia over Big Brother, a boom in surveillance cameras has made for lots of Little Brothers watching what's going on everywhere from banks to the border—and probably places you wouldn't expect.

Throw in the popularity of Web cams and cell phone cameras, and it leaves some people concerned about a growing, unchecked privacy problem.

Or has it just become part of life?

"They're everywhere," said Peter Vito of Peter M. Vito & Associates, a local security company, "and because of the technology, they're going to be better and more prevalent in society."

It's hard to put a finger on how many surveillance cameras are out there—one esti-   10
mate shows sales growing 16 percent a year.

But try paying attention once you set foot out the door in the morning.

Drop the kids off at Brierwood Child Care Center, where Web cams allow the parents to log onto a secured Web site and peek in on their children during the day.

"Parents have told us that was one of the main reasons they signed up with us," said Carol Vogel, co-owner of Brierwood.

Then stop for gas at Delta Sonic, which recently updated its security system to help prevent drive-offs, when customers leave without paying, and to aid in tracking thefts.

"We've always had a fairly substantial system, but we upgraded in the fall," said Brian   15
Stone, director of corporate loss prevention. "It's worked extremely well."

Better quality and affordability have made the technology more accessible for businesses, as well as homeowners, who are helping drive the market growth, said Wally Carriero, general manager for Sentinel Security and Communications in Depew.

But a greater public suspicion and angst have played a role in the camera phenomenon, too, said John Sperrazza, president of the Western New York Alarm Association.

"9/11 heightened it," said Sperrazza, who owns Advanced Alarm in Buffalo. "Not necessarily from a terrorist standpoint—but you really don't know who people are and who you're employing."

Drive to work along the Kensington Expressway, or portions of the mainline Thruway, Niagara Thruway, Scajaquada Expressway and Youngmann Highway, and fixed high above the road, 30-plus cameras cover roughly 25 miles of interstate.

"People think we use it to catch drivers speeding or see who's going where, but these   20
are all used for traffic management issues," said Michael Smith of the Niagara International Transportation Technology Coalition.

Park in a ramp or lot? Good chance there's a camera. Hop on Metro Rail? Cameras have been installed. Your office building? That's the first place to look.

In fact, covert cameras—installed in everything from exit signs to smoke detectors, lights and clocks—have become popular as employers try to get a grip on employee theft, Sperrazza said.

"A lot of businesses are going to remote cameras," said Sperrazza. "I can put a camera system in, go home and call those cameras up on a computer, then watch what my employees are doing."

The objective is being met.

25   Videotaped evidence in criminal cases is probably 10 times more common than a decade ago, said Erie County District Attorney Frank J. Clark.

"A case that would have been barely triable without it, becomes a lock with it," Clark said.

The American Civil Liberties Union doesn't deny the technology can serve as a crime deterrent in some cases. But it's concerned about the trend of more government- and law enforcement-operated cameras around the country, while there really are no laws governing their use.

"That's the big problem with them, there's really no regulation," said Jay Stanley, communications director of the ACLU's Technology and Liberty Project. "The laws that impose checks and balances to protect us are out of date, and in the worst case—as in the Patriot Act—they're being weakened when they should be strengthened."

Others say it has just become part of the culture.

30   "As time goes by, we've just gotten very accepting that cameras are watching us," said Carriero, from Sentinel Security.

Stop at the grocery store after work? Cameras.

The mall? Cameras.

The gym? Actually, locker rooms should be safe, especially now that many clubs have set up rules since cell phone cameras have become en vogue.

The YMCA of Greater Buffalo, for example, instituted a policy in December preventing patrons from using cell phones in locker rooms or other private areas, said Kyle Donaldson of the YMCA of Greater Buffalo.

35   "We just felt it needed to be addressed," Donaldson said.

Researchers at Carnegie Mellon University in Pittsburgh estimate there are more than 10,000 Web cameras displaying places across the country, said Michael Shamos, co-director of the university's Privacy Technology Center.

"We think the public has no idea how many cameras are really out there," he said.

Jeffrey Rosen

The Way We Live Now: Naked Terror

The *New York Times*, January 4, 2004

(This article is adapted from his book, *The Naked Crowd: Reclaiming Security and Freedom in an Anxious Age*.)

When the Bush administration raised America's antiterrorism alert status from yellow to orange over the holidays, some travelers became anxious, while others took the warning in stride. If and when another attack on American soil occurs, however, everything

Airport security in Indianapolis.

we know about the psychology of fear suggests that it will lead to extreme public panic that may be disproportionate to the actual casualties. The public responds emotionally to remote but terrifying threats, and this leads us to make choices about security that are not always rational.

After the 9/11 attacks, for example, officials at Orlando International Airport began testing a new security device. Let's call it the Naked Machine, for that's more or less what it is. A kind of electronic strip search, the Naked Machine bounces a low-energy X-ray beam off the human body.In addition to exposing any metal, ceramic or plastic objects that are concealed by clothing, the Naked Machine also produces an anatomically correct naked image of everyone it scrutinizes. The Naked Machine promises a high degree of security, but it demands a highsacrifice of privacy. With a simple programming shift, however, researchers at the Pacific Northwest National Laboratory in Richland, Wash., have built a prototype of a redesigned Naked Machine that extracts the images of concealed objects and projects them onto a sexless mannequin, turning the naked body into an unrecognizable and nondescript blob. This redesigned version of the Naked Machine—let's call it the Blob Machine—guarantees exactly the same amount of security while also protecting privacy.

The choice between the Blob Machine and the Naked Machine might seem to be easy. But in presenting the choice hypothetically to groups of students and adults since 9/11, I've been struck by a surprising pattern: there are always some people who say they would prefer to go through the Naked Machine rather than the Blob Machine. Some say they are already searched so thoroughly at airports that they have abandoned all hope of privacy. Others say those who have nothing to hide should have nothing to fear. But in each group, there are some who say they are so anxious about the possibility of terrorism that they would do anything possible to make themselves feel better. They don't care, in other words, whether or not the Naked Machine makes them safer than the Blob Machine, because they are more concerned about feeling safe than being safe.

In their willingness to choose laws and technologies that threaten privacy without bringing more security, the people who prefer the Naked Machine to the Blob Machine are representative of an important strain in public opinion as a whole. When presented with images of terrifying events, people tend to miscalculate their probability. A single memorable image—of the World Trade Center collapsing, for example—will crowd out less visually dramatic risks in the public mind. This explains why people overestimate the frequency of deaths from disasters like floods and fire and underestimate the frequency of deaths from more mundane threats like diabetes and strokes.

5   How can we protect ourselves from our psychological vulnerabilities? First, we can turn off the TV. A study of psychological responses to 9/11 found that, two months after the attacks, 17 percent of the American population outside New York City reported symptoms of post-traumatic stress related to 9/11. High levels of stress were especially notable in those who watched a lot of television. This anxiety is only heightened by cable networks, which have converted themselves into 24-hour purveyors of alarm.

         But cable TV isn't the only institution of democracy that has an incentive to exaggerate risks. We've seen the temptations for politicians to pass along vague and unconfirmed threats of future violence in order to protect themselves from criticism in the event that another attack materializes. Ultimately, our success in overcoming fear will depend on political leadership that challenges us to live with our uncertainties rather than catering to them. After 9/11, for example, Mayor Rudolph Giuliani understood that the greatest leaders of democracies in earlier wars did not pander to public fears; instead, they challenged citizens to transcend their self-involved anxieties, embracing ideals of liberty and justice larger than themselves. It is hard to imagine Franklin D. Roosevelt instituting a color-coded system of terrorist alerts.

         The vicious cycle at this point should be clear. The public fixates on low-probability but vivid risks because of images we absorb from television and from politicians. This cycle fuels the public's demand for draconian and poorly designed laws and technologies to eliminate the risks that are, by their nature, difficult to reduce. We have the ability to resist this dangerous cycle by choosing leaders who will insist on laws and technologies that strike a reasonable balance between freedom and security. What we need now is the will.

Katie Hafner

Where the Hall Monitor Is a Webcam

The *New York Times*, February 27, 2003

School camera, Jacksonville, Florida.

THEY look like small snow globes. The dozen inconspicuous cameras on walls and ceilings at the school campus at the center of this central California city capture video images of students as they enter and leave the two buildings, work in the computer lab, climb and descend the main staircase or relax outside.

Not only can the comings and goings of the 350 teenagers at the two public charter schools here be watched from a monitor in a small room next to the main building's reception area, but they can also be seen remotely over the Internet.

Every night, someone in Jackson, Miss., home of the company that installed the cameras, watches over the buildings half a continent away.

Sometimes the schools' executive director checks the cameras from her home. And if a crime occurs, the computers at the Fresno Police Department can display an immediate picture of what is happening.

As security becomes an ever more pressing concern, schools across the nation are seeking new ways to provide a sense of safety to students, staff members and parents.

"The reality is that today's educators face greater threats to safety than ever before," said Ken Trump, a school security consultant in Cleveland. "Threats range from bullying to school shootings, and now terrorism and war." 5

Security equipment can include two-way radios for school staff members and metal detectors and panic buttons with a direct connection to the local police department. A few schools with special concerns about abductions or terrorism are turning to identification cards that can hold bar-coded biometric information like fingerprints.

Mostly, however, schools are making use of increasingly sophisticated video cameras like those at the Fresno campus, home of the W.E.B. DuBois and Carter G. Woodson charter schools. The Web-connected cameras here are among the most advanced available, their images viewable by anyone with a computer, Internet access and the proper password.

Perhaps it is a reflection of how security-conscious the nation has become that remote monitoring of students has so far raised few concerns about privacy.

On the contrary, security experts and administrators who use the cameras say, students and teachers seem to appreciate the increased sense of security. And in some cases, administrators say, having cameras around has modified students' behavior.

The systems are expensive. A network in a single building can cost around $30,000 to install. Fresno's cost was $35,000, plus $350 a month for nighttime monitoring by CameraWatch, a company specializing in security systems for schools. Some school districts are buying much more extensive systems. Biloxi, Miss., for example, has spent $1.2 million to put a security camera in each of its nearly 500 classrooms. 10

While Biloxi may be an extreme case, "cameras are probably one of the better investments that most middle and high schools can make," said Mary Green, a security specialist at Sandia National Laboratories in Albuquerque who works with schools. She estimated that 30 percent of high schools and 15 percent of middle schools now have video cameras, although most are not as sophisticated as those used in Fresno. (Elementary schools have lagged behind, she added, with less than 2 percent using cameras.)

Security experts and even those educators who use the cameras acknowledge that no system can deter a person or group intent on violence. But that has not dampened interest in the systems. "I don't know that I've ever visited a school where they didn't immediately say, 'So, tell me about cameras,'" Ms. Green said.

For years, cameras that record video images on tape loops have been a fixture in stores and banks, intended for deterring crimes and as an aid in identifying suspects after a crime occurs. Some schools have been using them for similar purposes.

The Fresno cameras were installed in the hope of deterring graffiti vandals, who began defacing the buildings soon after the schools opened in 2000. Linda Washington, executive director of Agape, the company that runs the two schools, said that after the cameras began operating, petty crimes decreased, but graffiti vandals simply moved to areas not covered by the cameras.

15   Administrators, teachers and students quickly realized the cameras' value in helping create a greater sense of security. That feeling is generated in large part by the system's real-time remote-monitoring capabilities.

Ms. Green said that feature seems invaluable as the 1999 shootings at Columbine High School in Littleton, Colo., linger in the public memory. Security experts who have analyzed the Columbine shootings, in which two students killed 12 fellow students and a teacher before committing suicide, say that the police response was hampered because it was unclear where the shooters were.

"When you're thinking of the kind of horrible tragedy like what happened at Columbine, you need the real-time," Ms. Green said.

Gary Jones, assistant principal of the middle school in Reeds Spring, Mo., said it was the remote, real-time monitoring that he found most attractive when he was investigating camera systems.

"If something happened, I wouldn't have to go into the building to find out what was going on," Mr. Jones said. "We're a little more prepared."

20   Reeds Spring installed a system for the school district that monitors four buildings. To pay the $68,000 bill, voters passed a bond measure.

In most schools, cameras are placed sparingly in places known to attract crime or where security may be a concern: hallways, stairwells, common areas and parking lots. Cameras are customarily installed at entrances, too. At the Fresno campus, cameras are affixed to entrances, placed in hallways and positioned inconspicuously in computer labs.

Giving a friendly wave to what she took to be a camera (it was an alarm) above a hallway door, Leah Cherry, 18, a senior at W.E.B. DuBois, said the cameras' presence had changed her behavior and that of her schoolmates.

"You don't ditch your class," she said. "You don't try to smoke in the hallways and you don't bring illegal things to school, because you'll get caught."

Some schools are installing cameras in greater numbers, like those covering every classroom in the Biloxi school district.

25   The system, a fully digital version that the district paid for with bonds, state gambling revenue and money from a federal program to bring Internet access to schools, can store up to 20 days' worth of images. The cameras have real-time functions as well.

The Biloxi cameras, 800 or so in all, act as silent witnesses to any number of transgressions, including spitballs, theft, vandalism and bullying.

"Right now I can walk over to my computer and tell you what's going on in any facility in my district," said Dr. Larry Drawdy, the Biloxi superintendent of schools. The Biloxi Police Department has the same ability, he said.

Dr. Drawdy said that since the cameras were installed, students have occasionally confessed even before the cameras pointed a finger.

"We have kids coming up and admitting to things we don't even have on camera," Dr. Drawdy said.

30   Privacy concerns have for the most part been minimized. "Our teachers don't have a problem, the parents love it, and the kids all know it's there," Dr. Drawdy said. "We've had little or no question about it."

Nor have schools encountered much resistance to another kind of security technology that is beginning to make its way onto the premises: identity cards with two-dimensional bar codes containing information that can include photos, fingerprints, personal information and iris scans.

Preventing kidnappings is one reason schools buy the systems. "There's a huge issue now of child abductions, and schools are interested in combating that crime any way they can," said Chuck Lynch, a vice president at Datastrip, the company that supplies the cards and the portable scanners that go with them. Datastrip has sold the systems to a Jewish day school in New York and two schools in Florida.

"With all the recent events, terrorism and 9/11, and some of these children having parents who are fairly high-profile people, the parents felt this was something they wanted to pursue," said the principal at one of the Florida schools, a private middle school in the Orlando area. He requested anonymity to protect the privacy of families with children at the school.

The Orlando school has been using the cards for nearly three months. A total of 300 were issued to students, parents, nannies and anyone else authorized to pick up a child. Each card contains a color photograph and other identifying information. But plans to add fingerprints were delayed. "It felt too encroaching," said the principal. "We decided, let's get everybody comfortable with it, then reinvestigate that."

Public schools, on the other hand, generally must be more circumspect about security expenses. "With the way school budgets are going, they're lucky they have locks on doors," said Mr. Trump, the security consultant.   35

But for Ms. Washington of the Fresno charter schools, the choice was clear. "We can say we don't have money, but you have to put money into school safety," she said, "You have to find money in your budget."

However reassuring such systems may be, whether they discourage violent crimes is doubtful, say even those who have come to rely on them.

"The security may be false in some way," Dr. Drawdy said. Those who go to school and open fire on teachers and fellow students are looking for attention, not hoping to escape, he said. "You could put the National Guard out there and it might not deter them."

Despite the violence in Columbine's recent past, the school's own surveillance system remains limited. Before the shootings, the school had security cameras in the cafeteria for monitoring lunchtime activity. They have been replaced with a $30,000 system of 24 cameras throughout the school. There is no remote-monitoring capability. The cameras are used as a deterrent for small crimes, and for investigations.

Rick Kaufman, the director of communications for the Jefferson County public schools, of which Columbine is one, underscored Dr. Drawdy's point.   40

"Cameras aren't going to stop the kind of mayhem, chaos and murder that Eric Harris and Dylan Klebold did," Mr. Kaufman said, referring to the students who did the shooting.

He acknowledged that real-time remote monitoring might have helped during the incident. "But who foots the bill?" he added.

Ultimately, Mr. Kaufman said, no amount of technology can substitute for the human touch in stopping crime and violence in schools. "The greatest deterrence is students who report it," he said.

Bill Hendrick

Get Ready for Your Close-up; Some Cameras Will Focus on Drivers' Faces

The *Atlanta Journal-Constitution,* March 25, 2002

There's no need to say "cheese" when you spot one of about 875 traffic cameras aimed at cars on metro Atlanta's freeways and roads. Big Brother is watching, and taking pictures, but only of vehicles, not faces.

So far.

In the wake of September's terrorist attacks, 74 percent of Atlantans don't give a hoot about such camera surveillance, according to a survey of 2,400 people conducted for *The Atlanta Journal-Constitution's* Metro Poll.

They do bother 25 percent of us, including 13 percent who view the cameras as an invasion of privacy, and 12 percent who are annoyed about being watched.

5   Most of the cameras are operated by the Georgia Department of Transportation, which uses them to monitor and measure traffic flow and speed, and to spot wrecks, disabled vehicles and road debris. The DOT's 162 color and 701 black-and-white cameras can see inside cars and trucks but aren't used for speed detection or enforcement.

Ignorance can be bliss, because research shows drivers who are aware of road cameras tend to pay more attention to traffic laws.

"We don't pick up on how fast you're going, only average speeds across all lanes," says Marion Waters, DOT's state traffic operations engineer. "The cameras aren't out there to invade privacy. They're there for safety." Waters said the cameras are not used to pick up what's going on inside cars.

That may be the case for DOT's devices, but cameras at the intersection of Cobb Parkway and Windy Hill Road have been taking facial shots of drivers since a testing period began in 2000. Soon, they'll be used to nab scofflaws who run red lights, providing evidence to back up $70 tickets, says city official Warren Hutmacher.

The half dozen cameras will snap photos of violators' faces, their cars and license plates. Digital mug shots will be stored in computers until fines are paid or court appearances made, Hutmacher says.

10   "Our position is, we have an absolute right to catch you, and you have no right of privacy," he says. "The only people who'll wind up in the database are those who run red lights. It's not our intent to create divorces or see what you're doing while driving."

Decatur won't be far behind, though its system will shoot only cars and tags before sending out $50 tickets, says City Manager Peggy Merriss. Its two red-light cameras, at the intersection of Clairmont Road and Scott Boulevard won't be used for enforcement for several months.

Marietta is anxious to go live, Hutmacher says. Since testing began, cameras have monitored only one of 16 lanes and are spotting 10 to 15 violators a day, sometimes as many as 30.

"I've seen school buses that have run the red light two or three seconds after it turns red," he said. "There have been many near misses."

Toll Cheaters Watched

15   The only cameras in the state now used to send out tickets are alongside toll booths on Ga. 400 and are used to nab Cruise Card cheaters. State Tollway Authority official Terry Rogers says the toll delinquency rate has dropped from a high of 4 percent to .001 percent,

because most drivers know about the cameras.

Barbara Bilder, 75, of Peachtree City wishes more would be put up.

"I wish they'd get the road hogs and road ragers and nail 'em," she says. "If the cameras can help, I'm all for them, and I'm not worried about privacy."

The newpaper's poll found men, blacks and longtime metro residents are more apt than others to consider cameras an invasion of privacy.

Evelyn Cuthbert, a 44-year-old, self-employed Riverdale resident who's been in the metro area for several years, doesn't like the cameras.

"I'm not a criminal, and I don't think anyone should have the right to look inside my 20
vehicle anywhere to see anything," she says. " What's next, a camera inside my house to monitor my comings and goings?"

Deterrence can be a major benefit. An insurance industry study in Oxnard, Calif., the first of more than 50 cities to use cameras to monitor traffic or enforce laws, credits them with a 29 percent drop in injury-causing accidents.

"The debate over cameras has heated up since 9/11," says Patricia Wallace, a pecialist in privacy issues at Johns Hopkins University in Baltimore. "People are more willing to give up certain rights and freedoms than we had in the past to achieve more security."

Dr. Richard Winer, a Roswell psychiatrist, says men are more likely than women to feel cameras invade their privacy because they "like to feel they are more in control of their lives. As far as black individuals feeling more upset, it would seem that, based on past injustices that have happened toward blacks, that anything of this nature might be seen as one more way to try to keep an eye on them."

And longtime Atlantans may be more concerned than newcomers because "people get comfortable and know they can count on things being the way they have been, and this is a change."

Waters, who says four Georgians die every day in traffic accidents, is among 25
traffic engineers insisting the cameras are important. A study by the Insurance Institute for Highway Safety last year reported that between 1992 and 1996, red-light runners caused an estimated 260,000 crashes nationwide, killing at least 750 people.

Web Site Available

Waters invites anyone worried about privacy to visit its Web site at www .georgianavigator.com/traffic/. Click on "lists," then click on "cameras" for real-time traffic views seen by "war-room" personnel. The cameras can zoom in for tighter shots of drivers, but that's not how they are used in day-to-day monitoring, Waters says.

Occasionally the cameras, monitored around the clock, spot people illegally walking on the freeways, and are used to dispatch police officers to such hazards, he says.

"You can't imagine what we see in the road all the time," he says. "Chickens, cows, any kind of livestock you can imagine. We've seen jumpers, people throwing rocks." Georgia law doesn't allow images from traffic cameras to be used in the prosecution of crimes other than red-light violations or Cruise Card cheating.

There are about 300 miles of freeway in the Atlanta area; only 60 are watched by 30
cameras.

"It's silly to think we're invading anybody's privacy," Waters says.

Writing Prompts

1. Would you get on an airplane if you had to go through "the naked machine?" In three pages, argue why you would (or would not) and why others would.
2. How do you feel about cameras and face-recognition software? Using evidence from at least two essays, write an argument in favor of or against the use of such technologies.
3. Write a paragraph for each essay that summarizes the main points of that essay.
4. Using two essays, write your own three-page essay that synthesizes two sources such that your paper is able to clarify both of the authors' positions on the issue without taking a side yourself.
5. In science fiction, technology is often pictured as something both remarkable and slightly evil, or even antihuman. As our world seems more and more "modern" with our surveillance technologies, do you think the overall effect is antihuman? Write a two-page editorial in which you outline the appropriate role for advanced technologies in our lives.

What Is at Stake for Citizenship?

1. Is the "right to privacy" in the Constitution?
2. If only people guilty of wrongdoing are affected by cameras, aren't cameras a good thing?
3. Do we give up our right to or expectation of privacy when we walk out our front doors?
4. Would having to present a national ID card at checkpoints (subway stations, airports, important buildings, etc.) bother you?
5. Do you think there is anything wrong with having your face regularly scanned to see if it fits any known criminals?

EXPANDING VOCABULARY

Al Qaeda: From the Arabic words *al Qaida,* meaning "the base" or "the camp" (as in base of operations), Al Qaeda is a worldwide network of terrorists founded and run by Osama bin Laden. Al Qaeda's goals include the destruction of Israel, the elimination of all non-Muslims from Muslim countries, and the overthrow of governments in Muslim countries that Al Qaeda considers corrupt. Their goal is to replace these corrupt systems with governments that rule by Islamic law. Al Qaeda considers America its enemy because the U.S. supports Israel and because American troops are stationed in Muslim countries on the Arabian Peninsula. The September 11, 2001, hijackers were members of Al Qaeda, as was Richard Reid, the "shoe bomber."

Bin Laden, Osama: (1957–) This very wealthy Saudi and leader of Al Qaeda is thought to have planned the terrorist attacks of September 11, 2001. He has been involved in radical Islamic movements for many years, and he set up bases and training camps in Afghanistan after the withdrawal of the Russians in the late 1980s. In 1996 bin Laden called for a *jihad*, or holy war, against America—including its citizens and military around the globe. Although American forces have searched for him since the September 11, 2001, attacks, he has remained free, although in hiding. His capture would be more of a psychological than a strategic victory, as Al Qaeda is quite decentralized and can operate without his leadership.

Military draft: The system for choosing young men (but perhaps someday also young women) over the age of eighteen for military service. During Vietnam, in the summer of 1969, selection was based on birthdays, with individuals born on a specific day assigned a draft number between 1 and 365. Those with lower numbers were sure to be called up, while those with higher numbers often had a chance to avoid service. Today our armed forces are all volunteer, meaning they are completely staffed by volunteers. Because our military forces are so deeply committed around the globe fighting terror, some would like to bring back the draft, which would be a highly unpopular move.

Nation of Islam: An African American religious movement that grew out of early twentieth-century black self-improvement associations, the Nation of Islam combines tenets of more mainstream Islam and the social, political, and economic concerns of African Americans. In contrast with Christian civil rights leaders (like Martin Luther King) who called for integration and cooperation between black people and white people, members of the Nation of Islam rejected pacifism and called for equal rights "by any means necessary." Its primary leader was Elijah Mohammad, who preached that white people were the devil and called for a separatist state of America where only blacks could live. More recently there has been a split in the organization, resulting in two new groups: The American Muslim Association (led by Elijah's son Wallace Muhammad) stresses the tenets of Islam, while the Nation of Islam (led by Louis Farrakhan) stresses black nationalism.

Malcolm X: (1925–1965) Formerly known as Malcolm Little, this controversial civil rights leader later took "X" as his last name—in place of the African tribal name that was replaced by the name of white slave owners in America. While in jail, Malcolm X read the teachings of Elijah Muhammad and converted to Islam. He quickly became the leader of the Nation of Islam's New York mosque and a well-known supporter of black nationalism. Nation of Islam doctrine held that the white man was the devil, and thus the group stood apart from integrationists like Martin Luther King. After making controversial comments about the death of President John F. Kennedy, Malcolm X was asked to leave the Nation of Islam. While speaking in New York City, he was shot by gunmen thought to be associated with the Nation of Islam

Pearl Harbor: On December 7, 1941, Pearl Harbor (home of the U.S. Navy's Pacific Fleet) was attacked by carrier-based planes from the Japanese Imperial Navy, thus bringing the United States into World War II. Nearly three thousand people were killed or severely wounded in the attack. Eight battleships were sunk, while many other ships were severely damaged; nearby, nearly two hundred planes were destroyed before they could take off. Since the Japanese were still in negotiations with America to address areas of conflict between the two nations, the surprise attack was considered particularly underhanded and motivated American wartime hatred for the Japanese. President Roosevelt declared December 7 "a day that will live in infamy." The 9/11 terrorist attack is often compared to the attack on Pearl Harbor.

Pentagon: The headquarters for the U.S. Department of Defense is a five-sided building known as the Pentagon. Built from 1941 to 1943, the Pentagon is one of the largest office buildings in the country, providing workspace for over twenty thousand military and civilian employees. In September 11, 2001, the Pentagon was a target of terrorists who hijacked a plane and crashed it into the west side of the building, causing great damage and loss of life.

Reid, Richard (the "shoe bomber"): This alleged Al Qaeda member attempted to blow up a plane from Paris bound for Miami in December 2001. He had a bomb hidden in his shoe and was attempting to light a fuse when he was subdued by other passengers on the flight. Reid received a life sentence for his actions, and because of where he hid his bomb, airline passengers now take off their shoes as part of airport security checks.

Tenure: Originally describing the manner of tenants holding property in feudal England, today the term *tenure* primarily describes the rights of professors at colleges and universities to be protected from termination because of unpopular research, political views, or publications. Tenure is the foundation of academic freedom, allowing scholars to pursue their interests no matter what the political climate. Tenure is important but not bulletproof; many people have lost their jobs for just the sort of thing tenure attempts to override. After World War II, professors across the country were accused of having been communists in the 1920s and 1930s; many were fired. In the 1960s, some professors who became active in antiwar protests were fired for their desire to get the United States out of Vietnam. Today many political leaders feel that tenure is no longer useful, and they would like to eliminate it from public universities.

USA Patriot Act: An acronym for "Uniting and Strengthening America by Providing Appropriate Tools to Intercept and Obstruct Terrorism," the Patriot Act was passed in response to the September 11, 2001, terrorist attacks. It allows for further cooperation between intelligence agencies and gives those agencies more power to search, wiretap, seize, and detain persons of interest (particularly noncitizens) in terror investigations. While the Bush administration hailed it as a crucial law enforcement tool in the fight against terror, civil rights groups such as the American Civil Liberties Union claimed that the Patriot Act allows the government to violate our rights and our privacy.

World Trade Center: Although the 110-story twin towers were the most recognizable element of the design, the World Trade Center was actually a seven-building complex in Lower Manhattan. The twin towers were designed by Minoru Yamasaki and built by the firm of Emory Roth and Sons between 1966 and 1973. While the twin towers were built to withstand an impact from a commercial airliner, planes had substantially increased in size between 1966 and 2001. The commercial planes that hit the towers were also fully loaded with fuel. After being struck by the hijacked planes (flown by the 9/11 terrorists), the heat from the fires—caused by jet fuel—melted the steel supports of the buildings, causing both of the towers to collapse.

CHAPTER 10

Point of Contact:
Technology, Internet Culture,
and the Online Community

With today's technology, the pace moves fast. Just as you become comfortable with one way of doing something—how you vote, how you receive your news, how you communicate your political ideas—you discover that things have changed. One election, we vote by pushing a button or a lever, turning down a handle. The next election, we touch a screen and a light registers on a monitor. We have moved from physical to virtual. Where once we had a paper trail, we now have only an electronic count. What will be next? Will electronic voting be the only option at the next election? Or will a whole new technology come on the scene?

For many years, we read the newspaper and listened to network television for the news of the day. Now, we read our news online and listen to news from multiple channels and twenty-four-hour news platforms. Online, bloggers hold the mainstream media in check. Who will hold the bloggers in check? Will the balance be tilted? Will a whole new way of receiving the news come into being?

In the early days of the nation, when American citizens first gathered to discuss issues of governance, they came together in town hall meetings. Everyone had the opportunity to speak for or against a particular position. As towns grew into cities, hearing every personal voice on a political matter became impossible. Today, technology provides us the opportunity to return virtually to the town hall meeting. Once again, each of us has the chance through the Internet to connect with those we know and do not know, with those who share our concerns and those who adhere to different values. As we move forward in time, in some ways we are moving backwards to recapture those communal conversations that once shaped our system of government. Will the conversation continue online? At the next election, will we still use the Internet to find community with those who share our views?

This Point of Contact addresses issues of citizenship that we now confront through technology, the Internet culture, and the online community:

1. Electronic Voting: An Issue of Trust
2. Bloggers and Dan Rather: Shaping the Public Debate
3. Meetup.com and the 2004 Presidential Race

These clusters offer us a look at the debate surrounding issues that were all part of the 2004 presidential election. They can serve as a way to start thinking about how issues of technology and the Internet will make their way into the next presidential election. *Will all the problems that surround electronic voting be solved? Will bloggers still be keeping the mainstream media in check? Will websites like meetup.com be defunct or still very much a part of the 2008 presidential action?*

ELECTRONIC VOTING: AN ISSUE OF TRUST

In modern history, determining the winner of a presidential election has never taken as long as it did in the 2000 race between Democrat Al Gore and Republican George W. Bush. The candidate who won Florida would be the next president of the United States. The winner in Florida, however, could not be determined; cries of voting fraud were heard from the southern part of the state. The paper butterfly ballots failed, and "hanging chads" soon became a running gag in television prime time. Solving the complicated problem of contested votes was a high priority before the presidential election of 2004.

Enter technology. In this new century, registered voters already familiar with the ease of touch-screen computer monitors at local ATMs or airport kiosks would be comfortable, too, with electronic voting. Or so it seemed. In anticipation of the 2004 presidential election, states hurried to purchase new electronic equipment. Billions of dollars were spent, then the equipment needed to be tested, but the government was slow in establishing standards. The tests were made, in some cases by the people who made the equipment. Severe flaws were found in some of the software that ran the programs. As the election neared, computer scientists questioned security; they called for a paper trail backup system. On October 27, 2004, CBS's *60 Minutes* showed one electronic voting machine test in which a person pushed two tabs simultaneously and a third tab (one not pushed) lit up to claim the vote.

The collection of readings in this cluster is arranged chronologically—from six months before the 2004 presidential election until a few months after. About 30 percent of voters cast their ballots electronically—with no paper trail. In the opinions gathered here, some insist that a paper trail is essential. Some remind us that old machines with levers and hanging chads provided a flawed system, too. Some say it is a matter of trust. *After reading these various positions, how would you enter the conversation? What kind, if any, of electronic voting would you trust? Do you vote? Would your faith in technology make you more likely to vote?*

Dan Keating

Electronic Voting Still in Infancy, Critics Say; Security Is a Concern as Election Day Nears

Washington Post, May 5, 2004

Four years after the Florida presidential recount fiasco, opponents of electronic voting say a lack of security safeguards for the new technology could undermine voter confidence in this year's presidential election.

Problems in recent months—from crashed election computers in Fairfax to the Pentagon's scrapping of Internet voting plans because of security concerns—have given

Miami, Florida—Early touch screen voting at the Stephen P. Clark Government Center for the 2004 presidential election.

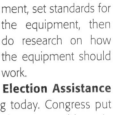

further ammunition to the opponents. And last week's decision by voting officials in California to decertify new touch-screen voting equipment has exposed the backward scheme of national election reform: lay out billions for new equipment, set standards for the equipment, then do research on how the equipment should work.

With six months to go before the presidential election, the **Election Assistance Commission** established by Congress is having its first meeting today. Congress put up $3.9 billion for election upgrades after the 2000 debacle and repeat problems in South Florida in 2002. States are to get the biggest chunk of the money in the next two months. But the commission, which was established to guide them, just came into existence, too late to help in buying decisions. And the federal research intended as the basis of the standards has not been financed, much less begun.

Meanwhile, Congress is ready to weigh in, with hearings to begin next week on several election-technology-related proposals.

"Tensions are so high and the scrutiny is so great that I would be very surprised if there were not some kind of election controversy leading up to or on Election Day," said Doug Chapin of www.electionline.org, a nonpartisan clearinghouse that monitors election reforms. "If you think of election problems as being like a forest fire, the woods aren't any drier than they were in 2000, but more people have matches. Advocacy and partisan groups are aggressively looking for problems."

Local officials are skittish about upgrading amid the growing controversy and changing standards. Localities that have not bought equipment are pleading for guidance. Early adopters who plunged ahead are fearful that the systems they bought will be declared unfit. On Friday, California Secretary of State Kevin Shelley did just that, decertifying 14,000 Diebold touch-screen terminals in four counties because of problems in the state's March 2 primary. He also decertified an additional 28,000 touch screens but said they could be used in November's election if several conditions are met, including giving every voter the option to use a paper ballot instead.

Shelley and secretaries of state in Missouri and Nevada said all electronic voting equipment must have a paper record confirmed by the voter. But manufacturers complain that the federal government has not adopted standards for those systems or even begun considering how to do so.

Vendors of the new equipment, many local officials and congressional sponsors of the 2002 **Help America Vote Act** that provided billions for reform are urging patience and faith in the new systems. The sponsors of the act have recommended waiting until the

5

Election Assistance Commission's technical committee is established and research begins before new rules are passed.

"The touch-screen controversy creates the impression that we have more problems than we do," commission Chairman DeForest "Buster" Soaries Jr. said.

10 People complaining about theoretical problems are forgetting that older technologies lost many ballots, said David Bear, spokesman for Diebold Election Systems, whose latest touch-screen equipment was decertified in California.

"The fact of the matter is that there are a lot, lot of voters who welcome the advancement of electronic voting," he said. "The fact is that we know cases where voters have been disenfranchised by the tens of thousands with lever and punch-card machines, but still we're only talking about potential scenarios with the security concerns" on new equipment.

Scot Petersen

E-Voting Underachieves; Starry-eyed Predictions Lag Behind Technical Realities

eWeek, July 26, 2004

From the digging through the archives department: "Soon every local, state and national election will be conducted online." Who was the fool who wrote that one? Answer: me, your friendly "E-Volution" columnist in the Jan. 3, 2000, issue of *PC Week* (five months before we changed our name to *eWEEK*). And for you Marv Albert fans, it came complete with the clever headline: "Online voting: Yes, and it counts!"

I could hardly be faulted for such wide-eyed optimism, could I? At the time, the stock market hadn't peaked. Everything was becoming dot-commed. Our parent company, Ziff Davis Media, took the PC out of our name for that very reason. "E" would be around a lot longer than PCs and would be a lot more relevant. If you had e-commerce, eBay and eTrade, why not e-voting?

That year, the Arizona Democratic Party held its presidential primary election over the Internet, and Alaska Republicans conducted part of their primary straw poll online. When the Florida ballot fiasco happened later that year, did we need any more proof that the nation's election systems badly needed an overhaul?

Internet voting has not caught on, due to security and business-model problems. But "electronic" voting has, thanks to the Help America Vote Act of 2002, which was enacted in the wake of the Florida recount. As Caron Carlson reported in our cover story last week, more than 30 percent of the presidential election ballots will be cast this year using touch-screen, kiosk-type machines. That's just behind the leading method, optical scanning. Almost 14 percent of voters still use the old-fashioned lever-style booths, and about 12 percent still use punch cards.

5 As Carlson reported, there are some teensy-weensy problems with the electronic systems. One, poor security, has been obvious for several years yet remains to be remedied. Two, the major suppliers of these machines, particularly Diebold and Election Systems & Software, have been dogged by allegations ranging from fraud to outspoken support of President Bush, which hardly engenders the confidence of those who are still sticking pins in their Jeb Bush and Katherine Harris dolls.

But those problems pale in comparison with the biggest shortcoming, which is that few of the systems contain a way to create a certifiable record of a person's vote. If a recount were again called where these machines are installed, it could make all of us long for the days of hanging and dimpled chads. Belatedly, Congress is holding hearings on VVPAT, or voter-verified paper audit trail, legislation, but nothing will be put in place for this fall.

As the Democratic National Convention kicks off this week in Boston, we can take note that politics has always had a kind of love-hate relationship with technology.

Voting system problems are nothing new. In the old days, ballots were stuffed, lost and cast by ghosts. Lever machines were forever getting jammed, losing who knows how many votes along the way. Even today's most reliable method of optical scanning is dubious, if you recall from your SATs how easy it is to mark outside the dot.

I was right about one thing in the 2000 column when I pointed out that people "will find in the Internet new ways to mobilize causes, raise funds and get out the vote." Indeed, Howard Dean's campaign and sites such as MoveOn.org proved this in spades last year, raising millions and getting people charged up, while John Kerry and others lagged behind.

But once the primary season came around, where was the Internet then? Dean fell   10
faster than Enron stock. As much as we'd like to believe that the distributed nature of the Internet is the great democratizing force in the world (and I've said that, too), the reality is that power is more concentrated and technology is less reliable than we are willing to admit.

When real change is warranted, though, we ought to be thankful that we still have the power to do the right thing, however imperfect the means, whether via paper, machine, touch-screen or browser. At the end of the day, it's better to have hanging chads than no chads at all.

Avi Rubin

An Election Day Clouded by Doubt

The *Baltimore Sun*, October 27, 2004

About 50 million Americans will cast their ballots for president on touch-screen terminals Tuesday.

If my experience as an election judge is any guide, voters will love these machines, which are generally easy to use and which easily accommodate voters who have disabilities or do not speak English.

And if my experience as a computer scientist is any guide, those voters will not realize just how dangerous it is to rely on these machines to conduct a free and fair election with a reliable result.

Voting on a direct recording electronic voting machine, or DRE, is in many ways similar to transferring money from one account to another at an automated teller machine. But there is one critically important difference: no receipt. There will be no physical record produced that could later be used by your local election board to prove how you intended to vote.

After you cast your ballot on a DRE, the only official record of your choices will be the   5
electronic record within the system itself. You will not be asked to look at a piece of paper

that confirms your candidate selections. You will not leave that piece of paper behind for use in case of a recount.

Why is this a problem?

Without paper ballots that can be physically examined, the only recount possible is a review of the votes recorded by the DRE system itself. And if those votes were recorded incorrectly, no recount will fix the error. The incorrect result could never be detected, much less corrected.

And incorrect results are entirely possible. Largely because of Florida's problems in 2000, there has been a headlong rush nationwide to adopt DRE voting. Touch screens will be used in this election despite numerous studies, by my colleagues and me and by others, showing that the machines from the leading manufacturer, Diebold Election Systems, are poorly designed, with lax security and programming errors.

All of Maryland except Baltimore City will be using the Diebold AccuVote-TS machines. Nationwide, about one-third of all ballots will be cast electronically.

10   Technical glitches and malfunctioning machines—the kinds of problems that occur with any computer system—could result in the loss of votes in unrecoverable ways. Worse, these fully electronic machines could be rigged—undetectably, because of the complexity of the software that runs them.

While we can never eliminate the possibility of tampering with elections, the impact of an attack on a DRE system would likely be more serious than the results of tampering with traditional mechanical voting machines or paper-based systems, such as optically scanned ballots. This is because a bug in the software of an electronic voting system, whether accidental or intentional, has the potential to skew results in more than an isolated polling place or two. It could impact the vote totals on many thousands of machines in hundreds of precincts.

Elections, by their nature, are adversarial. In a successful election, the loser should be as convinced as the winner that the outcome is legitimate, despite the potentially strong party loyalties of the people running the mechanics of the process.

One of our safeguards in the United States is that members of the two principal parties are present to watch each other through every facet of an election. The utility of this security measure is diminished when the votes are invisible and the counting is virtual. DREs reduce the transparency of the voting process, and traditional checks and balances become ineffective.

Even if, on Wednesday, this election appears to have been a success, there will be no way of knowing for sure whether the will of the people was accomplished.

15   And even if there is no problem Tuesday, that does not imply that the election was secure—only that no one chose that day to exploit the insecurity. If an apparent success in November leads to greater adoption of fully electronic voting in the future, then subsequent elections will be even more vulnerable, providing increased incentive to attackers and, at the same time, more avenues for attack.

For voters to have confidence in the election process, it should be as transparent as possible. When technology that is inherently opaque is used in elections, peoples' confidence in the process will be justifiably shaken.

There are ways in which DREs provide an apparent advantage over butterfly ballots and hanging chads. But there are other ways in which these systems, implemented without voter-approved paper ballots that allow meaningful recounts, are potentially much worse.

Our goal should be voting technology that is beyond reproach. That goal may never be fully attainable, but we must do better than this. The foundation of our democracy is at stake, and thus, ultimately, so is our freedom.

Avi Rubin is a professor of computer science at the Johns Hopkins University.

Andy Ihnatko

It's a Fun Idea, but Electronic Voting Doesn't Pass the Trust Test

Chicago Sun-Times, November 9, 2004

I'll keep three interesting artifacts from the 2004 presidential election. The first is the "I Voted Today" sticker that was pressed onto my lapel after I cast my vote. The second is the "I Donated Blood Today" sticker that was pressed onto the opposite lapel an hour or so earlier, after I drove to the wrong middle school in my voting district and got in the wrong line. The third is my copy of the Dumbold Voting Machine, a plug-in that brings real, fake electronic voting to the life-simulation game, **"The Sims."**

You can still download it from *www.originalsims.com/dumbold*. The Dumbold reproduces every weakness, both real and feared, of electronic voting machines. Your vote can be misread, polling data can be intentionally erased, a monkey can destroy the log, when P. Diddy offers you his challenge "Vote or Die!" the consequences of making the wrong choice are both tangible and immediate.

Parenthetically, you know, there's no reason why this couldn't be a mechanism for actual voting. What if we had a third voting system, in addition to traditional and absentee ballots: a secure and open standard for electronic remote polling? Just as Amazon.com allows anyone to conduct a secure financial transaction so long as they use software that conforms to a free, open and widely accepted standard (specifically, a Web browser that supports secure sockets) there could be a secure box in the state capitol that could accept connections from a properly registered piece of software, running on a networked computer.

So, I could vote from an ATM. Or through the remote to my cable box.

And, yes indeed, voting through a Web site would be possible. But it'd be cool if those   5
Sims voting machines actually worked and could send my vote through my broadband connection. Better yet, what if this voting protocol were wired into my favorite massive multiplayer online game?

I and the rest of my World War II light-infantry squad would liberate a small French village, after which we'd be free to get a shave and a hot meal, visit the bordello and then walk into the town's bombed-out post office and drop a ballot into a still-smoking box.

"Cool idea," you say, envisioning a slightly different implementation of that last idea. "But wouldn't such an uncontrolled system make it easy to fix an election?"

Not necessarily.

In fact, this sort of open standard might actually have an advantage, in that there's no single system to tamper with.

As for the possibility of hijacking a registered voter's record, well, honestly, is our current   10
paper balloting system all that secure?

Ideally, you wouldn't be able to vote remotely without using a **Smartcard,** biometric-input device, or some other method of proving that the vote's coming from a human and not a piece of illicit software. But even if all I had to do was tap in an identification number, it'd be an improvement.

Last Tuesday, anybody who (a) knew my name and street address and (b) got to my polling place ahead of me could have cast my paper ballot. No photo ID, no problem. Plus, who's to say that the same shadowy agency that would tamper with an electronic voting machine wouldn't tamper with the electronic box that scans my ballot?

But there's a clear danger to electronic voting. Paper balloting might be a flawed (and boring) system, but at least it's universally trusted.

Its weaknesses are well understood, and the voters believe that the results can be easily corroborated by a manual recount.

15   But in last week's election, many voters felt that they couldn't trust an entire fundamental nationwide technology. Hours after the polls closed, blogspace and my Inbox were jammed with graphs and first-hand accounts, each one "proving" that electronic voting irregularities skewed the results toward Bush. If not for the fact that John Kerry conceded the race 24 hours later, the process of declaring a winner in the 2004 election could have dragged on so long and so tenaciously that this time next year, we'd still be without a president, and we'd be begging the British to impose a colonial governor upon us once again.

As big a geek as I am, as committed as I am to the idea that a correctly applied technology can only create new opportunities rather than limit our potential, I have to be opposed to electronic voting. If you can't trust it completely, you shouldn't trust it at all.

Clean Election; Allegations of Massive Voter Fraud Turn Out to Be Unfounded, Fortunately

Editorial, *Houston Chronicle*, November 14, 2004

Many Americans feared that the election of 2004 would be tainted, manipulated, perhaps stolen outright. Among the suspects were Democratic voter registration drives that registered ineligible voters; GOP efforts to suppress minority votes or delete voters from the rolls; and hackers who could change the totals in electronic voting machines as easily as they enter government and corporate computers networks.

After the election, Internet bloggers seized on voting machine malfunctions and alleged widespread fraud. Adding gasoline to this tinderless and low-oxygen fire was the discrepancy between early exit polling and the actual vote count. The exit polling seemed to indicate that Sen. John Kerry would win handily; the opposite resulted.

The helpful principle that the simplest explanation for a phenomenon is apt to be the best explanation fully applies to postelection fears. It is easier to explain the inaccuracy of the exit polls—they have a large margin of error built in, and did not exceed that margin—than to prove or even plausibly allege massive voting fraud spread over at least two states and many voting jurisdictions.

The director of elections in Columbus, Ohio, said the wave of election fraud allegations on the blogosphere amounted to "a snowball of hearsay." He has a point. However, the miracle of the Internet helped to resolve and disprove the allegations it had cast over the Web. Objective election analysts countered the charges one by one.

This year's election was marred by real, admitted problems: long lines and voting 5
machines that went haywire and had to be fixed or sidelined. But the unthinkable, a
tilted election, apparently did not take place. As some analysts pointed out, the electronic
voting machines, though imperfect, are an improvement over the punch-card systems
they replaced, systems that routinely failed to count or discarded thousands of votes in
each state.

Anne Applebaum

In ATMs, Not Votes, We Trust

Washington Post, November 17, 2004

When the ATM asks whether I want a receipt, I usually say no. When a Web site
wants my credit card number, I usually say yes. When I pay bills online, there is no paper
record of the transaction. In my failure to demand physical evidence when money
changes hands, I am not very unusual. Most Americans now conduct at least some of
their financial transactions without paper, or at least sleep happily knowing that others
do. Yet when it comes to voting—a far simpler and more straightforward activity than
electronic bank transfers—we suddenly become positively 19th century in our need for
a physical record.

It is, if you think about it, quite inexplicable.

Two weeks after the election, the Internet rumor mill continues to spout stories of
computer-stolen votes. No sooner are they disproved than others appear. Some are
demanding an Ohio recount. Otherwise sober people are asking whether there can be
smoke without fire. Last weekend the *New York Times* published an editorial that found
"no evidence" of vote fraud but called electronic voting "a problem" all the same. After all,
the editorial noted, there is "no way to be sure" that votes weren't changed "by secret software" inside the machines. If you're tempted to believe that analysis is rational, just ask
yourself this question: Are you really sure that your bank isn't using secret software to steal
$9.72 from your retirement account every week? And if the answer is no, why aren't you
up in arms about that, too?

Given our reliance on computerized accounting, the explanation for the American
paranoia about computer voting cannot be rational. It must lie elsewhere, in some special
part of the national psyche. Plenty of other nations are prone to conspiracy theories, of
course: I've never forgotten a conversation I had with a Western-educated, business-suited
Jordanian who explained to me that the two blue stripes on the Israeli flag represent the
Nile and Euphrates rivers, the planned future borders of the Jewish state. But American
conspiracies have their own peculiar flavor. They tend to involve concrete, significant
historical events, and they almost always concern our own government, not external
cabals. There are few European equivalents, for example, to the decades of speculation
that have been devoted to the Kennedy assassination, which no government commission
and no historian has ever put to rest. Surely the post-Sept. 11 rumors will have an equally
long run: "The Bush administration knew in advance," "The Bush family is protecting the
Saudis" and "Did a plane really hit the Pentagon?" are all still fully current. There isn't any
reason why "They stole the 2004 election" shouldn't live forever, too.

5   Some of this may be attributable to a phenomenon observed a few years ago by a British psychologist: The larger and more significant the event, the larger the explanation the human brain seems to require. In a big country such as America, political cataclysms are inevitably large and significant. For that reason, there had to be a second gunman on the grassy knoll, and no bearded madman could possibly bring down the World Trade Center without inside help. By the same logic, the reelection of someone so widely loathed on the island of Manhattan could only be made possible by secret software.

Perhaps this country's distrust of its politicians plays a role too, as do our rarely acknowledged anxieties about the stability of our political system. All of the longest-running American conspiracy theories involve small groups of people inside the government who are secretly trying to pervert the system. They may spout the rhetoric of liberal democracy, but really they're trying to accrue personal wealth, or dominate the oil markets, or propagate some immoral cause, or steal the election. At this particular moment in history, the political left is more worried about anti-democratic cells operating in the U.S. government, but throughout the 1990s, an era of swooping black helicopters, the right was far more paranoid.

Perhaps it's a phenomenon that requires no special explanation. Maybe it's healthy that we have so much faith in our paperless financial system, and so little in our paperless voting machines. Not many democracies have lasted as long as ours, after all. Sometimes conspiracy theories do prove to be true, and it's important to remain vigilant.

Or maybe our anxieties are simply misplaced. Not long ago, I met a man who believes the U.S. financial system is an elaborate hoax perpetrated by the Federal Reserve. I laughed him off—but when I retire and find my bank account empty, I probably won't think it's so funny.

Step toward Election Standards

Editorial, *Los Angeles Times*, November 29, 2004

The Internet conspiracy theories that George W. Bush supporters stole the election by tampering with electronic voting equipment have finally died down, and for good reason. The new machines generally worked well, and there's no evidence that their data were corrupted in ways that could have swung the election.

That doesn't mean, though, that the nation's precincts should continue moving to the latest and most costly e-voting systems. The conventional wisdom now emerging—that the lack of evidence that e-voting systems improperly influenced the election means that fraud would have been impossible—is just as loopy as the cloak-and-dagger conspiracy theories it is replacing.

Touch-screen systems, which recorded about 30 percent of the nation's votes Nov. 2 (up from 12 percent four years ago), suffer from a host of security flaws that their manufacturers and local election officials have done little to correct. It doesn't take a conspiracy theorist to recognize the possibility of someone using a home computer, a modem and some hacker savvy to break into most of the touch-screen devices now on the market. The most obvious deterrent to such fraud is one that only Nevada managed to implement Nov. 2: a paper printout that scrolls under glass at the edge of the screen.

One way to fix the problem is simply to not use touch-screen systems. Voting-technology experts tend to favor optical scanners, like those used in Los Angeles County, which cost one-third as much and have been shown in some studies to produce lower voter error rates.

Regardless of what system is used, though, it will have a credibility problem until   5
Washington mandates national standards to guide how local precincts oversee voting technologies. Incredibly, the "independent" labs that local election officials hire to monitor software and hardware errors on e-voting systems are often paid by the makers of the machines. When those lab techs find problems, they are often prohibited by nondisclosure agreements from sharing them with election officials. Invitations to mischief rarely come clearer than that.

No one wants Washington to exert federal control over the ballot boxes, which state and local governments have governed since the nation's inception. But that doesn't mean Congress couldn't, or shouldn't, set basic certification and oversight procedures.

Last week, the **Government Accountability Office** took the first step toward establishing such standards. At Democrats' request, the GAO agreed to study how well both touch-screen and optical scan systems fared in the last election.

The audit should put useful pressure on the many local precincts that still haven't complied with open-records requests by those seeking to verify that everything was above board.

The conspiracy theories should be put to rest, but so should the complacency.

One Last Election Lesson

Editorial, *New York Times*, January 18, 2005

The November election may feel like ancient history, but it is still going on in North Carolina. The state has been unable to swear in an agriculture commissioner because a single malfunctioning electronic voting machine lost more ballots than the number of votes that separate the two candidates. The State Board of Elections, the candidates and the public are sharply divided on how to proceed. The mess North Carolina finds itself in is a cautionary tale about the perils of relying on electronic voting that does not produce a paper record.

When the returns came in for the agriculture commissioner race, two things were clear: the Republican, Steve Troxler, and the Democrat, Britt Cobb, were just 2,287 votes apart, and a voting machine in Carteret County had lost 4,438 votes. The machine had mistakenly been set to keep roughly 3,000 votes in its memory, which was not enough. And in a spectacularly poor design decision, it was programmed to let people keep "voting" even when their votes were not being saved.

There have been many suggestions for what to do next. The State Board of Elections initially wanted to have a revote limited to Carteret County, but a court struck that down. Then it scheduled a new statewide election, but that, too, was held to be improper. The elections board, which is bitterly divided along partisan lines, has been ordered by a judge to try again to find a way to resolve the election. But no one is predicting it will be easy.

"There are conflicting and little-used statutes and constitutional provisions that may not be consistent with each other," says Don Wright, the general counsel of the elections board.

In the meantime, both sides are promoting methods that appear designed to ensure that their candidate wins. Republicans want to count 1,352 affidavits recently collected by Mr. Troxler from Carteret County voters saying that they voted for him on the faulty machine. They say that if the affidavits were counted, it would be mathematically impossible for Mr. Cobb to win. Democrats say this would violate the principle of a secret ballot and open up the possibility of voter coercion. Some of Mr. Cobb's backers argue that the State Constitution requires that the race be decided by the state legislature, which just happens to be in Democratic hands.

5   North Carolina agriculture commissioner may not be the loftiest of offices. But if the same glitch had occurred in Washington, where Christine Gregoire was just elected governor by 129 votes, it would have destabilized the entire state government. If it had occurred in 2000 in Florida, where President Bush's margin was just 537 votes, it would have undermined an entire presidential election.

North Carolina's plight underscores a basic point about elections: because there are often problems, there must be a mechanism for a recount. If the Carteret County voting machine had produced a voter-verified paper record each time a vote was cast, these paper records could have been counted and the matter would be resolved. But electronic voting machines that do not produce paper records make recounts impossible.

The one positive thing to come out of the agriculture commissioner race fiasco is that it has prompted North Carolina to reconsider its use of paperless electronic voting. As the state ponders the issue, it should look to Ohio. Kenneth Blackwell, the Ohio secretary of state who did so many things wrong as elections supervisor last year, recently did one very important thing right. He directed all of the state's counties to adopt paper-based optical-scan voting systems. If Carteret County had voted on machines that produced a paper record, North Carolina would not have the constitutional crisis it has now—it would have an agriculture commissioner.

Writing Prompts

1. Make an argument for trusting electronic voting machines with no paper trail.
2. Looking at selections from before and after the election, how do the predictions of pundits hold up in the postelection comments?
3. Avi Rubin is a professor of computer science at Johns Hopkins University. He has concerns about the security of the software that runs the most popular brand of electronic voting machine. Because he is an expert in the field, how do his concerns carry more weight than those of the editorial writer for the *Houston Chronicle*? Or do they?
4. Search several commentaries for word choices that suggest emotionally loaded language. How does this language help the author argue persuasively for being skeptical of electronic voting?
5. Of all the pieces, which do you think has the most logically persuasive argument? Which is the most emotionally persuasive?

What Is at Stake for Citizenship?

1. If we cannot trust completely the accuracy of our vote count, how might this determine our respect for and trust in the declared winner?
2. Only a few years ago, experts in the technology field predicted that all local, state, and national elections would be conducted online. To date, that prediction has not come true, but it is now technically possible for this to be a reality. Do you believe that within the next few years, all of our voting will indeed be done online?
3. Do you think that the ease of online voting will increase the number of voters in local, state, and national elections? (In other words, if voting is easier, will more people vote?)
4. When some glitch appears in electronic voting, such as is described in the editorial about the North Carolina agriculture commissioner, what do you think is the best way to resolve the matter?
5. Do you believe that you are more likely to trust a paperless financial transaction than a paperless voting machine? What does this position have to do with your faith in a democratic nation?

BLOGGERS AND DAN RATHER: SHAPING THE PUBLIC DEBATE

The term "blog" is a conflation of "web log," and active Internet users know that blogs are a hybrid of what is happening in their real lives and in their virtual lives, a kind of modern diary or journal. For the purposes of this cluster, we will use the term "blog" in a political sense. Bloggers enter the world of journalism without the training or education of journalists. Bloggers check facts—or make them up. They may comment on the news by challenging or providing alternative views. A blogger may function alone or enter into a virtual conversation with another blogger. Bloggers don't need to know each other to enter into fierce corroboration or wild disagreement.

On September 8, 2004, *60 Minutes II* offered a segment on claims that George W. Bush was given preferential treatment during his days with the National Guard. Before the television show was off the air, bloggers had posted the first challenges to CBS and Dan Rather's report. The segment, which was based on four memos, was dubbed "Memogate" by some and "Rathergate" and "Fontgate" by others. The debate hinged on three specific areas of concern: the typography of the memos, the military terminology of the memos, and the recollections of those involved. Were those memos forged documents? The loudest bloggers claimed they were. The reputation of CBS News, also known as MSM (the mainstream media), took a hit, as did Dan Rather, who had been with CBS since 1962.

In the reading selections gathered here, the longest article appeared four months after the questioned *60 Minutes* segment in the *Columbia Journalism Review,* which, according to its website, refers to itself as "America's premier media monitor." The report challenges the alleged fact finding of the various bloggers. What all the selections seem to agree on is that blogging is putting the MSM on notice. *After reading the various pieces, where do you enter the conversation—about both Dan Rather and the work of bloggers?*

Corey Pein

Blog-Gate; Yes, CBS Screwed Up Badly in "Memogate"— But So Did Those Who Covered the Affair

Columbia Journalism Review, January/February 2005

Dan Rather signs off on his last televised CBS News Report, March 2005.

"The drama began when CBS posted forged National Guard documents on its Web site and, that same evening, an attentive 'Freeper' (a regular at the conservative FreeRepublic.com Internet site) named Buckhead raised suspicion of fraud. From there, intrepid bloggers Powerlineblog.com and Little Green Footballs, the Woodward and Bernstein of Rathergate, began to document the mounting signs of forgery."

—Chris Weinkopf in *The American Enterprise Online*

"The yeomen of the blogosphere and AM radio and the Internet took [CBS's 60 Minutes II] down. It was to me a great historical development in the history of politics in America. It was Agincourt."

—Peggy Noonan in *The Wall Street Journal*

"NOTE to old media scum . . . We are just getting warmed up!"

—"Rrrod," on FreeRepublic.com

Bloggers have claimed the attack on CBS News as their Boston Tea Party, a triumph of the democratic rabble over the lazy elites of the MSM (that's mainstream media to you). But on close examination the scene looks less like a victory for democracy than a case of mob rule. On September 8, just weeks before the presidential election, *60 Minutes II* ran a story about how George W. Bush got preferential treatment as he glided through his time in the Texas Air National Guard. The story was anchored on four memos that, it turns out, were of unknown origin. By the time you read this, the independent commission hired by the network to examine the affair may have released its report, and heads may be rolling. Dan Rather and company stand accused of undue haste, carelessness, excessive credulity, and, in some minds, partisanship, in what has become known as "Memogate."

But CBS's critics are guilty of many of the very same sins. First, much of the bloggers' vaunted fact-checking was seriously warped. Their driving assumptions were often drawn from flawed information or based on faulty logic. Personal attacks passed for analysis. Second, and worse, the reviled MSM often followed the bloggers' lead. As mainstream media critics of CBS piled on, rumors shaped the news and conventions of sourcing and skepticism fell by the wayside. Dan Rather is not alone on this one; respected journalists made mistakes all around.

Consider the memos in question. They were supposed to have been written by Lieutenant Colonel Jerry Killian, now dead, who supervised Bush in the Guard. We know Killian's name was on them. We don't know whether the memos were forged, authentic, or some combination thereof. Indeed, they could be fake but accurate, as Killian's secretary, Marian Carr Knox, told CBS on September 15. We don't know through what process they wound up in the possession of a former Guardsman, Bill Burkett, who gave them to the star CBS producer Mary Mapes. Who really wrote them? Theories abound: *The Kerry campaign created the documents. CBS's source forged them. Karl Rove planted them. They were real. Some of them were real. They were recreations of real documents.* The bottom line, which credible document examiners concede, is that copies cannot be authenticated either way with absolute certainty.

The memos that were circulated online were digitized, scanned, faxed, and copied who knows how many times from an unknown original source. We know less about this story than we think we do, and less than we printed, broadcast, and posted.

Ultimately, we don't know enough to justify the conventional wisdom: that the documents were "apparently bogus" (as Howard Kurtz put it, reporting on Dan Rather's resignation) and that a major news network was an accomplice to political slander.

What efforts did CBS make to track down the original source? What warnings did CBS's own experts provide to *60 Minutes II* before air time? These are matters for the independent commission, headed by Lou Boccardi, former chief of The Associated Press, and Dick Thornburgh, the former U.S. attorney general. But meanwhile, the dangerous impatience in the way the rest of the press handled this journalistic tale bears examination, too.

'It Isn't Just Rush Limbaugh . . . '

Three types of evidence were used to debate the documents' authenticity after Rather and *60 Minutes II* used them in the story. The first, typography, took many detours before winding up at inconclusive. The second, military terminology, is more telling but also not final. The third, the recollections of those involved, is most promising, but so far woefully underreported.

Haste explains the rapid spread of thinly supported theories and flawed critiques, which moved from partisan blogs to the nation's television sets. For example, the morning after CBS's September 8 report, the conservative blog Little Green Footballs posted a do-it-yourself experiment that supposedly proved that the documents were produced on a computer. On September 11, a self-proclaimed typography expert, Joseph Newcomer, copied the experiment, and posted the results on his personal Web site. Little Green Footballs delighted in the "authoritative and definitive" validation, and posted a link to Newcomer's report on September 12. Two days later, Newcomer—who was "100 percent" certain that the memos were forged—figured high in a *Washington Post* report. The *Post's* mention of Newcomer came up that night on Fox, MSNBC, and CNN, and on September 15, he was a guest on Fox News's *Hannity & Colmes.*

Newcomer gave the press what it wanted: a definite answer. The problem is, his proof turns out to be far less than that. Newcomer's resume—boasting a Ph.D. in computer science and a role in creating electronic typesetting—seemed impressive. His conclusions came out quickly, and were bold bordering on hyperbolic. The accompanying analysis was long and technical, discouraging close examination. Still, his method was simple to replicate, and the results were easy to understand:

> Based on the fact that I was able, in less than five minutes . . . to type in the text of the 01-August-1972 memo into Microsoft Word and get a document so close that you can hold my document in front of the 'authentic' document and see virtually no errors, I can assert without any doubt (as have many others) that this document is a modern forgery. Any other position is indefensible.

10   Red flags wave here, or should have. Newcomer begins with the presumption that the documents are forgeries, and as evidence submits that he can create a very similar document on his computer. This proves nothing—you could make a replica of almost any document using Word. Yet Newcomer's aggressive conclusion is based on this logical error.

Many of the typographic critiques were similarly flawed. Would-be gumshoes typed up documents on their computers and fooled around with the images in Photoshop until their creation matched the originals. Someone remembered something his ex-military uncle told him, others recalled the quirks of an IBM typewriter not seen for twenty years. There was little new evidence and lots of pure speculation. But the speculation framed the story for the working press.

The very first post attacking the memos—nineteen minutes into the *60 Minutes II* program—was on the right-wing Web site FreeRepublic.com by an active Air Force officer, Paul Boley of Montgomery, Alabama, who went by the handle "TankerKC." Nearly four hours later it was followed by postings from "Buckhead," whom the *Los Angeles Times* later identified as Harry MacDougald, a Republican lawyer in Atlanta. (MacDougald refused to tell the *Times* how he was able to mount a case against the documents so quickly.) Other blogs quickly picked up the charges. One of the story's top blogs, Rathergate.com, is registered to a firm run by Richard Viguerie, the legendary conservative fund-raiser. Some were fed by the conservative Media Research Center and by Creative Response Concepts, the same p.r. firm that promoted the **Swift Boat Veterans for Truth.** CRC's executives bragged to PR Week that they helped legitimize the documents-are-fake story by supplying quotes from document experts as early as the day after the report, September 9. The goal, said president Greg Mueller, was to create a buzz online while at the same time showing journalists "it isn't just Rush Limbaugh and Matt Drudge who are raising questions."

In order to understand "Memogate," you need to understand "Haileygate." David Hailey, a Ph.D. who teaches tech writing at Utah State University—not a professional document examiner, but a former Army illustrator—studied the CBS memos. His typographic analysis found that, contrary to widespread assumptions, the document may have been typed. (He points out, meanwhile, that because the documents are typed does not necessarily mean they are genuine.) Someone found a draft of his work on a publicly accessible university Web site, and it wound up on a conservative blog, Wizbang. The blog, citing "evidence" that it had misinterpreted, called Hailey a "liar, fraud, and charlatan." Soon Hailey's e-mail box was flooded. Anonymous callers demanded his dismissal.

Hailey is more restrained in his comments than other document examiners more widely quoted in the press. Of course, cautious voices tend to be quieter than confident ones.

Hailey wasn't the only one to feel the business end of a blog-mob. The head of one   15
CBS affiliate said he received 5,000 e-mail complaints after the *60 Minutes II* story, only 300 of which were from his viewing area.

The specific points of contention about the memos are too numerous to go into here. One, the raised "th" character appearing in the documents, became emblematic of the scandal, as Internet analysts contended that typewriters at the time of the memo could not produce that character. But they could, in fact, according to multiple sources. Some of the CBS critics contend they couldn't produce the specific "th" seen in the CBS documents. But none other than Bobby Hodges, who was Colonel Killian's Guard supervisor, thinks otherwise. He told *CJR*, "The typewriter can do that little 'th,' sure it can." He added, "I didn't think they were forged because of the typewriter, spacing, or signature. The only reason is because of the verbiage."

Hodges's doubts about the memo rest mainly on military terminology, and he has a list of twenty-one things wrong with the terms used in the CBS documents. He says he came up with the first ten in a couple of minutes. For example, he points to the use of "OETR" instead of "OER" (for Officer Effectiveness Report), and the use of the word "billets" instead of "positions." This helped close the case for some, but probably shouldn't have. Even preliminary digging casts some doubt on the evidence. For example, Bill Burkett was quoted in a book published last March using the term "OER," suggesting he would've known better had he forged the documents as Hodges and others implied in interviews. And newspaper stories and Air Guard documents indicate that the term "billets" was indeed used in the Air Guard, at least in the mid-1980s. Such small points don't prove anything about the memos. But they do suggest that the press should never accept as gospel the first explanation that comes along.

The Double Standard

As Memogate progressed, certain talking points became conventional wisdom. Among them, that CBS's producer, Mary Mapes, was a liberal stooge; that her source, Bill Burkett, was a lefty moonbat with an ax to grind. Both surely wanted to nail a story that Bush got preferential treatment in the National Guard. Still, there was a double standard at work. Liberals and their fellow travelers were outed like witches in Salem, while Bush's defenders forged ahead, their affinities and possible motives largely unexamined.

The Killian memos seem to have grown out of battles that began long before last September. In early 2004, Burkett had featured prominently in a book, *Bush's War for Reelection,* by the Texas journalist Jim Moore, who also co-wrote the Karl Rove biography *Bush's Brain. Bush's War for Reelection* included a story dating back to 1997, when Burkett worked as an adviser to the head of the Texas National Guard at Camp Mabry. In that role, Burkett says, he witnessed a plan to scrub George W. Bush's file of embarrassments.

When this came out, the press naturally turned to the people Burkett had named   20
in Moore's book. And those men—Danny James, Joe Allbaugh, John Scribner, and George Conn—all dismissed Burkett's story. That's four against one, but not necessarily case closed. Most reporters omitted some basic, and relevant, biographic facts about Burkett's critics.

For example, Joe Allbaugh was usually identified in press accounts—in *The New York Times,* the *Baltimore Sun,* and *USA Today,* to name a few—as Bush's old chief of staff. He is much more. In 1999 Allbaugh, the self-described "heavy" of the Bush campaign, told *The Washington Post,* "There isn't anything more important than protecting [Bush] and the first lady." He was made head of the **Federal Emergency Management Agency** after Bush's victory, resigned in 2003, and went on to head New Bridge Strategies, a firm that helps corporations land contracts in Iraq.

Danny James, a Vietnam veteran and the son of "Chappie" James, America's first black four-star general, is also a political appointee whose fortunes rose with Bush's. He had his own reason to dislike Burkett. Burkett's 2002 lawsuit in a Texas district court against the Guard claimed that the staff of then adjutant-general James retaliated against him for refusing to falsify reports. It was dismissed, like other complaints against James and the Guard, not on the merits, but because under Texas law the courts considered such complaints internal military matters. Without further investigation, we are stuck at he said, she said.

Many of the people defending Bush in February on the scrubbing story appeared again in September, when the alleged Killian documents appeared on CBS. Other defenders appeared as well, and rarely were their connections to the Bush camp made clear, or the basis for their claims probed.

Other pieces of context might have been helpful, too. For example, Maurice Udell, the former commander of the 147th Fighter Interceptor Group, in which Bush served, first came to Bush's defense in 2000 and was resurrected for the same cause in 2004. After Memogate he was a guest on *Hannity & Colmes* and was quoted in the *Fort Worth Star-Telegram,* saying the memos were "so totally false they were ridiculous." He also popped up in *The Richmond Times-Dispatch* and an Associated Press story. No one noted the cloudy circumstances of Udell's exit from the military (probably because the relevant clips are hard to find in electronic databases). In 1985, after an Air Force investigation into contract fraud, as well as misuse of base resources, Udell was ordered to resign. The initial probe included an allegation of illegal arms shipment to Honduras, but the charge came up dry.

25   Context was also lacking in quotes from Bush's old National Guard roommate, Dean Roome, who appeared with this old boss Udell on *Hannity & Colmes.* With one exception, Roome's press appearances have served a singular purpose: praise the president, attack the memos. The exception was notable and often reprinted. Last February, *USA Today* used a quote from a 2002 interview with Roome: "Where George failed was to fulfill his obligation as a pilot. It was an irrational time in his life." Roome says the comment was taken out of context, and emphasizes how great it was to fly with Bush.

In his office, Roome had taped up a printout of a September 16 *Washington Times* story in which the reporter asked Roome to speculate about who "the forger" was. Roome does not name Burkett but hints that it was he, without offering specifics. Roome also has a framed picture of President Bush signed, "to my friend Dean Roome, with best wishes." Another picture shows Roome and Bush on a couch. Roome says it's from this past March, when he attended a private party in Houston with Bush and about a dozen old friends. The meeting, Roome said, was a back-slapping affair, in which Bush told the group how he cherished his old friends from the Guard, Midland, and Dallas.

When the central charge is a cover-up, as it was in the CBS story, vigilance is required. Thus, the connections between Bush's old associates should have seen print. Together the men formed a feedback loop, referring reporters to one another and promoting a version of events in which Bush's service is unquestionable, even exemplary. With such big names and old grudges in play, journalists are obliged to keep digging.

The Memogate melee peaked in late September. On cable, Joe Scarborough of MSNBC held forth with hasty overstatements: "I'm supposed to say 'allegedly forged.' I think everybody in America knows these documents were forged." His guests threw in anything that sounded good: "You know, Dan Rather's being called on the Internet, 'Queen of the Space Unicorns,'" said Bob Kohn, author of a book on why *The New York Times* "can no longer be trusted." (The "Space Unicorn" line had first appeared on Jim Treacher's conservative humor blog, and quickly wound up on *The Wall Street Journal's* online opinion page.)

Conclusions were often hidden within questions, no matter how little evidence supported them. NBC's Ann Curry, hosting the *Today* show, asked a guest, who had no way of knowing: "Was CBS a pawn in a dirty tricks effort by the Kerry campaign to smear . . . President Bush? Can we go that far?"

No, we can't. But by the time Dan Rather announced on November 23 that he would step down from the anchor spot in March 2005, the bloggers' perceptions had taken hold. For example, the December 6 issue of *Newsweek* stated, incorrectly, that Rather had acknowledged that the *60 Minutes II* report "was based on false documents." The following week the magazine's "Clarification" was limited to what Rather had said, not to what *Newsweek* or anyone else could have known about the documents.

Dan Rather trusted his producer; his producer trusted her source. And her source? Who knows. To many, Burkett destroyed his own credibility when he told Dan Rather that he had lied about the source of the Killian memos. Still, many suppositions about Burkett are based on standards that were not applied evenly across the board. In November and December the first entry for "Bill Burkett" in Google, the most popular reference tool of the twenty-first century, was on a blog called Fried Man. It classifies Burkett as a member of the "loony left," based on his Web posts. In these, Burkett says corporations will strip Iraq, obliquely compares Bush to Napoleon and "Adolf," and calls for the defense of constitutional principles. These supposedly damning rants, alluded to in *USA Today, The Washington Post,* and elsewhere, are not really any loonier than an essay in *Harper's* or a conversation at a Democratic party gathering during the campaign. While Burkett doesn't like the president, many people in America share that opinion, and the sentiment doesn't make him a forger.

Jim Moore, who relied on Burkett for much of his book on Bush, says he initially called some of the generals who worked with Burkett to check his source's reputation—but didn't tell them what the story was about. They all said Burkett was honest and trustworthy. When Moore called them back, and described the accusations, only one of them, Danny James, then changed his opinion, calling Burkett a liar. George Conn, the ex-Guardsman who said he didn't remember Burkett's story of file-scrubbing, nevertheless told reporters Burkett was "honest and forthright."

Newsweek's Mike Isikoff has said that he interviewed Burkett last February and thought Burkett "sounded credible," but didn't use the Texan's story because he couldn't substantiate it. Good decision. CBS couldn't prove the authenticity of the documents in its story, and look at the results. Dan Rather has announced his resignation under a cloud and his aggressive news division is tarnished. And the coverage of Memogate effectively killed the story of Bush's Guard years. Those who kept asking questions found themselves counted among the journalistic fringe.

30

While 2004 brought many stories of greater public import than how George W. Bush spent the Vietnam War, the year brought few of greater consequence for the media than the coverage of Memogate. When the smoke cleared, mainstream journalism's authority was weakened. But it didn't have to be that way.

Jonathan V. Last

Prove It; The *Columbia Journalism Review* Finally Confronts CBS News, Rathergate, and the Blogosphere

The *Weekly Standard*, January 4, 2005

The *Columbia Journalism Review* has a long, proud history of ignoring the story of the forged documents used by Dan Rather and CBS News. You'll recall that the scandal first broke on September 9, 2004, when a group of bloggers publicly questioned the validity of the four CBS memos. In the ensuing media scramble to get to the bottom of the story, blogs and big journalistic outfits such as ABC News, the *Dallas Morning News,* and the *Washington Post* took turns breaking news about the forgery, and then about the real source of the documents.

In all of the hubbub, the *Columbia Journalism Review*—America's premier media criticism outfit—was notably absent. *CJR*'s blog did not mention the story until September 14, and then only in passing. Goaded by the blogosphere, they addressed the matter head-on later in the day, when managing editor Steve Lovelady wrote, ". . . we're not in the business of saying, 'You may be a bad boy; drink your medicine.' We're in the business of saying 'You are a bad boy; drink your medicine.' And, as of this moment, despite the flurry of charges and counter-charges, it's not clear whether CBS has been had by some under-cover operative intent on smearing the president, or whether the network itself is the victim of a smear campaign."

By that point, of course, the matter was nearly settled. Nevertheless, *CJR* refrained from saying much more about the story. (However Lovelady did send a letter to Jim Romenesko's media criticism website chiding other journalists for making much ado about nothing: ". . . come on, guys—try to get a grip. It's not Watergate. It's not even Rathergate. So far, it's no more than Fontgate.")

After CBS disavowed its forged documents and announced that it was conducting an independent investigation into the affair, *CJR* finally weighed in definitively, declaring that "There's nothing complicated about any of this. The real story here isn't political bias on the part of CBS or Rather. It's that of big news organizations still in the thrall of a scoop mentality that dates back to the 1920's . . ." And that was that.

5   But now *CJR*'s flagship magazine has waded into the fray, albeit four months late, with a long analysis of the story by Corey Pein.

Pein's article, "Blog-Gate," posits, somewhat counterintuitively, that the lesson of CBS's "forged" documents is that the media are allowing themselves to be manipulated by a throng of right-wing bloggers. Says Pein, "on close examination the scene looks less like a victory for democracy than a case of mob rule."

The case Pein makes against bloggers rests largely on one point: That the CBS documents were not forged. Pein says that the memos "it turns out, were of unknown origin."

"We don't know enough to justify the conventional wisdom: that the documents were 'apparently bogus,'" Pein says. He adds, "We don't know whether the memos were forged, authentic, or some combination thereof." (Authentically forged, perhaps?) And finding proof for Pein may well be impossible. "The bottom line," he says, "which credible document examiners concede, is that copies cannot be authenticated either way with absolute certainty." Which suggests that, to Pein's mind, it is actually impossible to prove that the documents are forgeries.

Having erected an insurmountable burden of proof, Pein then goes about trashing anyone who dared reach a conclusion about the memos, beginning with Joseph Newcomer.

One of the fathers of modern electronic typesetting, Newcomer wrote a definitive, 7,000 word explanation of why the memos must necessarily have been forgeries on September 11, 2004, back when *CJR* was still officially ignoring the story. Four months later, his essay is still considered definitive. By everyone save Corey Pein, that is. Pein labels Newcomer "a self-proclaimed typography expert" and allows that his work "seemed impressive." Yet Pein dismisses the 7,000 word proof out of hand in two sentences, maintaining that it was based on a "logical error." (Meryl Yourish has cleared Newcomer of this silly charge.)

Pein then moves on to the inconvenient Bill Burkett, the Texas man who fed the documents to CBS and fibbed about their origins. By the end of last September, Burkett's credibility was in tatters: He admitted lying to CBS and claimed that he had received the memos from a mysterious woman named "Lucy Ramirez" during a blind hand-off at a livestock show in Houston. He was calling himself "a patsy." *USA Today* reporters described their sessions with him: "Burkett's emotions varied widely in the interviews. One session ended when Burkett suffered a violent seizure and collapsed in his chair."

But just as he could not be persuaded that the memos were forged, Pein refuses to discount Burkett either. "Dan Rather trusted his producer; his producer trusted her source. And her source? Who knows." Pein's sympathies for Burkett go farther:

> . . . many suppositions about Burkett are based on standards that were not applied evenly across the board. In November and December the first entry for "Bill Burkett" in Google, the most popular reference tool of the twenty-first century, was on a blog called Fried Man. It classifies Burkett as a member of the "loony left," based on his Web posts. In these, Burkett says corporations will strip Iraq, obliquely compares Bush to Napoleon and "Adolf," and calls for the defense of constitutional principles. These supposedly damning rants, alluded to in *USA Today*, *The Washington Post*, and elsewhere, are not really any loonier than an essay in *Harper's* or a conversation at a Democratic party gathering during the campaign. While Burkett doesn't like the president, many people in America share that opinion, and the sentiment doesn't make him a forger.

So goes it at the *Columbia Journalism Review*. The university's motto may still be "In lumine Tuo videbimus lumen," but over at the j-school they have a new slogan: You can't prove anything.

Jonathan V. Last is online editor of The *Weekly Standard*. He also runs the blog Galley Slaves.

Art Buchwald

Caught in the Web

Washington Post, September 28, 2004

Last week the bloggers had a big win over Dan Rather—14-0. Who, you ask, are the bloggers? They are people who send their opinions out over the Internet on any subject they deem fit or not fit to print.

Bloggers come in all political flavors. They put information on their Web sites that other bloggers can read and reply to.

The captain of the team that gave such a drubbing to CBS was Carlton Doolittle, an all-American conservative blogger from Texas.

We met in a chat room.

5   "Congratulations," I said. "What an upset."

"It was a team effort," he typed back. "The conservative bloggers have been waiting for some time to get Rather and his team."

"How did you find out how weak their line was?" I asked.

He typed back: "As soon as Rather kicked off with the story on '60 Minutes,' I sent a message to Tex Hotrod, Charley Rov and Sam Flyswatter. Then all the papers picked it up and ran with it."

"Is that when Rather called 'time out'?" I asked.

10   "Yes, but he fumbled and lost control of the ball."

I wrote, "I saw it on television."

"Once the ball started rolling, bloggers from all over the country blitzed Dan. None of us could leave his computer. It was the biggest reaction we've ever had on the Internet. I've gotten e-mails asking me to be on Fox, the 'Today' show and 'Good Morning America,' and Peter Jennings wants to make me Person of the Week."

"Talk about fame. What do you need to be a blogger?"

"A computer and the Internet."

15   "Do your blogs have to be true and verified by two sources?"

"No," Doolittle wrote. "That is the beauty of it. Anyone can send a message and not worry whether it is reliable. The truth is in the head of the sender. Some of our best bloggers have a reputation for putting the most outrageous things on their Web sites and having other people believe it."

"What does your big win over Rather tell you?"

"Blogging is no longer a spectator sport. Kids now do it after school. Colleges vie for testimonials from celebrity bloggers. The world will never be the same after the Rather fiasco."

"Blogging is relatively new," I wrote.

20   "It started only a few years ago. Bloggers used their Web logs to meet other men and women on the Internet. Then one day someone sent out a political message. The other side responded. Pretty soon the messages got meaner and meaner. Both the right and the left discovered they had the power—and that's where we stand right now."

"There are a lot of people I would like to blog, but I'll check my sources first."

"It's not necessary. There are no rules. We lucked out against CBS. They tried to prove that George W. Bush was a lousy Air National Guardsman and it blew up in their faces."

"What now?" I typed.

"We're still blogging John Kerry's cowardly Swift boat acts in Vietnam."

"Thanks for joining me in the chat room. May I have your autograph on a fax?"   25

Doolittle replied, "Not if you're going to forge it."

Our Turn; There's No Denying Impact of Bloggers; Their Challenge to CBS News Makes It Increasingly Difficult to Dismiss Them as Simply Amateurs in Pajamas

San Antonio Express-News, September 16, 2004

Mainstream media often look with disdain on the burgeoning world of Web logs, better known as blogs.

But if anyone questioned the influence of the blogosphere, surely doubts have dissipated in the past week as bloggers have risen to challenge the credibility of a "60 Minutes II" report about President Bush's Air National Guard service.

Evidence they have accumulated offers a compelling case that the documents used by CBS to bolster the report were forgeries. Other networks and newspapers now are focusing not on the original story, but on the story about the story.

CBS and "CBS Evening News" anchor Dan Rather, clearly on the defensive, continue to stand by the accuracy of their initial report.

Jonathan Klein, a former executive vice president of CBS News, dismissed bloggers'   5
significance in a Fox News Channel interview: "You couldn't have a starker contrast between the multiple layers of checks and balances (at "60 Minutes") and a guy sitting in his living room in his pajamas writing."

Rather said there was "no definitive evidence" to prove the documents are forgeries. In a less than stellar endorsement of the network's checks and balances, Rather added: "If any definitive evidence comes up, we will report it." This fairly well inverts a standard rule of investigative journalism.

But bloggers already had burst into the media as an alternative to traditional sources of news and commentary in print and on television. They were instrumental in pushing questions about John Kerry's military service in Vietnam to the front page and evening news.

As with any medium, bloggers include purveyors of meaningful information and enlightening commentary, as well as recyclers and garbage dealers.

What has become clear is that serious bloggers are now helping shape the public debate and driving issues that the mainstream media might otherwise ignore.

The verdict on the accuracy of the "60 Minutes II" report may not be conclusive. The   10
growing impact of blogs, however, is undeniable.

La Shawn Barber

The Blogosphere's Smaller Stars

National Review, December 20, 2004

Things happen in real time on the web, and by now, "Rathergate" is rather old. But its early days marked a dramatic moment for bloggers, and a dark one for traditional journalism: one that Dan Rather will never forget. A nascent watchdog known collectively as the **"blogosphere"** had emerged from the shadows.

Earlier this year, CBS aired a now-infamous *60 Minutes* episode in which Rather presented typed memoranda supposedly written over 30 years ago by President George W. Bush's Texas Air National Guard commander, the late Lieutenant Colonel Jerry B. Killian. The documents purported to show that Bush received preferential treatment while serving in the military. Hours after the broadcast, well-known bloggers like Little Green Footballs, Power Line, and the widely known Instapundit—as well as NRO's Kerry Spot & The Corner—were casting doubt on the documents' authenticity. As the controversy grew, they posted frequent updates and became virtual clearinghouses of information.

The rest is well-documented history, so to speak.

The thing about history, though, is that the efforts of minor players often go unnoticed. During the scandal, high-trafficked bloggers were interviewed on radio and television and mentioned in countless news articles. Two appeared on the cover of *Time* magazine. But smaller, lesser-known, and lower-trafficked blogs that didn't get press coverage served a valuable function during Rathergate. By linking to well-known blogs, articles, documents, and one another, they made worthy contributions. A few even conducted their own independent, journalistic-style investigations (often scooping the professionals).

5   "It all happened organically, without any controlling influence at all, and it happened fast," says Jeff Harrell about the growth of the blogosphere-fueled controversy. A freelance writer from Texas, Harrell's blog, The Shape of Days, was frequently linked to by Instapundit as the story picked up steam.

Once the story caught on, it spread rapidly across the web, though some bloggers were skeptical at first. "It just seemed the type of thing that could make the blogosphere look bad if people jumped the gun and start[ed] crying 'forgery' without actual evidence," admits a blogger who goes by the name "Cassandra" and runs I Love Jet Noise.

Rusty Shackleford, a political-science professor who hosts MyPetJawa, says he followed the story very closely but urged bloggers to proceed carefully. "My original post was quoted all over the blogosphere as a word of caution to those boring full speed ahead on indicting the Killian memo."

He eventually joined the blogosphere's quest for the truth as he searched the National Archives to find out whether the U.S. Air Force had purchased a typewriter during the stated time frame capable of producing the memos.

Other bloggers saw the frenzy as political noise. "I despise partisan bickering," insists Harrell. "I thought this story was just another example . . . I dismissed it pretty early on."

10   Once the CBS memos seemed likely to be forgeries, some bloggers began investigating different aspects of the story. "Patterico," a prosecutor in California, fact-checked ABC News and posted the results on his site, Patterico's Pontifications. He said ABC News

falsely concluded that posters on FreeRepublic.com—the conservative news forum where the hoax idea germinated—were the forgers of the documents.

Patterico contends that ABC News's conclusion was based on a misreading of the time-zone stamp on the posts, which they had assumed to be Eastern time. "ABCNEWS failed to note that the time stamp was Pacific time. Based on this simple mistake . . . [the network] falsely concluded that internet (sic) posters had posted their doubts about the documents before the program had ended," he wrote. ABC News has since corrected the error on its website.

Additionally, Patterico interviewed "Buckhead" and "TankerC," the subjects of ABC's report and the first to express doubt about the memos. "I knew that these individuals would likely be the focus of some interest from the media, and that loonies would try to connect them to Karl Rove. I thought it would be interesting for them to get their real stories before the public."

Now that's journalism.

Like Patterico, Harrell used the power of the web to gather information and answer questions. "[W]hile the typographic evidence of forgery was pretty good, there was one hole I wanted to fill." It seemed that the IBM Selectric Composer, an expensive typewriter from the 1970s, might have been able to produce the memos. While that possibility had been dismissed, Harrell continued to investigate. The expert he tracked down, a Composer owner, confirmed it could not have produced the documents. "I wanted to rule it out conclusively," Harrell said.

While other bloggers parsed news reports and interviewed experts, Bill Dyer used his own expertise to add insight. A practicing lawyer in Texas who runs the BeldarBlog, Dyer verified and posted the professional credentials of lawyer bloggers pursuing Rathergate—such as Glenn Reynolds (Instapundit) and Hugh Hewitt—after Jonathan Klein, former executive vice president of CBS News, referred to bloggers as "a guy sitting in his living room in his pajamas writing." 15

The effect bloggers have had on traditional journalism as they become fact-checkers, disseminators of information, and "citizen journalists" is still in flux. But the paradigm has clearly shifted in determining what is news and who is qualified to cover it, and smaller bloggers are playing an important role. Tom Maguire, host of the blog Just One Minute, also frequently linked to by Instapundit, says that smaller bloggers can do research to uncover overlooked angles and connections.

Patterico believes smaller bloggers can be noticed. Although larger ones get the media coverage, smaller bloggers can still break stories. "[I]f your message is unique, there is still a good chance it will get attention."

Others see the importance of blogs and public interaction, particularly during Rathergate. "[B]y making the news cycle interactive, bloggers had essentially resurrected the front-porch aspect of civil life where folks used to gather to discuss the issues of the day," Cassandra says. Blogging is "revitalizing democracy."

At least one journalist seems to agree. Chris Satullo, editorial-page editor at the *Philadelphia Inquirer*, recognizes the role of bloggers but stressed that journalists are still necessary. "The idea is not that journalists know what the best result is; it's that democracy works best when issues get aired, real dialogue happens and ordinary people aren't shut out of the deal by elites. [A]ny card-carrying civic journalist is going to celebrate the blogosphere."

20   Including its smaller stars.

La Shawn Barber is a freelance writer from Washington, D.C., and hosts her own blog at www.lashawnbarber.com.

Russ Lipton

Blogging In

World Magazine, September 25, 2004

The word blog is still sometimes greeted by uncomprehending stares, but that's changing as writers of internet blogs (short for "web logs") have shown their importance once again by demonstrating that CBS and Dan Rather accepted as real evidently forged documents concerning President Bush's National Guard service.

Critics of bloggers say they are uncredentialed, but God has an odd habit of certifying opinion leaders uncredentialed in the sight of the professional classes. Thus, Joseph rose to prominence in Egypt, David in Israel, and Peter in A.D. Jerusalem.

Heaven cares nothing about man's credentials as such but cares only whether the speaker is telling the truth or offering his own opinion. Many of Israel and Judah's kings, priests, and prophets were duly appointed by one another, but their words proved false to the "what is" of moral and historic fact.

Blogs are a mixed bag, since most practitioners are private citizens on Internet soapboxes. We live in a culture that often believes mere anti-establishment sentiment is a mark of authenticity. Too often, blogging is narcissistic and self-referential. Then, again, so is mainstream media reporting.

5   Since the latter for many months did not pursue John Kerry's Vietnam narrative—or last year's misfeasance by a *New York Times* editor—was it unprofessional for the blogosphere to go after that story? Who are the journalists and who are the special pleaders?

CBS in essence said, "Trust us, we're CBS." But we should not trust without verification the credibility of political and media leaders or their critics. As human beings, we often rewrite our own histories to make ourselves look better, and sometimes (for dramatic purposes) to look worse in the past. Nor should we trust the big media leaders who set themselves up as impartial judges: The evidence of a tilt to the left is overwhelming.

Paradoxically, blogging has emerged as a trustworthy source precisely because bloggers wear their prejudices on their sleeves. Liberal and conservative bloggers deconstruct the mainstream media and then each other until the fool's gold of spin has been worn away. Often, a tiny, but valuable, nugget of factual gold emerges that is unchallengeable.

There's hope. *The New York Times* may live up to its ombudsman's recent, remarkable admission that it is (surprise!) a liberal newspaper: It's certainly time for it to surrender hypocrisy. And bloggers whose punditry is consistently spot-on to facts will be rewarded with the appropriate street-credential of a large, faithful readership.

—Russ Lipton is one of the "blogging pastors" on http://www.worldmagblog.com, which also provides up-to-date coverage of "Rathergate" and other breaking news.

Peggy Noonan

The Blogs Must Be Crazy

Wall Street Journal, February 17, 2005

"Salivating morons." "Scalp hunters." "Moon howlers." "Trophy hunters." "Sons of Sen. McCarthy." "Rabid." "Blogswarm." "These pseudo-journalist lynch mob people."

This is excellent invective. It must come from bloggers. But wait, it was the mainstream media and their maidservants in the elite journalism reviews, and they were talking about bloggers!

Those MSMers have gone wild, I tell you! The tendentious language, the low insults. It's the Wild Wild West out there. We may have to consider legislation.

When you hear name-calling like what we've been hearing from the elite media this week, you know someone must be doing something right. The hysterical edge makes you wonder if writers for newspapers and magazines and professors in J-schools don't have a serious case of freedom envy.

The bloggers have that freedom. They have the still pent-up energy of a liberated   5
citizenry, too. The MSM doesn't. It has lost its old monopoly on information. It is angry.

But MSM criticism of the blogosphere misses the point, or rather points.

Blogging changes how business is done in American journalism. The MSM isn't over. It just can no longer pose as if it is The Guardian of Established Truth. The MSM is just another player now. A big one, but a player.

The blogosphere isn't some mindless eruption of wild opinion. That isn't their power. This is their power:

1. They use the tools of journalists (computer, keyboard, a spirit of inquiry, a willingness to ask the question) and of the Internet (Google, LexisNexis) to look for and find facts that have been overlooked, ignored or hidden. They look for the telling quote, the ignored statistic, the data that have been submerged. What they are looking for is information that is true. When they get it they post it and include it in the debate. This is a public service.

2. Bloggers, unlike reporters at elite newspapers and magazines, are independent   10
operators. They are not, and do not have to be, governed by mainstream thinking. Nor do they have to accept the directives of an editor pushing an ideology or a publisher protecting his friends. Bloggers have the freedom to decide on their own when a story stops being a story. They get to decide when the search for facts is over. They also decide on their own when the search for facts begins. It was a blogger at the World Economic Forum, as we all know, who first reported the Eason Jordan story. It was bloggers, as we all know, who pursued it. Matt Drudge runs a news site and is not a blogger, but what was true of him at his beginning (the Monica Lewinsky story, he decided, is a story) is true of bloggers: It's a story if they say it is. This is a public service.

3. Bloggers have an institutional advantage in terms of technology and form. They can post immediately. The items they post can be as long or short as they judge to be necessary. Breaking news can be one sentence long: "Malkin gets Barney Frank earwitness report." In newspapers you have to go to the editor, explain to him why the paper should have another piece on the Eason Jordan affair, spend a day reporting it, only to find that all that's new today is that reporter Michelle Malkin got an interview with Barney Frank. That's not enough to merit 10 inches of newspaper space, so the *Times* doesn't carry what the blogosphere had 24 hours ago. In the old days a lot of interesting information fell off the editing desk in this way. Now it doesn't. This is a public service.

4. Bloggers are also selling the smartest take on a story. They're selling an original insight, a new area of inquiry. Mickey Kaus of Kausfiles has his bright take, Andrew Sullivan had his, InstaPundit has his. They're all selling their shrewdness, experience, depth. This too is a public service.

5. And they're doing it free. That is, the *Times* costs me a dollar and so does the *Journal*, but Kausfiles doesn't cost a dime. This too is a public service. Some blogs get their money from yearly fund-raising, some from advertisers, some from a combination, some from a salary provided by *Slate* or *National Review*. Most are labors of love. Some bloggers—a lot, I think—are addicted to digging, posting, coming up with the bright phrase. OK with me. Some get burned out. But new ones are always coming up, so many that I can't keep track of them and neither can anyone else.

But when I read blogs, when I wake up in the morning and go to About Last Night and Lucianne and Lileks, I remember what the late great Christopher Reeve said on "The Tonight Show" 20 years ago. He was the second guest, after Rodney Dangerfield. Dangerfield did his act and he was hot as a pistol. Then after Reeve sat down Dangerfield continued to be riotous. Reeve looked at him, gestured toward him, looked at the audience and said with grace and delight, "Do you believe this is free?" The audience cheered. That's how I feel on their best days when I read blogs.

15   That you get it free doesn't mean commerce isn't involved, for it is. It is intellectual commerce. Bloggers give you information and point of view. In return you give them your attention and intellectual energy. They gain influence by drawing your eyes; you gain information by lending your eyes. They become well-known and influential; you become entertained or informed. They get something from it and so do you.

6. It is not true that there are no controls. It is not true that the blogosphere is the Wild West. What governs members of the blogosphere is what governs to some degree members of the MSM, and that is the desire for status and respect. In the blogosphere you lose both if you put forward as fact information that is incorrect, specious or cooked. You lose status and respect if your take on a story that is patently stupid. You lose status and respect if you are unprofessional or deliberately misleading. And once you've lost a sufficient amount of status and respect, none of the other bloggers link to you anymore or raise your name in their arguments. And you're over. The great correcting mechanism for people on the Web is people on the Web.

There are blogs that carry political and ideological agendas. But everyone is on to them and it's mostly not obnoxious because their agendas are mostly declared.

7. I don't know if the blogosphere is rougher in the ferocity of its personal attacks than, say, Drew Pearson. Or the rough boys and girls of the great American editorial pages of the 1930s and '40s. Bloggers are certainly not as rough as the splenetic pamphleteers of the 18th and 19th centuries, who amused themselves accusing Thomas Jefferson of sexual perfidy and Andrew Jackson of having married a whore. I don't know how Walter Lippmann or Scotty Reston would have seen the blogosphere; it might have frightened them if they'd lived to see it. They might have been impressed by the sheer digging that goes on there. I have seen friends savaged by blogs and winced for them—but, well, too bad. I've been attacked. Too bad. If you can't take it, you shouldn't be thinking aloud for a living. The blogosphere is tough. But are personal attacks worth it if what we get in return is a whole new media form that can add to the true-information flow while correcting the biases and lapses of the mainstream media? Yes. Of course.

I conclude with a few predictions.

Some brilliant rising young reporter with a growing reputation at the *Times* or   20
Newsweek or *Post* is going to quit, go into the blogging business, start The Daily Joe, get someone to give him a guaranteed ad for two years, and become a journalistic force. His motive will be influence, and the use of his gifts along the lines of excellence. His blog will further legitimize blogging.

Most of the blogstorms of the past few years have resulted in outcomes that left and right admit or bray were legitimate. Dan Rather fell because his big story was based on a fabrication, Trent Lott said things that it could be proved he said. But coming down the pike is a blogstorm in which the bloggers turn out to be wrong. Good news: They'll probably be caught and exposed by bloggers. Bad news: It will show that blogging isn't nirvana, and its stars aren't foolproof. But then we already know that, don't we?

Some publisher is going to decide that if you can't fight blogs, you can join them. He'll think like this: *We're already on the Internet. That's how bloggers get and review our reporting. Why don't we get our own bloggers to challenge our work? Why don't we invite bloggers who already exist into the tent? Why not take the best things said on blogs each day and print them on a Daily Blog page? We'd be enhancing our rep as an honest news organization, and it will further our branding!*

Someone is going to address the "bloggers are untrained journalists" question by looking at exactly what "training," what education in the art/science/craft/profession of journalism, the reporters and editors of the MSM have had in the past 60 years or so. It has seemed to me the best of them never went to J-school but bumped into journalism along the way—walked into a radio station or newspaper one day and found their calling. Bloggers signify a welcome return to that old style. In journalism you learn by doing, which is what a lot of bloggers are doing.

Finally, someday in America the next big bad thing is going to happen, and lines are going to go down, and darkness is going to descend, and the instant communication we now enjoy is going to be compromised. People in one part of the country are going to wonder how people in another part are doing. Little by little lines are going to come up, and people are going to log on, and they're going to get the best, most comprehensive, and ultimately, just because it's there, most heartening information from . . . some lone blogger out there. And then another. They're going to do some big work down the road.

Writing Prompts

1. After you read Pein, argue that Last either does or does not build an effective argument against Pein.
2. Humorist Art Buchwald, known for his insightful political satire, creates a fictional "Carlton Doolittle" as a vehicle to explain a blogger's activity. Continue the satire by imagining what Doolittle might have said to Hotrod, Rov, and Flyswatter after his exchange with Buchwald.
3. Noonan offers an argument that bloggers provide a public service. Do you agree with her position? Is "public service" a helpful way to think about the activities of bloggers?
4. Bloggers have a tendency to work quickly to get their thoughts and positions, knowledge and opinions, posted to the blogosphere. Do you think that speed works for or against their credibility? Use information from a selection of the readings to support your position.
5. Bloggers are quickly changing the roles and rules of trained journalists. Based on what you read here, do you think bloggers are here to stay?

What Is at Stake for Citizenship?

1. A free citizenry depends on a free press. While bloggers might function as watchdogs on the mainstream media (MSM), how can we know that they aren't just pushing another agenda?
2. When blogging meets MSM, it is necessary that citizens be well informed so that they may weigh both sides being presented. What, then, is the challenge of educating ourselves responsibly? Where do we begin? Whom do we trust first?
3. When bloggers bring down icons from the MSM, what do these success stories suggest about the training and education of journalists?
4. The Internet gives bloggers the opportunity to act quickly, to reach the masses without any responsibility to authority. Is this instant reporting a positive or a negative?
5. Should bloggers be held to accountability when they weigh in on serious political issues that affect us as a democracy? Should they have to state by what authority they have come to their positions? Should they identify upfront their political agendas?

MEETUP.COM AND THE 2004 PRESIDENTIAL RACE

In 2000, Harvard professor Robert Putnam published a book called *Bowling Alone*, about the disintegration of community involvement and social interaction among neighbors. Scott Heiferman, successful dot-com entrepreneur, read Putnam's book and responded with a June 2002 debut of meetup.com, a website where individuals with specific pursuits might find others who enjoy their same interests. Within six months, meetup.com entered the political arena. Liberal-leaning, mostly white, middle-aged professionals went online to meet up with other people who shared their frustrations with the Bush administration. The people came to the candidates—especially to Howard Dean, in whom many found a voice that was expressing their views and their hopes. Soon all the Democratic presidential hopefuls saw that meetup.com could be a useful tool. From late winter 2003 through the summer, Dean's popularity continued to grow; a "campaign phenomenon" some called it. Was it the man or the medium that was attracting the attention and the interest of voters, the media, and those who study such occurrences?

Dean showed his competition that the Internet and specifically meetup.com could be used to raise money—more than $7 million within a few months. Meetup.com became the avenue, as well, for candidates to inform potential voters and recruit volunteers. Meetup.com showed the electorate how the Internet will matter in future elections.

In the readings offered here—from March 2003 through the start of 2005—we see that meetup.com is a website that can and will be used by both major political parties. It has and will make a difference in mobilizing supporters, fund raising, and getting out the vote. In the election of 2004, meetup.com involved thousands of individual citizens in active support of various candidates, providing a welcomed respite from "bowling alone." Meetup.com did not change the outcome of the election, but its potential for making a difference has been tapped. *After reading the selections on the role of meetup.com, where do you enter the conversation? What other uses do you see for such websites as meetup.com that have, as yet, been unexplored?*

Kathleen Hennessey
How Grass Roots Grab Hold of Presidential Race on Web

Sacramento Bee, March 16, 2003

Voters meet up in San Bernardino, California.

Never mind a former House leader, a trio of U.S. senators and the Rev. Al Sharpton. On one front of the 2004 election battle, presidential candidate Howard Dean's fiercest opponents are people who believe they were unicorns in a past life.

That far battlefield is the "Top Topics" list on Meetup.com, a

Web site that helps people of similar interests, zip codes—and, yes, reincarnations—meet face to face. Since it launched in June 2002, the site has primarily been a place to meet the freaks and geeks in your neighborhood; vampires, pagans, tarot readers and reincarnated unicorns had a lock on the most popular topics list. But in recent weeks, the politically minded have signed on en masse, using Meetup to organize get-togethers across the nation and drum up grass-roots support for their favorite candidates.

The users are primarily young, tech savvy, political newcomers who say memories of the 2000 debacle in Florida and opposition to Bush's foreign and military policies have motivated them to get active. The surge of early organizing is making the fledgling campaigns take notice, and raising questions about when and how in an Internet age a campaign should grab hold of its grass roots.

In a little over a month, some 7,274 people have signed up to attend a "meetup" for a 2004 candidate, according to the counter on the site. On Feb. 4, some 25 gathered in Chapel Hill, N.C., to talk about Sen. John Edwards. Another 15 met that same week in a bar in Minneapolis to talk about Dean. March 5 was National Howard Dean Meetup Day, bringing several hundred people to a restaurant in New York, Howard Dean being one of them.

5   "It's pretty cool. I mean, from the campaigns' standpoint, it's great. These people are mobilizing themselves," said Sue Burnside, the founder of Burnside and Associates, an L.A.-based consulting firm specializing in grass-roots organization and fieldwork. "Of course, at some point you need to take control of your campaign. If I were working for these campaigns I'd be watching them pretty closely."

So far, the campaigns that are watching them closely are the ones that can't afford not to. Volunteers who'll go door-to-door in places like Ames, Iowa, and Keene, N.H., are critical to any primary campaign.

But for Dick Gephardt, who has name recognition, grass-roots infrastructure in the all-important states of Iowa and New Hampshire, and a presidential campaign under his belt, a pack of young potential volunteers talking about his economic plan over lattes in San Francisco would not typically reach the radar of top-level campaign staff. For a former governor from Vermont making his national debut or a first-term senator from North Carolina, any meeting of 10 supporters who can find Iowa on a map doesn't just get watched—it gets ogled.

Meetup is 31-year-old CEO Scott Heiferman's third tour on the dot-com circuit. He sold his first company, an Internet marketing startup called i-traffic, for $25 million in 1999. After another venture failed, Heiferman dropped out of dot-com life, and took a job flipping burgers at McDonald's, as his Web site explains, "to help get back in touch with the real world . . . and because I deserved a break today." Heiferman's break ended in June 2002 when, inspired by Robert Putnam's *Bowling Alone*—an account of the deteriorating social ties in America—he launched Meetup.

The Web site boasts of practicing egalitarian principles, subverting hierarchy and promoting greater community ties. And company spokesman Myles Weissleder said they are happy to see candidates for office taking the spotlight away from the ex-Jehovah's Witnesses. But the change hasn't happened on its own. Meetup has done all it can to draw political types to the site, from encouraging campaigns to put a link to Meetup on candidate Web sites, to meeting with the Dean campaign to discuss a future partnership.

"We always knew what our potential was," said Meetup's political point man William   10
Finkel of the site's new incarnation. "I think we always envisioned this sort of use, I don't
think we knew it would be this early."

For many political junkies, the site has become a sort of straw poll tracking what candidates are getting the most buzz online. On that front, Howard Dean is leading the pack.
In addition to inspiring several Web logs and Yahoo groups, the Dean2004 meetup group
has 5,675 people signed on nationwide. Kerry is at 593; Al Gore has 333; and Edwards
has 410. Lieberman (24), Gephardt (40) and Bush (151) supporters all have meetups
scheduled. At least five people in one zip code must sign on for the meetup to actually
occur, a rule that forced the handful of John Kerry fans in San Francisco to cancel the party.

All these eager volunteers need to get started is an e-mail address and a zip code.
Once logged in, they can search for an existing topic, like, tarot cards or GaryHart2004. The
site tells them the date of the next meetup for that group. The topic, dates and time for
these groups are suggested by the users, but must be approved by Meetup. Visitors themselves vote on a location from a ballot of four restaurants, bars or coffee houses that have
paid to be listed on the site. One week before the meeting users get a reminder e-mail
revealing the winning location.

Then, they pack their cards or their '80s nostalgia and go meet. The company doesn't
send any representatives to the meetups, and there is no set agenda.

Ginny Franks, an eager young Democrat at the University of North Carolina in Chapel
Hill, used the site in January to find people who supported her favorite presidential candidate. At first, she said, the experience was slightly disorienting.

"It took me a moment to figure out if it was a site for, like, the Indigo Girls and Tori   15
Amos, or for John Edwards," she said.

Once she had that straightened out, Franks signed in, voted to meet at a coffee house
across the street from campus and showed up on a February evening. Like Franks, most
of the people there were already part of a Students of Edwards group on campus.

They were joined by a handful of others, an Edwards campaign volunteer coordinator
who'd learned of the event online and the local TV news crew she brought with her. Franks
said the group spent most of its time getting to know each other and talking about the
candidate's positions.

"There was just a lot of talking," said Bill Hulette, a 51-year-old engineer, one of the
few people over 30 at the meeting. Still, he was happy to make contact with a campaign
representative and plans to attend another meetup on March 4.

Franks also worried that the meeting was long on talk and short on planning. "It's
based on a sort of egalitarian Internet society, and the problem with that is: Who takes
responsibility for facilitating action?"

At a Meetup for Howard Dean in early February, a group of New Yorkers answered   20
that question quickly: whoever takes the initiative. John Miller and Dave Nir both found
Meetup.com through the political Web log, mydd.com. They met up with 15 other supporters at a hipster Greenwich Village bar. After one meeting the group started building its
own listserv, designing flyers to hand out at the Feb. 16 anti-war protests and planning its
next meeting independent of Meetup. Miller and Nir have since started a sort of unofficial
field office in New York, and launched their own Dean site, NewYorkforDean.com.

"I think at such an early stage people who wanted to get involved don't always have
a way to do it. There's no Dean office in New York without Meetup," said Miller, a

34-year-old techie for an Internet startup. Miller and a handful of Meetup recruits are hoping that their early involvement will give them a leg up in the organization once a New York office comes to town.

A Dean meetup in Oakland early this month was equally focused. The 20 people gathered at the Cyber Cafe made specific plans for printing bumper stickers, passing out fliers and making signs in preparation for Dean's appearance at State Democratic Convention. Some even talked about appointing volunteers to positions like campaign contact and media relations director.

Of course, all this activity happening independent of the campaign is a terrible tease for a consultant. "One of the big frustrations is knowing there are 2,000 people going to these meetings, and I don't have their e-mails," said Joe Trippi, Dean's campaign manager.

Meetup does not release the e-mail addresses of its members. So both the Dean and the Edwards campaigns have sent representatives to some of the meetings to scope out the groups and collect contact information. But Finkel said the company is hoping to develop partnerships with campaigns in which Meetup would send e-mails to users on the campaign's behalf and share demographic information in exchange for a service fee. Right now all of the site's revenue comes from the restaurants and bars that pay to have their establishments listed as possible locations for a meetup.

25   "We're helping them build their brand, or rally behind a cause, and there's value in that. We plan on extracting some of that value," said company spokesman Weissleder.

However, the Dean campaign said it's not thinking that far ahead.

"We love Meetup.com because they provide a service which we could not do ourselves," said a senior Dean advisor. "I don't know if we'd be willing to pay for it."

But experimenting with interactive efforts using corporate sites is new territory for campaigns. "I don't know of anything that's been done like this before," said Elaine Kamarck, who studies politics and Internet at Harvard Kennedy School of Government. "Campaign Web sites, up to this point, have essentially been Internet brochures."

Breaking out of that mold requires some careful steps by a campaign. The Federal Election Commission closely monitors corporate ties to presidential campaigns. Corporations are not allowed to give anything of value to presidential candidates—no discounts on pizza, no free advertising. However, the FEC does allow companies to put information about candidates on their Web sites provided that no one candidate is given preferential treatment. So, until Meetup and a campaign enter into a formal contract, a link to the Dean campaign Web site or greater visibility for a Kerry meeting could raise FEC attention.

30   Campaigns must also be careful that a site's commercial interest doesn't interfere with the campaign's message of public service. While Meetup doesn't post banner ads or use pop-up windows, its privacy policy allows the company to send e-mail to its users on behalf of advertisers and doesn't protect user information if the company merges or folds.

For a commercial site, this isn't unusual. But Mike Cornfield of the Institute for Politics, Democracy and the Internet at George Washington University said Meetup's political associations and the talk of free-form community mislead users into thinking the site is something other than a moneymaking endeavor.

"These people are data merchants disguising themselves as **communitarians**," said Cornfield, a self-described privacy hawk.

Users said that since Meetup only asked for their e-mail addresses and zip code, they were not concerned with privacy.

"My e-mail is already out there pretty heavily," said Bill Hulette. "Maybe I should be concerned, but I wasn't. I wanted to make contact with the campaign. That's why I was there."

This focus on action is perhaps a key difference between these new Meetup visitors and other Internet users who passively forward e-mail alerts and sound off in chat rooms.

"Sure, you can ask someone to send out a mass e-mail, blast the hell out of everyone, but it doesn't do any good unless people actually read it, get outside and show up at the train station, or the rally," said Burnside. These people, she said, have already proven they'll show up.

"These people are your precinct walkers."

Kathleen Hennessey is a student at the UC Berkeley Graduate School of Journalism.

Edward Miliband

Meet-up at the White House? All of a Sudden, the Anti-War Howard Dean Looks a Serious Candidate for US President

New Statesman, August 25, 2003

Flashmobs are the fad of the summer. Groups of young people, prompted by the internet, gather at a particular time and place to perform some mundane and meaningless action. For months, the Democratic presidential campaign of the former Vermont governor Howard Dean has been dismissed as a political flashmob: a passing fad soon to be forgotten.

After all, went the conventional wisdom, Vermont is one of the smallest states in the US, so his political experience will carry no clout. In any case, ran the argument, this guy—an opponent of war in Iraq, the first governor to sign legislation for gay civil unions, a proponent of universal healthcare—is far too liberal to win the nomination, never mind the presidency. And rather like the flashmob, Dean has built support through a website, www.meetup.com, which up to now has been used by people with hobbies, such as breeding chihuahuas or performing yoga, who want to meet like-minded people. "It's like watching my 13-year-old daughter instant-messaging," sneered the campaign manager for a rival candidate. "It's not particularly about politics and policy. It's almost like a reality show."

Dean meet-ups have indeed become a campaign phenomenon. On the first Wednesday in August, 481 events took place on the same day in every US state, with nearly 80,000 people attending (the next most popular meet-up Democrat, John Kerry, has 8,000 members). At one of three separate meet-ups in the Boston area, Maggie, a doctor at a local hospital, confirmed that Dean's innovative use of the internet is part of his appeal.

"I am here as much because of the campaign as the candidate," she said, sitting cross-legged on the floor of the bar where the meet-up was held.

Brief rallying speeches by local state representatives and a rather wooden video message from Dean were followed by the main business of the evening: the assembled supporters, about 100 of them, mostly young, writing personal letters to New Hampshire voters about why they should support Dean.

The extent of Dean's grass-roots network is unprecedented for this stage of a Democratic primary campaign, still five months before the first real vote is cast in Iowa. His supporters enabled him to raise more money ($7.5m) from more people (59,000) than any other Democratic candidate in the second quarter of the year, with much of it coming from small, web-based donations.

Moreover, there are reasons to believe that Dean's appeal can extend beyond his current support base to a wider Democratic audience. First, he sounds angry—angry at the war on Iraq, angry about George Bush's tax cuts. This resonates with Democratic voters, who still resent the contested 2000 election result. Second, he is an outsider in Washington, anything but slick, with a slightly herky-jerky speaking style. For many, this adds to his appeal as an honest and unspun guy who says what he thinks. The perception that he is plain-speaking gives credibility to his policy agenda, centered around a promise to move towards universal healthcare for children and then adults, based on his record as governor of Vermont.

So far, so liberal—liberal enough, at any rate, to prompt the Democratic Leadership Council to attack him as a throwback to the more unsuccessful liberal Democratic candidates of the past.

Yet Dean defies conventional labeling. He supports the death penalty. He opposes most further gun control, wanting the issue left to individual states. And he is a zealot for balanced budgets, which he delivered for 11 years in succession in Vermont. All this is precisely why the liberals at the Boston meet-up believe that Dean could win against President Bush—because, rather like Senator John McCain, who sought the Republican nomination in 2000, he can run as the straight-talking reformer who can't be typecast.

10 Yet the history of American politics is littered with people whose primary campaigns briefly surged and then fell away when they moved from media-charmed insurgent to scrutinized front-runner. If he is to avoid that fate, Dean has to meet three challenges.

He must show that his policies are robust, and so avoid the fate of Bill Bradley in 2000, whose plans for healthcare were taken to the cleaners by Al Gore. He must show that he is electable against Bush, particularly given that the action in Iraq enjoys majority public support and that his pledge to reverse all of Bush's tax cuts may leave him open to attack. Many are also asking whether a Democrat from Vermont, in the far northeast, can possibly appeal to the rest of the country, particularly the south. And it was clear from Democrats at the Dean meet-up that if he demonstrably cannot win, they may switch allegiance.

Finally, Dean has to hope that no other candidate can pick up momentum. Of these, John Kerry looks the best bet. He sounds far more presidential than Dean and has a war record to insulate him from charges of softness on national security. Kerry's challenge is to gain the enthusiasm as well as the respect of primary voters.

What is clear for now is that Dean has changed the shape and feel of this primary race. Democratic outsiders can win the nomination: Jimmy Carter and Bill Clinton, both of them state governors, pulled it off. Three months ago, people would have guffawed at such comparisons. Yet, all of a sudden, Dean looks like no joke.

Edward Miliband, on leave from HM Treasury, where he is special adviser to the Chancellor, is a visiting lecturer in government at Harvard University. miliband@fas.harvard.edu

Barb Palser

Virtual Campaigning

American Journalism Review, October 2003/November 2003

Munching a turkey sandwich in front of his laptop on July 28, Democratic presidential candidate Howard Dean saw that his three-day online fundraiser had reeled in more than $500,000, shooting past the total for the $ 2,000-a-plate luncheon Dick Cheney hosted the same day. Add that figure to the $5 million in online contributions collected by late July, plus more than 100,000 supporters registered with MeetUp.com to lead and attend Dean gatherings, and the case is made: The Internet will matter in 2004.

Yes, the Net also mattered in 1996, 2000 and the midterm elections in between, but mainly as a convenient resource for reporters and a last-minute primer for voters. With a few notable exceptions (such as Jesse Ventura's 1998 run for Minnesota governor and John McCain's post-New Hampshire online fundraising flurry in 2000), neither the media nor the campaigns behaved as though online stumping could turn an election.

This time, however, the politicians and the press seem to believe the Internet could actually make a difference in the sustained, mobilizing, money-raising, vote-getting sense. The spotlight is on Dean now, but the entire pack of 2004 candidates is putting on a good show. Months before primary season, their Web sites are already bursting with daily bulletins, snapshots from the campaign trail and invitations to donate, sign up, get involved. If the early interest is any indication, people will.

According to the **Pew Internet & American Life Project,** 8 percent of the online population visited candidate Web sites during the 2000 race. With a much larger potential audience this year, reporters need to start looking at those sites as more than press release repositories. They are a direct line of communication between candidates and voters. If the candidates are ready to treat the Web as a primary medium for their messages, the media should be prepared to cover it that way.

That means looking past the novelty of a folksy campaign journal and scrutinizing a site's content. In a 2002 report published by the Institute for Politics, Democracy and the Internet, author Albert L. May suggests that "Web watches" may soon become as common as today's "ad watches" in which journalists investigate the veracity of campaign ads. (The full report, "The Virtual Trail," is available at www.ipdi.org.) Tracking the online campaign is old territory for many online news sites, but seldom have those stories made print or broadcast news. In the Internet era, all audiences ought to know how a candidate handles his or her virtual campaign.

Does the candidate's site make claims that contradict his or her voting record or other public statements? Does the site present all of the candidate's campaign advertisements or only the positive, non-attack ads? If the site contains financial information, does it jibe with the Federal Election Commission's reports? Is personal information submitted to the site kept private, or shared with other organizations? If the site offers campaign journals or Weblogs, who writes them? (Dean's Weblog is mostly maintained by volunteers and staffers; despite the hype, the candidate rarely makes a personal appearance.)

In addition to monitoring the candidates' activities, the online media should take a good look at their campaign coverage. According to Pew, for example, e-polls rank among the favorite online activities of election news consumers yet in previous campaigns, we've seen that the results of online polls often don't correlate to those of scientific polls. And consider how a networked mob of enthusiastic supporters for a particular candidate could skew an online survey.

Most important, the media will be obliged to do an even better job of what they've done all along: provide the information, analysis and decision-making tools the candidates won't. While voters can tap position statements and rhetoric at the source, news sites should tell us whether the candidates' actions measure up to their words. They should help us track the money, dissect the ads and follow the promises.

The full-scale entry of campaigns and grassroots movements onto the Web has the potential to change political communication and participation in this country. Despite legitimate concerns about the wealthier, whiter demographics of the online population, Web campaigns are already reaching people who didn't get involved before. They can unite scattered voices into potent forces and expand the 30-second sound bite that typifies modern campaigning. They are also vulnerable to the same old manipulations we see in other media, and probably some new ones.

10   Whether or not the Web makes a clear difference in the 2004 vote and even if Howard Dean's virtual juggernaut turns out to be a flash in the pan, the way campaigns are waged and covered is about to change.

Jonathan Saltzman

Dean Activists Found to Be Party Core; Surveyor Finds Bulk Far from Disaffected

Boston Globe, November 20, 2003

If the thought of Howard Dean's grass-roots supporters conjures up a bunch of Volvo-driving, Starbucks-sipping, antiwar baby boomers who are new to political activism, you're right and you're wrong.

In what is being described as the first systematic analysis of Dean activists who attend nationwide coffee klatches set up by the online group Meetup.com, Bentley College government professor Christine B. Williams confirmed that Dean's supporters were largely white, middle-aged, upper-middle-class professionals who use the Internet several times a day.

But they were hardly alienated from politics before Dean's insurgency, she said. Indeed, they tended to be liberal Democrats who voted regularly, often volunteered on national and local political campaigns, and supported Al Gore for president in 2000.

They generally liked another past anti-establishment presidential candidate, former Democratic Senator Bill Bradley of New Jersey, and were evenly divided over two others, Ralph Nader of the Green Party and Republican Senator John McCain of Arizona.

5   Williams surveyed nearly 600 activists who attended the former Vermont governor's Oct. 1 "meet-up" at about 20 venues in 15 states, including five in Massachusetts. The findings, she said, challenge the notion that the Democratic front-runner's supporters are themselves "mavericks or political newbies."

"These people are strong Democrats, the people who vote in Democratic primaries, the Democratic core," she said at the Waltham campus.

Williams, who has studied the role of the Internet in politics and government, found that the average age of activists at Dean's meet-up was 44 (although it ranged from 12 to 88). Some 91 percent were white. They had an average household income of $67,000 a year.

Most said they followed the news every day in the newspaper and on television, radio, and the Internet. And 75 percent went online several times a day—no surprise, given the prominent role the Web had played in Dean's campaign to raise campaign funds and organize.

Some 84 percent said they voted in all or most federal, state, and local elections. Thirty-nine percent said they had volunteered on political campaigns before. About 71 percent described themselves as liberal or progressive, or both.

Jesse Gordon, the cofounder of MassForDean, a Boston-based group of Dean volunteers, who arranged for the surveys to be distributed from Missoula, Mont., to Norton, Mass., said the results confirm the impression people have of Dean activists, with the notable exception of dispelling the myth they were from outside the Democratic party.

"Most people perceive the Dean movement as filled with disaffected Democrats or people outside the party system, in other words Greens or independents, and that's not the case," he said.

Williams acknowledged that the results may say more about Dean activists who go online and attend monthly meet-ups than about his more casual supporters.

"What we don't know is how much is this about the candidate and the campaign, and how much is this about the medium and Meet up," said Williams, a native of Chicago who got a taste of political activism as a child in the early 1960s, when Democratic precinct captains handed out campaign buttons to children in her neighborhood.

She hopes to survey supporters of all candidates who hold meet-ups—virtually all the Democrats as well as President Bush—and compare them. The next group will be those attending the Dec. 1 meet-up for retired general Wesley K. Clark.

So far, about 142,000 people have signed up to attend Dean meet-ups, 44,400 for Clark meet-ups, 17,900 for Ohio Representative Dennis Kucinich's meet-ups, and 16,100 for Massachusetts Senator John F. Kerry's meet-ups, according to Meetup.com.

Meetup.com, a New York-based company, was co-founded in 2002 by Scott Heiferman, 31, a dot-com millionaire who had established two Internet firms in the boom years. The goal was to use the Internet to arrange face-to-face get-togethers of people with common interests instead of the faceless chat rooms that pass as communities in cyberspace.

Heiferman, a native of suburban Chicago, said he was influenced by *Bowling Alone*, a 2000 book by Harvard University professor Robert D. Putnam focusing on what he sees as the collapse of community spirit in America.

"Meetup was at its core really a simple idea—to connect people locally," Heiferman said in a telephone interview Tuesday from Las Vegas. "The traditional logic goes that the Internet makes things less local, but why couldn't it make things more local?"

Initially, Meetup.com expected the site would be used mostly by people with a passion for Elvis, or dachshunds, or Dungeons & Dragons. But the presidential candidates, particularly Dean, have harnessed them for their campaigns. Dean supporters, for example, attend meet-ups to exchange ideas, hand-write letters to New Hampshire voters, and distribute campaign literature.

Christine B. Williams and Jesse Gordon

The Meetup Presidency

Campaigns & Elections, July 2004

An organizing tool guaranteed to triple donations. Proven to increase campaign volunteers by 30 percent monthly. Ready-to-use in all 50 states. Another McCain-Feingold loophole? No, it's Meetup.com, the source of Howard Dean's and Wesley Clark's grass roots Democratic presidential primary surges, now poised to do the same for John Kerry in the general election.

The Internet came of age in the 2004 Presidential nomination contest. And it was not in the expected role of a new medium of communication destined to supplant television. Instead, the Internet proved its worth as the high tech equivalent of pre-television one-on-one campaign techniques long used by political parties to mobilize support for their candidates, largely through Meetup.com

We surveyed 1,500 attendees at Meetups from October 2003 through April 2004 to investigate how Meetups might work for Kerry.

How Meetups Helped Dean and Clark

Meetups are Internet-organized volunteer-run meetings of people who share a common interest, arranged through the Web site www.Meetup.com. The Dean campaign was the first presidential campaign to extensively use Meetup.com, beginning in December 2002. The Draft Clark movement and several other campaigns soon followed. Since then, "Politics and Activism" has become Meetup's largest category by far, with more than 60,000 people attending monthly at the peak of the primary season.

5   Dorie Clark, a press secretary for the Dean campaign, summed up the benefits.

"Meetup gets people invested in the campaign. They're not just passive supporters; they're active participants," she said. "The more connected people feel to a Dean community, the more likely they will volunteer, and the less likely they will be to change allegiance to another candidate."

John Hlinko, founder and leader of the "Draft Wesley Clark" movement, credits Meetup with allowing growth from one campaign Web site to 100 local chapters in 90 days. Kerry's Meetup numbers similarly increased fourfold from the time of the Iowa contest to the nomination wrap up in mid-March.

Meetups provide a link between the formal campaign and local grass-roots politics. Most people first attend Meetups and then become involved with the campaign, providing a local means to get further involved with the national campaign.

"Over 200,000 Americans have expressed interest in meeting with their neighbors to plan for an election many months away," William Finkel, Meetup's outreach manager, said. "That shows that Americans do care about their government."

The General Election, Meetups and Kerry

10   Steve Grossman, former chair of the Democratic National Committee and national finance chair of the Dean campaign, said he sees significant opportunity in Meetup.

"Meetup can be used by the Democrats to level the playing field . . . and truly bring back a commitment to participatory politics in America. That's the hallmark of the Democratic Party. Adapting Meetup as an organizational tool of choice addresses our core strengths and values."

The top three Meetup political categories are **Democracy for America** (the post-Dean organization), the Kerry campaign and the Democratic Party. A large majority of the political Meetups are for Democratic campaigns or liberal causes.

The majority of Meetup attendees first found their local Meetups because of campaign home page links. Local political Web sites could similarly direct viewers to their upcoming local Meetups, which would increase attendance and thereby increase support for Kerry.

Grossman said the Internet is a powerful tool, but must be used carefully.

"You can't simply look at the Internet as a fund-raising tool. For example, you can buy names to build your e-mail lists, and your campaign will still fall flat if you don't get those people on-board as stakeholders. Meetup is a tool for grass roots organizing, and small-donor fund-raising is a natural by-product of a Meetup-based campaign."

What type of people attend Meetups? Demographically, the profile of these survey respondents is mostly white, middle-class and older than the average Internet user.

While Meetups primarily reach one side of the digital divide, they should be considered a means of creating Kerry recruiters, not just creating Kerry voters. Most attendees (79 percent) invite others to attend subsequent Meetups.

"In addition to the monthly national action item of generating letters to early primary state voters and elected officials, Meetups were a springboard for the birth of hundreds of local and state Dean organizations," said Michael Silberman, who was Dean's national Meetup director.

Can the success of Dean and Clark Meetups be replicated for the Kerry campaign? Yes, if attendees feel empowered to take grass roots action and if the Meetup hosts receive appropriate support (supplies, tasks, campaign materials) from the campaign. Local Kerry organizers should draw on the large base of Meetup hosts who were formerly Dean and Clark supporters, and encourage them to lead Kerry Meetups and Democratic Party Meetups.

From anecdotal evidence, the Kerry campaign has not heavily focused on Meetups as a recruiting tool, and the Democratic Party Meetups are even less organized.

Meetup hosting is a relatively small investment with a potentially large return. Plan on some introductory activities and on addressing new supporters separately from those already onboard.

"When there's lots of new folks coming, they expect to be wooed for a bit, and to have a little cheerleading and fun before some real action items later on," Hlinko said.

How Meetups Will Change Politics

Meetup.com includes Senate, House and gubernatorial races. While the non-presidential Meetup listings remain small (the largest, Barack Obama, the Democratic U.S. Senate nominee in Illinois, boasts 1,300 registrants), registrations continue to grow, and Meetup.com anticipates wider use in 2006.

Survey respondents said they expect of Meetup usage primarily by future grass roots campaigns, as well as issue campaigns and statewide campaigns. We surveyed how Meetups would be useful to future campaigns. Attendees had three basic categories of motivation:

1. **Information-seeking.** Respondents came to Meetups "to learn more about the candidate and to see who else is interested in him. Also to learn what else we could do to get involved locally." Meetup hosts should provide information about the candidate's background, and make campaign materials readily available.
2. **Social interaction or community building.** The need for building "social capital" as expressed in books like "Bowling Alone," is the goal of Meetup.com's founders. Many respondents wrote comments like, "I like the informality and also the flexible, yet helpful structure provided by the host."
3. **Empowerment and task orientation.** The Dean campaign used Meetups for direct volunteer tasks such as writing personal notes to voters in other states, telling them why they supported Dean, or urging officeholders to endorse Dean. The monthly Meetups provide the only regular meeting-place for casual volunteers. One response: "Coming together with other concerned voters gives me a sense of community, empowerment and hope. It also directs our energies toward specific events for which we can volunteer."

25   By the November elections, perhaps a million people will have attended Meetups, and a cadre of several thousand will have hosted Meetups. The positive experience of these hosts and participants lead them to expect they would be repeat attendees.

Justin Gest

Bush Supporters Are Catching on to Internet Connection

St. Louis Post-Dispatch, October 17, 2004

One of the leaders of the St. Louis group is 2001 mayoral candidate Michael Chance, who said the group attracts anywhere from three to 24 people to its monthly meetings at Pat's in Dogtown.

The presidential campaign of Howard Dean made it popular. John Kerry expanded on it. And now, several George W. Bush supporters are warming up to it.

MeetUp.com

The Dean campaign used the nonpartisan Web site last year to organize those supportive or intrigued by the Vermont governor to physically "meet up" and discuss Dean, the Democratic Party, and the 2004 presidential election.

Beyond providing an outlet for the politically passionate, the Dean meet-ups by some 300 groups offered a place for volunteers to push their candidate and cheaply construct a grass-roots campaign.

5   Now, Bush supporters are borrowing a page from the Democratic playbook. Hundreds of Bush meet-ups are convening everywhere from Anchorage, Alaska, to Miami Beach, Fla.

Missouri is no exception. St. Louis' "Bush in 2004" meet-up boasts 52 members. Kansas City's has 47, Jefferson City's has 12, and Columbia's Bush meet-up has six people subscribed.

One of the leaders of the St. Louis group is 2001 Republican mayoral candidate Michael Chance, who said the group attracts anywhere from three to 24 people to its monthly meetings at Pat's Bar and Grill in Dogtown.

"Oftentimes, people don't know how to hook into a campaign and they usually just want to meet with like-minded individuals, and MeetUp.com gives you an opportunity to do just that," said Chance, a computer programmer and analyst for SBC Corp.

"We sit around and talk about the issues and criticize the latest, most outrageous ad from MoveOn.org and make fun of the latest dumb thing Kerry did."

Chance, a board member of the city's Republican Party, has also used the meetings   10
as a way to mobilize support for local Republican candidates—like his wife, Sandra Chance, who is running for state representative from the 63rd district.

St. Louis GOP chairman Ronald Sherill said he believes voter mobilization will determine the result of the November election, and that Dean campaign's initial idea can work for Republicans too.

"Any good idea is usable by both sides," Sherill said. "I think the clear distinction between George W. Bush and John Kerry will be bringing people out of the woodwork to vote. Meetup gives us an infinite amount of possibilities."

A further possibility is fund raising.

James Parmelee, the chairman of the political action committee Republicans United for Tax Relief, leads a meet-up just outside of Washington.

"I kept hearing about the Dean meet-ups, so I thought I'd go on the Web site and see   15
what it's all about," he said. "We figured, why not give it a try ourselves? We've met new people and recruited new people. This gives me around 300 new people who otherwise were not affiliated."

At its September meeting, Parmelee's group gathered at the Rock Bottom restaurant in Ballston, Va. Amid a happy-hour atmosphere, they chatted about everything from politics to their personal lives.

"With this election being so heated, I didn't want to sit it out," said Shye Kahan, who just moved from Pittsburgh. "This gathering is a beginning for me to meet people who feel the same way I do. Most of my friends are liberals, so it's nice to talk to someone who says, 'Yeah, right on,' instead of arguing with me."

Washington resident and meet-up member Peter Evans said meet-ups are an inherent part of the democratic process. "What it's doing is channeling my spare time and creativity into political activity," Evans said. "A lot of people within the U.S. think the government runs this country. But little meetings like this give us a chance to bounce ideas off of each other, and translate into our decisions at the polls."

Bush supporters have opened 330 meet-up groups nationwide with over 6,000 members. There are currently 849 Kerry counterparts with nearly 140,000 members.

And many Kerry supporters also belong to anti-Bush meet-ups, like the "Against Bush"   20
group (131 chapters), the "Republicans Against Bush" group (137 chapters), and even the "Impeach Bush" group (277 chapters).

In Washington, one Democratic front group called "Angry Drunken Leprechauns for Bush" also emerged on the MeetUp Web site.

The leprechaun movement seems to have had tough luck though.

It has one member.

How to join To join a MeetUp of your choice, log on to http://www.meetup.com/browse/. For a Bush 2004 MeetUp: http://bush2004.meetup.com/. For a Kerry 2004 MeetUp: http://johnkerry.meetup.com/.

Blogosphere Politics

Michael Barone

U.S. News and World Report, February 21, 2005

Going into the 2004 election cycle, just about everyone said the Internet was going to change politics. But no one was sure how. Now we know.

The first signs of change came from the Howard Dean campaign. His campaign manager, Joe Trippi, used the Internet and meetup.com and moveon.org to identify and bring together Bush haters from all over the country and raise far more money than anyone expected. Dean rose to the top in the polls and amassed an E-mail list of 600,000 names. When Democratic voters dropped Dean as unelectable and embraced John Kerry as the most readily available instrument to beat George W. Bush, Kerry inherited Dean's Internet constituency. No one expected the Kerry campaign to raise more money than the Bush campaign. But it did, because of the Internet.

The Democratic Internet constituency was and is motivated by one thing more than anything else: hatred of George W. Bush. To see that you only have to take a look at dailykos.com, run by Democratic consultant Markos Moulitsas, which gets 400,000 page views a day—far more than any other political weblog—and which received funding from the Dean campaign (which Moulitsas disclosed). It seethes with hatred of Bush, constantly attacks Republicans, and excoriates Democrats who don't oppose Bush root and branch. When four American contractors were killed in Iraq in April 2004, dailykos.com wrote, "I feel nothing over the death of the mercenaries. They are there to wage war for profit. Screw them." This repulsive comment produced no drop-off in page views. This was what the left blogosphere wanted. Kos was an early enthusiast for Dean's campaign for Democratic chairman and disparaged other candidates.

For 12 years, Democratic chairmen were chosen by Bill Clinton. He built a new generation of fundraisers who relished contact with the Clintons. Now the big money comes from the left blogosphere and Bush-hating billionaires like George Soros. Dean gives them what they want. As Dean says, "I hate the Republicans and everything they stand for." Hate. But Bush hatred was not enough to beat Bush in 2004—while Democratic turnout was up, Republican turnout was up more—and doesn't seem likely to beat Republicans in 2006 and 2008. The left blogosphere has driven the Democrats into an electoral cul de sac.

5   Media hatred. The Bush campaign, quietly, used the Internet to build an E-mail list of 7.5 million names and a corps of 1.4 million volunteers who produced more new votes than the Democrats. But the right blogosphere was different from the left. There was no

one dominant website and no one orthodoxy. Glenn Reynolds, the University of Tennessee law professor whose instapundit.com gets 200,000 page hits a day, supports Bush on Iraq but disagrees with him on abortion, stem-cell research, and same-sex marriage. The focus of hatred in the right blogosphere is not Kerry or the Democrats but what these bloggers call Mainstream Media, or MSM. They argue, correctly in my view, that the *New York Times,* CBS News, and others distorted the news in an attempt to defeat Bush in 2004.

The right blogosphere's greatest triumph came after CBS's Dan Rather on September 8 reported that Bush had shirked duty in the National Guard and the network posted its 1972-dated documents on the web. Within four hours, a blogger on freerepublic.com pointed out that they looked as though they had been created in Microsoft Word; the next morning, Scott Johnson of powerlineblog.com relayed the comment and asked for expert views. Charles Johnson of littlegreenfootballs.com showed that the documents exactly matched one he produced in Word using default settings. CBS defended the documents for 11 days but finally confessed error and eased Rather out as anchor. MSM tried to defeat Bush but instead only discredited itself. The Pew Center's post-election poll showed a sharp decline in the credibility of newspapers and broadcast TV and a sharp increase in reliance on cable news, especially Fox News, and radio.

So what hath the blogosphere wrought? The left blogosphere has moved the Democrats off to the left, and the right blogosphere has undermined the credibility of the Republicans' adversaries in Old Media. Both changes help Bush and the Republicans.

Writing Prompts

1. Using several selections here, what can we learn from the early popularity of Howard Dean on the meetup.com site that either party might want to replicate in the next presidential election?
2. If you have participated in a gathering of people through meetup.com, how would you describe your experience? Does it match any examples from the readings?
3. Based on what you read here, how do you see the Internet continuing to make a difference in future political elections?
4. Internet websites can be used to spur hatred just as easily as they can be used to promote positive feelings. Should a watchdog or blogger monitor and comment on such attitudes? Using selections from the readings, in what positive and negative ways were the meetup.com sites used in the election of 2004? Support your position with quotes from the reading.
5. According to Gest and Barone, the Republicans came late to the Internet and borrowed "a page from the Democratic playbook." From what you read, why is this the case? In the next presidential election, which political party will make the most use of such sites as meetup.com?

What Is at Stake for Citizenship?

1. What difference does it make if those citizens that use meetup.com are mostly white, middle-aged professionals?
2. What are some ways to encourage diversity among those who get involved in politics through meetup.com?
3. What is the connection between giving money and voting? Are people less likely to vote for a candidate if they give neither their time nor their money to that candidate?
4. How important to democracy is it that the Internet's role in our elections be relatively balanced in delivery—both positive and negative? Or does it matter if the Internet slants too heavily in one direction or the other?
5. Do you see yourself participating in future meetup.com gatherings for political candidates of your choosing?

EXPANDING VOCABULARY

Blogosphere: A term used to describe the interactive connection between bloggers (those who maintain logs or journals on the Internet) and mainstream media journalists (often abbreviated MSM).

Cabal: A secret scheme or plot; also, a conspiratorial group of those plotting some form of intrigue.

Communitarian: A member or supporter of a small cooperative community.

Democracy for America: According to their official website, "Democracy for America (DFA) is a political action committee dedicated to supporting fiscally responsible, socially-progressive candidates at all levels of government—from school board to the presidency. DFA fights against the influence of the far right-wing and their radical, divisive policies and the selfish special interests that for too long have dominated our politics." The group was inspired by the presidential campaign of Howard Dean.

Election Assistance Commission: This group serves as a national clearinghouse and resource for compiling information and reviewing procedures with respect to the tasks of federal elections.

Federal Emergency Management Agency (FEMA): Established in the aftermath of 9/11, FEMA is under the auspices of the Department of Homeland Security and is charged with the mitigation, preparedness, response, and recovery of any area declared a federal disaster area by the President of the United States.

Government Accountability Office (GAO): The investigative agency of the legislative branch of the federal office, GAO exists to help improve the performance of Congress and to make the federal government accountable to the American people.

Help America Vote Act (2002): This act established a program to provide funds to states to replace punch card voting systems, established the Election Assistance Commission to assist in the administration of federal elections and provided assistance with the administration of certain federal election laws and programs, and established minimum election administration standards for states and units of local government with responsibility for the administration of federal elections.

Pew Internet and American Life Project: According to their website, the mission of the project is to "produce reports that explore the impact of the Internet on families, communities, work and home, daily life, education, health care, and civic and political life. The Project aims to be an authoritative source on the evolution of the Internet through collection of data and analysis of real-world developments as they affect the virtual world."

Sims, The: The best-selling PC game in history, it is a strategy/simulation game designed to let the player create and control the lives of virtual people.

Smartcard: A credit card–sized plastic card with an embedded microchip that can be loaded with data, allowing the card to do an assortment of sophisticated technological transactions.

Swift Boat Veterans for Truth: This organization formed after John Kerry's use of Swift Boat veterans in his 2004 presidential campaign. As this group challenged Kerry's military record, others challenged theirs. Right or wrong, though, the group was influential in calling into question Kerry's war record.

Expanding Vocabulary: Historical, Rhetorical, and Genres

Historical: Cases, Speeches, Organizations, Events, Legal Terms, and People

Affirmative action: A program undertaken by government, employers, and educational institutions to redress the effects of past discrimination. The long-term goal is gender-free and color-blind laws bringing equal opportunity, but such a program may involve quotas, policies, and recruitment that recognize minority candidates who have been historically denied opportunity.

Alexie, Sherman: (1966–) A Spokane/Coeur d'Alene Indian and a graduate of Washington State University, Alexie is the author of poetry, short stories, novels, and screenplays. Alexie received the Washington State Arts Commission Poetry Fellowship in 1991 and the National Endowment for the Arts Poetry Fellowship in 1992.

American Civil Liberties Union (ACLU): On the organization's website, it states: "The ACLU is our nation's guardian of liberty. We work daily in courts, legislatures, and communities to defend and preserve the individual rights and liberties guaranteed to every person in this country by the Constitution and laws of the United States. Our job is to conserve America's original civic values: the Constitution and the Bill of Rights." ACLU was founded in 1920.

American Family Association (AFA): On the organization's website, it states: "The American Family Association represents and stands for traditional family values, focusing primarily on the influence of television and other media—including pornography—on our society. AFA believes that the entertainment industry, through its various products, has played a major role in the decline of those values on which our country was founded and which keep a society and its families strong and healthy." AFA was founded in 1977.

Americans United for Separation of Church and State (AU): On the organization's website, it states: "Americans United for Separation of Church and State was founded in 1947 by a broad coalition of religious, educational, and civic leaders. At that time, proposals were pending in the U.S. Congress to extend government aid to private religious schools. Many Americans opposed this idea, insisting that government support for religious education would violate church–state separation. The decision was made to form a national organization to promote this point of view and defend the separation principle. The organization worked to educate members of Congress, as well as state and local lawmakers, about the importance of maintaining church–state separation."

American Veterans Standing for God and Country: A part of the American Veterans in Domestic Defense, this subgroup took control of the tour for Roy Moore's Ten Commandments' rock. Dates and places for the tour are not posted after March 2005.

An American Dilemma: The Negro Problem and Modern Democracy: Written by **Gunnar Myrdal,** this landmark effort probes the contradictions in a nation committed to justice, freedom, and opportunity for all yet simultaneously discriminates against its black citizens.

Angelou, Maya: (1928–) As a poet, educator, historian, author, actress, playwright, civil rights activist, producer, and director, Dr. Angelou has authored twelve best-selling books, including *I Know Why the Caged Bird Sings.* In January 1993, she became only the second poet in U.S. history to read at a presidential inauguration.

Black Like Me: Written by **John Howard Griffin,** the story of this white man's travels as a black man through the pre–civil rights South.

Blogosphere: A term used to describe the inter-active connection between bloggers (those who maintain logs or journals on the Internet) and mainstream media journalists (often abbreviated MSM).

Brando, Marlon: (1924–2004) Considered by many other actors as the actor who taught them the most about freedom, Brando mastered the "method approach" in which an actor draws on the motivations of the character to determine what actions should be emphasized. His career fluctuated between brilliance—in such roles as Stanley Kowalski in Tennessee Williams's *A Streetcar Named Desire* and as the Godfather—and disappointingly squandered talent.

Brown v. Board of Education of Topeka: On May 17, 1954, the U.S. Supreme Court ruled unanimously that segregated schools are unconstitutional, putting an end to the doctrine of "separate but equal."

Bush, George W.: (1946–) Forty-third president of the United States. He was president during the September 11, 2001, terrorist attack on America, and initiated an aggressive retaliation on those who perpetrated the attack.

Cabal: A secret scheme or plot; also, a conspiratorial group of those plotting some form of intrigue.

Charles, Ray: (1930–2004) Born in poverty and blind at seven years old, Charles went on to win twelve Grammys and be named to the Halls of Fame in Rhythm and Blues, Jazz, and Rock and Roll.

Cheney, Lynne: (1941–) Married to Vice President Richard Cheney since 1964, Mrs. Cheney has a Ph.D. in English from the University of Wisconsin. She has served as chair of the National Endowment for the Humanities (1986–1993) and has been a force in writing and speaking about the importance of historical knowledge in the education of children.

Child Evangelism Fellowship (CEF): According to their organization's website, its purpose is "to evangelize boys and girls with the Gospel of the Lord Jesus Christ and to establish (disciple) them in the Word of God and in a local church for Christian living." CEF was founded in 1937.

Civil rights movement: Beginning in 1954 with the U.S. Supreme Court's unanimous passage of *Brown v. Board of Education,* the movement rallied black and white citizens to direct action to improve conditions for black citizens living in the southern states. The modern civil rights movement ended with the assassination of Martin Luther King, Jr. in April 1968.

Communitarian: A member or supporter of a small cooperative community.

Cosby, Bill: (1937–) Cosby has followed a career that has spanned the entertainment industry—as a comedian, television star, director, and other roles. He returned to school to obtain his Ed.D., which has given credibility to his public talks about education.

Court-appointed attorney: Every defendant has the right to legal counsel. Court-appointed attorneys are hired by the courts to defend those without means to hire a lawyer.

Democracy for America: According to their official website, "Democracy for America (DFA) is a political action committee dedicated to supporting fiscally responsible, socially progressive candidates at all levels of government—from school board to the presidency. DFA fights against the influence of the far right-wing and their radical, divisive policies and the selfish special interests that for too long have dominated our politics." The group was inspired by the presidential campaign of Howard Dean.

Du Bois, W. E. B.: (1868–1963) Du Bois was one of the founders of the Niagara Movement, which became the NAACP. He was also editor of *The Crisis,* the NAACP journal, which promoted the creative work of young black talent. A scholar, scientist, and lifelong activist for civil rights, Du Bois was the first African American to earn a Ph.D. at Harvard.

Edwards, John: (1953–) A United States senator from North Carolina and former personal injury lawyer, Edwards was the Democratic vice presidential candidate in 2004.

Election Assistance Commission: This group serves as a national clearinghouse and resource for compiling information and reviewing procedures with respect to the tasks of federal elections.

Eminem: (1972–) Born Marshall Mathers, Eminem burst onto the rap scene in the late 1990s, exploiting his poor, white background as the subject matter for his lyrics. His *The Marshall Mathers LP* won a Grammy for Best Rap Album in 2001, selling nearly 2 million copies in the first week.

Equal Access Law: Passed in 1984, this law applies to public high schools that receive federal funding and already have at least one student-led non-curriculum club that meets outside of class time. The rules dictate that attendance at the club is voluntary and student-initiated. The club should not be sponsored or attended by any school employee, not disruptive to the community, and not open to persons from the community. While originally backed by conservative Christian groups for the purpose of Bible Clubs, the law has become popular with gay/lesbian/bisexual support groups and atheist and Goth clubs.

Fahrenheit 9/11: Directed by Michael Moore, a controversial filmmaker, who intentionally wanted this film about Bush's presidency to be a part of the anti-Bush movement during the campaign of 2004.

Federal Emergency Management Agency (FEMA): Established in the aftermath of 9/11, FEMA is under the auspices of the Department of Homeland Security and is charged with the mitigation, preparedness, response, and recovery of any area declared a federal disaster area by the President of the United States.

Fellowship of Christian Athletes (FCA): On the organization's website, it states: "Since 1954, the Fellowship of Christian Athletes has been challenging coaches and athletes on the professional, college, high school, junior high, and youth levels to use the powerful medium of athletics to impact the world for Jesus Christ. FCA is the largest Christian sports organization in America. FCA focuses on serving local communities by equipping, empowering, and encouraging people to make a difference for Christ."

Freedom Forum First Amendment Center: Founded in 1991, the Forum is a non-partisan foundation dedicated to free speech, free press, and free spirit for all people. The foundation focuses on three priorities: the "Newseum," the First Amendment, and newsroom diversity.

Free rider: Describes the phenomenon within a free society where compliance is preferred or even required but not enforceable. The free rider takes advantage of everyone else's compliance.

Good News Club: Under the auspices of the Child Evangelism Fellowship, this club, according to the CEF website, is for "boys and girls ages 5 through 12 to gather with their friends to sing interesting visualized songs. They enjoy playing games that help them memorize a verse from God's Word. Through the missionary time they learn of children around the world who are following Jesus. The visualized Bible story applies God's Word to what is happening in their lives. They play review games that help them remember what was taught. An opportunity to receive Jesus Christ as Savior is given. Activities that help them grow in Christ are presented."

Government Accountability Office (GAO): The investigative agency of the legislative branch of the federal office, GAO exists to help improve the performance of Congress and to make the federal government accountable to the American people.

Griffin, John Howard: (1920–1980) White author of the 1961 book *Black Like Me;* turned his skin dark and traveled throughout the South as a black man.

Groupthink: A reductive pattern of thought within problem-solving groups that forces agreement over correct solutions.

Harjo, Joy: (1951–) A member of the Muscogee tribe, Harjo is the author of numerous collections of poetry, including *She Had Some Horses* and *The Woman Who Fell From the Sky.* She received her M.F.A. in creative writing from the University of Iowa in 1978.

Help America Vote Act (2002): This act established a program to provide funds to states to replace punch card voting systems, established the Election Assistance Commission to assist in the administration of federal elections and provided assistance with the administration of certain federal election laws and programs, and established minimum election administration standards for states and units of local government with responsibility for the administration of federal elections.

Hemings, Sally: (1773–1835) Thomas Jefferson's Negro slave, who historians believe gave birth to several of his children. Some of the black and white descendants of Jefferson today remain at odds with each other over the legitimacy of the birth claims.

Impeachment: According to the Constitution, the House of Representatives has the charge of impeaching high-ranking government officials when they abuse the powers of their office. Impeachment is not dismissal from office; it is accusation. The Senate has the power to dismiss. Two presidents have been impeached— Andrew Johnson and William Clinton; neither was dismissed from office. Impeachment proceedings began for Richard Nixon, but he resigned from office before the proceedings could follow their natural course.

Jackson Advocate: Since 1938, Mississippi's oldest African American newspaper has published stories not covered significantly or sufficiently by white-owned presses. It has been the target of numerous acts of vandalism and has been firebombed at least three times, the latest incident occurring in 1998.

Jefferson, Thomas: (1743–1826) The third president of the United States, whose work on our country's founding documents was essential to establishing how we see ourselves as a nation.

Jim Crow: (1870s to 1950s) Named for an old slave character (who embodied negative stereotypes about blacks) who appeared in an 1829 minstrel song (sung by whites in blackface), Jim Crow was the system of laws that enforced the segregation of public spaces and places as "white only" and "colored only" in the American South. These laws were applied to all facets of southern life—including but not limited to schools, transportation, restaurants, parks, drinking fountains, and restrooms.

Johnson, Andrew: (1808–1875) The seventeenth president of the United States and the first president to be successfully impeached. He remained in office by a slim one-vote margin.

After Lincoln's assassination and the end of the Civil War, Johnson was at odds with congressional leaders, who wanted to control the southern states.

Johnson, Lyndon B.: (1908–1973) Thirty-sixth president of the United States (1963–1968). During his administration, most of the important civil rights legislation became law.

Jordan, Barbara: (1936–1996) A three-term congresswoman from Texas who came into the national spotlight for her televised speech during the impeachment proceedings of Richard Nixon. She delivered the keynote address at the Democratic National Convention in 1976 and 1992.

Kennedy, Robert F.: (1925–1968) Attorney general in his brother John Kennedy's administration and senator from New York; assassinated in June 1968 when he was campaigning for president.

King, Martin Luther, Jr.: (1929–1968) The most well known spokesman for the civil rights movement (1954–1968). His televised speeches riveted a nation, and his written words remain a powerful statement for justice and freedom. King was assassinated on April 4, 1968, in Memphis.

Kingston, Maxine Hong: (1940–) The daughter of Chinese immigrants, she is a teacher and the author of both fiction and nonfiction primarily focused on the Chinese American experience. She earned her bachelor's degree from Berkeley in 1962.

Lee, Harper: (1926–) Author of the Pulitzer Prize–winning novel (1960) *To Kill a Mockingbird,* her only book.

"Letter from a Birmingham Jail": Martin Luther King's powerful statement, written from his jail cell in the spring of 1963, in answer to white clergymen who asked him if he would just wait. He eloquently explained that waiting always meant "no" from the white establishment.

Liberty Counsel: On the organization's website, it states: "Liberty Counsel is a nonprofit litigation, education, and policy organization dedicated to advancing religious freedom, the sanctity of human life, and the traditional family.

Established in 1989, Liberty Counsel is a national organization headquartered in Orlando, Florida, with branch offices in Virginia and hundreds of affiliate attorneys in all 50 states." The legal team has close ties with Jerry Falwell and the conservative religious right.

Lincoln, Abraham: (1809–1865) The sixteenth president of the United States, who served during the trying days of our country's War Between the States. He was assassinated at Ford's Theatre in Washington by John Wilkes Booth.

Lynching: To hang or otherwise execute as punishment a presumed criminal for a cultural (racial) offense, carried out by mobs, without any due process of law. Lynchings were most common in the South, and after the Civil War the victims were almost exclusively African Americans. Lynchings were a tool to support white supremacy and subvert civil rights.

Manifest Destiny: The American philosophy that explains America's thirst for expansion in the nineteenth century and presents a defense for America's claim to all new territories.

> ". . . the right of our manifest destiny to over spread and to possess the whole of the continent which Providence has given us for the development of the great experiment of liberty"— John O' Sullivan

Milgram, Stanley: (1933–1984) American psychologist famous for his human experiments exploring issues of obedience in the early 1960s.

Miranda v. Arizona **(1966):** Landmark U.S. Supreme Court case that ruled that police officers were required to inform suspects of certain legal rights, commonly known as Miranda rights.

Mistrial: A judge declares a mistrial in criminal court when errors or events in the trial are such that the trial cannot proceed, or when a jury cannot agree on a verdict. A mistrial is the ending of one proceeding with the option to go to trial again, often without double jeopardy being attached.

Moore, Michael: (1954–) Moore won his first Academy Award for best documentary in 2003 for *Bowling for Columbine*. His *Fahrenheit 9/11*,

a stinging rebuke of President George W. Bush, was the first documentary to gross over $100 million.

Morrison, Toni: (1931–) Winner of the 1993 Nobel Prize for Literature (the only African American to do so), Morrison is the author of award-winning novels, plays, and critical essays; she has served as an editor for Random House and teaches at Princeton University.

Myrdal, Gunnar: (1898–1987) A 1974 Swedish Nobel Prize winner in economics who was commissioned in 1938 by the Carnegie Corporation to study the "American Negro Problem." His findings were published in 1944 as *An American Dilemma: The Negro Problem and Modern Democracy.*

National Association for the Advancement of Colored People (NAACP): Since its founding in 1909, the organization has been among the champions for equal rights for black Americans.

Niagara Movement: Organized in 1905 and the forerunner of the NAACP, the leaders called for full and equal rights for black Americans.

Nixon, Richard: (1913–1994) The thirty-seventh president of the United States, Nixon's involvement in the coverup of the Watergate scandals of 1974 ultimately forced him to resign the presidency. He was later given a full pardon by President Gerald Ford, who believed we needed to put Watergate to rest and move forward with other business of the country.

No Child Left Behind Act (NCLB): Passed into law in 2002, this act affects public education from kindergarten through high school. It is built on four principles: accountability for results, more choices for parents, greater local control and flexibility, and an emphasis on doing what works based on scientific research.

Paley, Grace: (1922–) The daughter of Russian Jewish immigrants, Paley is a well-known political activist and the first recipient of the Edith Wharton Citation of Merit; she is also the highly acclaimed author of three collections of short fiction and three collections of poetry.

Pew Internet and American Life Project: According to their website, the mission of the project is to "produce reports that explore the impact of the Internet on families, communities, work and home, daily life, education, health care, and civic and political life. The Project aims to be an authoritative source on the evolution of the Internet through collection of data and analysis of real-world developments as they affect the virtual world."

Queen Latifah: (1970–) Born Dana Elaine Owens and winner of one Grammy, Queen Latifah at the start of the twenty-first century is the most well-known female rapper.

Racial Privacy Initiative: A 2003 California Ballot Measure that would, if passed, prevent government agencies in California from classifying individuals by race, ethnicity, color, or national origin for any purpose pertaining to public education, public contracting, or public employment.

Rainbow/PUSH Coalition: A merger of Operation PUSH (1971) and the National Rainbow Coalition (1985). Headquartered in Chicago, the founder and president is Jesse Jackson, Sr. The organization fights for social, racial, and economic justice with a multiracial, international membership.

Reagan, Ronald: (1911–2004) The fortieth president of the United States (1981–1989); his legacy is his contribution to the fall of communism and the swelling of the ranks of government bureaucracy after he declared that "government is the problem."

Reconstruction: The reorganization and reestablishment of the seceded states in the Union after the American Civil War.

Reconstruction Acts: In the spring of 1867, the South was divided into military districts and the states that had seceded from the Union had to agree to certain conditions to be reinstated. Among the requirements was the ratification of the Fourteenth and Fifteenth Amendments to the Constitution.

Reservations: The result of vast expansion in the West by non-native settlers, reservations are tracks of land specified by treaty—between the tribe in question and the U.S. government—that determine where Native Americans may live and preserve their language and culture beyond many local and state laws and restrictions. While the original object was separation,

today most Native Americans do not live on the reservation, and whites may live on leased reservation land.

Simpson, O[renthal] J[ames]: (1947–) One of the most famous running backs in football history remembered for his murder trial, where he was accused of killing his ex-wife, Nicole Brown Simpson, and her friend Ron Goldman in 1994. The trial began in January 1995, and Simpson was found not guilty in October 1995. In a later civil trial he was found guilty on both counts.

Sims, The: The best-selling PC game in history, it is a strategy/simulation game designed to let the player create and control the lives of virtual people.

Smartcard: A credit card–sized plastic card with an embedded microchip that can be loaded with data, allowing the card to do an assortment of sophisticated technological transactions.

The Souls of Black Folks: The 1903 classic by W. E. B. Du Bois that best explains what it means to be black at the beginning of the twentieth century in America.

Southern Poverty Law Center: On the organization's website, it states: "Today, the Center is internationally known for its tolerance education programs, its legal victories against white supremacists, and its tracking of hate groups." The Center was founded in 1971 in Montgomery, Alabama, as a small civil rights law firm.

Stanton, Edwin: (1814–1869) The secretary of war under President Andrew Johnson, who removed him from office and spurred the House of Representatives to begin impeachment proceedings. Congress wanted Stanton to stay in office so that the military rule of the South after the Civil War would continue without interruption. Johnson was in violation of the Tenure of Office Act.

Swift Boat Veterans for Truth: This organization formed after John Kerry's use of Swift Boat veterans in his 2004 presidential campaign. As this group challenged Kerry's military record, others challenged theirs. Right or wrong, though, the group was influential in calling into question Kerry's war record.

Tenure of Office Act: The president was not to remove any federal officeholder without the approval of the Senate. Johnson dismissed Edwin Stanton, and the legislative branch went up in arms. The act was eventually declared unconstitutional.

Watergate: This complex in Washington, D.C., housed the Democratic National Committee's headquarters. With ties to the highest level of the Republican Party, five men broke into the headquarters, and thus began a series of scandals—known as "Watergate"—that eventually forced Richard Nixon to resign, the first sitting president in our country's history to do so.

Whitman, Walt: (1819–1892) A New York native and one of America's most famous poets, Whitman was not successful in his own time. In his struggle to support himself, he worked as a printer, teacher, self-taught writer and journalist, and later a government clerk, but he also served as a volunteer nurse for Union forces (including his own wounded brother) during the Civil War. He released several editions of *Leaves of Grass,* a collection of poems and a preface, beginning in 1855, but wouldn't receive substantial royalties until the 1882 edition.

Winfrey, Oprah: (1954–) Talk show host and actor, she is famous for her award-winning, nationally syndicated television program.

Youth for Christ (YFC): On the organization's website, it states that YFC communicates a "life-changing message of Jesus Christ to young people." Founded in the mid-1940s, Billy Graham was its first full-time worker. It has grown into an international organization, presenting mass rallies to introduce young people to Christian principles.

Expanding Vocabulary: Rhetorical

Abstract: Having intrinsic value, but lacking a tangible form.

Alliteration: Two or more words close together with the same initial sounds.

Allusion: An indirect reference to a person or place in one text that solicits thoughts of that person or place in its original context.

Analogy: A likeness that draws two usually unlike things together.

Anecdote: Usually a personal and amusing incident.

Annotate: To add critical commentary or explanatory notes to an existing text.

Aristotle's three appeals: When writers want to make a point or further an argument, they use specific rhetorical strategies to appeal to their audiences. Aristotle divided such strategies into three distinct appeals—**ethos, pathos,** and **logos.**

- **Ethos—the ethical appeal.** This rhetorical strategy is based upon the character of the speaker and is designed to appeal to the readers' shared values.
- **Pathos—the emotional appeal.** This rhetorical strategy is directed toward the feelings and emotions of the reader and is designed to move the audience on a visceral level.

- **Logos—the logical appeal.** This rhetorical strategy is directed toward the readers' intellectual capabilities and is designed to privilege reason supported by evidence.

Audience: The person or group of people to which a piece of writing is directed.

Beliefs: Systems of values rooted in a person's faith community; tenets or creeds.

Brainstorming: A method of sharing ideas and possibilities in a spontaneous manner; done collectively in a group or alone with a computer or a pen and paper.

Comma splice: The use of a comma (instead of a semicolon) to separate independent clauses in a sentence.

Concrete: A tangible or pictorial representation.

Connotation: A meaning that suggests more than the word explicitly stated.

Cubing: Looking at subject matter through a variety of lenses: describing, comparing, associating, analyzing, applying, and arguing.

Denotation: A dictionary definition.

Diction: Word choice.

Didactic: Intended to teach a moral lesson.

Figures of speech: The various means by which we use language creatively.

Fragment: A word group trying to pass as a sentence, but missing either its subject or its verb.

Free writing: A stream-of-consciousness type of writing used to get whatever you may know about a topic down on paper or the computer.

Genre: A distinctive type or style of composition.

Hyperbole: An exaggeration or overstatement.

Invention: The process by which ideas are transformed into argument.

Judgments: Weightier opinions based in a system of beliefs, usually arrived at by discernment.

Map or cluster: A visual means of linking ideas on paper with the use of circles and lines.

Metaphor: A figure of speech in which one word is used in place of another to suggest similarity between the two.

Metonymy: The use of an associated feature to suggest something not stated.

Modes: System of organization that categorizes context-specific forms of language.

- **Description:** This mode primarily employs sense perceptions to quantify and qualify a person, a place, or situation.
- **Narration:** This mode relies upon the qualities and expectations of story.
- **Example:** To give an example is to employ the tools of representation and sample where one thing suggests many.
- **Definition:** By stating a precise significance or meaning, making clear and distinct the meaning of language, action, or situation, you create definition.
- **Classification:** Classification separates items into classes or groups based on shared characteristics or traits, thus designating what something is based on what group or subset it belongs to.
- **Comparison/contrast:** The examination of two or more items, events, actions, or situations in terms of each other expresses meaning through the presence and/or absence of difference.
- **Cause and effect:** Considering two or more items, events, actions, or situations in terms of the chronology they share, with a focus on the ways in which the first thing

precipitated the second, is to establish a cause-and-effect relationship.

- **Argument:** Unlike exposition, which explores and informs, argument seeks to prove a point and convince an audience.

Narrator: The voice in a story or poem; the narrator can often be a character who relates the events that make up the plot to the reader.

Opinions: What a person may think about something, usually based in stereotypes, whim, or mood; insubstantial in argument.

Outlining: A listing of points contained in a prose piece; suggests order, context, and connection of ideas to each other. An outline may be used either before or after writing.

Paraphrase: Restating another's words in your own unique fashion while giving the author credit.

Personification: The representation of an inanimate object with the qualities of a living being.

Proofreading: The activity of making corrections to a piece of writing.

Purpose: In a writing assignment, the reason to do so and its intended goal.

Reader: The person who reads the assignment for a grade; the reader and audience may well be different people.

Rhetorical strategy: Any conscious choice—including but not limited to issues of vocabulary, form, voice, and construction—intended to strengthen an argument and better convince a reader.

Run-on sentence: Also called a fused sentence; two sentences together without punctuation trying to pass as one sentence.

Simile: A figure of speech in which two unlike things are compared with the use of *like* or *as.*

Spheres of communication: Communication can be categorized by the sphere—the area, conditions, and audience—it occurs within, primarily the public, the private, and the technical spheres.

- **The public sphere** includes such things as speeches, press releases, web logs, media articles and editorials, advertisements, and slogans on T-shirts. If the message is directed at the general public, it's in the public sphere—the content can be specific, but the audience is as wide as possible.

- **The private sphere** is much more limited in scope and audience, and it includes such things as personal letters, private thoughts or feelings shared with another select person, and intimate details. Private communication is based upon and usually stays within a relationship: a friendship, a marriage, or a family. It can also take place between a lawyer and a client, a doctor and a patient, a member of the clergy and a follower of that faith.
- **The technical sphere** of communication covers all means of technical or specialized conversation. It's how experts in any given field—from astronomy to coal mining to medical research—talk to one another in their shared, specialized language. Technical communication involves complex, specific vocabulary that is shared among those experts and crucial to the sharing of technical information.

Stanzas: A group of lines forming a division of a poem.

Stereotypes: Something that one group of people believe about others who are different; may be partly true.

Summary: Reducing the whole of another's work by carefully reading and restating the main idea of each paragraph into a sentence. An effective summary is objective, not evaluating how or why something is written but comprehending what is written.

Syllogism: A three-part logical scheme used in developing an argument in which the major and minor premises yield a certain conclusion, based on the truth of the premises.

Synecdoche: Using one part of something to signify the whole.

Thesis: A position maintained by a sustained argument; a controlling idea.

Tone: The sound of words, which conveys a meaning that might add to or take away from the words themselves; the attitude of a piece of writing; style or manner of expression.

Transitional markers: Specific words used to show the connection and/or relationship of one paragraph or sentence to another.

Treatise: A systematic exposition or argument.

Voice: Deliberate choices in diction and syntax to support **purpose.**

Expanding Vocabulary: Genres

Column: A feature article that appears regularly in a newspaper or periodical, which offers opinions and facts about current events, politics, or lifestyle topics.

Congressional debates: Persuasive short speeches delivered on the floor of both the House and the Senate for the express purpose of influencing colleagues' voting positions.

Editorial: An opinion piece that appears in newspapers and newsmagazines; attempts to sway the reader toward a particular point of view.

E-mail: An electronic communication between two or more computer users.

Eulogy: On the occasion of someone's death, a tribute offering praise or commendation.

Free-verse narrative poem: A poem, usually in multiple stanzas, that tells a story in unrhymed lines.

Government document: Supporting proposal or policy signed by appropriate government officials.

Humor column: Writing, either fiction or nonfiction, whose purpose is to entertain through the use of jokes and/or humor.

Inaugural poem: A poetic tribute written expressly for the occasion of the inauguration of the president of the United States. In recent history, only John Kennedy and Bill Clinton have asked poets to write and deliver something for their inaugurations.

Interview: Nonfiction writing that involves two voices—the narrator who conducts the interview and direct quotes from the subject of that interview.

Lyrics: The words of a song.

Lyrical poem: A lyrical poem tends to be short, lacks a cohesive or definite narrative, and clearly expresses a specific emotion or feeling.

Memoir: An autobiographical account of the personal experiences of the author. Often about a specific period of time, event, or topic.

News feature story: A signed news story that slants the news toward the writer's bias.

News story: A journalistic story that delivers the who, what, when, where, and how of an event with as much objectivity as possible.

Review: A critical report on a new artistic work or performance.

Short story: A narrative form of fiction, shorter than forty pages, that has characters and a plot in which they act or exist.

Speeches: Spoken opinions, judgments, and facts combined to sway an audience to the speaker's position.

Service Learning

THINKING AND READING ABOUT SERVICE LEARNING: INITIAL STEPS

It would be impossible to place a date on the first time somebody went into a community and helped someone out—and learned something in the process. But organized service-learning activities connected with educational institutions date from the nineteenth century. In the early twentieth century, John Dewey and William James penned the philosophical bases for service learning. Since the late 1960s, experiential education, community action programs, volunteer opportunities, and service-learning offices have been a presence on college campuses across the nation. They have facilitated both extra- and co-curricular programs. Depending on the orientation of the college or university, name-specific programs have gained acceptance and often reflect the mission statements of institutions. For example, many engineering colleges offer a program called EPICS, or Engineering Projects in Community Service. EPICS classes usually combine writing about, speaking on, and designing site-specific projects that are helpful to both student and company (the client or agency with which the students will work). Church-related institutions may involve their students in programs that produce servant-leaders for lifelong learning. Service-learning opportunities may be specific to an individual course or university-wide. At some institutions, service learning or similar activities are a requirement for graduation with the hope that the volunteer spirit will last a lifetime.

To embrace the spirit and the content of this book, aspects of service learning are offered in the hope that writing assignments may be paired with off- or on-campus volunteer opportunities that are directed at helping you to become a more responsible citizen.

Find out the names of the offices on your campus that have service-learning programs. Many students go through four years of undergraduate education and never know that their schools offer such a program as international service learning or others in which they might have been interested. *Once you identify the centers or offices that exist, make a list of opportunities that interest you. Arrange the program possibilities by category, suggesting ways that each category could help you grow in citizenship. Begin now to read and think about how you might volunteer for something that will shed more light on an area in which you have an interest.*

Here are some ideas to get you started. You might want to volunteer for a few hours a week at one of the following:

- A political campaign office
- A voter registration table on campus

- A speaking program to encourage other students to register to vote
- A tutoring center for young children or high-schoolers who are learning English
- A food bank
- A single-parent care facility

TALKING AND WRITING ABOUT SERVICE LEARNING: LEAVING THE CLASSROOM AND ENTERING THE COMMUNITY

The examples here concern issues of justice between and among those of us who call ourselves Americans. A half-century removed from the civil rights movement of the 1950s and 1960s, we have returned in many ways to segregated communities. While American citizens are more open to living in integrated communities—and may even desire the richness that such diversity adds to the human experience—we are most likely to draw our friends from among those who share our ethnicity, our political positions, our religious persuasions. We gather with others like ourselves.

En route to service-learning involvement, talk with your classmates about exploring the community surrounding your college campus. Take the bus or some other form of public transportation to various parts of the city within five or ten miles of your campus. Visit places where the people vary in socioeconomic levels. With justice as your theme, tour the courthouse, city hall, capitol building, jails and juvenile detention centers, and other buildings where the work of government is carried out. What agencies help the homeless? Where do runaway teenagers congregate? Where are the food banks? Who frequents them?

If you go to school in rural America, visit places that appear to hold the heart of the community: churches, community socials, high school athletic events, grange meetings, town meetings, council meetings. Are questions surrounding the theme of justice more difficult to access in rural America?

Before leaving on your bus, train, or car trip, write a paper predicting what you expect to find. Upon your return, write a reflection paper on what you did discover. From the journey, what one place are you curious about knowing more? Talk with a classmate about before and after experiences. About what issues surrounding justice do you want to know more?

BEFORE AND AFTER SERVICE LEARNING: OUT OF THE AGENCY, INTO THE NEIGHBORHOOD

The examples we have used address the importance of honoring and respecting the ways democracy plays out in our daily lives—from the importance of understanding history so that we might have a larger frame of reference to draw upon to questions of growing disparities between the rich and the poor. Earlier, you were asked to become familiar with the neighborhood of your campus.

Our focus here is to bring that neighborhood up close and personal for each of you. Service-learning activities often take students into various community agencies for volunteer experiences in hopes that the student will understand more deeply how the agency accomplishes its goals. If you go to work in an agency, you are usually assigned a specific task; it often can be a rather humbling task. Even the most humbling task offers you the opportunity to participate in and contribute to an agency's usefulness to its community. But inside the agency, you are less in control of what you get to do and how you will spend your time. In other words, the creativity of your involvement often lies in the hands of another.

When you leave the agency and go into the neighborhood itself to bring something to the people who live there, you get to guide the activity toward its planned-for end. Often people who need services do not know what is available for them. The best thing you can take to the people who live near your campus—or somewhere in your town or city—is information.

First, do your research. Are there free services available that will help the poor? The temporarily disadvantaged? The research works both ways. Sometimes you may simply go to the door and offer information. Other times you will find out from the people what they need, and then you can serve as the person who figures out how to meet that need. Research is rarely a stagnant activity, where you do your homework and then you don't have to do it anymore! Research continues—you determine what information is relayed and discover new paths to explore.

Talking with people you do not know at their front door can be both humbling and frightening. Before blindly going to the front door on behalf of an agency, you need to do practical research. Have you anything to say to whoever answers the door? What kinds of questions will you ask? When might your presence overstep its bounds? When is it simply too much?

The process of going door-to-door in the neighborhood puts you in the tradition of direct action, a popular strand of the civil rights movement, when young college-aged students canvassed the neighborhoods to find out who wanted to register to vote. This activity may well be worth pursuing again today.

The activities you will need to accomplish before leaving campus are the following:

- Have a clear understanding of the geographical limits of the neighborhood you will canvass.
- Decide on either teams or partners with whom to make your calls.
- Study the materials you will deliver and prepare your talk should you find someone at home.
- Know how you will return answers to questions you might be asked.
- Commit to a certain number of hours each week that you will be available to approach those who live in the neighborhood you are canvassing.

Your agency (and your instructor) should receive a written report from you that tracks your successes, frustrations, and failures. You might want to develop an assessment tool you can use to can measure your effectiveness in delivering necessary information.

All service-learning activity should conclude with a written report in which you reflect on your contributions. The agency also needs to make use of what you learn so that it can be more efficient in the work it does for your community. Service learning is a two-way enterprise.

SERVICE LEARNING: FROM THE AGENCY TO YOUR COMPUTER

Service learning is a way for you to join new communities and participate in the lives of your fellow citizens. As already discussed, there are many forms of community service and many opportunities for you to offer your time and enthusiasm. Often college students serve as tutors at a local school or work at a food bank or mission. There are also opportunities to work with the developmentally disabled or focus your efforts in support of the environment. The choice is yours, but it's always best to volunteer for an agency or organization that works on something that interests you.

Service learning is a lot more than work; it's your way of taking your place among the leaders of your community and exerting your efforts in a worthy cause. But service learning doesn't happen in a vacuum. When you share your time and effort with people you would otherwise not meet and further a cause that needs your help, everyone involved is changed by the experience.

One way you can measure this change—in yourself and in those around you—is by writing about your service-learning experience. Below you will find several writing prompts—opportunities to explore and consider your service-learning community experiences. You might try responding to the prompts twice—once before your service-learning experience and once after.

1. *Consider the relationship between the individual and the community. What is important about being an individual, and what is important about being in a community? Which would you rather be, an individual or part of a community? Is it possible to be both at once? Is one more important than the other? Use your own experiences to support your discussion.*

2. *Compare/contrast a time in your life when you needed guidance or assistance with a time where you offered help or assistance to another. What did you need? Were you able to give what was needed? Did one experience inform the other? Which is easier, to ask for help or to give it?*

3. *Argue what the greatest need in your community is today. How do you know about this need? Are you involved in the problem or in the solution, or are you just an observer? What are the best ways to meet this need? How might you get people involved in possible solutions?*

4. *Tell the story of your service-learning experience. Include the before and after—what you knew and what you learned. Do you recommend service learning to others? Would you be willing to try volunteering outside of the classroom setting? How might you motivate others to participate?*

Index

Chapter 1

Maxine Hong Kingston, Excerpt from *The Woman Warrior: Memories of a Girlhood Among Ghosts,* Knopf Publishers.

"The Loudest Voice," from THE LITTLE DISTURBANCES OF MAN by Grace Paley, copyright © 1956, 1957, 1958, 1959 by Grace Paley. Used by permission of Penguin, a division of Penguin Group (USA) Inc.

Toni Morrison, "Black Matters," from *Playing in the Dark: Whiteness and the Literary Imagination.* Viking Publishers.

Toni Morrison, "Recitatif," from *Confirmation: An Anthology of African American Women.* Harper Collins.

George Will, "Dropping the 'One-Drop Rule'," from *Newsweek,* March 25, 2002. Reprinted with permission.

"The Reluctant Spokesman," by Erik Himmelsbach, as appeared in the *Los Angeles Times,* December 17, 1996. Reprinted by permission of the author.

Maya Angelou, "On the Pulse of the Morning," Random House.

Joy Harjo, "Remember" originally appeared in *She Had Some Horses,* Thunder's Mouth Press.

Brant Ayers, "Can We Laugh Now?" May 20, 2001, *Anniston Star.*

Rebecca Rodriguez, "Hispanics Not Laughing at Humor Column," February 7, 2003

Chris Rock, The 77th Academy Awards, February 27, 2005.

Chapter 2

From BLACK LIKE ME by John Howard Griffin, copyright © 1961 by John Howard Griffin, rnwd 1989 by Elizabeth Griffin-Bonazzi, Susan Griffin-Campbell, J.H. Griffin, Jr., Greg Griffin, Amanda Griffin-Sanderson. Used by permission of Dutton Signet, a division of Penguin Group (USA) Inc.

Roland S. Martin, Editor, "Thumbs Up to the Sisters at Spelman," April 22, 2004. *Black America Today.* Reprinted with permission.

Richard Kim, "Emimem—Bad Rap" February 23, 2001. Reprinted with permission from the March 5, 2001 issue of the *Nation.* For subscription information, call 1-800-333-8536. Portions of each week's *Nation* magazine can be accessed at http://www.thenation.com.

Cynthia Fuchs, *Emimen: The Marshall Mathers LP,* Popmatters.com.

Chris Massey, *Eminem: The Marshall Mathers LP.* Popmatters.com.

Marshall Mathers, "Criminal," rap lyrics, Universal Music Publishing Group.

Queen Latifah, "Sleeping on the Sidewalk," rap lyrics (Queen), Queen Productions.

Korn, "Faget," rap lyrics, Sony Music.

Alice Childress, "Health Card" from *Black on White: Black Writers on What It Means to be White.* Random House.

Adam Goodheart, "Change of Heart," May/June 2004. *AARP, The Magazine.*

Gloria Naylor, "A Word's Meaning Can Often Depend on Who Says It," from "Hers" column, February 20, 1986. The *New York Times.* Copyright © 1986 by The New York Times Co. Reprinted with permission.

Halle Berry, Oscar Acceptance Speech for Best Actress, March 24, 2002.

Mark Pino, "If Hispanics Want a Voice, They Must Vote," May 16, 2004, the *Orlando Sentinel.* Reprinted with the permission of the *Orlando Sentinel.*

Don Babwin, "Bill Cosby Gets a Little More Off His Chest," July 2, 2004. Associate Press.

William Raspberry, Excerpt from "America, Ray Charles Style," July 25, 2004. The *Washington Post.* Reprinted with permission.

George Yates, "America's 'Four Freedoms' Aren't Quite so Robust this July 4," July 4, 2004, the *Ashville Citizen-Times.* Reprinted with the permission of the *Asheville Citizen-Times.*

Ellen Goodman, "A Forty-Year Search for Equality," June 26, 2004, the *Washington Post.* © 2004, The Washington Post Writers Group, Reprinted with permission.

Chapter 3

Bich Minh Nguyen, "Toadstools," *Dream Me Home Safely: Writers on Growing Up in America,* Ed. Susan Richards Shreve, 2003. Houghton Mifflin.

Annette Gordon-Reed, "Was the Sage A Hypocrite?" July 5, 2004. *Time* magazine.

Anne Applebaum, "What Would You Do?" © 2004, the *Washington Post,* reprinted with permission.

"The Week," and "Moore and His Friends" July 26, 2004. *National Review.*

Mary Corliss, "A First Look at 'Fahrenheit 9/11'" May 17, 2004. *Time* magazine. Reprinted with permission.

Jonathan Alter, "The Art of the Closing Argument," July 19, 2004. *Newsweek* magazine.

Alice Walker, "The First Day (A Fable after *Brown*): A Short Story"

Erin Cox, "Our Pop Culture Doesn't Want Musical Artists to Actually Have Something to Say," July 29, 2004, the *Asheville Citizen-Times.* Reprinted with the permission of the *Asheville Citizen-Times.*

James Kilpatrick, "Free Gifts, Old Adages," July 25, 2004. Universal Press Syndicate. Reprinted with permission.

Chapter 4

Harper Lee, Excerpt from *To Kill a Mockingbird,* Harper Collins.

Shirley Jackson, "The Lottery." Farrar, Straus, Giroux.

Anna Quindlen, "The Great Obligation," April 19, 2004. *Newsweek.* Reprinted with permission.

Marina Krakovsky, "Teaching Apathy?" Sept/Oct. 2004. Stanford Alumni Association. Reprinted with permission.

Stanley Milgram, 2004. *Microsoft Encarta Encyclopedia* Entry.

Amy Herdy, "Teaching the Silent Treatment," August 8, 2004. The *Denver Post.* Reprinted with permission.

John Edwards, "Juries: 'Democracy in Action,'" December 15, 2003. *Newsweek* magazine.

Barney Gimbel, "Twelve Anonymous Men," April 19, 2004. *Newsweek* magazine.

Peter McEntegart, "One Angry Man," April 12, 2004, *Time* magazine. © 2004, TIME Inc., reprinted by permission.

Mike Colias, "Winfrey, Jury Convict Man of Murder," August 18, 2004. Associated Press.

Chapter 5

Rebecca Winters, "No Longer Separate, but Not Yet Equal," May 10, 2004, *Time* magazine. © 2004, TIME Inc., reprinted by permission.

Keith Naughton, "A New Campus Crusader" 12/29/03-1/5/04. *Newsweek* magazine. Reprinted with permission.

Candace Warren, "How to Survive When You're the Only Black in the Classroom." Reprinted with permission.

Katherine S. Mangan, "In Search of Diversity on Law Reviews," September 5, 2003, Copyright 2003, the *Chronicle of Higher Education.* Reprinted with permission.

Diane Carman, "Tough Love on Culture, Progress," May 18, 2004. The *Denver Post.* Reprinted with permission.

Peter Schmidt, "New Admissions System at U. of Michigan to Seek Diversity through Essays," September 5, 2003, Copyright 2003, the *Chronicle of Higher Education.* Reprinted with permission.

Ernie Suggs, "Cosby: Blacks Own Enemy," November 20, 2004. Cox Newspapers. Reprinted with permission.

Anna Brown, "Search Widens for Carjacking Suspect," October 26, 1994, the *Union Daily Times.* Reprinted with permission of the *Union Daily Times.*

Richard Lacayo, "Stranger in the Shadows," November 14, 1994. *Time* magazine.

Tom Turnipseed, "Continuing Saga of Sex, Murder, and Racism: Susan Smith is Still Scheming in Prison," September 14, 2000, Common Dreams News Center. Reprinted with permission of Common Dreams News Center.

Charles L. Warner, "Mother's Actions Not Seen as Racially Motivated," November 4, 1994. Union South Carolina *Daily Times.* Reprinted with permission.

"S.C. Town Still Coping with Child Killings: Susan Smith Case," Amy Geier Edgar, October 24, 2004. The *Denver Post.* Reprinted with permission.

"Interracial Intimacy: White-Black Dating, Marriage, and Adoption Are on the Rise," Randall Kennedy, December 2002 (Volume 290, p. 103). The *Atlantic Monthly.* Reprinted with permission.

"Three Case Studies: Matthew, Sidney, and Claudette," Ursula M. Brown, in *Growing Up Black/White, Racially Mixed in the United States.* Praeger.

Tamar Jacoby, "An End to Counting by Race?" June 2001. *Commentary* magazine.

Beverly Yuen Thompson, "Memories from a Mixed Childhood," from *Iris: A Journal about Women,* Spring 2002. University of Virginia's Women's Center.

Scott Minerbrook, "The Pain of a Divided Family." Copyright 1990, *U.S. News & World Report,* L.P. Reprinted with permission.

Ann Blackman, Wendy Cole, Michele Donley, Timothy Roche, Megan Rutherford, and Jacqueline Savaiano, "Multi-Colored Families: Racially Mixed Households Face Their Own Challenges", May 3, 1999, *Time* magazine. © 1999, TIME Inc., reprinted by permission.

Chapter 6

"The Next Question," September 30, 2004, p. 8. The *Oregonian.* Reprinted with permission.

Jennifer Mena, "'Dream Act' Offers Hope for Immigrant Students," September 19, 2004. The *Los Angeles Times.* Reprinted with permission.

Nancy Mitchell, "Students Speak Out on Behalf of Their Undocumented Friends," February 15, 2005, 17A. *Rocky Mountain News.* Reprinted with permission.

Kate Taylor, "For These Top Students, Dreams Falter," June 8, 2004, B1. The *Oregonian.* Reprinted with permission.

Nurith C. Aizenman and Amy Argetsinger, "Virginia Order Decried by Immigrant Advocates; State Turning Colleges Into Police, They Say," © 2002, the *Washington Post,* reprinted with permission.

Editorial Desk, "Punishing the Innocent," October 1, 2004, B10. *LA Times,* The Times Mirror Company.

Bill and Jacki Dahl, Michael Scott, Dae Yoon, Randle C. Sink," Letters to the *Times:* Deportation or Education?" October 6, 2004, B10. *LA Times,* The Times Mirror Company.

Nina Bernstein, "Immigrants Lost in the Din: Security v. the Dream," September 20, 2004, B1. The *New York Times.* Copyright © 200 by The New York Times Co. Reprinted with permission.

Kevin Sullivan, "An Often-Crossed Line in the Sand: Upgraded Security at U.S. Border Hasn't Deterred Illegal Immigration from Mexico," © 2005, the *Washington Post,* reprinted with permission.

Ruben Navarrette, Jr., "What Really Matters in the Debate on Immigration," March 2, 2005, Pg. B7. The *San Diego Union-Tribune.*

Alex Pulaski, "Legislation Helps Both Farmers, Laborers," February 11, 2005. The *Oregonian.* Reprinted with permission.

Maria Anglin, "Immigration Comic Glams up Danger," January 10, 2005, *San Antonio Express-News.* Reprinted with permission of *San Antonio-Express News.*

Michael A. Fletcher, "Bush Immigration Plan Meets GOP Opposition: Lawmakers Resist Temporary-Worker Proposal," © 2005, the *Washington Post,* reprinted with permission.

Linda Chavez, "Take off the Blinders on Illegal Immigration," December 16, 2004, 23A. The *Baltimore Sun.* Reprinted with permission.

Yeh Ling-Ling, "Bush's Unwise Immigration Proposal," November 29, 2004 B7. The *San Diego Union-Tribune.*

John Downes, "US Envoy Tries to Reverse Decline in J1 Student Visas," January 18, 2005, Page 1. The *Irish Times.*

By John Hughes. Reproduced with permission from the January 12, 2005 issue of the *Christian Science Monitor* (www.csmonitor.com). © 2005 the *Christian Science Monitor.* All rights reserved.

Chimamanda Ngozi Adichie, "The Line of No Return," November 29, 2004, Page 1-21. The *New York Times.* Reprinted with permission.

Olivia Winslow, "Growth Reverses; Surveys: Fewer Foreign Students in US Colleges," November 12, 2004, Page A20. *Newsday.*

Mark Bixler, "Foreign Student Ranks Decline; Stricter Security after 9/11 Cited," November 10, 2004, page 1F. The *Atlanta Journal Constitution.*

Randy Furst, "Caught in the Details of Immigration Law: A Decade after Dropping Out of College, Mohammed Haider is Fighting a Series of Events that now Has Him Slated for Deportation to Bangladesh," the *Star Tribune.* Reprinted with permission.

Hernán Rozemberg, "An Education in Red Tape; Foreign Students are Learning that Visa Applications are not an Easy Test to Pass in Post 9-11 America," October 28, 2004, *San Antonio Express-News.* Reprinted with permission of *San Antonio Express-News.*

Christopher Grimes, "Colleges Get a Hard Lesson in Making the US More Secure," April 29, 2004, the *Financial Times.* Reprinted with the permission of the *Financial Times.*

Chapter 7

Todd Starnes, "Revival at Public School Stirs 100 Students to Conversion," May 9, 2000. *Christianity Today.*

Bruce Nolan, "Christian Groups Rejoice in Fervor at Public School," May 28, 2000. The *Albany Times Union.* Reprinted with permission.

Unsigned, "Cecilia Student Sues after School Denies Bible Club," March 3, 2001. Associated Press.

"The Wall between Church and State," Editorial, June 16, 2001, the *Buffalo News.* Reprinted with the permission of the *Buffalo News.*

Dave Condren, "Staff Problems Keeping Church Groups from Elementary Schools," June 19, 2001, the *Buffalo News.* Reprinted with the permission of the *Buffalo News.*

John McElhenny, "Federal Rule Aids Student Lawsuit; Bible Club Fights Ban on Messages," March 2, 2003. the *Boston Globe.*

Matthew D. Staver, "Federal Court Upholds Student Right to Dispense Candy Canes," March 18, 2003. Junto Society for Legal Issues.

Stan Bailey, "Moore: Will Seek Blessings of God," January 16, 2001, the *Birmingham News.* Copyright, the *Birmingham News,* 2005. All rights reserved. Reprinted with permission.

Paul Greenberg, "Dueling Symbols," August 12, 2001. *Arkansas Democrat-Gazette.*

Lee McAuliffe Rambo, "The Ten Commandments: Halt Judge's High-Handed Campaign to Push Religion," July 24, 2003. The *Atlanta Journal Constitution.* Reprinted with permission.

Megh Duwadi, "High Court Refuses to Hear Ten Commandments Case," November 4, 2003. The *Houston Chronicle.* Reprinted with permission.

Cal Thomas, "Tough Questions in Alabama," August 27, 2003. Tribune Media Services.

Natalie Hopkinson, "Beliefs Carved in Stone; Christians, Atheists Gather at Ten Commandments Rock," © 2004, the *Washington Post,* reprinted with permission.

Deb Price, "A Progressive Church Serves God by Welcoming Differences," December 23, 2004. *Asheville Citizen-Times.*

Leonard Pitts, "Sleaze, Yes; God's Love, No," December 13, 2004. The *Charlotte Observer.*

Nancy Ellett Allison and Nathan King, "Who is Beyond God's Reach?" December 13, 2004. The *Charlotte Observer.*

Joseph Loconte, "Houses of Worship: Exclusion and Embrace," December 3, 2004. The *Wall Street Journal.*

Peter Steinfels, "In Rejecting a Church's Ad, Two Networks Provide Fodder for a Different Debate," December 18, 2004. The *New York Times.* Copyright © 2004 by The New York Times Co. Reprinted with permission.

Tim Feran, "Networks Air Dirty Laundry, Not Church Ad," December 13, 2004, the *Columbus Dispatch.* Reprinted with permission of the *Columbus Dispatch.*

Chapter 8

Priscilla Pardini, "The History of Sexuality Education," from *Rethinking Schools* Online-*Let's Talk About Sex.* Reprinted with permission from *Rethinking Schools,* Volume 12, Number 4. www.rethinkingschools.org.

Joel Mowbray, "Abstinence Works: The Evidence," April 11, 2002. *National Review* Online.

"Sex Education," by Wendy Stock from THE READER'S COMPANION TO U.S. WOMEN'S HISTORY, edited by Wilma Mankiller, et al. Copyright © 1998 by Houghton Mifflin Company. Reprinted by permission of Houston Mifflin Company. All rights reserved.

Paul M. Weyrich, "The Value of Abstinence Education," February 4, 2004, Free Congress Foundation. Reprinted with permission.

Ceci Connolly, "Some Abstinence Programs Mislead Teens, Report Says," © 2004, the *Washington Post,* reprinted with permission.

Priscilla Pardini, "Two Approaches to Sexuality Education," *Rethinking Schools* Online. Reprinted with permission from *Rethinking Schools,* Volume 17, Number 2. www.rethinkingschools.org.

Suzanne Woods Fisher, "The Stay-at-Home Dad: Why Some Christian Couples are Choosing to Reverse Roles and How it Affects their Marriage," Copyright © 2000. This article first appeared in *Marriage Partnership* magazine (Fall 2000), published by Christianity Today International, Carol Stream, Illinois. Reprinted with permission.

Peg Tyre, "Ms. Top Cop," April 12, 2004. *Newsweek.*

Alisa Weinstein, "Single Father from the Start," October 26, 2003. The *Denver Post.* Reprinted with permission.

Vanessa Juarez, "Out of Bounds," March 8, 2004. *Newsweek.*

Promise Keepers, "Fact Sheet," Copyright 2005. Reprinted with permission.

Cate Terwilliger, "Father Superior: Promise Keepers Glorify God—and Resurrect the Patriarchy," the *Colorado Springs Independent.* Reprinted with permission of Cate Terwilliger and the *Colorado Springs Independent.*

"Staying at Home," 60 Minutes, 10/10/04. www.cbsnews.com/stories/2004/10/08/60minutes/main648240.shtml. CBS News.

David G. Hackett, "Promise Keepers and the Culture Wars," *Religion in the News,* Summer 1998, Vol. 1, No. 1. Reprinted with permission of The Leonard E. Greenberg Center for the Study of Religion in Public Life, Trinity College.

"The Case for Gay Marriage," February 26, 2004, the *Economist.* © 2004, The Economist Newspaper Ltd. All rights reserved. Reprinted with permission. Further reproduction prohibited. www.economist.com.

Kathleen Parker, "Upsetting the Natural Order," Tuesday, November 25, 2003. Tribune Media-Services.

Cal Thomas, "Should Gays be Allowed to Marry? NO: It's an Affront to Tradition," November 23, 2003. Tribune Media-Services.

Richard Cohen, "Should Gays Be Allowed to Marry? Yes: They May Rescue Institution," © 2003, The Washington Post Writers Group, Reprinted with permission.

Robert P. George, "One Man, One Woman," November 28, 2003. The *Wall Street Journal.*

David Crary, "Fresh Look at Nuptials Urged: Gays' Push Spurs Wider Scrutiny," November 22, 2004, The Associated Press. Reprinted with the permission of The Associated Press.

Chapter 9

Ward Churchill, "Some People Push Back" from "On the Justice of Roosting Chickens," originally appeared in *Pockets of Resistance* #11. Dark Night Press.

Scott Smallwood, "Anatomy of a Free-Speech Firestorm: How a Professor's 3-Year-Old Essay Sparked a National Controversy," February 10, 2005. Copyright 2005, the *Chronicle of Higher Education.* Reprinted with permission.

Kirk Johnson, "Incendiary in Academia May Now Find Himself Burned," February 11, 2005, the *New York Times.* Copyright © 2005 by The New York Times Co. Reprinted with permission.

John C. Ensslin, "Free Speech Can Cost Profs; Outspoken Faculty Have Paid Price in Loss of Jobs, Tenure," February 12, 2005. *Rocky Mountain News.*

Jim Spencer, "Whom Does Churchill Work For?" February 11, 2005. The *Denver Post.* Reprinted with permission.

Dave Curtin and Howard Pankratz, "Governor Renews Call for CU Regents to Dismiss Churchill," February 10, 2005. The *Denver Post.* Reprinted with permission.

Reggie Rivers, "Can't Governor Be Offensive, Too?" February 11, 2005. The *Denver Post.* Reprinted with permission.

David Harsanyi, "CU Hiding Behind Tenure," February 1, 2005. The *Denver Post.* Reprinted with permission.

"The Freedom to Discuss; Americans Can Question Ideas, but the Right to Debate Them Should Always Be Protected," February 7, 2005, the *Buffalo News.* Reprinted with the permission of the *Buffalo News.*

Phillip Swann, "Is Your Television Watching You?" March 3, 2003. *Television Week.*

John Jerney, "Is Big Brother Watching You While You Surf?" January 25, 2005. Reprinted with permission of the author.

Salim Muwakkil, "Forgotten Freedoms," January 7, 2002. *In These Times.* Institute for Public Affairs.

Kate O'Beirne, 'Congress's Patriotic Act: This is a Law That Defends America and, Yes, Preserves Civil Liberties, Dammit," September 15, 2003, © 2003 by National Review, Inc., 215 Lexington Avenue, New York, NY 10016. Reprinted by permission.

Reid J. Epstein, "University Warns Students of Patriot Act Disclosures; Government Can Get Medical Records," December 18, 2004. *Milwaukee Journal Sentinel.* Reprinted with permission.

Charlie Brennan and Karen Abbott, "Did Civil Liberties Fall with the Twin Towers? Ramifications of the Patriot Act Still Being Argued," September 11, 2004. *Rocky Mountain News.*

Eleanor J. Bader, "Thought Police: Big Brother May Be Watching What You Read," November 25, 2002. *In These Times.* Institute for Public Affairs.

Edward Epstein, "GOP Makes Time for Patriot Act Vote; Leaders Successfully Beat Back Challenge by Extending Roll Call," July 9, 2004, the *San Francisco Chronicle.* Reprinted with permission of the *San Francisco Chronicle.*

Susan Murray, "'Queer Eye' for Big Brother," reprinted by permission of the author.

Robyn E. Blumner, "Cards Spell End of Privacy," October 10, 2004. *St. Petersburg Times.*

Mark F. Bonner, "Parish Gets Money for Street Cameras; ACLU's Concerns Fail to Dissuade Sheriff," July 24, 2004, © 2005 The Times-Picayune Publishing Co.

All rights reserved. Used with permission of the *Times-Picayune.*

Jay Rey, "Privacy at a Premium/Think You're Alone? Think Again. Security Cameras are Popping Up Everywhere," the *Buffalo News.* Reprinted with the permission of the *Buffalo News.*

Jeffrey Rosen, "The Way We Live Now: Naked Terror," January 4, 2004. the *New York Times,* Article was adapted from his book, *The Naked Crowd: Reclaiming Security and Freedom in an Anxious Age,* Random House, 2004.

Katie Hafner, "Where the Hall Monitor Is a Webcam," February 27, 2003. The *New York Times.* Copyright © 2005 by the New York Times Co. Reprinted with permission.

Bill Hendrick, "Get Ready for Your Close-Up; Some Cameras Will Focus on Drivers' Faces," March 25, 2002. The *Atlanta Journal Constitution.*

Chapter 10

Dan Keating, 'Electronic Voting Still in Infancy, Critics Say; Security Is a Concern as Election Day Nears," May 5, 2004. The *Washington Post.*

Scot Petersen, "E-Voting Underachieves: Starry-eyed Predictions Lag Behind Technical Realities," July 26, 2004. *eWeek.*

Avi Rubin, "An Election Day Clouded by Doubt," October 27, 2004. The *Baltimore Sun.*

Andy Ihnatko, "It's a Fun Idea, but Electronic Voting Doesn't Pass the Trust Test," November 9, 2004. *Chicago Sun-Times.*

Editorial, "Clean Election; Allegations of Massive Voter Fraud Turn Out to Be Unfounded, Fortunately," November 14, 2004. The *Houston Chronicle.* Reprinted with permission.

Anne Applebaum, "In ATMs, Not Votes, We Trust," November 17, 2004. The *Washington Post.* Reprinted with permission.

Editorial, "Step Toward Election Standards," November 29, 2004. *LA Times,* the Times Mirror Company.

"One Last Election Lesson," January 18, 2005. The *New York Times.* Copyright © 2005 by the New York Times Co. Reprinted with permission.

Corey Pein, "Blog-Gate; Yes, CBS Screwed UP Badly in 'Memogate'—But So Did Those Who Covered the Affair," January/February 2005. *Columbia Journalism Review.*

Jonathan V. Last, "Prove It: The Columbia Journalism Review Finally Confronts CBS News, Rathergate, and the Blogosphere," January 4, 2005. The *Weekly Standard.*

Art Buchwald, "Caught in the Web," September 24, 2004. The *Washington Post.* Reprinted with permission.

"Our Turn; There's No Denying Impact of Bloggers; Their Challenge to CBS News Makes It Increasingly Difficult to Dismiss Them as Simply Amateurs in Pajamas," September 16, 2004. *San Antonio News Express.*

La Shawn Barber, "The Blogosphere's Smaller Stars," December 20, 2004. *National Review.*

Russ Lipton, "Blogging In," September 25, 2004, *World* magazine.

Peggy Noonan, "The Blogs Must Be Crazy," February 17, 2005. The *Wall Street Journal.*

Kathleen Hennessey, "How Grass Roots Grab Hold of Presidential Race on Web," March 16, 2003. *Sacramento Bee.*

Edward Miliband, "Meet-up at the White House? All of a Sudden, the Anti-War Howard Dean Looks Like a Serious Candidate for US President," August 25, 2003. *New Statesman.*

Barb Palser, "Virtual Campaigning," August 25, 2003. *New Statesman.*

Jonathan Saltzman, "Dean Activists Found to be Party Core; Surveyor Finds Bulk Far from Disaffected," November 20, 2003. The *Boston Globe.* Reprinted with permission.

Christine B. Williams and Jesse Gordon, "The Meetup Presidency," July 2004, Campaigns and Elections.

Justin Gest, "Bush Supporters Are Catching on to Internet Connection," October 17, 2004. *St. Louis Post-Dispatch.* Reprinted with permission.

Michael Barone, "Blogosophere Politics," February 21, 2005. *U.S. News and World Report.*

Photo Credits